The New Bourgeoisie
and the Limits of Dependency

The New Bourgeoisie
and the Limits of Dependency:
Mining, Class, and Power
in "Revolutionary" Peru

David G. Becker

Princeton University Press • Princeton, New Jersey

For
Dad, Mother, Dan, and Paul
David Ballón
and
Victoria

Contents

List of Tables   ix
List of Figures   xi
Glossary of Acronyms   xiii
Foreword, *by Richard L. Sklar*   xvii
Preface   xxi

PART I: Introduction

1. Development, Class, and Dependency   3
2. Peru: *Un País Minero*   17
3. Mining Policy and Policymaking after 1968   49
4. World Industries and World Markets in Nonferrous Metals   72

PART II: Mining Transnationals and the Peruvian State   95

5. Southern Peru Copper versus an Assertive State: The Cuajone
   Project   97
6. The Decline and Fall of Cerro de Pasco   132

PART III: Institutional Foundations of the Peruvian Mining
Bourgeoisie   169

7. The Medium-Mining Subsector   171
8. Parastatal Enterprise in Peruvian Mining   201

PART IV: Mining and Development: A Class Analysis   235

9. The Bourgeoisie and Middle Class of the Minería   237
10. The Mining Industry and the Claims of Labor   279

Conclusions

11. The New Bourgeoisie and the Limits of Dependency   323

Appendices

A. Miscellaneous Data   345
B. Mining Policy Guidelines and Legislation of the Military
   Regime   354
C. A Comparison of Key Provisions of the Toquepala and
   Cuajone Basic Agreements   361
D. Statutory Rights and Privileges of Peruvian Mine Workers   365

Bibliography   371
Index   409

List of Tables

2.1 Indicators of Development for Peru 18
2.2 Peruvian Exports by Product, 1960 and 1980 23
2.3 Peruvian Exports and Imports by Destination or Source, 1962 and 1980 24
2.4 Southern Peru Copper: Net Earnings and Contributions to Owners' Consolidated After-Tax Profits, 1960-1969 38
3.1 Southern Peru Copper Corporation: Financial Performance, 1956-1970 54
5.1 Members of the Chase Manhattan Banking Consortium for Cuajone, with Their Contributions 115
5.2 Cuajone Long-Term Copper Sales: Final Contractual Disposition 121
5.3 Financing of the Cuajone Project: Final Summary of Funding Sources and Recuperable Investment 124
5.4 Southern Peru Copper: Proportion of Sales Income Spent in Peru, 1971-1980 126
5.5 Southern Peru Copper: Earnings Statements for Toquepala and Cuajone, 1977-1980 129
6.1 Cerro's Production of Refined Metals in Peru, 1950-1968 144
6.2 Financial Performance of Cerro's Peruvian Mining and Refining Operations, 1950-1968 144
6.3 Comparison of Centromin's Financial Performance, 1974-1980, with That of Cerro's Peruvian Mining and Refining Operations, 1969-1973 156
6.4 Centromin's Production of Major Refined Metals, 1974-1981 157
6.5 Comparative Size Measures for Cerro and Certain Other Major Corporations in 1973 162
7.1 Gross Value of Production, Economic Rent, and Fixed Assets of the Peruvian Mediana Minería, 1967-1979 173
7.2 The Companies of the Peruvian Mediana Minería, with Financial Indicators for 1979 177
7.3 Directorial Interlocks between the Mediana Minería and Other Sectors of the Peruvian Economy 188
7.4 Ratio of Long-Term Debt to Shareholder Equity for the Mediana Minería and Selected Subdivisions, 1967-1979 195
7.5 Returns on Invested Capital for the Mediana Minería and Selected Subdivisions, 1967-1979 196
9.1 Earnings of Selected Groups Employed in the Peruvian Minería 244
9.2 Mining Society Membership, 1950-1980 259

9.3 Opinions of Mediana Minería Managers and Staff Respecting
   Aspects of Government Mining Policy in the 1968-1974 Period   265
9.4 Opinions of Mediana Minería Managers and Staff Respecting
   Issues of Class Interest   267
10.1 Evolution of Employment in Peruvian Mining, 1967-1979   286
10.2 Strikes in Peru, 1967-1979   301
10.3 Indicators of Strike Intensity in Peru, 1967-1979   302
10.4 Strike Intensity Indicators by Enterprise, 1969-1979   303
A.1 Average Annual Exchange Rate of the Peruvian Sol, 1950-1980   345
A.2 Peruvian Consumer Price Index, 1950-1980   346
A.3 Volume of Production of the Peruvian Minería, 1950-1980:
   Major Nonferrous Metals   347
A.4 Value of Production of the Peruvian Minería, 1950-1980:
   Industry Total and Major Nonferrous Metals   348
A.5 Gross Value of Peruvian Mine Production by Subsector, 1963-
   1980   349
A.6 International Price Quotations for Major Nonferrous Metals,
   1950-1980   350
A.7 Major Western World Copper Mine Producers, 1977   352
A.8 Major Western World Primary Refined Copper Producers, 1977   353
B.1 A Comparison of the Mining Policy Objectives of the Plan Inca
   (1974) and the Plan Túpac Amaru (1977)   354
B.2 Principal Mining Legislation of the Military Regime   356

List of Figures

1. Outline map of Peru, showing the country's division into geographical regions and the locations of the principal mining centers.   20
2. Outline map of Peru, showing the country's political subdivisions, departmental capitals, and major population centers.   26
3. Diagram showing the ownership structure of the Peruvian gran minería as of 1970.   42
4. U.S. Producers' (Domestic Refinery) and LME Settlement copper prices, 1950-1979.   83
5. Distribution of Southern Peru Copper's sales among the principal world copper markets, 1961-1977.   128
6. Economic indicators for the mediana minería by corporate nationality, 1967-1979.   192
7. Combined GVP of the "big seven" Peruvian-owned-medium mining groups as a percentage of the GVP of all nationally owned firms of the mediana minería.   194
8. Real wages (money wages deflated by the cost-of-living index) in the Peruvian minería and in metropolitan Lima.   305
9. Ratio of empleado average salary to obrero average wage for Southern Peru Copper, Cerro-Centromin, and metropolitan Lima, 1967-1977.   306

Glossary of Acronyms

ADEX   Asociación de Exportadores: a trade association of Peruvian manufacturers who produce principally for export

AMAX   American Metal Climax Corporation, now formally known as AMAX: a major nonferrous metals transnational corporation

APRA   Alianza Popular Revolucionaria Americana: a political party founded in Peru in 1924; once radical, it could now be described as "centrist"; much of its support comes from the working and middle classes; it is institutionally linked to Acción Democrática of Venezuela

BICC   British Insulated Callender's Cables: an importer of copper and producer of finished copper goods

BID   Banco Interamericano de Desarrollo: the Inter-American Development Bank, an international financial agency

CADE   Conferencia Anual de Empresarios: an annual conference of Peruvian business executives, sponsored by IPAE (q.v.)

CAEM   Centro de Altos Estudios Militares: Center for Higher Military Studies, an advanced staff school with civilian participation, in which the Peruvian military's developmental ideas have been worked out and propagated

CGTP   Confederación General de Trabajadores Peruanos: General Confederation of Peruvian Workers, one of the four labor centrals and a loose affiliate of the PCP (q.v.)

CIPEC   Conseil International des Producteurs et Exporteurs de Cuivre: International Council of Copper Producers and Exporters, a cartel of Third World copper-exporting countries

CNT   Confederación Nacional de Trabajadores: National Confederation of Labor, another of Peru's labor centrals and formerly an affiliate of the now-defunct Christian Democratic Party

COAP   Consejo de Asesoría a la Presidencia: Presidential Advisory Council, an institution peculiar to the military regime; composed of senior officers without ministerial portfolios, it established broad policy outlines and approved major legislation

COCOMI   Comunidad de Compensación Minera: Mining Compensation Community, an institution charged with receiving profit-sharing contributions from all Peru-based mining companies and distributing the proceeds among all workers of the sector

COFIDE   Corporación Financiera de Desarrollo: Development Finance Corporation, a state development bank

COMEX   New York Commodities Exchange

COMMSA   Consultores Minero-Metalúrgicos S.A.: a mining and metallurgical engineering firm; it is a subsidiary of Centromin, a parastatal mining enterprise

CTP   Confederación de Trabajadores del Perú: Confederation of Labor of Peru, an affiliate of the APRA (q.v.)

CTRP   Confederación de Trabajadores de la Revolución Peruana: Confederation of Workers of the Peruvian Revolution; the newest of the country's four labor centrals, it was organized by the military regime with the intent of setting up an "officialist" labor movement; it soon began to operate independently of the state and does so today

DGM   Dirección General de Minería: General Directorate of Mining, the agency within the Ministry of Energy and Mines that exercises direct supervisory authority over the mining sector

ECLA   Economic Commission for Latin America: an agency of the United Nations with headquarters in Santiago, Chile

ER   Economic rent from resource exploitation: a measure of firm or industry performance, it is equal to GVP (q.v.) less payouts to sectors other than mining (principally, purchases of goods and services and non-income taxes); it is the contribution of the firm or industry to gross domestic product

FTMMP   Federación de Trabajadores Minero-Metalúrgicos del Perú: Federation of Mine and Metallurgical Workers of Peru; many local unions in the Peruvian mining sector are affiliated with it, but some are not; its strength is mostly in Southern Peru Copper and MineroPeru; it frequently cooperates with the CGTP (q.v.) but is not formally associated with any of the four labor centrals

GVP   Gross value of production: the value of mine, smelter, or refinery production at market prices as of the time when produced, regardless of whether sold or retained as inventory

IBRD   International Bank for Reconstruction and Development: the World Bank

IFC   International Finance Corporation: an arm of the IBRD (q.v.) which makes loans to, and equity investments in, development projects in Third World countries; unlike the IBRD itself, it lends to private entities and does not demand government guarantees

IIM   Instituto de Ingenieros de Minas: Institute of Mining Engineers, a Peruvian engineering guild association

IMF   International Monetary Fund

IMI   Imperial Metals Industries: a British manufacturer of copper goods

INCITEMI   Instituto Científico y Tecnológico de la Minería: Mining Industry Scientific and Technological Institute, a parastatal research and development entity; founded by the military regime, it was later merged with the Geological Institute to form INGEMMET (q.v.)

INCO   International Nickel Company, now formally known as INCO: a transnational nickel duopolist (nearly) based in Canada, its mines and refineries also produce considerable quantities of copper and other nonferrous metals

INGEMMET   Instituto Geológico, Minero y Metalúrgico: Geological, Mining, and Metallurgical Institute, a parastatal research and development entity supported by a 1 percent tax on mining company profits

INP   Instituto Nacional de Planificación: National Planning Institute, the government agency charged with responsibility for indicative economic planning and for acquiring and analyzing the data on which national development plans are based

IPAE   Instituto Peruano de Administración de Empresas: Peruvian Institute of Business Administration, a private, nonprofit agency whose mission is the improvement of organizational and managerial technologies; one of its principal activities is to assist companies to set up in-house managerial training programs for their employees

IPC   International Petroleum Company: a Peruvian subsidiary of Standard Oil of New Jersey (now Exxon), controlled through its Canadian subsidiary; its abusive practices and defiance of local law made it a nationalist *cause célèbre* and led to its expropriation without compensation during the military regime's first week in power

LME   London Metals Exchange

OECD   Organisation for Economic Co-operation and Development: an association of developed nations that seeks to promote development and the study thereof

PCP   Partido Comunista Peruano: this is the "official" Peruvian Communist party, in the sense that its policy orientation hews closely to that of the Soviet Communist Party (CPSU)

SNI   Sociedad Nacional de Industrias: National Society of Industries, formerly—until its charter was revoked by the military regime because of its strenuous opposition to property reforms—the main Peruvian association of manufacturers; it remains in existence, having dropped "nacional" from its name

UNI   Unión Democrática Popular: Popular Democratic Union, a small political front that combines a number of still smaller political parties and factions of the radical Left; its major component, Vanguardia Revolucionaria, is often described as "Maoist"; it has close links to the labor movement in the southern mines and to the FTMMP (q.v.)

UNI   Universidad Nacional de Ingeniería: the National Engineering University, where the vast majority of Peruvian mining engineers and managers received their undergraduate education

Foreword

by Richard L. Sklar

INDUSTRY is the great arch of modern civilization. In all societies, material culture is molded, like putty, by the driving force of industrial development. The underlying and constitutive principles of industrial organizations are political as well as economic. In newly industrializing countries the political foundations of an industrial order are clearly visible. Industrial civilizations are reared upon systems of government and law which facilitate the mobilization of labor, training of specialists, taxation, accumulation of capital, fiscal management, foreign exchange, and many other processes of industrial construction. These requirements are common to all industrial orders regardless of whether they are constructed according to capitalist or socialist economic principles.

Despite these commonalities, every country's industrial transition is distinctive and largely unpredictable. However large or small, populous or sparsely populated it may be, each country's own mixture of economic assets, cultural artifacts, and leading personalities will result in a national experience that is unlike that of any other. In Peru, the political power of a capitalist oligarchy, based mainly upon landholding and mercantile interests, was displaced in 1968 by a military government motivated by nationalistic, populist, and developmental beliefs. The nation's chief economic asset is a metal mining industry which currently ranks fourth, after Chile, Zambia, and Zaire, among Third World copper-exporting countries, and first among such countries in proved and probable copper reserves. As in the nineteenth-century "age of guano," twentieth-century Peru is endowed with a "bonanza" in the form of copper and other nonferrous metals. Unlike its conservative predecessors, however, the current generation of Peruvian leaders views the mineral "bonanza" as an instrument of economic and social reconstruction. Hence David G. Becker's concept of "bonanza development" to characterize Peru's transition to its industrial destiny.

The main agencies of bonanza development are transnational corporations and Peruvian state mining enterprises. Their presence is felt most strongly in the gran minería, a large-scale mining subsector which accounts for more than four-fifths of all copper exports in addition to the export of iron ore. Since the government does not pursue a policy of nationalization for its own sake, state enterprise in Peru is a purely pragmatic instrument of economic development. Leaders of the "revolutionary" military governments of 1968-

1980 decided to avoid the costs of symbolic nationalizations undertaken to inflate their national *amour propre*. If the mining goose lays golden eggs, they reasoned, why should the state incur expenses and other problems just to become responsible for its care and feeding?[1] One wonders whether the Peruvians drew negative conclusions from the heroic but expensive nationalizations of copper mines in Zaire and Zambia between 1967 and 1973, as they did from the Chilean experience of the sixties and early seventies.

Professor Becker's examination of Peru's mining policy and practice includes a fascinating tale of two companies. Chapters 5 and 6 could become classic contributions to industrial historiography. They compare the fortunes of two American mining ventures, namely, Southern Peru Copper Corporation and Cerro Corporation, which exemplify contrasting corporate types. Southern, managed and mainly owned by Asarco, Inc. (a New York-based metals enterprise) earned acceptance in Peru as a "good corporate citizen." By contrast, Cerro was an old-style "colonial-type" company, which could not adapt to the changing conditions of assertive and developmental nationalism.

We learn that Asarco/Southern greatly expanded its operations in Peru and strengthened its position as a world-class producer by virtue of its ability to negotiate mutually beneficial and satisfactory agreements with the government. On one side, the company and its financial associates bowed to the wishes of the government with respect to various sensitive issues. On the other, skilled government negotiators were informed and mindful of the corporation's global interests. These approaches to bargaining are consistent with my notion of a "doctrine of domicile," which is an idea about the behavior of multinational corporations. It means that the local subsidiaries of international business groups will seek to operate in accordance with the policies of states in which they are domiciled. The chief aim and purpose of such local adaptation is to promote the interests of the transnational enterprise as a whole.

Unlike Asarco, Cerro functioned on the "fringe" of transnational business, but it was deeply rooted in Peru. Cerro inaugurated modern mining in the high Peruvian Andes; over the years, it made an immense contribution to the growth of an impressive corps of Peruvian geologists, mining engineers, and mining managers; it promoted the establishment of related Peruvian industries; it provided on-the-job education for an astonishing "30 to 40 percent of the top managers of the [present-day] mining sector." But Cerro, reared on cheap labor and thick with the pre-"revolutionary" oligarchy, had a "social debt" to pay. Its archaic paternalism and political insensitivity resulted in its expropriation by an exasperated and indignant government. No tears were shed at its demise by the Peruvian professional mining establishment, which said, in effect, "Thanks for the memories, but what have you done for us lately?"

The "doctrine of domicile" is an alleged maxim of transnational corporate

[1] For a generalized formulation of this question, see Raymond Vernon, *Storm over the Multinationals: The Real Issues* (Cambridge: Harvard University Press, 1977), p. 168.

action, a likely tenet of ideological belief for those who plan and rationalize the future of transnational corporate expansion. Becker has further developed the idea by adducing the distinction drawn by John Kenneth Galbraith between "entrepreneurial" and "mature" forms of corporate organization. Becker's research led him to this significant finding: that Cerro's "entrepreneurial" style of management and type of organization "fell outside the conceptual reach of the doctrine-of-domicile idea." So Asarco's subsidiary survives as a private enterprise in Peru while Cerro's has become a state enterprise.

My heart goes out to Cerro, and especially to its sometime chief executive, Robert Koenig, who incurred the wrath of Peruvian nationalists by investing in Chile for an idiosyncratic reason: he could not resist the challenge of geological and topographical problems which had "repeatedly stymied other would-be developers of [a particular] property." Koenig personifies the spirit of traditional entrepreneurship. By contrast, Becker's viewpoint is entirely modern. With Frits Wils, he criticizes Joseph Schumpeter's conception of the "heroic" entrepreneur as a species of "economism," which "undervalues the political dimension of organized social life." This viewpoint is in accord with the political logic of the "doctrine of domicile." Furthermore, Becker cites the Peruvian objection to Cerro's Chilean venture to show that transnational corporations will come under pressure, applied by the assertive governments of countries in which they have invested, to forgo other investment opportunities in hostile neighboring states. I am inclined to question the efficacy of such pressures. In all parts of the world, truly transnational corporations defy national antipathies and straddle the sovereign states of regions that are torn by political conflicts.

Since it is an element of transnational business ideology, the "doctrine of domicile" draws attention to the actions of ideological groups. It implies, for the analyst, a social rather than institutional or systemic frame of reference: a disposition to look "behind" corporations and governments to the group and class bases of their actions. For Becker and myself, this tenet of ideology is significant chiefly because it smooths the relationship between the corporate bourgeoisies of the industrial capitalist countries and the bourgeoisies of those Third World countries that are newly developing but, as yet, narrowly industrialized. Transnational class alliances may also signify the coming transcendence of the nation-state by an international bourgeoisie.

Two additional, related concepts also guide the argument of this book. "Postimperialism" is an idea about transnational class domination on a global scale. From that standpoint, Becker breaks with "dependency theory" (*dependencismo*) in all of its forms. Only so can he comprehend the developmental role of the corporate bourgeoisie—both American and Peruvian—in the era of transnational enterprise. Whereas "postimperialism" is an idea about the order of things, its cousin, "post-dependency," is an idea about the order of thought. Its exposition in this book marks the emergence of a new way of thinking in international studies: an early formulation of a theory of world development that is neither state- nor system-centered but class-based. As Becker contends, a theory of "late-capitalist development" will have to be "built up inductively on a groundwork of empirical studies." His case for the "post-dependency" orientation presented in this pathbreaking study is persuasive; yet, we have been forewarned by Thurman Arnold that "old gods always thrash around . . . violently before they die."[2]

Los Angeles
August 1982

[2] Thurman W. Arnold, *The Folklore of Capitalism* (New Haven: Yale University Press, 1937), p. 119.

IN this book I advance the contention that the 1968-1980 period of military rule in Peru coincided with the emergence of a "new bourgeoisie" as the nation's dominant class stratum. That ascendant class element has one of its primary bases of support in the country's key mining industry. Since mining also engages the interests of transnational and of parastatal enterprises, we find a core industry in which three forms of capital participate. This fact, together with the centrality of mining to the national economy, makes Peru an apt case through which to examine afresh processes of late-capitalist industrialization in resource-export-dependent developing countries.

The so-called Peruvian "revolution" was rather less than revolutionary, for which reason I place the term within quotation marks throughout the book. It was assuredly no social revolution: although the character of the bourgeoisie was transformed after the remnants of landed and commercial-financial oligarchic power had been destroyed, there was no overthrow (not even a serious threat of one) of bourgeois political power and social control. Indeed, I will show that both were modernized and strengthened. Neither was this a true organizational revolution—one where, without change in the basic nature of class relationships, a new set of economic and political institutions is put into place for the purpose of meeting new challenges to class domination. To be sure, major societal institutions—the state, business corporations, trade associations, labor unions—underwent great changes in their internal structures and in their relationships with each other. Nonetheless, the process of change consisted almost entirely in reinforcing and/or redirecting institutions which had been gradually developing for some time. State economic planning and large-scale parastatal enterprise, two conspicuous innovations of the Peruvian military regime, were present some years before in incipient form—in the latter instance, in fact, for much of this century. Workers' comanagement and "social property" *were* significant institutional novelties; but the first is a sickly child of the "revolution," and the second was essentially stillborn.

Yet, I hold that this nonrevolution has had extremely important consequences for the future Peruvian political order. I will argue that the military *docenio* (twelve-year reign) ushered in a form of late-capitalist development which offers promise for the establishment of a fairly stable bourgeois democracy *and* for the political and material advance of at least some of the popular sectors. I maintain that the recent evolution of transnational corporate interests and behavior has conditioned the process in generally positive ways. This may not be so where the transnational presence is concentrated in economic areas other than resource extraction. But it does seem to be so in Peru and, quite possibly, in other less-developed countries whose economies revolve around mine or petroleum production for export.

By taking such a stance, I place myself in direct opposition to the ideas of the now-popular dependency school. I do so deliberately. For some time there has been uneasiness about the accuracy of dependency's underlying assumption: that in less-developed countries, political dependency and capitalism are inextricably linked. Doubters have long pointed, e.g., to Cuban political and economic dependence upon the Soviet Union; while I do not denigrate the very real accomplishments of the Cuban Revolution, I remain unhappy both with the continued absence there of participatory democracy and with ideologically motivated attempts to prove that, in Cuba, authoritarianism and dependency do not exist—or somehow take on a different, less malign aspect. Immanuel Wallerstein approaches the problem of "socialist dependence" imaginatively, redefining the Soviet state as a "national capitalist" and thereby justifying his lumping of it together with the other "core" powers of an all-embracing "world-economy." I fear, however, that this is but a Ptolemaic solution: it "saves the appearances," but the requisite theoretical epicycles painfully obfuscate reality. In reality, Soviet-type systems of domination differ from the Western in that domination is politically rather than economically based. It is possible, I am sure, to develop a single set of class-analytical tools which could be brought to bear with equal facility for comprehending the nature of domination in either system. But I see no useful purpose in pretending that these two manifestly different modes of social control are one and the same.

If dependency is not always an outcome of capitalist development, is it farfetched to suggest that capitalist development need not invariably produce dependency? I do not think so. However, to make this suggestion does not at all entail a claim that international capitalism *never* envelops less-developed countries in bonds of dependence and external control. It merely implies that such bonds have been outgrowths of an earlier, neocolonialist phase of capitalism, one that is now drawing to a close; and that, where dependency relationships are yet found, they are consequences of particular national development experiences. In fact, one reason why I have chosen to treat an instance of mineral-export-based development is that dependency analysis tends to focus on another form: import-substitution industrialization, fueled by capital accumulated from agricultural exports. One cannot assume a priori that dependent outcomes inevitably result from capitalist development qua capitalist, irrespective of gross differences in host-country economic structures and in modes of articulation with the international economy.

The last assertion makes clear that I view with disfavor approaches to understanding development that ignore historical contingencies and seek to explain everything of importance by invoking grand theory: the "laws of motion" of the world capitalist system. All that grand theory offers is weak, teleological explanation at best (e.g., the Peruvian military took power in

1968 because it "had to" in order for the system of domination to persist); it offers tautology at worst. "Men make their own history," Marx tells us, even if they are constrained in so doing by "circumstances directly encountered, given and transmitted from the past." Abstract social structures are real, but their reality is theoretical rather than existential. In restricting the scope of autonomous human action, they do not eliminate it; they do not act—living human beings do; they have no unlimited power to influence human conduct in a manner that promotes system maintenance.

Having said all this, I hasten to laud dependency ideas—especially in their historically concrete version as propounded by Fernando Henrique Cardoso and others—for their valuable contribution to the normative side of development studies. The dependency school has restored to the concept of development the norm of social justice—a norm largely missing from the "modernization" school which preceded it in the evolution of North American social science. *Dependencismo* emphasizes the unevenness and inequities of capitalist development, and it reminds us that bourgeois liberalism stresses political rights to the exclusion of economic and social rights. That is all to the good.

It happens that in the present work I do not join in the normative critique of capitalist development to any great extent—though not because I am out of sympathy with it. Much to the contrary, I feel it to have become so widely recognized and firmly grounded that further elaboration is less useful in this context than is the working out of certain other ideas and concepts. In particular, I prefer to concentrate on the question of political domination—loss of control—rather than on that of economic exploitation. The two are *not* the same. Popular classes in society can win a measure of power even when economically exploited; and they can then use their power to improve their lot by confronting the dominant class with a situation in which a degree of accommodation becomes the better part of valor. Much of the dynamic of capitalist development comes from the dialectic of popular-class resistance to domination. In my opinion, one of the greatest weaknesses of dependency approaches has been their relative neglect of this dialectic; it is no wonder that, having omitted it from consideration, they see Third World capitalism as stagnant. Still, it should be possible to reinsert into theory the neglected element, to revise outmoded teachings about the nature of transnational corporate action, and to find that capitalist development in certain less-developed countries has dynamism, without abandoning *dependencismo*'s progressive value premises. I believe I have done that in this work.

It is as certain as tomorrow's sunrise that there will be those who, finding little sense of imminent capitalist crisis in these pages, and noting my heterodox argument that economic relationships with transnational resource enterprises can be constructive and mutually beneficial, will insist that I am putting forth a mere warmed-over version of the Rostovian "stages of economic growth." I do no such thing. Indeed, my discussion of the Peruvian model, "bonanza development," implies that there are *no* universally valid stages of growth, that there is instead a variety of national paths to development—even within a capitalist framework. What is more, I make plain that Peruvian development is contradictory, not unilinear. I simply posit that its inherent contradictions are as yet a long way from sharpening or exploding into crisis. If I am right, should we not face the truth squarely? Does scholarship gain by pretending, as so many progressives have done for so many years, that the ultimate crisis lies just around the corner?

None of us can do more than speculate about the long-term future of Peruvian development. The task I have set myself is the more modest one of looking to the near future, where there is some power of prediction based on an extrapolation of currently observable tendencies. To find that within this time frame some less-developed countries, Peru among them, can develop capitalistically, does not require me to accept that capitalism is the predestined end of social evolution. Nor does it require me to believe that capitalism, wholly free of internal contradiction, can go on forever.

In short, the approach taken herein is Marxian in that it deals with classes as the primary unit of analysis; in that it regards class conflict as the motive force of societal change; and in that it views class conflict as a struggle for social control, a struggle in which control of the means of material production is a chief (yet, not an exclusive) instrument. But it is openly revisionist, owes no allegiance to ideological orthodoxy, rejects determinism, and is avowedly anti-Leninist. It is, I feel, a return to Marx's original vision of the progressiveness of capitalist expansion into the Third World, this vision in no way signifying that the process has a uniformly positive impact on all whom it touches. If there is still room for a dynamic capitalism in parts of the Third World, the final systemic crisis will be further delayed. We need not conclude, however, that it will be delayed for eternity. In the interim, the task facing scholars of development is to indicate how the subordinate classes of less-developed societies can best act to secure for themselves a fairer share of development's rewards, albeit in a less-than-ideal capitalist milieu; to preserve and extend democratic institutions, no matter how limited their present scope and effectiveness; and to attain a greater degree of solidarity and ideological autonomy—the last a time-consuming effort that depends on capitalist development itself and that cannot be incubated artificially. Upon completion of this task rests the likelihood that, come the appropriate moment, the people at large will press forward successfully the transition to a truly democratic socialism.

All quotations from Spanish-language sources were translated by myself; my translations are fairly literal, but I have taken the few liberties necessary to provide a smoothly flowing English syntax without altering the original meanings. I should also call brief attention to three usages which, while conceptually unimportant, may appear unusual to U.S. readers.

In order to avoid excessive repetition, I have alternated the adjective "U.S." with "North American." I avoid the commonplace "American" out of deference to the sensibilities of our neighbors to the south, for whom the U.S. habit of employing "American" strictly as a form of self-reference is an ethnocentrism. Canada and Canadians are always addressed by name.

Peruvians, like many Hispanics, routinely carry the matrilineal surname in addition to the patrilineal. In Peru, however, patrilineal surnames are often themselves compounds, as in the cases of Francisco Morales Bermúdez (Cerutti) and Jorge Fernández Maldonado (Solari). Here, parentheses indicate matrilineal surnames, which are generally dropped in familiar or repeated address; but no Peruvian would refer to these two gentlemen as "Morales" or "Fernández." I have respected local custom in my use of Peruvian names and would urge any who quote from this work to do likewise.

Lastly, a few words of justification are in order concerning my employment of "dependencismo" and "dependencista." In Chapter 1 I remark in a footnote that both are derived from the Spanish *dependencia*. I make no apologies for labeling the dependency idea an "ism"; to my mind, this merely conveys the notion that, like the Marxism to which it has a strong affinity, *dependencismo* is a coherent body of thought with a definite normative-ideological component in addition to a conceptual-analytic one. "Dependencista" is then the corresponding term of reference for one who adheres to this body of thought, just as "Marxist" is. (Latin Americans, it may be noted, frequently utilize *tercermundista* in much the same sense and without embarrassment; but I found the English equivalent, "Third Worldist," too clumsy for repeated use.) Although far from expert in Spanish etymology, I can claim some modest acquaintance with that language. To my ear, "dependen*c*ismo/dependen*c*ista," not "dependen*t*ismo/dependen*t*ista," are the proper derivations from the base word, *dependencia*; however, I will happily stand corrected if someone can supply a good argument for the rejected choices.

This work might never have seen the light of day had it not been for several intellectual mentors and a larger number of friends and colleagues who gave freely of their time and energies in furnishing indispensable "inputs": knowledge, advice, timely information, constructive criticism. One of my mentors, Richard L. Sklar, hardly needs mention here, for his formidable presence is apparent in notes and cited quotations throughout the book. Less evident in these pages yet every bit as important to me is Edward Gonzalez, chairperson of my doctoral committee at UCLA. Ed has helped me in many ways that go far beyond his official duties. Most tellingly, his own work has served me as a model of honest, thorough, critical scholarship; to the extent that such qualities find pale reflection herein, they derive in good part from his stellar example. He and Dick Sklar, valued friends both of them, were united in sharing with me their profound respect for liberty and democracy along with their dedication to the ideal of social justice. Their intervention impelled me toward the realization that the third must be achieved without sacrifice of the first two, lest it be diminished.

Charles R. Nixon, in his course and in many private conversations, has influenced my thinking about the nature of political inquiry in general and about class, civil society and the state, and the political-economic order in particular. I have been further enriched by direct exposure to the ideas of, among others, Roman Kolkowicz, Susan Kaufmann Purcell, Francine F. Rabinovitz, and David Wilkinson. And I have benefited also from the comments of Peter Evans, Brown University; of Charles T. Goodsell, Southern Illinois University; of H. Jeffrey Leonard, Princeton University; of James Scarritt, University of Colorado; of Waltraud Morales, University of Central Florida; of David Baldwin, Richard Joseph, Nelson Kasfir, Ian Lustick, Gene Lyons, Roger Masters, and Richard Sterling, Dartmouth College; and of several of my students at UCLA, of whom Lawrence Jones and—especially—Jonathan Rosenberg merit special mention. The contributions of these and of the others too numerous to name stand out in the following pages. As for errors of omission and commission, they are mine alone, and I accept full responsibility for them.

Many people in the United States and Peru contributed as interviewees and in other ways to the acquisition of the information and data which are the foundations of this study; but some made extraordinary commitments of time and effort. Foremost among them, without the slightest doubt, is my dear friend, Ing. David Ballón Vera. I can only say that he is almost single-handedly responsible for the success of my Peruvian research endeavors. More than that, his forward-looking ideas, sincere concern with the well-being of the less privileged, and high sense of duty to his country have served as a constant inspiration; I have taken heart from his firm dedication to Peru's future and his deep appreciation for its historical and cultural traditions. The unstinting friendship of David, Ruth, Carlos, Oscar, and Ruthie was more than once a vital sustenance in time of need.

A second dear friend as well as contributor is Marcia Koth de Paredes, director of the Peruvian Fulbright Commission (Comisión para el Intercambio Educativo entre los Estados Unidos y el Perú). From her and from the entire staff of the commission I received encouragement, logistical and research support, and, most importantly, *simpatía*. I daresay that no Peruvianist in recent years who has sought out the services of the commission has come away disappointed; it is gratifying to know—and useful to remind ourselves, at a time when the essential work of this and similar international interchange programs is coming under budgetary assault—that there are such individuals and organizations whose aid is available to any scholar willing to repay his debt to the host country by diffusing the knowledge which he or she has obtained.

Alberto Benavides de la Quintana, president and board chairman of the Compañía Minera Buenaventura, went well beyond the limits of a research relationship in his assistance to me. Mario Samamé Boggio, president of INGEMMET and a member of the board of the Fulbright Commission, charmed me with his graciousness and was the first to direct my attention to the significance of the Peruvian-owned medium-mining companies. Robert Andrew Nickson, a British government-United Nations advisor to the Ministry of Commerce, provided much valuable information regarding commercial aspects of the *minería*.

Certain individuals were in a position to extend institutional in addition to personal assistance in the gathering of information. David Ballón made available the specialized library of the Banco Minero del Perú and arranged for the cooperation of the Ministry of Energy and Mines. Alberto Benavides set up a tour of one of his company's mines. The directors and officers of the National Mining and Petroleum Society graciously allowed me access to the Society's data files. What is more, Róger Arévalo Ramírez, chief of the Society's Department of Economic Studies and Statistics, placed at my disposal the full resources of his bureau; he and his staff devoted a great deal of their time to data analysis for this project, and it would have been difficult or impossible to bring the information up to date without their help. Arthur G. Beers, senior vice-president of the Southern Peru Copper Corporation, was largely responsible for the excellent working relationship that I was able to establish with Southern. Thanks to him and to its president, Frank Archibald, the company supplied me with data unavailable elsewhere; acted as a most courteous host during the time spent at its installations; gave me full access to those installations and their personnel for research purposes; and, in general, left me entirely free to investigate as I wished. I also received the full cooperation of the Empresa Minera del Perú (MineroPeru) and its then-president, Luis Briceño Arata. I thank these people and their institutions for having helped to make an arduous research effort less so.

Andrés Bravo Bresani, a warm human being as well as an acknowledged expert in his field, favored me with multitudinous insights gained during his many years as a mining engineer, manager, and chief of the General Directorate of Mining.

This study is based in part on research performed in Peru during 1977-78 and the summer of 1981. Funding for this and associated efforts was received from the U.S. Department of Health, Education, and Welfare, Office of Education, in the form of a Fulbright-Hays Dissertation Research Abroad fellowship; from the UCLA-Meiji University Pan-Pacific Studies Program, administered by the Council on International and Comparative Studies at the University of California, Los Angeles; from the Department of Political Science, University of California, Los Angeles; and from the School of International Relations, University of Southern California. The last two further contributed by way of employment. My thanks go out to Charles R. Nixon and Andrzej Korbonski, former chairpersons of the UCLA Political Science Department; and to Michael G. Fry, director of the USC School of International Relations. I only hope that, in some way, I have justified the faith and expectations of these institutions and individuals.

An early supporter was Sanford G. Thatcher of Princeton University Press. I am grateful to Sandy for having stood behind the book on the questionable basis of an early draft of the manuscript; for his guidance and help in the preparation of the final version; and for his tolerance of the usual delays in completion. Marilyn Campbell's patient editorial labors, though sorely tried on occasion, never faltered.

Karin Erika Zimmermann made a unique, central contribution to the success of this study. She located several of the most important research contacts. She assisted directly with aspects of the research, notably the sociological investigation of the workers of Southern Peru Copper. She maintained an excellent photographic record of our visits to the Southern facilities. She stimulated my thinking and offered useful suggestions. And, by no means the least, she helped to organize, revise, and edit drafts of the manuscript.

I am fortunate to be blessed with an involved, emotionally supportive family. My father and mother, Bernard and Madeline Sadowitz; my brothers, Daniel and Paul Sadowitz; my sister-in-law, Jo Sadowitz; my aunts and uncles, Morris and Sylvia Weiner and Alvin and Sybil Greenfield; and my cousins, Michael and Eve Greenfield—all provided a stimulus that greatly facilitated my change from a career in the physical sciences to a new and (for me) uncharted course. However others may judge the fruits of that decision, I thank those who so lovingly encouraged it for the personal happiness and fulfillment it has brought me.

Still others have come to occupy honored places in my heart and spirit as a result of this whole experience: Javier and Elena Buenaño, together with Elena *hija*, Alejandro, Javier *hijo*, and Isabel; Mollie Copeland, Nancy Gusten, Lila Merritt, and Clare Walker of UCLA, who made my work infinitely less burdensome than it might have been; Craig and Linda Loftin of the Portage Project, Portage, Wisconsin, who provided such solid friendship. Finally, there is a most wonderful, special person whose struggle to find freedom and contentment mirrors in microcosm that of her people; her example will remain forever an undying source of warmth and inspiration. . . .

D.G.B.
Los Angeles
March 17, 1982

PART I

Introduction

CHAPTER ONE

Development, Class, and Dependency

T HIS is a study of political power and social control in Peru. The much-discussed "revolution from above" imposed by the military from 1968 to 1980 forms the backdrop against which it is set. Its major aim is to show how the organization, distribution, and uses of power have been affected by the country's chief export industry, nonferrous metal mining. But that is not all. The industry produces for the international market and has long been shaped by direct foreign investment. Consequently, the study is also a vehicle for comprehending the nature and significance for national development of the interaction between external economic forces—transnational mining companies and the world metals market—and an industrializing Third World polity.

In recent years the field of development studies has been graced by a swelling output of scholarly works, many of them carefully researched and cogently argued, whose viewpoints have been influenced by dependency "theory," or *dependencismo*.[1] Their authors persuasively press the core *dependencista* thesis: that the global interests of metropolitan capitalist classes have always determined development processes and power relationships in countries like Peru, to the clear detriment of these countries.[2] Dependencismo, however, is much more than a telling critique of imperialist exploitation inflicted in the past upon the Third World by the developed nations. It indicts metropolitan capitalism for continuing its exogenous conditioning of Third World development, albeit in novel ways that depend less than formerly on

[1] I here place the word "theory" within quotation marks (I shall not repeat the usage) out of deference to prominent upholders of dependency ideas who insist that dependency is not a theory in the sense generally understood by North American social science. These same thinkers are also uncomfortable with the term "paradigm," which, however, I do consider apt. The Spanish noun, *dependencismo*, and its corresponding adjective, *dependencista*, better capture the sense that dependency is primarily a world view and an approach to the study of development; they also render due homage to the Latin American origins of many who have made major contributions to the intellectual development of the dependency viewpoint. For further discussion see Cardoso (1977).

[2] The historical development of dependencismo is described and discussed by Corradi (1977), Kahl (1976), and Palma (1978); the last work is particularly useful, in large part because it clarifies the sometimes ambiguous relationship between dependencismo and Marxism. For reviews of the extensive dependency literature see, among others, Caporaso (1978); Caporaso and Zare (1981); Chilcote (1974); Moran (1978); Packenham (1978), a very acerbic critique; and the Valenzuelas (1981). I have also been helped to better appreciate certain of the issues by Castells (1977).

the use of force. One such way, it is held, is the penetration of Third World societies by transnational firms and the resultant subjugation of the host countries' economies to metropolitan requirements. This is a grave accusation.

As Richard L. Sklar has observed, development has a political aspect: it is "the improvement of a society's ability to control the rate and direction of change. The concept of control is crucial to this definition, as it implies the ability to formulate and implement strategies for solving problems and achieving goals."[3] If the dependencista indictment is upheld by the evidence, a transnational corporate presence in a key economic sector (e.g., Peru's mining industry) tends to deprive the host country of this vital control capability. At worst, development is rendered impossible, and one finds instead the "development of underdevelopment."[4] At best, development can occur solely in a distorted form—Fernando Henrique Cardoso has coined the phrase, "associated-dependent development," to describe it[5]—where the host country abandons its indigenous values and practices to acquire a second-rate version of metropolitan capitalism and where the benefits of "development" flow disproportionately to small, privileged elites affiliated with transnational enterprise.

There results, in other words, a new form of foreign domination that is subtler than the overt imperialism of previous epochs. The new dominators are no longer the military and administrative minions of a colonial power. Rather, dependency erodes national independence from within, by promoting a structure of preeminent socioeconomic interests inside the host society which responds preferentially to external demands. Dependency, as Cardoso writes, thus represents "a structural pattern of relations that 'internalize[s]' the external and create[s] a state which [is] formally sovereign and ready to be an answer to the interests of the 'nation,' but which [is] simultaneously and contradictorily the instrument of international economic domination."[6]

The Issues at Stake

Issues of power and control are amenable to a class analysis. However, the analysis and supporting research must take into account the actual class formation processes and practices of present-day, semi-industrial Peruvian capitalism, rather than imposing a ready-made scheme of social relations derived from other epochs and national experiences. The current realities of Peruvian capitalism will be shown by this study to include: (1) the economic preeminence of the modern, oligopolistic business corporation which, like its developed-country counterparts, is largely self-financed out of retained earnings and is controlled by professional managers whose positions in the cor-

---

[3] Sklar (1975:179).
[4] This concept was originated by Frank (1966, 1969). A convincing empirical refutation has been offered by Warren (1973).
[5] Cardoso (1973).
[6] Cardoso (1977).

porate hierarchy, and power, depend much more on expertise than on considerations of juridical ownership;[7] (2) a state that not only provides welfare benefits and a degree of income redistribution but also engages directly in industrial development and capital accumulation as well as in macroeconomic planning and management; (3) the presence of a new leading element of the local bourgeoisie—the "new bourgeoisie" of managers and technical specialists—whose members are based in both the private and public sectors and which has evolved into an ever more significant socioeconomic and political force; (4) transformed middle classes, most of whose integrants now fill middle-level professional, technical, and supervisory-administrative posts—class positions likewise determined by expertise gained through education—and have come to perceive greater opportunities than before for promotion into the bourgeoisie proper; and (5) a modern-sector working class that is far more skilled and secure in its conditions of employment,[8] far better organized, and far more active politically than was the case a decade or so ago.

The class analysis presented in this work will address the following questions: How has foreign investment in Peruvian mining affected class formation, class practices, and interclass relations? What kinds of relations does the "new bourgeoisie" maintain with other local bourgeois elements, with other classes, and with international capital? Are these sufficient to establish and maintain "new bourgeois" political dominance? If so, what form is that dominance apt to take, and why? Does the "new bourgeoisie" perceive a class interest in autonomous capitalist development in Peru under its aegis? Or are its international ties and concerns such that it uses its power to fortify foreign domination? Are the transformed middle classes sufficiently attracted by the upward mobility opportunities and other privileges available to them under the late-capitalist order that they will acquiesce in bourgeois sociopolitical hegemony? Or are they frustrated enough by "blocked ascent" and by an overweening foreign economic presence that they could be enlisted into a class alliance opposed to the existing system of domination? Is the modern-sector working class likely to use its relatively greater security and capabilities to become a leader, or a major component, of a radical socialist movement that could create serious problems for the capitalist status quo? Or do its members undergo a process of "embourgeoisement" in which they, too, become affiliated with a capitalist societal consensus in exchange for material benefits, some mobility chances, and a measure of political participation?

[7] Berle and Means (1932) were the first to call attention to these features of corporate organization in the modern age. Note that to accept this view of the nature of corporate control need not commit one to the position that managers' interests contradict those of juridical owners or their representatives, the corporation's directors; cf. Zeitlin (1974).

[8] This assertion obviously runs counter to the common belief that corporate enterprise in the Third World subsists on the basis of exploitation of cheap labor; that the highly capital-intensive production methods introduced there by transnational firms are designed to simplify tasks so as to reduce job skill requirements; and that, given low skill levels, wages are held down by the existence of a huge "industrial reserve army" of urban marginals. Nonetheless the assertion is accurate in Peru's case, as I will document in Chap. 10.

The state is the key institution through which political power is organized and social control exercised. Hence, no examination of power and control can afford to overlook the character of the state and its relationship to socioeconomic structures and institutions both local and external. The recent advances in the theory of the capitalist state make it impossible to go on treating the latter as either a monolithic "state-for-itself" or a mere executive committee of a dominant class. Rather, the state is "relatively autonomous," in the sense of possessing some initiative vis-à-vis the particular (especially short-run) interests of any private institution, class, or class stratum, and at the same time is itself an arena of class conflict whose actions manifestly affect class interests and power.[9]

Inasmuch as the state is not a simple instrumentality of a "ruling" class, it is not enough to ask who controls the state and to whose benefit does it act. We must also inquire as to changes in the state's institutional capabilities for organizing and controlling both internal politics and external relations on behalf of a set of interests that it attempts to project ideologically as being the general interest of Peruvian society.[10] Specifically, we must ask whether the transnational corporate presence results in a weakening or a strengthening of the state's control capabilities (including the will as well as the capacity to exert control) versus foreign and domestic forces.[11]

Documenting the inequities of capitalist development in Peru will not be a major theme of this book, since that task has already been performed by others.[12] It must not be forgotten, however, that capitalist development also produces counterforces, embodied in the subordinate but majoritarian classes of society, which are capable under certain conditions of exercising political power sufficient to impel the amelioration of some of the worst capitalist

[9] The nature of the capitalist state has been analyzed in these terms by Miliband (1969, 1973, 1977), Poulantzas (1969, 1973, 1975, 1976, 1978), and Gold et al. (1975).

[10] The role of the capitalist state in helping to project the interests of the bourgeoisie as the general interest of society, thereby legitimating bourgeois social dominance and laying the basis for consensus politics in capitalist society, is one of Antonio Gramsci's principal themes and is central to his concept of hegemony. I shall make frequent use of that concept in this work. Note that in addition to ideological projection, a hegemonic class needs an ability to accommodate to the most urgent demands of subordinate classes without a perceived loss of ultimate social control. Developed-country bourgeoisies have such ability; it is attested to by their acceptance of labor unions and the welfare state. On hegemony see Gramsci (1971, 1973), Adamson (1980), and Femia (1979).

[11] The dependency literature has not generally considered that the transnational presence may generate counterpressures as host states seek mechanisms enabling them to reassert control in the face of this relatively new challenge—which, of course, they would not have done had the challenge not appeared. One author who does recognize the importance of this reaction is Stepan (1978:234ff), who writes with particular reference to Peru. See also Ramirez and Thomas (1981).

[12] See Larson and Bergen (1969), Maletta (1978), Matos Mar et al. (1970), Petras and Havens (1979), and Quijano (1977). Note that the critique of Peruvian capitalist development began in the late twenties and early thirties with the writings of Mariátegui (1971) and Haya de la Torre (1936, 1956). Another reason why I will not dwell on this subject is that capitalism's production of gross socioeconomic inequities is hardly limited to Peru or to the present, but has been observed everywhere and in every epoch; so we are reminded by Adelman and Morris (1978) and by Ahluwalia (1976).

excesses. The appearance of these counterforces is another important part of the process of capitalist development in its political aspect. By examining their growth and effectiveness we may move beyond static description to embrace the issue of the immanent tendencies and probable future course of development in Peru.

Questions of popular power cannot be divorced from that of the internality or externality of political power. Now and for the foreseeable future, the political action of subordinate popular groups is and will be confined to the national stage. If, as dependencistas assert, the locus of power in less-developed societies like Peru's resides in the capitalist metropoli, then the popular sectors are excluded from the arena and have no possibility for successful political activity within its existing structures.[13] If, on the contrary, the locus of power is internal, then the relevant arena is one in which the popular sectors do have at least a potential for political self-help. Thus, the pressing issue with regard to the lot of the majority faced with capitalist exploitation is not whether capitalism intrinsically improves it—to all events an improbability. It is, instead, whether the course of development bids fair to propitiate the formation of a local political arena in which an effective popular-class practice is feasible; of popular classes capable of such practice; and of a dominant class or class element capable of accommodating to it without a perceived surrender of fundamental interests.

In this context, liberty and democracy are of vital concern. Marxists used to argue that bourgeois liberal democracy was progressive. Political liberties, though limited in scope by the nature of civil society and by the doctrine of individualism, would provide many more opportunities for the popular classes to gain political awareness and strength than would authoritarian rule. But it has lately become fashionable in some Leftist quarters to deprecate both liberal democracy and the liberal conception of individual rights with the claim that these are empty ideological devices for disguising capitalism's unpleasantries.[14] Yet, any real improvement in the quality of life of the people at large—

[13] For which reason many dependencistas urge a complete and immediate break with world capitalism, a rapid transition to "socialism," and autarkic development; see, for instance, Dos Santos (1977). Unfortunately, there is seldom much of an attempt to discover whether the social basis for such a new course exists; its presence is too often assumed a priori.

[14] An example is the discussion by Rubio and Bernales (1981) of Peru's 1980 constitution. To be sure, late-capitalist bourgeoisies may find less value for themselves in democratic political forms than did their market-capitalist predecessors; on this point see Jessop (1978), who concludes that there remains an objective bourgeois interest in democracy but of a corporatist rather than a liberal kind. The case against the liberal conception of individual rights is that it overlooks "social rights" deriving from, and/or necessitated by, membership in a social collectivity. However, as individual humans are real, sentient beings whereas all social structures and institutions are abstractions, there is a sense in which any humanistic, progressive conception of rights must always be referred back to the individual person. I fully agree, on the other hand, with Marx's tireless assertion—see, e.g., Marx (1975b), Avineri (1968:87-95)—that we are all social beings by nature and that a true human life outside of society is inconceivable: thence, "social rights." The problem with the liberal conception is only that it is incomplete.

the very definition of "development"[15]—depends upon their own political efforts, not the altruism of those in power. These efforts include not only revolutionary ones but also (and often, simultaneously) those aimed at forcing an accommodation from the system of power. Both kinds of effort can succeed only if there is high social cohesion and political-organizational capability among the popular majority. Those are much more likely to arise and to flourish where there is some freedom of association and communication and where a modicum of political participation exists.

For these reasons I shall try to discern whether Peruvian processes of capitalist development may bring forth new near-term possibilities for liberal-democratic stability, or whether the more probable outcome is some variant of authoritarian political monopoly.

Dependency versus "Post-Dependency"

The issues raised above are not of a sort that can be elucidated using state-centered analytic frameworks. Of the available frameworks which partake of the dependency paradigm in greater or lesser degree, the one that is most plainly ruled out by this criterion is the world-system theory associated with the name of Immanuel Wallerstein.[16] True, Wallerstein's framework links internal structures to external forces. It concentrates, however, upon expli-cating the relative positions of *states* within the "world-economy" according to the classification scheme, core-semiperiphery-periphery. For Wallerstein, a class analysis of "peripheral" societies is of secondary interest, since the class structures of those societies have already been specified from first prin-ciples once their "peripheral" status has been established.[17]

What I take to be the main body of present-day dependencismo offers two principal strands of thought from which we may draw. The first is essentially institutional. It strives to demonstrate how and why transnational corporate interests in profit, market share, and managerial control make impossible a capitalist strategy of development that would advance the quality of life of the majority of the population or transform and modernize the economy as a whole.[18] The problem with this approach is that it is quite easy to document the accuracy of the description; but it is exceedingly difficult at the institutional level of analysis to move beyond simple description in order to prove that what has occurred was inevitable and cannot be altered short of a drastic change in the system itself. Still, the study of institutional behavior is a

[15] Sklar (1975:179); also, Sklar (n.d.).

[16] Wallerstein (1974a, b, c).

[17] For Wallerstein, a location in the periphery of the "world-economy" necessarily entails reliance on coerced labor, implying class structures and relations adapted to coercive labor control. Critiques of Wallerstein's conceptions of class relations and of capitalism itself have been offered by, among others, Brenner (1977), Laclau (1971, 1977), and Skocpol (1977). Also see Sklar (1977) for an objection to the manner in which Wallerstein has conceptualized class.

[18] Examples of the genre include Barnet and Müller (1974), Evans (1971), Girvan (1970), Hymer (1972), Müller (1974), and Sunkel (1969, 1972). Also recommended is the case study of Brazilian development by Evans (1979).

necessary prelude to class analysis, for class interests and practices are most straightforwardly revealed in the character and conduct of institutions in which the various classes are involved. Key Peruvian mining-sector institutions are treated in this work. The treatment is empirical. It does not just confirm institutional forms and behaviors that have in reality been assumed a priori on the basis of "laws of motion of dependent capitalism."

The second strand consists in the search for a higher degree of sophistication in the class analysis of dependency. Modern dependencista class analysis, having surpassed simplistic "comprador" formulations,[19] generally argues that the key to external control is found in the fractionalization by late-capitalist development of each domestic class. Some class strata become associated with the modern, internationally linked capitalist sector, while others remain rooted in the traditional national sectors: agriculture, small-scale manufacturing, much of the service economy.[20] Fractionalization enables the state to attain a larger amount of "relative autonomy" with respect to civil society.[21] But state technocrats tend to share values and interests with private-sector managers, both domestic and foreign. Moreover, they realize that state revenues and economic (thence military) power—which they want to maximize— are basically dependent on the modern part of the economy, and that its health in turn depends on continuing inputs of capital and technology from abroad. Thus, a triad of state officials (including military officers), transnational corporate managers, and domestic manager-entrepreneurs captures the heights of the political economy. They are supported by those members of the middle classes who consume the kinds of durable goods that the transnationals specialize in producing and who aspire to upward mobility into the managerial-technocratic bourgeois stratum. Other class elements—the traditional national bourgeoisie, whose backward firms cannot compete with modern capitalist enterprise; and the popular classes, whose ability to consume has to be held in check in order to foster the high rate of capital accumulation which "associated-dependent development" requires—are pushed into opposition. The dominance of the triad is maintained by resort to authoritarian rule (necessary because the ruling coalition is numerically small) and by the diversity of interests among the opposition.[22]

[19] "Comprador" originally referred to indigenous merchants who cooperated in the early Spanish-Portuguese colonization of Africa in exchange for the profits they made once colonial trade came to be channeled through their hands. The word has since come to refer to any ruling group whose interests lead it to cooperate with foreigners who seek to dominate its country economically. Latin Americans usually prefer the term *entreguista*—from the verb *entregar*, meaning "to hand over."

[20] This thesis, set forth in great detail by Sunkel (1973), also animates the work of Cardoso (1973), Cardoso and Faletto (1979), and Dos Santos (1970).

[21] Bamat (1977) claims that the Peruvian state has become almost wholly autonomous of local class forces—which fact enables it to better serve as the handmaiden of foreign interests. I shall dispute both contentions in later chapters.

[22] This analysis is largely based on case studies of Argentina and Brazil, particularly the latter; see Cardoso (1972, 1973) and Skidmore (1973). The idea of the triad of power is due to O'Donnell (1978).

I am in full agreement with Cardoso and others that the central issues of Third World development must be studied in concrete social-historical settings; that the analysis must not predetermine the nature of the external-internal interaction; and that it must deal with the subject society in terms of structured conflict. Many, perhaps most dependencistas now agree and have ceased the pursuit of a will-o'-the-wisp "general theory of dependency."[23] But even concrete, historically grounded dependencista class analyses appear to suffer from four serious deficiencies:

1. Although it may be evident that late-capitalist development causes severe social and economic dislocations which harm large segments of the population, it still must be demonstrated why these change processes are correctly qualified as "dependent," viz., externally determined and implying a loss of control by the nation over its own future. The dependency literature has mostly failed to locate the "taproot of dependency"[24] directly in class practices observed in Third World societies. Instead, it has had to fall back upon very abstract, structuralist economic formulations that overlook both political and social dimensions as potential causal factors. It is posited that, due to the absence of extensive capital-goods sectors and the resultant inability to generate their own productive technologies, less-developed economies are subject to the external economic structures in which they must enmesh themselves in order, as Cardoso puts it, to "complete the cycle of capitalist reproduction."[25]

My case study presents, in Chapters 7 and 8, some evidence suggesting that this structuralist proposition understates the Peruvian capacity for capital goods and technology production. Surely, any attempt to offer the proposition as a general law of economic development would seem to be contradicted by the existence of smaller economies—Switzerland's, say, or Denmark's— which, though they do not autochthonously generate anything like the full range of goods and technologies required for the expanded reproduction of capital, can hardly be labeled "dependent" in the usual sense of the term. Further, the assertion that a national bourgeoisie fractionated into international-modern and national-traditional elements cannot lead a process of autonomous capitalist development is rarely supported by empirical research on the practices of the bourgeois class—particularly, its relation to state power and to the popular classes.

2. It is proper that the class analysis of "dependent" societies treat issues of national unity, cohesiveness, and autonomy. Nevertheless, there is little justification for populist antagonism, as found in much of the dependency literature, toward social changes implying the transference from abroad of

---

[23] Cardoso (1977), Cardoso and Faletto (1979:vii-xxv), and Palma (1978). There are, of course, those who have not abandoned the chase: e.g., Amin (1974, 1976). For a devastating critique of Amin's effort see S. Smith (1980).

[24] I use this term with apologies to Hobson (1938), who wrote in a similar spirit of the "taproot of imperialism."

[25] Cardoso (1972). Dos Santos (1970) has a near-identical view of the "taproot of dependency" in the modern age.

new values, ideas, and social models. *Ideas and values, in and of themselves, have no nationality*. As to social models, Latin America has long been part of a broadly Western political, cultural, and social tradition. Were it not, it would still not be self-evident that the local adaptation of many originally Western socioeconomic, political, and cultural modalities means a loss of national identity; nor does their mere presence confirm that they have been externally imposed and do not answer to local needs. This is especially so, I submit, with respect to the rise of a late-capitalist "new bourgeoisie," a principal topic of this book. Absent the evidence, one cannot properly regard technocracy and managerialism as foreign imports without domestic roots— as, for example, Guillermo O'Donnell has done in his discussion of the origins of "bureaucratic-authoritarianism."[26]

In addition, Latin American dependencistas have frequently put forth the claim that no capitalist state in their region can be legitimate if it is not explicitly concerned with the promotion of national socioeconomic integration and with the revindication of popular demands.[27] These, it is true, are functions which the late-capitalist Latin American state performs fitfully at best. It is also true that the "Iberic-Latin" political tradition is neither liberal nor individualist and probably does emphasize these functions more than is customary in the political systems of the developed West.[28] However, political traditions are not immutable. At a minimum, research must remain open to the possibility that the societal changes wrought by the implantation of late capitalism have established a new basis for political legitimation.

3. Several authors have recently remarked upon the lack of attention to the nature of *working-class* formation and practice that typifies much of dependencismo.[29] Even though this is a surprising weakness for a body of thought that claims a sympathy with Marxism and an allegiance to socialist alternatives to capitalist development, the criticism is, in my opinion, valid. Working classes are commonly *assumed* to be socialist and revolutionary—the assumption being based, like as not, on such tenuous foundations as labor leaders' *pronunciamientos*.[30] Or the opposite tack is taken: the modern-sector working class is dismissed with the pejorative phrase, "labor aristocracy,"

[26] O'Donnell (1973:30ff, 75-82). Since, in his view, technocracy represents no national need, technocrats can only retain political power and socioeconomic privilege by restructuring their societies so that it does. And, for the same reason, that restructuring lacks a wide constituency and thus has to be carried out under authoritarian protection and control.

[27] O'Donnell (1979) is specific on this point. Cardoso is less so. Yet, he is clearly concerned with what he believes to be the "denationalizing" propensities of the "new dependency." He has written, e.g., that ". . . as the process of internationalization of dependent nations progresses, it becomes difficult to perceive the political process in terms of a struggle between the Nation and the anti-Nation. . . . The anti-Nation will be inside the 'Nation'—so to speak, among the local people in different social strata. . . . [T]he Nation is an occupied one. . . ." Cardoso (1972). See also the quotation reproduced on p. 4 above.

[28] On the illiberal nature of the "Iberic-Latin" tradition see Wiarda (1973).

[29] See Henfrey (1981) and Sofer (1980).

[30] This approach is taken by Quijano (1972, 1973, 1977) when he writes on Peruvian labor.

and the mantle of socialist consciousness and revolutionary fervor is placed instead on the shoulders of the masses marginalized by development.[31]

To concentrate upon bourgeois "fractions" to the exclusion of empirical examination of working-class formation and practices is to engage in elite, not class, analysis. It is to view the political process as a "circulation of elites," ignoring the dialectics of conflict and change. What is more, the marginalized masses are a weak reed indeed on which to rest hopes and strategies for the transcendence of capitalism. History teaches that these are as likely to form the backbone of popular support for fascism and other capitalist "regimes of exception."[32]

4. In terms, finally, of research methodology, a litmus test for the absence of dependency cannot consist of cultural "purity," economic autarky, socialism, and/or total freedom of national action, as dependencismo seems to imply. *Every* instance of successful development has entailed a borrowing of "alien" ideas and strategies for extended periods of time. Nor can the foregoing "test" anything, since all nonautarkic and nonsocialist development becomes "dependent" *by definition.*[33] The real test of dependency can only be the existence of a "dominant" class which exercises proximate control over the society and profits from the political and economic decisions adopted by the local state, but which has minimal real influence over the externally imposed choice of development strategies and cannot control more than details of their implementation. *It is no proof of the existence of this sort of passive bourgeoisie that private entrepreneurs do not behave in a Schumpeterian manner*; i.e., that they rely heavily on state guidance and protection, and/or on specific arrangements with foreign investors, for much of their earnings.[34] What matters is whether or not they define and pursue their interests in a way that encompasses a progressive transformation of the nation of which they are a part.

It may be that these problems and deficiencies of the dependency paradigm have to do with very recent changes in the international capitalist order, which may no longer be structured as dependencismo says. If so, a new paradigm, not just a modified analytic framework, is called for. Sklar has challenged dependencista thought from a class-analytic standpoint that attempts to revise the orthodox Marxist-Leninist teachings about imperialism.[35] He argues that

---

[31] The *locus classicus* is Fanon (1963). Amin (1980a, b) proceeds similarly.

[32] Such was, as is well known, the opinion of Marx (1963b).

[33] This is one of the core arguments advanced by Packenham (1978).

[34] The point is made by Wils (1979) in his examination of the conduct of Peruvian entrepreneurs. Earlier, Gerschenkron (1962) noted and explained a correlation between the tardiness of development and the degree to which state, rather than private, institutions guided the development process. He did not, however, find a relationship between the extent of state involvement and the *success* of development strategies in attaining their goals. The contrasting view of the "heroic" entrepreneur whose private initiatives transform society is found in Schumpeter (1935, 1942).

[35] Sklar (1976).

potentially "geocentric" transnational firms[36] have begun to integrate the world economy in a manner that is overcoming the structural limitations of Lenin's day—limitations that led to interimperialist rivalry among metropolitan states.[37] The shift in corporate perspectives from a national to a global plane has been marked by a concomitant process of transnational class formation. Sklar perceives a cosmopolitan international bourgeoisie, the product of transnational corporate action, whose interests transcend the political interests of its members' home states. Furthermore, the international bourgeoisie has found the means for harmonizing its global interests with the national aspirations of the various countries in which transnational subsidiaries operate; its ideological *doctrine of domicile* posits "that there is no necessary inconsistency between the properly defined claims of foreign ownership . . . and uncompromising loyalty to the [host] government on the part of those who are collectively responsible for the [subsidiary's] performance."[38] Accordingly, the stage has been set for the emergence in less-developed countries of dominant class strata which *do* have a class interest in national development but which simultaneously participate as junior partners[39] in the international bourgeoisie.

Unlike the compradors who preceded them, these dominant classes can ideologically identify their concerns with widely held national goals, so that the parochial aspects of their interests are concealed. Late-capitalist forms, culture, and values *are* imposed, but in a different way from the dependencista conception. The leading bourgeois strata interact with both metropolitan and local societies, since they have interests in each. In interacting with the former they partake of Western, capitalist values; and in interacting with the latter they impose metropolitan values *because to do so is in their self-interest*. Succinctly stated, the leading strata are the economic and political hinge points between local societies and the metropoli. Yet, inasmuch as these strata need no longer opt for *either* national *or* metropolitan concerns, they can be nationalist and developmentalist without contradicting their international interests. As their dominance is not narrowly self-serving, it does not need to rest on coercive force and can coexist with formal democracy. The reality, Sklar suggests, is a new, "postimperialist" phase of capitalist development shorn of paleo- and neo-colonialism.

"Postimperialism" or "post-dependency," as a paradigmatic conception, appears to improve on the deficient dependencista grasp of domination without

[36] The term "geocentric" was coined by Perlmutter (1970).

[37] Lenin (1933); cf. Hobson (1938).

[38] The idea of the "doctrine of domicile" is expounded by Sklar (1975:182-88). On p. 184 (whence the material quoted in the text) he goes on to say that "[i]n general, the doctrine maintains that affiliates of international business corporations are truly able to conform to the policies and national interests of their host governments irrespective of the policies and interests of other governments, *including the governments of those relatively powerful countries where parent companies are likely to reside* [emphasis added]."

[39] The imagery is deliberate. A junior partner is less powerful and influential than a senior partner but is, nonetheless, far more than a dependent or servant.

sacrificing dependencismo's progressive value commitments. This study will test the "post-dependency" hypothesis.

The Tools of Analysis

Since a number of the core concepts to be employed in this work are habitually approached differently by different authors, it behooves me to specify at the outset my understanding of power, development, and class formation.

I hold that power, conceived as a capacity for social control, derives from monopolization of scarce societal resources, most—but not all—of them economic. Alternative power resources are distinguishable in theory yet inseparable in political practice. Specifically, economic power *is* political.[40] On the other hand, control of the means of production is not the sole source of power. Control of the state's "monopoly of the legitimate use of force in the enforcement of its order" is assuredly a power resource.[41] Another is technological, managerial, or administrative expertise. Even the job skills of blue-collar workers can constitute a power resource if the latter cannot then be readily replaced, if they are employed in a sector on which the health of the whole economy crucially depends, and if they can organize so as to be able to threaten the massive withdrawal of their labor.

Development, as I have previously stated, consists in an improvement in the quality of life of the people at large. So conceived it is inherently multifaceted; for "quality of life" embraces not just material well-being but the enjoyment of nonmaterial goods as well. The most vital of these is freedom: the ability to exercise control over the directions of one's life and to participate as an equal in the making of authoritative decisions binding upon the collectivity of which one is a member.

I have already described the political aspect of development. There are also economic and social aspects. The first is conventionally defined as the harnessing of science to productive technology, with the result that a given expenditure of labor time by the society produces an ever-increasing volume of more varied goods with a higher technological content. In effect this means industrialization. The second aspect, the social, entails the reorganization of human relationships—partly to accommodate the requisites of new modes of production; and partly to vitalize new societal norms stressing progress, freedom, and personal fulfillment over stasis, ascriptive authority, and conformity to tradition.

The aspects of development are interdependent. However, their interde-

---

[40] See Lynd (1943).

[41] The phrase quoted in this sentence is from Weber (1978:1:54). Sklar (1977, 1979), following Ossowski (1963), proposes that class power can derive from control of the means of production *or* compulsion *or* consumption. The last two refer to the state and political system: the former obviously so; the latter in regard to the economic planning, redistributive, and welfare functions of the modern state.

pendence is better expressed as a dialectical, tensive accumulation of actions and reactions rather than as a unilinear causal series.

Class formation relates to the capacity for collective action on the part of structured societal groups. The key determinants of class are those which create *interests* that are amenable to pursuit via collective political action and not those which merely define a *position* in a socioeconomic structure. The fundamental interest of any class always lies with political power and social control, as these are the means for securing all other advantages and privileges.

Classes are theoretician's constructs with no real existence beyond that of the individual men and women who compose them.[42] What makes them relevant categories for political analysis is the fact that their integrants tend to flock together socially and to act together politically in pursuit of their common interests, employing for the purpose their common, pooled power resources. Therefore, I shall concentrate in this study on those aspects of class which most closely pertain to interest-based, purposive collective behavior: to wit, class identification, cohesion, organization, and political practice,[43] all of which represent forms of class action. (*Class* action is that which tends to enhance the social control exercised by a dominant class, if the latter is the actor; or to weaken it, if a subordinate class is the actor.) I shall treat abstract, static aspects of class determination only to the extent that seems necessary for a sound understanding of the politically more central class phenomena.

As delimited by the nature of my concerns, then, class formation is the process by which individuals (1) become aware that they share specific interests and a specific orientation toward the existing mechanisms of power and control; (2) form social bonds on the basis of that mutuality of interest and commonality of orientation; (3) organize to secure more effectively advantages for themselves; and (4) collectively employ their political assets to that end. (In some instances, particularly when dealing with the formation of a dominant class, it is useful to think of elites rather than individuals as the units which participate in this process.) Class formation as herein defined corresponds generally to the Marxian idea of a transition to the condition of a class *für sich*.[44] The purpose of the empirical investigation of class formation is to comprehend the basis and character of class domination and practice. This is an especially important analytic task when confronting the politics of a developing country like Peru, where, as a consequence of development itself, class structures and relationships are in a state of flux.

[42] Cf. Poulantzas (1973, 1975). In Poulantzas's "structural Marxist" theory, classes are the reality, and their human integrants are described merely as "bearers" of systemically defined class relationships. His disclaimers to the contrary notwithstanding, Poulantzas verged closer in his conception of class to Platonic Idealism than to the materialism which most Marxists hold as their philosophical and epistemological underpinning.

[43] These concepts are discussed by Sklar (1977).

[44] Marx (1963a).

The book is organized into four parts and a separate concluding chapter. Part I, including the present chapter, furnishes the background for the study. Chapter 2 describes Peru's economy, geography and geology, political system, and mining industry organization and economic role. Chapter 3 treats the nature, objectives, and formulation of the military regime's mining policies, relating them to the regime's other political and economic goals. It also discusses the minor changes that have been introduced by the civilian administration which returned to power on July 28, 1980. Chapter 4 examines the world nonferrous metals industry, its effect on the behavior of the firms, and its underpinning of transnational class formation.

Part II is an institutional analysis of the principal transnational mining companies operating in Peru and of their interactions with the state. Chapter 5 takes up the successful adaptation of one firm to a new political environment after 1968; Chapter 6, the decline and fall of another, as well as its progress after its expropriation. These chapters reveal why one firm was better able to defer to local policy dictates than the other; and why the state responded to each of them as it did. The two chapters also compare institutional dependency and "post-dependency" propositions relating to the transnationals' supposed ability to force host-state compliance with the desires and preferences of foreign capital.

Part III investigates the economic foundations of the Peruvian mining bourgeoisie. Chapter 7 examines medium-scale local and foreign private enterprise; Chapter 8, state (parastatal) enterprise. These chapters document the technical-managerial character of the class element, its links to capital ownership, and its nationalism-developmentalism. They critically evaluate dependency propositions which imply the subservience of local entrepreneurship to transnational capital.

Part IV details the formation, structure, ideology, and practices of the "new bourgeoisie," middle class, and working class of the mining sector. Chapter 9 treats the bourgeoisie and middle class, with emphasis on the former's class character, international ties, relations with the middle class, and potential for ideological hegemony. Chapter 10 treats the formation, character, and practice of the working class, showing why current working-class aspirations can be met within the reformed capitalist order. Both chapters discuss the role of transnational enterprise in class formation.

Chapter 11, lastly, suggests an alternative way of conceptualizing local class dominance and class-state relations in a Third World increasingly under the sway of transnational late capitalism. It points up the prospects and limitations of the Peruvian mode of development and considers its applicability to other national situations.

CHAPTER TWO

Peru: *Un País Minero*

A nation of 18 million people in possession of the third largest political subdivision of South America, Peru is one of the three Andean countries (with Bolivia and Ecuador) where pockets of Inca-era peasant culture can still be found. That fact has endeared it to tourists and anthropologists alike. It has also conjured up in many minds an image of an urban-based, mostly white, culturally Western elite riding herd over a far larger rural, mostly Indian, culturally traditional mass. Such an image was quite valid thirty years ago.[1] It has since become far less so.

Modern Peru is a racially mixed, urban-centered society that may well be less culturally heterogeneous, on the whole, than is the United States. Waves of internal migration have brought the sons and daughters of upland peasants to the coastal cities and mountain mining centers, where they have become *cholified*—that is, have adopted Western ways, Spanish speech, and the predominant "criollo" culture. Some descendants of earlier arrivals have recently risen to membership in the nation's political and economic elites. Less than 41 percent of the economically active population is currently employed in agriculture (much of it still quite traditional), whereas 33.7 percent finds employment in the modern sector: in manufacturing, mining, construction, transport and communications, and commerce.[2] Human development, as measured by school attendance, adult literacy, and infant mortality rates, has been rapid, particularly since 1960.[3] Industrial output has risen steadily during the last twenty or so years; if we exclude the small countries of the region that began from an exceptionally low base, the only Latin American nation with a higher industrial growth rate for 1960-1977 is Brazil.

However, this undeniable progress has been insufficient to elevate the country from its status as a politically weak, economically underdeveloped member of the Third World of "peripheral" nations. Table 2.1, a summary

[1] On social structure and culture in the Peru of the fifties and sixties, see Bourricaud (1966, 1970) and Larson and Bergen (1969).

[2] Wilkie and Reich (1980:167).

[3] In 1960, 89 percent of children in the appropriate age group were enrolled in primary schools, 18 percent in secondary schools; adult (over seventeen years of age) literacy was 61 percent. The comparable figures for 1970 were 115, 41, and 72 percent (where "adult" now refers to anyone over fifteen years of age). The mortality rate among children 0-4 years of age was 15.7 per thousand inhabitants in 1960-1962, the fifth highest in Latin America; by 1970 it had declined to 7.9 per thousand inhabitants, giving Peru the twelfth highest rate in the region. Wilkie and Reich (1977:31, 32).

of some commonly accepted indicators of development, shows not only that Peru still lags far behind the United States on all per capita development indices but also that its progress in recent years has been slower than that of other nations of the region. Value added in manufacturing has generally constituted a lower proportion of gross domestic product than the Latin American average. Worse, GDP per capita grew at an average annual rate of but 1.7 percent from 1966 to 1976, placing Peru thirteenth in economic growth among the twenty Latin American republics—whose combined average GDP per capita growth rate in the period was 3.8 percent per year. Life expectancy at birth in 1975-1980 was 57.2 years, lower than in all save the most backward countries of the hemisphere: Bolivia, Haiti, Honduras, and Nicaragua.[4]

A principal reason for Peru's persistent inability to "take off" economically is the stagnation of agriculture. For many years it suffered the worst maldistribution of landholdings in all of Latin America and probably in the world: 83.4 percent of the individual holdings were *minifundios* of five hectares or less, totaling 5.8 percent of the land under cultivation; whereas the 0.1 percent of the holdings in estates greater than 2,500 hectares monopolized 60.1 percent of the cultivated land.[5] The large landholdings in the irrigated valleys along the Pacific coast were given over by their absentee landlords, many of them domestic and foreign agribusiness corporations, to the capitalist production of cash crops—sugar, cotton, rice—and agroindustrial derivatives for export. These agribusinesses earned good profits because they were modern and efficiently managed. The haciendas of the Andean highlands were not. They were, with few exceptions, semifeudal manors whose peasants produced food crops, wool, and a little meat with techniques and forms of work relations not much changed from those of the Inca. An extensive land reform, begun

TABLE 2.1 Indicators of Development for Peru (*Data are for 1975 unless otherwise noted*)

Indicator (per Capita)	Peru	USA	Peru's Rank in Latin America	
			1975	1960
Number of radios	0.131	1.882	8	6
Number of automobiles	0.018[a]	0.434	9	8
Newsprint consumption (kg/yr)	4.7	45.3	4	1
Steel production (met.tons/yr)	28.4	496.3	6	7
Energy consumption (kg coal equiv./yr)	682	10,999	8	8
Electric power consumption (kwh/yr)	531	9,370	9	8

SOURCES: Wilkie and Reich (1977:44, 271-72); (1980:55-64, 164, 217, 238, 253).
[a] Datum is for 1974.

[4] Wilkie and Reich (1980:6, 259, 283).
[5] Wilkie and Reich (1977:61). The data are for 1961.

in 1969, wrought major alterations in the nature of land distribution but was unaccompanied by sufficient technical assistance, agricultural credit, and market price incentives for the new proprietors. Consequently, per capita food production in 1977 had fallen 15.7 percent below the level attained in 1966. No other Latin American country's agricultural sector has performed worse than Peru's in terms of food production.[6]

GEOGRAPHY AND GEOLOGY

The Inca empire was able to support a population of some 5 millions in the highlands of present-day Bolivia, northern Chile, Peru, and Ecuador, but solely by dint of effective social organization and rigid regimentation of the entire populace. Peru's geography and climate have been even less kind to the development aims of a latter-day civilization that has generally lacked the first, that has never attempted the second, and that has compounded its difficulties by aspiring to a standard of living of which the Inca never dreamed.

The Andean cordillera, traversable only by a few secondary roads, two rail links, and one all-weather highway, divides the country into three zones (Fig. 1). The coastal strip is a harsh desert unsuited to agriculture except in a few widely spaced river valleys (one being the Rímac basin in which the capital, Lima, and its port, Callao, are located); however, most of the population resides there, and all modern manufacturing activity other than mining and the processing of mine products is located there. The Andean uplands, or sierra, are the home of the traditional peasantry, which farms the steep hillsides much as its pre-Columbian ancestors did; the extreme altitudes (the *floors* of the main valleys lie above 3,500 meters), fragile ecology, broken terrain that resists agricultural mechanization, and short growing season conspire to keep agricultural productivity low. The trans-Andean zone, the selva, has become the source of most of Peru's oil but is almost completely unpopulated (save for aboriginal tribes) and undeveloped except along the eastern slopes of the mountains—the *ceja de selva*—which are farmed for maize, tropical tubers, fruits, coffee, and coca. This region offers tremendous prospects for future development (the Peruvian military is especially anxious to establish a stronger national presence there lest neighboring Brazil cast a covetous eye on the oil reserves), but they will not be realized until transport and communications improve enough to integrate the area into the national market.

However unfavorable the topography and climate, they are compensated for by a geology unusually well endowed in minerals of commercial importance. Indeed, there is no part of the Andean chain that does not contain at least one active mine or mineral deposit of commercial value. The country has the largest yet-undeveloped copper reserves (proved and probable) of any Third World nation. The Marcona mine, in the coastal region not far from

[6] Calculated from Wilkie and Reich (1980:197).

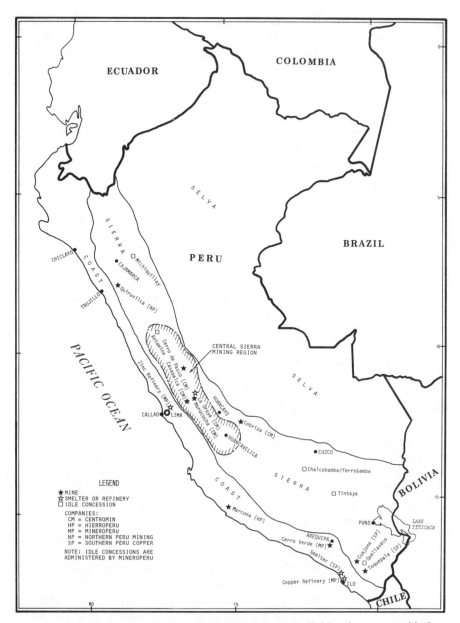

FIGURE 1. Outline map of Peru, showing the country's division into geographical regions and the locations of the principal mining centers.

the famous Plains of Nazca, has iron ore reserves sufficient for more than a century's worth of steel production at current or probable future levels; coking coal, while not as abundant, is available and could be developed more thoroughly than it has been. The sierra is dotted with polymetallic mineral deposits rich in lead, nickel, silver, tungsten, zinc, and all sorts of minor industrial metals (Peru is the world's largest producer of one of these, bismuth). Current prices have made gold mining and dredging worthwhile. There are few known mineral deposits that are not being actively mined, and it is thus understandable why Peruvians refer to their country as *un país minero*. But Peru need not remain forever a mineral storehouse supplying industries elsewhere. The Andean topography provides great hydroelectric potential, and the recent petroleum discoveries represent another important source of energy. With its existing resource endowment and given further energy development, the country could easily become a regional center of heavy industry, a kind of South American Ruhr Basin.

THE ECONOMY

The Nature of Economic Organization

The country's economy is capitalist. In the 1969-1975 period some private businesses were nationalized and a number of new parastatal enterprises were established. There were experiments in worker comanagement and industrial cooperativism, or "social property."[7] The haciendas expropriated in the 1969 agrarian reform were reorganized as collective farms rather than being distributed to peasants as private property.[8] None of this, however, seriously altered the economic preeminence of private capital. Moreover, the "social property" experiment has since been abandoned, and the civilian government elected in 1980 has begun to float proposals for breaking up and privatizing the agricultural collectives.

Private industrial capital in Peru is owned by a minuscule number of individuals and families. Most are former members of the large-landlord class or of a class element of commercial-financial capitalists allied with them; they were known collectively as "the oligarchy." In industrial investment oligarchs have acted as passive rentiers, turning the management of their firms over to professionals (of whom there is no local shortage). The concentration of money capital in few oligarchic hands has produced an industrial economy characterized by a small number of modern corporations in command of the "heights," a far larger number of artisan workshops in the "lowlands," and

[7] See Jiménez (1974) and Knight (1975) for details. Comanagement is discussed at length and in comparative perspective by Stephens (1980).

[8] Bourque and Palmer (1975); and Harding (1975).

a paucity of intermediate-scale, owner-managed enterprises in between.[9] One sign of this disparity is that Peru ranks fourth in Latin America in the proportion of professionals and technicians (middle managers) in the economically active population, but only seventeenth in the proportion engaged in business management.[10]

Whereas most of the larger Latin American countries experienced a boom in import-substitution industrialization during the 1930s, widespread industrialization did not really get under way in Peru until some twenty years later. But it has since advanced at an accelerating pace—most notably after 1968, when active state promotion of industrial development became the keystone of economic policy. Industrial production increased at a 9.1 percent average annual rate in 1969-1975; this may be compared to the 1960-1969 average of 7.2 percent, starting from a much lower base.[11] In 1977, industrial activities (mining and manufacturing) contributed 29.9 percent of GDP, while agriculture's contribution was just 15.2 percent.[12] The bulk of manufactured goods are destined for the domestic market, although Peruvian manufacturers, thanks to state subsidies, perceived limitations of the internal market, and the stimulation of the Andean Common Market,[13] have lately shown more of an interest in export promotion. Industrial development has not proceeded far enough to eliminate economic extraversion, however. Peru must still import many consumer durables in addiṭon to most of her capital goods and a significant proportion of her industrial raw materials and intermediate goods. She pays for these by exporting primarily metals, minerals, and agricultural products.

Tables 2.2 and 2.3 outline the principal dimensions of Peruvian foreign trade. Mineral exports (including petroleum) increased their share of total export value by more than 34 percent from 1960 to 1980, during which time a correspondingly dramatic falloff in agricultural and marine commodity exports was registered. These data, as well as the increase in "other" exports (many of which are manufactured goods), are another indicator of the country's industrial advance.[14] Peru has succeeded in diversifying her trade partners. As Table 2.3 indicates, this has mainly been accomplished by shifting sales and purchases away from the United States and the European Economic

[9] Artisan industries employing one to four persons made up 92 percent of the industrial establishments in the Lima-Callao metropolitan area (where the nation's industries are concentrated) in 1966 but accounted for just 1.8 percent of industrial output (Instituto Nacional de Planificación, 1966). Later data, were it available, would probably show some decline in the first figure and a greater decline in the second.

[10] Wilkie and Reich (1977:192).

[11] My computation, based on data in Wilkie and Reich (1980:219).

[12] Economic Commission for Latin America (1978:395).

[13] Peru was the primary instigator of the Pact of Cartagena that established the Andean Common Market and has consistently been the pact's most avid supporter.

[14] Because mine products only leave the country after undergoing a good deal of industrial processing, in many cases to refined metal. Note, however, that the precipitous fall in agricultural export percentages between 1960 and 1980 reflects the general decrease in agricultural output that was mentioned earlier.

TABLE 2.2 Peruvian Exports by Product, 1960 and 1980

Product	1960 A	1960 B	1980 A	1980 B
Petroleum products	4.1	—	21.9	—
Major mine products	43.9	45.8	42.6	54.6
Copper	21.9	22.9	17.6	22.5
Iron ore	7.6	7.9	2.5	3.2
Lead	5.1	5.3	2.7	3.5
Silver	5.6	5.8	14.8	19.0
Zinc	3.7	3.9	5.0	6.4
Major agricultural products	44.2	54.2	10.7	13.7
Coffee	4.3	4.5	3.7	4.7
Cotton	16.9	17.6	2.0	2.6
Fishmeal	12.0	12.5	4.7	6.0
Sugar	11.0	11.5	0.3	0.4
Other products	7.8	8.1	24.8	31.7
Total	100.0	100.0	100.0	100.0

SOURCE: Computed by the author from data furnished by the Banco Central de Reserva del Perú and by the Departamento de Estudios Económicos y Estadística, Sociedad Nacional de Minería y Petróleo.
NOTE: Columns A = percent of total value; columns B = percent of total value excluding petroleum products.

Community (in percentage terms; absolute trade value has risen in both instances) and toward such nontraditional trading partners as Japan, the Soviet bloc, and, especially, other Latin American nations. Finally, Peru has not been a victim of secularly declining terms of trade; rather, her terms of trade have fluctuated irregularly with metals prices and show a long-term tendency toward stability.[15]

The economy is further characterized by a heavy foreign investor presence, most of it in the guise of local subsidiaries of transnational corporations.[16] The oligarchy, which dominated Peruvian politics until the military *coup d'état* of 1968, was less interested in protecting domestic industry and more interested in free trade than a dominant class of industrial entrepreneurs would

[15] The argument that the economic development of Latin America has been held back by secularly declining terms of trade is associated with the U.N. Economic Commission for Latin America (ECLA), which began to analyze the problem in the 1950s; see Prebisch (1963). FitzGerald's (1976:14) data show an improvement in Peru's terms of trade from 1960 to 1972. ECLA (1978:404) data indicate that 1977 terms of trade were very slightly lower than those in 1973, an extraordinarily good year for metals prices.

[16] Wils (1979:28) states that foreign ownership of 51 percent or more is found in 37 percent of all medium- and large-scale industrial enterprises in the Lima-Callao area and in 54 percent of the thirty-nine largest (in terms of gross production value) industrial companies.

TABLE 2.3 Peruvian Exports and Imports by Destination or Source, 1962 and 1980 (*Percent of total value except as noted*)

Country or Region	Exports		Imports	
	1962	1980	1962	1980
United States	34.9	30.0	39.6	28.9
Canada	0.4	0.7	2.2	2.4
Latin America	10.0	16.0	9.9	30.3
Britain	9.7	3.8	6.4	4.3
EEC countries (excluding Britain)[a]	31.6	16.2	25.7	14.6
Japan	6.5	12.0	5.4	7.4
OPEC nations	0.0[b]	0.0[b]	0.0	0.0
Soviet bloc	0.4	9.9	0.3	1.3
Other	6.5	10.8	10.5	10.8
Total	100.0	100.0	100.0	100.0
Total trade value ($ millions)	539.4	1,665.8	537.4	1,598.3

SOURCE: Computed by the author from data furnished by the Banco Central de Reserva del Perú and by the Departamento de Estudios Económicos y Estadística, Sociedad Nacional de Minería y Petróleo.
[a] Denmark and Ireland added to 1962 data (they were not then EEC members) in order to provide an equivalent data base for both years.
[b] Less than 0.1 percent.

have been. In consequence, economic policy was much less nationalistic and protectionist than was the case, say, in Argentina, Brazil, Chile, or Mexico. Not only domestic private enterprise but also state enterprise was and is less of a contributor to industrial output than is so in these four other nations.

Money and Monetary Policy

The monetary unit is the sol. There was in Peru a traditional preoccupation with the soundness of the currency. Policy strove, even (if necessary) at a sacrifice of economic growth, to keep the value of the sol stable and high in relation to the U.S. dollar and to do so without resort to exchange controls. Devaluation became unavoidable by 1967, however, at which time controls were applied. The military government continued them in force and resisted further devaluation for a number of reasons, not the least being the widespread belief that the value of the sol was a matter of national prestige.

In 1975 the country began to be shaken by the same sort of structural inflation that has long gripped many of the more industrialized Latin American economies; since then, all efforts to stabilize the currency have proved futile. Except for very brief periods, though, the government has steadfastly rejected IMF strictures against currency controls. Instead, the sol is devalued daily, but under control, so that the official exchange rate stays close to the free-market rate. The rate has fallen from S/38.7 to the dollar in 1967-1974 to S/200 in 1978 and to S/800 as of late 1982.

Table A.2, in Appendix A, reveals how inflation has affected the average consumer price index. After rising by only 8 percent per year from 1968 to 1973, the index increased more rapidly each year thereafter. In 1980 the rate of inflation reached 69.4 percent.

Wherever possible I have converted financial data from soles to current dollars at the average rate of exchange for the year in question. The principal exceptions are wages and salaries, which mostly remain in soles. I have done this to avoid misleading impressions, for it is notoriously difficult to compare purchasing power of wages in two national economies as different as those of Peru and the United States.

THE POLITICAL SYSTEM

The Peruvian political system functioned until 1980 under a constitution written in 1933. Both the 1933 and 1980 constitutions provide for government institutions that are highly centralized in the French manner. The country is subdivided into twenty-four departments (Fig. 2), each headed by an appointed prefect who answers to the Ministry of the Interior, thence into provinces and districts (each with a subprefect), and finally into *municipalidades* governed by elected *alcaldes* (mayors) and councils.[17] There is a bicameral legislature (it did not sit during the years of military rule) and a quasi-independent judiciary. The president of the republic is elected for a five-year term.[18] He appoints a Council of Ministers headed by a prime minister and composed of the heads of the functional executive departments. Military presidents during 1968-1980 were also assisted by a Presidential Advisory Council—the COAP—made up of senior officers of the armed services; its approval was required for all major legislation and policy initiatives. As in France, the president is empowered to rule by decree in emergencies, and his cabinet is always responsible to him alone. All legislation adopted by the military regime was promulgated in the form of decree-laws under the emergency provisions of the 1933 constitution.[19]

In reality the powers of Peru's civilian presidents are considerably weaker than those of their counterparts in the French Fifth Republic. There are three reasons for this debility. The first is the political independence of the armed forces, whose responsibility, according to both constitutions, is primordially owed to the abstract concept of the nation rather than to the civil authority of the state. The armed forces deposed civilian presidents three times since 1933 (in 1948, 1962, and 1968) and, it is clear, will do so again should the

[17] Under the military regime these officials were appointed.
[18] He can be reelected, but only after a lapse of one complete term. The provisions of the 1933 constitution were the same except that the presidential term was six years.
[19] The 1980 constitution restricts the president's use of emergency powers.

FIGURE 2. Outline map of Peru, showing the country's political subdivisions, departmental capitals, and major population centers.

president seem incapable of maintaining civil order, support policies or parties apparently opposed to the essential interests of the military establishment, or fail to protect adequately the sovereignty of the state against foreign economic or political pressure—this an innovation that first appeared with the 1968 coup.

The second reason is the absence of securely institutionalized political parties. Scores of parties have arisen and disappeared in the course of Peruvian history; few of them have been more than coalitions of the moment or vehicles for advancing the political career of a specific individual.[20] The programmatic parties, such as the Communists and the Christian Democrats, have not had the necessary following seriously to contest national elections. The one exception is the Alianza Popular Revolucionaria Americana (APRA), founded in 1924 and led continuously until his death in 1979 by Víctor Raúl Haya de la Torre. An amazingly complex man, the APRA's *jefe máximo* was, simultaneously or by turns, a charismatic populist leader, a socioeconomic and political theorist, and a cynical political tactician. His party was for many years the only true popular political movement in the country. It was able to hold that position because Haya cleverly adapted his early Marxism to Peruvian realities, emphasizing middle-class leadership of the popular classes and the necessity of living with foreign investment until a higher level of capitalist development was reached.[21] Unfortunately for him and his party, Haya's choice of tactics was less clever. An initially insurrectionary stance promptly alienated the military (which otherwise came to share many of the APRA's ideas about economic development), with the result that every one of the three coups referred to above was undertaken in part to prevent the APRA from assuming power. Later he switched to a policy of tactical cooperation with the dominant Right in exchange for favors that were intended to improve the party's future electoral chances. But the policy did not attain any of its ends; it merely drove out the party's ideologically radical wing, whose ex-members have since swelled the ranks of the "New Left."

The third reason has to do with the ability of the oligarchy to exploit political institutions for its own behalf. The franchise used to be confined to literate adults over twenty-one years old[22]—which had the effect of disenfranchising most of the peasantry, making a popular electoral coalition impossible, and forcing the president (if reluctant to move there of his own accord) into the arms of the Right. The election of the congress by single-member districts assured the landed class a disproportionate voice, since *hacendados* had little difficulty in manipulating the electoral process in the sparsely populated (in

[20] The 1980 presidential elections were contested by fifteen parties and party alliances. Just four of these had ever before run candidates for executive office, and only five were in existence before 1968 (Roncagliolo 1980).

[21] On the policies and tactics of the APRA, see Haya de la Torre (1936, 1956); Kantor (1966); and, with a different view, Hilliker (1971).

[22] It was extended to the eighteen-to-twenty-year-old age group by decree-law in 1978 and to illiterates by the 1980 constitution.

terms of eligible voters) rural districts. That, together with the lack of real
national parties, deprived the president of political leverage over congress-
persons and compelled him to defer to the wishes of the landlords' congressional bloc. Of course, the same system favored the election of conservative
presidents, most of them members in good standing of the landed or commercial-financial elites. If, perchance, the president fell prey to reformist
notions, the congress could always block his initiatives; if the reforms could
be accomplished administratively without enabling legislation, the president
could still be brought to heel by withholding approval of his budget. The
landed class preferred a weak central government: since the peasantry was
generally docile, a large, expensive repressive apparatus was not needed to
keep it in its place; if organized labor in the industrial sector became restive,
the landed class was happy to quiet it with concessions (as it did not have to
pay for them); and, besides, a strong central government might have been
tempted to increase taxes on large private wealth accumulations and to promote
industry to the detriment of landed, agro-export interests.[23]

Thus it was that the nation limped into the last third of the twentieth century
with a weak, poorly institutionalized political system; a cumbersome, inefficient state administration staffed for the most part by corrupt, inept, woefully
underpaid civil servants; and an outmoded, inadequate, regressive system of
taxation. Presidents were unable to adopt and follow through with any policy
initiative that threatened any interest, no matter how immediate or minor, of
the propertied classes, nor could the state maintain the minimal autonomy
from dominant class interests that a stable capitalist political order requires.[24]
Whereas murmurs—occasionally, rumbles—of economic nationalism were
heard elsewhere in the hemisphere, the Peruvian door remained wide open
to foreign investors, who were assured of generous and nondiscriminatory
treatment in all particulars. Peruvian foreign policy faithfully followed the
U.S. lead except in a few affairs of direct local concern, such as the boundary
disputes with Chile and Ecuador and the defense of the 200-mile limit of
territorial waters.

The Gobierno Revolucionario de la Fuerza Armada that came to power
after the 1968 coup was a very different animal from its predecessors. Its
first president, Gen. Juan Velasco Alvarado, was a mestizo of humble origins
who knew how to use that fact for mass appeal; but he remained a *primus
inter pares* in the military establishment and never emerged as a true dictator
in the mold of Oscar Benavides (1933-1939) or Manuel Odría (1948-1956).

[23] Congress could also harass the executive by interpellating—questioning—individual ministers, who could then be subjected to votes of no confidence. This congressional power remains
under the 1980 constitution but has been hedged with restrictions: once three ministers appointed
by a sitting president have been subjected to successful no-confidence votes, the president may
dissolve the congress and call for new elections. Nor can the congress any longer obstruct the
executive by withholding approval of the budget; instead, the budget becomes law automatically
in the form initially presented if it is not approved by December.
[24] Miliband (1969).

On the other hand, the military had no intention of just setting up an interim junta to rule until a suitable civilian candidate could be found. From the first they declared as their aim a thorough restructuring of the state, the economy, and the political system, proclaiming that they would stay in power until all of those objectives had been irreversibly secured.[25]

We can briefly characterize the political orientation of the military regime as nationalist, developmentalist, technocratic, pro-capitalist but with a strong populist thrust, and not at all repressive as military governments go; its key programs have been extensively discussed in the literature,[26] and we need not review them yet again. However, it is relevant for our purposes to note that a major preoccupation of the regime was to strengthen the state, particularly its administrative machinery, which was seen as essential if development planning were to be implemented and foreign investor activities controlled to produce greater local benefits. To that end, the clumsy multifunctional ministries of the pre-coup cabinet (such as the Ministry of Development and Public Works) were broken up into leaner entities with clearer functional responsibilities (such as the Ministry of Energy and Mines). The National Planning Institute (INP) was enlarged and its director raised to cabinet rank. Salaries in the state administration were increased and the old clientele networks loosened with the appointment of new department chiefs from among the military and the technical-managerial corps of the private sector. (The institutional reforms adopted by the military government have been enshrined in the new constitution, which, in addition, provides for a stronger executive than before.) We shall find that this drastic improvement in the capabilities of the state apparatus, along with the expertise and zeal of the technocrats who entered it after 1968, had much to do with the state's success in implementing a new mining policy. Yet, it would be incorrect to assert that the military created a new state technobureaucracy. The civilian and military department heads proved far better policymakers and administrators than most of their predecessors *when they were able to deal personally with affairs*. But their staffs, though enlarged, were composed in their majority of the same mediocre bureaucrats as formerly. Bold new policies frequently bogged down when the time came to translate them into routine.

Let us quickly summarize what we have learned of Peru's economy and political system. The country is semi-industrialized—less so than such larger states of the hemisphere as Argentina, Brazil, and Mexico but more so than much of Latin America, all of the Middle East outside of Israel, and all of Africa north of the South African border. Industrial capital ownership is highly concentrated; much more capital is foreign-owned, and much less state-owned,

---

[25] On the character of the Peruvian military and the nature of the military regime, see Einaudi and Stepan (1971); Einaudi (1976); Bourricaud (1970); and Villanueva (1962, 1969).

[26] Regime policies are discussed in depth by the contributors to Lowenthal (1975) and to Chaplin (1976). None of these contributions, however, deals with the class content of policy other than peripherally. That subject is treated by Cotler (1969, 1970), and by Quijano (1971); I do not agree with their analyses.

than is typical of Latin America. The country's resource endowment creates exciting possibilities for the development of heavy industry but is not especially favorable for agriculture. A traditional Indian peasantry remains only as a shrinking minority of the population, and race per se has ceased to represent much of a barrier to upward mobility. The civilization is urban-centered, with a proportion of urban residents almost identical to the Latin American average.[27] The political system was historically weak, poorly institutionalized, and subject to manipulation by the oligarchy and by a military that has never acknowledged the supremacy of civilian authority.

After 1968 a military regime moved with alacrity to reinforce the power and improve the capabilities of the central state, and the changes it instituted have been largely preserved under restored civilian rule. Like military regimes everywhere, however, it was uninterested in, and incapable of, restructuring the mechanisms of political participation that are necessary for the long-term survival of a political regime without the constant deployment of repressive force. That is one reason why the military did not continue in office; the unfinished task of institutionalizing participation remains for the current civilian government.

THE PERUVIAN MINING INDUSTRY

The origins and early evolution of the mining industry in Peru, as well as the changing impact of mining on the local economy and society, have been discussed at some length in the literature.[28] The following discussion, therefore, is limited to the briefest of overviews; its purpose is to introduce the principal institutions and actors with which the later chapters of this study will be concerned.

While the Inca mined copper for weapons and implements in addition to gold and silver for ornamentation, the colonial industry revolved around monetary metals. The industry declined in the late eighteenth century and languished during the first fifty-odd years of independence.[29] It only revived at the end of the nineteenth century, when it was resuscitated on the basis of industrial metals—the world demand for which was increasing rapidly, thanks to the booming electrical industries. European experts came to Peru to explore for nonferrous metals. One of them stayed on to found and direct a college of engineering that had graduated 206 Peruvian mining engineers by the time

[27] In 1975 the population of Peru was 44.6 percent urban (residing in population centers of 20,000 or more); the comparable percentage for all of Latin America was 45.0 (Wilkie and Reich 1980:77).

[28] Samamé (1974, 1979); Purser (1971); and, on the colonial period, Fisher (1977). Those interested in the historical evolution of the industry's economic impact will find useful Thorp and Bertram (1978).

[29] The reasons were economic, political, and technological; they have been reviewed in the literature (n. 28).

of his death in 1909.[30] A new mining code designed to stimulate private investment in the industry was adopted in 1901 and marks the beginning of Peruvian mining in its modern form.[31]

The Cerro Corporation

In the meantime, wealthy North Americans were bestirring themselves to investigate new investment opportunities in Latin American raw materials.[32] In 1896 a group of New Jersey investors formed the Backus and Johnson Company, which gained title to a small copper mine at Casapalca, in the Rímac valley,[33] and constructed a smelter there. One year later, a North American engineer, William A. McCune, arrived in the central sierra in search of copper. He found it aplenty amid the nearly exhausted silver ores of an old mining district known by the name of its principal town—Cerro de Pasco. He also found the local mine owners willing to sell out. After McCune had documented the value of his find, he returned to the United States to line up financial backing for a Peruvian copper venture. A syndicate was put together in 1900-1901 by James B. Haggin and J. P. Morgan.[34] Named the Cerro de Pasco Investment Corporation, it was initially capitalized at $10 million.

The venture needed a more hospitable legal regime in Peru, and this was provided by the 1901 Mining Code. It swept away at a stroke a 350-year-old tradition of state ownership of mineral rights and substituted an imported tradition for the convenience of foreign interests. The indigenous tradition would one day reassert itself; but for the moment, mineral rights lost their special status and became just another form of property, capable of being used, mortgaged, or disposed of at will. Any "resident" of Peru (a local office was sufficient proof of residency) was thenceforth eligible to own title to mineral rights, subject to only minor restrictions.

The first Cerro copper smelter was constructed in 1906 near Cerro de Pasco town. In the next year Cerro formed a subsidiary to acquire additional concessions in the area, and in 1915 it reorganized itself as the Cerro de Pasco Copper Corporation. It bought out Backus and Johnson's mine holdings in 1919. Cerro's concessions, which had originally totaled about sixty hectares, grew to over a thousand hectares by 1920.

The 1901 Code stimulated other investments besides Cerro's. Within a short time there were a half-dozen or so foreign-owned mining companies in operation. All of them, however, remained far smaller than Cerro (the only

[30] Samamé (1974:1:93); the individual in question was Eduardo Juan de Habich, a Polish engineer under contract to the French and Peruvian governments. At least five members of this early crop of graduates went on to become important mining entrepreneurs.

[31] Samamé (1974:1:202-203).

[32] This was the era when the outward expansion of U.S. capitalism began. The process does, it seems to me, conform reasonably well to Lenin's (1933) model.

[33] Conveniently located along the line of the Central Railway joining Lima and Callao with the sierra town of La Oroya.

[34] Among the other noteworthy participants were Henry Clay Frick, William Randolph Hearst, and the Vanderbilt heirs.

company to operate more than one mine), and only one—the French-owned Compagnie des Mines Huarón—still exists. A few Peruvians established small mining firms, several of which have continued to the present. By 1915 the mineralized area under active exploitation had increased fourfold from what it had been in 1890.[35]

Cerro's volume of ore production soon reached a point where the construction of a large central smelter to process the output of all of its mines was justified. The new copper smelter, located at the rail junction town of La Oroya, was completed in 1922. Additional processing facilities and ancillary installations were added over the years—smelters and refineries for lead, zinc, and minor metals; a copper refinery; service shops; and support facilities— converting the once-sleepy town into a heavy industrial complex.

Cerro's was a *custom* smelter: the process could be altered to accommodate ores of different metallic composition and impurity content.[36] The custom capabilities of the Cerro smelter quickly became an important economic asset. A smelter always functions most efficiently (viz., at the lowest cost per ton of throughput) when it runs at full capacity. Since Cerro's could accept ore from any source, full-capacity operation could be maintained at all times— even in the face of strikes, mine accidents, and declining ore grades—by the simple expedient of buying ores from the independent mining enterprises in the zone. The company could offer its smelting services more cheaply than local miners could obtain them abroad; and by blending ores from different sources it could often reduce impurity levels enough that it did not have to charge impurity penalties.[37] Therefore, local miners were usually happy to keep Cerro supplied with additional ore as needed, and Cerro in turn could realize extra profits from the collection of smelting and (eventually) refining charges from them. The company further increased the profitability of its operations by entering into a contract with the British (later Canadian)-owned Peruvian Corporation, operator of the Central Railway: in return for a 15 percent discount on shipping charges, Cerro agreed to ship all of its production to Callao by rail. It is hardly surprising that other smelters in the country could not compete and had to close, leaving Cerro after 1931 with a total monopoly over the smelting and refining of nonferrous metals in Peru.[38]

Except during World War I, Cerro sold much of its production in Europe;

[35] Samamé (1974:1:51-53).

[36] Custom smelting was necessitated by the fact that each of the company's mines produced ores with different properties. Custom smelters are more complicated to build and operate than are those tailored to just one kind of ore; but in this era, low Peruvian labor costs, together with the value of recovered byproducts and improved yields, made the Cerro smelter competitive with the specialized installations then being constructed in the United States, Chile, and Africa.

[37] The smelting process becomes more difficult and expensive if certain impurities (notably, antimony and arsenic) are present in the ores in more than a specified minimum concentration. Hence, processors add a penalty fee to the processing charge they exact when purchasing ores with higher-than-minimum levels of these impurities. If, however, the impure ores are first mixed with others of exceptional purity, the resulting blend may show a net impurity concentration lower than the limit and may, therefore, be exempt from penalty.

[38] Purser (1971:203); and Ocampo (1972).

it did not build refining or fabricating plants in the United States, and it never became a full member of the North American copper oligopoly. If Cerro's entry into Peru tied the country's mining economy to some extent to the economic fortunes of the United States, the effect was far weaker than in Chile—where Anaconda and Kennecott developed their mines as nearly exclusive suppliers to North America.

Local employment increased apace. Cerro employed 5,166 Peruvian laborers—fully a third of the country's mine labor force—by 1908, and this number grew to 7,800 by 1920 and to almost 13,000 by 1929 (it would peak at about 18,000 some years afterward).[39] But the company was more than Peru's largest private employer; for, twenty years after its founding, it became the country's largest landowner.

Ores of copper, lead, and zinc are compounds of the metals with sulfur. In the smelting process a chemical reaction liberates the former and causes the latter to combine with oxygen, forming sulfur dioxide gas. When discharged into the atmosphere through the smelter's stacks, sulfur dioxide is a particularly noxious pollutant: foul-smelling and irritating to the mucous membranes, it unites with atmospheric moisture and forms sulfuric acid—which, upon condensing out of the air, kills crops and livestock. Almost immediately after the Cerro smelter went on stream, nearby landowners started to complain of serious crop and livestock losses. They brought suit; and, as invariably happens in Peru, the courts proved sympathetic to the claims of local propertied citizens against a foreign enterprise. The company settled the judgment against it by agreeing to purchase the damaged lands and, thus, found itself the owner of some 320,000 hectares of cropland and pasture. Shortly afterward Cottrell precipitators were installed in the stacks, removing most of the sulfur emissions and enabling the newly acquired lands to become productive once more. Cerro, the new *hacendado*, joined the National Agrarian Society and became a political ally of the oligarchy. However, it broke with semifeudal patterns of landlord-peasant relations in order to implement modern farming methods. Most of the land was given over to scientific sheep husbandry; the company's herds became world-famous for the quality of their wool. Meat from slaughtered sheep was sold to mine workers in the company stores; while the markup was small, the "fringe benefit" of cheap meat helped to keep wages down. Cerro introduced enclosure to prevent the local peasants' herds from contaminating the prize-winning ovine bloodline. With the fencing of the pastures, peasants lost their traditional usufruct rights to grazing lands (some of which were without doubt the legal property of peasant *comunidades* that had been usurped in the past). Deprived of their livelihood, they became miners or salaried shepherds for the company, or else moved away.[40]

The further expansion of private mining investment in Peru awaited a new mining code, since, in the face of changing economic conditions and the increasing costs of new mine development, foreign mining firms were de-

[39] Flores Galindo (1974:36-37).
[40] A history of the Cerro haciendas has been written by Kapsoli (1975).

manding more favorable treatment than the 1901 Code provided.[41] They got it shortly after the nationalist-reformist administration of José Bustamante y Rivero (1945-1948) was overthrown by the Odría dictatorship. Finding that Odría was eager to stimulate foreign capital inflows to the mining sector, Cerro's president, Robert Koenig, thoughtfully brought forward a proposed text for the new law that he had written. It was enacted in 1950 after only minor reworking. Needless to say, many of its articles, such as one providing for a long-sought depletion allowance, were lifted intact from the U.S. Code.[42]

Peruvians expected that Cerro, as the author and principal beneficiary of the 1950 Mining Code, would expand the scope of its local operations. Those expectations went unfulfilled. The company entered into two joint mining ventures with Peruvian firms and set up seven manufacturing joint ventures to produce materials required by the mining industry and some copper wire,[43] but its total capital outlay for these was less than $3 million. Koenig, who had assumed the Cerro presidency in 1949, recognized that his firm could not long survive as a mere neocolonial outpost in an era of transnational capital and globally integrated production. Accordingly, the company began to funnel its Peruvian profits into the acquisition of copper fabricators in the United States and a copper mine in Chile. It expanded laterally into aluminum fabrication and oil exploration and, in conglomerate fashion, bought a trucking line, a real estate developer, and a stereo tape club. It symbolically deemphasized its *peruanidad* by changing its name to Cerro Corporation. With the diversification program exerting a priority claim on corporate profits, there could be little new mining investment in Peru. Only one new mine was opened in the fifties and sixties—the Cobriza copper mine. Built at an unusually low cost of $20 million, it paid for itself in just three years, lending weight to accusations that it was "highgraded" (i.e., mined for only the richest ores) so that the investment in it would be tied up for the shortest possible time.[44]

[41] Their principal objection to the 1901 Code was that it taxed export value rather than net profit; the formula for computing the export tax had not been revised to account for changed international price levels, with the result that by the late forties the tax burden was coming to seem onerous. The companies also complained that taxation of export value, as it cannot be predicted in advance of actual production and sale, made corporate planning much more uncertain. A secondary issue was that the 1933 constitution had reaffirmed the state's ultimate ownership of all mineral rights. By now foreign companies were accustomed to operating under a regime of concessions without absolute privatization of their reserves, but they feared that the contrary provisions of the 1901 Code might one day lead the Supreme Court to declare it unconstitutional. They were, of course, wise enough not to press for a constitutional amendment to resolve the issue—which would have become a nationalist *cause célèbre*.

[42] Koenig confirmed this version of the 1950 Code's authorship during a conversation with me in September 1981.

[43] Wils (1979:75) describes the manufacturing industries set up by Cerro as "the joint product of the oligarchy and foreign export companies, who shared not only an economic relationship in export production, but also relationships in the social, political, and ideological realms." Although local shareholdings in these firms were considerable, the fact that they were promoted by Cerro raised fears among nationalists of a North American economic octopus.

[44] This accusation, though often heard in some Peruvian mining circles, cannot be proven and was vehemently denied by Koenig in my interview with him (n. 42). The best evidence supporting it is that Cerro's parastatal successor, Centromin, has found it quite worthwhile to exploit lower-

In 1973, the last year in which it operated as a private concern, Cerro (Peru) employed 14,816 persons, generated $228.3 million in exports, and paid taxes of $34.1 million to the Peruvian state.[45] Despite the diversification program, Peruvian mining contributed 61 percent of the corporation's worldwide earnings.[46]

If Cerro was laggard in grasping the opportunity held out by the 1950 Mining Code, Peruvian miners were not. A number of modern Peruvian mining corporations were founded during the twenty years that the code was in force (we will look at them in Chapter 7). There was also a trickle of foreign investment into smaller mines, initially from the United States and Britain but later from Japan. However, the greatest impact of the code was in making possible the development of three huge open-pit mines: the Toquepala and, later on, the even larger Cuajone copper mine, built by the Southern Peru Copper Corporation; and the Marcona iron mine, a project of the Marcona Mining Company.

Large-Scale Mining: Southern Peru Copper and Marcona

The Southern Peru Copper Corporation is a joint venture of four North American firms in which Asarco, Inc. (formerly the American Smelting and Refining Company) holds a controlling interest.

Asarco was for many years a mainstay of the Guggenheim industrial empire.[47] In its early days it operated lead and copper smelters and a few mines in Mexico, but it was not long before the Guggenheim interest extended further south. In 1921 the family established the Northern Peru Mining Company as a wholly owned subsidiary to operate a copper mine at Quiruvilca, in the northern Andes east of the city of Trujillo. Elsewhere, however, its mining investments were usually limited to minority partnerships; its aim was not managerial control of the mines but obtaining long-term smelting and refining contracts on favorable terms. Integrating forward into fabrication, it acquired operating control of the General Cable Corporation, the Revere Copper and Brass Company, and the Federated Metals Corporation, a reducer of copper scrap. While Asarco's interests in copper grew, it fortified its position as a producer of lead, zinc, and silver by purchasing control of the Federal Mining and Smelting Company from John D. Rockefeller and by absorbing the National Lead Company. Subsequent expansion has made Asarco the largest smelter and refiner of nonferrous metals in the United States and one of the largest integrated producers in the Western world.[48] We will examine its position in the world industry more closely in Chapter 4.

---

grade ores than Cerro did; and that the cutoff grade used by Cerro in planning the mine, 2.2 percent, is extremely high for Andean copper deposits.

[45] Consolidated declaration of the company for 1973 (see n. 66).

[46] Datum from Cerro's annual report for 1973.

[47] On the Guggenheim family see Hoyt (1967). Asarco's authorized corporate biography is by Marcosson (1949).

[48] In 1980 Asarco was the 199th largest U.S. industrial corporation ranked by total sales (*Fortune*, 4 May 1981, pp. 322ff), making it the third largest nonferrous metals producer (behind

Southern Peru Copper evolved out of corporate infighting between Cerro and Asarco for control of three enormous copper deposits of the southern sierra and, through them, of the heights of the Peruvian mining industry. Cerro derived all of its copper from relatively high grade underground mines which could be exploited profitably with cheap labor and little capital; but its mine output was declining, making the company's copper production dependent on purchased ores. Asarco, in contrast, had the opposite problem: having begun as a processor of ores mined by others, it became eager to expand its mining interests and to protect its copper supplies against future exhaustion of the Quiruvilca orebody. Now, the three copper deposits in question are associated orebodies lying in close proximity to each other. Cerro controlled the northernmost, Cuajone, under concession since the 1930s. Asarco, through Northern Peru Mining, held the central orebody, Quellaveco. The southernmost, Toquepala, was by 1937 in the hands of a Peruvian, Juan Oveido Villegas. Cerro took an option on the property in that year but relinquished it in 1940. In 1941 the option was taken up by Northern. This was a threatening development from Cerro's point of view. The exploitation of Quellaveco would pose problems for Northern, as a river ran through the orebody and would have to be diverted if an open-pit mine were to be constructed. With Toquepala under its control, however, Asarco's subsidiary would be in possession of the lion's share of the region's copper reserves and could begin their exploitation at Toquepala, where there were far fewer engineering difficulties to be overcome.

Cerro sued Northern in order to protect its interests, but it lost.[49] Once the concessionary rights were secure, Asarco immediately undertook exploration and preconstruction activities necessary to plan the Toquepala mine, spending $6 million between 1948 and 1952. It had intended from the beginning to obtain U.S. government aid in financing the Toquepala project and was counting on the fears of a coming copper shortage raised by the 1950 Paley Report[50] to get it. Authorization was eventually issued for an Export-Import Bank loan of $100 million at 5⅛ percent interest. Asarco was required to contribute at

AMAX and Kennecott). In the Western world as a whole it was also outranked in terms of total sales by five other non-U.S. producers, one of which was the Zambian state (*Fortune*, 10 August 1981, pp. 205ff).

[49] Its suit demanded a 50 percent interest in Toquepala on the ground that Cerro's earlier agreement with Oveido had included his partner, who, it was alleged, had not participated in the transfer of the option to Northern. The case dragged on for seven years and was finally decided by the Peruvian Supreme Court in Northern's favor in November 1948.

[50] President's Materials Policy Commission (1952). The Paley Commission erred seriously in its prediction of a great increase in U.S. dependence on imported copper. For example, actual 1975 U.S. copper mine production was 1.28 million metric tons, versus the Paley Report's forecast of 0.75 million. U.S. consumption of refined copper in 1975 was 1.40 million metric tons, whereas the report had predicted 2.27 million. On the other hand, the report grossly underestimated the growth of copper consumption outside the United States: non-U.S. Western world refined consumption was 4.08 million metric tons in 1975, compared to the report's forecast of only 1.86 million. (Production and consumption data for 1975 are from World Bureau of Metal Statistics, *World Metal Statistics*, January and May 1977).

least $95 million in corporate funds, which could not be borrowed. While the Washington financing negotiations proceeded, Asarco went about writing a special development contract with the Peruvian government under the terms of the freshly enacted 1950 Mining Code. To meet the government's preference that subsidiaries of foreign mining companies be locally incorporated, Asarco chose to organize Toquepala separately rather than utilizing Northern as its vehicle; in 1952 it incorporated Southern Peru Copper for the purpose. The Peruvian negotiations went smoothly, for, as was previously noted, President Odría wanted Peru to receive new foreign investment and was willing to assent to any terms suggested by Asarco that were within the law. A contract was signed in November 1954. Its terms were extremely favorable to the company: income tax rates were as low as the law allowed and were guaranteed not to change until five years after all invested capital had been recouped out of after-tax profits.[51] Quellaveco was included in the contract in a peripheral way; Southern was under no obligation to develop it, but if it should decide to, the same provisions of the Toquepala agreement would presumably apply.

The successful completion of Asarco's financing and contract negotiations sunk Cerro's hopes of independently developing its Cuajone property—which it had, in fact, been seriously considering. In 1952 Cerro had formed a partnership with Newmont Mining Corporation, turning over to it a 20 percent (raised to 25 percent in 1953) interest in Cuajone in return for its assuming the entire cost of exploration and preconstruction work. The Newmont agreement, however, called for each partner to shoulder its proportionate share of these costs beginning in 1954. Cerro, as we have seen, was heavily engaged in expansion elsewhere and could not spare the financial resources for Cuajone. Neither could Newmont. The Export-Import Bank would not consider another large mine development loan for the same area of the same country, and no private bank would expose so much of its funds in a politically risky Third World environment unless protected by U.S. government participation. With loan financing thus ruled out, Cerro and Newmont approached cash-rich Phelps-Dodge, the biggest U.S. domestic copper producer, but the latter would agree to participate only if all three orebodies were placed under the control of a single corporate entity.[52]

Having forced Cerro out as a competitor, Asarco next maneuvered to bring it and its allies back as partners. Asarco, too, recognized the manifold advantages of placing all three orebodies under one corporate roof—if it were to control the resulting organization. In addition, it did not wish to expose more than $40 million of its own capital in the project and would be willing to accept partners able to furnish the balance of the required $95 million equity investment. Cerro itself would not make such a contribution; but if it

---

[51] Meaning that funds deducted for depreciation, depletion, and loan amortization, even though considered capital recuperation by any accounting definition, were *not* charged against it.

[52] Ballantyne (1976:32).

were to come in, Newmont and Phelps-Dodge would as well, and the latter did have the cash to invest. Perhaps to urge matters along, Asarco began to purchase stock in Cerro; its holdings reached 14.9 percent of Cerro's outstanding shares by 1955.[53] Cerro, finding itself outmaneuvered at every turn, capitulated.

Southern Peru Copper was officially transformed into a joint venture of Asarco, Cerro, Phelps-Dodge, and Newmont in September 1955. Each partner's share in the venture was proportional to its contribution to Southern's cash investment except for Cerro, which was credited with a 16 percent share in exchange for signing Cuajone over to Southern.[54] Each partner was authorized to purchase the same percentage as its ownership stake of Southern's annual copper production.

For a total investment in the project of $237.1 million, the four firms created one of the largest, most modern, and most profitable copper mining and smelting installations (the project did not include a refinery, as all of the partners except Cerro owned ample refinery capacity in the United States) in the world.[55] Table 2.4 shows the mine's net earnings in its first ten years of operation and the contribution of those earnings to the aggregate profits of

TABLE 2.4 Southern Peru Copper: Net Earnings and Contributions to Owners' Consolidated After-Tax Profits, 1960-1969 (*Net earnings in millions of dollars; contributions in percent*)

| Year | Net Earnings | Contribution | | | |
		Asarco	Cerro	Phelps-Dodge	Newmont
1960	15.9	18.6	37.6	7.1	9.2
1961	19.1	27.9	86.7	8.0	11.7
1962	11.7	15.3	47.3	4.8	6.1
1963	16.0	19.3	28.0	6.6	8.7
1964	18.7	15.8	16.0	5.4	6.2
1965	32.4	22.1	25.0	7.8	7.9
1966	67.6	38.4	34.1	13.2	10.2
1967	70.1	50.6	46.7	22.0	15.3
1968	53.6	35.1	36.8	13.4	10.9
1969	62.1	31.7	33.7	11.1	9.9

SOURCE: Compiled by the author from data presented in Southern's consolidated declarations and in the annual reports of the other firms.

[53] Ballantyne (1976:32n).

[54] Cerro was not satisfied with this share and sued; in 1960 it agreed to accept additional Southern stock in return for a small cash payment to Asarco, raising its holding to 22.25 percent.

[55] Of the total investment, $119.6 million was lent by the Export-Import Bank, $32.6 million was equity capital invested by the partners, $74.8 million was in cash advances from the partners (interest-free loans that Southern had to repay out of profits), and $10.1 million was in supplier credits (Mikesell 1975a:48).

each owner. All of them benefited handsomely from the venture. As is to be expected, Asarco, with 51.5 percent ownership and managerial control, was a prime beneficiary. Cerro, because its overall profit margins were lower than Asarco's, came to depend even more on Southern's contribution to its consolidated profit (with consequences to be examined in Chapters 5 and 6). Phelps-Dodge and Newmont earned less, but both acquired access to important copper reserves and thereby improved their positions in the world market.

Southern's total employment in 1973 was 3,850. In that year it generated $221.4 million worth of exports and paid $68.7 million in Peruvian income taxes, making it the country's biggest taxpayer.[56]

The Marcona iron deposits were discovered by a Peruvian engineer in 1905.[57] Local investors, including Alfredo Gildemeister (of one of the most powerful oligarchic families), Augusto Leguía (president of Peru from 1919 to 1930), Roberto Letts (later a founder of a major domestic mining firm), and the Prados (also oligarchs; Manuel Prado was president of Peru in 1939-1945 and 1956-1962), gained control of Marcona but were unable to develop it for lack of sufficient capital. In 1943, however, President Prado decided that state assistance might overcome this difficulty. His administration chartered the Corporación del Santa, a parastatal enterprise, to promote decentralized development by bringing a steel industry and other investments to the valley of the Río Santa, in northern Peru near Trujillo. The iron ore to feed the projected steel mill would come, naturally, from the Marcona mine in which the president and some of his political allies had a financial interest. The corporation was given title to the Marcona deposits in 1945, subject to production royalty payments to the former private owners. Over the next six years it invested some $2 million in Marcona, most of it to improve the nearby port of San Juan. But it exhausted its resources before it could bring the mine into production.

There matters stood until 1951, when the Utah Construction Company (now Utah International), attracted by the convenient coastal location, the availability of a deep-water port, and the liberal investment climate of the time, proposed to develop the mine for the Corporación del Santa. A contract was let on terms basically identical to those suggested by the North American firm in February 1952. It called for a mine capable of producing more than 500,000 tons per year of high-grade iron ore. Utah would be permitted over the twenty-year life of the contract to export up to a third of the mine's proved reserves, plus half of any newly discovered reserves. The Corporación del Santa would be able to buy up to 300,000 tons per year at a reduced price and would earn royalties on all production. Upon contract expiration the Corporación del Santa would receive full title to the permanent installations and an option to buy the machinery and other moveable assets.

[56] Consolidated declaration of the company for 1973 (see n. 66).

[57] The discussion of Marcona in this and the following paragraphs draws heavily upon García Sayán (1977).

Utah obtained an Export-Import Bank loan for the project in 1953 and incorporated Marcona as an 80-percent-owned subsidiary, with Cyprus Mines the minority partner. As construction was getting under way, planners found that they could materially increase the usable reserves by blending. So the company built a blending plant; and to make its now-larger investment more secure, it solicited and received a contract amendment extending the term to thirty years and enlarging the area of concessions under its control. Next Marcona decided to expand further by setting up a facility to concentrate the low-grade ores, which increased the usable reserves by a factor of twenty. Just under half the cost of the concentrating facility was financed by another Export-Import Bank loan. Simultaneously, a second port was constructed a few kilometers up the coast at San Nícolas.

Marcona sought still more legal protection for its position in Peru as its investment grew. It insisted on an absolute property right to the San Nícolas port installations, along with the right to appropriate for itself a portion of the higher-grade ores set aside for national use (which it would replace with an equivalent amount, in terms of metal content, of low-grade ores). As was habitual, the Corporación del Santa supinely acceded to these demands.[58]

Marcona, feeling more secure, continued its program of incremental investments. To the ore concentrator were added a magnetic separation plant and a "pelletizing" plant (it converts concentrated ores into pellets rich in iron and uniform in composition). Japanese mills liked the pellets so much that Marcona became their biggest supplier of imported iron ore (20 percent of annual Japanese imports). The original pelletizing plant was joined by a second in 1964. By the end of the sixties Marcona was exporting 80 percent of its annual output of some 10 million tons to Japan.[59] Its cumulative investment, originally $6 million, then stood at $71.5 million.

The firm employed 2,815 persons in 1973. Its iron ore exports earned Peru $60.7 million in foreign exchange—much less in proportion to material mined than Cerro or Southern because of the lower unit value of iron as compared to the nonferrous metals. Marcona's profits were correspondingly low; accounting losses were registered in half of the years between 1968 and 1975, and the net result for the eight-year period was a loss.[60] Peruvians were deeply disturbed by this outcome, especially inasmuch as Utah was reaping sizable profits from its construction activities, and as Marcona's Panamanian shipping subsidiary was earning large sums transporting the ore to Japan.

The 1950-1968 expansion of large-scale Peruvian mining represented by

[58] Goodsell (1974:51) correctly observes that the successive revisions of the Marcona contract gave the Peruvian government greater shares of the project's profits—which, however, were never very large (as will be seen below). But it was in the crucial dimension of *control* where Marcona won out, since the revised contracts gave it more power to determine the nature and directions of the project's development.

[59] *Peruvian Times*, 24 December 1971, p. 5.

[60] Consolidated declarations of the company for the years in question (see n. 66). Export data are from Dirección General de Minería (1976).

far the greatest commitment of new mining investment capital to the Third World during that period by transnational resource corporations headquartered in the United States. In 1950 Peru had been host to $145 million of U.S. direct private investment (3.1 percent of the total for Latin America), of which $55 million, or somewhat over a third, was mining and metallurgical investment (almost all accounted for by Cerro and Northern). By 1968 total U.S. private investment in Peru had nearly quintupled, to $692 million, and had risen to 6.6 percent of all such investment in Latin America. Mining and metallurgy's share stood at $421 million, or 60.8 percent of the Peruvian total, having increased more than sevenfold since 1950. In 1950 Peru had hosted 10.4 percent of all U.S. foreign investment in mining and metallurgy; the corresponding figure for 1968 was 34.5 percent.[61] In other words, the real expansionary thrust of U.S. capital in Peru in those years was in mining, not manufacturing. After Chile nationalized her mines, Peru became far and away the largest Latin American recipient of U.S. mining and metallurgical investment; its current share is 74.5 percent.

The Present Organization of the Mining Industry

The Peruvian mining industry is divided into three subsectors. The *gran minería*, or large-mining subsector, consists of enterprises that use high-volume mining technologies; until 1981 it also included all firms that smelted or refined metals, irrespective of the size of their mines. Employment per firm in the subsector varies widely, as we have seen—from 2,500 (Marcona) to 15,000 (Cerro). The *mediana minería*, or medium-mining subsector, includes corporations that mine in lesser volume (and, until 1981, that did not process their ores beyond the concentrates stage). Employment per firm ranges from a low of about 75 to a high of just under 2,000; only one firm in this subsector (it is domestically owned) operates more than one mine. Lastly, the *pequeña minería*, or small-mining subsector, is comprised of very small firms, which must be locally owned and which are often no more than the owner himself and a few helpers. This small-business subsector, important nationally only in gold production, survives on the basis of special subsidies justified by the myth of the "lucky strike." Unfortunately, the availability of subsidies has had the effect of inhibiting a few of the firms from increasing their scale of operations and advancing into the mediana minería.

Prior to 1970 the active gran minería was made up of Cerro, Southern, and Marcona and was thus wholly foreign-owned. (Other transnational corporations held title to concessionary rights but had not developed them.) Figure 3 details the ownership of these three and their interests in Peru as of that year.

In 1970 the Peruvian government set up a new parastatal enterprise, the Empresa Minera del Perú (MineroPeru) to refine copper and zinc and to

---

[61] Calculated from Wilkie and Reich (1978:367-69).

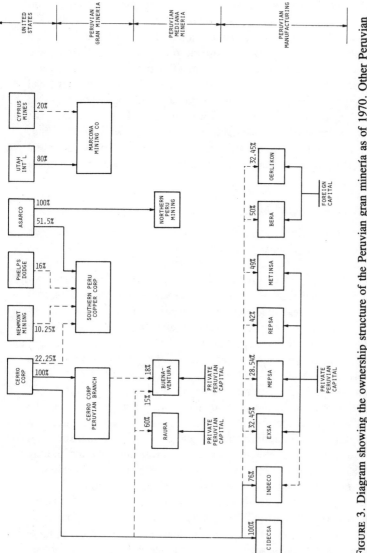

FIGURE 3. Diagram showing the ownership structure of the Peruvian *gran minería* as of 1970. Other Peruvian mining and manufacturing holdings of the transnational corporate owners are also shown. Percentages indicate ownership shares; heavy solid lines, managerial control. Note that the later expropriation of the Cerro Corporation (Peruvian branch) did not affect the other Peruvian holdings, carried in the name of the Cerro Corporation of New York. The diagram omits Cerro's and Southern's sales subsidiaries, incorporated in the United States; Cerro's hacienda holdings (expropriated in 1969), organized as the company's Livestock Division (División de Ganadería); and Marcona's Panamanian ore-shipping subsidiary, San Juan Carriers Ltd.

develop some of the larger unworked mineral deposits. It currently operates one open-pit copper mine and is developing a second. Cerro was nationalized in 1974, becoming the Empresa Minera del Centro del Perú (Centromin); the following year the same fate befell Marcona, which became the Empresa del Hierro del Perú (HierroPeru). Thus, today's gran minería consists of one transnational firm—Southern—and the three parastatals. Southern's ownership has changed slightly and currently stands as follows: Asarco, 52.3 percent; the Marmon Group of Chicago (it absorbed Cerro's remnants in 1976), 20.8 percent; Phelps-Dodge, 16.2 percent; and Newmont, 10.7 percent. Its latest mine, Cuajone, is a joint venture in which Billiton N.V. of the Netherlands, a metal-fabricating subsidiary of Royal Dutch/Shell, holds an 11.5 percent share. Figure 3 explains what happened to Cerro's various other Peruvian holdings after nationalization; its minority share in the domestic Buenaventura firm was sold in 1978 to the French government's Bureau de Recherches Géologiques et Minières.

The gran minería's earnings come mainly from the production of copper. This subsector has made Peru the fourth largest copper exporter in the Third World behind Chile, Zambia, and Zaire.

There are presently seventy-one firms active in the mediana minería. Fifteen of these are under effective foreign control and the rest are domestically controlled. Foreign owners range from giant transnationals like Asarco and Mitsui to very small firms with no other holdings of importance. Some of the Peruvian firms are small, obsolescent, and barely surviving; others, however, are as large, modern, and profitable as any of the foreign subsidiaries. There have been no nationalizations in this subsector, although the state has acquired interests in a number of medium mines through equity investment, foreclosure, or abandonment. (It was the policy of the military regime to support employment in the subsector by taking over and operating mines that would have otherwise been closed down by their private owners.) The subsector competes in the same international markets as does the gran minería. It produces some copper and contributed 12.9 percent to the country's 1977 mine production. But its principal contribution has been and is in lead (63.2 percent of national mine production in 1977), zinc (56.9 percent), and silver (74.7 percent).[62]

The pequeña minería is economically and politically insignificant. Many of its mines are worked only on a part-time basis, or when metals prices are exceptionally high. Its limited scale of operations and backward technologies are not propitious for growth, except for a very few firms that should be part of the mediana minería but that deliberately hold their output below the legal limit so as to qualify for small-mining subsidies. Resort to advanced prospecting technologies has severely reduced the likelihood of an individual prospector discovering a major addition to national reserves—once the prin-

[62] Data from the Ministry of Energy and Mines.

cipal justification for special assistance to this subsector. Even in gold, where the pequeña minería contributed 44 percent of Peru's 1977 production,[63] the subsector's significance will decline once larger-scale mining projects now being promoted by MineroPeru get under way. It seems fairly clear, therefore, that subsidies to the pequeña minería survive solely to avoid the political alienation of small business. Due to its lack of significance, small-scale mining will not be further discussed in this study.

Tables A.3 through A.5, in Appendix A, show the historical evolution of Peruvian nonferrous metal mining in terms of volume of production, gross value of production, and contribution of each subsector to gross value.

Most of the capital equipment and some of the supplies and process inputs needed by the mining sector are imported. Government regulations regarding these purchases were revised during the 1970s at the urging of domestic industrialists, so that they now require mining firms to buy locally wherever possible. But none of the heavy equipment or spare parts used by the gran minería is domestically produced, and medium-mining managers, complaining of low quality and poor after-sale service in the local product, have sometimes gone to great lengths to circumvent the regulations. Nevertheless, the "buy-local" policy has been effective, if major capital goods are excluded from the evaluation. In 1977 the gran minería bought 72.5 percent of its small equipment and process inputs locally, spending for the purpose $214.5 million. The mediana minería spent $67 million locally, representing 74.8 percent of its noncapital purchases. By way of contrast, in 1970 the mediana minería made 66 percent of its purchases in Peru but the gran minería only 37 percent.[64]

The low incidence of local purchases in former years by the large foreign mining firms meant that the gran minería was disarticulated from the rest of the national economy, since the subsector is not linked to it on the output side. The IPC affair—the unsuccessful effort of the first Belaunde administration (1963-1968) to regularize Peru's relations with a Standard Oil of New Jersey subsidiary[65]—was the proximate cause of the military takeover, but behind its specifics lay the historical tendency of foreign-owned extractive industry in the country to organize itself in disarticulated "enclaves." A phenomenon of the early twentieth century, the extractive enclave produced exclusively for export and used imported goods and services in the production process; manual labor was the only significant item locally supplied. As foreign administrators and technicians poured in to manage and supervise its operations, the enclave actually took on aspects of extraterritoriality. Facilities

[63] Data from the Ministry of Energy and Mines.

[64] Data for 1977 are from the Ministry of Energy and Mines; for 1970, from Ocampo (1972). Note that the 1977 figures probably give an overoptimistic picture of local purchases, since many of the locally purchased goods may well have had a significant import content. Moreover, the shift of gran minería purchases from imports to local products is largely explained by Peru's increased petroleum output, which since 1975 has eliminated the need to import heavy fuel oil— a major cost item in smelter operation.

[65] The affair is discussed at length by Pinelo (1973).

and lifestyles, except for laborers', came to look more like those of Suburbia, U.S.A., than those of the *sierra peruana*; they were maintained that way by the massive importation of U.S.-made consumer goods. Physical access to the mining zones was controlled by company police, who, during Cerro's early years, also assumed full responsibility for maintaining civil order in the area. Although many of the worst features of the extractive enclaves had disappeared by 1968, their vestiges, along with a historical legacy that time could not extinguish, attracted nationalist resentment. The military took power determined to do away once and for all with the remnants of the enclave mode of production, viewing it as an obstacle to broadly based development and as an insult to national integrity. In this they were supported by the overwhelming majority of Peruvians.

Metals used to be marketed by each company as it saw fit: foreign firms sold to their overseas parents or to third parties via their in-house sales subsidiaries, while the domestic firms used the services of independent metals traders. (Cerro Sales also acted as a sales broker for some medium enterprises.) Then in 1970 the military government declared a state monopoly over mine product export sales in order to eliminate the potential for price manipulation and to promote diversification of export outlets. Minero Peru Comercial (Minpeco), another parastatal entity, was set up in 1974 as the government's sales agency. State control of sales has made possible the development of markets in China, the Soviet bloc, and India, where the transnationals and private traders lacked contacts. In other respects Minpeco has had more than its share of problems. While it never interfered very much with the customary sales practices of the gran minería, domestic medium companies complained from the start that its lack of market expertise and general business acumen was causing them to lose sales income. After several reorganizations these problems seem to have been overcome. But the civilian government acceded to pressures from the domestic industry and abolished Minpeco's monopoly in 1980. Now only the parastatal firms must use it as their sales broker; to get other business it has to compete with the independent traders.

The state operates a mining promotion bank, the Banco Minero del Perú. It offers loans for working capital, makes occasional mine development loans, arranges for foreign debt financing, furnishes technical and managerial assistance, and trades in precious metals. Its clients are limited by law to domestic firms of the mediana and pequeña minerías; but bank officials have promoted a few joint ventures in which foreign investors hold majority interests. The military regime greatly enlarged the lending capital available to the bank and established several mining development funds which it administers.

The activities of the enterprises of the sector are supervised by the General Directorate of Mining (DGM), since 1969 a bureau of the Ministry of Energy and Mines and before that a dependency of the Ministry of Development and Public Works. It is headed by a civil servant, normally a mining engineer

with private-sector experience. The parastatal enterprises are nominally independent and responsible to the mining minister alone. There is also a quasi-
independent research institute known as INGEMMET, which is charged with
the acquisition, development, and diffusion of new geological, mining, and
metallurgical technologies. The DGM plays a much more active role in sectoral planning and in overseeing the operations of private firms than does,
say, the U.S. Bureau of Mines. It requires each company to submit annually
a lengthy "consolidated declaration" of its finances, production, investments
planned and in progress, labor utilization and relations, mining camp conditions, and shareholders of record.[66]

Conclusions

The Peruvian mining sector is the linchpin of the national economy, whose
health depends on the export of metals and mineral products. Copper is the
chief export, and Peru ranks fourth in the Third World as an exporter of the
red metal. But, unlike any other principal Third World copper producer, the
nation also exports significant amounts of lead, zinc, and silver. Peru is, in
addition, the only one of the top four Third World copper exporters that has
not nationalized the entire large-mining subsector and the only one in which
privately owned domestic mining firms, some of them as large and well
organized as are smaller foreign subsidiaries, participate to a major degree
in export production.

The gran minería was established by foreign corporations and operated for
many years as a set of disarticulated enclaves tied more closely to overseas
economies than to Peru's. Extremely liberal laws allowed that condition to
continue. They also set taxes at very low levels (by Third World standards)
and did not interfere with the companies' profit repatriations or sales and
pricing policies. All of this was possible because the political system was
dominated by an oligarchy, consisting of a landed class and an associated
rentier plutocracy, that had no interest in using the state to promote the
development of a more broadly based, internally oriented industrial capitalism.
The development of the gran minería from 1950 to 1968 was the principal
Third World mining investment activity by U.S.-domiciled transnational resource corporations in those years. At the end of the period, Peru was host
to over a third of all U.S. private direct investment in Latin American mining
and metallurgical processing.

Large mining enterprises in Peru have been of two kinds. Cerro, which
appeared on the scene just after the turn of the century, operated several small
(by modern criteria) mines, its techniques of production in all but two of them
being essentially identical to those employed in the mediana minería. Its

---

[66] These "consolidated declarations" (see nn. 45, 56, 60) are an invaluable source of information on all phases of company activities and are available for all years since 1967. I have
drawn on them extensively during the course of this study.

position in the national industry was therefore due more to its sheer size and its smelting-refining monopoly than to the scale and character of its mining technologies. Cerro was also the only large, foreign-owned mining firm to branch out into other activities, which it did by becoming a great landowner and by investing in and managing local manufacturing operations related to the mining industry. These brought its interests into harmony with those of the oligarchy. Lastly, Cerro did not become a true transnational mining enterprise, understood as one that integrates operations in several political jurisdictions on the basis of global profit maximization. Until the fifties it was a Peruvian concern with head offices in New York; after that—its U.S. expansion having been fueled by profits earned in Peru—it was more of a loose conglomerate than an integrated nonferrous metals producer. Southern and Marcona, both of which entered Peru some fifty years after Cerro, were high-volume producers utilizing the latest mining and metallurgical technologies. Both confined their local operations to mining and partial processing. However, these two differed in their places in the world mining industry. Southern unites three (now four) large transnational enterprises and Cerro, and is managed by one of the world's principal integrated producers of nonferrous metals. Marcona, in contrast, was under the majority ownership of a firm whose main business is mine and refinery construction and which does not manufacture or sell steel.

We are now in a position to set forth three general propositions about the Peruvian mining industry:

1. The operations of the companies have impacted differently on the formation of both a local bourgeoisie associated with the industry and a local working class of the mines. Due to technological similarities and business relationships entailed in the refining and marketing of mine products, Cerro was more tightly linked than the rest of the gran minería to the domestic medium firms. In consequence, it may well have had a stronger impact on bourgeois class formation. Cerro's influence on local politics and class formation may also have been affected by its mutuality of interests with the oligarchy; it alone of the large foreign mining firms was structurally tied to that group.

2. The companies have defined their interests differently because of their different forms of organization, technologies, and market situations. As a result, they have had differing effects on local economic development; have responded differently to Peruvian policy in the sector; and have differently affected relations with external forces. These effects will surely prove to have been greater in Cerro's and Southern's cases than in Marcona's, since the latter has not figured nearly as prominently in the country's employment structure, tax revenues, or export base. For that reason, the balance of this study can safely focus on the first two firms.

3. In most Third World mineral-exporting countries, the only local bourgeois element directly supported by the mining industry is a small managerial

group associated with parastatal enterprise and the state apparatus. Otherwise the interests of a local bourgeois class in the industry are limited to the best use of its tax payments, profits (if there is state ownership), and foreign exchange earnings to promote capital accumulation elsewhere in the economy. This interest is present in Peru, too. But there is also a private-sector bourgeois class element that depends on mining for its class position. Its direct connection to the fulcrum of the national economy may have significance for bourgeois hegemony. Its ability to influence policy toward this key economic sector is an indicator of the degree of "relative autonomy" enjoyed by the state.

The three propositions are the point of departure for the rest of our study.

CHAPTER THREE

Mining Policy and
Policymaking after 1968

O UR purpose in this chapter is to review the mining policy goals and framework adopted by the military government—the first step in comprehending why it acted as it did in the situations that we will examine later on. (We will also review the minor policy changes adopted by the civilian government after 1980.) Policymaking in the mining sector was primarily influenced by three factors, and we shall discuss each of them in turn. They are: (1) the historical evolution of the process of Peruvian development and of the mining industry's role therein—particularly, the failure of the industry to perform as anticipated during most of the sixties; (2) the institutions and personnel responsible for sectoral policy formulation after 1968; and (3) the nature of the military's interest in industrialization. Then we shall look at policy content. I will show that the military's policy framework included both inherited practices and certain radical departures to accommodate new goals: more rapid industrial development, and the regime's broader sociopolitical aims—e.g., securing its legitimacy in power and furthering the ''revolution's'' attempted modernization of Peruvian capitalism. Policy output entailed both change and constancy: change, in that the state's role in the industry was greatly expanded and the prerogatives of foreign investors cut back; constancy, in that the interests of private Peruvian mining capital continued to be protected and nurtured.

To all intents and purposes there was no development planning of any sort in Peru before 1968. The oligarchy professed an ideological preference for ''free market'' capitalism. In reality the market was hardly free, given the high concentration of capital and land ownership; what the oligarchic preference actually signified was openness to foreign investment in any form and avoidance of government interference with the vested rights of property. The power and political influence of the various oligarchic elements were denoted by the expression *fuerzas vivas*, signifying that they, and not ''superstructural'' politics, determined policy outcomes; they were deployed to block every reform that might have infringed in the slightest on the group's business or political interests. Treasury ministers, usually selected from the oligarchy itself, saw their duty as defending the value of the currency; maintaining a low taxation pressure, especially on incomes, so as not to discourage private investment; balancing the budget; keeping the state's economic profile to a minimum; and preserving a stable investment climate. Government credit was never used to support domestic enterprise—with the exception of the cotton industry, in which oligarchs had sizable interests.[1] Fiscal policy favored mining but did not distinguish in any way between domestic and foreign firms: "Preferential treatment was extended to all existing mining enterprises regardless of whether they undertook new investments. No *quid pro quo* was asked by the government in exchange for the tax revenues which it was proposing to forego." A 1959 industrial promotion act granted additional tax forgiveness to industry (most of the benefits went to mining and agricultural exporters), with the effect that the income tax take was further reduced and the weight of regressive, indirect taxes increased.[2] Macroeconomic policy was unplanned and ad hoc, its content circumscribed by the short-run concerns of the *fuerzas vivas*.

The military, well before the 1968 coup, had already signaled their dissatisfaction with this laissez-faire approach to national development: one of the few substantive acts of the junta that briefly ruled in 1962-63 was the establishment of the National Planning Institute, which was charged with drawing up an indicative plan of national development.[3] During the first Belaunde administration the INP undertook the task of macroeconomic forecasting, analyzed the causes of underdevelopment (its thinking paralleled that of ECLA, the U.N. Economic Commission for Latin America),[4] and assisted in the preparation of the state budget. It eventually issued a development plan;[5] but the plan contained little more than a compendium of investments proposed by the private sector and a set of macroeconomic projections based on them.

From the start the "revolution" aimed to implement meaningful, centralized economic planning; the military dreamed of rapid economic development and were convinced that market forces alone were inadequate to stimulate it.[6]

[1] Frankman (1974). The laissez-faire character of oligarchic economic policy is documented by Bourricaud (1967:194-203).

[2] See Frankman (1974), who is the source for the lines quoted in this paragraph; see also Webb (1972a). Foreign mining companies had to pay an income tax surcharge of 30 percent, but it was in lieu of a tax that domestic companies paid on dividend distributions.

[3] It should be noted that the existence of such a plan was a requirement for receiving aid under the Alliance for Progress. Nonetheless, most writers are of the opinion that the Peruvian military's dedication to planning was sincere. Certainly, their acts when in charge of the state after 1968 confirm that conclusion.

[4] The ECLA approach to underdevelopment and dependency is expressed in the writings of, among others, Prebisch (1962, 1963); he is usually considered to have been the intellectual parent of these ideas. See also Furtado (1970:205-11 and passim). ECLA's analysis of the problem is institutional, suggesting that appropriate policy choices by Latin American governments can do much to overcome conditions of dependency. This, of course, is a quite different position from that taken by the more structurally oriented dependency literature referred to in Chapter 1.

[5] Instituto Nacional de Planificación (1967).

[6] This was not merely an obvious deduction from recent Peruvian history. ECLA development theories emphasizing the importance of economic planning for bringing about development in Latin America permeated the economics courses taught at the Centro de Altos Estudios Militares (CAEM). On the role of the CAEM in the political-ideological formation of Peruvian officers see Einaudi and Stepan (1971); and Villanueva (1972).

Development, in the military's view, required the state to assume new powers and to become the director of the process. This would be accomplished in part through state entrepreneurship, since state enterprises could be commanded to take on development projects irrespective of risks or the absence of short-term profitability. In part it would be accomplished by the expansion of credit under state control: much of the banking system was nationalized, and the state set up a new development bank, the Development Finance Corporation (COFIDE), to make debt and equity investments in government and private development ventures. However, inasmuch as the regime neither nationalized all private capital nor took systematic control of the commanding economic heights, planning remained largely indicative. Economic policy derived from the development plan still had to influence private decisionmakers via fiscal and credit incentives.

The novelty of these reforms left the regime, for a while, with an unusual measure of autonomous control over the content of economic policy once the stranglehold of oligarchic power had been broken, but this should not be interpreted as structural autonomy from class interests. There was no baseline of prior experience with which to judge the probable reactions of the private sector to various kinds of policy initiatives involving an economically active state. Until some moves were made and the responses thereto evaluated over time, policymakers could not know what was possible and what impossible under a restructured capitalism and thus were relatively free to experiment. Private industrial capital had been caught off guard by the rapidity of change and would need time to emplace new networks of political power and influence to replace those ruptured by the "revolution." As regards the mining sector, we shall see that there was a precedent in the years just prior to the 1968 coup for bourgeois support of stronger measures to control the activities of foreign mining companies.

THE HISTORICAL BACKGROUND TO MINING POLICY

Since the military produced no thoroughgoing social revolution, its mining policies had to take into account some of the same interests served in the past and could not radically depart from previous practice. Rather, those policies sought to revitalize and bend to new purposes an idea about the political role of mineral exports that had been handed down from the earliest days of the Peruvian republic.

In the preceding chapter we observed that the oligarchy had no need of a powerful central state to assist it in accumulating capital and enforcing social control. But there was a problem. As gradual socioeconomic change brought forth social strata with growing aspirations, private coercion alone could no longer be counted on to stem unrest. If the rising groups were to find a unity based on their common situation of "blocked ascent," the status quo would be severely endangered. Therefore, a divide-and-conquer strategy toward them was adopted. Known as "segmental incorporation,"[7] it consisted in selectively admitting the best-organized and most cohesive subordinate strata to a measure of economic privilege and limited political participation while continuing to repress those popular groups that seemed less capable of mounting a threat. This kind of co-optation necessitated financial resources and a state to administer and channel them. The former were found initially in the export "bonanza" of the nineteenth-century "age of guano."[8] By allowing foreign investors to rationalize the fertilizer trade while assuring a flow of royalty revenues into its and the state's coffers, the oligarchy was able to eat its cake and have it, too: a state large and competent enough to undertake segmental incorporation, yet one that did not have to depend for its fiscal support on taxing domestic wealth. The means of co-optation, meanwhile, were tailored to the rising stratum in question. Military *caudillos*, the first, were coopted by putting them on the state payroll—a procedure repeated many years later in the case of middle-class groups, who were also offered legal protection of white-collar employee rights and a series of social insurance programs. Industrial entrepreneurs, the second, were given tax exemptions, some subsidies, and a small amount of tariff protection (never so much as to infringe upon the oligarchic interest in free trade). When, eventually, it came the turn of organized working-class and underclass elements, they were accommodated through public works programs and the gradual extension to them of employee rights and insurance benefits.[9]

The exhaustion of guano reserves by the latter part of the nineteenth century, followed by the loss of mineral nitrate deposits to Chile in the settlement that ended the War of the Pacific (1879-1883), necessitated the discovery of a new exportable resource. Copper and other nonferrous metals then became the fount of the new "bonanza" and remain so today. The 1901 Mining Code was enacted for the specific purpose of fostering their large-scale exploitation by foreign investors, exactly as had been done earlier on with fertilizers; and when burgeoning cooptative claims on the metals "bonanza" began to overburden it, investment incentives were liberalized still further with the promulgation of the 1950 Code. However, the size of the "bonanza" was also a function of world metals prices—not only directly but in that mining companies' investment plans responded as much to price trend projections as to incentives held out to them. Whenever prices fell sharply the "bonanza" shrank, leaving the state with an uncomfortable choice: to reduce cooptative benefits and slow segmental incorporation, or to run budgetary and balance-of-payments deficits. Inasmuch as oligarchic sound-money policies foreclosed

[7] The term comes from Julio Cotler (1967-68).

[8] This period is discussed and its policies analyzed by H. Bonilla (1974a, 1977); Cotler (1978:85-114); Greenhill and Miller (1973); Hunt (1973); and Miller (1976).

[9] The approximate time periods corresponding to the attempted cooptation of the several groups are as follows: for the *caudillos*, 1845-1875; for the entrepreneurs, 1895-1925; for the middle classes, 1945-1965; for the urban underclass, 1950 to the present; and for the organized working class, 1950 to the present but with emphasis on the years after 1969.

the second option, the first was invariably selected. The resulting popular unrest was then contained by switching from incorporation to overt repression, as occurred from 1933 to 1939 and from 1948 to 1956. Resort to repression was not a favorite oligarchic measure. It enlarged the powers of the state and led to their exercise by generals who, though subject to oligarchic influence, enjoyed an independent institutional basis of power and thus were less compliant than civilian governors. It was, simply, the lesser evil.[10]

By the 1960s the "bonanza" political economy was coming under new stresses. The capitalization of agriculture was expelling more and more peasants from the haciendas and feeding the explosive growth of the urban underclass. The long-dormant peasantry itself was becoming restive. At the same time the mining sector was stagnating after its growth spurt of the previous decade.[11] New foreign investment in Peruvian mining could no longer be stimulated by additional incentives, since the 1950 Mining Code was already one of the most liberal in the Third World; they would only reduce the size of the existing "bonanza." The sole alternative was to move in the opposite direction: to compel the transnational resource firms already on the scene to contribute more in taxes and capital inflows than they had been doing. Hence, the oligarchy and the political authorities started to cast a jaundiced eye in the direction of the privileges enjoyed by the mining industry under the 1950 Code.

A particular sore point was the economic performance of Southern Peru Copper, detailed in Table 3.1. As the table indicates, Southern's profit flows had turned into a veritable flood by 1966. Its shareholders' investment was fully amortized in that year, well ahead of schedule.[12] And yet, the company went on benefiting from guaranteed low taxes under its Toquepala contract with the Peruvian state, for two reasons: (1) as has been mentioned (Chapter

[10] The connection between the 1901 Code and the need for a new "bonanza" is explained by Purser (1971:97-100) and by Basadre (1961-1968:7:3105-16). The clearest example of a "bonanza stagnation crisis" leading to the institution of political authoritarianism is probably the decline of Bustamante y Rivero's reformist government (1945-1948) and its overthrow in a military coup headed by Gen. Manuel Odría; on the events of the period see Cotler (1978:266-72) and Pike (1967:280-88). But Odría's dictatorship partook of many populist elements (MacLean y Estenós 1953; Bourricaud 1964; Collier 1976:55-72). His effort to build a personal following among the urban underclass and other popular sectors required him to extend cooptative benefits and gave him a strong interest in revitalizing the "bonanza"—the reason for his approval of the 1950 Mining Code.

[11] The rise of underclass political activity is described by Collier (1976); Dietz (1969); and Michl (1973). On peasant unrest in the 1960s see the works by two leaders of peasant rebellions: Hugo Blanco (1972) and Héctor Béjar (1969); see also the analysis by Handelman (1975). As for mining during this period: except for Cobriza, Cerro's modern underground mine, no new large projects were initiated; and the mediana minería was badly hurt by falling lead and zinc prices (Thorp and Bertram 1978:219).

[12] The reason is that copper prices had been projected at a very low level in planning the mine, on the assumption that they would plummet after the end of the Korean War. In fact, they rose. With production costs of only 9¢/lb when it opened in 1960 (14¢ in 1968), Toquepala is considered one of the cheapest of the world's major open-pit copper mines to operate (Mikesell 1975a:48).

TABLE 3.1 Southern Peru Copper Corporation Financial Performance, 1956-1970
(*Profit in percent; cash flow in millions of dollars*)

Year	Profit on Sales	Profit on Equity	Cash Flow to Shareholders[a]	
			Annual	Total
To 1955			(13.9)[b]	(13.9)[b]
1956			(31.0)	(44.9)
1957			(29.0)	(73.9)
1958			(19.5)	(93.4)
1959			(14.0)	(107.4)
1960	12.7	28.2	0.0	(107.4)
1961	14.9	36.1	14.4	(93.0)
1962	10.5	21.0	13.5	(79.5)
1963	13.3	17.8	16.1	(63.4)
1964	15.0	20.8	15.7	(47.7)
1965	23.5	27.0	15.4	(32.3)
1966	38.6	64.3	41.9	9.6
1967	59.6[c]	116.3[c]	46.5	56.1
1968	25.1	45.0	43.5	99.6
1969	23.5	50.7	55.0	154.6
1970	17.2	36.1	45.1	199.7

SOURCES: Profits data computed by the author from information in the consolidated declarations of the company; cash flow data from Mikesell (1975a:74).
[a] Dividend payments, amortization of shareholder advances, plus sums reinvested in other mines; less advances by shareholders.
[b] Sums in parentheses are negative.
[c] Includes extraordinary profit of $28.1 million, consisting of depletion reserves transferred to ordinary income less income taxes paid thereupon.

2, n. 51), certain accounting items that should have been counted against investment recuperation were not; and (2) tax stability had been guaranteed not for the actual time it took to recoup the investment, but for a fixed term of years predicated upon the company's original—and very pessimistic—recuperation time estimate. To make matters worse, the special advantages which Southern received had been based on an article of the 1950 Mining Code authorizing additional incentives for the exploitation of "marginal" mineral deposits. Peruvians naturally understood "marginal" to mean that such deposits could not be profitably worked at all without the extra incentives. Southern had argued, and the Odría regime had agreed, that Toquepala should be considered marginal because its average ore grade was "only" 1.3 percent copper. It did not publicize the fact that ores of considerably *lower* grade were even then being exploited quite profitably in open-pit mines in the United States and Canada.

It was the congress, controlled by conservative forces, and not the "reformist" Belaunde administration that led the attack on Southern's "superprofits." When a powerful congressional committee published a report highly critical of the company,[13] Southern decided to stop beating into the wind. It volunteered to abrogate its special contract two years early, meaning that it would pay income taxes at the regular rate of 54.5 percent (its special rate had been 30 percent) starting in 1968 rather than 1970 as originally scheduled. Nevertheless, the congress repealed the article of the 1950 Code under which the contract had been let, substituting far stricter qualifications and more limited incentives.

A second sore point was that foreign investors had not moved to develop Peruvian mining to anything like the extent that had been anticipated when the 1950 Code was promulgated. It had been the dream of the code's supporters that Peru would become host to several open-pit copper mining installations on the scale of the great Chuquicamata (Anaconda) and El Teniente (Kennecott) mines in rival Chile. The reserves were there: eight important concessions had all been carefully explored by their holders and contained proved and probable reserves amounting to nearly 20 million fine metric tons of copper.[14] The development of any one of them would require huge investments in infrastructure and mine construction—but that, after all, was what the incentives in the mining code were supposed to make feasible. Only Southern's Cuajone property was under any sort of active development by 1966, however. In view of the number of concessions it held idle (five) and its long tenure in the country, Cerro's performance was particularly disappointing. Due notice was taken of the fact that Cerro *had* made a major investment in a new copper mine—in the territory of Peru's historic enemy to the south.

Thus the military, upon assuming supreme power, inherited a "bonanza" politics based on the underwriting of a cooptative-repressive state by foreign extractive enterprises. The military regime was not in a position to do away with this sort of politics entirely, since its "revolution" was partial. It did not eliminate all of the propertied elements that had benefited from the old politics. Furthermore, it was intended as a "revolution with order," a neat surgical excision of oligarchic power without unleashing popular forces. Therefore, the process of cooptation and segmental incorporation of mobilized lower strata had to be continued and extended. But too much of the "bonanza" was leaking away in profits repatriated by the transnationals, just as pressures from below against the existing order were steadily increasing. In view of

[13] Comisión Bicameral Multipartidaria (1967). It is significant in light of later events that, according to the commission's conclusion, much of the controversy could have been avoided had the government exercised proper oversight of both the company's financial estimates used in its contract proposal and its operations later on.

[14] My calculation, from data presented by Rodríguez Hoyle (1974). The concessions in question were: Cuajone and Quellaveco, held by Southern; Cerro Verde, held by the Andes Exploration Company, an Anaconda subsidiary; Michiquillay, held by Asarco via Northern Peru Mining; and Antamina, Chalcobamba-Ferrobamba, Tintaya, and Toromocho, all held by Cerro.

the past history that we have examined, the generals had every reason to believe that more active state policies designed to correct the problem would not further alienate the Right and might actually prove attractive to the industrial bourgeoisie.

POLICYMAKERS AND INSTITUTIONS

The military's concern with the size of the "bonanza" did not stem entirely from perceptions of its political utility. Peruvian generals were convinced of the need to spur industrialization, with a new emphasis on basic heavy industry—not only to provide the ultimate solution to the country's persistent social and economic problems, but also out of narrowly military considerations.

This was an armed force that had fought two full-scale wars in the recent past with its neighbors, Chile (1879-1883) and Ecuador (1940-1941), both of which had resulted in major territorial realignments.[15] Consequently, it was highly sensitive to the nation's geopolitical situation and to the regional power balance. It had a firm sense of its own military tradition, with its French—not North American—origins.[16] Like most Latin American military establishments of the fifties and sixties it had concentrated on improving its internal security capabilities; but it remained conscious of the lessons of history and continued to emphasize traditional territorial defense.[17] Its strategic doctrines took full cognizance of the importance of a modern economic, especially heavy industrial, base to the conduct of sustained military operations. They counseled the wholesale improvement of Peru's economic base (as well as an arms buildup, which the "bonanza" would also have to finance) so that Chile would cease to be the hegemonic power of western South America.[18]

In spite of the tremendous economic significance of mining, neither the military presidents nor the COAP involved themselves very much with the sector's affairs. Their presence was most in evidence when a sectoral policy

[15] The War of the Pacific ended with the loss to Chile of Peru's three southern provinces (the northernmost, Tacna, was returned pursuant to a 1929 arbitration by the United States). Peruvians still complain that Chile has never complied with provisions of the arbitration agreement obligating it to allow Peruvian trade to pass duty-free through the ex-Peruvian port of Arica and to build a railroad at its expense linking Arica with the city of Tacna. In the Ecuadorian war Peru seized a huge tract of Amazonian territory almost equal in extent to Ecuador's current land area. Ecuador has on several occasions repudiated the 1942 treaty that ended the war; armed conflict has broken out numerous times along the frontier, most recently in early 1980. The disputed territory's strategic importance has increased tremendously, as it contains nearly all of Peru's petroleum reserves.

[16] The modernization and professionalization of the Peruvian army took place beginning at the turn of the century with French assistance (North 1966).

[17] Einaudi (1970:7-8).

[18] See Mercado Jarrín (1974); the prologue to his book leaves no doubt that his views reflect the official thinking of the military establishment. The post-1968 Peruvian military buildup is detailed to some extent (the data are secret) in *Aviation Week and Space Technology*, 2 December 1974, pp. 21-22.

threatened to create a negative image of the Peruvian investment climate in the eyes of prospective foreign investors and lenders whom the regime wanted to attract; when it might have had adverse foreign-policy implications; or, when it came into conflict with policy in other sectors.[19] Otherwise, the making and implementation of mining policy was left to the relevant ministries, although drafts of proposed legislation were always reviewed by the whole Council of Ministers and the COAP. The ministries, however, were not free to do as they pleased; their actions had to conform—or be made to appear to conform—to the guidelines set down in the regime's master plans. There were two of these: the Plan Inca, first published in 1974 but claimed to have been circulated privately among the generals since before the coup; and the Plan Túpac Amaru, which superceded the former in 1977.[20] The mining policy guidelines of both are summarized in Table B.1, Appendix B.

The INP never became an effective voice in the making of high economic policy and had relatively little impact on policy vis-à-vis the mining industry.[21] It produced a series of reports on the nature of property ownership and the organization of investment and production in the minería, but these seem to have been consulted more by scholars than by policymakers.[22] That the military wanted to confine the INP largely to the monitoring of policy implementation is clear from the fact that its director was a colonel, outranked by the senior generals and admirals on the Council of Ministers. Moreover, the policy recommendations contained in INP reports, many of them prepared by academic economists who were Marxist or radical nationalist by training and inclination, were often well to the left of what the regime was ready to accept. Above all, the INP had no day-to-day contact with the private sector and, thus, little political sensitivity. In proportion as the influence of private capital on economic policy reasserted itself, that of the INP waned.

Hence, most of the burden of mining policy formulation fell to the mining ministry and, within it, to the DGM. The significance of this lay in the fact that the flow of power and influence through the DGM was bidirectional. On the one hand, the bureau was the supervisor of mining company operations and the enforcer of the sector's laws and regulations. On the other, it was the principal contact point between the state and private mining capital; and

[19] Intersectoral conflict often broke out between the ministers of mining and of industries, most commonly over the issue of mandatory local purchases of machinery and equipment by the mining industry. Each minister assiduously advanced the interests of private capital associated with his area of competence. There was also occasional conflict between the mining and economy ministries over the former's proposals for state expenditures in the resource sector.

[20] Gobierno Revolucionario de la Fuerza Armada (1975); and Presidencia de la República (1977). Zimmermann Zavala (1974) is the primary source for the claim of pre-1968 authorship of the Plan Inca; see also Stepan (1978:145).

[21] The only "hard" INP role in mining policy that I could discover lies in the agency's issuance of priorities for state and parastatal capital projects. The INP cannot dictate to, say, MineroPeru how and where to invest; but by withholding a priority it can prevent the project from being included in the state's current capital investment budget, thereby delaying it.

[22] INP reports and analyses are listed in the bibliography.

as one of the DGM's duties was to promote mining development, it acted as the spokesperson for the industry within the state apparatus. In its administrative reform the military regime had been careful not to alarm local mining capital by depriving it of its voice inside the state—institutionalized not only in informal contacts and relationships but also in private-sector representation on the Superior Mining Council, an interagency consultative body that advises the minister. Under these circumstances it was extremely unlikely that mining policy would ever ignore the interests and desires of the domestic companies, whatever its effects on foreign interests (foreigners did not have as effective an institutional voice). The locus of policy initiative became blurred: If the minister were determined and knowledgeable in the affairs of the industry; if he could persuade the companies that his policies were in their long-range interest; and if the industry were economically healthy and its owners and managers content—then the minister could initiate policy. If these conditions were not met, there was every likelihood that, be it via threats and confrontation or via cooptation of the minister and his staff, the locus of initiative would shift to domestic private enterprise.

The first mining minister (he held the portfolio from its creation in April 1969 until September 1975) was well equipped to be an active initiator of sectoral policy. He was Gen. Jorge Fernández Maldonado Solari, one of the planners of the 1968 coup and an early confidante of President Velasco. Fernández Maldonado had made a study of the mining industry while a student at the CAEM (Center for Higher Military Studies) and had taken a personal interest in the issue of natural resources and their role in national development. A self-professed Social Christian, he disliked untrammeled free-market capitalism, which oppressed workers and divided society into hostile camps. A preferable system, he believed, would not abolish private property but would encourage private interests to defer voluntarily to the national welfare; classes would cooperate for the attainment of national goals under the guidance of a "moralized" state acting to eliminate extremes of wealth and poverty.[23] He was, in addition, attuned to the dependencista critique of foreign resource investment, opining that the open door to foreign investors had produced an insufficient degree of exploitation of workable deposits, a loss of national wealth in excessive profit remittances, a distorted and disarticulated enclave economy, and a neglect of the human dignity of the mine worker. However, he did not wish to eliminate all foreign investment in mining; in his view, only transnational resource corporations could make up Peru's domestic deficiencies in regard to investment capital and metal-processing technology. As long as this were so, the transnational presence would have to be accepted and its abuses controlled through a greater state economic activity in the sector, better state supervision of private enterprise, and the scaling back of

[23] These are the classic ideas of Latin American Catholic corporatism. Their origins, evolution, and implementation are reviewed by Stepan (1978:27-72); see also Schmitter (1974) and Wiarda (1973).

incentives to the minimum demonstrably necessary to attract new resource investment.[24]

The effectiveness of a minister depends in good part on his relations with the civil servants under his direction, and Fernández Maldonado's were excellent. The senior career officials of the DGM found his policies echoing most of their preferences and were impressed by his comprehension—rare for a nonspecialist—of the details of mining industry affairs. He, in turn, respected their loyalty and professionalism, deferring to them in matters where informed judgment rested upon technical expertise.

Now, the DGM staff was and is something of an exception from the run-of-the-mill Peruvian bureaucracy. The chief of the agency has usually been an experienced mining engineer drawn in laterally from the private sector (since there was until recently no state mining enterprise where the requisite technical background could be gained). Most chiefs have enjoyed a fairly long tenure in office and have thus been able to build up cadres of well-trained subordinates from among their associates in private industry and the National Engineering University. This is possible despite notoriously low salaries in state service because Peruvian administrative tradition is relatively unconcerned with conflict of interest. Consequently, bureau heads and their subordinates are free to retain shareholdings in private firms of the sector and even to earn second salaries as part-time private managers. Many have also been instructors of mining engineering, yet another source of outside income and social status for them. Still, there is no evidence that these men and women have crassly favored in their official duties the firms with which they were personally connected—which, of course, does not exclude a general sympathy with the interests of domestic private mining capital as a whole.

We will examine the class character of the state mining "technobureaucracy" and its linkages with other bourgeois and middle-class elements in Chapter 9. It is already apparent, however, that this is no autonomous (from dominant economic interests) ruling group as posited by theories of "revolution from above":

A bureaucratic state apparatus can be considered autonomous when those who hold the highest civil and military posts satisfy two conditions: (1) that they are *not* recruited from the dominant landed, commercial, or industrial classes, nor do they have personal vested interests in the dominant means of production; and (2) such bureaucrats are not controlled by or subordinate to a parliamentary or party apparatus which represents the dominant interests.[25]

[24] Interview with Fernández Maldonado, July 15, 1978. He told me that he "could have had his pick of high positions in the military regime" and that the choice of the mining portfolio was his own. I was also favored with opportunities to discuss these issues frankly and openly with several of Fernández Maldonado's former civilian aides and immediate subordinates. That the general was one of the "progressives," or "radical colonels," who planned the 1968 coup has since been widely acknowledged; see Zimmermann Zavala (1974) and Stepan (1978:145).

[25] Horowitz and Trimberger (1976). The theory of "revolution from above" is due to Trimberger (1972, 1978), who applies it to Peru (among other cases) in the latter work.

The military establishment—arguably—meets these criteria. But the officer corps could not spare the manpower to occupy all policymaking positions in the central state. In the mining ministry, only the minister himself was a military officer; all other top officials were civilians, whose technical expertise gave them a significant input in the determination of policy. The civilian "technobureaucracy" met the second criterion (after 1968) but not the first.

Some of the younger DGM staff members during the late sixties and early seventies were ideological Leftists who hoped to place obstacles in the path of new and existing foreign investment, in the belief that this would promote local socialism. Most, however, were "moderates"—meaning, in this context, that they supported a capitalism in which private property rights were subject to regulation in the general interest, with the state actively redressing inequities and securing the welfare of the less privileged. They were quite conversant with strategies of state ownership in the resource sector as practiced in other countries. None of them believed (or feared) that nationalization of natural resources had to do with establishing socialism; they understood it, accurately, as a sometimes-useful mechanism for making the resource industries contribute more to local development. But a full-scale state monopoly over resource exploitation was not, in their view, a mechanism needed in Peru. The country could already boast of a mining entrepreneuriat and a sizable group of technical specialists and other professionals like themselves. With such human resources available in the private sector, total state control of the resource economy would actually be counterproductive in that it would absorb too much of the state's revenues and personnel, bring bureaucratic inefficiencies in its wake, and, if achieved by expropriating existing foreign firms, cause further conflict with the developed West—all this without lessening national dependence or speeding economic development. That, they thought, was the lesson of Allende's Chile. On the other hand, they did not eschew nationalization altogether; they merely reserved it for the ultimate sanction to be used against foreign mining companies that could not or would not play the role being laid out for them.

A preferable development strategy, in the eyes of the "moderates," was something that they styled (incorrectly) as *el modelo japonés* (after the economic policy of the Meiji regime). The strategy envisioned state promotion of private capital accumulation by means of carefully managed relationships with foreign enterprise, macroeconomic planning, and the stimulation of an oligopolistic private economy characterized by close institutional ties among companies and between them and the state. The plan of development would utilize foreign investment in extractive industry to speed local capital accumulation: a large share of the economic rent from resource exploitation would be appropriated by the state through taxation and directed toward undercapitalized economic sectors. State entrepreneurship in mining would be fostered but would complement, not replace, private investment. It would intervene in projects useful or essential to mining development in which private capital was uninterested or in which foreign control would entail too great a measure of dependence. The state would also seek to open up opportunities for local private investment in the supply of raw materials and equipment to the mining industry and in semifinished manufactures based on locally refined metals.

MINING POLICY IN PERU AFTER 1968: "BONANZA DEVELOPMENT"

We have seen that the development plans of the military regime called for continuing reliance on a minerals export "bonanza." Unlike oligarchic policy, however, the "bonanza" was no longer to be used solely for political purposes and for enriching the ruling elite and its allies. Rather, it was to become as well—without abandoning its political function—a principal source of new capital and scarce foreign exchange for a program of vastly accelerated industrialization under state guidance. Evidently, the "bonanza" could not possibly bear the burdens imposed on it unless it were greatly enlarged. That in turn demanded that the stagnation of mining investment during the 1960s be overcome and that additional foreign investment be attracted. But the generals were good nationalists, as were the DGM technocrats. For both the prime requisite of mining-sector policy was that it not increase, and that it preferably decrease, Peru's external dependence even as foreign investment in the country's key economic sector was growing. How were these apparently contradictory objectives to be attained?

1. First and foremost: even though the state would not take over the entire mining industry, it would play the main directing role in sectoral affairs and would cease to be the sector's *gran ausente* ("great missing member"). Only it could meet the most elementary prerequisite of a national minerals policy— a full accounting of reserves. Only it could authoritatively define the national interest in resource development, fashion a strategy to secure it, and assure that each actor—foreign enterprise, domestic private enterprise, parastatal enterprise—complied with its appointed function.

2. State approval would henceforth be required for all foreign investment activity in mining, including reinvestments and irrespective of scale. The state would begin to employ disciplinary sanctions in addition to positive incentives as a means to induce foreign-owned firms to conduct their operations in harmony with the national interest. Corporate discretion over marketing, production volumes, and levels of local processing would be restricted or eliminated; firms would not be permitted any longer to sit on concessions, not developing them but blocking others from doing so.

3. Peru's export dependence was acknowledged, and it was accepted that there was no realistic alternative for ending it in the near future without bringing industrialization to a grinding halt. Export dependence, it was thought, would come to an end gradually, as an industrialized domestic economy evolved into the principal generator and consumer of national wealth. In the

interim Peru would diversify her market outlets so as to become less dependent on the economic fortunes or political actions of any one of her customers.

4. The gran minería, being dependent in any event on markets controlled by the transnational resource corporations, could accept more foreign investment without that, in itself, worsening national dependency. Nor would its arrival preempt domestic business opportunities, since local mining enterprise was not in any condition to undertake such huge mining projects alone. A capital-intensive gran minería would be encouraged, as it would result in lower costs of production and, therefore, higher "bonanza" returns. The deleterious effects of mining enclave formation would be eliminated by the use of the "bonanza" to underwrite industrial development elsewhere, thereby substituting for direct economic linkages to the rest of the nation's economy. But the state would still promote such linkages by requiring mining firms to patronize local equipment and raw materials suppliers wherever possible, and by insisting that they make their output preferentially available to local refineries as feedstocks and to industries as inputs. Taxation of the industry's profits, naturally, would be raised to the limit of what the traffic would bear (the income tax rate for foreign firms was raised to 68 percent, where it remains today).

5. The state would not dissipate its newly formed or borrowed capital[26] by plowing all of it back into the gran minería in competition with foreign enterprises or in paying compensation for nationalized properties. The state might find it politically or economically useful to enter into joint ventures with foreign capital. But it would avoid contributing cash capital to joint mining ventures and would not borrow on its own credit for the purpose. Neither would it commit any portion of its borrowing capacity to guaranteeing loans for privately financed mining projects.

6. Most of the constraints confining the gran minería to an indirect development role mediated by the state were not applicable to the mediana minería. It could prosper despite its lower capital intensity by exploiting high-grade ore veins too small to interest transnational mining companies, and/or by mining precious metals. It would be encouraged to expand, since it offered a greater employment potential per unit of output. It was also an important training school for national entrepreneurial and managerial talent. It might even be possible in time for stronger Peruvian companies to participate in

[26] Foreign borrowing was always an intrinsic part of the development plan. It was assumed that acceptance of new foreign resource investment, and the growth of Peruvian nonferrous metal exports, would enhance the nation's creditworthiness abroad, especially in the evaluation of private banks. Loans from private banks in Europe, furthermore, would compensate for U.S. actions in cutting off aid and Export-Import Bank financing in the wake of the IPC affair (Pinelo 1973). The intent was to use most of the loan proceeds for capital investments that would generate the income to amortize the loans with interest. In practice, though, the bulk of Peru's overseas loans were contracted for political purposes: to cover current budget deficits resulting from consumption subsidies to popular groups and from an unwillingness to further antagonize the bourgeoisie by raising taxation pressure. See FitzGerald (1979) and Stallings (1979).

large mining projects, alone or in association with state or foreign capital, thereby ensuring a greater degree of national control with a lesser commitment of state resources and personnel. Thus, a core element of mining policy was the care and feeding of the Peruvian-owned medium-mining firms via favorable tax treatment and more incentives than those extended to foreigners.

7. Peruvian refinery capacity would be significantly expanded. Besides capturing more local value added, domestic refineries could take advantage of cheap energy and low-cost labor to offer mining companies lower processing charges than they were paying abroad. That would enhance the international competitiveness of the mediana minería, which would especially benefit from a local refinery for zinc—one of its principal products. Domestic refining would also decrease market dependence by increasing the number of potential buyers of Peruvian mine products.[27]

Policymakers did not feel that scaling back large-mining investment incentives would hinder the realization of these policy objectives. As will be shown in the next chapter, such incentives were not really of much value in stimulating transnational firms to enter Peru. The country already possessed a number of comparative advantages: a national transportation network; good port facilities not too far removed from the mining districts; cheap energy; and, as befits a país minero, cadres of well-qualified engineers and skilled workers. In any event, all Third World producer nations were limiting the privileges of foreign investors, so Peru was under no pressure from its competition to increase them.

Interpreting Peruvian Mining Policy

Industrializing state elites, in searching for successful development models to emulate, are often drawn to "socialist mercantilism" as practiced in the Soviet Union under Stalin.[28] The Stalinist strategy of state-guided semi-autarkic heavy industrialization on the basis of capital accumulated coercively from agriculture stands as the most prominent such effort of all time. Except for its coercive element, it has much in common with the autarkic, statist development strategies that some dependencistas recommend—which, given the social character of the post-1968 Peruvian ruling elite, the nature of elite objectives, and the fact that the elite is known to have been influenced by

[27] The preceding has been my own synthesis based on Ballón (1974); my interview with Fernández Maldonado (n. 24); and conversations during 1977-78 with some thirty mining engineers, mine managers, and bureaucrats of the DGM—among them, two former DGM chiefs and the 1978 director of mining promotion. The last point regarding market diversification needs a bit of amplification. When ores or unrefined metals are exported, the only conceivable buyers are refineries, which are few in number (around sixty in the case of copper) and are concentrated in the metropolitan countries. Refined metals, in contrast, can be sold to hundreds of thousands of fabricators throughout the world, an increasing number of whom are located in countries— notably, the semi-industrialized Third World nations—which are not among Peru's traditional trading partners.

[28] The phrase "socialist mercantilism" is due to Sklar (n.d.), who has drawn upon Wheeler (1957) in formulating the concept.

dependency ideas,[29] makes it relevant to our discussion. However, no non-revolutionary state, and few revolutionary ones, can count on the total autonomy from class forces in civil society that is needed to implement this strategy. The Soviet Union was uniquely fortunate (or unfortunate) in that a weak prerevolutionary civil society, a highly authoritarian political tradition, and the ruin of civil war combined to give the Stalinist state an exceptional degree of autonomy.

If, on the other hand, these state elites find that their country has available to it the sort of resource "bonanza" that Peru does, another alternative presents itself: to make the "bonanza" serve in place of agriculture as the original source of large-scale industrial capital. This strategy demands the assistance of transnational resource firms, who alone can supply the huge investments necessitated by natural resource exploitation on a modern scale. That in turn means that capitalist development is tolerated, though not necessarily applauded or even openly proclaimed. In the resource sector itself, capitalist relations of production are inevitably implanted (along with highly capital-intensive production modes) regardless of the character of juridical ownership or of regime ideology, since ruling elites' interest in the sector revolves around productive efficiency to maximize the "bonanza." Yet, if the capital accumulated through resource exploitation is not to be merely exported by the transnationals or reinvested solely in ever more resource development—if, that is, it is to be used to foster industries in other sectors, some of which may not presently exist—the state must capture it and redirect it in the desired manner. What results is a distinctive strategy of development, which I term *bonanza development*. I suggest that it is a strategy with many parallels in other resource-rich Third World countries ruled by modernizing elites who do not wish to remain, as an old Peruvian saying has it, "beggars seated on a pile of gold."[30]

Bonanza development consists in using the resource "bonanza" for financial support of the state and for purposes of cooptation, as we have discussed; but *coupling these to greatly expanded state activity oriented toward industrial promotion*. In such a strategy, mineral production and export are valued primarily as sources of capital and foreign exchange. The enclave character of the minerals industries in Third World countries—the fact that they employ relatively few persons, export their product, and do not foment local industries to supply them with inputs[31]—ceases to be a problem, as the absent linkages

[29] Stepan (1978) points out that this was one of the first Latin American governments formally to embrace dependency ideas and to incorporate them in policy.

[30] I have analyzed bonanza development in a recent paper (Becker 1982), where I argue that it also has relevance to mineral-export-based development strategies observed in Nigeria (Schatz 1977) and Zambia (Sklar 1975). Other countries that might be considered examples of bonanza development include, most prominently, the OPEC nations and especially those six which are (or were, until very recently) governed by modernizing elites: Algeria, Ecuador, Iran, Iraq, Libya, and Venezuela. Mexico, since its petroleum boom, is potentially another example.

[31] The negative political consequences of enclave formation are discussed by Cotler (1979).

to the local economy are substituted by the state's capture and redistribution of the lion's share of the surplus that they generate.[32] Surplus is captured by the state through taxation, royalty payments, direct claims on profits (where the state is part or full juridical owner of the enterprise), and/or forced transfer payments. The industries that are promoted may be state- or privately owned. In either case their dependence on state-supplied capital (or subsidies, in which event the "bonanza" compensates the state for the outflow of funds or loss of tax revenue) enables the state to enlist them as well in the political task of cooptation. They are ordered or encouraged to pay higher salaries and to create more jobs than would be justified by narrowly economic criteria, thereby passing some of the benefits of their subsidies on to workers and middle-class staff.

Bonanza Development, Nationalism, and Class Forces

The omission from the policy guidelines of an explicit commitment to nationalization of foreign resource subsidiaries, and bonanza development's reliance on transnational capital in the resource sector, may raise questions about the nationalist bona fides of the regime. There also seems to be a too-obvious parallel between Peruvian bonanza development and the "agro-export"-based economic policy of the oligarchic epoch. Nonetheless, the new policy was, in fact, profoundly nationalist. In Part II we will discover that the military and the mining ministry technocrats were on solid ground with their claim regarding the sufficiency of improved state oversight of corporate operations for ensuring that resource development responded to local needs. Meanwhile, let us attempt to clarify the issues by looking at some of the ramifications of the bonanza development concept itself.

I have elsewhere stated that

> . . . it has become common practice to regard "primary product exports," agricultural and mineral, as all of a piece. This is a serious error. . . . [M]inerals production is an eminently *industrial* activity. . . . Consequently, the exclusion of an agricultural export base from the bonanza development concept is probably necessary. It is unequivocally necessary when agricultural export production depends on traditional peasant labor or on forms of coerced labor in a low-technology context.[33]

In other words, bonanza development based on mining (or petroleum) exports, *because it is a form of industrialization* and introduces capitalist relations of production, is likely to appeal to different class interests and to have different effects on class formation than does dependence on agricultural exports. In Peru bonanza development dissected the "agro-export bloc" into its com-

---

[32] On the other hand, bonanza development has one great weakness: it does not encourage an increase in local savings rates. FitzGerald (1979) documents the low Peruvian rate of domestic saving and capital formation.

[33] Becker (1982).

ponent parts. The oligarchy, its domination resting on a plantation and traditional agriculture which by 1969 had already become economically marginal thanks to the far greater dynamism of mining exports, was politically destroyed by that year's agrarian reform.[34] In contrast, the bloc's industrial component, resting upon corporate enterprise, was elevated to a central place in the new scheme of development. The linkup of mining to industrialization, furthermore, created a basis for unifying the interests of the manufacturing and mining elements of the bourgeoisie, whose mutual hostility and bickering over incentives had kept the class divided and weak during the oligarchic period.

Secondly, under bonanza development the state remains free, despite its preoccupation with efficiency and surplus maximization in the resource sector, to pursue limited noneconomic objectives that do not conflict with efficiency goals. One objective of this sort is the indigenization of enterprise management, which has clear nationalist appeal and which may, under some circumstances, enhance local control. True, the policy guidelines make no explicit mention of indigenization. But none was necessary in Peru's case; for, as we shall detail later on, expatriate personnel were found in the mining industry only at the very topmost levels of transnational corporate hierarchies and in a few of the most highly technical and specialized middle-management slots. What is more, the establishment of parastatal enterprises in the gran minería, all of them staffed with Peruvians from top to bottom, further increased the preponderance of local nationals in the sector's superior management.

Finally, a national capitalism demands, as was posited in Chapter 1, a local state that is relatively autonomous of particular and short-range bourgeois interests in the private economy. The same requisite applies to bonanza development. It will serve the long-range interest of the domestic resource bourgeoisie, if there is one, by building up the industry and placing it at the strategic center of the national development program; but this bourgeois element would prefer to keep more of its capital under its own control, reinvesting it in the resource field. The strategy will also serve the long-range interest of the domestic industrial bourgeoisie—but not necessarily the interests of existing entrepreneurs, who are apt to find themselves facing new, powerful competition as industrial development proceeds.

A relatively autonomous local state with a capitalist and, at the same time, nationalist-developmentalist character does not arise out of thin air, however. It appears when and if the rising class forces of society need it to realize their interests and succeed in installing it to help secure their dominance. It follows that bonanza development is a nationalist development strategy *to the degree that it propitiates the formation and consolidation of a nationalist bourgeois class with a structural interest in development under its aegis*. In Part III we

[34] Bourque and Palmer (1975); Harding (1975).

will investigate whether Peruvian bonanza development did indeed affect class formation and consolidation in that way.

Post-1975 Mining Policy

The discussion to this point has implied that the military regime's mining policy was more than just a reflection of the personal predilections of some army officers and technocrats. It has suggested instead that the implementation of bonanza development responded to a series of thoroughgoing changes in the Peruvian polity and society. If this view is accurate, it is to be expected that bonanza development has been institutionalized; that, passing beyond a mere policy option to be adopted or countermanded by the government of the day, it has arrived as an indispensable fixture of the country's political economy.

Fortunately, events allow us to investigate this question. There was a major reorientation of the military regime in 1975, when a "coup-within-the-coup" ousted an ailing General Velasco from the presidency and installed in his stead the far less colorful and more conservative Gen. Francisco Morales Bermúdez Cerutti; within a year all of the "progressive" generals, including Fernández Maldonado, had left the government. On July 28, 1980 the military regime handed over the reins of government to a newly elected civilian administration headed by the same man whom the generals had deposed twelve years before. Do the mining policies of the Morales Bermúdez and second Belaunde administrations represent departures from bonanza development?

In the case of the "second phase" military regime ushered in with the events of 1975, the answer is that there was an observable shift of policy emphasis, but one that did not signify an abandonment of the bonanza development framework. Prior to that date, the principal policy thrust had been the buildup of the state's oversight capabilities and of a parastatal mining enterprise, and the institutionalization of the new rules of the foreign investment "game." The regime had protected its legitimacy by refraining from actions that might have been called *entreguista* by its opponents; its perception was that foreign investment was in public disfavor.[35] After 1975, the lengthening shadows of an economic crisis limited the state's policymaking flexibility. Falling metals prices impacted heavily on the profits of the Peruvian-owned mining companies, making them more vociferous than ever in their demands for nurturing and protection. That, together with Fernández Maldonado's departure from the mining ministry and his replacement by less knowledgeable generals (none of whom served for more than two years), permitted a resurgence of the influence of local private mining capital within the state. The main objectives of policy changed to those of supporting the

[35] A 1966 opinion poll showed that 75 percent of Lima residents queried, up from 39 percent in 1961, favored the nationalization of some or all foreign enterprise. Goodsell (1974:112-15) discusses this and other indications of the declining public acceptance of foreign investment in Peru in the sixties and early seventies.

mediana minería, improving the efficiency and profitability of (rather than further extending) parastatal enterprise, and otherwise raising private-investor confidence.[36] A comparison of the mining policy guidelines contained in the 1974 Plan Inca with those in the 1977 Plan Túpac Amaru (Table B.1, in Appendix B) makes evident that the shift, though subtle, was unmistakable. Still, this shift of emphasis is quite consistent with the capitalist nature of bonanza development and can equally well be explained as a sign of the *success* of pre-1975 policy in achieving its immediate goals. As a matter of fact, foreign mining capital made no further inroads under Morales Bermúdez, nor were existing foreign firms granted any additional privileges. Indeed, they, too, suffered under the emergency taxes on "traditional" exports that the regime enacted in hopes of balancing its budget and staving off the deflationary measures demanded by the IMF.[37]

In his campaign for the presidency, Belaunde had attacked the "statism" of the military regime and had promised a more sympathetic official attitude toward private enterprise. After his election he chose for his prime minister Manuel Ulloa, an industrialist who, as finance minister in the last years of the first Belaunde administration, had instituted very conservative economic policies. For a time there were frequent rumors of the impending privatization of the parastatal enterprises founded by the military government, as well as of the restoration of expropriated foreign assets to their former owners. Some expropriated *Peruvian*-owned businesses—the communications media and several manufacturing plants—were reprivatized. A few exiled ex-oligarchs who had become vocal opponents of military rule were invited to return. There can be no doubt that the present civilian administration is committed to capitalism and has no intention of furthering structural reform.

But the government's spokespersons have since confirmed on a number of occasions that there will be no privatization of parastatal enterprise in mining or petroleum. What is being demanded of the parastatals is that they do without operating subsidies and pay their own way; bonanza development does not contemplate that parastatal enterprises in natural resources will operate at a loss! Due to the financial weakness of MineroPeru and the currently depressed state of the international metals markets, the government feels that "new arrangements" will have to be sought to entice more foreign mining investment into the country. However, they will entail novel joint-venture agree-

[36] The policy shift was pushed by local private enterprise not out of *entreguismo* plain and simple, but for other reasons. Thorp and Bertram (1978:296) describe them: "In a case where foreign capital comes into conflict with and drives out a dynamic national capitalist class, it may be reasonable to suppose that the exclusion of foreign capital would be a sufficient condition for a revival of local capitalism. Where foreign capital enters as an ally of local capital . . . , no such conclusion can be drawn. An attempt to exclude foreign firms, far from clearing the field for local initiative, may serve rather to discourage local capitalists . . . and to damage the general confidence of private investors."

[37] On the economic crisis and the actions of the IMF, see Petras and Havens (1979); Roël (1976); *Business Week*, 21 March 1977, pp. 117-18; and *Actualidad Económica* (various issues, esp. February and April 1978).

ments that offer greater security to foreign capital and *provide for local private capital participation*.[38] There has been no general effort to open the door wider to foreign investment in resources nor to weaken state oversight of operations. Moreover, the state continues to prohibit private claim denouncements in large areas of the national territory while it completes a comprehensive geological survey now in progress.

Perhaps the best clue to the intentions of the civilian government is its newly promulgated (in 1981) General Mining Law, which replaces one enacted by the military regime in 1971.[39] It provides no lower taxes and very few investment incentives beyond those in the old law; the benefits are, if anything, slightly more skewed in favor of domestic mining enterprise. It derogates the state monopoly over export sales that the old law had confirmed. But Minpeco remains, with strengthened organizational capabilities and an ongoing institutional role (see Chapter 2). It still has the right to require the preferential sale of ores and concentrates to Peruvian refineries; and if the state-owned refineries and the mine operators do not agree on charges and terms in direct dealings, it can impose terms of its own with no right of appeal.

Furthermore, the new law eliminates the old formal distinction between gran minería and mediana minería that was left over from the days when this was also a distinction between foreign and domestic capital. That action ratifies the maturity of the domestic mining industry and makes it easier for it to enter into smelting and refining. More importantly, it guarantees that special incentives will no longer be effectively reserved for foreign capital on the basis of project scale, as was the case with the incentives for "marginal" deposits under the 1950 Code.

In sum, the new government's mining policies appear to be entirely consistent with bonanza development. They seek to further strengthen domestic mining corporations relative to their foreign competition and do not countenance any major retreat of the state from the mining sector. Hence there is no decrease in the state's ability to appropriate the "bonanza" or to control

[38] Interview with Fernando Montero, vice-minister of energy and mines, August 19, 1981. He specifically confirmed the "no-reprivatization" official line. The new joint-venture agreements are designed to entice foreign investors to supply the majority of exploration capital for deposits whose development feasibility has not yet been sufficiently documented. If the venture proceeds to exploitation, the foreign interests will be able to obtain up to a 45 percent share on the basis of their prior exploration investment and some input of new capital; MineroPeru will hold a 25 percent share; and the remaining 30 percent will be sold to domestic private investors to raise additional capital. Government officials feel that, as joint ventures always operate independently of the global strategies of their owners (necessary to reconcile differences of interest), and as state and domestic private capital together control a majority interest, the bonanza development concerns of the nation in regard to such joint ventures are adequately protected.

[39] A high official of Southern, interviewed on August 13, 1981, told me that the government had solicited the company's suggestions for reform of the old law. He went on to say, however, that the drafting and promulgation of an entirely new General Mining Law took the company quite by surprise, adding that Southern received "only about half" of the changes it was hoping for.

the purposes to which it is put. National control of resource development in general has not been materially weakened. Significantly, the new General Mining Law has been highly praised by one of the prominent technocrats responsible for drafting the military regime's sectoral policies.[40]

CONCLUSIONS

The military establishment saw the economic dimension of development as synonymous with the development of heavy industry—feasible in view of the country's resource endowment. Heavy industry would increase Peru's potential as a regional power, enabling her to resolve her border disputes and preserve her sovereign prerogatives. Industrialization was also seen as the sole answer to the country's long-term political and economic problems, born as they were out of underdevelopment and "dualism."

The military view of the political aspect of development derived from the self-imposed limitations of its "revolution." The "bonanza" politics received from the past had to be continued but was coupled to a program of state-guided industrialization in which an expanded "bonanza" provided the capital and the state directed it as needed. Much of the "bonanza" was to be generated by transnational corporate subsidiaries, but they came under greater state control in order to ensure that they contributed more to the development program. State entrepreneurship complemented their activities rather than displacing them. Domestic private industry was promoted. Some of the state's increased revenues were to be used to continue the traditional process of segmental incorporation, forestalling any challenge from below to the limits of the "revolution," and private employers were to be enlisted in the process. Consequently, development would be painless; private industry would go on benefiting from tax exemptions and subsidies; civil order would be maintained without extreme repression or thorough social restructuring; and foreign investment—the "bonanza"—would pay the bills. "Bonanza development" is an appropriate term to describe this vision of "easy" capital accumulation and minimally disruptive capitalist development.

Because bonanza development was aimed at building up the nation's power potential, this strategy was firmly nationalist in a way that distantly echoed Stalinism. As under Stalinism, economic development came to be seen as a job to be planned and guided by expert technicians; ideologically motivated, voluntary popular participation in the delineation and implementation of development policy was discouraged in favor of an apolitical, technocratic approach. In its fundamentals, though, the stategy had little in common with Stalinist statism but a great deal in common with capitalist corporatism.[41] The new capitalism would resemble the old in being based on corporate oligopoly in the private economy and on close structural and institutional ties

[40] David Ballón Vera, interviewed on August 13, 1981. Ballón is not connected with the current government nor with any of the political parties that support it.

[41] See Schmitter (1974); and, especially, Panitch (1977).

between domestic capitalists and the state. But it would differ in that the domestic industrial capitalist class would necessarily become the leading national class, the interests of manufacturers and industrial (mining) exporters having been unified at last and definitively separated from those of the agro-export oligarchy. It would differ as well in that the new relationship between the state and the private economy would be a relationship of equals.

This partnership arrangement, along with the nature of the state "technobureaucracy" that administered one end of it, rules out any claim that the Peruvian state after 1968 was autonomous from domestic class forces—meaning, changes in the relationship between the state and foreign capital will have to be interpreted as at least a partial reflection of the interests of a domestic dominant class. The arrangement left open the question of which partner would predominate. The organization of policymaking was such as to leave fluid the locus of policy predominance. Initially it tended to lie with the state; in time, however, it shifted in the direction of the private sector.

Alfred Stepan, in his analysis of Peruvian corporatism, maintains that the following variables determine the relative ability of the corporatist state to control the action of foreign capital within its territory: (1) the internal strength of the state elite and its commitment to control; (2) the capacity of the elite for technically and managerially evaluating the desired role of foreign capital in the national development plan; (3) state administrative and political capacity for monitoring the ongoing activities of foreign capital, which is determined by the effective technical and administrative skills at state disposal; (4) the state's and the nation's capabilities to generate technological know-how, gain access to machines and techniques, and organize socially to put these to use; (5) the state's and the nation's capacity for saving and investment.[42] It is apparent that bonanza development correlates positively with all of these variables except the last. What remains to be seen is whether bonanza development is merely an outcome, the values of the variables having determined it and having been determined in their turn by other factors; or whether bonanza development is a causal factor in the relationship, operating to affect the class structure of society and the nature of the state and thereby influencing the values that the variables take on.

Also remaining conspicuously unanswered is the response of foreign investors to the new arrangements. Would they supinely accept the new "rules of the game"? Would they resist and seek to restore the status quo ante? Would they simply walk away and refuse to play the part that the generals had written for them? That would depend on whether their interests were such as to permit them to accommodate to this kind of capitalist development without the sacrifice of more encompassing global concerns; and on the cleverness of Peruvian authorities in convincing them that they had much to gain from continued access to the country's natural resources and from a stabilization and modernization of her system of domestic capitalism.

[42] Stepan (1978:238-42). He also mentions four other variables, all of which relate to the structural situation of the economy and need not concern us here.

CHAPTER FOUR

World Industries and
World Markets in Nonferrous Metals

NEITHER Peruvian policymakers, nor transnational mining companies, nor the smaller firms of the mediana minería are free to act just as they please if they hope to secure their respective interests. Instead, the field of action realistically available to any of these actors is bounded by the institutions, structures, and practices of the international mining and metals industries and their markets. The latter-day OPEC experience surely points up the unwisdom of assuming that these fields of action can be specified in the abstract on the basis of supposed world capitalist system-maintenance exigencies. On the other hand, government policymakers in particular will doubtless have to go on treating industry and market practices for some time to come as given data. Unlike the situation of petroleum, metropolitan dependence on Third World sources of nonferrous metals is not absolute. Japan and many West European nations lack an adequate domestic mine production in many of these metals, but "safe" sources in the United States, Canada, and Australia are theoretically capable of making up most of their deficit. That much of their supplies—and, indeed, a portion of those of the mineral-rich United States—come from the Third World has more to do with mining company cost and profit calculus, and with environmental protection policies, than with irreplaceable need. It has to do as well with international politics. None of the consuming nations wants to be dependent on a single foreign source, no matter how apparently "safe": single-sourcing is but an invitation to political arm-twisting (if the source does not depend vitally on its mineral exports), and the U.S. government has not exactly refrained from such tactics in the past. It is thus in the interest of the metropolitan metal-importing countries to develop diversified sources; here is where the mines of the Third World are indispensable.

In this chapter I shall give the main emphasis to copper, since it is by far the most important nonfuel mineral in both general international trade and "North-South" trade.[1] But I shall discuss in addition the situations of lead, zinc, and silver, as these make major contributions to Peruvian bonanza development. Throughout the remainder of the chapter and the book, "non-

[1] Gluschke et al. (1979:1, 7); Mikesell (1979:37). "North-South" trade refers, of course, to trade between the less-developed countries and the metropoli.

ferrous metals'' is used as a shorthand designation for these four materials, thereby excluding aluminum and tin from the definition. While this restrictive usage is not the industry standard, it is useful inasmuch as the four metals share commonalities that do not extend to aluminum and tin. They are often found in nature in close association with each other; their ores are chemically similar; and similar metallurgical processes and technologies are employed in extracting and purifying them.

The chapter has three principal objectives. One is to clarify the meaning and significance of certain industry practices that figure prominently in the developments to be discussed later on. A second is to learn whether the structure of the nonferrous metals industry fundamentally contradicts host-country interests in using it as the foundation-stone of bonanza development. A third is to discover whether or not the nature of the industry is propitious for the coalescence around it of an international bourgeois class element of the sort posited by the "post-dependency" paradigm.

OWNERSHIP, CONTROL, AND COORDINATION IN THE WORLD COPPER INDUSTRY

The world copper industry has been aptly described as a "homogeneous oligopoly with [a] relatively large competitive fringe" over which transnational resource corporations exercise a "limited domination."[2] The central oligopolists are a group of about ten private firms and three Third World states (see Table A.7, in Appendix A), who together account for 76.8 percent of Western world mine production (the private firms alone account for 64.1 percent).[3] Seven of the leading private firms are domiciled in the United States, one in Canada, one in Britain, and one in South Africa. Seven are transnational firms in the accepted definition (Phelps-Dodge is a marginal

[2] Labys (1980:42).

[3] In assembling Table A.7 I used Berle and Means's criterion of effective control—"the actual power to select the board of directors" (1932:66)—to group certain companies together into units. This criterion is more realistic than that of majority control, since most modern corporations can be easily controlled through minority share blocks. Using the majority control criterion, Mikesell (1979:28-33) finds that in 1974, the four largest private mine producers accounted for less than a 19 percent share of the market; the ten largest, for less than 35 percent; and government-owned enterprises, for 34 percent. He contrasts this to the situation in 1947, when the four largest mine producers held 60 percent of the market, in order to be able to claim that corporate concentration in copper has declined drastically. Yet, even he will not commit himself to the proposition that the industry is competitive rather than oligopolistic (pp. 106-11). Labys's concentration data (1980:27) for 1975, using the same control criterion as Mikesell, indicate that the four largest mine producers held a 34.0 percent market share; the eight largest, 50.4 percent. It is quite true, as Mikesell maintains, that monopolistic behavior—whose clearest form is holding back on new investment even in the face of rising demand in order to save capital and force prices up—is not observed; and it is also useful to contrast the case of copper with that of, say, nickel, where two firms account for 50 percent of the world market (Gluschke et al. 1979:14). Even so, the oligopolistic character of the copper industry is well established, in my opinion. Furthermore, the combined concentration data (Mikesell's for 1974, Labys's for 1975, and mine for 1977) reveal a recent trend toward further consolidation of control.

case; its only foreign mine holding is its minority interest in Southern Peru Copper).[4] On the "competitive fringe" of the industry are found a large number of small mining and fabricating companies as well as secondary producers (reducers of cuprous scrap).

Such evidence as can be gleaned from company reports and the financial press strongly suggests that ultimate control of the world's major private mining firms is held by institutional investors; that many of these firms, hoping to protect themselves against uninvited acquisition, have been purchasing their own shares—which conveys control to (self-)appointed managers in charge of corporate treasuries;[5] and that ownership is increasingly international. International ownership is not new: AMAX, for instance, has had a high proportion of Britons and Europeans among its shareholders since its foundation. But in recent years it has advanced by leaps and bounds. Asarco and AMAX now list their shares on both the New York and the London exchanges. British Petroleum has gained control of Kennecott through its Standard Oil of Ohio subsidiary. Consolidated Gold Fields, a member of the Anglo-American Group based in South Africa, is in the process of taking an important equity position in Newmont.[6] The recent restructuring of Asarco's relationship with its Australian subsidiary (n. 5, this chapter) introduces Australian shareholders into the parent corporation.

Many of the central oligopolists have diversified horizontally into the other nonferrous metals. Vertical integration in the copper industry is also found, but it lags well behind what has been achieved in aluminum, steel, and oil; vertical integration from mining to smelting and refining and on into fabrication is much more common in the United States than elsewhere.[7] The integrated producers do not dominate the industry, however. There are also *custom refiners*, who process concentrates and smelted metal ("blister copper") purchased from others; most are integrated forward into fabrication. (Do not confuse custom refin*ers* with custom refin*ing*, discussed in Chapter 2 in relation to Cerro. Unfortunately, both usages are industry norms.) In-

---

[4] Mikesell (1979:38-44) briefly describes the principal transnational mining firms. The qualification with regard to Phelps-Dodge applies only to its status as a mine producer; the company owns twenty-four fabricating subsidiaries outside of the United States, distributed among eighteen countries.

[5] In the last several years, cash-rich oil companies have been gaining control of mining firms by purchasing their shares on the open market or by making tender offers—a fate that has befallen the two biggest copper oligopolists, Kennecott and Anaconda, as well as a smaller miner of ferrous and nonferrous metals, Cyprus Mines. A recent advertisement in *The Economist* (17 October 1981, p. 55) informs us that Asarco's own Australian subsidiary, M.I.M. Holdings Ltd., has just purchased 16 percent of the parent's outstanding shares; and not long before that the Asarco corporate treasury bought back a block of shares that had been held by the Bendix Corporation. Asarco has frequently been mentioned in the financial press as a tempting takeover target.

[6] *Wall Street Journal*, 8 October 1981, p. 28; 16 October, p. 8; 22 October, p. 9.

[7] McMahon (1964) and Elliot et al. (1937) explain why this is so. Mikesell (1979:32) states that eight vertically integrated companies account for 88 percent of U.S. copper production; eleven, for 97 percent.

dependent fabricators continue to compete with the fabricating subsidiaries of the integrated producers and custom refiners.[8] Some very large mining companies lack refineries of their own. Small mining firms can survive on the "competitive fringe," if their ore grades are rich enough, by selling concentrates to custom refiners.

Note that the distinction between integrated producer and custom refiner, though important, is imprecise. The former generally buy some refinery feedstocks from non-owned mines, and many of the latter supply part of theirs from small mines under their control or—more commonly—from the output of joint mining ventures in which they hold minority shares. Asarco is an example of an integrated producer that still refines a greater amount of metal than is produced from its own mines.

A position as a central oligopolist depends upon control of mine production, as it is here that entry barriers are highest, investment requirements greatest, and concentration of ownership most extreme.[9] Yet, the custom refiners have not been forced out. They have, in fact, reinforced their position in recent years by utilizing a new tool that the economics of the industry has pressed into their hands: financial aid to new mining ventures. In proportion as the costs of new mines have escalated, custom refiners have become sources of capital for mine development. Sometimes they purchase an equity share in a joint venture. More often they extend loans, or underwrite bank loans, in exchange for long-term contracts entitling them to a certain percentage of the new mine's output for a number of years. By either method they assure themselves of a guaranteed flow of feedstocks at costs no higher than what the integrated producers bear.

The potential for substitution by aluminum or plastics is a powerful deterrent to monopolization in copper because it limits the ability to earn monopoly rents by raising prices far above the levels determined by supply and demand.[10] Substitutive inroads are already so great that copper is used only where its unique properties are irreplaceable; its market grows no faster than the average

[8] About a third of U.S. wire and brass mills are controlled by integrated producers; but this includes four of the seven largest brass mills and four of the eleven largest wire mills (Charles River Associates 1969:57-58). On the other hand, the majority of the "independent" mills are actually subsidiaries of such huge manufacturing firms as General Motors and Westinghouse. Their economic power is important in limiting further vertical integration from copper mining to fabricating.

[9] The reference is to very large mines working low-grade ores of from 0.5 to 2 percent copper— the typical oligopolist's installation. These operations involve the movement of enormous amounts of rock for a given metal output, and also the use of expensive machinery to concentrate the raw ores before smelting. The trend of entry barriers at the mining stage is clear upon comparing Southern Peru Copper's 1969-1976 investment in its Cuajone mine, $4,400 per ton of annual metal production capacity, with its 1954-1960 Toquepala investment of $1,800 per ton. For a general analysis of entry barriers, see Charles River Associates (1969:91-101); and Bain (1956). Entry barriers are high in smelting and refining, too, but they remain low for *small* mines with high ore grades (Mikesell 1979:108-109).

[10] The aluminum and plastics industries are themselves oligopolies with entry barriers even higher than for copper; hence, copper oligopolists cannot solve their substitution problems by moving into direct production of the substitutes.

GNP growth rate of the metropolitan economies, and analysts predict little change in that trend for the foreseeable future.[11] No firm or group of firms will expend the resources and energies to gain monopoly control of an industry with so few possibilities for dynamic growth or for upward price manipulation.

Mechanisms of Coordination

Since the number of major integrated producers, custom refiners, and heavy consumers is small, economic rationality and the interest of all in predictable profits over the long haul counsels mutual coordination of policies and strategies to avoid ruinous competition. Mine producers need to be assured of outlets for any excess production beyond their smelting and refining capacity. Custom refiners, who operate most efficiently at 100 percent capacity and with continuous throughput, need assured feedstock supplies. Fabricators need to be able to secure stocks of refined raw copper in appropriate volume to meet their production plans. All of them need to sell their products dearly enough, and to purchase their inputs cheaply enough, that they can finance new and replacement capital investment and still earn surpluses for their shareholders. Over the years the industry has developed a series of mechanisms and practices designed to effectuate the sort of coordination that must be achieved in order to attain these objectives:

1. Many companies make it a habit to hold small amounts of each others' capital shares. Asarco, for example, has at various times owned 5-10 percent of the outstanding shares of Anaconda, Kennecott, and Cerro, while Cerro has been known to invest in Asarco shares.[12] Berle and Means defined financial control of an enterprise as a shareholding sufficient to authorize the holder to name the firm's board of directors.[13] Holdings the size we are speaking of are too small for that. However, there is an indefinite grey area in which a shareholding, though insufficient to establish financial or managerial control, nonetheless gives its owner considerable influence over the other firm's policies; a 5-10 percent holding is probably well within the range for most large, diffusely held corporations. Furthermore, the dividends paid on the minority shares help to stabilize the oligopoly by allowing the minority owner to share in the other firm's successes and failures.

2. Interlocking directorates provide companies with "listening posts" inside each other's domains. Interlocking directorates are frequently found in the copper industry and do not stop at national frontiers. Newmont, one of

[11] Strauss (1978a); and *Copper Trends 1970-1980* 5 (October 1977).

[12] American Smelting and Refining Company's annual reports for the years 1950-1973; Cerro Corporation's annual reports for the same years. In addition to the instances mentioned in the text, AMAX holds 17.5 percent of Copper Range; Anglo-American holds 31 percent of Falconbridge and 12 percent of Noranda. Anaconda held 28 percent of Inspiration Consolidated, but it was reported (*Wall Street Journal*, 9 March 1979, p. 5) that the U.S. government demanded divestiture as a condition of approving Anaconda's absorption by ARCO, the oil company.

[13] See n. 3, this chapter.

the parents of Southern Peru Copper, participates in such linkages; it interlocks with AMAX and with INCO of Canada.[14]

3. Joint ventures, long usual in the industry, have become more so as costs of new mining projects rise beyond the financial resources of even the biggest individual corporations. Joint ventures are useful risk-sharing devices, particularly with regard to political risks in Third World countries. Although the normal procedure is for one partner in a joint venture to exercise formal managerial rights, efficient operation obviously requires a high degree of policy coordination among the owners. Nor can coordination be limited to matters of parochial concern to the joint venture. It is customary for the partners to apportion the output of the jointly owned mine among themselves and to market it through their sales operations—which means that some coordination of overall marketing strategies is needed as well.

The firms most likely to participate in joint ventures are one-time custom refiners such as Asarco, who find this the least expensive path to becoming integrated producers; and smaller mine producers like Newmont, who thereby attain access to additional mine production without having to supply all of the capital to develop it. There are about seven major joint copper mining ventures that are currently producing in the Third World. Every one of them except Southern has parents domiciled in more than one country. Southern's new Cuajone mine, however, is itself a joint venture in which Billiton N.V. of the Netherlands has the minority share.

4. Debt financing linkages (loans by one company to another unsecured by equity holdings) and sales agency agreements (by which one firm markets another's production and receives a commission thereupon) are frequent. The former are risk-sharing devices similar in their effects to joint ventures. The latter relieve certain firms of the necessity of establishing their own sales networks and trading expertise. They are an important link between the custom refiners—who have very far-flung sales outlets and who are thus most likely to assume the part of agent—and the integrated producers, who thereby gain additional sales outlets besides their own subsidiaries.

Asarco smelts, refines, and markets the output of Duval's North American mines. Noranda does the same for a number of independently owned Canadian mines. Newmont transfers its share of Southern Peru Copper's output to AMAX for final sale.[15]

Stabilization Practices in the Marketplace

The mere existence of coordinating mechanisms is no guarantee that they will be so utilized. The proof that they are lies in the fact that the industry

[14] But Sklar (1975:181) points out that, in the absence of formal financial control, the mere existence of interlocking directorates does not permit the conclusion that there is a "harmony of interests and uniformity of purpose among distinct corporate groups. . . . The degree of solidarity or conflict involved in any such relationship is always a matter for strictly empirical determination." For a contrasting view see Sonquist and Koenig (1976).

[15] American Bureau of Metal Statistics (1978); and Sánchez (1975).

is characterized by a variety of traditional, customary practices whose persistence cannot be explained by competitive forces alone. In addition to verifying that coordination exists, these practices act to supplement the mechanisms we have described above and to institutionalize further the limits on competition within the industry.

Most sales are in large lots under long-term contracts. The pattern of sales is not random but is governed by buyer-seller relationships that have been built up over many years (possible because of the small number of firms at each end of the transactions and their collective interest in security of disposition or supply). Custom requires buyers to avoid cutting purchase volumes right away when facing a declining demand for their products; until supplies are reduced by producer action at the mine end, consumers must shoulder a part of the expense of stockpiling surpluses—a cost they bear in return for an understanding that producers will not rush to increase prices when supplies are tight. Producers, on their side, stabilize the market during periods of high demand by rationing available supplies among all customary buyers instead of compelling the latter to outbid each other; buyers are allotted fractions of their usual purchase volumes when this type of rationing is imposed.[16]

The large producers also stabilize the market by selling and buying both refined copper and intermediate products (concentrates and "blister") to and from each other and by including the custom refiners in these transactions. Such interchanges make up for the imperfect vertical integration of the large producers (none of whom is so fortunate that the output of each stage of production under its control exactly matches the input requirements of the next stage). They enable a producer to compensate for temporary production shortfalls that would, if not overcome, force its usual customers to turn elsewhere. And they create yet another interest linkage between the integrated producers and custom refiners.

Hence it is that, even though Asarco's refining capacity still exceeds its mine production, and even though Newmont and Cerro, two of Asarco's partners in Southern Peru Copper, do not have excess refinery capacity of their own, Asarco has never sought to capture for itself the right to refine all of Southern's "blister" production. Much of it has been sold to Norddeutsche Affinerie of Germany, Metallurgie Hoboken-Overpelt of Belgium, BICC and IMI of Britain, and the Japanese refiners.[17]

The recent evolution of the industry has introduced another factor tending to ensure that these kinds of coordination will continue and spread. This factor is the rise of the international banking establishment to a preeminent role in the financing of enormously expensive new projects. It is the practice of the banks to secure their investments by insulating them from the vicissitudes of

---

[16] These and other commercial practices are discussed by Charles River Associates (1969) and by Banks (1974).

[17] A list of the Western world's principal copper refiners will be found in Appendix A as Table A.8.

any one national economy; they do so by insisting that mine production be distributed under long-term contract among most or all of the principal metropolitan consuming nations. (In most cases, this international distribution of output complements an international distribution of participant banks.) In consequence, new mines in the Third World, even when owned by a single parent or by partners of the same nationality, are not free to direct all of their production to their owners' home market, as Anaconda and Kennecott used to do with their Chilean mines. The requirement for international distribution of production naturally makes it still more difficult for integrated producers to keep their mine output "in-house."

The Mining Industry and International Class Formation

This overview of industry institutions and structural relationships is pregnant with implications respecting the class character of the metropolitan bourgeoisie associated with the great transnational mining firms. The institutional nature of ownership and control is such as to signify that we are dealing with a primarily "managerial" or "organizational" class element, not with one based on traditional private entrepreneurship. It is, moreover, in the process of becoming an *international* bourgeoisie, as is posited in the "post-dependency" paradigm. Remember that the nationality of a class element, as with all other class characteristics, is determined to first order by its integrants' interests; while the members of this group unquestionably retain their separate linguistic and (up to a point) cultural identities, their interests are eminently international. Not only that: as the pursuit of these interests entails a high degree of conscious coordination among the members, it promotes the sort of communications and interactions that breed class cohesion.[18]

Third World parastatal enterprises are also found among the central oligopolists. They participate in some of the linkages that were reviewed—joint ventures and sales agency agreements most of all—and play by the oligopoly's rules. This suggests that bourgeois elements in the producer countries are affiliated with the international bourgeoisie of the industry. We are not yet ready to specify the nature of the affiliation, however; we need to know if it is an equal membership or something less, and whether the affiliation implies "denationalization." For that we shall have to wait until we have examined in greater detail class formation and class practices in the Peruvian mining industry.

The "Japanese Contradiction"

The Japanese have a rather different set of interests from the remaining oligopolists. They represent a contradiction within the world oligopoly, a

---

[18] The conclusion should be thought of as tentative, not definitive. Further research into the political practice and ideology of the putative international class element is needed for confirmation.

contradiction that will be seen in subsequent chapters to have had important ramifications for the Peruvian industry in the years after 1968.

Japan's economy, as everyone knows, is extremely dependent on imported raw materials. What is more, its dependence has increased much faster than that of any other metropolitan region: Japanese copper demand grew at an average annual rate of 11.7 percent from 1964 to 1968, seven times faster than for the whole of the West; the Japanese share of the copper trade among OECD countries rose from 9.5 to 19.1 percent between 1964 and 1969; and Japanese dependence on imported copper currently stands at around 80 percent.[19] Meanwhile, rapid population and industrial growth in the home islands has created severe problems of environmental pollution and excessive energy consumption. In order to solve them, the Japanese are willing to shift polluting, energy-intensive processing industries abroad, with security of supply taking precedence over the profitability of any particular investment:

> Overseas investments in resource-processing industries are viewed as one important instrument to facilitate industrial restructuring of the Japanese economy toward a less energy-consuming and bulk-resource-dependent entity, while still enabling it to retain the necessary supply sources of processed materials. . . . In addition to assuring the supply sources of vital resources, overseas ventures in resource-processing industries *also create opportunities to export a large volume of capital goods.*[20]

The contradiction resides in the fact that Japanese foreign investment responds to a different set of interests from those motivating transnational mining investment from the United States and Europe. It does not require close attention to price considerations and world supply-demand relationships. For, when Japanese refiners invest in overseas ventures, they need only take into account "considerations of the macroeconomic requirements of their home economy rather than . . . considerations of rivalry relationships with other . . . multinationals, the primary oligopolistic motif of Western corporations."[21]

In pursuit of this strategy the Japanese have been investing avidly in Latin American extractive industry. The region has absorbed 18.1 percent of Japan's $12.7 billion stock (as of 1974) of direct foreign investment and 14.6 percent of her $3.6 billion stock of extractive investment.[22] In addition, Japanese

[19] Ozawa (1979:159-62); and Gluschke et al. (1979:128).

[20] Ozawa (1979:138, emphasis added). See also Gluschke et al. (1979:127-41), who note that, despite its lack of mine production, Japan smelts more copper than any other nation except the United States and the Soviet Union; and that, whereas about 60 percent of world trade in copper involves refined metal, three-fourths of Japan's imports are unsmelted ore concentrates.

[21] Ozawa (1979:138). Gluschke et al. (1979:131) describe the Metal Mining Agency of Japan, a government entity that subsidizes mine exploration costs for Japanese firms. Founded in 1963, it extended its activities to overseas mining concessions in 1968.

[22] My computation from data tabulated by Ozawa (1979:23). This may be contrasted with the investment behavior of U.S. mining firms. U.S. direct investment in Third World mining increased by 44.3 percent between 1960 and 1976, most of the increase coming before 1973.

firms have been much more amenable to Third World host-country preferences for state ownership and local private capital participation in mining and met-allurgical ventures. They will often extend loans to such ventures in return for a guaranteed share of the output—something that U.S. and European mining and refining transnationals never do.[23]

PRICING INSTITUTIONS AND PRACTICES[24]

We need to look briefly at the way that international market prices are established, as these institutions and practices are of great concern to less-developed countries seeking to maximize their "bonanza." A distinctive feature of the copper industry is that, whereas there is a unified world oli-gopoly, there are two price systems—a U.S. system administered by the major domestic producers; and another based on market mechanisms, which reigns outside the United States.

The U.S. Producers' Price

If free-market prices are the hallmark of competition, the *producers' price*, established by fiat, is the classic symbol of tight oligopoly control. The North American firms have operated a successful producers' price system since the end of World War II. It is based on reports of negotiated sales compiled and published by the journal, *Metals Week*.[25] The system works because of the large size and small number of North American producers and consumers.[26] Its success also has not a little to do with the copper stockpiling policies of the U.S. government. From 1953 until 1974, the United States maintained a strategic stockpile of the red metal. Its purpose in theory was to meet U.S. defense production needs in the event of military interdiction of transoceanic commerce. In practice, it served as a price-stabilizing buffer stock, since stockpile purchases were made at moments of slack demand and releases to the open market when the supply situation tightened.[27] The government wanted to stabilize prices at a high enough level to assure profits to the producers (thus, incentives for new mine investment) but low enough to counteract inflation and protect the interests of the consumers. That, needless to say, harmonized nicely with the interests of the producers themselves.

Indeed, Southern Peru Copper's Cuajone mine absorbed over half of *all* capital expenditures by U.S.-owned (51 percent or more) Third World mining subsidiaries in 1973-1977. Meanwhile, during the same 1960-1976 period, U.S. direct investment in mines in *developed* countries (mostly Canada and Australia) increased by 236.6 percent. See Mikesell (1979:249-51).

[23] Ozawa (1979:159-62); and Mikdashi (1976:28-29).

[24] These are reviewed by Mikesell (1979:81-93); Labys (1980:98-102); and Gluschke et al. (1979:9-12).

[25] The U.S. Producers' price is published under the name "Domestic Refinery" and is quoted FOB New York.

[26] See nn. 7 and 8, this chapter.

[27] The stockpiling of copper was authorized by the Strategic and Critical Materials Stockpiling Act of 1946, an authority later expanded by the Defense Procurement Act of 1950. On the evolution of stockpiling policies and their role in market stabilization, see Newcomb (1976).

There is a U.S. free market (i.e., one where prices are determined by arm's-length trading rather than private negotiation): the New York Commodities Exchange (COMEX). It had been until recently merely a small supplementary market. But since the end of government stockpiling, it has taken on more importance as an indicator that helps the producing companies to decide on the "correct" producers' price level.

The LME Price

The truly important world free-market price is the one quoted on the London Metals Exchange (LME). The LME price has long been standard for copper deliveries to Europe, where the industry is not sufficiently concentrated to allow price administration; and to Japan, where the smelting and refining industry, though concentrated, is not integrated backward into control of mine production and so cannot influence supply-demand balances. The LME's importance is unrelated to the amount of metal traded on it; it, too, is essentially an indicator, since physical deliveries of copper pursuant to sales on the LME amount to under 10 percent of annual European consumption and less than 1 percent of world consumption.[28] Instead, its importance stems from the absence of any other mechanism by which customers and producers in the less tightly oligopolized European market can obtain readings of the supply-demand relationship. What has happened, simply, is that the LME price has become the price specified in all *privately negotiated* sales contracts.

The biggest defect of this system is that prices are far less stable than in the United States. LME prices fluctuate wildly with minor changes in supply-demand equilibrium (see Fig. 4) due to the small amount of copper actually traded on the exchange. When large consumers enter the LME in times of high demand—which they do when they are no longer able to cover their needs from contracted orders—their purchases powerfully affect this small volume of metal and drive prices up more rapidly than the actual supply-demand balance warrants. Conversely, large consumers desert the LME in times of slack demand, causing prices to fall lower than they otherwise would. These swings are further amplified by the effects of speculation.

Figure 4 indicates that, while neither price exceeded the other more *often*, on the average, between 1950 and 1980, the price *difference* has generally been greatest when the LME was the higher of the two. In other words, over this thirty-year span it would have been more advantageous for a Third World producer nation to export at the LME price than at the U.S. Producers' price. (In mathematical terms the advantage, or extra profit, is equal to the total area between the two curves when the LME price was higher, less the total area when the U.S. price was higher.) This, as Moran has documented, was one reason for Chilean resentment against Anaconda and Kennecott. Both exported almost all of their Chilean production to the United States at the

[28] Charles River Associates (1969:119-20). The metal traded on the LME is that produced by small mining firms, along with occasional surpluses being disposed of by the large oligopolists.

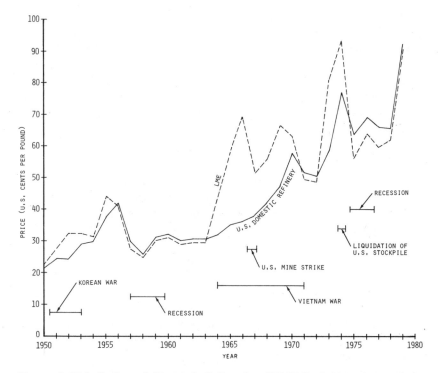

FIGURE 4. U.S. Producers' (Domestic Refinery) and LME Settlement copper prices, 1950-1979. Plotted from tabulated data in Appendix A, Table A.6.

U.S. Producers' price; but some of the metal was then reexported to Europe or Japan (or replaced domestically produced U.S. copper sold abroad). The frequent result was a lower profit for the Chilean subsidiaries but a greater one for the companies in the United States, thanks to the effect of the price differential.[29] In view of the Chilean problem, it is significant that the bulk of Peru's copper has always been exported at the LME price; this particular source of friction did not arise there.

Deviations from the Price Standards

Price quotations are given for refined copper. The prices of intermediate products are established as the refined price less a discount equal to the cost (including profit) of processing them to the refined state. But these costs are quite variable; they depend on the prices that each processor pays for labor and fuel, on whether he has outstanding amortization obligations, and on his acceptable profit level. As a result, the prices actually paid for "blister" and concentrates are variable. The only rule is: the less the degree of processing of the intermediate product, the greater the room for price bargaining between

[29] Moran (1974:47-54, 76-78, and passim).

buyer and seller, and the greater the deviation of the end price from that set by the market. This departure from price regularity is accepted by all parties because it occurs *within* the structure of the industry, is understood by all, and is essential for reconciling the interests of custom refiners with those of mine producers. Still, it has been a cause for worry on the part of Third World governments, for it admits the possibility of price manipulations designed to shift profits out of the reach of the former's ability to tax them.

LEAD, ZINC, AND SILVER

The market structures and institutions involved in the production, sale, and consumption of these three metals are quite similar to those for copper. The North American market is dominated by vertically integrated producers, whereas the rest of the Western world markets are less tightly integrated and controlled. Since lead and zinc are smelted and refined much as copper is, most of the custom refiners—and the integrated producers who, like Asarco, began as custom refiners—deal in all three. The other integrated producers (i.e., those whose competitive strength always lay in the control of mines) are diversified or not according to the nature of the mineral deposits that they work.[30] A comparison of the principal privately owned lead and zinc producers with those of copper would entail dropping Kennecott, Phelps-Dodge, and Duval from the ranks (see the listings in Tables A.7 and A.8, in Appendix A); demoting Anaconda and Newmont; and adding St. Joe Minerals, Homestake Mining, the French-Spanish Peñarroya Group, and Australia's Broken Hill Proprietary.

Pricing institutions for lead and zinc are almost identical to those for copper: a producers' price system in the United States, and reliance on the LME as the price authority for Europe and Japan.[31] There is one exception, a significant one for us: zinc concentrates are bought and sold everywhere via private negotiation, there being no posted price for this material. Since most of Peru's zinc production has been exported as concentrates, the Peruvian government and local mining companies have no accepted yardstick close to hand by which to measure the fairness of the received price. Therefore, the state and the domestic mining firms have been particularly anxious to expand the country's zinc refining capacity. Even if some exports of concentrates continue, a greater Peruvian refining capacity would provide firsthand local knowledge of refining costs and thus improve the domestic firms' bargaining position in concentrate sales to metropolitan refineries.

Lead and zinc, both much more abundant than copper, carry low prices per unit. They are also subject to a comparable threat of substitution, which

[30] Mining companies specialized in low-grade, diffuse copper deposits, which rarely contain much lead or zinc, are usually less integrated into these metals than are those with underground mines (now or in the recent past), whose veins are likely to contain all three.
[31] Strauss (1977).

further keeps prices low. The metals are mined in sufficient quantity in North America and Europe that the major producers have had less of an incentive to develop sources in the Third World. Moreover, Third World lead and zinc mines are intrinsically less profitable for them than copper mines, because transportation costs become a large percentage of the value of the metals. In Peru, U.S.- and Europe-domiciled companies are active in lead and zinc mining only if (1) the metals are byproducts of copper mining or are present in mines whose copper ores are played out (Cerro and Northern Peru Mining); (2) exceptional ore grades, unusual geology, cheap labor, and/or investment incentives combine to make production costs especially low (St. Joe's Santander mine, Homestake's Madrigal mine, and, to some extent, Cerro); or (3) the mine is very old, its investment long since recuperated (Peñarroya's Huarón mine). Other lead and zinc mines developed by North American and European interests have been sold off to Peruvians.

The Japanese are another story. For the reasons outlined above, they are eager to establish secure sources of supply of lead and zinc without too much consideration of cost. Since the mid-sixties they have been the leading foreign developers of Peruvian lead-zinc mining.

The absence of a strong foreign concern with these two metals has been important to Peruvian mining-sector development, in that it has left a vacuum for domestic mining companies to fill.

Silver's situation is in many ways the diametric opposite of lead's and zinc's; it is, of course, a relatively rare metal and commands a very high unit price. Most of the West's silver is nowadays produced from traces in ores of copper, lead, and zinc. High-volume modern mining and efficient refining practices make this possible and compensate for the exhaustion long ago of the world's rich silver veins. Yet, the high price of the metal permits even small-scale mining to be profitable; most of the profits of Peruvian lead-zinc mining firms now come from the silver "byproduct." The ability to compete in world silver markets without large capital expenditures is one of the principal factors accounting for the present health of the country's mediana minería.

Silver prices are established by competitive market forces, though most sales are through private brokers rather than exchanges. These brokers publish daily quotations. The prevailing U.S. price is the one quoted by Handy and Harman, a broker headquartered in New York and Toronto. Elsewhere silver is bought and sold at a price published by four London brokers and known as the London 999 Fine Silver price.[32] Table A.6 (in Appendix A) shows that, unlike the cases of the other three nonferrous metals, the price differential between New York and London has never been significant in the postwar epoch.

[32] The numbers refer to the standard purity of 99.9 percent.

OLIGOPOLISTIC COMPETITION AND "BONANZA" MAXIMIZATION

The members of the nonferrous metals oligopoly are mostly large corporations, thoroughly bureaucratized, controlled by professional managements, and dependent on long-range planning to ensure their profitability. The ability to plan is proportional to the amount of control that can be exercised over exogenous variables. We have found that a fundamental variable—price—cannot be fully controlled but can, with care, be stabilized and rendered more predictable by coordination of action. Coordination must extend to control over reserves of the metals, so that world supply comes to bear a constant relation to long-term demand. The management of the supply-demand equilibrium is economically rational for the companies because it tends to stem tendencies toward a costly investment race—a scramble to open new mines and refineries or to incorporate marginally more efficient technologies in existing facilities. As market pressures do not allow "superprofits" to be earned, an investment race would force the companies to jeopardize their managerial independence by turning even more to outside financing than they already have.

On the other hand there is no monopoly, and coordination is insufficient to suppress all competition within the industry. Students of oligopoly agree that oligopolistic competition replac s price competition with efforts to protect and stabilize, and then (if possible) to extend, market shares.[33]

Oligopolistic competition explains an otherwise perplexing phenomenon, most apparent in the case of copper. Why is it that the major producers send exploration teams around the world to locate and secure concessionary rights to new deposits but actually develop very few of them? The answer is that their development is very expensive and, if not planned in coordination with world supply and demand, would destabilize prices. However, there will eventually come a time when demand begins to exceed current supply. Then, protection or extension of one's market share demands that one not delay in bringing a new mine into production. The only logical conclusion, therefore, is this: *each company explores in order to create for itself a "strategic reserve" of mineral deposits that can be held off the market (and denied to others) but then quickly tapped when conditions are ripe.*

Asarco officials explain that planning groups study the potential development of each concession more or less continuously, adjusting calculations of required investment, expected rate of return, etc., with every significant change in the world market situation. These constantly updated contingency plans enable the company to know at all times which of its idle concessions is the best prospect for development, and they permit it to compute a metal price at which the development of that best prospect is feasible. But with so many factors, some subject to unpredictable fortuities, to be weighed, corporate

---

[33] On the theory of oligopolistic competition as a competition for market shares, see Vernon (1977:59-101); also Mikesell (1979:220).

planners make their projections on the basis of highly pessimistic estimates of future costs and prices. As the tendency is to err on the conservative side, the real operating returns of a new mine frequently turn out to be much greater than anticipated in the plan. We observed in Chapter 2 how this happened in Peru with Toquepala.

Investment Incentives and Their Failure

Transnational mining corporations are not racing to develop new mines. Whatever may have been the case earlier in this century, they do not now press reluctant governing elites for the right to invest in the Third World. Instead, the desire for new foreign resource investment is expressed first and loudest by host governments that have or want bonanza development, and it is the companies who are hesitant to seize hold of the incentives laid out to attract them. Attacks on private corporate action in the mining sectors of less-developed countries have been aimed exclusively at ongoing operations, never at proposed new ones.[34]

Dearest to the hearts of host governments is the development and enlargement of mines—the fastest route to increasing the total value of the metal export "bonanza" available for financing economic development. A close second priority is to expand local processing of mine products. For refineries mean: factories; work experience and training that are more adaptable to other manufacturing fields than is mining experience; and inputs for local metal-fabricating industries. Tertiary but still useful is investment directed toward improving the physical conditions of mining camps and assisting a local mining supply and equipment industry to get started. If "unproductive" from a company viewpoint, such investment is seen by the host country as a part of the "bonanza" (since it rewards and pacifies local workers and business-people at no cost to the state) and as its just due in compensation for past colonialist or neocolonialist economic exploitation.

For many years the host countries sought to attain these ends by extending financial and property incentives to prospective foreign resource investors, which Peru did with her 1950 Mining Code. The content of the incentive program was normally determined by the investors, whose shopping list of "indispensable" incentives was then written into law. The key incentives were guaranteed perpetual tenure over mining claims and low taxation.[35]

[34] This is explained by the concept of the "obsolescing bargain" put forth by Vernon (1971); see also Labys (1980:51). The latter also notes (pp. 97-98) that capital-short Third World countries must have large inflows of foreign capital to develop their mineral wealth and will seek to create a good investment climate (in resources) to attract it. I would add, however, that a good investment climate in natural resources (I discuss its requirements further on) need not entail *entreguismo* toward foreign direct investment, either in this sector or in general.

[35] Also, the taxation of income rather than export value, as used to be done in Peru before 1950. The reason is that the United States allows a write-off of foreign income taxes against the U.S. income tax bill but credits other forms of foreign taxes only as business-expense deductions from gross revenues. If the host country's total tax take is greater than the United States' but the host country's direct income tax bill is lower, there has been a double taxation (Behrman

What we have learned of the nature of oligopolistic competition in the industry is sufficient to predict the failure of investment incentives based on guaranteeing easy access to and permanent tenure over mining claims. They neatly coincide with the companies' desire to control *nonproducing* "strategic reserves" and do nothing to induce the companies to bring these reserves into production. Production and reserves data do indeed indicate that Peru was being used as a "strategic reserve" by most of the mining firms that held concessions there—this in spite of the fact that Peruvian mining costs are among the lowest in the world.[36]

Low rates of taxation are overrated as incentives. When the home government allows a tax credit for income taxes paid abroad, as does the United States, low income taxes merely reduce the size of the "bonanza" and shift the tax take to the home country without affecting the total tax burden borne by the company. Besides, transnational firms, when investing in a new mine, want to maximize *worldwide* return on investment over a long time frame; if there is a choice, it may pay them to invest in country A, where immediate returns *on that particular investment* are lower than in country B, if A's deposits can be brought on stream more quickly, entail lower transportation costs to market or fewer political risks, and so forth.

No economic incentives that Third World countries can provide will suffice to encourage transnational investment in local refining—except in the case of the Japanese. There are no process efficiencies to be had in locating refineries close to overseas mines rather than close to metropolitan markets. Much of the metropolitan refinery capacity, though still serviceable, is old—hence, fully depreciated and able to offer low processing charges because relieved of the necessity of amortizing investment out of profits. Nor do the mining companies wish to threaten the custom refiners of the developed West with new competition at just the moment when their contribution to new mine financing is becoming critical.[37] Third World countries seeking to expand local refinery capacity would therefore do well to concentrate on exploiting the "Japanese contradiction."

Are there incentives that a host country *can* provide to attract new foreign mining investment without sacrificing its own economic interests? The mining executives with whom I spoke listed the following as essential: a stable

1971). Wells (1971) suspects that U.S.-domiciled mining companies are "anti-taxation," perhaps for ideological reasons; i.e., they insist on bargaining for still lower host-country income tax rates than those which would just offset their U.S. taxes. Mining incentive programs around the world as of the late fifties, when incentives were yet very generous, as a rule, in most Third World countries, have been reviewed by Ely (1961).

[36] Among the countries ranked as major present or potential copper producers (I define the category in terms of total reserves, i.e., those being mined plus those known but unexploited to date, exceeding 12 million tons copper content), Peru's 1977 ratio of reserves under active development to total reserves, 40.7 percent, is the lowest except for Panama—where the copper deposits are quite recent discoveries. (My calculation from data presented in Gluschke et al. 1979:51.) For comparative production costs in different countries see Mikesell (1979:122-23).

[37] Radetzki (1977).

political order of whatever ideological stripe that is capable of carrying out its agreements with the company and of assuring labor peace;[38] the right to recoup invested capital and to repatriate profits; noninterference with prevailing marketing practices, patterns, and prices (the companies claim not to engage in shady transfer-pricing maneuvers and are willing to accept government oversight to verify the fact); tax *stability* (i.e., constant rates rather than low rates), which promotes investment planning; and, because labor productivity is more of a cost factor than the actual wage rate in capital-intensive mining operations, a work force trained (or readily trainable) in the operation and maintenance of heavy machinery and inured to industrial discipline. These incentives are entirely compatible with recent Peruvian mining policy as analyzed in Chapter 3.

Joint Venture Strategies

Risk-sharing joint ventures have become the rule in the industry. Mining firms have also become amenable to host-country participation in them.[39] Such participation may be the only means by which the company can obtain access to the resource; for it reconciles private investment in mining with the ideological imperative of national ownership of natural resources. With its participation assured, the host government may be willing to guarantee repayment of third-party loans to the project; private banks, increasingly concerned about the security of their bulging portfolios of outstanding loans to the Third World, are starting to insist on official guarantees of this kind. Governments alone can solicit low-interest development loans from international agencies such as the IBRD (World Bank) and the BID (Inter-American Development Bank) or from other governments; and interest expense may figure significantly in a mining project's investment budget. In short, adequate financing may simply be unattainable without host-country equity participation. On the host-country side and apart from ideological considerations, an ownership share is seen as more firmly securing the "bonanza" and as a logical prelude to eventual full national ownership.

Another nonideological reason why host countries find joint ventures attractive is that even in the absence of state participation they promote "good corporate citizenship" on the part of the jointly owned subsidiary. In the vast majority of cases, the owners are domiciled in different countries, thus loosening ties between the subsidiary and a particular foreign state. In any event a joint venture can never be as closely controlled by its majority parent as

[38] The fact of Gulf Oil's continuing cooperation with the Marxist government of Angola, in direct contravention of U.S. policy toward that nation, is a powerful reminder of this truth.

[39] Mikesell (1979:246). A host-country ownership share may entail a capital contribution, which is always useful. If not, host-country entitlement to a proportionate share of mine output simply means to the private owners that they must mine more material in order to obtain the same amount of metal they would have had without it—which is, in effect, a calculable addition to production costs. Naturally, this cost factor will be considered in evaluating the economic feasibility of the project.

can a wholly owned subsidiary. (Recall that owners share in production as well as profits; hence, management details liable to affect production are of concern to all of them.) The majority owner usually does not try. Rather, a good deal of power is delegated to the subsidiary's local management. The result is that key decisions are more likely to be made from the perspective of the subsidiary's position in the host country instead of being dictated by a remote parent.

CONCLUSIONS

The world nonferrous metals industry is no monopoly bent on oppressing the less-developed countries. There is no sign that the companies are tightly tied together by linkages of outright control. Even if they were, or could be, the potential rewards for monopolization are simply not there. Substitutive pressures place an effective ceiling on the prices that can be charged, a ceiling low enough to preclude monopoly "superprofits." The market lacks dynamism and growth potential. High entry barriers at the mining stage (in copper; they are lower in lead and zinc and practically nonexistent in silver) give a certain advantage to the integrated producers—most based, for historical reasons, in the United States—who control the ultimate source; but the advantage is in no way overwhelming. The custom refiners have, in fact, improved their competitive position, for they have become an important source of new mine financing.

However, the industry is sufficiently concentrated to be considered an oligopoly. That the actions of any one of the larger members of the industry can affect the economic environment of all of them; that metals prices are too low as is to permit them to be driven still lower by untrammeled competition; and that the members are mostly "mature" corporations with an institutional interest in environmental stability and predictability—these are all factors tending to make coordination of action both economically rational and practicable. Coordination is generally informal but is promoted by a number of institutional mechanisms and customary practices. It involves a few short-run sacrifices for some; yet, it rewards all by eliminating the threat of an expensive investment race and by fostering the mutual interest in stability. There is one unresolved contradiction, though, in this picture of oligopolistic coordination. It is the investment policies of the Japanese, which respond purely to Japan's national aspirations rather than to the long-term profit calculus of the other oligopolists.

The nature of the world industry creates some notable opportunities for producers in the Third World but also imposes some limitation upon them. There are vacuums resulting from lack of interest on the part of transnational mining firms that can be filled by mining on a scale sufficiently small to interest private Third World capital; Peru is especially fortunate in that her polymetallic geology enables her mediana minería to fill the lead-zinc vacuum while simultaneously profiting from the high unit price of the silver "by-product." Economic and political conditions have encouraged the transnationals to accommodate to joint-venture participation by host governments, resolving the contradiction between the desire for bonanza development with foreign capital assistance and the ideological imperative of national ownership of natural resources. The large producers' and custom refiners' lack of concern with expanding local processing can be countered by exploiting the "Japanese contradiction." For Japanese transnationals *do* have such an interest; it lies in security of supply and sales of capital equipment rather than in refining profits, and it is therefore quite compatible with 100-percent host-country ownership of the facility (with supplies to Japan guaranteed by long-term sales contracts tied to financing). But in order to grasp these opportunities, a Third World country must be ready to act the part of a good oligopolist, respecting the norms and customary practices that the private members have worked out for themselves. Nevertheless, there is no reason why conformity to these requirements need result in the exploitation or domination of the country, any more than the private oligopolists are exploited—*provided* that government policymakers, parastatal managers, and domestic private entrepreneurs demonstrate business acumen.

Solid business acumen is particularly necessary for avoiding economic exploitation in the sale of intermediate products, as deviations from the posted prices (and the absence of a posted price for zinc concentrates) make possible below-market transfer pricing. There is no indication, however, that the profits of the transnationals *depend* on maneuvers of that sort. It is almost certainly the case that the transnationals will engage in them if they are convinced that the rewards are very great and the odds of getting caught very slight. But they are unlikely to jeopardize their long-term relations with the host government by doing so if the chance of being discovered is less than remote. This counsels improved state oversight to shift the odds in the desired direction; the transnationals accept it, inasmuch as it removes a cloud of suspicion from them and stabilizes their position in the typically nationalist Third World political environment. Also counseled is an effort to engage in local refining operations, so that the processing cost factor in price deviations can be independently evaluated.

I suggest that the ability of the industry to organize itself around mutual interests shared by all of the members regardless of nationality, and to work out so many formal and informal coordinating mechanisms to secure these mutual interests, lends powerful empirical support to the concept of an international bourgeoisie in formation around this nucleus. Very importantly, the fact that Third World parastatal enterprises and joint ventures with partial state (and/or local private) capital participation function in the oligopoly, together with the fact that Third World private mining enterprise can function within the "competitive fringe," implies that certain bourgeois elites of the less-developed countries *are incorporated into this class element on a somewhat equal basis.*

That host countries have often been less than successful in persuading the transnational mining companies to act in the interest of bonanza development appears to have more to do with an inapposite choice of policies than with a firm network of external domination. Tax and concession-tenure investment incentives failed because they stimulated just the opposite kind of corporate behavior from what policymakers hoped for. These incentive programs, it is true, *were* urged upon Third World states by the transnationals, for obvious self-serving reasons. Yet, there is no proof that more restrictive, better-designed incentives would have been met by a refusal of foreigners to come in, nor is there any that the incentive packages adopted after World War II by politically sovereign host countries were forced upon reluctant local elites by external pressure. Actually, the incentives that transnational resource firms seem to desire most—economic and political stability, a state strong enough to carry out its agreements, a disciplined and trainable work force—would appear very much to serve the host country's own interest in domestic development without requiring it to assume an externally predetermined value system or political ideology.

PART II

Mining Transnationals and the Peruvian State

In Part I we made our acquaintance with the principal actors, institutions, and structures that have influenced the impact of the Peruvian minería on national development. We discovered that after 1968 the military regime sought a rapid increase in the volume and value of mining exports as the key to a bonanza development strategy focused on heavy industry. At the same time the strategy called for segmental incorporation of certain popular sectors—those most likely to go over into opposition, and to make their opposition effective, if not economically mollified—to be continued and extended. We have seen that the military intended to attain its political and economic goals by separating the interests of the mining bourgeoisie from those of the once-dominant agro-exporters; by reordering the system of incentives and sanctions with the aim of attracting new foreign capital to Peru, but under conditions where new and existing investment would contribute more to development than it had in the past; and by furthering the protection and nurture of Peruvian mining capital. The regime calculated that this last policy aspect would disarm the most important domestic source of potential opposition to its development plan for the minería. That is to say, a positive state attitude toward domestic mining enterprise would deter the sector's bourgeoisie from perceiving either the tightening of the rules of the foreign investment ''game'' or the expansion of the state's entrepreneurial functions as a threat to its interests.

Innovative (as compared to prior national practice) policies of this sort were feasible in the wake of the ''revolution,'' because the regime enjoyed a fair measure of political autonomy—for a while—and was thus free to experiment. But its concern with both bourgeois and popular responses to its policies shows that the extent of the ''revolutionary'' state's relative autonomy from class forces was distinctly limited.

We also argued that nothing in the structure of the world nonferrous metals oligopoly precluded a priori the ability of transnational mining firms to accommodate to the altered, post-coup political and economic environment. On the contrary, foreign mining investors might find this environment more to their liking, to the degree that the military could provide a stronger, more stable system of government than what had typified Peru until then. But we further observed that the two most important foreign investors, Asarco/Southern and Cerro, were structurally and institutionally dissimilar in a number of ways. Those dissimilarities could well affect the manner in which the managements of the two firms defined their interests within oligopolistic constraints and, thereby, their willingness to do what the military regime expected of them.

In Part II we take up this question of the institutional behavior of the large foreign mining corporations and the reformed Peruvian state as they attempted to adjust their traditional relationship to new circumstances. We do so because the behavior of institutions provides the clearest evidence respecting the interests and practices of the class elements that control them (or contest for their control); and because the network of institutional relationships helps to structure the socioeconomic and political-ideological arenas in which classes act.

We will test the proposition that local subsidiaries of transnational mining corporations tend to act like "good corporate citizens" of the host country, as the doctrine of domicile (Chapter 1) predicts; and that, if they do not, the host state has the capability to discipline them at minor cost to itself—just as it would discipline individual asocial behavior. The test does not require that corporate behavior in conformity with local development needs and policies be voluntaristic to the point of altruism. All it asks is whether, once the state has authoritatively defined the behavioral content of "good corporate citizenship" and has backed its definition with appropriate coercive sanctions for misbehavior, the corporations comport themselves within the limits of the definition such that the sanctions do not actually have to be applied.

Part II is composed of two chapters. In Chapter 5 we test the proposition with respect to Asarco/Southern; in Chapter 6, with respect to Cerro.

CHAPTER FIVE

Southern Peru Copper
versus an Assertive State:
The Cuajone Project

T HE Southern Peru Copper Corporation and its majority parent, Asarco, had been since the 1950s the stellar representatives of modern, oligopolistic transnational mining capital in Peru. They had entered the country at a time when neocolonialism, though still present in the form of oligarchic social supremacy and political-economic domination, was on the wane with the rise of industrialization and medium-mine development. Their operations, highly capital-intensive from the start and physically located in a desert region where few peasants lived, had little direct impact on local populations. (We will see later on that the bulk of Southern's small work force was recruited from the department of Puno, well to the east, whose agricultural economy was chronically depressed and where migration of peasants from countryside to urban centers was already well under way.) Wages were high and working conditions good by local standards; indeed, the installations were run hardly differently from comparable ones in the United States. Furthermore, Southern stood entirely aloof from domestic capital in the minería, neither preempting business opportunities within the latter's reach nor even entering into dealings with it. In consequence of all this, the Gobierno Revolucionario de la Fuerza Armada could feel relatively free to treat with Southern and Asarco purely on the economic basis of "bonanza" maximization, without worrying very much about the impact of these dealings on societal forces.

Peruvian "good citizenship" demands on Asarco and Southern revolved around their proposed investment in a huge new mine, Cuajone, that was to be larger than Toquepala. From the first, Southern had regarded the three copper concessions under its control—Toquepala, Quellaveco, and Cuajone— as forming a single mining complex; in fact, the Toquepala development contract had so stated. The three were geologically and metallurgically similar. Being close together geographically, they could be served by the same in- frastructure network. When fully developed they could produce in the neigh- borhood of 500,000 fine metric tons of copper per year, a figure comparable to the annual output of Chile's vast Chuquicamata mine.

Toquepala had always been thought of by its owners as the initial step in a long-term sequential development of the whole three-mine complex. Sequential development meant that less new venture capital would have to be committed in the later stages, which would be paid for in part out of the cash flow from the first mine. Operating experience gained at Toquepala would minimize planning uncertainties for Cuajone and Quellaveco. Additionally, ore grades would be held uniform over a longer period of time (since the gradual decline in the richness of ores from the first mine would be balanced out by the richer initial grades of the next, and so on), obviating the need for frequent adjustments in the concentrating and smelting processes. The selection of Toquepala as the first phase of the project had been made on the basis of lowest cost: it had the least amount of sterile overburden to be removed and lay closest to the natural road and rail right-of-way to the port of Ilo. All installations associated with Toquepala had been planned from the beginning to allow for expansion or extension as needed to accommodate the other mines.

The military regime knew of Southern's plans for Cuajone from its first day in office, since negotiations over the project had begun some six months previously under the Belaunde administration. The regime planned its entire mining-sector policy under the assumption that Cuajone would go forward. It expected the project to do much more than nearly double the size of the mining export "bonanza." Besides that, it would reestablish Peru's bona fides with the international investment community; prove that the expropriation without compensation of the International Petroleum Company (IPC) had been, as government pronouncements insisted, a "special case" rather than a trend-setter in the area of natural resources;[1] and demonstrate that at least four major foreign investors (Southern's parents) could adapt to the new rules of the Peruvian investment "game." On the other hand, state policymakers were determined to sacrifice as little as possible of their newfound assertiveness and internationally nonaligned stance[2] for the sake of an agreement.

This chapter examines the negotiations between the two parties over development incentives, project financing, sales, the extent of government supervision, and allied issues. It also evaluates the impact of the project, both in terms of Peruvian bonanza development and with respect to Asarco's role in the world nonferrous metals oligopoly. We will thus determine whether this transnational resource corporation was able to act like a "good corporate citizen" of Peru; and whether the requirement to do so was consistent with the company's global interests and objectives.

Let us note at the outset that the company, once having cleared away the resentment engendered by Toquepala's early "superprofits" (Chapter 3), could call on a number of valuable assets to help it through its adjustment to a changing Peruvian environment. Asarco had years of experience in dealing

[1] The state's position is set forth and argued in Empresa Petrolera del Perú (1969).

[2] The nature of Peru's new foreign policy in this period is analyzed by Dodd (1975); cf. Peruvian Government (1972).

with the Mexican variant of Latin American nationalism.[3] Drawing on that experience, Southern had historically held itself apart from the U.S. Embassy in Lima and had never resorted to diplomatic channels in its occasional disputes with the Peruvian government; neither had it ever acted as a spokesman for broader U.S. interests.[4] And inasmuch as Southern was formally a joint venture, its management was accorded a great amount of autonomous decision-making power with respect to Peruvian affairs.

THE BASIC CUAJONE AGREEMENT

Under Peruvian mining law, new large-scale foreign investment enters pursuant to a development contract between the investor and the state. This contract spells out the rights and obligations of both parties in regard to the project, and it lays down the rates of taxation and other concessionary privileges that the investor will enjoy. (In these areas the Mining Code's provisions are limiting rather than prescriptive.) Unlike the situation prevailing in many less-developed countries without fully elaborated mining codes, in Peru the development contract reigns only for a limited time period keyed to investment recuperation; thereafter the contract lapses, and the project falls under the general provisions of the code—which, of course, the government can alter at will. Nevertheless, the military regime was not content to wait for that to happen; it, like Southern, wanted a basic contract that would secure its interests from the start. It also wanted one that could serve as a precedent for relations with other investors. The negotiation of the basic agreement was thus of equally vital importance to both sides and would shape their relationship in all that followed.

The Concerns of the Peruvian Government

Since they had made Cuajone the keystone of their mining policy, the generals wanted a contract that would be politically palatable both initially and in the future. Palatability, to them, meant the ability to go on labeling the old order as *entreguista* without being tarred by the same brush. Their first concern lay with the fact that Southern was extremely anxious to proceed with negotiations immediately, implying that a lengthy delay to write a new mining code applicable to the project could well sink it. Therefore, negotiations would have to go forward under the 1950 Code as amended in 1964 and 1968. The amendments had tightened up on available incentives, but the old code was still seen as a symbol of an earlier era. The government's

---

[3] Asarco had operated continuously in Mexico since the latter part of the nineteenth century. It weathered the Mexican Revolution quite well and managed to maintain a good working relationship with the various revolutionary and postrevolutionary regimes (Marcosson 1949).

[4] Interview with Frank Archibald, president and board chairman of Southern Peru Copper, April 1, 1978. Earlier interviews with the U.S. commercial attaché and with employees of the Economic Section of the U.S. Embassy in Lima confirmed this; all were singularly uninformed regarding Southern's activities in the country.

strategy, then, had to be one of extending lesser incentives than the maxima allowed by law (and solicited by Southern in its project proposal). A difficult sequence of negotiations lay ahead if the strategy were to succeed, but the rewards would be worth it: there could not be a more dramatic contrast with the origins of Toquepala—or, for that matter, with the position of the civilian administration overthrown by the 1968 coup, which had been on the verge of accepting Southern's Cuajone proposal as written.

Beyond these political-ideological considerations, however, the military were concerned to institutionalize and render stable their bonanza development model. To do this they needed a Cuajone agreement flexible enough to adapt automatically to unforeseeable contingencies, such as wide swings in international copper prices, without unduly privileging either party to the contract. Specifically, a repetition of Toquepala's "windfall" profits had to be guarded against.

There were also the general requirements of sectoral policy to be considered. The government wanted:

1. An enlargement of the "bonanza" and the elimination of the worst enclave aspects of large-scale mining. The first meant higher taxation than had been levied on the gran minería in the past and, if possible, other forms of wealth transfer from the company to domestic interests. Progress toward the second could take the form of more local procurement of goods and services. Even were these limited to local assembly of imported, knocked-down kits (as with motor vehicles) and to the channeling of other imports through local merchants, the situation would have been improved in comparison to Toquepala—where everything had been directly imported to Southern's Ilo wharf with no local economic contact of any sort.

2. The placing of more of the country's copper production in markets other than those of the United States, in order to reduce export dependency via market diversification. When Toquepala had gone on stream, the U.S. market had been receiving slightly less than half of Peruvian copper exports. But Southern's owners exported preferentially to themselves in the United States, and by 1969 copper exports to that destination accounted for 75 percent of the national total. The government thought that it could attain its diversification objective without entering into a dispute with Southern over Toquepala sales practices by arranging for most or all of Cuajone's output to go to non-U.S. markets.

3. The refining of at least some of Southern's "blister" copper production in Peru. In addition to the benefits of more domestic industrial employment and value added, a Peruvian refinery would extend potential export markets beyond the sixty-odd metropolitan refineries to encompass thousands of independent fabricators, some of them in Third World countries with which Peru very much wanted to increase trade.

What about direct state participation in the Cuajone endeavor? Here, government officials were hesitant. There were indications—but, as we shall see in a moment, misleading ones—that Southern would absolutely refuse such a demand. More importantly, state participation might entail an input of state capital to the project in violation of policy guidelines and without yielding effective control. In any case, state ownership was not, as we found in Chapter 3, a high-priority political or ideological goal. DGM technocrats had concluded that their neighbor's experiment with "Chileanization" of the gran minería[5] had failed. In their opinion, conformity to the national interest could be assured as effectively and much more cheaply by a well-written basic agreement, sensible taxation, stronger legislation, and careful use of the state's oversight and enforcement powers on the part of a trained bureaucracy.[6]

The Interests of the Company

Cuajone was every bit as critical to the global strategy of Asarco as it was to the Peruvian government. Asarco's long-range plan for cementing its status as an integrated producer and extending its market share was crucially dependent on being able to proceed in a financially sound manner with the development of the Toquepala-Cuajone-Quellaveco complex. But to do so it needed to secure its managerial control over the complex for years to come. It was stated in Chapter 4 that transnational mining firms are frequently not averse to nationalization, for a variety of reasons. That argument, though, applies only to installations in being whose investment has already been recovered—usually, many times over. Companies feel quite differently when they are thinking of committing enormous amounts of capital to new projects; they will contemplate no such action unless they themselves are in a position to control the course of the investment.

Furthermore, Asarco was not sanguine about the prospects for retaining control of market disposition after a nationalization. Marketing rights were highly important to it, since it is one of the world's premier metals traders and has proven particularly adept at taking advantage of the extra profit opportunities presented by the two-tier price system and by refining-charge deductions from posted prices. It had to worry about the availability of Peruvians experienced in the mediana minería and in Cerro who were knowledgeable about international metals marketing. Their presence raised the fear that Peruvians would not funnel the output of the nationalized mines through Asarco but rather would assume the marketing function themselves.

Asarco and Southern officials told me that they had secretly decided to accept state equity participation in extremis, if this were the only way to get an otherwise-satisfactory basic Cuajone agreement. Thus, what they needed was an "insurance policy" to protect against any government move to replace

---

[5] On Chilean mining policy see Novoa Monreal (1972), also Moran (1974).

[6] Interview with David Ballón Vera, president of the Banco Minero and former chief of the DGM, August 7, 1977.

their management with its own.[7] It could be provided by continuing to offer Peru the one resource that an alternative state management could not: ready access to investment capital in quantity. Much of it would be borrowed, and the foreign banks would insist on guarantees of managerial continuity; the state would not dare to violate them, since its international credit rating would thereby be jeopardized. What is more, access to capital unavailable to the state could be parlayed afterward into the follow-on development of Quellaveco. In that manner, the "insurance policy" would be effective for the sum of the construction and investment recuperation periods of both mines— perhaps as long as twenty years. The Peruvian government never knew that its ownership participation in the project was possible. On the other hand, the company never knew that the government would raise such a demand only as a bargaining counter.

Clearly, the company's preference for borrowing heavily to finance Cuajone and for committing proportionately less of its own venture capital than it had with Toquepala was a response to its perceptions of a higher level of political risk than had existed in 1952.[8] But this preference created a dilemma in that interest expenses would increase the total cost of the project and reduce the rate of return on invested capital, at least for the first few years. Furthermore, outside financiers were sure to restrict Southern's right to distribute profits to its owners as dividends until the loans were fully amortized. Thus, the company had its reasons for negotiating tenaciously over tax rates and other investment incentives. Still, as it was facing a government determined to achieve the opposite, the company might have to choose between increasing its capital exposure in a risky environment in order to maximize potential returns on investment; or, alternatively, settling for a lower rate of return in order to attain more securely its market-share objective.

Where company and government interests stood in total opposition was in regard to a copper refinery to go with the new mine. Southern had no interest whatsoever in a local refining facility. The increased cost of the project was a minor objection. Far more worrisome was the fact that the existence of a Peruvian refinery would inhibit the company's flexibility for trading in intermediate products, a flexibility which, as we just observed, was important in its profit picture. It could be predicted with absolute certainty that even if the refinery were 100 percent company-owned, political pressure would be used to compel Southern to refine locally all of its mine production.[9]

---

[7] The concept of "investment insurance" obtained via a network of international political and economic alliances is due to Moran (1973).

[8] Interview with Arthur G. Beers, senior vice-president of Southern, August 13, 1981.

[9] It has been alleged by Brundenius (1972), Bossio Rotundo (1976), and several others that Southern's resistance to refining copper in Peru was due to its desire to "give away" the gold and silver content of exported "blister" copper, profits on which were then taken by the owners outside of Peru; that the "blister" was being sold to the owners at below-market prices, further transferring profits out of the country; and that refining-charge deductions were applied to "blister" sales without justification, since the product is pure enough to be used without refination. All three charges are ill-informed. "Blister" sales always provide (as I verified by examining Southern's sales contracts) for full payment for assayed gold and silver content, paid at the

Process and Outcome of the Cuajone Negotiations

The actual negotiating process got under way on November 20, 1968 with the company's submission of a formal proposal and draft contract.[10] The proposal included a marketing analysis and preliminary financing plan. Knowing that no loan could be obtained from the U.S. Export-Import Bank at that time due to the precarious state of U.S.-Peruvian relations, and believing that the negotiations would be facilitated if Peruvian desires for market diversification were met at the outset, Southern suggested that European and Japanese governments and private banks would offer financial support in loans and credits if tied to long-term commitments of copper exports to their countries. The marketing analysis backed this idea by demonstrating that future copper supplies would be much tighter in Europe and Japan than in the United States. The proposal therefore outlined a plan according to which, in exchange for financial assistance, about 90 percent of Cuajone's annual output would be allocated under long-term sales contract to Britain, Germany, Japan, and the Netherlands in equal shares. The remaining 10 percent would be available for sale to Southern's owners or to others on a "spot" (one-time instantaneous sale) basis.

Southern knew that if copper production were distributed in this way, U.S. banks, too, would be willing to lend to the project. Since the United States was self-sufficient (with assured supplies from Canada) in copper, private North American banks would analyze Cuajone solely in terms of security and return on investment—which they would make from their swollen Eurodollar holdings in overseas branches. And all lenders would be pleased by the fact that copper sales would directly earn the various currencies in which the loans would be repaid, thus insulating loan repayment from the uncertainties of fluctuations in currency exchange rates.

The company, naturally, framed its draft contract so as to take maximum advantage of the promotional legislation then in effect. The draft included these guarantees:

    a. An income tax rate of 40 percent during the investment recuperation and loan amortization period, with only net earnings to be charged against recuperation;

---

quoted market prices. Southern's owners have granted themselves marginally better terms in their purchases of the subsidiary's production, but the deviations from terms of sales to unaffiliated buyers are slight and are not set by fiat without relation to market conditions. The purity of Southern "blister," 97 to 98 percent, is insufficient for direct use except, perhaps, for a few crude manufacturing applications; the predominant applications of copper for electrical or heat conduction and for alloying into brass and bronze require purities on the order of 99.9 percent, which can only be attained by electrolytic refining.

[10] The draft and proposal were located in the files of the Ministry of Energy and Mines. The proposal consisted of three volumes of description and technical data. A fourth volume containing Southern's financial analysis was not received in the ministry until October 27, 1969—by which time its contents had been revealed to the government piecemeal. In a letter from the company to the chief of the DGM dated March 4, 1969, the former apologized for the delay in completing the financial proposal, attributing it to unexpected difficulties in projecting estimated labor costs and market prices.

b. Tax stability at the same rate for a further six years after the end of the recuperation period;

c. Exemption from all other taxes during the combined period of tax stability;

d. Accelerated depreciation, and the right to revalue assets on books to account for changes in the value of the sol against the dollar;

e. Unrestricted access to all foreign exchange earned from export sales;

f. Duty-free unrestricted importation of all capital equipment and supplies required for the construction *and operation* of the mine;

g. A blanket waiver of statutory restrictions on the hiring of expatriate labor and the employment of foreign contractors and consultants.

In return, the company promised to complete the project (at an estimated total cost of $355 million) within seven years. Knowing that the Peruvians would insist upon one in any event, Southern additionally volunteered to incorporate a "Calvo clause" in which *it renounced all right of appeal through any non-Peruvian court, international tribunal, or diplomatic channel.*[11] But as it had done with the Toquepala contract, the firm added a clause stating that Cuajone and Quellaveco, by virtue of their close physical proximity, were to be considered "a single economic and administrative entity." Its intent was to protect its rights to the last part of the three-mine complex and to ensure that contractual terms for the third phase of the overall development of the complex would be no less favorable than those arranged for Cuajone.

Disagreements arose from the moment that the Southern draft was placed on the table. The government offered faster depreciation write-offs in exchange for a higher initial income tax rate, balanced so that the total tax burden in the early years of the project would not change. Southern, thinking in terms of returns over the long haul, refused; the mine would one day be fully depreciated, but the higher tax rate would apply forever. It also refused a government demand that it pay a small but symbolically significant surcharge on its ground rent for the Cuajone and Quellaveco concessions—an admission, if accepted, that the company had been laggard in starting their development. If the state's only concern had been with the size of the "bonanza," these conflicts could have been quickly resolved by the splitting of differences. We have noted, however, that the state had *political* objectives at stake as well. It needed to be able to grant fewer incentives than the legal maxima and to prevent any tax-free "windfall" profits later on; neither could it yield on the ground-rent surcharge issue, which it saw as a symbol of the government's ability to adopt and impose its own mining-sector policies without clearing them in advance with the large foreign corporations. Having learned its lesson

[11] "Carlos Calvo (1824-1906) was an Argentine diplomat who wrote a treatise on international law. . . . The Calvo Doctrine, drawn from his work, . . . asserts that foreigners are to be treated on a plane of absolute equality with the nationals of a given country. Foreigners should not lay claim to diplomatic protection or intervention by their home countries since this would only provide a pretext for frequent violations of the territorial sovereignty and judicial independence of the less powerful nations" (Sigmund 1980:20-21).

from Toquepala, the government further insisted that not merely net profits but also sums deducted for depreciation, amortization of mine preparation costs, payment of loan interest during the construction phase, and freely disposable corporate reserves be charged against investment recuperation; and that any funds derived from Toquepala's depletion reserve and reinvested in Cuajone, as Southern was doing, be excluded from investment to be recuperated.

The company was willing to meet all of the government's demands regarding recuperation, since it, too, wanted to avoid a repetition of the negative publicity attendant upon Toquepala's "windfall." Where it would not compromise was on taxation issues.

Government representatives responded by requisitioning all of the economic forecasts, earnings projections, and supporting data that Southern had employed in preparing its proposal. These materials were turned over in August 1969 and were submitted to the DGM staff for review and recommendations. The documents gave government negotiators some useful ammunition. Southern had projected future copper prices at a constant 40¢/lb for the first ten years of operation. Government analysts, though, recognized this figure as unduly pessimistic; 50¢/lb, they suggested, was a more realistic but still conservative price.[12] If the lower figure were accepted and a 40 percent income tax imposed, and if copper prices were to rise much above 50¢/lb, the Peruvian tax take might not even fully offset U.S. income taxes. Peruvian technocrats calculated that U.S. income taxes on Cuajone profits, taking account of depletion allowances and the reduced rates available under the law to a Western Hemisphere Corporation, would be assessed at an effective rate (i.e., the ratio of income tax to gross earnings before deductions and exclusions) of 26.4 percent. They therefore recommended a Peruvian tax rate of 47.5 percent, equivalent to an effective rate of 31.6 percent. The difference between the U.S. and Peruvian effective rates, they reasoned, would serve as a safety margin in Peru's favor, assuring that U.S. taxes would continue to be fully offset if (as then seemed probable) U.S. laws were changed to reduce the depletion allowance.[13]

With this analysis in hand, government negotiators hardened their position. They now insisted on a tax rate of not less than 47.5 percent during the recuperation period and an even higher rate of 54.5 percent during the succeeding six years of tax stability.

It was on the reefs of the refinery issue that the negotiations threatened to founder, however. The government pressed very strongly for the inclusion of a refinery in the project; Southern, just as strongly, refused to consider it.

[12] They were right; see Table A.6, in Appendix A.

[13] Ministry of Energy and Mines internal report dated August 1969 and signed by David Ballón Vera, director of mining promotion. It is a tenet of resource policy everywhere in the Third World that local taxes on the income of transnational subsidiaries should fully offset home-country income taxes whenever the home country allows a credit for income tax paid abroad (Mikesell 1975a:29 and passim; 1975b).

The company was pointedly warned that the refinery was an all-or-nothing proposition as far as Southern was concerned. In other words, should the contract be signed without provision for a refinery and should Southern later decide to build one after all, the state would neither amend the Cuajone contract for the purpose nor issue a separate one. This amounted to a thinly veiled challenge: If the company continued to balk, the state might itself build the refinery and then compel Southern to supply it with "blister" copper; the company would then find itself refining copper in Peru anyway, but without control over refinery management and costs. Southern regarded this as an empty threat and persisted in its refusal. But, hoping to move the talks off dead center, its representatives attempted to finesse the issue by claiming that they lacked negotiating authority with respect to the refinery question. That tactic proved counterproductive. The government side promptly broke off the discussions, insisting that it would not reopen them unless the agents for the company were given full power to negotiate all outstanding issues.

This juncture called for consultation between the DGM technocrats who had been representing the state and Fernández Maldonado. All agreed that the state should concede nothing further on the points of greatest interest to it. But since the company was showing no signs of bending, it appeared to the mining minister that political pressure would have to be applied. An adverse (from Southern's perspective) alteration of the legal environment, with the promise of more adverse changes to come, would make it to the company's interest to settle sooner rather than later. To that end the government promulgated decree-law D.L.17792, only its second venture into mining legislation, in September 1969. The new law prohibited foreign investors from holding idle concessions in "strategic reserve" and required them to submit firm calendars for the development of all such concessions by the end of 1970; failure to comply was punishable by *caducidad* (forfeiture) of the concession without compensation. One of its targets, obviously, was Cuajone. It constituted a plain warning to Southern not to drag out unduly the negotiating process. Yet the stick was applied gently: the law stated that any project undertaken with state participation or under a special development contract—Cuajone's status—could receive a deadline extension at government discretion. A second new law, D.L.17793, reduced the surface area of concessions that could legally be combined into "a single economic and administrative entity." Its effect was to split Quellaveco away from Cuajone definitively, denying the former any protection under the Cuajone agreement and threatening it with *caducidad* unless developed simultaneously. In this case the stick fell with force.

Southern got the message; shortly after the new legislation had been enacted, the talks were resumed at a higher level. The Peruvian government was henceforth represented by Fernández Maldonado, Treasury Minister Morales Bermúdez, and Prime Minister Montagne. Across the table from them sat Frank Archibald, Southern's president and board chairman, and two senior vice-presidents. The talks were sometimes acrimonious, but a tentative compromise was hammered out and a second draft contract prepared. The provisions of significance for us were these:

a. The sole tax would be an income tax, guaranteed stable at 47.5 percent during the recuperation period and at 54.5 percent for six years thereafter;

b. Unrestricted foreign exchange access would be allowed, but subject to a complicated system that would permit the Central Reserve Bank of Peru to monitor all transactions;

c. Toquepala depletion reserves could be reinvested free of tax in Cuajone, Quellaveco, a refinery, or any other activity related to Peruvian mining, but any such sums invested in Cuajone would be excluded from recuperation;

d. Deductions for depreciation (less new investment), depletion, amortization of mine preparation costs, loan interest payments (where included as part of invested capital), and corporate reserves would be charged against investment recuperation in addition to net profits;

e. All recuperation-period benefits would lapse in ten years or upon completion of recuperation, whichever came first; and the recuperation schedule could be renegotiated at the initiative of either party whenever the international price of copper varied more than ±10 percent from the company's planning projection;

f. The company would conduct a feasibility study for a 100,000 tons-per-year refinery but would not be obligated to build it;

g. The company would be allowed marketing freedom and would not be required to service any market at a price lower than in the market where most of the metal was sold;[14] but if the company should sell metal at below-market prices, the higher (market) price would be used in computing its income for tax purposes;

h. Depreciation deductions would be lowered automatically if necessary to avoid a U.S. tax obligation;

i. Duty-free imports would be permitted only if competing local products were adjudged—*by the company*—inadequate as to quality or function, or were priced more than 25 percent above the CIF value of competing imports. The government would have the right to an expert review of the project plans by its own personnel, who could recommend design changes to maximize the use of locally produced equipment;

j. The company would be deemed to have complied with the law in regard to the time schedule for development of Cuajone and Quellaveco and, thus, would pay no ground-rent surcharge;

k. While the government would support the company's solicitations for loans from foreign governments and international agencies as well as its

[14] This provision was included because of Southern's concern that the Peruvian government might, for political reasons, order sales to China, Eastern Europe, and/or the Soviet Union at prices lower than the LME.

application for investment insurance from the U.S. government, it would not assume any guarantees or other financial obligations;

l. The company would have eighteen months in which to begin construction, during which time it could secure the outside financing it needed.[15]

Southern accepted the importation clause *i* because it was allowed to be the sole judge of the "quality" and "functional adequacy" of what it was being asked to procure locally. It had never opposed the stricter recuperation clauses *d* and *e*, although it did not volunteer them in its own draft. This second draft hewed to the government's tax proposals but traded off the issue of the ground-rent surcharge.

The new draft, like the old, was next submitted to the DGM staff for its advice. The technocrats generally approved but expressed two key reservations. First, they adamantly opposed exempting the company from the ground-rent surcharge, as this would, in their view, symbolically undercut official policy with respect to the idle concessions. Secondly, and for the same reason, they objected to the allowable eighteen-month lapse prior to project startup as a violation of the spirit of D.L.17792. Instead, they suggested, Southern should be required to begin work no later than April 4, 1970 and to make an initial investment of not less than $25 million during the first eighteen months of construction; that would give it sufficient time to concert the financing but would require it to demonstrate good faith in cash. To protect further the interests of the state should the financing not work out, the technocrats additionally asked that the maximum project completion time (seven years in the company's proposal) be shortened by six months and that failure to comply with all provisions as to starting date, termination date, financing deadline, and/or initial cash investment be grounds for abrogation of the contract and forfeiture of the Cuajone concession.[16]

The draft then went to the Council of Ministers, along with the DGM recommendations. The ministers accepted the latter on all points but took the further step of objecting to the clauses relating to the refinery. They had concluded in the interim that there would probably be no refinery unless the state were to build it; naturally, their concern thus shifted to denying any implied authorization for Southern to construct a competing facility once the state announced its plans. Hence, they struck clause *f* from the draft.

The revised second draft was approved by the Council of Ministers in November 1969 and was resubmitted to Southern. The company knew that there would be no evading the ground-rent surcharge, and it was pleased to have gotten out from under the refinery problem. Only one point remained to obstruct ratification. The new requirement for a minimum initial cash

[15] Draft located in the files of the Ministry of Energy and Mines and dated December 17, 1969.

[16] Ministry of Energy and Mines internal report dated October 7, 1969 and signed by David Ballón Vera, director of mining promotion; César Polack Romero, ministry legal officer; Wilfredo Heraita Núñez, director of mining concessions and finance; and Pablo Ribeyro Ibáñez, chief of the legal division.

investment and an early startup date meant that the company would have to make a larger-than-anticipated commitment of its own funds to the project, a commitment that might grow burdensome if financing arrangements could not be completed as soon as hoped. This commitment of company funds would help to cement those arrangements, since lenders would view it as Southern's vote of confidence in the project. But there was a hitch: although any cash outlays by Southern's owners (other than those derived from the Toquepala depletion reserve) would be repaid as soon as borrowed capital began to flow in, the need to make such outlays in the first place might result in an interruption of Southern's dividend payments to its owners. This was a price that Asarco was quite willing to pay. Yet Cerro, the largest minority shareholder, vigorously objected.

Cerro, not a central oligopolist, had little interest in controlling a greater volume of "blister" copper in international commerce. Its principal interest in Southern, rather, was the flow of dividend income it produced—a substantial contributor to Cerro's overall cash flow (see Table 2.4). Cerro had some influence with the other two minority owners, Newmont and Phelps-Dodge, who together controlled 26.25 percent of Southern's capital shares and who, lacking their own experience in Peru, were wont to listen carefully to the advice of the U.S. firm with the longest local operating record. Asarco, for its part, preferred to govern by consensus even though, as majority owner, it had the right to impose its will. It happened that the issue was resolved by the fact that Cerro was beginning to encounter problems with the Peruvian government and was not proving very adept at resolving them—as we shall see in the following chapter. In the end this weakened Cerro's voice within the owners' councils. Phelps-Dodge and Newmont decided to accept Asarco's lead, and Cerro went along reluctantly.

The final text of the contract was approved by Supreme Decree on December 19, 1969 and was signed by government and company representatives at a brief ceremony held the same day. Fernández Maldonado used the ceremony as an occasion to justify the regime's desire to go ahead with the agreement against anticipated criticism from the nationalist Left. He observed that the new military government had announced, as early as two months after its installation in office, that the development of Cuajone (and of Madrigal, a smaller lead-zinc mine that was being built by Homestake Mining) were among its short-term objectives. Restructuring the legal regime and economic relationships of the mining sector so that the state could play a greater role in it was most certainly a medium-term government objective and one that, admittedly, Cuajone did not seem to advance. But, he averred, what was needed first of all—and to which Cuajone would unquestionably contribute— was to "reactivate the national economy in the shortest possible time in support of the process of national transformation, the fundamental objective of the Peruvian Revolution." Nor should the signing of the agreement be interpreted as a backing away from an earlier commitment, supposedly implied by the

IPC seizure, to expel all foreign interests from the resource sector. For in truth,

> the Revolutionary Government has not rejected at any time the participation of private enterprise in the mining industry, nor that of foreign enterprise in particular; what is demanded is that foreign investment respect the legal order in force and, especially, that it serve the development of the country.[17]

The provisions of the Toquepala and Cuajone contracts of greatest interest in the present context are summarized and compared in Appendix C. It is obvious that the new contract conforms far better to Peruvian national interests than the earlier one. The award of a larger piece of the economic pie to the state is only a part of the story;[18] of still more importance is the way in which the later contract recognizes a tremendously expanded range and scope for the legitimate exercise of state power vis-à-vis a major foreign resource investor compared to what was acknowledged in 1954. Whereas the Toquepala contract was overwhelmingly concerned with guarantees to the company— which is to say, with *limiting* the exercise of state power—the Cuajone agreement ratifies the broadened oversight and supervisory powers that the new regime was already asserting on behalf of a strengthened state apparatus. In so doing, it makes the state more than an equal partner in the new agreement; for, on the basis of the historical record it can be assumed that any adjudication in the Peruvian courts of a dispute over contract interpretation will almost inevitably conclude by favoring the local interest. The investment recuperation provisions of the later agreement are also much fairer and less likely to lead to subsequent conflicts.

Moreover, because the Peruvian state of 1969 had a much better and more detailed perception of its interests than did its antecedent of 1954, it was able to write into the later contract certain other provisions of value to it, provisions to which Southern was essentially indifferent but which it would hardly have suggested on its own initiative. In this category can be placed clauses such as the requirement for state-supervised personnel training programs, for company purchases of electrical power from the state, for state access to heavy equipment no longer needed after the construction phase, and—most notable of all—for increased local purchases of machinery and supplies. The sole benefit awarded to the company in the later contract but missing from the earlier one is the six years of tax stability after completion of investment recuperation; however, it is offset by the shorter recuperation time that the Cuajone agreement contemplates.

Above all, the state's position triumphed in three of the four areas of greatest contention: Quellaveco, where the state's freedom of future action was pre-

---

[17] My translation of a transcript of the speech published in Southern's house organ, *Mensajes*, no. 10 (December 1969).
[18] But not a negligible part; the tax rate applied to Cuajone was the highest ever levied on a new foreign resource investment.

served and the company prevented from acquiring a vested interest beyond reach of the new policy of forcing idle concessions into development; the ground-rent surcharge, where the same policy was again ratified with the company's tacit admission that it had indeed been laggard in developing the concessions under its control; and income tax rates, where the state obtained the largest "bonanza" ever and demonstrated its power to scale back incentives to foreign investors below the maxima permitted by law. The refinery issue alone was resolved in favor of Southern; we shall see, though, that it would not be long before this apparent setback for the state was converted into another victory.[19]

Why was it possible for Peru to obtain so much more from contract negotiations with Southern in 1969 than it could in 1954? One reason is that the company, having had the benefit of fifteen years' worth of prior experience and now able to draw on a better-educated local work force as well as a local pool of trained technicians and middle managers, faced fewer uncertainties to bedevil its project planning and could therefore accept a somewhat lower rate of return.[20] Another can only be that, when the chips were down, Asarco (and also Newmont and Phelps-Dodge) decided in good oligopolist fashion that securing and extending their share of the world copper market was in fact more important as an immediate goal than Cuajone's return on investment per se. A third is that the state in 1969 was more willing to fight for its interests and less fearful of the consequences. Although Odría, the Peruvian dictator of 1954, would have profited from a more intensive milking of the Toquepala "bonanza"—it would have allowed him to expand further the public works programs on which his personal image and policy of segmental incorporation depended—neither he nor his advisors had any clear idea of how hard they could push without risking Asarco's withdrawal.

This last point suggests that more important than the state's will was its skill. The more proficient state mining bureaucracy of 1969 was well schooled in the problems of mine development *as seen by the private investor*. Knowing how private mine developers think and plan—for many of them had done so themselves—state technocrats were positioned to exploit Asarco's and Southern's points of vulnerability while maintaining the dialogue on an economic plane to which the latter could relate.

[19] Some Peruvians have insisted that the country would have gained more by delaying the signing of the Cuajone basic agreement until after the enactment of the 1971 Mining Code, whose provisions regarding incentives for foreign investment were more restrictive than those applicable in 1969. In the text it was already noted that Southern might have dropped the project in that case. Moreover, the Peruvian economy was in a recession when the generals took power in 1968, and they had staked their reputation as governors on their ability to end it quickly—which, as they saw it, required Cuajone to proceed without delay. In my conversation with him on July 15, 1978, Fernández Maldonado stressed these points. When I asked him specifically whether the decision to sign the Cuajone basic agreement while the 1950 Code was still in effect was a violation of the regime's mining policy, he replied: "We knew that the existing legislation was defective and wanted to replace it, but we were not going to be dogmatic about it."

[20] See Bosson and Varon (1977:139-43).

What one notices immediately upon reviewing the documents making up the record of the Cuajone negotiations is that state officials did not try to counterpose overtly political or ideological arguments against the economic arguments coming from the company side. Neither did they fall back upon that artifice of last resort, the adoption of an extreme opposite position in the hope that some vague bargaining calculus would produce an outcome splitting the differences. Rather, state negotiators used their knowledge of the company's operations and of the international copper market to comprehend how Southern defined its global interests. Armed with this insight they could proceed to delineate the Peruvian national interest in the project without denying legitimacy to the company's overriding concern with profitability, investment recuperation, and disposition of production.[21] Keeping the discussion within the purely economic realm in which Southern's interests lay, they could bring forth counterproposals, based on the same data and modes of analysis that Southern itself used, with the claim that they were designed to secure the legitimate interests of *both* parties—and, in consequence, were not negotiable. It thus proved impossible for company representatives to define the Peruvian case as "political" (i.e., nonquantifiable) and to dismiss it by reference to the "hard, practical facts of economic life."[22]

THE FINANCING OF CUAJONE

The primary responsibility for concerting the project financing rested with Asarco as Southern's majority owner. Asarco "had a friend at Chase Manhattan" Bank, with which it had maintained a relationship of long standing. Chase Manhattan, as is widely known, considers itself something of a specialist in Latin America; long experience in the area enables it to evaluate and accept apparent risks that deter many of its less experienced competitors. Furthermore, the bank had remained on very good terms with the Peruvian military regime. The generals had expropriated Chase Manhattan's Peruvian branch in 1970 along with the rest of the foreign banking establishment in the country. But, knowing that its favor could greatly facilitate government plans to finance development projects with loans from private overseas banks, they had paid it an extremely generous compensation settlement.[23]

[21] In his study of transnational corporate action in Brazil, Evans (1979:193) makes the point that pressures applied to the corporations by nationalist regimes on behalf of their interests are most likely to yield the desired results if they run parallel to the pressures of oligopolistic competition and do not fundamentally deviate from the logic of profitability. What we see here is totally consistent with his observation.

[22] Goulet's comments (1977:73) regarding the attitudes and behavioral dispositions of transnational managers are relevant here. He notes that these individuals, as a rule, have little respect for "academic generalizers" or for ideologists; they much prefer to deal with opposite numbers whose profit and/or power goals are made manifest.

[23] Peru's dealings with Chase Manhattan are discussed by Hunt (1974); with it and the rest of the international banking establishment, by Stallings (1979). These authors report that the compensation award was 3 times higher than the book value of assets and 5½ times higher than the selling price of the branch's shares on the local stock exchange. As the regime treated no

The Cuajone Banking Consortium

The $200 million loan requested by Asarco for Cuajone represented too much of an exposure even for Chase Manhattan, especially inasmuch as the risks were magnified by the absence of any direct involvement of an international or quasi-governmental lending agency and by the refusal of the Peruvian state to offer a formal guarantee of the loans. Therefore, Chase Manhattan set about assembling an international consortium of private banks to share the risks.[24]

Asarco, as we saw, had already determined that private bank loans would have to be secured by committing most of Cuajone's production for sale under long-term contract to refiners in the countries whose banks participated in the financing arrangements. Now Chase Manhattan laid down four conditions that these sales had to meet: (1) Delivery contracts would have a minimum term of fifteen years, to ensure that they would remain in force during the entire period of investment recuperation and loan amortization (with a suitable margin of safety). (2) Sales commitments could not favor any one country and, since much Toquepala copper was being exported to the United States, should preferably be directed toward Europe and Japan. (3) The only acceptable buyers were to be major custom refiners and fabricators whose volume of business and lack of access to alternate sources of supply left no doubt of their ability to meet their purchase obligations over the full fifteen years. (4) Purchasers of copper were to assist in financing the project in every way possible: by persuading their bankers to join the consortium, by urging their home governments to support the consortium, by lending to the project on their own account, etc. Home-government cooperation was anticipated by all parties, for the long-term copper sales program would ensure that their economies enjoyed for years a steady supply of the metal at prices lower than what would be paid on the "spot" market in periods of high demand.

Asarco was not overjoyed at the prospect of having to commit contractually so much of Cuajone's production to firms unaffiliated with Southern for such a long span of time. In fact, the company had heretofore made it a matter of policy not to accept sales contracts with a duration longer than eighteen months—for the reason that industry custom requires sellers to offer price discounts in return for longer-term purchase commitments. However, Asarco clearly had no choice in this instance but to accede to Chase Manhattan's conditions. Its maneuvering room in marketing affairs was thus circumscribed to the possibility that the volume of production required to be committed would be sufficiently less than the mine's total output as to leave an "excess production" surplus of reasonable size that could be disposed of in a more customary manner. Increasing the amount and keeping discretionary control

other foreign investor so generously, one can only assume that in this case it was hoping to cultivate a new relationship with the bank.

[24] The growing role of consortium banking in international finance is discussed by Spero (1977) and von Clemm (1971).

of this "excess production" became a major Asarco preoccupation from then on.

Another condition of the loans was that Southern accept a number of restrictions on its managerial prerogatives. Its total outstanding debt could not exceed $404 million without a special waiver from the consortium. It had to maintain a large balance of current assets over current liabilities. It could not use any of its profits to repurchase its own capital shares. And it was prohibited from paying dividends until its debt were substantially reduced.[25] It is worth reiterating that Asarco/Southern's willingness to accede to these conditions and to bear the interest charges for such large amounts of borrowed capital signals that its interest in Cuajone was more one of oligopolistic market-share competition with minimal risk than of short- to medium-term profit.

The members of the banking consortium put together by Chase Manhattan are listed along with their contributions in Table 5.1. The list reads like a veritable *Who's Who* of international finance. Some dependencistas might leap to the conclusion that the involvement of such a constellation of international banks in the Cuajone project reinforces Peru's external dependency. It is difficult to take that argument seriously, however. The loans were made not to the state but to a transnational enterprise, and the only responsibility accepted by the state was the tacit one of honoring the provisions of the basic Cuajone agreement. It in turn was entered into freely and knowledgeably by a nationalist government which believed that its interests had been adequately protected. Observance of the agreement does entail a surrender of sovereign prerogatives, in the limited sense that the state has committed itself to a course of future action that cannot be altered for some years to come. But all states, including the world superpowers, routinely bind themselves in this way when there are advantages to be gained. A nation is not dependent solely because, by virtue of its own prior decisions, it does not enjoy absolute freedom of action at every instant.

A fringe benefit for Peru—and a more direct one for those countries whose banks joined the consortium—was a degree of trade diversification on the import side. Had Cuajone been wholly U.S.-financed, all of the capital equipment and supplies for the project would have been procured in the United States—which is what occurred with Toquepala. Instead, some non-U.S. members of the consortium tied their loans to the purchase of equipment and supplies from providers in their home countries. Many of these purchases were made in Britain, giving a boost to that nation's ailing capital-goods industries.[26] The Germans and Japanese, for their part, won most of the vehicle supply contracts.

[25] Asarco's "10K" report for 1976, filed with the U.S. Securities and Exchange Commission.

[26] The importance of equipment supply contracts to the British was singled out by the head of the metals purchasing division of British Insulated Callender's Cables Ltd. He was interviewed on May 20, 1977 by Robert Andrew Nickson, a member of an advisory team to the Ministry of Commerce that was sponsored by the United Nations and funded by the British Government Technical Cooperation Programme. I thank Mr. Nickson for making available a transcript of that interview.

TABLE 5.1 Members of the Chase Manhattan Banking Consortium for Cuajone, with Their Contributions (*Contributions in millions of dollars*)

Country or Area	Name of Bank	Contribution
USA	Bank of New York	5
	Bankers' Trust Company	10
	Chase Manhattan	30
	Chemical Bank	10
	Citibank N.A.	15
	Marine Midland Bank	10
	Morgan Guarantee Trust Company	15
	USA TOTAL	95.0
Canada	Bank of Montreal	5
	Bank of Nova Scotia	5
	Canadian Imperial Bank of Commerce	5
	Royal Bank of Canada	7.5
	Toronto Dominion Bank	5
	CANADA TOTAL	27.5
Japan	Chuo Trust and Banking Company Ltd.	5
	Kyowa Bank Ltd.	5
	Long-Term Credit Bank of Japan Ltd.	5
	Mitsubishi Bank Ltd.	5
	Mitsui Bank Ltd.	5
	Nippon Fudusan Bank Ltd.	5
	JAPAN TOTAL	30.0
Europe	Atlantic International Bank Ltd.	2
	Credito Italiano	1
	Girozentrale Vienna	5
	Japan International Bank of London	5
	Libria Bank Ltd.	6.5
	National Westminster Bank Ltd.	3
	Orion Termbank Ltd.	5
	Österreichische Kommerzialbank AG	5
	Rothschild International Bank Ltd.	5
	Société Financière Européenne	5
	West Deutsche Handelsbank Girozentrale	5
	EUROPE TOTAL	47.5
	GRAND TOTAL	200.0

SOURCE: Southern Peru Copper Corp., private documents.

Participation by International Agencies and the U.S. Government

It will be recalled that the requirements imposed on the disposition of Cuajone copper gave Asarco/Southern a new interest in increasing the mine's "excess production." The easiest way to do this was simply to enlarge the mine so that its originally planned annual output of 120,000 metric tons (fine copper content) could be raised to 150,000. The decision to do so was taken in 1972 (the mine was already under construction), after a report by the firm supervising the construction work revealed that the increased output could be had for a less-than-proportionate increase in construction costs.[27] Nonetheless, total construction costs would rise. At about the same time it was discovered that considerably more sterile overburden than planned would have to be removed to develop the Cuajone open pit—another cost escalation factor. And, as if this were not enough, by 1972 the metropolitan economies were suffering a serious bout of inflation, which rapidly drove up the prices of capital equipment far beyond the project estimates. In 1973 the cost for completing the project was reestimated at $551 million, including allowances for further inflation and contingencies—an increase of 55 percent over the originally estimated $355 million. Additional financing had to be found in order to complete Cuajone on schedule.

Fortunately for the company, the so-called Mercado-Greene Agreement between Peru and the United States, which resolved all outstanding controversies stemming from Peru's expropriations of U.S. property in 1968-1973, was signed early in 1974.[28] Relations between the two countries took an immediate turn for the better, and, for the first time in over five years, Export-Import Bank loans were once again obtainable for Peru. Chase Manhattan was pleased: Export-Import Bank participation would further add to the security of the consortium's loan exposure. The Peruvians were not. They were concerned that the Export-Import Bank would interfere with their market diversification plans by requiring that more of Cuajone's production be sold in the United States. Their planned counterstrategy—feasible now that Southern was fully committed to Cuajone—was to use the state monopoly over mineral and metal export sales to shift an equivalent amount of Toquepala production away from the North American market.

The Export-Import Bank loan of $75 million was insufficient to make up the financing shortfall. Southern's owners contributed $40.4 million in additional equity capital. Billiton N.V., the Royal Dutch/Shell metals subsidiary, was brought in as a joint-venture partner with an equity contribution of $27.4 million.[29] But more was still needed. Therefore, the International Finance

---

[27] This decision was not in itself unusual; much the same was done with Toquepala (Mikesell 1975a:42) and with other large open-pit mines around the world, since planning tends to be conservative until preliminary construction work reveals the full extent of the ore deposit.

[28] Sigmund (1980:204-207).

[29] Southern's agreement with Billiton gives the latter priority over the former's owners in regard to all cash distributions until the $27.4 million investment has been paid back. Then Billiton is to receive distributions equal to a 10 percent annual return on its investment until dividend payouts to Southern's owners equal their original equity investment in Cuajone. Thereafter all of the participants share in dividends in accordance with their equity holdings. The first obligation to Billiton was fulfilled in 1980. Note that Southern's willingness to convert Cuajone

Corporation, an arm of the World Bank, was solicited as a possible participant. The IFC expressed interest, suggesting a contribution of $22 million: $10 million in a loan at 11½ percent annual interest and the rest in equity shares. All of the private lenders were delighted, for IFC involvement represented ironclad investment insurance: Peru would never dare to antagonize the World Bank by moving against a venture in which it held an equity interest. The IFC was both quick and undiplomatic in reminding the Peruvian government of its leverage. It warned that, as an equity participant, it would have an interest in the continued unrestricted export of Cuajone copper even after the end of the investment recuperation period.[30] In effect, it demanded that the state sales monopoly, then being activated, be kept out of Cuajone forever. Not even Chase Manhattan had gone that far; it had promised to give the sales monopoly access to Cuajone's "excess production" as soon as the recuperation period had ended.

The DGM staff strenuously lobbied for state disapproval of IFC equity participation, irrespective of the effect of such a rejection on the future of the project. These technocrats were convinced that the World Bank would attempt to impose additional conditions on the project that would be antithetical to Peruvian interests and, possibly, in violation of Peruvian law, pointing to its demand regarding sales as an indication of what might be expected.[31] They were especially disturbed at the likelihood that the World Bank would seek to force abrogation of the "Calvo clause" in the basic agreement. Fernández Maldonado, as usual, took their advice and pressed it upon Treasury Minister Morales Bermúdez, whose portfolio had jurisdiction in the matter. He in turn took a hard line with the IFC; he stressed that the government preferred for its participation to be limited to a loan and that the government would veto any IFC equity ownership unless the latter put into writing that neither the rules of the World Bank nor any other relationships between it and the Peruvian state would be allowed to supersede or alter the provisions of the basic Cuajone agreement in the slightest. The IFC chose not to belabor the point. It restricted its involvement to the $10 million loan.

THE LONG-TERM COPPER SALES

Asarco had assumed that it alone would negotiate with prospective buyers the conditions of the contracted sales of Cuajone copper. As much as the company disliked having to sell so much metal in advance under long-term contract, it disliked even more the idea of having its market disposition determined for it by the newborn Peruvian state sales monopoly. It hoped

---

into a joint venture with an outsider is a further sign that it was more concerned with risk minimization than with profit maximization in the narrow sense.

[30] Letter from the IFC to Fernández Maldonado, dated February 26, 1974; original found in the files of the Ministry of Energy and Mines.

[31] Ministry of Energy and Mines internal memorandum dated April 16, 1974 (not signed).

that the sales restrictions imposed by the banking consortium would be enough to keep the state's nose out of its marketing business.

Company representatives began by approaching five major European consumers. Two British firms, British Insulated Callender's Cables (BICC) and Imperial Metal Industries (IMI), were the first to come to a tentative agreement. This agreement was not very advantageous to Asarco/Southern, who, because they desperately needed the sale to secure the financing for their mining project, were negotiating from a position of weakness. Both buyers demanded and received a sizable discount from the LME price, one that would increase still further on a sliding scale should the price later rise. It was anticipated that basically identical terms would be extended to all other potential buyers. But before they had signed up, the Peruvian government once more intervened.

Even as the negotiators of the basic Cuajone agreement were thrashing out the refinery issue, state officials were secretly exploring the construction of their own refinery with two Japanese firms, Mitsui and Furukawa Electric.[32] When the plans were finally announced, Asarco/Southern realized to their regret that their opposition to a Peruvian refinery had painted them into a corner: they were uncomfortably certain that the state would compel Southern to deliver "blister" copper in sufficient quantity to keep the new refinery operating at full capacity. To make matters worse, the refinery's appetite would be huge; it was to have an annual production capacity of 150,000 metric tons, expandable later on to 300,000 tons. Toquepala alone could not supply "blister" in such volume. At least some of Cuajone's production, then, would also be refined in Peru; and all involved could not but agree that the wording of the "free product availability" clause in the basic agreement would not prevent the state from requiring local refination, so long as its charges for the service were equivalent to those obtainable from the principal overseas refiners.

What is more, the advent of the state refinery unraveled the company's plans for keeping the state out of the Cuajone sales picture. The state sales monopoly was administered by MineroPeru (Minpeco was not "hived off" as a separate entity until 1974), which would also operate the refinery. In other words, the government's interests in controlling export sales and in assuring a continuous supply of refinery feedstocks were institutionally wedded. Meanwhile, MineroPeru had been acquiring sales expertise. It had cleverly begun by negotiating sales of Toquepala "blister" to China, Poland, the German Democratic Republic, and Yugoslavia—all markets that Asarco had never tapped and where, consequently, the parastatal enterprise could operate without subjecting itself to invidious comparisons with an established, transnational rival. Once having demonstrated its value to the state by opening new markets for Peruvian metal exports, MineroPeru started to display an

[32] The reasons for the Japanese interest are those discussed in Chapter 4 in the context of the "Japanese contradiction" in the world copper oligopoly.

active interest in Cuajone. It lobbied with Fernández Maldonado for the right to supervise the long-term sales. Its interests were threefold: to prevent the disposition of Cuajone copper from adversely affecting supplies to its refinery; to complete its monopoly; and to secure its yet-uncertain institutional existence by proving its value to the state and by stemming heated criticism of the sales monopoly from a dubious mediana minería—all of which it could accomplish, it felt, by working out better conditions with the long-term copper buyers than Asarco itself had been able to get.

In view of the changed circumstances, Asarco conceded that there might be some advantage in admitting MineroPeru to a role in the negotiations, and Chase Manhattan was of like mind. MineroPeru's presence would resolve a doubt as to whether the sales contracts would still be honored if the investment recuperation period ended in less than fifteen years.[33] It would also overcome the resistance of German and Belgian consumers, whose home banks were unwilling to back their purchase commitments without their governments' official support—in turn contingent upon a guarantee of the sales arrangements by the Peruvian state.

Since its intrusion was now seen as useful, MineroPeru was able to win a promise from Chase Manhattan regarding the disposition of Cuajone's "excess production," all of which was originally to be sold to Southern's owners. However, the bank agreed that the owners' right to acquire the "excess production" would reign solely during the recuperation period and that thereafter, MineroPeru could purchase all of it. Its participation in the project having thus been ratified by the principal international sponsor, MineroPeru suggested that it should negotiate the sales contracts and become the seller of record vis-à-vis the consumers under a system of "back-to-back" contracting. (That is, MineroPeru would sell the copper to the end purchasers under conditions laid down by Chase Manhattan and would turn around and buy it from Southern on identical terms.)[34] The parastatal's profit would be limited to a small commission, but, as the seller of record, it would enhance its international reputation and gain more valuable marketing experience.

In order to prove that it could obtain a better arrangement than Asarco had been prepared to settle for, MineroPeru attacked the price discount clause in the tentative agreements with BICC and IMI. It succeeded in instituting a different type of discounting system whose benefit to the buyers—estimated by experts as 0.4-1.0¢/lb[35]—was less than under the old system. It also

[33] The Japanese, concerned as they were with security of supply to their resource-short national economy, were the most worried. They had gone so far as to seek an equity participation in Cuajone in order to guarantee supply security over the long haul, but their offer was refused by Southern and vetoed by the Peruvian government. Cablegram dated April 4, 1973 from Ueda Company Ltd. (MineroPeru's representative in Japan) to MineroPeru, located in the files of the Ministry of Energy and Mines.

[34] Letter from the president of MineroPeru to Fernández Maldonado, stamped as received on April 16, 1973 and located in the files of the Ministry of Energy and Mines.

[35] Internal MineroPeru working document dated January 25, 1974, from the files of the Ministry of Energy and Mines. The document attributes the datum to the (British) Commodities Research

convinced BICC and IMI to reduce the refining-charge deduction from the posted price that they had proposed to levy. MineroPeru was able to accomplish what Asarco could not because it possessed additional bargaining leverage; it did not have a direct stake in Cuajone's financing, could afford to be patient, and was supported by the coercive powers of the state. Chagrined Asarco officials grumbled that the changes were insignificant. But their real opinion of the revised BICC-IMI sales agreement was revealed by their petition, submitted in February 1974, that Cuajone's "excess production" be sold during the recuperation period to Southern's owners on identical terms.

A final controversy arose over the "excess production" issue. The magnitude of this uncommitted volume of metal had increased from the 10 percent of total annual output estimated in Southern's original proposal to a full 41 percent. Some of the increase was due to the expansion of the mine; the rest resulted from a decision by prospective West German buyers to opt out of the deal, whereupon Chase Manhattan permitted their share to be reconsigned as part of the "excess production." As the Peruvians had feared, the Export-Import Bank was now asking that a "substantial portion" of Cuajone copper be exported to the United States. Using this demand as a bargaining tool, Southern sought a guarantee from the Peruvian government that its owners would have free access to the "excess production" for fifteen years, without going through MineroPeru and without being obligated to have the metal locally refined. Fernández Maldonado rejected the solicitation out of hand,[36] but there was still the Export-Import Bank demand to be taken care of.

Again it fell to the DGM staff to work out an analysis supporting the state's position. The technocrats argued that the primary concerns of the state should be assuring availability of refinery feedstocks; preventing any of the long-term purchasers from diminishing Southern's profits (taxable in Peru) by applying excessive refining-charge deductions; and guaranteeing that the state monopoly could take over the marketing of Cuajone's "excess production" as soon as practicable. They also wanted to make sure that the "excess production" was sold at the highest possible price, generally the LME. Some compromise with the market diversification goal could be accepted if all of these other objectives were attained. Their specific recommendations were these: (1) All sales to Southern's owners should be guaranteed only for the recuperation period and should carry price terms at least as favorable to Southern as those in the long-term sales to unaffiliated buyers. (2) After the recuperation period ended, the owners' portion should be totally taken over by the state sales monopoly, which could, at its sole discretion, either reassign it to the owners or dispose of it elsewhere. (3) The owners should be made

---

Unit. A comparable figure was given to me by Simon D. Strauss, Asarco's vice-chairman and a recognized international authority on metals marketing, in a conversation on August 10, 1978.

[36] Letters from Frank Archibald, Southern's president and board chairman, to Fernández Maldonado on March 14 and April 3, 1974; copies found in the files of the Ministry of Energy and Mines.

to agree to have at least 75,000 metric tons, and preferably all, of their portion refined in Peru. MineroPeru would initially charge them the same fees that BICC and IMI were entitled to deduct from the posted price in their contracts. (4) Asarco and MineroPeru should work together to convince as many of the unaffiliated buyers as possible to agree to have their allotments refined in Peru. (5) Southern should be made to enlarge Toquepala by 30 percent and to commit all of the new output to be refined locally.

These recommendations were cleared without alteration by the Council of Ministers and were presented to Asarco/Southern as the state's final, non-negotiable position. As they did with the basic agreement, Asarco/Southern yielded when they recognized that all possibilities for further maneuver had been exhausted. The arrangements for financing Cuajone were still in abeyance after four years, and any additional delay might result in a failure to complete the project on time—in which event the state could invoke the penalty clause it had written into the basic agreement and take over the almost-completed installation. The Peruvians had shown by their tenacity in all phases of the bargaining process that they might well do just that.

The final sales contracts, signed simultaneously in Geneva on September 19, 1974, are identical to each other except for minor details. They produce the distribution of Cuajone production shown in Table 5.2. I have examined the texts of the contracts and find that their key provisions are well within the limits of industry custom for agreements of this type; indeed, they differ

TABLE 5.2 Cuajone Long-Term Copper Sales: Final Contractual Disposition

Buyer	Fine Short Tons	Percent of Total	Form	Time Period
BICC (Brit.)	15,000	8.45	Blister	15 years
IMI (Brit.)	15,000	8.45	Blister	15 years
Billiton (Neth.)	30,000	16.89	Refined[a]	15 years
Enfield (Brit.)	10,000	5.63	Refined[a]	15 years
Europe Total	70,000	39.41		
Japanese[b]	30,000	16.89	Blister	15 years
Non-US Total	100,000	56.31		
Owners (US)	77,600[c]	43.69	Refined[a]	[d]
GRAND TOTAL	177,600	100.00		

SOURCE: Compiled by the author from texts of the sales contracts.
[a] At MineroPeru's Ilo refinery.
[b] Consortium consisting of Dowa, Furukawa, Mitsubishi, Mitsui, Sumitomo.
[c] Estimated; actual quantity ("excess production") equals total production less other commitments.
[d] From commencement of operations until owners have recovered their investment.

little from similiar provisions in existing contracts for Toquepala copper sales. Prices are tied to the LME (the discounts are obtained by the buyers' selection, within limits, of the days on which the price quotation is applied) and are thus subject to ready verification. Refining-charge deductions in those contracts specifying delivery of ''blister'' are determined by published formulae[37] so that they can also be independently verified by Peruvian authorities. The Peruvian government is guaranteed the facilities and access it needs to supervise assaying and weighing of all shipments. Hence, below-market transfer pricing is precluded if the state properly exercises its responsibilities.

QUELLAVECO: A FOOTNOTE

The Quellaveco concession, having been separated from Cuajone, was subject to the legal requirement that a calendar of development operations and proof of financing be submitted by the end of 1970 on pain of *caducidad*. Southern could not, of course, meet the deadline with Cuajone in progress. In order to avoid losing the concession it filed a series of administrative appeals. These did not prosper, and Quellaveco reverted to the state.

Since the Quellaveco orebody lies midway between Toquepala and Cuajone, it is unthinkable that it could be developed without being intimately connected to the infrastructure associated with its two sister mines. Thus, Southern will unquestionably be given another chance at it after its Cuajone investment has been recovered. However, it will then have to bargain for concessionary rights, which it did not have to do with Cuajone. It is probable that MineroPeru, which now administers Quellaveco, will have to be taken in as a joint venture partner. If that happens, the state will have established an entrepreneurial presence in the last segment of the gran minería where it does not yet have one; it will have done so without a conflictual expropriation, without the expense of compensation payments, and, quite likely, without having to make a contribution of cash equity.

On the other hand, Southern officials have informed me that they will not move on Quellaveco unless investment incentives are increased. Yet they are realistic as to how far that can be done. When in 1980 the new civilian government asked the company for its suggestions for possible amendments to the Mining Code, the latter replied informally that it would ideally prefer a system of variable income tax rates designed to provide a constant internal rate of return (or discounted cash flow rate; the two are identical) of 11 percent; but it understood the political impossibility of the request and did not formally submit it. These same officials feel, however, that the investment incentives contained in the 1981 Mining Code are in line with what other less-developed countries are currently offering—which implies that they will favorably con-

---

[37] The formulae are based on the published energy and labor cost indices of the countries in which the recipient refineries are located, each multiplied by a constant factor representing the ponderance of the item in the overall refining cost.

sider such incentives as a basis for going ahead eventually with Quellaveco.[38] The real question is that of international metals prices. Quellaveco's development would entail severe engineering problems (as a river now runs through the site) and could cost as much as $1 billion. With MineroPeru as a joint venturer, Southern would need a copper price of as much as $1.80/lb to assure itself of an "adequate" internal rate of return.

THE RESULTS

Cuajone came on stream in October 1976, just in time to meet the completion deadline written into the basic agreement. The final cost of the project (see Table 5.3) was almost $670 million, not including provision for working capital. (In order to meet the added costs, Southern had to solicit an additional $53.4 million loan from the consortium.) About three-fourths of the project's cost exclusive of interest, or $506.4 million, is recuperable investment in the contractual definition.

The mine is very capital-intensive and employs the latest automation technologies in all phases of operation.[39] Total employment at the end of 1980 stood at 1,573 at all levels, of whom 37 were expatriates.[40] Copper production for the year was 150,800 metric tons fine content, or 95.9 metric tons per worker. In contrast, Toquepala—which, being older, is far less automated—produced only 108,500 metric tons with its 2,647 workers (including 41 expatriates), a productivity of but 41 metric tons per worker.[41] One can legitimately bemoan the inappropriateness of this ultra-advanced technology in a country where some 45 percent of the urban population is un- or underemployed. Yet, even if Toquepala's fifteen-year-old technologies had been reproduced at Cuajone, the gain in employment would not have made a measurable dent in the nationwide situation. Meanwhile, a part of the earnings that actually went toward tax payments, and that were thus available in theory for the benefit of all Peruvians, would have been captured privately by a tiny group of additional workers. Provided that sizable profits are realized and are then taxed at a high rate, capital-intensive production of this kind is entirely

[38] Interview with Arthur G. Beers, senior vice-president of Southern, on August 13, 1981. He made specific reference to Art. 157 of the 1981 Code, which authorizes essentially the same incentives that were contained in the Cuajone basic agreement.

[39] A dramatic example of the degree of automation installed at Cuajone is the use of radio control for the railroad trains which haul ore from the open pit to the concentrator. This enables each train to be operated by a single individual, the engineer. When the train arrives at the unloading chute, the engineer dismounts from the locomotive cab and positions himself alongside the chute. Using a back-carried radio pack, he remotely advances the entire train until an ore car is properly positioned by the chute; stops the train; dumps the car; and advances to the next. At Toquepala the same procedure requires an engineer, a brakeman, and a dump operator.

[40] The expatriate workers all occupy technical middle-management positions where specific and extensive prior experience is necessary; the manager of the Cuajone installation and his immediate staff are Peruvian.

[41] Total Southern employment in 1980 was 6,541, including 130 expatriates. All employment data are taken from Southern's annual report for 1980.

TABLE 5.3 Financing of the Cuajone Project: Final Summary of Funding Sources and Recuperable Investment (*Millions of dollars*)

1. Debt Financing:	
Chase Manhattan consortium	200.0
U.S. Export-Import Bank	75.0
International Finance Corp. (IFC)	10.0
Supplier credits	54.0
Long-term copper buyers' credits and loans	65.0
Supplementary loan from Chase consortium	53.4
Bank credits for working capital	50.0
TOTAL DEBT FINANCING	507.4
2. Equity Financing:	
Billiton N.V. equity investment (11.2 percent in Southern Common	
stock)	27.4
Southern owners' purchases of additional Southern common stock	20.0
Southern owners' purchases of new issue of Southern Class A	
preferred stock	20.4
TOTAL EQUITY FINANCING	67.8
3. Toquepala Depletion Reserves	163.4
4. GRAND TOTAL	738.6
5. Recuperable Investment:	
Total cost of project	738.6
Less: provision for working capital	(68.8)
Less: Toquepala depletion reserves	(163.4)
TOTAL RECUPERABLE INVESTMENT	506.4

SOURCE: Compiled by the author from private documents furnished by the Southern Peru Copper Corp.

consistent with the intended role of the gran minería in a bonanza development strategy.

Bonanza development also requires that the resource sector make a major contribution to foreign exchange earnings. Cuajone's 1979 copper output of 183,500 metric tons fine content represented 45.8 percent of Peru's exports of the red metal in that year. The mine generated net copper sales of $361 million (all paid for in hard currencies), or 50.1 percent of the total value of the nation's copper production in 1979. In the first four years of full operation (1977-1980), it earned $1.06 billion in hard-currency sales, as compared to $604 million earned by Toquepala. It should also be noted that since Cuajone's share of Peruvian copper value was actually somewhat greater than its share of exported production, the average price received for Cuajone copper had to have been above the national average. This is an indication, though not conclusive proof, that the long-term sales conditions are fair and in line with general market practices.

The available data do not allow us to determine precisely what proportion of Cuajone's annual revenues remains in Peru and what proportion is exported as dividends, interest, and investment recuperation. We can, however, paint an approximate picture. Table 5.4 reveals how Southern's revenues were distributed during the years 1971-1980. We expect that after Cuajone came on line there was a larger net outflow of funds than before from Peru; the question is, how large has the effect been? The table demonstrates that, indeed, the percentage of Southern's revenues remaining in Peru dropped suddenly in 1977 and 1978 when the Cuajone outflows started. But since then the trend has reversed. By 1980 Peru was receiving a bigger share of the combined revenues from Toquepala and Cuajone than it had received from Toquepala alone in 1971-1973, despite the fact that Toquepala (its investment fully recovered several years before) was operating under the general regime of the Mining Code rather than under a special agreement. Clearly, any claim that Cuajone is a pump sucking capital out of Peru along with copper simply ignores the important contribution that the mine is making to the local economy.

This contribution appears as wages, local purchases of goods and services, interest paid to local banks on short-term borrowings, and taxes. It is not possible to compute what fraction of the contribution takes the form of "bonanza" benefits to the state, since taxes are only one part of the "bonanza"; also included are interest charged by state-owned banks and the profit earned by MineroPeru from the sale of refining services to Southern. I calculate that Cuajone alone accounted for 6.4 percent of the Peruvian government's total revenues from income taxes in 1980; Southern as a whole contributed 12.8 percent—much more than any other taxpayer. It also appears that Minero-Peru's refining charges have been running higher than those assessed by metropolitan refineries. Inasmuch as Southern was effectively made to patronize the local refinery through the use of political pressure, the company has thus been compelled to make transfer payments to the state. Their amount can be estimated to first order as the difference between what MineroPeru charges and what refining services could be bought for in the metropoli. Southern's president claimed in 1978 that, due to underutilization of refinery capacity in Europe, the company was receiving offers from custom refiners to limit charges to $160 per ton, whereas MineroPeru was charging $200 per ton. If that difference held true throughout the year, the forced transfer payment would have amounted to $6 million on the basis of the 150,000 tons of Southern "blister" that MineroPeru refined.

The 1980 abolition of the state metal sales monopoly decreed by the new civilian government will not adversely affect refining operations, as these are contractually guaranteed. Once the contracts lapse the state will continue to be assured of refinery feedstocks from Toquepala and Cuajone by provisions to such effect in the 1981 Mining Code. Moreover, although Minpeco is no longer a marketing monopolist, it has the power under the new code to set refining charges and other conditions unilaterally if MineroPeru and Southern

TABLE 5.4 Southern Peru Copper: Proportion of Sales Income Spent in Peru, 1971-1980

	Net Sales Income	Total Local Expenditures		To Peruvian-Private Sector[a]			To Peruvian Government[b]		
		A	B	A	B	C	A	B	C
1971	120.1	67.8	56.4	31.1	25.9	45.9	36.7	30.5	54.1
1972	123.7	77.5	62.7	45.0	36.4	58.1	32.5	26.3	41.9
1973	215.7	137.2	63.6	48.3	22.4	35.2	88.9	41.2	64.8
1974	190.5	154.7	81.2	82.2	43.1	53.1	72.5	38.1	46.9
1975	93.4	100.2	107.3	89.6	95.9	89.4	10.6	11.4	10.6
1976	108.1	130.5	120.7	104.2	96.4	79.8	26.3	24.3	20.2
1977	244.9	180.8	73.8	147.2	60.1	81.4	33.6	13.7	18.6
1978	293.4	164.1	55.9	130.9	44.6	79.8	33.2	11.3	20.2
1979	549.9	330.8	60.2	158.4	28.8	47.9	172.4	31.4	52.1
1980	517.6	375.5	72.5	200.5	38.7	53.4	175.0	33.8	46.6
1971-80[c]	2,457.3	1,719.1	70.0	1,037.4	42.2	60.3	681.7	27.8	39.7

SOURCE: Computed by the author from data presented in Southern Peru Copper Corporation's annual report for 1980.
NOTE: Net sales income and columns A, millions of dollars; columns B, percent of net sales income; columns C, percent of total local expenditures.
[a] Wages, materials, purchased services, financing charges by local banks.
[b] Income and ad valorem export taxes.
[c] Net sales and columns A, totals for the period; columns B and C, averages for the period.

are unable to agree to them in direct dealing. Is there any question as to which side Minpeco's decision would favor?

While Peru did not attain its goal of having most or all of Cuajone's production sold outside of the United States, market concentration had not taken place up to 1977 (detailed export breakdowns for later years were not yet available in late 1981). Figure 5 plots the geographical distribution of Southern's sales over its entire productive existence. Cuajone has obviously arrested the precipitous decline in the U.S. share of Southern's exports but has not reversed it. The reason is that Minpeco, as Southern's uninvited sales agent, has directed more Toquepala copper (much of it refined by MineroPeru) to non-U.S. markets as compensation.[42]

Table 5.5 summarizes Cuajone's earnings statements for the first four years of operation and compares them to Toquepala's. The new mine has consistently earned higher dollar profits, thanks to its larger output and much lower operating costs, even though it is burdened with high interest expenses and charges for investment recuperation. But return on invested capital is less. Company officials compute their internal rate of return as 3 percent, which they regard as unsatisfactory.[43] Although Cuajone, like Toquepala before it, is one of the world's lowest-cost mines of its epoch, it nevertheless requires a copper price of 80¢/lb (in 1977 dollars) to recover its investment with interest, and a price of 97¢/lb to yield an after-tax annual return on investment of 15 percent. Even so, Asarco/Southern do not regret their decision to go ahead with the project. By 1980 the first obligation to Billiton had been discharged;[44] the outstanding long-term debt had been reduced to 40 percent of the amount originally borrowed; and dividend payments to the owners were resumed. Almost $350 million had by then been applied toward investment recuperation;[45] if recuperation proceeds at the same average annual rate, it will be completed within six years of startup—two years earlier than the company had estimated in its project proposal. Tax stability will be enjoyed for another six years, until 1988.

Cuajone contributed nearly 19 percent of Asarco's consolidated profit for 1980. More significantly, its output had the effect of increasing Asarco's market share in the world copper oligopoly by a factor of 50 percent.[46] The company's general opinion of its Peruvian experience is betrayed by its effort to negotiate by January 1982 an agreement with the government for a $400

---

[42] Southern did not protest Minpeco's actions, since sales were shifted in a way that did not disrupt markets or customer relationships and that conformed to the customs of the world oligopoly.

[43] According to an official interviewed on August 13, 1981, an 11 percent internal rate of return is regarded as satisfactory. Note that this disagrees with Mikesell's statement (1979:129) that mining companies operating in less-developed countries insist on an internal rate of return (discounted cash flow) of 20 percent or more.

[44] See n. 29, this chapter.

[45] The figure is obtained by summing the deductions for depreciation, depletion, and amortization and the net profits shown in Table 5.5 for the years 1977-1980.

[46] My computation, based on 1977 production figures.

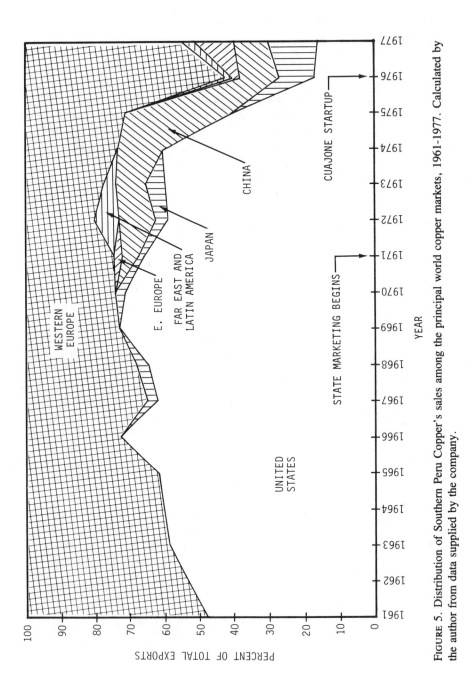

FIGURE 5. Distribution of Southern Peru Copper's sales among the principal world copper markets, 1961-1977. Calculated by the author from data supplied by the company.

TABLE 5.5 Southern Peru Copper: Earnings Statements for Toquepala (T) and Cuajone (C), 1977-1980 (*Millions of dollars except as noted*)

Item	1977 T	1977 C	1978 T	1978 C	1979 T	1979 C	1980 T	1980 C
Net Sales Income	107.9	160.3	95.5	213.9	195.0	376.3	205.3	312.3
Cost of Sales	115.2	71.9	72.1	92.2	92.1	105.5[a]	106.5[b]	115.4
Gross Cash Inflow	(7.3)	88.4	23.4	121.7	102.9	270.8	91.8	196.9
Interest Expense	3.3	39.2	7.7	40.2	7.6	40.7	7.4	31.2
Deductions[c]	(22.7)[d]	59.5	6.9	31.0	6.2	34.4	6.4	32.6
Worker Profit-Sharing	(0.2)[d]	—	0.3	0.7	7.3	10.0	7.6	5.6
Other Expenses (Income)	(12.6)	(10.3)	(5.5)	1.9	(2.7)	3.4	(4.3)	(8.2)
Pretax Profit (Loss)	24.9	(10.3)	14.0	47.9	84.5	182.3	81.7	135.7
Income Tax	10.6		2.1	25.9	55.3	78.2	60.5	59.5
After-Tax Profit (Loss)	14.3	(10.3)	11.9	22.0	29.2	104.1	21.2	76.2
Distribution of Profit:								
Owners	14.3	(10.0)	11.9	18.0	27.3	93.0	19.3	66.1
Billiton N.V.	—	(0.3)	—	4.0	—	6.0	—	6.4
Workers' shares	—	—	—	—	1.9	5.1	1.9	3.7
Cash Dividends Paid:								
To owners	—	—	—	—	—	—	—	42.4
To Billiton N.V.	—	—	—	—	—	—	—	27.4[e]
Effective Income Tax Rate[f]	42.6	—	15.0	54.1	65.4	42.9	74.0	43.8
Copper Produced[g]	97.8	162.4	107.0	176.0	107.6	183.5	108.5	150.8

SOURCE: Southern Peru Copper Corporation's annual report for 1980.
[a] Includes $9.4 million in refining charges. [b] Includes $12.1 million in refining charges.
[c] Depreciation, depletion, amortization. [d] Adjustments from previous years.
[e] Fulfills contractual obligation to Billiton N.V. and permits resumption of dividend payments to owners.
[f] Percent. [g] Thousands of metric tons fine content.

million investment in enlarging Toquepala and Cuajone—which it will proceed with even if the internal rate of return is somewhat less than "adequate."
It has already sunk some tens of millions into a molybdenum separation plant
for Cuajone.

CONCLUSIONS

The Peruvian government was not able to achieve every one of its policy
objectives in the development of Cuajone. It was, however, able to secure
all of its key *political* objectives. It entered into a well-written basic agreement
that could not be construed as *entreguista* except by the most rabid nationalists
opposed to foreign resource investment in any form. It furthered its bonanza
development strategy by extracting a greater share of the economic pie than
any local regime had ever before managed. It eliminated some of the enclave
features of the project. It got itself a long-wanted copper refinery and compelled Southern's patronage. It protected its sales monopoly and enhanced its
international reputation. And, by removing Quellaveco from Southern's grasp
without jeopardizing Cuajone, it created the conditions whereby it can probably gain a direct participation in the company's future operations without
spending a cent.

Asarco/Southern, on their side, were able to secure their key *economic*
objective: an opportunity to expand their world market share, and local government ratification (backed by suitable international "insurance" to make
sure that it sticks) of their right to go on operating in Peru—a right that has
become crucial to the company's status in the world copper oligopoly. There
was no inherent incompatibility between the two sets of objectives in the view
of the parties who held them. Hence, corporate behavior in the Cuajone
episode was as the doctrine of domicile predicts; our proposition regarding
the "good corporate citizenship" of local subsidiaries of transnational resource corporations, stated in the introduction to Part II, is confirmed. Furthermore: although the Peruvian state has become a far more potent bargaining
adversary than it used to be, company officials remain committed to the
country and have emerged from the affair with the perception that the political
risks are manageable.

This mutually satisfactory outcome was not produced by any altruistic
dedication to Peru's welfare on the company's part. It resulted because the
state could call upon local technical expertise to reinforce its bargaining
position, and because, as Stepan argues, the very presence of transnational
investment gave it an interest in doing so.[47] DGM staff members were concerned to advance Peruvian national interests and always knew what they
wanted to accomplish, for they had written or recommended most of the
military regime's mining policy. Due to their origins in and ongoing con-

[47] Stepan (1978:235-36).

nections with the private sector, they were able to confront Asarco/Southern head-to-head on economic grounds. They prevailed for the reason that they understood the company's global interests almost as well as their own. The converse was not true, however. That is, if government negotiators could pursue political-ideological objectives by operating wholly within the economic plane, company representatives could not do the opposite; they were incompetent to pass judgment on the host state's political-ideological claims and did not try to. In this sense the company's economic power was offset to a degree by the state's greater flexibility of maneuver.

Equally important to the outcome was the state's wise use of its coercive powers. In spite of the authoritarian character of the regime, these were always exercised with appropriate regard for the formalities of due process. Legislation and official decrees designed to influence the bargaining environment were invariably structured to accord with the constitution and were never applied ex post facto. These careful procedures made it less likely that the company could have found sympathy for anti-Peruvian confrontational tactics within U.S. government circles. Even had it wanted to get around the "Calvo clause" in the basic agreement, nothing that the Peruvian government had done would have been deemed to be in violation of accepted principles of international law.

Finally, the Cuajone story rebuts dependencista claims that international finance and transnational capital work hand-in-glove to enforce host-state compliance with their need for an open international economic order. The financiers allowed and, up to a point, encouraged a monopolistic state sales agency to intrude into the project. They did not interfere with host-state use of political pressure with respect to the refinery issue. They did not support Asarco/Southern's effort to keep the state away from the "excess production" for a full fifteen years. They went so far as to acquiesce in the state's decision to protect its sovereign prerogatives by vetoing World Bank equity participation. One can only assume that they acted in this way because their concerns, as good capitalists, lay with the profitability and security of their loans—best assured by seeking good relations with Peru—and not with preserving the structure and legitimating ideology of a world capitalist system for which they bore no responsibility. When the Marxian analysis of national capitalism is broadened to encompass the international system, this fundamental difference must be kept in mind: At the national level, the state is there to oversee capitalism's system-maintenance and legitimation requirements, but no comparable organism exists in the international sphere.

CHAPTER SIX

The Decline and Fall of
Cerro de Pasco

THE experience of Southern Peru Copper shows that it was possible in certain circumstances for a transnational mining company to work out a mutually acceptable *modus vivendi* with Peru's "revolutionary" military regime. However, the Southern experience was not universally replicated. At the same time that it and the government were feeling their way toward an accommodation, Cerro was finding it much harder to do likewise. In the end, all chance for accommodation disappeared, and the foreign company with the longest record of continuous operation in the country was expropriated. We now know that the Peruvian military establishment was not doctrinally committed to a policy of nationalization in natural resources but was prepared to accord a central role in bonanza development to foreign mining investment, existing as well as new, provided that foreign-owned corporations operated so as to serve national objectives. If we look at foreign mining investment in general (i.e., including that in the mediana minería, where, as will be seen in the next chapter, several transnational oligopolists have local subsidiaries), we must conclude that in terms of relations with the state, Cerro—not Southern—represents the exceptional case. In this chapter I will explain what made it exceptional. I will also compare the two cases in order to gain a deeper understanding of the doctrine of domicile and of foreign-capital/host-state relations under conditions of bonanza development.

It will be found that Cerro management was not wholly averse to the nationalization of its Peruvian assets, if it could be made to take place in a way that would be to the corporation's advantage. What were its interests? Did Cerro anticipate that it would be allowed to exercise exclusive or preferential marketing rights on behalf of a nationalized entity? Or did it feel that nationalization with appropriate compensation would relieve it of unprofitable assets and present it with the wherewithal to invest in more remunerative activities? One author has made just this argument. She posits that Cerro's nationalization represented a restructuring of capital to the advantage of the transnationals and the disadvantage of the Peruvian state. The latter took on the responsibility for continuing to service metropolitan markets from obsolescent facilities whose low capital intensity and large, unruly work forces limited their surplus-generating capabilities; whereas the former were left free to concentrate on the sort of capital-intensive mining operations that spell success and preeminence in the world nonferrous metals oligopoly.[1] If she is right, the nationalization, far from being a triumph for the state, merely deepened Peru's dependency. I propose to elucidate this issue by examining the company's strategies and tactics, the nature of the act of expropriation, and the progress of Centromin in the years since it took control of the Cerro installations.

I begin by discussing the character of Cerro's management, which is of greater relevance here than was so in the instance of Asarco/Southern. I then take up, first, Cerro's situation in Peru at the advent of the military regime; and next, the sequence of events that led up to this conjuncture and that influenced management's perceptions of the options available to it. With this background in place, I turn to the actual process of the company's decline and fall; and to a determination, based on what has occurred since, of whether Peru benefited from it or suffered an extension of dependency. Finally I consider the meaning of these events in light of Sklar's doctrine-of-domicile idea and draw out an explanation for the differences between Southern's relations with the "revolutionary" state and Cerro's.

THE CHARACTER OF CERRO MANAGEMENT[2]

In the preceding chapter, Asarco and Southern Peru Copper were spoken of, for the most part, as institutions. This is, in fact, the only way to comprehend them and their actions. It is not that individuals do not matter: the personality of Frank Archibald, Southern's chief executive, has certainly impressed itself on the company and, most assuredly, on the Cuajone negotiations that we have just finished reviewing. Like the majority of large corporations, however, Asarco/Southern are bureaucratic structures of authority. The impact of a particular person at the top is limited and softened, as it is in any bureaucracy, by these structures' fixed long-term interests, their established planning modalities, their standard operating procedures, and so forth.

Cerro was a different animal. For many years a tightly held private syndicate, its shares were never widely distributed.[3] It was a far smaller and less far-flung operation than is Asarco: prior to its belated diversification it functioned in Peru alone, excepting solely its headquarters and sales offices in

---

[1] Dore (1977).

[2] For much of the material in this section I am indebted to Alberto Benavides, with whom I had many discussions in 1977-78 and in 1981; and to Robert Koenig, interviewed on September 3, 1981.

[3] In 1955 Cerro had fewer than 6,000 shareholders, an unusually small number for a major public corporation. The number rose as the company issued new shares of capital stock and offered them in exchange for the shares of firms taken over in its later acquisition drive. Even so, there were under 11,500 shareholders in 1959 and slightly less than 20,000 in 1966. (Data are taken from annual reports of the Cerro Corporation for the years in question.) I will compare the diffusion of Cerro share ownership with that of some other corporations at the end of this chapter.

New York. Cerro's Peruvian mines were not only much more central to its overall profit picture than was Southern to Asarco's; they were also wholly owned, as Southern is not. In consequence of these two factors, authority in Cerro over Peruvian mining was never delegated to officials on the scene. All planning decisions, as well as many operating decisions—those entailing capital expenditures greater than $5,000, and also those involving hiring at salary levels greater than $10,000—were the province of New York head-quarters;[4] and within the headquarters staff, decision-making power was concentrated in the office of the chief executive. Cerro could thus become—and did—an extension of the personality of whoever occupied this office, his power further augmented by control of the largest block of capital shares. From 1950 to 1970 the individual in question was Robert Koenig; from 1970-71 to 1973, C. Gordon Murphy. The company's history over these years and its ultimate expropriation are closely bound up with the actions of those two men.

Koenig, trained in mining engineering and geology, was a member of the Cerro staff in Peru during the 1920s. He rapidly acquired a working knowledge of Spanish and a solid grasp of Peruvian politics and elite culture. It was not long before he counted a number of prominent oligarchs among his personal friends; the oligarchy accorded him an honor rarely visited upon foreigners—membership in the prestigious Club Nacional. The geologist in Koenig took a keen interest in the still largely unexplored central sierra, and he satisfied his curiosity by prospecting in his spare time. But curiosity led him afoul of higher-ups in the company, and he was dismissed in 1927 on the ground that he had violated his employment contract by engaging in a private mining endeavor.[5] He returned to the United States to enter the coal-mining business, where he pioneered in the application of geological science (in place of the "seat-of-the-pants" methods then in common use) to mine planning and output maximization. In this way he raised his company to third-place ranking among U.S. coal producers. Koenig had not, however, forgotten Cerro or Peru. He sold his interest in the coal firm at a handsome profit and invested the proceeds in Cerro shares, becoming the largest shareholder. On the strength of this ownership stake and of his intimate knowledge of the Peruvian situation, he returned to Cerro as its president.

Given the nature of his interests and experience, Koenig expected to, and did, take a direct hand in the firm's Peruvian operations. As a result, the centralization in New York of control over Peruvian affairs increased during his tenure. Until the early sixties he took personal charge of governmental relations (we observed in Chapter 2 his role in the drafting of the 1950 Mining Code) and was a familiar figure around the presidential palace. Then, soon

[4] See Goodsell (1974:69). He notes, too, that all staff appointments down to the level of department chief had to be reviewed by New York headquarters.
[5] One of Koenig's most prized mementos from his Cerro days is the letter of dismissal, now framed; it declares that he is to be forever barred from reemployment with the firm.

after the 1963 election of President Belaunde, he started to turn some of these responsibilities over to locally based representatives, but they could take few initiatives without his express authorization. Government officials understood this. They continued to prefer treating with Koenig himself and attempted to do the same with his successor.

After twenty years at the helm, Koenig felt that it was an hour for him to relax a bit, to move up to the less demanding post of board chairman. It also seemed to him that Cerro had evolved to a point where it needed to be guided by someone more skilled than he in the integration and management of a highly diversified corporation. Since there was no one within the ranks who satisfactorily filled the bill, an outside search for a new chief executive was undertaken.

Murphy arrived at Cerro a product of this executive search; he and Koening had never previously met. He had built his reputation in the presidency of Litton Industries, a conglomerate corporation with important interests in defense production and electronics; Litton then had some export business but was not a transnational enterprise in the full meaning of the term. Thus, Murphy's background included expertise neither in Peru nor in mining. But on paper, at least, his qualifications as a conglomerate manager were excellent, and he was hired for that reason. The lacunae in his resumé did not seem a problem, for Koenig would still be there to plug the gaps.

The relationship between the two quickly became troubled, then acrimonious. Koenig claims to have been unimpressed with Murphy's methods and to have found him clumsy in his dealings with Peruvian authorities.[6] Murphy, meanwhile, shored up his position with other major shareholders. Just seven months after his appointment as chief executive, he and the board chairman had a final falling out. Having tried and failed to get Murphy removed, Koenig resigned from Cerro and sold his shares.[7] The outcome was that the company had to face its most difficult moment in Peru without anyone in top manage-

[6] He illustrated the point by relating the following: Believing it imperative that Cerro's chief executive have a working relationship with the president of Peru, he had successfully established one with President Velasco in spite of his distaste for the military regime and its reforms. Upon Murphy's accession he was concerned to see that such a relationship would continue; and he therefore set up a meeting between Murphy and Velasco—their only one, as it turned out—with himself as translator. At the meeting Murphy made several statements that Velasco was sure to adjudge undiplomatic, perhaps insulting. Koenig did not accurately translate them. Velasco, unfortunately, caught the gist of what Murphy was saying and detected (but with appreciation) Koenig's mistranslation. As the meeting was breaking up, Velasco took Koenig aside and, speaking to him as if he were still in absolute command at Cerro, told him never again to send Murphy (to whom he referred not by name but with a vulgarism) to Peru in a representative capacity.

[7] Koenig's side of the story is that he sought a vote from the board of directors for Murphy's ouster, thinking that he could get its approval by virtue of his position as the largest single shareholder. However, his shares did not constitute a majority. Murphy, he claims, made a secret deal to sponsor the second largest holder as a replacement board chairman in return for that individual's support in the controversy over the presidency. The two of them were then able to bring over to their side enough of the other directors to carry the day.

ment who was a true expert in the country's mines and politics. And it had to do so with an authority structure that had not been designed to compensate for lack of knowledge at the top by feeding up information and counsel from below.

GROWTH, CHANGE, AND PROBLEMS, 1950-1968

The October 1968 expropriation of the International Petroleum Company by the newly installed military regime left Cerro as the most visible example of direct foreign investment in Peru. Its work force, down slightly from the peak of a few years before, amounted to 16,634 workers and close to a thousand managers and other professionals. It controlled six metal mines and a coal mine in the central sierra departments of Pasco, Junín, Lima, and Huancavelica. The original copper smelter at La Oroya had grown into a formidable metallurgical complex which produced refined copper, lead, silver, and zinc along with smaller quantities of antimony, arsenic, bismuth, cadmium, gold, indium, selenium, tellurium, and tungsten. Sulfuric acid was manufactured there, too, as were copper tube, rod, and wire for domestic consumption. Cerro was a participant in two joint mining ventures with Peruvian capital and controlled eight industrial firms (Fig. 3) that together accounted for 10 percent of Peru's output of basic chemicals, 35 percent of her clay construction materials, 15 percent of her semifinished iron and steel products, 93 percent of her semifinished nonferrous metal products, and 10 percent of her light machinery.[8] The company had sold off certain of its extensive landholdings but still retained title to 250,000 hectares of good pasture land, on which grazed the Cerro sheep herd. Under Koenig's management, Cerro's sheep husbandry had returned to a modest profitability through scientific animal care and selective breeding; its haciendas became famous for their high-grade wool, and its animals won many prizes at international agricultural fairs.

Conglomerate growth had modified Cerro's position in the world nonferrous metals markets without fundamentally transforming it. The Mining Division (a profit center whose earnings included those from Cerro's share in Southern Peru Copper, from other joint ventures, and from Chilean mining in addition to those from the company's Peruvian business) still brought in half or more of the firm's consolidated profit. Vertical integration did not advance; the U.S. manufacturing subsidiaries purchased their raw materials from unaffiliated suppliers, while metals refined in Peru were mostly sold in Europe—to which, however, Cerro was but a minor supplier. Unhappily for a would-be growth conglomerate (whose success depends upon high earnings on invested capital to generate cash for future acquisitions), 80 percent of total

---

[8] See Ocampo Rodríguez (1972). According to the Cerro Corporation's annual report for 1965, the total amount invested in these ventures was just $3.1 million.

fixed assets—those in Peru—contributed only 38.2 percent to consolidated sales and 29.6 percent to consolidated profits.[9]

But these signs of weakness cannot be permitted to obscure the fact that in the late sixties Cerro affected, directly or indirectly, more Peruvian lives than any other private enterprise in the country—doubtless many more than IPC, which had caused such a political furor. At the level of the economy, it accounted for 18.1 percent of annual copper production, 55.9 percent of lead, 46.7 percent of silver, and 23.3 percent of zinc.[10] It retained its local monopoly over metal refining. The refineries, though aging, were very advanced technologically; from the complex polymetal ores of the region they extracted not only the main constituents but also the long list of industrial metals given above, and they did so with exceptional purity.[11] Gross sales typically amounted to around a third of the gross value of production of the nation's minería. Income tax payments were exceeded only by Southern's and, in some years, by IPC's. Local wage and salary payments in 1960-1968 totaled $129.6 million; when taxes and local purchases (including ores and concentrates bought from the mediana minería) are added thereto, it appears that 70 to 75 cents of each sales dollar remained in Peru.[12]

At the level of social structure, Cerro's hacienda operations and its work force recruitment (examined in Chapter 10) were among the earliest penetrations of capitalist relations of production (even, on occasion, of modern market relations) into the central sierra. These penetrations had wrought enormous socioeconomic changes throughout a geographical zone stretching across the Andean cordillera to the *ceja de selva*. Commerce in agricultural and manufactured goods had expanded; wealth distributions and class structures had undergone irreversible alteration. While the pace of change had since slackened, the effects remained fresh: most of those who had benefited or suffered because of them were still alive to tell the tale and pass the memory on to their descendants. The beneficiaries, however, were not always members of the same societal group; rather, their identity varied as the company grew, introduced new processes and technologies, or otherwise altered the character of its operations.[13] Its actions, then, were motivated by its profit calculus as interpreted by management, not by a desire to build up a consistent set of alliances with other propertied groups based in the zone—except, as will be

[9] Cerro Corporation's annual report for 1968.

[10] My computation from data presented in Tables 6.1 and A.3.

[11] It was Koenig's boast that the zinc produced by "his" refinery had a purity of "five nines" (99.999 percent)—which, he claimed, was a world record for commercial-scale production.

[12] My estimate is based on data derived from DeWind (1977), Hamilton (1967), Ocampo Rodríguez (1972), Rodríguez Hoyle (1972), and Cerro's consolidated declarations for 1967-1970. I assume that local purchases of noncapital equipment and goods during 1960-1968 were the same in each year as in 1967-68: $32.7 million. I further assume that the 1968-1970 annual average of ore purchases from the mediana minería bore the same dollar relationship to total sales—22.8 cents per dollar of sales income—throughout 1960-1968.

[13] Mallon (1981).

seen, with the mediana minería. Cerro was more efficient in creating enemies than in making friends.

Cerro's Development in the Koenig Era

In the opinion of the many Peruvian mine owners and managers who know him, Koenig never lost his sincere desire to foster the country's economic development and retained his belief that the biggest private firm in the nation had a special obligation to do so. Two factors affected the orientation and limitations of the means adopted for expressing that will. The orienting factor was this: for Koenig, fundamental decisions as to where, when, and how economic development ought to be promoted lay fully in the province of private capital. His attitude rested, I am convinced, on ideological principle, but it was reinforced by his long experience with a succession of Peruvian regimes which forswore any firm guiding role for the state. The limiting factor was that Koenig, no altruist, was dedicated above all else to his primary responsibility, the future of the company. Therefore, what he would or would not do had to answer first and foremost to the question of Cerro's present health and eventual prospects.

He was ever prepared to invest in Peru relatively small amounts of capital in strategic projects designed to produce significant profitability returns at low cost. Thus, one of his earliest decisions was to go ahead with the introduction and gradual enlargement of a zinc refining capability so as to capture for the company refining profits reaped by others from Cerro's output of zinc concentrates. His planning, however, was conservative: refining capacity was added in three stages over a ten-year period from 1955 to 1965 and was never permitted to approach the firm's capacity for zinc concentrate production. In other words, Koenig made quite sure that his refinery would be able to operate at 100 percent throughput on the basis of his own mines' output, much of which would continue to be exported in unprocessed form; and that he would not have to rely on zinc purchases from the mediana minería, as he was having to do with copper. A later decision of the same kind was to construct the Cobriza mine in order to increase the firm's "in-house" production of copper ore. It was noted in Chapter 2 that this rich but difficult-to-work deposit was brought in with an extremely small investment of $20 million. Yet, Koenig had initially attempted to reduce the requisite capital outlay even more by incorporating Cobriza as a separate entity and selling shares in the venture to local investors; his plan failed because the latter preferred to put their cash into the mediana minería, where they enjoyed real managerial influence. Thanks to conservative planning aimed at exploitation of the richest ores as well as to high capital intensity,[14] the company recouped its investment in a mere three years.

But Koenig's supreme objective was to modernize Cerro, to make it over into an advanced corporation that could either survive and prosper in the

---

[14] Cobriza is the only highly mechanized underground mine in Peru.

presence of the industry's giants or, failing that, arrange a friendly merger on favorable terms with a bigger partner. And he did not feel that the investment required to accomplish this should be directed toward Peru. Firstly, Cerro had been seriously debilitated by the low metals prices of the Depression and war years. The 1950 revision of Peruvian taxation and a $50 million loan extended a few years afterward by the U.S. Export-Import Bank for the zinc refinery had helped to set it on its feet. They did not, however, fill Cerro's coffers with the sums needed to begin full-scale development of its five idle concessions. Furthermore, Cerro's defeat at Southern's hands over ownership of Cuajone, while it resulted in a useful dividend flow, had demonstrated how difficult it could be to proceed with major mine development while a more powerful competitor with better outside financing was doing the same in the same country. Secondly, modernization meant diversification in terms of both geography and lines of business. Cerro would have to fortify its position in the United States by entering into production there of fabricated nonferrous metal products as well as into unrelated areas should the opportunities arise. It would also have to protect itself against political disruption as it enlarged its mine output, and the best way to do that was to develop mining properties in other countries—preferably, ones with a better history of political stability than Peru's. To this end the firm became a minority joint venturer in a couple of Canadian mines and developed the Río Blanco mine in Chile.[15] Thirdly, were stress to be placed on modernizing the existing Peruvian mines, there would have to be major work force reductions. That would give rise to conflicts with the mine unions and might be rejected by the government.

The inescapable conclusion was that *profits earned in Peru would have to be used to finance development elsewhere*. Koenig was experienced enough to know that this would cause his company to lose the sympathy of the Peruvian government. He therefore faced the task of defusing that powder keg, of protecting his flanks by shoring up local alliances, and, if it could be simultaneously managed, of avoiding "cognitive dissonance" between the investment strategy and his values regarding Cerro's place in Peruvian development. To carry out the task he undertook the following:

1. Promotion of mediana minería development under local auspices. Cerro offered generous loans, sometimes secured by equity interests, to founders of medium mining firms.[16] More than that, it offered free technical assistance to Peruvian mine managers. It tried, in so far as it could without jeopardizing

---

[15] Chile was an attractive site for copper mine investment at this time. It had a long record of relatively high political stability and had recently promulgated its Nuevo Trato legislation, which, like the Peruvian Mining Code of 1950, reformed the system of taxation and introduced various incentives for foreign investment (Ely 1961; Moran 1974:89-98; Novoa Monreal 1972:19-22).

[16] There were five such cases, although in one of them the project was never launched. In two of the remaining four, Cerro initiated the projects and then sold out to local investors. In a third, the case of Buenaventura (to be discussed in Chapter 7), it took a minority equity share. In the fourth, Raura, it retained majority ownership but left management in Peruvian hands.

its own profits, to extend liberal terms for ore purchases from the mediana minería. It sold hard-to-get or used equipment and spare parts from its stocks to the smaller firms on request, charging a minimal markup or none at all. In this way, it was hoped, Peruvian medium-mining entrepreneurs would feel a debt of gratitude to Cerro and would, when necessary, use their considerable political influence on its behalf.

2. Promotion of manufacturing industries linked to mining. Cerro took the lead in setting up eight manufacturing enterprises and furnished their technological expertise. Oligarchic capital and local management were brought in at an early stage and were given effective control.[17] The aim was to forge alliances with the dominant element of Peruvian society and to further the politically popular goal of industrialization, all while avoiding heavy financial commitments.

3. "Peruvianization" of staff and local management. In 1944 there were exactly two local citizens in staff positions with managerial responsibilities and very few in lower-level administrative posts. Between 1951 and 1960 the number of Peruvian foremen, administrators, and middle managers increased by over 130 percent; it rose another 65 percent in 1960-1968, reaching 3,048 in that last year. Upper management ranks were said to be 27 percent Peruvian in 1968 and 80 percent in 1971.[18] Twelve annual postgraduate scholarships were established for staff members, who could use them for advanced study anywhere in the world.[19] "Peruvianization" stood to save the company money in the long run, since training costs would be outweighed by the reduction of "hardship" salaries, living allowances, and bonuses customarily paid to expatriates. But it also represented a significant contribution to the development of local "human capital"—Koenig ranks it as one of his three great contributions—as well as a potential alliance with those middle-class elements which were starting to form the "new bourgeoisie."

"Peruvianization" reached its fullest flowering in the appointment of Peruvians to Cerro's local board of directors—which additionally functioned to involve politically well-connected locals in the running of the firm's affairs. The first such appointee (in 1956) was Augusto Wiese. Not only was his Banco Wiese the only private financial institution that loaned to the mediana

---

[17] CIDECSA, a wire and cable manufacturer shown in Fig. 3 as 100 percent Cerro-owned, was set up with the idea that it would also be an independent entity under Peruvian management and with Peruvian capital participation. As had happened with Cobriza, however, local investors were by the sixties no longer interested in going into partnership with Cerro.

[18] The first figure is given by Goodsell (1974:67); the second was estimated for me by Alberto Benavides.

[19] These scholarships were far more generous than is customary: they provided a stipend sufficient to allow the scholar's spouse and children to accompany him abroad and to maintain their previous standard of living. Koenig adds that the company sometimes went to great lengths to further the professional careers of its Peruvian staff members even when their advancement took them out of Cerro. In one instance, that of a senior Peruvian geologist who was offered a position on the Harvard faculty, the individual was given a consultantship and other financial aid to compensate him for the lower professorial salary.

minería for new mine development; what is more, he was a good friend of President Manuel Prado (1939-1945, 1956-1962) and of Prado's influential treasury minister, Pedro Beltrán Espantoso.[20] Three more prominent Peruvians were added to the board in 1960.

Wiese resigned in 1963, to be replaced the following year by Alberto Benavides de la Quintana. Benavides, whom we shall meet again in the next chapter, began his career as a geologist on the Cerro staff—he was one of those two Peruvian staff members of 1944—and later left to become the president and a part-owner of what has since become the largest local mining company (Cerro financed him and took a minority interest in his firm). He was known as a thoroughly modern businessman, was sympathetic toward the reform objectives of the recently elected President Belaunde, was widely thought to be the president's personal friend, and was related by marriage to the APRA leader, Víctor Raúl Haya de la Torre.[21] Besides, he was a close friend of Koenig's. On the strength of these credentials he was appointed to the chairmanship of the local board, the first (and only) Peruvian so honored. Although the position had no real authority in view of Cerro's centralized management structure, Benavides had some influence through his friendship with the chief executive. He seemed the ideal local spokesperson at a time when winds of political change were starting to blow.

Nevertheless, the Cerro strategy contained several flaws and contradictions, some of which later came back to haunt the firm. Let us examine the most important of them.

First, Cerro had accumulated a heavy "social debt" (Benavides's phrase) owed to the popular sectors—a debt compounded out of contempt toward the Peruvian worker and peasant shown too freely by an earlier generation of gringo foremen; out of hacienda ownership and enclosure practices, which stripped peasants of their traditional usufruct rights; out of past wage exploitation, coercive labor controls, and intolerance toward labor unions; out of overcrowded, unhealthful mining camps; and out of having made no provision until quite late for workers' salary advancement and promotion. Benavides, who has always understood the political and social aspects of development, continually pressed Koenig to liquidate the "social debt"; the measures he proposed were disposing of the haciendas and upgrading the camps. However, Koenig, who regarded the "social debt" as a historical

[20] The Beltráns owned one *latifundio* and were partners in a second; Pedro was a prominent member of the National Agrarian Society, a center of oligarchic power. Pedro Beltrán was also the owner of Lima's second largest newspaper, *La Prensa*; though it had a reputation for rather greater objectivity in news coverage than did its equally conservative competitor, *El Comercio*, it was a strident editorial advocate of laissez faire, of liberal treatment for all forms of foreign investment, and of the other interests of the *fuerzas vivas*. Beltrán was sent into exile by the military regime and currently lives in San Francisco. His brother, Felipe, is a prominent industrialist who holds shares in, *inter alia*, two important medium-mining firms. See Malpica (1976:91).

[21] The APRA was at this time the stronger member of the majority coalition in the congress. What is more, most observers were predicting that Haya would win the presidential election scheduled for 1969.

inevitability, resisted: partly because he viewed development in narrowly economic terms, partly because investment in the camps would bring no returns in higher profits, and partly because he feared that new owners of the Cerro lands would revive the smoke damage suits that had led the company to acquire them in the first place.[22]

(It can be plausibly argued that Koenig's lack of concern with the "social debt" issue had grave political consequences for Peru. His determined four-year battle against Belaunde's modest agrarian reform program[23] undermined the president's credibility as a reformer, stiffened the anti-reform attitude of the landed oligarchs, and helped convince both the military and the public at large that reformist goals were inconsistent with legalism and political moderation.)

Second, Koening did not realize that, no matter how worthy his objectives and how successful his actions in fostering industrial development, Peruvian nationalists and developmentalists would resent these activities. They implied that control over the development process was being exercised by foreigners. They seemed to be taking place *in lieu of* more intensive mining and refinery development, an area where Cerro could and should be a leader. Inasmuch as they were undertaken by what was already the country's largest enterprise, they raised the specter (as newer transnational entrants to the manufacturing sector did not) of a monopolistic foreign octopus spreading its tentacles into every vital sector of the national economy.

Third, in spite of the fact that he by now considered himself *medio peruano*, Koenig had little conception of Peru's national interest defined in political rather than economic terms. For instance, he never understood the Peruvian desire for a larger local refining capacity, which struck him as unwarranted on economic grounds.[24] Far worse, however, was his incomprehension of the century-old regional rivalry that had divided Peru and Chile. The less radical among Peruvian nationalists were not as antagonistic as they might have been toward Cerro's use of locally earned profits to expand in the United States; but no nationalist could countenance the diversion of those profits to a Chilean mining venture—particularly inasmuch as the company held so many idle yet rich concessions in Peru, and as the investment in Río Blanco ($154 million)

---

[22] The acquisition of the haciendas was discussed in Chapter 2. Renewal of the lawsuits could well have caused Cerro to pay out large sums in damage claims and/or fulfill, at considerable expense, pollution-control requirements imposed by the courts or the government.

[23] Belaunde's agrarian reform administration proposed in 1964 the nationalization of just one 40,000-acre parcel of Cerro land, for which the company would be fully compensated. Cerro fought the proposed nationalization in the courts and, thanks to Belaunde's concern for due process, was able to delay the measure until March 1968. The court battle had the effect of holding up the rest of the agrarian reform; not only did it cause a loss of prestige for Belaunde and Acción Popular, but it also caused Cerro to be popularly perceived as the oligarchy's advance guard in the anti-reform struggle.

[24] Mario Samamé Boggio, a technocrat, medium-mine manager, author (see Samamé Boggio 1974, 1979), and current president of INGEMMET, reported conversations with Koenig to this effect when I interviewed him on August 20, 1981.

was nearly eight times what had been spent on Cobriza. Ominous for Cerro was that the military, focused as they are on the Chilean threat, were well aware of the Río Blanco investment: it came up regularly in CAEM courses as a stellar example of the way in which certain foreign interests callously disregarded Peruvian security requisites.[25]

Fourth, Koenig did not fully recognize at that time—though he ruefully admitted it later on—that the "Peruvianization" of Cerro's staff and management, necessary and desirable as it was for its own sake, was making foreign control ever more dispensable to host-country interests in the company. Indeed, Peruvian managers and staff members were beginning to express unhappiness over the concentration of planning and control functions in New York headquarters (to which none of their number had ever been promoted); many of them started to view their inability to get on-the-job training in these areas as a classic instance of "blocked ascent." It was suggested in Chapter 4 that a transnational mining firm can protect its indispensability by promising the host country major inputs of new capital. But that is just what Cerro's growth and diversification strategy ruled out.

Fifth, the strategy was predicated on the assumption that, with minimal new investment, Cerro could at least hold the line in Peru. That is, it could keep metals production constant, or even increase it somewhat, and could also preserve its profit margin by realizing various small economies—essential if the funds needed to back the strategy were to continue to flow in. Table 6.1 gives the evolution of Cerro's 1950-1968 production of refined metals. Levels of output were successfully kept up or increased, thanks to Cobriza, the steady expansion of the zinc refinery, and process improvements which raised the yield of the silver and industrial metal "byproducts." However, these advances had to be bought at a cost over 1960-1968 of $130 million in reinvested profits,[26] which cut into the resources available for financing acquisitions in other countries. In Table 6.2 we see what happened to profits. These rose in absolute terms, particularly after 1960. Yet, most of the rise was due to favorable international prices (as is apparent upon comparing sales revenues with production figures), a situation that could reverse itself at any moment for reasons entirely out of the company's control. More importantly, profits declined as a percentage of sales; the economies attainable within Cerro's self-imposed expenditure limits were clearly not enough to offset

[25] Koenig admitted to me in our conversation that his failure to take account of the rivalry between the two countries was his greatest error as Cerro's chief executive. He notes that Anaconda erred similarly by not developing its Cerro Verde copper deposit in spite of the fact that it had been thoroughly explored and was known to be an economically feasible endeavor. He feels that the Anaconda refusal to invest was interpreted by the generals as a deference to Chilean preferences, and that its refusal was a major factor behind the decision to expropriate all idle concessions.

[26] My calculation from data in Hamilton (1967) and in the Cerro Corporation's annual reports for 1958 and 1968.

TABLE 6.1 Cerro's Production of Refined Metals in Peru, 1950-1968
(*Metric tons fine content*)

Year	Copper	Lead	Silver	Zinc	Minor Metals[a]
1950-54[b]	22,814	48,229	242	6,449	410
1955-59[b]	26,120	62,321	269	22,640	527
1960-64[b]	35,020	77,719	531	43,122	934
1965	40,994	86,807	605	62,932	1,143
1966	36,841	88,762	561	63,450	1,233
1967	35,613	81,818	567	63,352	1,180
1968	38,500	86,421	528	68,032	1,283

SOURCE: Compiled by the author from data presented by Samamé (1974:1:547-60).
[a] Combined totals: antimony, bismuth, cadmium, indium, and selenium.
[b] Data for these years are annual averages.

TABLE 6.2 Financial Performance of Cerro's Peruvian Mining and Refining Operations, 1950-1968 (*Millions of dollars except as noted*)

Years	Total Sales	Average Annual Sales	Total Profits	Average Annual Profits	Profits on Sales[a]
1950-54	233.1	46.6	30.52	6.1	13.1
1955-59	299.2	59.8	21.52	4.3	7.2
1960-64	391.8	78.4	27.44	5.5	7.0
1965-68	541.8	135.4	31.85	8.0	5.9

SOURCE: Compiled by the author from data presented in Hamilton (1967).
[a] Percent.

increasing costs—especially (and crucially, given the firm's relatively low capital intensity) labor costs.[27]

As the new military government prepared to embark upon its program of sweeping reform, it was already evident to Cerro officials that their strategy had failed.[28] There seemed to be but three alternatives open to them. One would have been to reverse course and concentrate on development in Peru, pouring in the large amount of capital needed to convert to fully mechanized operations and thus lowering production costs per unit of output. This was

[27] I compute, from data presented by Ocampo Rodríguez (1972), that the net cash flow to Cerro from Peruvian mining and refining operations in 1960-1968 was $94.9 million; I include depletion, depreciation, amortization, set-asides for other corporate reserves, and after-tax profit. This is less than 62 percent of the cost of the company's Río Blanco mine in Chile.

[28] One indication of their failure was that successive efforts to merge with Studebaker-Worthington, Bethlehem Steel, and Standard Oil of Indiana had all come to naught.

never seriously considered, however. A second was to dispose of the Peruvian assets by selling them to the state, the most likely buyer. Provided that a good price could be obtained, the revenue from the sale could be plowed back into new mining projects—quite possibly in Peru, based on one or more of the idle concessions—which would be planned from the start to be capital-intensive and efficient. This was the alternative preferred by Koenig. Then there was the third possibility: to proceed on the hope of a negotiated sale but in the interim to economize by eliminating all local reinvestment of profits and cutting routine upkeep and maintenance expenses to the bone. In this way the flow of repatriated profits could be maximized in the short run, albeit at the risk that the deteriorating facilities would command a lesser price if the sale were delayed. It could be argued on the basis of other nationalizations, though, that the eventual price would be determined politically in any event.

The third option was not likely to appeal to a manager with a personal belief in the company's historic mission in Peru, such as Koenig had. But it could well appeal to Murphy, and it did.

From Negotiation to Expropriation

The arrival of the "revolution" had immediate consequences for Cerro, all of them negative. The whole system of alliances with the oligarchy, as well as the links that had been cultivated between the local directorate and the presidential palace, disappeared like a puff of smoke; only the alliance with the "new bourgeoisie" remained, and its value was untested and uncertain in the changed environment. Nor did the ruling generals allow themselves to be drawn into a comparable web of alliances: even seemingly innocuous gestures toward them by the company were repulsed as potentially compromising.[29] The military's reformist drive turned the Cerro "social debt" into a further handicap. Koenig was sufficiently wise this time around to let pass without objection the uncompensated 1969 expropriation of all of the haciendas; for the measure was unstoppable, the direct financial loss to the company small, and the prospect of the long-feared renewal of pollution damage suits negligible.[30] But it so happened that the haciendas were not the primary liability in the "social debt." Far more important was the legacy of maltreatment of workers, which (1) encouraged labor to seek and, with support from a sympathetic state and public, win large wage increases (thereby making it impossible to hold the line on production costs); and (2) estranged the Social Christian mining minister. Fernández Maldonado's nationalism set him more firmly against Cerro after the approval of the Cuajone basic agreement with

[29] For instance, Fernández Maldonado refused a Cerro offer to send him at company expense on a "get-acquainted" tour of the Peruvian minería soon after he assumed the mining portfolio.

[30] Because the reformed haciendas were to become government-sponsored collective farms; it could be assumed that a government interested in industrial development, as this one was, would not support a lawsuit to advance agricultural interests at the expense of industrial ones.

Southern. He did not want to compromise his reputation as a progressive by seeming to favor *two* foreign mining enterprises at the same time.

However, the core of Cerro's dilemma was that the regime's bonanza development plans put a premium on a mining firm's willingness to invest new capital. Cerro, moreover, was the most exposed target of demands for expanded investment, since it controlled more idle concessions than any other company. From its perspective the world had suddenly been turned upside down. Its strengths—carefully cultivated political alliances—were reduced to worthlessness; its signal weakness—capital investment—stood elevated to primacy.

Koenig's Effort at Negotiating an Arrangement

Koenig, as we saw, was ready to sell off the older, less efficient assets but did not wish to abandon Peru altogether. Beyond that, he felt that a plan to develop one or more of the idle concessions, in addition to enabling the company to be restructured on the basis of the higher capital intensity of open-pit mining, would constitute valuable bargaining leverage in negotiations with state authorities over a selling price.[31] As Cerro's financial resources were insufficient for self-financing such a project (even if it were to sell all of its existing Peruvian mining assets and receive their full $112 million book value), and as loans from the U.S. Export-Import Bank had been shut off after the uncompensated IPC expropriation,[32] the necessary financing would have to be found in Europe and would probably entail the establishment of a joint venture. Conversations were entered into with some of the major European metals firms, among which the Swedish Gränges, the French Péchiney, the British Charter Consolidated, and the South African Anglo-American Group expressed interest.

Before these discussions could proceed very far, the government promulgated the law requiring the immediate filing of development and financing plans for all idle concessions on pain of *caducidad* (D.L.17792; see p. 106). Cerro's negotiating leverage had now evaporated, and it instead confronted the prospect of having to complete an agreement with the Europeans solely to protect its existing interest in its concession holdings. Acting under the rigid time constraint imposed by D.L.17792, the company hurriedly threw together a plan for a consortium of itself and the four named European firms with Gränges the technological leader and project manager.[33] There was not enough time to secure financial commitments nor even to concretize ownership distributions and management details; these were left in abeyance until later. The one firm decision was that the consortium would undertake the devel-

[31] Cf. Kennecott's strategy as it confronted Chilean desires for national control (Moran 1974:129-36).

[32] In Chapter 5 it was seen that this was also a problem for Asarco when it sought to obtain financing for Cuajone.

[33] Interview with C. G. Burenius, the Swedish consul general in Peru, October 12, 1977. See also González Vigil and Parodi Zevallos (1975).

opment of four Cerro concessions: Antamina, Chalcobamba-Ferrobamba, Tintaya, and Toromocho. A sequential development scheme was proposed, just as Southern had planned for Toquepala-Cuajone-Quellaveco and for the same reason—minimizing the new capital outlay needed to get the program under way. Work would start with Tintaya. The cost of the first phase was tentatively estimated at $350 million. Despite the lack of detail and hard analysis, a letter of intent embodying the proposal was rapidly drafted and forwarded to the DGM, which received it in April 1970. It requested a temporary option on the properties to allow time for completion of the consortium arrangements.

Southern, when it began negotiating with the military regime over the Cuajone question, had the advantages of a detailed plan and a stable set of corporate interests; it was thus able to stay abreast of new legislative initiatives that affected it and was only bested after a series of arduous struggles. Cerro had neither. In consequence, each new law caught it not only unawares but also unequipped to respond properly. In the same month that the letter of intent was submitted, the regime promulgated decree-law D.L.18225, the so-called "normative law for the mining sector." It established the state metal sales monopoly, founded MineroPeru, reduced the incentives available to foreign investors, and declared that the state must receive a minimum 25 percent ownership share in any new gran minería venture. This legislation was rushed to enactment (a new comprehensive mining code would not be ready for another year) ahead of, and because of, the Cerro consortium plan; it ensured that after Cuajone, no more large mining projects could legally proceed under the pre-1968 legislation which the generals had repeatedly attacked as *entreguista*. If Cerro had expected to retain the right to market the output of its refineries and older mines subsequent to their sale, the establishment of the state monopoly disabused it of that notion. The issue became instead one of corporate survival. So, the company had to go on pressing the consortium idea in spite of lesser investment incentives and other adverse provisions of the statute. Its letter of intent was withdrawn, amended to include a state participation of 25 percent, and resubmitted.[34] Shortly thereafter Sumitomo Mining agreed to join the consortium.

It soon became apparent that Cerro's haste left ample room for misunderstandings to arise out of the obscurities in its proposal. Consortium members thought that the state was to secure its partnership by supplying a proportionate share of the financing; but state officials intended no such contribution, as D.L.18225 had specified that Peru was entitled to its share in return for making available a part of the national patrimony—the deposits—for exploitation. Besides, the DGM was displeased at the sequential development plan (recall that it had also disliked Southern's) and was worried by the vagueness of the financial arrangements. Since Southern had just signed the Cuajone agreement and Marcona had pledged itself to a $25 million investment, there was every

[34] *Wall Street Journal*, 6 May 1970, p. 40.

reason to believe that foreign investors in general had not lost interest in Peruvian mining. Were the Cerro consortium to be granted its option, other offers to develop any of the four properties would have to be refused while it went about organizing itself and acquiring its financing. And should it stumble in either effort and be compelled to drop the plan, who could be sure that the sponsors of the rejected alternate offers would assent to resurrect them?

The DGM staff recommended that the consortium's ability to proceed be tested by laying down still tighter regulations governing plans for idle concessions. Decree-law D.L.18368, promulgated in August 1970, obliged concessionaires to file more detailed development schedules and to show proof of financial backing by the end of the year. Faced with these requirements, the consortium collapsed. Cerro lamely attributed its breakup to "disagreement with Peruvian administrative practices" and to "delays experienced in negotiation with the Peruvian government, particularly having regard to recent decrees affecting . . . mining concessions which still require clarification. . . ." It said that it would continue "conversations" with the government on these points and that the consortium might be reassembled if there were indications of progress toward mutually satisfactory terms.[35]

None of this was believed in government circles. By its haste in placing its proposal on the table before it was really prepared to do so, Cerro had generated a chain of events which convinced the generals that it had been insincere from the outset—an inaccurate deduction, as it happens, but one that seemed fully justified from the information at the state's disposal. The whole episode looked to them like a maneuver designed to play for time, to delay the scheduled forfeiture of the company's concessions.[36]

It was at this critical juncture that Murphy replaced Koenig in the Cerro executive suite.

The Descent to Expropriation

Murphy wasted no time in putting into effect his plan for Cerro's Peruvian future. Capital expenditures fell from around $16 million in 1968 to $1.35 million in 1971.[37] While the installations were deteriorating from lack of investment in upkeep, the LME copper price (as luck would have it) began to fall. After-tax Peruvian profits slippped correspondingly, from $10.2 million in 1969 to $4.4 million in 1970 and to a net loss of $3.8 million in

[35] *Wall Street Journal*, 31 August 1970, p. 3.

[36] Unfavorable comparisons were drawn between Cerro's actions and Asarco's in regard to Michiquillay, an enormous copper reserve located in a remote area of Cajamarca department. Knowing that it had no hope of raising the $500 million or more needed to develop Michiquillay while simultaneously attempting to finance Cuajone, Asarco voluntarily surrendered the concession without waiting for the statutory deadline to arrive. By so doing it enabled the state to enter into immediate discussions with Japanese mining firms, who were then showing considerable interest in developing Michiquillay. Interview with Simon D. Strauss, Asarco executive vice-president, August 10, 1978.

[37] Cerro Corporation's annual reports for 1968 and 1971.

1971—the first since Depression days. Nonetheless, the company stepped up the flow of cash dividends remitted to New York. Whereas in 1967 and 1968 all after-tax profits had been locally retained for possible future reinvestment, $15.2 million was remitted in 1969, followed by another $4 million in 1970 and $1.8 million (from past retained earnings) in the loss year, 1971. The Peruvian retained profits reserve dropped from $20.2 million in 1969 to a scant $2.4 million in 1971. The company remitted in full the accelerated depreciation allowed on the Cobriza mine. Yet another device for stepping up cash remittances was an arrangement whereby $28 millions' worth of Peruvian assets were transferred to the parent corporation and "loaned" back to the subsidiary; yearly interest payments on the "loan" averaged $1.5 million.[38] These measures enabled the company to stabilize the ratio of total remittable earned surplus (net profit plus tax-free deductions for depletion, depreciation, amortization, and certain corporate reserves) to total sales at 16.9 percent for 1969-1971, a slight improvement over the 1960-1968 average (16.5 percent) despite poor 1971 sales.

Trouble, as the old saw has it, comes in threes. On top of the falloff in the rate of profit and the 1971 loss, Murphy now had to handle his problems without the advice of the two people whose breadth of knowledge could best compensate for his inexperience in Peruvian affairs. One was Koenig, of course. The other was Benavides. He had been willing to go on pushing for repayment of the "social debt" even though Koenig would not bend: the two were friends, and Benavides was listened to in many other matters. However, Murphy's accession meant the virtual end of his influence, and he was distressed at Murphy's apparent lack of interest in Peru's welfare. He therefore resigned in 1971. The third difficulty was Southern's decision to reduce and finally suspend dividend payouts from Toquepala in order to be able to plow its earnings back into Cuajone. Cerro's share of these dividends, $11.1 million in 1968 and $13.9 million in 1969, declined to $7.8 million in 1970; to $6.6 million in 1971; and to $3.5 million in 1972, after which the suspension took effect.[39] (Table 2.4 shows how important these dividends had become.)

Did Murphy mistake a short-term loss, the consequence of a temporarily unfavorable price situation, for a long-term trend? Perhaps. What is known is that, when a rough workup in January 1972 of the previous year's earnings statement showed that the company had undoubtedly finished the year in the red, he suddenly got in contact with Fernández Maldonado and proposed that they begin negotiations for the sale of all of Cerro's Peruvian assets to the state.[40] One month later, after no reply had been received, he broadened the offer to include the possibility of the state purchasing a 51 percent interest.

[38] Cerro's consolidated declarations for 1970-1973.

[39] Cerro Corporation's annual reports for 1968 and 1972.

[40] This action, coming immediately after a loss had been registered, is obviously inexplicable if the aim was to sell out at the highest possible price. It is for that reason that the suggestion in the first sentence of this paragraph is plausible.

In that event Cerro would supply management services under contract for as long as the government might wish.

The generals were caught off guard by these proposals. They were uninterested in the suggestion of a joint venture managed for a time by Cerro; however, they assumed that Murphy could not have known this and that his enlargement of the original offer confirmed his eagerness to get rid of the properties. On the other hand, they were wary of being enticed into concrete discussions before they had had time to weigh what the state's bargaining power would be and what sort of deal they should try to strike. Their reaction was to resort to delaying tactics. Murphy was informed that the government was definitely interested but that formal negotiations would have to wait until it could prepare a proper counteroffer. The latter would be revealed as soon as an expert commission had completed an appraisal of the firm's current net worth and future business prospects. A commission was in fact appointed and set about its investigation—after having been discreetly informed that there would be no objection if its work were to proceed in an unusually desultory fashion.

In January 1973 the earnings statement for 1972 was drawn up and showed that red ink had ceased to flow. It may have been the company's return to profitability that caused Murphy to change his mind about selling out, or he may have taken umbrage at the government's procrastination. In any case he withdrew his offer—a fatal error. He had behaved as if he were dealing with another private enterprise, as if he could enter into discussions, alter their context, and break them off according to changing business conditions, without ill will and without obligation so long as no contract had been signed. He had not reckoned with a sovereign state capable of using legal authority or coercion to achieve its ends. His actions had driven home to the generals that he was not to be trusted either to run Cerro in a manner consistent with Peruvian interests or to negotiate honestly for its subsidiary's transfer. They therefore decided to expropriate the company. Moreover, they calculated that Murphy was not very clever and could be readily overcome in any struggle over expropriation.

They made their preparations by promulgating a decree-law which prescribed minimum housing accommodations for mining camps. According to its provisions Cerro had a large deficit of adequate housing; a deduction from any compensation award of the $65 million needed to erase it was acceptable under international law. A second decree-law declared that mining businesses were thenceforth to be appraised on the basis of discounted future cash flow, not book or market value of current assets. In theory it was intended to facilitate mortgage financing in the mining sector. In practice it could also serve as a legal grounding for a low compensation payment.

Next the government put Cerro in a financial vise. After an incensed Murphy had threatened outright noncompliance with the housing statute, the DGM held up its normally routine approval of the company's plans for the disposition of its depletion reserve—an act which effectively froze several million dollars of corporate funds. The Central Reserve Bank abruptly refused to move on company requests to convert local currency into dollars for remittance to New York. (Currency controls were in operation; the company had no other way of repatriating its profits.) Corporate headquarters retaliated by withholding dollars received in New York in payment of export sales rather than sending them on to Peru. However, Cerro was legally obligated to credit to its account at the Central Reserve Bank all dollar earnings from Peruvian exports, an obligation guaranteed by the company's local commercial bank. As soon as this bank realized that it would have to make good on its guarantee, it froze Cerro's accounts. The Peruvian subsidiary was thus shut off from access to its working capital and could not meet its payroll. Desperate corporate officials in Lima asked Prime Minister Mercado Jarrín and Fernández Maldonado to intercede, which they did by authorizing the state-owned Banco Popular to extend short-term financing of current operating expenses. Cerro's funds were still frozen, and it was now subject to the mercy of a state financial institution. The government had demonstrated that Cerro could only operate in Peru at the pleasure of local authority; that it could be deprived of this privilege without its installations being touched; and that its retaliatory power was virtually nonexistent.[41]

On July 5, 1973 Cerro released an announcement stating that it was re-opening negotiations for the sale of its Peruvian subsidiary to the state. Agreement was quickly reached on two points: that Cerro's ownership share in Southern would be excluded from the sale (at the behind-the-scenes insistence of Frank Archibald, who had always rejected government efforts to become his partner), and that the joint-venture idea would not be pursued.[42] But the issue of price became a sticking point. Cerro demanded $175 million, its estimate of fair market value. The government offered $12 million, its estimate of market worth in terms of discounted future cash flow less the $65 million required to bring housing standards up to statutory norms.

Here each of the adversaries was confronted with an external event around which his strategy might be shaped. In August a special commission appointed by President Nixon and headed by his personal representative, James R. Greene, arrived in Lima armed with the power to negotiate a settlement of all outstanding claims resulting from the expropriations of North American businesses from 1968 to 1973.[43] Nixon's evident desire to improve U.S. relations with Peru seemed sufficiently strong in the eyes of the generals that

[41] The information on which this paragraph is based derives from the contents of a confidential Cerro internal memorandum.

[42] *Metals Week*, July 20, 1973. The *Peruvian Times* reported on August 24, 1973 that a management contract for the soon-to-be-nationalized Cerro installations would be awarded, if at all, either to Selection Trust or to Rio Tinto-Zinc.

[43] Hunt (1974). Greene was executive vice-president of Manufacturers' Hanover Trust.

he would not, they believed, let himself be deflected by the Cerro matter.[44] The U.S. government would probably acquiesce in a low compensation award, and such an outcome might be furthered if the Cerro question were brought into the framework of the Greene discussions. Murphy chose to play a riskier game. Knowing now that the company was at a gross disadvantage at the bargaining table, his one hope for improving the balance was to enlist the U.S. government as his ally. This he planned to accomplish by provoking Peru into a precipitous expropriation that would jeopardize—or better yet, wreck—the agreement that Greene was trying to hammer out. The United States would then be forced to adopt a harder line on the compensation issue, and Cerro would be the beneficiary.

Murphy's gambit consisted in gratuitously insulting the Peruvian government. Without prior warning he caused to be published in *La Prensa* and in the *Wall Street Journal* a communiqué couched in notably undiplomatic language and carrying his signature.[45] In it he announced that he was breaking off all negotiations for Cerro's transfer; that he was withdrawing his on-again-off-again offer to sell; and that he would reinstate it only if the government agreed in advance to drop its $12 million counteroffer. He went on to charge Peru with failing to bargain in good faith; with having presented "unacceptable proposals equivalent to expropriation"; with threatening to take over the properties first and discuss compensation after the fact; with imposing unfair taxation not contemplated in the 1971 Mining Code; and with having conducted an anti-Cerro publicity campaign throughout 1973.[46] He ended by reiterating his strenuous objection to the new housing ordinance, to which he added a complaint about the expropriation of the idle concessions nearly two years before—an act that had drawn no such protest from him or from Koenig when it occurred.

The tactic did not work. The Ministry of Energy and Mines issued a carefully worded reply rebutting Murphy's charges point by point but saying nothing about planned countermoves. President Velasco left the impression at a scheduled news conference that nothing had yet been decided. He also spurned an opportunity, presented by a questioner, to link Cerro's actions to "U.S. imperialism," making plain that there would be no official protest to the United States and that the Cerro affair would be treated as a private matter

[44] They undoubtedly remembered that he had resisted applying the Hickenlooper Amendment after the 1968 IPC expropriation and had withstood pressure from the U.S. Congress, strongly supported by W. R. Grace and Company, to cut the Peruvian sugar import quota. Too, the Allende regime was still in power in neighboring Chile and seemed to be becoming increasingly radical; that situation represented another incentive for Nixon to shore up relations with Peru.

[45] *Wall Street Journal*, September 25, 1973. The Murphy communiqué appears as a paid advertisement on p. 32; there is also news coverage on p. 12.

[46] The reference to taxation had to do with an emergency export tax levied in 1971 at a rate of 2 percent ad valorem; but the law provided that export tax payments would become a deferred credit against income taxes due. With respect to the supposed publicity campaign, Murphy went to the extreme of denouncing Chancellor (foreign minister) de la Flor by name for remarks made by him at a news conference (reported in *El Comercio*, August 30, 1973).

apart from U.S.-Peruvian relations—which would proceed on their conciliatory course.[47] October 9, the fifth anniversary of the seizure of IPC's refinery and oilfields (since commemorated as a national holiday, el Día de la Dignidad Nacional), would have been an auspicious occasion for proclaiming the passing of the last "imperialist" foreign company in the resource sector. But Velasco used the occasion to preach moderation once more:

> [The Cerro issue] is a delicate problem because of its undeniable political implications—which should be viewed from the perspective of the nationalist policies of the Peruvian Revolution, with good judgment . . . , without haste. We must balance diverse factors, but we are sure that the Armed Forces will totally support their government in whatever course of action it undertakes.[48]

With the Greene negotiations on track and with the Peruvian refusal to reply in kind to Murphy's provocation, the military could be confident that Cerro had lost whatever sympathy the U.S. government might have had for its plight. The road was almost open for the company to be unilaterally expropriated, leaving Greene to work out the compensation details as part of the package then being assembled; it was evident that he would agree to a figure much lower than the company's asking price.[49] Only the obstacle of the still-incomplete Cuajone financing barred the way, for the generals could not take the risk of their actions putting the international banks to flight. This obstacle proved evanescent: in November an agreement between Southern and the Chase Manhattan banking consortium was finalized.

The decree-law expropriating Cerro was promulgated on December 30 and took effect on January 1, 1974. Government officials doffed the mask of moderation and donned that of strident nationalism, trumpeting the expropriation as the latest victory of the Peruvian nation over the forces of imperialism. Reminding the people of Cerro's "social debt," Fernández Maldonado told them:

> All of us remember how Cerro used to buy consciences, authorities, senators, deputies, newspapermen. . . . [I]n collusion with other large resource companies such as IPC, it shared in the booty that the old Peru represented. . . . Cerro was no longer just a company. It was a name, a symbol, an evil and repudiated way of life . . . that pierced Peru's heart. Cerro . . . was a cancer.[50]

[47] Pease García and Verme Insúa (1974:2:620-21).
[48] Pease García and Verme Insúa (1974:2:636-37).
[49] Sigmund (1980) observes that the U.S. government, whenever it has been drawn into investment disputes in Latin America in recent times, has reneged on its commitment to "prompt, adequate, and effective" compensation by acquiescing in—and, sometimes, negotiating—awards for much less than the companies' asking prices based on fair market value. Fair market value is the official standard of "adequate" compensation.
[50] Ministerio de Energía y Minas (1974:29-30).

That florid rhetoric ushered into history the last of the neocolonialist foreign enterprises that had arisen and prospered on the foundation of oligarchic *entreguismo*. Still, the rhetoric must not obscure the essentially moderate nature of the act. Cerro's interest in Southern was exempted from the expropriation decree, as the government was not eager to antagonize the firm which was in the midst of the biggest mining project ever. Other properties held in the name of Cerro's New York parent were also exempted—specifically, most of the joint-venture holdings in the mediana minería and all of the industrial joint ventures.

Bereft of its negotiating leverage and its properties, there was nothing left for Cerro to do but trust in James Greene to obtain the best compensation settlement that he could. The government's final valuation of company assets less legal claims against them was $58 million. Greene wanted the figure raised to $67 million. The Peruvians assented: they had already agreed to pay $76 million in compensation moneys into a fund administered by the U.S. government, which would then distribute it among those claimants with whom Peru did not wish to deal directly; now they had merely to acknowledge tacitly that $9 million from the general compensation fund would go to Cerro in addition to the $58 million direct payment. As a matter of fact, Cerro would not even receive the entire award in cash; for Peru had submitted, and Greene had approved, a counterclaim to $38.5 million in hard currency due Cerro's local subsidiary but blocked in New York.

On February 19, 1974 the Greene Agreement was ratified by both governments as a full settlement of all claims against Peru by U.S. firms which had lost assets to expropriation up to the end of 1973. On the same day Cerro received its $58 million (the remaining $9 million was disbursed later in the year) and transferred the blocked $38.5 million to the Central Reserve Bank of Peru. Thus, for a net out-of-pocket cost of $28.5 million—of which $9 million would have been spent in any event as part of the general settlement—the Peruvian state became the sole owner of the largest polymetal mining and refining complex in the Third World; of huge unsold stocks of minerals and refined metals; and of the liquid assets and working capital needed for carrying on its business.

If this was a restructuring of capital, it assuredly did not redound to Cerro's benefit. The corporation did not have to write off the entire $175 million market value as a loss, since victims of expropriation are entitled to special U.S. tax relief. However, its net gain, including both that relief and the compensation payment, was but $21.4 million—not nearly enough to set up other mines or refineries to replace those lost and hardly enough to affect its overall financial condition. And it was now out of the nonferrous metals business (the Río Blanco mine had been nationalized a year or so before by the Allende regime); its truncated remains consisted of two copper fabricating subsidiaries with no internal sources of supply and a variety of activities unrelated to each other and not especially profitable. The wounded corporation became easy pickings for corporate vultures: in 1976 it was bought out and merged into the Marmon Group, a diversified enterprise operated as a family business by the Pritzkers of Chicago. One of the new owners' first acts, I am told, was to oust Murphy and most of his associates.

I will end this part of the story by appending the observation that no significant Peruvian socioeconomic group protested the expropriation. The applause of the popular classes was perhaps to be expected. So too was that of the middle classes—but not that of the members of Cerro's own staff, most of whom joined in the widespread approbation. The national industrial bourgeoisie, though engaged at the moment in a vigorous ideological defense of private property and free markets against the "revolution's" reforms, chose not to regard the expropriation as a danger to itself and remained mute. Not even the carefully cultivated mining bourgeoisie lifted a finger on Cerro's behalf. Most mining managers and entrepreneurs, more intimately familiar with the company's situation than the average Peruvian, had deduced that nationalization must come, due largely to the "social debt." Typical was the comment of an offical of a transnational entity engaged in medium-mine promotion and metals marketing: "Cerro de Pasco's problem was that it belonged to an era of colonialism. It tried to change its policies in the last ten years, but it couldn't escape the image it had built up. *There is no possibility whatever of good financial returns when popular dislike is this great.*"[51]

THE AFTERMATH OF EXPROPRIATION: AN APPRAISAL

Were Cerro no more, in truth, than a dilapidated relic with little potential for dynamic capital accumulation, a mere transfer of ownership from private to state hands ought not to have improved its financial performance very much. We should, rather, anticipate a continuing stagnation or a further decrease in profitability, intensified by disruption of managerial continuity and, perhaps (if the experiences of many other Third World extractive parastatals are any guide), by the introduction of bureaucratic inefficiencies. In Table 6.3 the sales and earnings of Cerro's successor, Centromin, can be compared to the results obtained over the final five years (Table 6.2 extends the series further back in time) under private ownership. An equitable comparison demands an adjustment for the impact of the burdensome tax levied on export value beginning in 1976; Cerro labored under no such burden.[52] I

[51] Interview with Fernando Núñez Barclay, September 14, 1977.

[52] This tax was introduced in July 1976 at a rate of 15 percent ad valorem, raised in 1978 to 17.5 percent. Unlike the 1971 export tax (n. 46), which remained in effect, the new one cannot be credited against incomes taxes due. Since it comes "off the top," as it were, and is independent of production costs, it is considered especially unwelcome by the mining companies. Cuajone is exempt from the export tax because the basic agreement gives it tax stability, but parastatal firms are not. Cerro paid export taxes in the years prior to 1950. However, there was no income tax at that time.

TABLE 6.3 Comparison of Centromin's Financial Performance, 1974-1980, with That of Cerro's Peruvian Mining and Refining Operations, 1969-1973 (*Millions of dollars, except profits on sales in percent*)

Year	Total Sales	Gross Operating Profit	Net Profit	Unadjusted Profit on Sales	Adjusted Profit on Sales[a]
1969	162.8	39.4	10.2	6.3	—
1970	165.7	26.2	4.4	2.7	—
1971	133.9	(3.8)	(3.8)	(2.8)	—
1972	149.0	22.0	7.9	5.3	—
1973	264.6	71.4	20.7	7.8	—
1974	282.5	80.3	38.1	13.5	—
1975	246.4	17.0	10.8	4.4	—
1976	302.4	17.6	9.7	3.2	6.5
1977	325.0	51.4	33.7	10.4	15.1
1978	302.1	38.1	11.9	3.9	14.4
1979	552.3	169.4	64.7	11.7	16.7
1980	714.0	137.2	68.0	9.5	11.7

SOURCES: Compiled and computed by the author from data presented in Centromin's annual reports and in Cerro's consolidated declarations.

[a] Based on the profit that would have been earned had no ad valorem export tax been assessed.

have therefore added a column indicating what Centromin's rate of profit would have been had the export tax not been in effect.[53] By either the adjusted or the unadjusted measure, Centromin's profit performance has been clearly superior to Cerro's. The former's average rate of profit on sales during its first seven years of existence was 8.7 percent, or 15.6 percent after removal of the export tax load; the latter's, in contrast, was 5.0 percent over the seven years from 1967 to 1973. (The very capital-intensive Southern does still better—its profit on sales for 1974-1980 was 12.9 percent without adjustment for export taxation—but the gap is narrowing.) Between 1976 and 1980 Centromin's profit per ton of ore mined increased by nearly 47 percent.

The state treasury realized from this performance an average of $59.3 million per year in taxes. Southern remained the more important generator of state revenues, its tax payments averaging $72.1 million per year. But Centromin contributed much more than Cerro had: an average of $10.9 million

[53] My computation consists in adding export tax payments to pretax profits and then calculating subtractions for income taxes and mandatory contributions (to worker profit sharing and IN-GEMMET) at the same percentage rates that were in fact applied (these rates are not dependent on the size of the pretax profit when one is working in this dollar range). The result is the net profit that would have been obtained without the export tax.

annually between 1967 and 1973. The parastatal's success can in no way be attributed to government favoritism in matters of taxation.

Was Centromin merely the beneficiary of fortuitous trends in international prices? Only in part. Table 6.4 gives annual production figures for the four principal refined metal products. Lead output declined slightly for a time and then returned to pre-expropriation levels (cf. Table 6.1); zinc output held steady; meanwhile, production of refined copper and silver rose significantly. (Good fortune played its role in that the increased silver output appeared just in time to catch the metal's 1979-80 price rise.) Mine production measured in fine metal content also rose after the expropriation: 1981 lead production was 7.8 percent greater than in 1974; zinc production, 9.2 percent greater; and silver production, 15.8 percent greater.[54] These data, like those for profits, are testimony to the competence of Centromin's management and to the smoothness of the transition to state ownership—possible because the staff was already largely Peruvian; there was no noticeable disruption caused by the departure of expatriates and their replacement by inexperienced locals.

I can conceive of no inherent reason why private management could not have performed similarly *had it wanted to*. The difficulty with Cerro, in other words, was unrelated to the intrinsic nature of the mining business and the company's place in it. Cerro was never a relic—at least, it did not need to be one. It had been reduced to that condition solely because its managers preferred to devote its resources to other things (Koenig), or preoccupied

TABLE 6.4 Centromin's Production of Major Refined Metals, 1974-1981
(*Metric tons*)

Year	Copper	Lead	Silver	Zinc
1974	38,951	80,090	549	68,518
1975	36,589	70,967	555	61,975
1976	50,327	74,070	598	64,381
1977	55,019	79,241	671	66,950
1978	51,895	74,255	650	62,857
1979	53,919	85,108	793	68,191
1980	54,105	81,973	740	63,826
1981[a]	45,091	79,361	717	66,450

SOURCE: Compiled by the author from data presented in Centromin (1981).
[a] Estimated on the basis of production for the first two quarters.

[54] Copper production declined by 3.8 percent, but this was a continuation of a long-term trend: the copper content of ores mined by the company had been decreasing since the 1940s. Since the stated production increases were attained without opening new mines or striking rich veins in older ones, they must be attributed to greater productive efficiency (in tons of ore mined per man-hour worked) rather than to changes in ore grades. The data are taken from Centromin (1981).

themselves with squeezing out short-term profits in disregard of long-term prospects (Murphy). The restructuring-of-capital argument thus falls for lack of a foundation. Indeed, such a restructuring could have been accomplished far more advantageously, from the standpoint of international capital's putative interest in control, by merging the company into a stronger competitor— let us say, one of the transnational oligopolists. Koening was ready to sell as early as the mid-sixties, a time when the Peruvian investment climate was still extremely hospitable to foreign investors. Moreover, the corporation was sufficiently small and weak that it could probably have been forced into a merger against its will. Yes, the new owners would have had to assume the "social debt." But they would not have been intimately identified with it and stood a good chance of being able to clear it with moderate investment in the camps and a modern approach to labor relations.

The projects undertaken and proposed by Centromin are proof positive that lurking below the surface was an untapped potential. As of 1981 parastatal management had increased mine and concentrator capacity by 10.6 percent over prenationalization figures. It had thoroughly modernized two of the oldest mines, Morococha and Yauricocha: whereas in 1974 both of them had barely broken even, in 1980 they were the second and third most profitable Centromin mines per unit of output. It had enlarged the capacity of the copper refinery and had measurably improved the metal recuperation rates of the existing facilities—another tribute to its skills, given that the refineries are technologically complex and were already considered efficient in spite of their age.[55] (Some of the new copper refining capacity is being used to refine concentrates imported from Spain, in competition with European custom refiners.) It had also launched the following major modernization projects:

    a. A 40 percent expansion of the Casapalca mine, another one of the oldest;

    b. A fourfold expansion of Cobriza—lending further credence to the claim that the mine's original plan had been extremely conservative;

    c. Expansion and upgrading of the zinc refinery;

    d. Installation of a water treatment plant at the Cerro de Pasco mine that will not only recover an additional 5,400 fine metric tons of refined copper annually but also reduce pollution of the Mantaro River, the zone's principal source of irrigation water;

    e. Modification of the lead processing facility to increase output and reduce air and water pollution;

    f. A new open-pit mine at Tintaya, in partnership with MineroPeru (Chapter 8).

The total cost of these six projects, including Centromin's 45 percent share in Tintaya, is $487.6 million; adding the cost of the completed projects brings total new investment to around $500 million. Much of the needed capital has

[55] Recuperation rates increased by 17.2 percent for silver; 9.9 percent for lead; and 9.2 percent for copper. The zinc refinery, being the newest and most efficient, could not be made to yield a higher percentage of metal inexpensively (Centromin 1981).

been borrowed from international sources.[56] However, the enterprise's retained profit stream has contributed as well. Its ratio of long-term debt to stockholder equity stood in 1980 at 0.277, which is quite typical of the debt burden customarily borne by the transnational mining majors. Most of the projects, furthermore, went or are going ahead on the basis of "in-house" engineering. Centromin has not become a vehicle for increasing Peru's technological dependence.

Lastly, the parastatal enterprise is dynamically expanding beyond its traditional geographic range and scope of operations. Tintaya, located in Cuzco department, is one such step. Explorations and feasibility studies are also under way for a gold mining project in the department of Madre de Dios, a polymetal mine with high molybdenum content in Tacna, and a copper mine with significant amounts of cobalt—a strategic metal of which the United States imports large quantities—in Ica. All four departments have been generally overlooked by the mining industry in the past (although Toquepala is in Tacna and Marcona in Ica, neither is host to other large or medium mines); the first two are economically underdeveloped even by Peruvian standards and will benefit greatly when the projects begin.[57] Possibilities for industrial development in the central sierra will be enhanced by Centromin's current effort to enlarge its capacity for electrical power generation and to tie its private generation and distribution network into the national power grid.

Centromin's strategy for success has thus rested on the perception that declining profits in Cerro's last years were due to a shortage of new investment and inadequate maintenance. Parastatal management recognized that many of the existing facilities could be upgraded and rendered more efficient with a relatively small expenditure aimed primarily at incrementing the metal recuperation rate at every stage of the production process. In this way the enterprise was rapidly restored to solid profitability, after which it has proved possible to seek and obtain outside financing for projects of larger scale without mortaging Centromin's future to the international banking establishment.

[56] As a state-owned enterprise, Centromin has the advantage that it can obtain state guarantees for loans from the World Bank and the Inter-American Development Bank—a privilege denied to private firms. However, the loans received from these sources have not been large; most of the borrowed capital has come from private banks. It is interesting that Canadian banks have been in the forefront and that support has been received from that country's Export Development Corporation (equivalent to the U.S. Export-Import Bank). Most of the Canadian loans have been used to finance the purchase of mining machinery produced in Canada. In consequence, this lending activity serves to stimulate that country's capital-goods sector: the expanded market helps to encourage the sector's growth and thereby contributes toward reducing capital-goods dependence on the United States. Here is another example of the way in which relations of economic dependence can be and are being overcome through cooperation among developing countries.

[57] The projects in Cuzco and Madre de Dios should also make contributions to political stability and national integration. Cuzco department is populous but has been bypassed by industrial development; it has a high unemployment rate and is a center of political radicalism. Madre de Dios is a remote Amazonian province whose economy is now linked only tenuously to that of the rest of the nation.

The strategy has also given attention to the human dimension. Action has been taken to liquidate the "social debt" (Chapter 10), thereby demonstrating that there was no fundamental contradiction between the goals of advancing worker welfare and of restoring the enterprise to health. Communication between labor and management has been improved. Workers' productive efficiency has been stimulated both by appeals to patriotic duty and by a new system of merit pay raises. As for the staff, high salaries and avoidance of politically motivated appointments and promotions have enhanced morale and reduced turnover. Nationalist appeals have been utilized here as well.[58]

Conclusions: Cerro and the Doctrine of Domicile

On its face, Cerro's behavior in Peru during the sixties and seventies stands in direct contradiction to the doctrine of domicile. Local government efforts to introduce moderate reforms impinging but peripherally on the company's interests were vigorously resisted. Later Peruvian desires for new mine and refinery investment and for repayment of the "social debt"—all appropriate matters of local policy and all deemed essential to national development by the political authorities—were persistently ignored, turned aside, and/or treated with less seriousness than they deserved. Routine upkeep of the Peruvian installations, a most elementary necessity for safeguarding their value to the host country's economy, was neglected in the last years. Peruvian acquisition of the company's local assets was explored by management only in a high-handed, take-it-or-leave-it manner; there was none of the cooperation that Sklar observed when the Zambian government moved to take over the local subsidiaries of Anglo-American and Roan Selection Trust. Still another important divergence between the Cerro case and the Zambian relates to the ability of the corporation to harmonize its global interests with the regional interests of the host country: whereas Anglo-American contrived to operate in both Zambia and South Africa but attended carefully to the former's hostility to the latter on grounds of antiracialism, Cerro completely ignored the Peru-Chile conflict of long standing and employed profits earned in the first to support development in the second.[59]

Koenig, it is true, did evince a belief in the worth of industrialization in Peru, manifesting it in Cerro's industrial activities and in backing the mediana minería. But his approach can only be described as colonialist. It was not for the Peruvian government as a sovereign entity to determine what policy of industrialization it would follow, nor for the company, as a "good corporate citizen," to accede to the requirements of that policy. Rather, the foreign

[58] Interview with Guillermo Flórez Pinedo, president of Centromin, August 22, 1981. He adds that there has been no exodus of upper staff members (whose qualifications are high enough to enable them to find jobs abroad) in spite of the erosion of the purchasing power of their salaries occasioned by the rampant inflation of 1979-1981. This signifies a high degree of identification with the enterprise.

[59] See Sklar (1975) for the observations on the Zambian case.

company arrogated to itself both the right to decide what kind of industrialization Peru should have and the power to establish how, if at all, it would contribute toward providing it.

Let us reexamine the doctrine of domicile and the determinants of Cerro's conduct in order to see if the apparent contradiction can be resolved. Our reexamination will be carried out on two planes: the plane of ideology, and the plane of corporate interests.

The Ideological Plane

Sklar presents the doctrine of domicile as an element of transnational managerial ideology whose intent is to justify corporate interests and to reconcile the transnational parent's pursuit of global profit with the subsidiary's ability to behave like a "good corporate citizen" of the host country. In a later work he unambiguously associates this ideological doctrine with the "mature" business corporation characterized by autonomous managerial authority,[60] bureaucratic organization, and rationalized internal planning:

> At the supranational level, the old issue of autonomous managerial authority becomes crucial to calculations about the potential exercise of corporate statesmanship in world affairs. In particular, it relates to the often vaunted ability of corporate managers to act in accordance with broad political and social values in addition to their economic objectives. John K. Galbraith has argued that the principled pursuit of noneconomic goals by a "mature corporation" is entirely consistent with its concurrent pursuit of overriding economic and technological goals. In fact, he [Galbraith] contends, social goals for the corporation are needed to maintain the loyalty and morale of the many mental . . . workers who serve it.[61]

By implication, a corporation which is *not* "mature" in Galbraith's terms may not seek the ideological justification for its actions that the doctrine of domicile represents.

Now, Galbraith does not regard all corporations as "mature" and, in fact, distinguishes between two forms of corporate organization: "mature" and "entrepreneurial." The former is typified by large size, which makes bureaucracy and rationalized planning necessary (since the size of the organization exceeds the span of control of a small management cadre); and by diffuse ownership, which insulates planning modalities from the potentially irrational, conflicting, and immediate demands of shareholders. Galbraith's examples of latter-day "entrepreneurial" corporations include Ford under the elder Henry and Montgomery Ward under Sewell Avery. Both men's behavior was oriented toward "individualism . . . [and] competition," not toward

---

[60] Managerial autonomy is here to be understood as autonomy not with respect to shareholders but to the state; it stems from the corporation's character as a "nonstatist political institution" (Berle 1954:60; 1959:17-24).

[61] Sklar (1976); his citation is of Galbraith (1967:169-78).

"accommodation to organization [and] intimate and continuing cooperation"; both adopted highly idiosyncratic management styles; and both insisted on centralizing power and authority in their own hands.[62] But the use of Henry Ford as an archetype of an "entrepreneurial" manager does not mean that owner-entrepreneurs are alone free to adopt such a style. Indeed, Avery was, as Galbraith points out, a minority (but large) shareholder in "his" firm— exactly as Robert Koenig was. Entrepreneurship denotes not ownership but a mode of behavior: one emphasizing risk-taking and innovation and tending to justify itself in its own terms (thus, having no need of a social ideology for the purpose).[63] It is hostile to bureaucracy and planning because both inhibit the flexibility of action that entrepreneurial behavior requires. I suggest that an "entrepreneurial" management can survive and prosper in the absence of majority financial control of the firm if (1) the firm is small enough that the span-of-control problem is not severe, and (2) the financial performance of the firm is good enough to satisfy a relatively small group of controlling shareholders.

Table 6.5 compares Cerro as it was in 1973 to the two largest U.S. corporations, both "mature" in every Galbraithian sense; to Kennecott, then still independent and the largest U.S. nonferrous metals corporation; and to Asarco. We see at once that Cerro was by far the smallest on all measures and was much more closely held as well. This does not require that Cerro's manage-

TABLE 6.5 Comparative Size Measures for Cerro and Certain Other Major Corporations in 1973 (*Financial measures in millions of dollars*)

Company	Sales	Rank[a]	Assets	Net Profit	Shareholder Equity	Number of Shareholders
General Motors	35,798	1	20,297	2,398	12,567	1,283,260
Exxon	25,724	2	25,079	2,443	13,718	722,549
Kennecott	1,395	120	1,977	159	1,307	77,583
Asarco	1,068	157	1,149	113	774	62,900[b]
Cerro	637	252	660	49[c]	346	22,689

SOURCES: Compiled from data in *Fortune* (May 1974):230-57; Cerro Corporation's annual report and "10K" report to the U.S. Securities and Exchange Commission for 1973; "10K" report of Asarco for 1975; "10K" reports of the other corporations for 1973.

[a] *Fortune* ranking of U.S. industrial corporations by total sales.

[b] Datum for 1975.

[c] Before deduction of expropriation loss; profit after loss deduction was $3.6 million.

[62] Galbraith (1967:31-34, 59-77, 92); the quoted material is from p. 92.

[63] Schumpeter (1942:132 and passim) regarded entrepreneurship as capable of dispensing with legitimating ideology for the reason stated.

ment have been "entrepreneurial" in style, but it implies that such a style would have been consistent with the firm's survival and continuing prosperity.

Our discussion above of the nature of Cerro management leaves no room for doubt that its style was indeed "entrepreneurial." Managerial authority was tightly concentrated in the hands of the chief executive officer: Koenig, then Murphy, made all of the key decisions; not a few of these (e.g., to proceed with Río Blanco)[64] were idiosyncratic, risky, and innovative; there was no deference to corporate planning committees nor even to the advice of knowledgeable presidential appointees. In brief, Cerro's managerial organization and style lie outside the conceptual reach of the doctrine-of-domicile idea. Its managers could have shared that ideological disposition anyway, of course, as a matter of personal belief; but they were unlikely to insofar as they actually acted like entrepreneurs, and the record of their actions makes manifest that they did not so believe.

The Plane of Corporate Interests

If the doctrine of domicile is regarded as necessary to the successful operation of transnational resource firms with subsidiaries in Third World host countries, it is because these face the chore of reconciling host-country interests with global profitability requisites. However, *Cerro was not a transnational resource corporation at all*. Setting aside its nonintegrated U.S. subsidiaries and looking only at its nonferrous metals business, we find that, right to the end, *it was a Peru-based, foreign-owned exporting and holding company*. It could, with justice, be described as a "colonial company." Like others of its ilk, it originated in what Manuel Castells defines as the second of three phases of metropolitan capitalist relations with the Third World: the phase of "[c]ommercial [i]mperialistic [d]ependency correspond[ing] to capitalism in its stage of free competition," when foreign investment in the hinterland "center[ed] its efforts on the exploitation of natural resources obtained at low cost through the mechanisms of unequal exchange."[65] Unlike the others, though, it did not expand out of its colonial enclave and "transnationalize" itself before World War II, when lower entry barriers allowed such expansion at reasonable cost. Being an international fringe competitor, its survival depended not on protecting a market share but on exploiting richer-than-average mineral veins with a small capital investment and cheap labor. Therefore, it *could not* conform to Peruvian insistence on higher levels of investment and liquidation of the "social debt" without losing exclusive control of its assets and becoming a weaker partner in a joint venture. Indeed, it might well have expired earlier were it not for its good fortune in having been able to participate as a junior partner in Southern Peru Copper.

[64] Koenig has said that his eagerness to become involved with Río Blanco was stimulated by a desire to overcome serious geological and topographical difficulties that had repeatedly stymied other would-be developers of the property.

[65] Castells (1977).

Still, Cerro contributed a great deal to Peru's development in a previous epoch, before the country had evolved a local dominant class with an interest in rapid industrialization and a state capable of directing the task. It trained the Peruvian engineers who would eventually come to run both it and MineroPeru; it gave sustenance to an independent Peruvian entrepreneuriat and manageriat in the mediana minería; it founded industries in which Peruvian capital participated and which Peruvians managed; and it made an indirect contribution, via the enhanced status its presence gave to the professions of geology and mining engineering, to the constitution of a competent mining technocracy. That Cerro was latterly a "bad citizen" and yet impacted positively on development in a former phase is not as much of a paradox as it seems, however. It has been the fate of colonial institutions everywhere to promote the rise of just those native classes and interests which, in time, render such institutions obsolete. With the coming of political independence—or, in the case of Latin America, of true national assertiveness—under the aegis of domestic dominant classes, colonial economic institutions ceased to serve a purpose and became mere parasites. Then their fate was sealed; for, exactly as occurred in Peru, *the very domestic bourgeoisies which they helped to create turned against them.*[66]

One last bit of unfinished business relating to the doctrine of domicile calls out for attention; it has to do with the question of the meaning for transnational corporate behavior of local interstate rivalries in which the host country is engaged. In the instance examined by Sklar, the rivalry was in no sense a power competition between two roughly equal less-developed states—one in which a small absolute increment by one of them in the economic foundation of power, especially if achieved at the other's expense, could tip the balance. He thus found that if Anglo-American conducted its Zambian and South African affairs separately from each other in all respects save for the pooling of profit streams at the top, there was no conflict between its profit-maximizing activity and the national interests of either state. The Peru-Chile rivalry, in contrast, *is* one between two states approximately equal in economic and military power, both of them excruciatingly sensitive to their power balance and to the effect thereupon of each one's processes of development. Cerro's experience, along with the Braden/Anaconda "nonexperience" of Peruvian investment, teaches that where such a rivalry exists, transnational resource corporations may be forced to choose to do business on the territory of one *or* the other country. They may not be able to deal simultaneously with both— most especially if the reinvestment of pooled profits is perceived as favoring one over the other.

This situation is a common one in today's Third World: the examples of

---

[66] See Sklar (1975:36, text and n. 14). He observes that in Africa, "colonial companies" are not necessarily more prone to nationalization than are others—because there, nationalization responds to an ideological imperative affecting all foreign investment more or less equally. However, they are more likely than others to be expropriated without compensation.

Algeria-Morocco, Iran-Iraq, and India-Pakistan are three that leap readily to mind. So long as it persists—so long, that is, as the Third World remains organized into sovereign states with no supreme political authority over all of them—transnational resource firms may find that certain combinations of investments are foreclosed to them. The international state system continues to challenge the economic power of international capitalism,[67] and that fact limits the efficacy of the doctrine of domicile as a tool for legitimating corporate interests.

[67] Cf. Gilpin (1975).

PART III

Institutional Foundations of the
Peruvian Mining Bourgeoisie

T HE two preceding chapters have dealt with the nature of relations between the Peruvian state and transnational (in the formal definition) mining enterprises. We discovered that the position of a foreign mining corporation in the world nonferrous metals oligopoly significantly affects its ability and willingness to harmonize its global interests with "good corporate citizenship" on the part of its local subsidiary. Nonetheless, it remains within the host government's capabilities to adopt a definition of "good corporate citizenship" in law and administrative regulation and to sanction deviant corporate conduct, just as is done with regard to individuals. Colonial companies—those which arrived early in this century in order to exploit cheap local resources (including labor) and which did not later evolve into integrated transnational oligopolists—were found to be the most likely to exhibit deviant behavior under modern conditions and to be sanctioned for it. Unlike the central oligopolists, their interests are not consonant with a host-country interest in national development.

Because they are labor-intensive and less technologically oriented than the central oligopolists, colonial companies often provide more upward mobility opportunities for more members of the domestic middle strata and nascent bourgeoisie. Yet, they do not—at least, not in Peru—purchase the loyalty and dedication of those social groups by so doing. The bourgeoisie of the private sector holds itself increasingly apart from the colonial company as the latter approaches obsolescence in terms of its potential contribution to national development. Bourgeois elements in the state, meanwhile, become its active opponents. These bourgeois groups are in no way hostile to all foreign investment on principle. But they are matricidal toward that form of it which did the most to birth and nurture them. Explaining this selectivity toward different forms of foreign investment is a major aim of Part III.

Chapter 7 treats the mediana minería of Peru, provider of the economic sustenance and definer of the interests of an important indigenous bourgeois class element. The study of the mediana minería is of particular value because the domestic firms in it have interacted with foreign capital at two levels: at the gran minería level (before 1974), via ore and concentrate sales to Cerro and the occasional purchase of refining services from Cerro; and within the medium-mining subsector, where foreign subsidiaries and domestic firms coexist. Despite its evident importance, the subsector has been all but totally neglected in the literature—necessitating, therefore, research into its organization and structure. My investigation addresses questions such as: Are bourgeois interests in the subsector subservient to those of foreign capital in large or medium mining? Are the domestic firms autonomous but too weak to compete effectively? Is the nature of the subsector such as to encourage entrepreneurial dynamism on the part of domestic bourgeois elements? or, does it tend to reduce them to a passive rentier or comprador role?

Chapter 8 examines parastatal enterprise in the Peruvian gran minería—an innovation of the military regime. Parastatal enterprise, depending on the class character of its control and the manner in which its interests and goals are delineated, may be a prop for an indigenous bourgeoisie. It can provide that service by subsidizing private business activity; by representing bourgeois class interests within the state; or by more successfully (because larger and better organized) countering the competition of transnational mining corporations, thus enabling local private enterprise to grow stronger in its shadow. On the other hand, Peruvian parastatal mining enterprise, being a late and *nonmonopolistic* entrant to a once foreign-dominated gran minería, may end by hitching its wagon to the foreign star and becoming still another avenue for foreign capital penetration and policy influence. Or, a third possibility— one that cannot be dismissed out of hand in view of the regime's proclaimed intent to construct a *democracia social de participación plena* (a fully participatory social democracy)—is that parastatal enterprise represents socialism a-borning ''in the bosom of the beast.'' It may be a check on and counterweight to bourgeois economic power in the mining sector and a potential vehicle by which politically mobilized popular groups can begin to exert some control over the nation's economic life.

In Part II we tested dependency propositions claiming that transnational enterprise exercises preeminent *institutional* power over host states and found them wanting. In Part III the analysis is still predominantly institutional, but from a different perspective: we now look at the institutions and structures of the domestic industry in terms of their direct impact on bourgeois class formation. We test propositions derived from class analyses of dependency— propositions claiming that no Third World indigenous bourgeoisie, and no public economic institution not subject to the control of a party-state with an explicit ideological commitment to Marxist socialism, can be anything other than subservient to metropolitan capital.

CHAPTER SEVEN

The Medium-Mining Subsector

P ERU stands alone among the major less-developed mineral-exporting countries in having an economically significant element of medium-scale private enterprise, much of it locally owned, operating in the resource industry. Chile has a national mediana minería, as does Mexico. But Chile's produces mainly coal, iron ore, and nonmetallic minerals for domestic consumption and is in any event swamped by the great size of her gran minería; while Mexico's is relatively small in comparison to the indigenous manufacturing sector. In contrast, the Peruvian mediana minería produces mostly nonferrous metals for export, exactly as the large mines do. Moreover, the nation's smaller industrial base gives medium mining a greater relative weight as a sustainer of the domestic industrial bourgeoisie.

The mediana minería is not entirely a local capital preserve, however; small subsidiaries of transnational mining corporations operate in it as well. Nor can we accept at face value, without further investigating the matter, any claim that the survival of domestic mining capital constitutes prima facie evidence of entrepreneurial dynamism. For, the state has fostered capital accumulation in the subsector since 1950, when the new Mining Code simplified and reduced corporate taxes and eliminated import duties on imported mining machinery and supplies; since 1969, the state has become a still more active nurturer of domestic mining capital.[1] We must keep in mind as well that the modern origins of the mediana minería at around the turn of the century coincided in time with the consolidation of oligarchic power; and that it used to be common practice for analysts to lump mining together with the other anti-developmental interests that once dominated Peru's economic and political life. The domestic mining bourgeoisie may turn out to be a progressive, expanding indigenous economic force. Alternatively, it may be found stagnant and subservient to external capital (or suffered by the latter to subsist as a sop to influential local allies); or else it may be an oligarchic remnant which merely testifies to the incompleteness of the Peruvian "revolution."

This chapter examines the institutions, structures, and economic perform-

---

[1] It has extended aid in the form of financial assistance through the state mining bank (the Banco Minero) and COFIDE; increased technical assistance through the Banco Minero and INGEMMET; and marketing support through Minpeco—although this last has been regarded by managers of the sector as of dubious value.

ance of the subsector in order that we may decide which of these three alternatives is most nearly correct. It opens with an overview of the subsector's recent performance—the object being to discern whether it is and will likely remain a viable locus of capital accumulation, or whether its future is to be marginalized, as was the pequeña minería, by larger-scale capital. Then the subsector's institutions—the individual firms and their controlling interests— are looked at in more detail. The chapter next analyzes the connections between the subsector's capital and capital in other sectors, which provides some clues regarding the character of the mining bourgeoisie and answers the question about its relationship to the oligarchy. It proceeds to compare the disaggregated economic performance of key groups of firms; by evaluating their performance diachronically it reveals where the sources of entrepreneurial dynamism lie, what the structural factors for the realization of this dynamism are, and what kind of future evolution can be expected. The last task assumed in this chapter is a consideration of the sources and development of the subsector's technologies, with an eye toward the issue of technological dependence.

THE VIABILITY OF THE MEDIANA MINERÍA

The mediana minería cannot be a viable foundation for a local bourgeoisie if it is economically stagnant. Stagnation would most probably be caused by competition from larger, more capital-intensive, and more efficient firms, whose activities would progressively displace the smaller entities of the medium-mining subsector.[2] It would be revealed in the failure of the subsector's production, earnings, and/or assets to grow.

I use three statistics to measure the economic performance of the mediana minería. *Gross value of production* (GVP) requires the least data to compute and interpret; it is the total amount of new value produced in a year and is equal to total sales plus additions to unsold inventory valued at current prices. *Economic rent from resource exploitation* (ER) is the income earned by the firm (or group of firms) as a whole after payments to other economic sectors; it measures contribution to gross domestic product and is the pie that will be divided among workers as wages and salaries, government as income taxes, equity investors as profits, and other investors as loan interest and royalty payments. Mathematically, ER equals GVP less payouts and deductions for purchased consumables and noncapital goods, indirect taxes on goods and services, loan amortization, and depreciation (which is ultimately paid out to suppliers of capital equipment). *Book value of assets net of depreciation* indicates in its temporal evolution whether the subsector is capitalizing and reinvesting its earnings, as it must do if it is to remain competitive in its markets.

---

[2] Biersteker (1978:104 and passim) provides a useful formal analysis of displacement.

Table 7.1 gives the magnitudes of the three statistics for the whole subsector in each year since 1967, when the detailed data needed to calculate them first became available on a regular basis.[3] Fixed assets net of depreciation rose 274 percent in the 1967-1979 interval—a dramatic increase in investment in new plant, equipment, and mine development. Most of the increase came after 1970, by which time the military regime had promulgated a new mining code, taken steps to enlarge the lending capacity of the Banco Minero (which the locally owned firms rely on for their primary outside financing of capital expenditures), and otherwise reassured the local private mining industry that it had nothing to fear from the new political order. GVP and ER also tended strongly upward in these years: between 1967 and 1978 the former rose by 141 percent and the latter by 183 percent.[4] Considerable year-to-year fluctuation in both GVP and ER is expected, since both depend on variable international price levels in addition to production volumes. This is indeed

TABLE 7.1 Gross Value of Production (GVP), Economic Rent (ER), and Fixed Assets of the Peruvian Mediana Minería, 1967-1979

Year	GVP		ER		Assets	
	A	B	A	B	A	B
1967	116.9	—	60.4	—	48.7	—
1968	115.3	−3.0	66.6	10.3	46.5	−4.5
1969	139.2	20.7	74.0	11.1	33.1	−28.8
1970	149.0	7.0	72.0	−2.7	38.0	14.8
1971	139.3	−6.5	65.5	−9.0	52.5	39.2
1972	160.0	14.9	83.8	27.9	43.2	−17.7
1973	284.3	77.7	140.0	67.1	61.7	42.8
1974	325.8	14.6	184.1	31.5	74.3	20.4
1975	288.6	−11.4	119.0	−35.4	124.6	67.7
1976	242.9	−13.7	125.8	5.7	120.2	−3.5
1977	261.4	7.6	150.8	19.9	166.5	38.5
1978	286.5	9.6	171.0	13.4	171.7	3.1
1979	549.3	91.7	363.8	112.7	182.0	6.0

SOURCES: Compiled by the author from data presented in the consolidated declarations of the companies and furnished by the Departamento de Estudios Económicos y Estadística, Sociedad Nacional de Minería y Petróleo.
NOTE: Columns A = millions of dollars; columns B = percent change from previous year.

[3] Fortunately, 1967 is a convenient beginning year for our analysis. It establishes a comparison baseline in almost two pre-"revolutionary" years and permits coverage of the entire "revolutionary" period.
[4] I here use 1978 as the comparison year because it can be argued that the 1979 data, having been inflated by exceptionally high silver prices, are atypical.

observed. Yet the fluctuations tend to be smaller than those of any one nonferrous metal price (see Table A.6, in Appendix A, for comparison). The reason is that the mediana minería is a polymetal industry producing copper, lead, silver, and zinc and is not absolutely reliant on any one of them. This fact helps to stabilize the industry by insulating it from some of the consequences of sharp international price reversals. Note too that ER has increased faster than GVP, meaning that the industry has become more efficient in its utilization of purchased goods and services. The same is definitely not true of Peruvian industry as a whole.[5]

Hence, all indications are that the mediana minería is lively and enjoys good economic health. However, it remains to be seen whether that health results predominantly from the activities of national or foreign capital in the subsector. We also need to know which group has captured most of the benefits of the subsector's recent growth. The answers await the specification of the organization and control of capital.

THE ORGANIZATION AND CONTROL OF MEDIUM-MINING CAPITAL

Capital in the subsector is organized without exception in the form of limited-liability corporations. By studying the ownership of corporate shares and the nature of interlocking directorates we can describe the control of capital along three dimensions: concentration versus diffusion, national versus foreign, and private versus state.

An understanding of the nature of ownership requires the correlation of shareholder data for all firms of the subsector. Historical practice, encouraged until recently by claim denouncement regulations, has been to organize a separate corporate entity for each mine. The procedure is useful to controlling owners in that it enables them to solicit support from outside equity investors for new mine development without having to admit them to a share of mining assets already in being. It may also produce lower tax bills than if earnings from several mines were aggregated for tax purposes. We can consequently expect that some nominally independent firms are actually controlled by the same ownership interest.

Considerable care must be taken in determining the nationality of the controlling interest. Extreme nationalists have argued that most of the firms of the subsector are under "direct or indirect" foreign control.[6] However, their

---

[5] Schydlowsky and Wicht (1980) document the fact that Peruvian manufacturing industry engaged in a veritable orgy of capital expenditures during the "revolutionary" years, which left it with considerable idle capacity. (The reason was that the regime's enterprise reforms were designed to stimulate reinvestment and did so with a vengeance; firms could stave off the approach of full worker comanagement by reinvesting profits, and many did so for that purpose alone.) The authors regard this as the major structural problem facing the country's industrial sector in the 1980s.

[6] Espinoza Uriarte (1970); Espinoza Uriarte and Osorio (1971); and Brundenius (1972), who, rather arrogantly in my opinion and with no further evidence than the data presented by the two

position rests on three assumptions, all of which are indefensible on either theoretical or empirical grounds. One is that interlocking directorates are an indication of control, which is false if presented as a universal fact; as I have earlier remarked (see Chapter 4, pp. 76-77 and n. 14), these may be maintained as "listening posts" within another's camp and are likely to be in an oligopolistic industry such as mining. A second is that any nonnegligible equity holding by foreign interests conveys to them control of the enterprise; this is simply wrong and can only be justified by ideologically imputing some innate superiority of power to foreign capital per se. The third, equally wrong for the same reason, is that a pattern of regular business dealings between a national and a foreign enterprise—for instance, the sale of concentrates by medium-mining firms to Cerro—"proves" the subservience of the former to the latter.[7] It may, of course, *indicate* a subservient relationship; but subservience cannot be proven except by obtaining negative replies to these questions: Were the dealings at issue entered into voluntarily in terms of the local firm's desires and interests in accumulation of capital? Is the national enterprise free to alter or terminate the relationship at its sole discretion, with no insurmountable cost to itself? Is the exchange a fair one, in that the values exchanged are determined with reference to market forces unmanipulated by either party and are not fixed by one party's fiat? Every one of the large number of medium-mine managers whose firms used to sell concentrates to Cerro answered all three questions affirmatively, adding that they would do business with it only insofar as it offered them better terms and conditions than they could get from independent metals traders.

These errors can be avoided by adopting a nonideological and unambiguous standard of control. As I did in Chapter 4 when discussing the world mining industry, I use the standard enunciated by Berle and Means, viz., "control lies in the hands of the individual or group who have the actual power to select the board of directors, (or its majority), either by mobilizing the legal right to choose them . . . or by exerting pressure which influences their choice."[8] I operationalize this standard as follows: Control is said to be vested in whomever (1) controls fifty percent plus one of the firm's outstanding equity shares; or (2) controls the largest block of shares, if there is no obvious majority. The controlling interest need not be owned by one person or one family; it can be and usually is represented by a group of unrelated shareholders

---

preceding authors, dismisses the national bourgeoisie of the subsector as "a joke." The Espinoza arguments have been given wider currency via their propagation in government documents, e.g., Oficina Intersectoral de Planificación (1976).

[7] The fallacy originates with Espinoza Uriarte and Osorio (1971:90) and is incorporated by Brundenius (1972). Apart from the theoretical error the three authors stumble into an empirical one. DeWind (1977:130-33) shows that in 1968-1970 only five of the sixteen firms claimed to be "directly controlled" by Cerro, and only eight of the eighty-four claimed to be "indirectly controlled" *primarily on the basis of ore and concentrate sales*, actually sold ores and concentrates to the North American firm. On the other hand, six other local firms not listed as "controlled" in any sense also sold ores to Cerro.

[8] Berle and Means (1932:66).

who, however, can be expected to vote their shares en bloc. It is not always easy to decide what constitutes a block of shares. In the difficult cases attention must be given to other business relationships maintained by the members of the putative controlling group; to the identity and outside interests of the board chairperson, who invariably represents the controlling interest; and to the character of corporate management.

In my definition the controlling interest is national or foreign according to the nationality of the person or corporate entity exercising control, with two exceptions: (1) if the controlling entity is domiciled abroad but is in turn controlled by Peruvians,[9] control is local (the converse, naturally, also holds); and (2) if a minority foreign shareholder has management rights under contract, or if his presence is contingent upon contractual arrangements that limit managerial prerogatives (e.g., by obligating the sale of the product to a particular dealer or export customer), control is foreign.

Table 7.2 lists the active medium-mining companies as of December 31, 1979. The table is organized on the basis of control. Whenever two or more firms are controlled by the same interest, I have collected them together into a corporate group named for the controlling interest. All corporate groups and individual firms are classified by nationality. The table also gives three indicators of relative size and economic weight: fixed assets at cost, paid-in capital, and 1979 gross sales.

The National Firms

A quick inspection of Table 7.2 discloses that seven locally owned firms and groups stand out from the rest in terms of size. They are: the Arias-Ballón Group; the Benavides Group; the Brescia Group; the Castrovirreyna-Volcán Group; the Picasso Group; the Rizo Patrón Group; and Atacocha.[10] The three largest—Arias-Ballón, Benavides, and Picasso—all originated with the medium-mining "boom" that followed the enactment of the 1950 Mining Code, although the Picassos had long owned small mines. Atacocha, the oldest of the "big seven," dates from 1936; Castrovirreyna-Volcán and Rizo Patrón,

---

[9] Several cases were found of Peruvians having set up holding companies in foreign tax havens and having transferred their mining shares to them.

[10] The Arias-Ballón companies are owned outright by Jesús Arias Dávila and the heirs of Alfonso Ballón Eguren, both of whom can be described as self-made "new men." The Benavides Group is controlled by Alberto Benavides de la Quintana and members of his immediate family; he is a cousin to an old landowner family but is a professional geologist and owes his personal fortune entirely to the mining business. The Brescia interests are owned by two multimillionaire rentier brothers of that name whose wealth derives from urban real estate and construction. The Castrovirreyna-Volcán Group is controlled by a collection of ten or so individuals and families, who include mining entrepreneurs, manufacturers, and rentiers. The Picasso Group's controlling interest is held by the Picasso Peraltas, an old landed family; however, they act as rentiers, leaving mining affairs in the hands of Ernesto Baertl Montori, Peru's second most powerful (after Benavides) mining manager. The Rizo Patróns are an old mining family; they control their companies in association with some of the principal Castrovirreyna-Volcán holders (though the link between the two groups is not a controlling one) and have manufacturing interests. Atacocha is controlled by the Gallo family, who are old but lesser landowners.

TABLE 7.2 The Companies of the Peruvian Mediana Minería, with Financial Indicators for 1979 (*Indicators in millions of dollars*)

Name	Type[a]	Nation-ality[b]	Fixed Assets	Paid-In Capital	Gross Sales
Arias-Ballón Group	P	N	17.6	5.1	21.2
La Virreyna			1.2	0.2	3.0
San Ignacio de Morococha (SIMSA)			16.4	4.9	18.2
Benavides Group	C	N	27.2	9.7	56.5
Buenaventura			26.1	9.2	52.3
Caudalosa			n/a	n/a	n/a
Colquirrumi			1.1	0.5	4.2
Brescia Group	C	N	25.3	8.7	50.4
Alianza			14.4	4.5	26.0
Minsur			10.9	4.2	24.4
Castrovirreyna-Volcán Group	C	N	13.5	5.9	31.9
Castrovirreyna (Cía. Minera)			7.5	2.6	20.9
Volcán			6.0	3.3	11.0
Del Castillo Group	P	N	1.1	0.3	2.5
Colquiminas			1.1	0.3	2.5
Minera del Hill			n/a	n/a	n/a
Fernandini Group	P	N	10.5	4.9	7.6
El Brocal			10.5	4.9	7.6
Farallón			n/a	n/a	n/a
Flórez Pinedo Group	P	N	0.8	0.1	3.7
Caridad			0.5	0.1	1.9
Chuvilca			0.3	0.0	1.8
Galjuf-Ukovich Group	P	N	1.5	0.5	3.5
Cerro (Cía. Minera)			n/a	n/a	n/a
Chungar			1.3	0.4	2.3
Vinchos			0.2	0.1	1.2
Gubbins Group	P	N	0.7	0.9	1.6
Sacracancha			0.1	0.3	0.5
Santa Rita			0.6	0.6	1.1
Hochschild Group	C	F	26.0	9.9	37.7
Arcata (Minas de)			13.1	4.9	19.0
Condoroma			4.1	1.6	8.3
Huarato			0.2	0.1	0.0
Locumba			2.5	1.3	2.3
Pativilca			5.6	1.3	7.7
Tamboras			0.1	0.5	n/a
Turmalina			0.4	0.2	0.4

(TABLE 7.2 cont.)

Name	Type[a]	Nation-ality[b]	Fixed Assets	Paid-In Capital	Gross Sales
Loret de Mola Group	P	N	4.5	1.6	7.0
Cercapuquio			0.2	0.2	0.4
Huámpar			4.3	1.4	6.6
Mitsui Group	C	N	16.1	2.1	21.6
Katanga			3.6	0.3	3.3
Santa Luisa			12.5	1.8	18.3
Picasso Group	C	N	39.0	19.1	61.0
Castrovirreyna (Corp.)			5.3	3.3	19.0
Milpo			30.4	13.8	32.2
Pacococha			3.3	2.0	9.8
Proaño Group	P	N	1.7	0.8	11.6
Austria Dúvaz			1.7	0.8	11.6
Tamboraque			0.0	0.0	n/a
Rizo Patrón Group	C	N	11.6	6.9	21.1
Río Pallanga			9.0	5.7	15.7
Sayapullo			2.6	1.2	5.4
Unaffiliated Firms					
Aguila	c	N	17.7	4.9	d
Algamarca	P	N	1.0	0.6	12.3
Atacocha	C	N	18.7	6.5	40.0
Atalaya	P	N	2.6	0.4	2.7
Canaria	P	N	n/a	n/a	n/a
Cata	e	N	n/a	n/a	n/a
Caylloma	P	N	4.1	0.7	10.9
Centraminas	P	N	2.7	0.0	8.3
Chapi (Cobre de)	f	N	3.4	1.3	5.3
Chavín	C	N	1.8	0.7	5.6
Cobre S.R.L.	e	N	n/a	n/a	n/a
Colquipocro	P	N	n/a	n/a	n/a
Condestable	f	N	0.6	0.4	4.1
Cóndor	e	N	n/a	n/a	n/a
El Altiplano	P	N	n/a	n/a	n/a
El Barón	P	N	0.4	0.0	1.1
Gran Bretaña	C	N	5.1	0.8	5.3
Huarón	C	F	18.6	8.1	37.6
Los Mantos	P	N	1.7	0.7	2.2
Los Rosales	P	N	1.0	0.1	1.9
Madrigal	C	F	12.7	4.0	14.7
Málaga Santolalla (Neg.Min.)	P	N	3.6	0.5	3.7
Millotingo	P	N	1.5	1.1	16.9
Northern Peru Mining	C	F	9.2	4.9	31.9
Ocoña	C	F	1.0	0.4	4.1

(TABLE 7.2 cont.)

Name	Type[a]	Nation-ality[b]	Fixed Assets	Paid-In Capital	Gross Sales
Puquio Cocha	P	N	0.4	0.7	0.1
Raura	C	F	22.6	8.5	34.2
San Juan de Lucanas	f	N	n/a	n/a	n/a
San Nícolas	P	N	n/a	n/a	n/a
Santa Fe	P	N	0.7	0.1	1.0
Santander	C	F	3.8	1.7	9.3
Santo Toribio	P	N	1.1	0.2	4.5
Yauli	P	N	0.9	0.5	9.5

SOURCE: Compiled by the author with the assistance of the Departamento de Estudios Económicos y Estadística, Sociedad Nacional de Minería y Petróleo.
[a] C = corporation, defined as a firm with ten or more unrelated shareholders; P = personal business, a firm with less than ten unrelated shareholders. (Note that all firms are formally organized as limited-liability corporations.)
[b] F = foreign-controlled; N = nationally controlled.
[c] Joint venture of the Peruvian state (via COFIDE) and local private capital; the latter holds a 60 percent interest and exercises management rights.
[d] Mine under construction in 1979.
[e] In bankruptcy; operated by an administrative committee appointed by the Ministry of Energy and Mines.
[f] Acquired by the state through bankruptcy or abandonment.

from the forties (again, their current controlling shareholders were involved earlier on in smaller mining firms). The Brescia Group differs from the others in that it is relatively new (1971) and in that it was based not on new mine development but on the acquisition of financial control over existing companies. The "big seven" are so much larger and, for the most part, more dynamic than the others that they deserve to be considered separately.

Apart from sheer size, the "big seven" have some features in common that are not found to a comparable extent in the rest of the Peruvian firms. All are rationally organized, professionally managed corporations. They thus enjoy a wide span of control and true immortality, both conducive to dynamism and growth. (Traditional family firms, in contrast, are limited in growth by the family's personal span of control—assuming, as is usually the case, that the family is reluctant to yield even routine operating control to outsiders—and by the fact that inheritance provides new generations of competent managers by sheer accident at best.) Most are characterized by more widely diffused shareholding than is typical in Peru, where capital ownership is concentrated in very few hands. Buenaventura, the core member of the Benavides Group, has over 1,500 unrelated shareholders—probably more than any other Peruvian firm whatever; Milpo, the core of the Picasso Group, about 600; Atacocha, about 600. These three have raised venture capital by selling shares to the general public and are listed on the Lima Stock Exchange.[11] Finally, all of the "big seven" are principally lead-silver-zinc miners, a more profitable activity (in most years) for lesser firms than is copper mining. Buenaventura's preeminence stems from the fact that it is the country's largest silver producer, outranking even the foreign firms. Atacocha ranks second only to Centromin in national lead production.

Peruvians supplied the entrepreneurial initiative in the founding of five of the "big seven."[12] The exceptions are Castrovirreyna-Volcán and Brescia. The former was assembled in the thirties and forties by James L. Rosenshine, a North American speculator and mine promoter who at one time owned a string of small mines in Peru. He began to sell off his shares to Peruvians in the fifties, a process afterward accelerated by his heirs; control passed to the Peruvian holders between 1965 and 1968. The two Brescia companies were originally set up by French and by British interests (in 1904 and 1960, respectively) and were acquired by W. R. Grace and Company[13] in 1967. Three years later, its extensive agroindustrial holdings having been expropriated, Grace decided to withdraw completely from Peru; it sold the Alianza mine to the Brescia brothers and the Minsur property to the Peruvian "fishmeal czar," Luis Alberto Banchero. Shortly after this purchase Banchero was assassinated, and his estate sold Minsur to the Brescias.[14]

As might be expected in view of its size, the Benavides Group has become the premier Peruvian mining entrepreneur. It sells management services to beleaguered family firms[15] and has set up subsidiaries to build roads and electric power grids in the regions where it operates. Its board chairman, Alberto Benavides de la Quintana, has established a reputation as one of the country's most progressive business leaders. Under his direction the company

[11] Buenaventura is particularly concerned to diffuse its shareholdings and has sought to keep the per-share price within reach of the smaller investor. To that end it instituted in 1978 a seven-for-five stock split—an innovative and extremely rare maneuver in the context of Peruvian corporate life.

[12] Buenaventura's founding was helped by a $200,000 loan from Cerro, which also purchased a third of the new firm's capital shares; but the initiative for setting up the company came from Benavides (at the time he was a Cerro employee) and his partner, Bruno Tschudi, who between them owned its first mineral deposit and a majority equity interest. (Some of the Cerro shares passed to the Peruvian government, which still holds them, when the U.S. company was nationalized; the balance was sold off by Marmon, Cerro's successor, to the French government's Bureau de Recherches Géologiques et Minières.) W. R. Grace and Company bought into Atacocha for a time; but that was in the sixties, long after the company's foundation, and Grace never acquired a controlling interest.

[13] Grace's interests in Peru were far-flung and extended to every sector of the economy; company officials used to boast that no Peruvian could live out a year without coming into contact with their company or with one of its products. On the Grace role in Peru see Burgess and Harbison (1954).

[14] See Peruvian Times, 30 April 1971; also Pease García and Verme Insúa (1974:1:253). Banchero was a notorious financial manipulator who, at the time of his death, stood accused of large-scale bribery and fraud. His murder has never been solved, nor has the motive for it been satisfactorily explained.

[15] It has recently taken over the management of the faltering Fernandini Group's El Brocal mine (it is a mercury producer and has operated more or less continuously since the Spanish Conquest) and has purchased an 11 percent equity interest in it.

has begun to play a pioneering role in regional development;[16] and whenever (as has occurred with some frequency in recent years) state authorities want to explore national capital's possible participation in large mining projects, they look to Benavides to organize it. Buenaventura has also provided the entrepreneurial initiative, some of the equity capital, and managerial counsel for mining projects in Ecuador and Venezuela. This activity, facilitated by the Andean Pact,[17] has made Buenaventura the first transnational firm to be domiciled in Peru and controlled by Peruvians. Moreover, it is the only medium-mining firm that operates several mines under a single corporate roof.

All of the remaining national groups and most of the unaffiliated national firms originated in what might be termed the "early modern" period of Peruvian mining—lasting from the enactment of the 1901 Mining Code to its supercession by the 1950 Code. Only one, Chavín, was founded by a foreigner. Most of these older firms have all but exhausted their mineral reserves; many will either convert themselves into holding companies for other investments or will close up shop. Inept family management has contributed to the problems of more than a few of them. On the other hand, there are several small firms which represent new entrepreneurial endeavors by younger Peruvians—among them, the Del Castillo and Flórez Pinedo groups (the owner of the latter is currently president of Centromin) and Centraminas. Their owners have found that, if technologically proficient, they can break into the mining business with a small initial investment by taking over the operation of older mines under contract and by offering occasional contractor services to the larger firms.

[16] Benavides has paid close attention for many years to the social effects of mining camp life as revealed by the research of Peruvian sociologists, and he is aware of the way in which poor camp conditions can exacerbate a firm's labor problems. It was noted in Chapter 6 how he used his position as a Cerro officer to press for improvements in the company's treatment of its workers, and how he resigned his directorship in protest when his advice was rejected. As Buenaventura's president and (since 1980) board chairman, he has made this long-time concern a formal commitment of his firm and has consistently sought means for making the traditional mining camp contribute more than it has to the development of the sierra. When the firm decided to add new worker housing for one of its mines in Huancavelica department, Benavides ordered the construction of a complete city—Santiago de Cocha Ccasa—at company expense. His aim is to overcome the occupational unidimensionality of the typical mining camp and to create in its stead a socially and economically diverse community; to offer his employees residences physically removed from their workplace; and to draw into this underdeveloped area a variety of small manufacturing, commercial, agricultural, and artisanal businesses. The company is therefore providing business as well as residential and municipal facilities, all of which will be occupant- or community-owned. At its Uchucchacua mine in Lima department, the workers' new townsite is being planned with an eye to beauty as well as function, and care has been taken to stimulate economic linkages with the nearby town of Oyón. Benavides has persistently opposed the prevailing tendency of mining firms to design their electrical power systems and service roads solely for their own needs, arguing that these should be planned from the start to service local communities as well.

[17] The Andean Pact, formally known as the Cartagena Agreement, unites Peru with Venezuela, Colombia, Ecuador, and Bolivia in a regional common market. For discussion and analysis see Tironi (1978a, b); also, Mytelka (1978, 1979).

State Capital in the Mediana Minería

The state has maintained a low entrepreneurial profile in the subsector. It does not want its presence to threaten or antagonize this politically and economically important sector of local private capital, whose nurturing has been a persistent feature of mining policy. Several new medium-mining projects were promoted by state officials after 1968, but only in one—Mina Aguila, a large (by the subsector's norms) copper project—has the state entered as a joint venturer. It did so through the mechanism of a COFIDE equity investment rather than through MineroPeru, which ensures that the management of the enterprise will remain in the hands of the private partners. The Mina Aguila project also includes a copper smelter, the first in the mediana minería and the first to be controlled by private Peruvian interests.[18] The other mines under state ownership were acquired when their private owners went into bankruptcy or otherwise abandoned their properties.[19] These properties have been managed in a way that once again displays the regime's need to placate class forces in civil society. All of the bankrupt or abandoned mines have been kept in operation in order to preserve jobs, as demanded by the miners' unions. On the other hand, early conjecture that they would be used as vehicles for establishing "social property" in the mining sector—a property reform[20] that has never been implemented in the industry—ended in 1978 when one of them, Santo Toribio, was returned to its private owners.[21] We are reminded that bonanza development conduces to capitalist relations of production in natural resources.

In sum, the state may have created propitious conditions for the foundation and growth of a local mediana minería, but most of the firms are monuments to private Peruvian initiative. The rest began as foreign endeavors or as foreign-local joint ventures. However, Peruvians had no difficulty in taking them over as soon as their capital resources and managerial skills enabled them to do so—irrespective of whether foreign capital was individual, small corporate, or transnational. The presence of the "big seven" shows that ownership in the local industry is tending toward concentration, a tendency that the state has done nothing to impede. Significantly, a high degree of

[18] See *Lima Times*, 5 October 1979. Fifteen percent of the capital for the project has been provided by Venezuelan investors.

[19] Two of Mitsui's properties, Condestable (1976) and Chapi (1980), were disposed of in this way; see Table 7.2. In both cases the mines were small and their ore grades were declining; both had been Mitsui's earliest mining investments in Peru. Technically they were sold to the Peruvian government when their parent lost interest in them, but in actual fact they were given away. Mitsui's action in the matter has been wholeheartedly approved by the Peruvian government and will certainly not harm any later effort by the Japanese giant to move into the gran minería.

[20] "Social property" is a form of extended cooperativism in which ownership is vested not in the workers of a particular enterprise but in all workers of all enterprises in the "social property" sector. At various times during the "first phase" of the "revolution" (1968-1975) it was touted as the preferred model for productive property ownership in general. See Adizes (1975a) on the theory of "social property"; on Peruvian practice see Knight (1975) and the brief comment by Gorman (1978).

[21] *El Comercio*, 24 February 1978.

directorial interlocks is observed among the "big seven," but there are few linking them to the smaller firms.[22]

The Foreign Presence

All but one of the fifteen foreign-controlled medium-mining firms are minor subsidiaries of oligopolistic transnational corporations. In this category are found Asarco's Northern Peru Mining, Homestake Mining's Madrigal, St. Joe Minerals' Santander, Marmon's Raura, Peñarroya's Huarón, the Mitsui Group's Katanga and Santa Luisa, and the various mines belonging to the Hochschild Group. The Asarco and Peñarroya investments are both quite old: each was an early effort by its parent at global integration of production; each is now dwarfed by later, larger-scale investments of the parent; and each continues in operation solely because returns on the original investment (which, of course, has long since been recovered) remain adequate.[23] Mitsui's medium mines (they are actually joint ventures with Nippon Mining) were acquired for the usual Japanese purpose of securing long-term sources of supply for the home economy. They were attempts to test the unfamiliar Peruvian waters on a small scale before investing more heavily in the gran minería; they also provided a low-risk opportunity for investigating the adaptation of Japanese mining and metallurgical technologies to the complex composition of Peruvian polymetal ores. Homestake's and St. Joe's projects are best thought of as profitable outlets for small amounts of excess corporate capital, since neither one contributes very much to the world market shares of their highly integrated parents. Ocoña, the one foreign firm whose parent is not a transnational enterprise, is jointly owned by two small Canadian resource companies.

Left to be discussed is the Hochschild Group, which is important for the reason that it represents the only external force in the subsector with a real potential for bringing about denationalization. "Don" Mauricio Hochschild, the group's founder, was until his death in 1965 an internationally renowned mine financier and metals trader. He also enjoyed a good measure of notoriety as one of the Bolivian "tin barons," but with the 1952 revolution he was stripped of his properties and expelled from the country.[24] He later organized

[22] Investigation shows that these interlocks are of the "listening-post" type and do not entail share ownership. They obviously serve to improve policy coordination among the "big seven"; to promote the constitution of joint ventures—which has not yet occurred but is likely to as a vehicle for "big seven" participation in the gran minería; to help present a united front to the state; and (though here, the conscious intent of the parties does not enter) to promote class solidarity.

[23] Their owners might well prefer to liquidate them, but only in exchange for cash payments at least equal to book value of assets—an improbable occurrence. There is reason to believe that Peñarroya wants to retain Huarón in order to keep its fingers on the pulse of the Peruvian minería with minimal risk; logically, Homestake, St. Joe, and Mitsui could well be thinking along similar lines.

[24] The Bolivian events are discussed by Alexander (1958) and Malloy (1970). "Don" Mauricio had a checkered career of high-profile political involvement in Bolivia. Said to have been a principal conduit of U.S. influence, he negotiated a U.S.-Bolivian tin-pricing agreement that was, apparently, quite disadvantageous for the latter. He was also the victim of a sensational political kidnapping and was implicated in at least one *coup d'état* (Andrade 1976:114-21 and

his now far-flung investments as South American Consolidated Enterprises, incorporated in Panama; since his death its ownership has passed to a closed trust incorporated in the Indian state of Assam, which has the effect of making its management wholly independent of shareholder concerns. (It also shields the corporation to the maximum possible degree from the taxation and financial disclosure requirements of the major capitalist powers.) Although South American Consolidated Enterprises is extremely secretive about the financial aspects of its operations, I was able to obtain a copy of its balance sheet and earnings statement for 1976. They show total assets of $319 million, total consolidated sales of $343 million, and a consolidated net profit for the year of $19.2 million earned by subsidiaries—metal traders, processors, and fabricators—in every continent of the globe. Its board chairman at the time, the Honourable Donald M. Fleming (now deceased), was an illustrious member of the international financial elite.[25]

Hochschild's interests in Peruvian medium mining are similar to those of the larger transnational oligopolists. That is, it is less concerned with mining profits in themselves than it is with protecting its market share and integrated-producer status through the control of an appropriate amount of mine production. Mine ownership in Peru has been acquired in one of two ways. In the cases of Arcata, Pativilca, and a few other firms since sold off to local citizens, ownership came as a byproduct of metals trading: the Hochschild trading subsidiary extended advance payments to the mine owners secured by the latter's capital shares and then took over the mines by foreclosure when the original shareholders were unable to repay the advances.[26] In the cases of the five other Hochschild mines, investment was organized *ab initio* in the form of joint ventures with local participation; all were designed to utilize Hochschild technology and to feed their output into the Hochschild worldwide sales network.[27] Local capitalists, most of them owners of other

---

passim; also Frontaura Argadoña 1974). Note that he was not related to the Hochschilds who are prominent in AMAX.

[25] While the final manuscript was being prepared, it was revealed (*Wall Street Journal*, 22 December 1981, p. 22) that Anglo-American Group will acquire a 40 percent holding in South American Consolidated Enterprises. This will make it the second major European mining transnational to stake out a claim in Peru; Rio Tinto-Zinc plans a joint gold-mining venture with a Peruvian mining and metal-trading group.

As for Mr. Fleming: a Canadian citizen, his career included service as finance minister and justice minister under John Diefenbaker; chairmanship of the OECD; and membership on the boards of governors of the World Bank and the IMF. He retired from public life in 1963 but reemerged four years afterward to contest for the leadership of Canada's Progressive Conservative party. While board chairman of the Hochschild Group, Fleming was also managing director of the Bank of Nova Scotia Trust Company and a director of numerous other firms (*Who's Who 1979*).

[26] There is little reason for viewing this as a deliberate strategy for gaining control. Borrowing from traders in advance of sales is a common way of raising working capital for production at low rates of interest. The borrower's risks—that prices will have fallen by the time that the production has to be sold to repay the loan, or that unforeseen contingencies may eat up the loan proceeds without there being sufficient production—are well understood in the industry.

[27] Interview with Fernando Núñez Barclay (a Hochschild official), September 14, 1977.

mining firms, own a majority of every one of the five, but all are managed by Hochschild under contract.

This strategy is a clever one for a small transnational enterprise like South American Consolidated to adopt, as it greatly minimizes economic and political risk. Dependable sources of ores and concentrates have been acquired with the outlay of much less new capital than would be needed for full financial control; most of the capital is instead raised locally, by Peruvians.[28] All of the mines, being under nominal Peruvian ownership, are "insured" against nationalization and are eligible for all benefits limited to locally owned companies. Hochschild comes to share through the joint venture arrangements a set of immediate economic interests held in common by local mining capitalists, assuring it of powerful allies in any dispute with the government. Meanwhile, efficient operation of the mines is guaranteed by managerial control, ready access to international expertise and finance, etc.

Hochschild is the only foreign entity which maintains a significant number of directorial interlocks with local firms. The majority of these are incidental to its joint ventures. However, it is also Hochschild policy to provide outside directors (i.e., directors who do not represent an ownership interest) to Peruvian companies requesting them. Some smaller ones do, for they see this as a way of obtaining free access to transnational technology and managerial knowledge without having to deal with an overwhelming foreign presence. (Hochschild's operations are highly decentralized, and its personnel who serve as outside directors are Peruvian nationals; consequently, the recipient firms have less reason to fear that their outside director responds to external commands.) From Hochschild's point of view, the stationing of one of its managers on the board of an unaffiliated company creates a propensity for the latter to employ Hochschild metal-trading services (if the terms are otherwise competitive) in preference to independents; we have seen that gaining access to sources of supply is a major Hochschild preoccupation.

Note that no Hochschild personnel are found sitting as outside directors on the boards of the "big seven." These stronger national firms do not need its advice and want to remain as free as possible to negotiate their own sales arrangements.

It appears, then, that the structure of the Peruvian mediana minería is not such as to make the national institutions of the subsector subservient to foreign ones. From 1968 to 1980 not a single locally owned firm fell under foreign control, but there were seven instances in which once-foreign entities—wholly owned mines or majority-owned joint ventures—were transferred to local ownership. Although Hochschild's peculiar blandishments receive a certain response from some small mine owners, the "big seven" are unaffected by them.

---

[28] Peruvian investors have been historically reluctant to enter into joint ventures with foreign mining interests, since there are good opportunities locally available which do not vest control in a distant management. Hochschild's decentralized operations serve to ameliorate local investor worries on this score.

MEDIUM MINING'S TIES TO OTHER BOURGEOIS ELEMENTS

Peru's political and economic history encourages us to think of her national bourgeoisie as consisting of four principal components. There is, first, an urban-industrial or modern-sector class element centering around manufacturing, civil engineering and construction, and communications. (I exclude the manufacture of expendable inputs to the mining industry, as these activities are controlled by mining interests.) It used to define its interests narrowly in terms of the domestic market, but it was never powerful enough to win a government commitment to highly protected import-substitution industrialization under national auspices. However, it has shown greater dynamism since the early seventies and has succeeded in extracting government export-promotion assistance.[29] Its opposite pole within the bourgeoisie was, until the 1969 agrarian reform, the agro-export element. Existing in close alliance with a traditional landed class of an undeniably precapitalist character,[30] the agro-exporters were themselves owners of vast estates; they were neither nationalist nor developmentalist, avidly supported laissez faire, and formed the mainstay of the oligarchic order.

The gap between these two poles was filled by finance capital. Yet, this third bourgeois class element was hardly a neutral arbiter between the previous two. Local finance capital had originated with the "plutocracy of guano" and with agro-export surpluses and was closely linked by both economic interests and social-familial relationships to the agro-exporters and to foreign capital. Hence, it too formed a part of the oligarchic order, a part to which the urban-industrial bourgeoisie was made to defer.

The fourth and final class element is the mining bourgeoisie, whose position with respect to the others has heretofore been regarded as somewhat ambiguous: its core economic interests are export-oriented, and its origins (in time and also in family lineage) parallel those of the agro-exporters; but the nature of its operations and of its labor control system give it more in common with the urban-industrial element. We need to clear up this ambiguity in order to get a better picture of the role of mining within the whole bourgeoisie. The best way of doing so is by examining ownership ties between mining and the other bourgeois activities. Since share ownership data outside of mining are notoriously difficult to come by, I shall proceed indirectly by assuming that mining company directors who represent nonmining interests owe their board presence to an ownership stake; my argument is that few if any nonmining activities would have need of "listening posts" inside the industry, nor would mining firms be concerned to obtain "expert counsel" from individuals who lack industry expertise.[31]

[29] Principally by way of the CERTEX program, which offers tax rebates to exporters of "nontraditional" export goods.

[30] Long (1975) discusses the elaborate systems of labor control—few of which bear much of a relation to capitalist wage labor—in the Peruvian agricultural sector prior to land reform.

[31] It might seem that outside directors representing banks could have been valuable. However, all but four "Peruvian" banks were controlled by foreign interests before their nationalization;

Strong linkages between the mining and urban-industrial sectors would tend to suggest the presence of a cohesive national industrial bourgeoisie. That is to say, intrabourgeois relationships founded on common social origins, social interaction and affective ties, mutuality of outlook, and so forth would be more firmly cemented by the powerful influence of manifestly common economic interests. The result *might* be a unified class committed to national capitalist development and industrialization.

Linkages between the mining and oligarchic sectors—agriculture and finance—are another story. The agricultural and financial bourgeoisies were destroyed as socioeconomic groupings by the land reform and the nationalization of most of the banking system, but many of the former integrants of both still reside in the country. It is to be anticipated that their values, ideology, and way of doing business, all formed in the oligarchic mold, will not have changed very much in a mere ten or so years. Indeed, the circumstances of their demise may well have produced a defensive hardening of reactionary attitudes. According to Carlos Malpica, whose well-known studies of the Peruvian oligarchy[32] depend heavily on surname identification, the oligarchy had gained control of most of the mediana minería by the late sixties. If he is right, ex-oligarchs should still control it; for expropriation of their agricultural and banking properties did not affect their mining shareholdings, on which they would naturally be even more economically dependent than before. Their anti-national, anti-developmental values would then express themselves through the actions of the medium-mining firms.

The linkages that I discovered are schematized in Table 7.3, where the symbol *o* denotes a link present in 1968 but gone by 1975-1977, and where *x* denotes one that was maintained throughout the seven- to nine-year interval. (There were no observed instances of new linkages appearing during the period.) We see that the domestic mediana minería has never been closely linked with finance capital or with the civil engineering-construction industry. But some ties to manufacturing exist, and there were a significant number of linkages to agriculture before the land reform.

Upon further investigation it was found that only one of the links to manufacturing was entrepreneurial in character. In other words, except for that one instance the links were not there because an industrial entrepreneur had founded a mining firm, or vice versa.[33] What is more, none of the ownership interests represented by these directorial interlocks appeared to be controlling,

---

these foreign-owned banks would occasionally extend routine short-term credits to mining companies, but they regarded other investments in the domestic minería as excessively risky. The state-owned Banco de la Nación felt that mine finance was the province of the Banco Minero. The Banco Minero lent to mining companies but was undercapitalized (prior to the early 1970s) and had a limited lending capacity. The Banco Popular, controlled by the Prado family, usually lent only to the family's many enterprises. The Banco Wiese, alone among the private, truly Peruvian banks, did finance mines; the few observed financial-sector interlocks involved this institution.

[32] Malpica (1976, 1980).

[33] The exception is the Rizo Patrón Group, whose controlling interest, an old mining family, later branched out into the manufacture of cement.

TABLE 7.3 Directorial Interlocks between the Mediana Minería and Other Sectors of the Peruvian Economy (*o* = *1968 and before, x* = *1975-1977*)

Mining Company or Group	Other Sectors[a]			
	A	B	C	M
Algamarca	o			
Atacocha	o			
Brescia Group	o		x	x
Castrovirreyna-Volcán Group	o	o		x
Caylloma				x
Fernandini Group	o	o		x
Gubbins Group	o			
Hochschild Group	o	o		x
Picasso Group	o		x	x
Rizo Patrón Group	o			x
Yauli	o			

SOURCES: Compiled by the author from information presented in the consolidated declarations of the mining companies and in Malpica (1976), supplemented by additional data supplied by private sources.
[a] A = agriculture, B = banking and finance, C = construction, M = manufacturing.

inasmuch as none of them involved a board chairman, a chief executive officer, or an identifiable controlling shareholder. My conclusion, therefore, is that the links to manufacturing are representative of noncontrolling rentier investment in both sectors by the same moneyed individual or family. These results are consistent with information gleaned from interviews, industry publications, and other sources. They imply that the mining industry, while dynamic, directs essentially all of its entrepreneurial energies toward its own growth and toward specialized industrial activities associated with mining. That is less a reflection on the quality of the subsector's entrepreneurship, however, than it is a verification that the subsector itself still offers ample opportunities for further capital accumulation; so long as it does, one ought not to expect mining entrepreneurs to venture abroad into areas where they lack expertise.

When the former linkages to agriculture are probed in more detail, it turns out that every case where a landed oligarch served as a mining company director can be traced back to his or her family's ownership of an important block of the company's capital shares. There were no instances in which prominent oligarchs served on mining firm boards without holding more than 5 percent of the outstanding equity. On the one hand, this indicates that it was not the custom of the mining companies to appoint oligarchs as outside directors—which, presumably, would most likely have been done to take advantage of their social prestige, influence with the financial sector, or political "clout." On the other hand, it does not indicate that the oligarchy exercised effective control. I pursued the question of effective control by studying management tenure, practices, and policies. Only in the cases of Algamarca, the Fernandini Group, and Yauli—all small entities by current subsectoral standards—did I find evidence of the exercise of decision-making executive power on the part of ex-oligarchs. Thus, ex-oligarchic investment in the mediana minería is also of the rentier type.

There is no mystery as to why the mediana minería became a preferred outlet for passive investors with idle cash and why so many of them were of the oligarchy. A few *latifundistas* of the sierra discovered mineral deposits on their lands, denounced them, and then arranged for mining professionals to develop them. The more prosperous owners of coastal *latifundios* needed investments that would support their high-consumption life styles by protecting their cash surpluses against inflation and devaluation of the sol (since most of the luxury goods that they consumed were imported).[34] Mining shares are an investment that meets these requirements.

Notice that oligarchic capital was not generally invested in foreign-controlled firms other than Hochschild's. (Cerro had tried to marshal local capital for new mining projects during the sixties but did not succeed.) In manufacturing, Peruvian rentiers have preferred to invest in transnational subsidiaries because they feel that the transnationals' possession of better technologies, large financial resources, protected trademarks, marketing expertise, etc., makes their investments more secure. The perception in mining is different. The profits and security of investment of a well-managed local firm are comparable to those of the transnational subsidiaries. And the passive investor need never be concerned that a foreign management will decide to close down the mine or limit production because costs are lower or ore grades higher somewhere else.

Fortunately for the domestic industry, this oligarchic desire for secure local investments dovetailed neatly with the need of early mining entrepreneurs for capital—which they could rarely obtain abroad and only with great difficulty from local banks.[35] Inasmuch as the oligarchic investors had no mining expertise, the mining entrepreneurs could feel safe in accepting equity contributions that would not deprive them of effective control.

None of the above should be read as implied support for the doctrine of managerialism—the claim that the professional managers who run the affairs of business firms have interests fundamentally different from those of passive investors and that, in consequence, there is no unified bourgeois class interest. On the contrary, all the evidence suggests that mining managers are as concerned to maximize profits and to accumulate capital as are the rentiers. (Neither is there a conflict over dividend distributions versus retention of

[34] Since their agricultural fortunes were based on the exploitation of peasant labor, they had no need to reinvest earnings in agricultural capitalization. They showed little knowledge of industrial operations and tended to be educated in high-status occupations such as the liberal professions rather than in those with practical business applications. See Astiz (1969); Bourricaud (1970); and Larson and Bergen (1969).

[35] See n. 31, this chapter, with regard to the lending activities of local banks.

profits, since the rentier interest lies with holding shares as an inflation and devaluation hedge; reinvested profits tend to increase the market value of shares.) It additionally suggests that the latter do not contest for control because they receive greater economic benefits when they allow expert managers to go about their jobs unimpeded.[36] But the issue of the managerial or rentier character of control cannot just be waved away, for it says a good deal regarding the nature of bourgeois class practice, including political-ideological action. The significance of managerial control in mining will be more fully explored in Chapter 9.

THE DYNAMICS OF THE MEDIANA MINERÍA

We are now in a position to evaluate the relative dynamism and competitive advantages of the key firms of the subsector. This will be done by studying their economic performance over time, beginning (for reasons stated earlier; see n. 3) in 1967. The aim of the study is to reveal how effective these economic units have been in accumulating and utilizing capital, and whether that effectiveness has required the presence of outside factors, e.g., finance capital. A diachronic evaluation of firm performance will enable us to discern important trends for the future of the industry and of the bourgeois class element that it supports.

Given that a central preoccupation of the class analysis of Peruvian society is the question of possible national-bourgeois subservience to foreign capital, the analysis will focus on comparing the performance of the national firms with the foreign subsidiaries—these last partially disaggregated by nationality so as to show up any systematic differences which derive from the parent's country of domicile and/or its status in the world oligopoly. The treatment of the Peruvian firms takes into account the discovery of a domestic "big seven," firms that differ notably from their smaller brethren. It measures the preeminence of the "big seven," regarding tendencies toward concentration in the national industry as a positive competitive factor vis-à-vis foreign capital.

Concentration means the agglomeration of smaller, independent enterprises into fewer, larger economic units and the tendency of the latter to grow at a faster rate than the former; it is not to be understood as the mere disappearance of smaller units, leaving the larger ones unchanged. Its progression in the Peruvian mining industry has no negative impact on employment, since geology, not company size, limits the degree of capital intensity that can usefully be introduced. Nonetheless, it results in the realization of other economies of scale: increased administrative efficiency, bigger purchase volumes (with

[36] The issue of managers versus rentier investors as an aspect of class composition is taken up in theoretical terms by Zeitlin (1974) and by Zeitlin and Norich (1979). Their conclusion agrees with mine, although I differ with them (their work specifically concerns the United States) as to their belief that managers do not constitute a distinguishable bourgeois class element.

more price leverage in the buyer's favor), pooling of mine production to earn superior large-lot prices and to obtain better transport and insurance terms, and so on. An economic unit with greater total assets and a greater amount of paid-in capital finds it much easier to concert outside financing when needed. Above all, size conduces to the introduction of the corporate form of enterprise and to reliance on skilled professional management. The historical record of the industry demonstrates beyond doubt that in today's market the one-person or family firm can barely survive; and, insofar as its survival depends on an economically inefficient exploitation of exhaustible natural resources, it is a drain on the nation's nonrenewable wealth.

Moreover, it is certain that the fewer, more powerful firms in a highly concentrated industry are better placed to resist the inroads of foreign investment than would be a large number of weak, widely scattered firms. The state, which wants to increase mining exports and will accept foreign investment to accomplish its purpose, will be more resistant to foreign requests for grants of access if it perceives that enterprises of the domestic private sector are large and efficient enough to undertake the projects that it has in mind.

Figure 6 displays the changing weight of foreign-controlled medium-mining firms in the production of the subsector's wealth. The upper part of the figure, designated as Fig. 6a, plots the percentage of the entire mediana minería's GVP that was generated by foreign companies between 1967 and 1979. The military regime was ready, for the sake of bonanza development, to allow some new medium-scale foreign investment in mining, so long as it did not preempt opportunities claimed by locals. Japanese investment was particularly encouraged in the interest of investment-source diversification; it was hoped that, if given the chance to gain local experience in medium mining, the Japanese would eventually invest in the gran minería. Figure 6a shows that foreign capital's share of the subsector's GVP rose for a time due to this influx of new foreign investment. But its share never became majoritarian; and after peaking in 1976, it declined rapidly to around 26 percent. To put it otherwise, the domestic industry was able to accommodate significant amounts of new foreign investment without being displaced, and at the end of the "revolution" it emerged with a greater share of GVP than it had at the start.

In Fig. 6b the foreign contribution is disaggregated according to its two predominant nationalities, North American and Japanese (this part of the figure shows ER as well as GVP). Clearly, the hoped-for diversification of investment sources has not been reflected in firm performance. Although new investment activity during the period increased for a while the Japanese share of GVP produced by all foreign firms and proportionately lowered the North American share, by 1979 both had returned essentially to where they stood in 1967. This does not mean that the role of U.S. capital in the mediana minería has expanded; in fact it has contracted, inasmuch as the North American bite now comes out of a smaller slice of the overall pie. It does mean

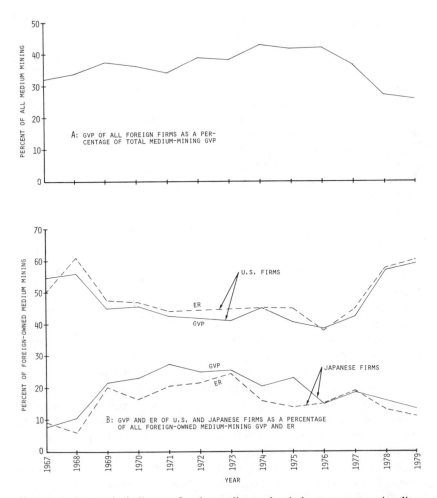

FIGURE 6. Economic indicators for the mediana minería by corporate nationality, 1967-1979. In (a), GVP of all foreign-controlled enterprises as a percentage of sub-sector's total GVP. In (b), GVP and ER of U.S. and Japanese firms as percentages of GVP and ER for all foreign firms. Computed in part by the author and in part by the Departamento de Estudios Económicos y Estadística, Sociedad Nacional de Minería y Petróleo, from data furnished in the companies' consolidated declarations.

that the performance of the Japanese companies has not been the success story elsewhere associated with them. According to my informants, Japanese mining investment in Peru has suffered severely from an incomprehension of local regulations, practices, and customs. Production has been especially plagued by labor problems, which are said to be the worst in the subsector. Local executives admit that their difficulties with labor have stymied their progress in the country; they attribute them to their unpreparedness to face the enormous differences between local labor relations and those in the home country.[37]

Figure 6b also indicates that the Japanese share is somewhat smaller, and the U.S. share correspondingly larger, when measured in terms of ER rather than GVP. It follows that subtractions from GVP which yield ER are proportionately larger in the Japanese case than in the North American. Recall that these subtractions are composed of payouts to other industries. Pursuing this clue, I closely inspected the consolidated declarations of the Japanese and U.S. firms for the years in question; as anticipated, I discovered that the Japanese have regularly applied against gross income larger deductions for loan amortization and, above all, depreciation than have their U.S. counterparts. As depreciation pays for the replacement of fixed capital consumed in production, I conclude that Japanese mining investment has been designed to promote sales of mining machinery from the home country to a greater relative extent than has the North American. This is consistent with the view of Japanese interests in overseas mining that was presented in our discussion of the "Japanese contradiction" in Chapter 4. In the case of the mediana minería, Peru's attempt to exploit the "Japanese contradiction" for increasing exports and diversifying investment sources has a price attached—less of the new value produced remains in the country.

Figure 7 charts the value produced by the "big seven" as compared to the combined GVP of all local firms. In GVP terms, concentration in the local industry has advanced spectacularly: the "big seven" increased their share of GVP from 46 percent at the beginning of the period to around 70 percent at the end. (The dip in 1973 resulted from that year's copper price rise; it benefited other local firms more than the "big seven," who mine mostly lead, silver, and zinc.) The growth of the "big seven" relative to the universe of national firms is verified by other data as well: their share of the domestic companies' net fixed assets rose from 17 to 71 percent between 1967 and 1979; and there was an increase in their share of paid-in industry capital, from 43 to 75 percent.[38]

The progress of the "big seven" does not come at the cost of pushing smaller firms to the wall in a competitive squeeze. Internal competition within the industry is simply nonexistent, and a small mining company blessed with a rich deposit can continue to prosper in absolute terms (and in terms of return on the owners' investment) even though its proportion of the subsector's production and profit is becoming less. True, that proportionate decline weakens the smaller firms' voices in government councils. But this would only be

[37] The problems have been exacerbated by Japanese insistence on using home-country personnel down to the middle-mangement level rather than making better use of the Japanese-Peruvian community—which has produced a fair number of mining professionals. One might also hypothesize that the earlier and more extensive Japanese experience in Brazil led them to believe that anywhere in Latin America they could count on a state able and willing to control labor for them.
[38] The 1967 percentages were computed from data in the consolidated declarations of the companies; those for 1979, from the data in Table 7.2.

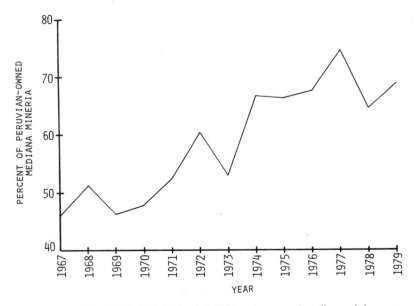

FIGURE 7. Combined GVP of the "big seven" Peruvian-owned medium-mining groups as a percentage of the GVP of all nationally owned firms of the mediana minería. Data sources are the same as for Fig. 6.

a problem for them should the "big seven" decide, with respect to some contentious policy matter, to throw in their lot with the foreign firms against the interests of their weaker compatriots. No such thing has happened during the time period covered by this study, and the nature of the industry makes it unlikely that it will.

Does the growth of the "big seven" depend on financial support from abroad, as does that of the foreign firms? (Some of the large local companies maintain lines of credit with major U.S. banks.) Could their growth therefore make them "front men" for foreign penetration? Table 7.4 gives the standard accounting measure of the corporate debt burden—the ratio of long-term debt to shareholder equity[39]—for the whole subsector and for various breakdowns of firms. By way of comparison, transnational mining corporations seem to carry consolidated debt-to-equity ratios in the 0.1-1.0 range, although the ratio can be higher if they are in the midst of financing a major new project.[40] The average debt-to-equity ratios of all national firms and of the foreign subsidiaries in Peru lie within this range. What is remarkable is the exceptionally low debt burden borne by the "big seven"—this despite the fact that they have added appreciably to assets in these years. *The growth of the "big seven" has been almost entirely self-financed out of retained earnings and*

[39] Long-term debt is defined as debt obligations amortizable over more than one year; shareholder equity is the excess of total corporate assets over total liabilities.

[40] My computation, using data in the 1973-1976 annual reports of Asarco, Newmont, and Phelps-Dodge as the sample.

TABLE 7.4 Ratio of Long-Term Debt to Shareholder Equity for the Mediana Minería and Selected Subdivisions, 1967-1979

Year	Total Subsector	All National Firms	National "Big Seven"	All Foreign Firms
1967	.437	.453	.005	.397
1968	.307	.226	.047	.496
1969	.215	.112	.024	.439
1970	.357	.119	.002	.917
1971	.455	.282	.080	.808
1972	.334	.128	.098	.727
1973	.258	.230	.039	.305
1974	.160	.119	.023	.226
1975	.293	.342	.072	.214
1976	.542	.283	.141	.234
1977	.427	.258	.111	.186
1978	.268	.806	.043	.130
1979	.197	.585	.065	.049

SOURCE: Computed by the author from data in the consolidated declarations of the companies and provided by the Departamento de Estudios Económicos y Estadística, Sociedad Nacional de Minería y Petróleo.

reserves. Self-financing to such an extent implies a high degree of earnings retention and a correspondingly low degree of dividend distribution. Whatever else one wishes to say about the Peruvian mining bourgeoisie, its leading element cannot be accused of squandering its capital by diverting it to personal consumptive use.[41]

Self-financing is only possible, needless to say, if there is a steady flow of profits to reinvest. It is thus worthy of note that during the years from 1967 to 1979 the return on invested capital realized by the "big seven" consistently outperformed the average of all national firms and, in eight of these thirteen years, even outperformed the foreign firms; see Table 7.5. As a group the "big seven" continued to earn profits in times of depressed metals prices, such as 1975—an exceptionally bad year for the foreigners.

Let us now sum up. The overall picture is one of an economic subsector in excellent health as seen from the point of view of a national entrepreneurial bourgeoisie. The subsector has been penetrated by foreign capital, but foreign economic power within it has not become preponderant. One group of foreign investors, the Japanese, has been quite unsuccessful in establishing itself as

[41] Interestingly, one reads in today's U.S. financial and popular press a growing chorus of complaints that excessive dividend payouts are one cause of the increasing weakness of U.S. industry vis-à-vis its Japanese and European competition. U.S. managers reply that high dividends are necessary to protect the value of their shares in the market.

TABLE 7.5 Returns on Invested Capital for the Mediana Minería and Selected Subdivisions, 1967-1979 (*Percent*)

Year	Total Subsector	All National Firms	National "Big Seven"	All Foreign Firms
1967	37.2	33.4	41.8	50.6
1968	55.2	55.5	62.6	54.6
1969	56.6	54.8	43.4	60.7
1970	23.6	24.5	16.7	22.0
1971	-1.7	-3.0	2.1	0.4
1972	1.6	3.4	7.6	-1.0
1973	23.8	10.6	39.3	48.2
1974	26.3	24.8	36.4	28.7
1975	-15.3	-11.1	1.8	-22.9
1976	-0.8	2.2	14.9	-8.9
1977	4.3	3.6	8.1	5.9
1978	22.0	22.0	24.4	22.3
1979	43.8	40.0	44.4	62.2

SOURCE: See Table 7.4.

a force to be reckoned with, in spite of considerable effort. On all measures the "big seven" have moved forward in the face of the foreign presence, giving the subsector, on balance, more of a national complexion than it had before the "revolution." The structural changes which made this progress possible have developed autochthonously and were not imposed by the state. They have strengthened the industry through concentration of more of its activities in the hands of larger economic units. The biggest national firms have evolved into highly modern corporations in both organization and behavior, which has helped them to withstand such adversities as occasionally depressed international metals prices. They grow by reinvesting their earnings and are independent of outside financing. That keeps them autonomous. However, it may also limit their future growth potential.

MEDIUM MINING AND TECHNOLOGICAL DEVELOPMENT[42]

The Peruvian firms of the mediana minería make use of mining technologies that originated in Europe and the United States. In this sense the industry depends on "imported" technology. But it is not technologically dependent to any serious extent.

Although the scale of these companies' mining operations does not conduce to the effective utilization of the latest high-volume technologies, that is an

[42] Much of the information in this section was obtained from an interview with Mario Samamé Boggio, director of INGEMMET, on August 20, 1981.

advantage for a developing country like Peru. It makes it possible for local industry to develop and prosper using technologies appropriate to the national factor endowment—specifically, its labor surplus and relative shortage of energy. It also does away with many of the problems cited in the literature with respect to technology transfer,[43] since the technologies in question are standardized and are available free of charge. (In the few instances where royalties must be paid, as in the local manufacture of certain mine machinery items under license, the amounts involved are said to be minimal.)

As is to be expected in an industrially developing capitalist economy, the existence of a viable, growing national mining industry has stimulated the local production of tools and equipment to supply it. The country now produces flotation machinery (used in the process of concentrating ores), mills for ore grinding, air-powered rock drills, and the like. Because the mining firms earn large enough profits that they can afford to import foreign-made machines even if import duties must be paid, the local capital-goods industry has faced competitive pressure to improve its product. I am told that it has indeed done so in recent years, thanks to the introduction of better welding techniques and a better understanding of the need for quality control. The skills acquired by the manufacturing industry in supplying the mining sector should stand it in good stead when it begins to undertake the local production of a wider range of capital goods.

On the other hand, the complexity of Peruvian polymetal ores mined in the mediana minería creates challenges for technological innovation in ore chemistry and metallurgy. Each mining company has had to learn how to tailor its processing methods to the composition of its particular ores, as well as how to adjust the process as ore composition changes. Local medium-mining firms are currently experimenting with variations of the new "lixi-viation" technique[44] for separating ore constituents and improving metal yields.

This strategy for technological and industrial development, admittedly, cannot be replicated everywhere, for it requires the prior existence of a tool-using industry which is largely under national control. Nevertheless, it is noteworthy that, given the necessary prerequisite, the competitive forces of international capitalism have acted to further the strategy's success rather than to impede it—the dependencista conception. They have done this in two ways: (1) By compelling the domestic mining industry to accept internationally determined prices for its products, they have divorced the mining bourgeoisie's

---

[43] A listing of the extensive literature on this topic will be found in Lester (1974). Policy issues are reviewed in OECD (1974). Goulet (1977) has studied the problem in depth, considering its ethical dimension as well as its socioeconomic aspects. A useful counterweight to the generally critical tone adopted in most of this literature is the more optimistic discussion by Arrow (1962).

[44] This technique entails the leaching of metallic constituents from the ores with acids, after which the metal-rich acidic solution is combined with liquid "lixiviating agents." These are chemical compounds or bacterial flora which have the effect of selectively attracting different metal ions in the solution. The purified metal-bearing solutions are finally drawn off and the metals extracted by electrodeposition. The technique is attractive because air pollution is greatly reduced, costs are low, and metal extraction takes place (except for the final stage) in a continuous-flow process.

interest in capital accumulation from any desire to acquire the latest and most elaborate technologies regardless of cost. The industry has no choice but to borrow and/or develop moderate-scale technologies appropriate to its economic and geological situation if it wishes to survive. (2) By creating effective but not overwhelming competition for the domestic manufacture of mining machinery, they have spurred domestic manufacturers to improve their product until it becomes a sound alternative to imports.

CONCLUSIONS: ENTREPRENEURS, NOT COMPRADORS

The bourgeoisie of the Peruvian mediana minería is not being displaced by foreigners, in spite of the fact that its apparent competition comes from transnational subsidiaries—with the usual advantages of direct access to markets, technology, and financing that transnational linkages provide. Neither can it be validly described as a comprador class. Expecting those few of its members who have chosen to invest in the Hochschild joint ventures, it does not encourage partnerships with foreign interests; it does not agitate for government action opening the door wider to foreign investment, yet it does not clamor for protection; and it is not subordinate to anti-national domestic groups. Instead, the class element has utilized the economic insitutions under its control to accumulate capital entrepreneurially—i.e., through a process of continuous reinvestment and self-fueled growth. Its integrants founded the vast majority of the local firms and consolidated them; now they are advancing into new projects of larger scope and are making profitable investments elsewhere in Latin America.

The progress of the mediana minería has not been an outgrowth of a conscious struggle to overcome foreign preeminence. Consequently, there is little in the actions of these firms or in the behavior of their owners and managers to suggest an overt and strident nationalism. Still, my conversations with them convince me that they *are* nationalist; they strongly believe that the proper role for foreign investment in mining is solely to do what they themselves cannot. They would prefer that foreign capital limit its future activities to the gran minería, and even there they are beginning to demand opportunities to make equity investments in new projects. They also defend those aspects of mining law that discriminate in favor of domestic enterprise.[45] And they oppose the extension of incentives for which only foreign-sponsored projects can effectively qualify.[46]

The state's nurturing role in the capitalist development of the subsector has been useful but minor and does not fundamentally account for the success of the more dynamic local firms. Indeed, it can be argued that the state's principal

[45] For example, the limitation of Banco Minero and INGEMMET services to locally owned firms; and the lower income taxes that local firms pay.

[46] They have obtained a victory on this issue with the enactment of the 1981 Mining Code. As was noted in Chapter 3, the new law does away with the formal distinction between gran and mediana minería; in so doing it assures that future investment incentives will not be reserved for projects of very large scale and scope that only transnational enterprises can attempt.

contribution to that development lies in what it has *not* done. It has refrained from attempting to implement "social property" in the subsector and, by so doing, has given the bourgeoisie no cause to retard its rate of reinvestment or otherwise behave as if it feared for the future. It has also done nothing to slow or reverse the process of concentration on which the competitive strength of the domestic industry depends.

There is a structural problem in the isolation of the subsectoral economy and of its leading bourgeois from the larger industrial scene. Whereas medium mining has provided a vital stimulus to the local production of capital goods, the subsector continues to export nearly all of its output in an unfinished condition. Were the managers of the "big seven" prepared to sacrifice short-term profits for the sake of national development, they might begin to consider forward integration and to channel some of their retained earnings into extending the local fabrication of semifinished products—copper cable, tubing, lead battery plates, dry cells, etc.—for domestic consumption and for export to other industrializing Third World countries. (Some progress has been made in the local production of zinc die castings, however.) But the export markets and competitive conditions there are unfamiliar to Peruvian mining people. Few of the industry's entrepreneurs are prepared yet for bold ventures of this sort.

In brief, the bourgeoisie of the medium-mining subsector does appear to exhibit a good deal of entrepreneurial dynamism in business affairs and has proven that it can define its interests on the basis of national realities, independently of the concerns of foreign capital. Nonetheless, the class element displays few signs of Schumpeterian "heroism"—that is, an entrepreneurial vigor so unlimited and all-encompassing that it radically transforms national economic, social, and political institutions such as to clear the path for autonomous capitalist development.[47] Instead, this radical transformation—if that be an accurate characterization of Peru's course under military rule—had to be implemented by proxy, much as José Nun describes in his discussion of the "middle-class military coup."[48]

The adoption of "heroic" standards of bourgeois performance obviously serves the ideological purposes of defenders of capitalism, enabling them to go on portraying it as a progressive force in the history of human development *and* as one that liberates individual human energies. Less obvious but equally true is that it is of ideological value to the dependencista Left as well; since the standard is one to which today's bourgeoisies of the world "periphery" plainly do not measure up, the conclusion can be drawn that capitalism in the "periphery" lacks in practice this potential for progress. One suspects that a standard so adaptable to diametrically opposed ideological ends and so out of touch with observed class practice cannot be terribly useful for un-

[47] Schumpeter (1935, 1942).
[48] Nun (1967, 1968, 1973).

derstanding and interpreting present-day capitalist reality. The point is well made by Frits Wils, who writes with Peru in mind.[49]

Wils argues that the Schumpeterian standard offers a distorted view of the capitalist development of the West and ahistorically ascribes to all bourgeoisies qualities that were actually possessed by just a few. It neglects the roles played by other societal groups (Wils mentions "ideologues," organized labor, the middle strata) in shaping the nature of capitalist development. Most of all it ignores the independent role of the capitalist state, which often leads the process of transformation (the more so the later the process begins, according to Alexander Gerschenkron)[50] rather than issuing from it. The "heroic" image of the bourgeoisie, then, undervalues the political dimension of organized social life. When invoked by liberals it expresses their preference for attributing political outcomes to the workings of economic forces in civil society. When invoked by Marxists the error is the same, although here we might better characterize it by the term "economism" as it is used in Marxian theory: viz., the belief that the political "superstructure" lacks autonomy, so that what takes place in it is mostly epiphenomenal and is really determined by forces acting in the economic "infrastructure." "Economism" is coming under increasing attack from within the Marxian intellectual tradition.[51]

By abandoning "economistic" orthodoxies we may see the Peruvian mining bourgeoisie as a *potential* force for "progressive" capitalist development.[52] Yet we can simultaneously recognize that the realization of this potential is contingent on factors other than those relating to entrepreneurial performance: the relationship of the bourgeoisie to the state; its political-ideological class practice; the character and practices of contending classes. These topics will be taken up in the chapters to follow.

[49] Wils (1979).

[50] Gerschenkron (1962).

[51] See, for instance, Mouffe (1979); and Block (1980). The writings of Miliband (1969, 1973, 1977) come close to taking the same anti-"economistic" position; but like many Marxists he prefers to remain with the idea of economic determinism "in the last resort."

[52] I here use the term "progressive" in the sense that Marx did with reference to capitalism— the best-known example being that of the *Manifesto* (Marx and Engels 1932). The term does not imply that capitalism answers to deep human needs or that it improves human life; it signifies that capitalism amplifies the forces of production and uproots humans from traditional social allegiances, all of which are progressive developments in that they are preconditions to the species's further advance.

CHAPTER EIGHT

Parastatal Enterprise in
Peruvian Mining

T HE object of our concern in this chapter is the effort of the Peruvian state to fill the economic space left vacant in the mining sector by the private domestic firms, whose financial resources have limited their further expansion; and by the transnational oligopolists, who, except for Asarco, have not hurried to invest in the country.

Other Third World mineral-exporting countries have turned to state entrepreneurship for the realization of political and ideological objectives: cementing central state control over the national territory (Zaire), eliminating vestiges of racism and promoting socioeconomic equality (Zambia), or attacking inequitable aspects of the world economic order (Chile).[1] In one sense, Peruvian objectives were more modest in that they were narrowly economic: to enhance the sector's contribution to bonanza development by maximizing, within the limits of external constraints regarded as given data, its ability to earn foreign exchange and generate tax revenues. That modesty; the fiscal weakness of a state facing new popular demands unleashed by the "revolution"; the high capital outlays required for mine and refinery development; the limited Peruvian experience with state enterprise[2]—all were factors counseling a go-slow approach to the state's assumption of a new economic role. In another sense, though, Peruvian objectives were ambitious indeed in that they aimed at substantial *additions* to the nation's mine and refinery capacity and proposed to acquire them, if need be, even without the cooperation and participation of transnational capital. These conflicting considerations caused the state to move cautiously as it first became a mining entrepreneur. But, once having committed itself, it exhibited a boldness not matched, in my opinion, by mineral resource development under state auspices in any other Third World country. Whether that boldness paid off in political and/or economic terms, or whether it deserves to be relabeled recklessness, are issues that this chapter will examine and explain.

[1] State enterprise in Chilean mining is discussed by Moran (1974); in Zambian mining, by Sklar (1975). Lukoji (1975) offers one of the very few discussions of Zairois mining to be found in the literature.

[2] The history of state enterprises in Peru is briefly reviewed by FitzGerald (1979:190-91), who finds that "[i]n no sense was the . . . public enterprise sector before 1968 a dynamic one, let alone a central element in the economy."

There are, since the nationalizations of 1973-1975, three parastatal enterprises operating in Peruvian mining: MineroPeru, Centromin (formerly Cerro), and HierroPeru (formerly Marcona). This chapter will deal almost exclusively with the first, although it will touch upon the experience of the second where relevant. One reason for choosing MineroPeru for detailed study is that, as a new entity whose actions have been less constrained by an accumulation of established interests and behavior patterns, it is both the purest embodiment of the military's hopes and plans for the mining sector and a tabula rasa on which its management has been free to write. A second reason is that MineroPeru is sui generis among the state enterprises organized to manage natural resource exploitation in the various less-developed countries around the world. It is, to my knowledge, the only one to have been formed *ex novo* for a specifically entrepreneurial purpose—that is, not only to operate existing mines and refineries but also to build them first. (Note that it was set up in 1970, well before the government knew that it would come to control, via expropriation, established enterprises of the gran minería.) For a historically weak, underdeveloped country to attempt to construct from nothing an organizationally and technologically advanced mining enterprise (the adjectives do apply) is an act ranking high in initiative and optimism. The dimensions of the act swell further when it is remembered that in a scant eleven years of existence, and with a 100-percent Peruvian management, MineroPeru has become a force of sorts in the world nonferrous metals industry. It controls an annual refined copper production of 150,000 fine metric tons, soon to double; it produces annually some 100,000 fine metric tons of electrolytic zinc—more than Asarco's new refinery at Corpus Christi, Texas; it mines about 30,000 fine tons of copper per year and hopes to more than triple its output in the near future; and it has proved and probable reserves larger than those of any mining firm in the Western world. In addition, it has become a major supplier of sulfuric acid to Peruvian industry.

MineroPeru's success has been far from unqualified. Still, its progress bespeaks the presence in Peru of entrepreneurial and technological talents and energies whose release required nothing more than the military's reforms—a phenomenon that testifies in turn to the possibility of real capitalist development in at least some Third World countries.

The Political Analysis of Parastatal Enterprise

No one but the most doctrinaire liberal would seriously maintain today that Peru has instituted socialism by the sole act of having given the state an entrepreneurial role in the economy. Whatever relevance such a view might have had when nineteenth-century market capitalism was the norm, it has little or none in a late-capitalist epoch typified everywhere by close institutional ties between a largely corporate private economy and an economically active state. Certainly, Marxists have regarded the bourgeois state, in its entrepreneurial function, as a mere "collective capitalist"; for them, parastatal enterprise is perfectly compatible with the preservation of a capitalist social formation.[3] The real issue is whether the presence of parastatal enterprise eases or inhibits a later transition to socialism. Put otherwise, does it weaken or reinforce bourgeois dominance and hegemony?

Much of the Marxist thinking on this subject has been based on the situation of parastatals in developed capitalist societies. There it can logically be argued that—since stable capitalist systems are evidently in being—parastatal enterprise is a contributor to system stability.[4] However, the premise of system stability is not axiomatic for less-developed countries, and so the argument collapses. Nicos Poulantzas's structural argument is also unhelpful when the object of reference is parastatal enterprise in the Third World. He posits that the capitalist character of the parastatal enterprise form is betrayed by its exploitation of wage labor, extraction of surplus value, and accumulation of capital.[5] All this is quite true. Yet, surplus must be extracted from the direct producers if there is to be any development. And, if the experience of all present-day "socialist" countries is any guide, surplus extraction and accumulation at low initial levels of development always entail wage-labor exploitation (perhaps supplemented by direct requisition) under the control of elites.[6] The conclusion, therefore, is that development is everywhere capitalist. This may be accurate, but it does not answer to the future of Third World capitalism.

Dependencistas approach the problem in a more sophisticated fashion, one which looks at Third World parastatal enterprise in the context of international capitalism. For them the potential contradiction between national and international capital is central. It is possible that parastatal enterprise lessens or makes more difficult foreign capital penetration. If so, it does not do away with capitalism at the national level, but it is nonetheless progressive in its effects because it weakens the international system—which needs to be able to penetrate new markets in order to survive. However, this is not a comfortable conclusion from a dependencista viewpoint; for it implies that "pe-

[3] It should be noted that the Marxist doctrine of "state monopoly capitalism" (Kissin 1972) represents an exception to this statement; it posits that state enterprise is a kind of socialist embryo growing in the womb of capitalism. (It appears during capitalism's "highest stage," signifying both that the transition to socialism is approaching and that it may be a peaceful one.) However, the doctrine has not received much currency outside official Soviet Marxism, whence it emerged during the heyday of détente.

[4] This position is taken by Mandel (1975:553-54); see also the extensive discussion of the state's economic role by Poulantzas (1978:163-89). It suffers from the usual epistemological weakness common to all "functionalist-Marxist" teleological arguments: the emergence of state enterprise is only "explained" abstractly and weakly, by imputing to it purposefulness in terms of system maintenance.

[5] Poulantzas (1978:175). He adds that state enterprise makes possible a transfer of accumulated capital to the private sector.

[6] Kolakowski (1978:2:381-98) demonstrates that the Leninist denial of the Communist Party's elite status, which underlies the "classlessness" claimed by all present self-described "socialist" states, is a matter of pure ideology.

ripheral'' capitalist states are autonomous enough to adopt an economic measure that strikes at one of international capitalism's core interests. Consequently,
dependencistas have tried to show that *in practice*, Third World parastatal
enterprise operates in partnership with private capital, and particularly with
foreign capital.[7] They attribute this tendency toward partnership to the bourgeois class character of the "peripheral" state and of parastatal management
itself, as well as to the superior competitive assets of capital domiciled in the
metropoli.

These are empirical questions to be examined afresh with each national
case study. We have no basis other than ideology for assuming that what was
observed in, say, Brazil will be replicated in Peru. Nor, as I argued in Chapter
1, is there a nonideological basis for dismissing the empirical issues on the
ground that a "general theory of dependency" suffices to explain them; no
such theory exists. Our task, then, is to investigate the institutionalization
and organization of control over Peruvian parastatal mining enterprise; the
class character and interests of those who exercise control; and the meaning
of parastatal behavior, with especial reference to relations with local and
foreign capital.

Two conceptual matters relating to enterprise control and objectives need
to be cleared away before we begin. First, there is no intrinsic reason why a
capitalist state could not use its regular administrative mechanisms to pursue
economic ends, but there are a number of advantages offered by the enterprise
form of organization.[8] They include greater flexibility and freedom of action;
a separate legal existence (so that, *inter alia*, contractual obligations are not
those of the central state); exemption from statutory limitations on the permissible uses of public moneys; and more leeway for structuring internal
organization, staffing, and networks of authority and discipline.[9] Not as frequently mentioned is that there is also a political advantage for the state caught
in the crossfires of contending class forces: parastatal enterprise has an ideological Janus face. The countenance it presents to the Right is that of a
quasi-independent institution similar in appearance, functioning, and goals to
a private business; while to the Left it presents a mystique of public service
and of dedication to general rather than self-interested aims.

Parastatal enterprises additionally allow their managers a greater degree of
autonomy relative to the political impositions of ministers and other central
state officials. Thus, it becomes easier for managers to ignore larger socio-

---

[7] See, for example, Evans (1979).

[8] As defined by Adizes (1975b), an enterprise is "an organization which conglomerates labor,
capital, and natural resources and is primarily geared towards the achievement of economic
results as measured by economic indices, such as the rate of return on investment, profits in
absolute terms, profit margin on sales, etc." One of its chief characteristics is that "[t]he economic
rewards for work done are determined mainly via the market mechanism as perceived by management."

[9] Wernette (1964:422-23).

economic and political objectives and to pursue narrowly economic ones—
if they are otherwise so inclined.

This brings us to the second matter, which is the classification of enterprise
goals. Renato Mazzolini identifies two kinds: the profit goal (to which may
be subsumed a goal of growth, as parastatal growth is usually fueled by
profits), and what he calls "tool" goals—specific state expectations regarding
parastatal performance which go beyond the profit-and-loss statement of the
entity and on behalf of which the state obligates and constrains parastatal
management.[10] The dynamic of competition between profit and "tool" goals
is conceived by Mazzolini as an equilibrium whose center of gravity favors
the former unless a contrary external pressure is applied: "When the company
is left on its own, it responds to market forces and behaves as any firm . . .
to maximize its own economic performance." On the other hand, external
pressure is never enough to cause the profit goal to disappear entirely; for,
"[e]arnings are regarded as a measure of success—a criteria [sic] of efficiency.
More importantly, they are a means to an end; without earnings the company
would fail and the tool goal itself would thereby not be attainable."[11]

These considerations suggest that we inquire into the question of managerial
autonomy; the degree of deviation from the profit goal; and the extent to
which that deviation is the result of central state imposition, as Mazzolini
believes, rather than managerial option.

INSTITUTIONAL FACTORS IN PERUVIAN PARASTATAL MINING ENTERPRISE

The military regime's plan for mining development, as was observed in
Chapter 3, saw MineroPeru as supplementing, not supplanting, private investment. When it was incorporated in October 1970, the transnationals had
already been given time to decide what projects they would undertake under
the new rules of the game. The Cuajone basic agreement had been signed; it
was understood that Southern Peru Copper would not build a refinery on its
own account; and the other transnationals had surrendered their idle concessions rather than accede to the government's insistence that their tenure be
conditioned on compliance with the standard of *amparo por el trabajo* ("work
it or lose it"). These developments served to define the original area of state
entrepreneurship in the sector; it consisted of whatever economic space remained after local and transnational private enterprise had staked out their
territories.

The act of incorporation made MineroPeru responsible for: (1) the assumption of the state's entrepreneurial and managerial functions "in all min-

[10] The term "tool" goal is intended here to convey the idea that the enterprise is thought of
as an instrument for carrying out broad national policies in the general interest.

[11] Mazzolini (1979:24-26 and passim). Gillis (1980) adds that externally imposed goals rarely
conflict in fact with the profit goal and may be useful to management in that they can serve to
justify losses.

ing, including activities such as the economic exploitation of intermediate products to the degree of processing deemed appropriate within an integrated activity''; (2) action as the state's fiduciary in "special" and "associated" mining enterprises (joint ventures; i.e., MineroPeru and not the central state would be the holder of record of the state's share in any joint venture with foreign or native private capital);[12] (3) the execution of programs of mine and refinery development assigned to it by the Ministry of Energy and Mines, utilizing "such resources as may be allotted for the purpose"; (4) the performance of mining and metallurgical research and development; and (5) the assumption of, "in general, all kinds of industrial and commercial [not until 1974 was this last split away to Minpeco] operations relating to the mining industry."[13] MineroPeru was also charged with administration of a new state monopoly over the refining of nonferrous metals in Peru, subject (after 1974) to an understanding that some of this responsibility was to be delegated to Centromin.

MineroPeru's mission stressed from the start its promotion of bonanza development by bringing as many as possible of the idle concessions into production as rapidly as possible. Of course, it was anticipated that these projects would turn profits, as bonanza development presupposes; there was never any requirement that the parastatal aim at noneconomic social objectives (except for those relating to workers' welfare, which are demanded of private firms as well), and in this sense it could be said that no "tool" goal was imposed. On the other hand, there was ample room for contradiction between *short-term* profitability and the pace of development. A prudent private enterprise that regarded the profit goal as primary would probably confine itself initially to a single, relatively low-cost project, husbanding its resources until experience was gained and a cash flow from the first project was available for reinvestment in later and larger ones. But the gradual development of natural resource wealth, with revenues reinvested in the same activity over a lengthy span of time rather than being used for other purposes, is not at all what bonanza development contemplates. It can thus be said that bonanza development itself was a "tool" goal. In our exposition of MineroPeru's approach to project development we shall seek to discover whether or not this "tool" goal had to be externally enjoined against the preferences of a reluctant management.

The fourth area of responsibility—research and development—might contradict the profit goal if it were interpreted as a license to plunge ahead with untried new technologies when designing projects. We may learn more about

[12] An "associated" mining enterprise is one in which MineroPero holds at least 25 percent of the equity shares and other local entities (private or public) the balance; a "special" enterprise is the same, except that the balance is held by foreign interests. The 1981 General Mining Law drops this distinction and instead employs the term "special enterprise" in reference to both cases.

[13] The quoted phrases are my translation of the text of MineroPeru's charter, decree-law D.L.18436.

the nature of the mining bourgeoisie by seeing how this potential contradiction was resolved.

Enterprise Organization

MineroPeru is a dependency of the Ministry of Energy and Mines, which appoints four of its nine directors[14] (two are designated by its employees and one each by the ministries of Economy and Finance, Industry, and Transport and Communications); its president, chosen by the directors—who seem to have few other duties of consequence—reports to the mining minister, bypassing the ministry's internal chain of administrative command. It is held to the same accounting standards as are private firms and is liable for payment of the same taxes. But in other respects it is a different creature. It is exempt from some of the provisions of *derecho de la empresa privada*. And, as item (3) above implies, its financial independence is less than complete.

Also less than complete is the independence of MineroPeru's management, whose powers and prerogatives are limited by its charter as follows: No contracts related to debt financing, long-term hiring of subcontractors, or major capital-goods acquisitions can be entered into without the approval of the Council of Ministers. Activities undertaken pursuant to principal objectives of the sectoral development plan require the approval of the mining minister. Ministerial approvals are required for the parastatal's own short- and medium-range strategic plans; for its operating budget, investment budget, and payroll; for all contracts entailing expenditure commitments above S/20 million; for opening branches and forming subsidiaries; and for portfolio investment in other firms. Management must supply the ministry with copies of its quarterly and annual earnings statements and general balances, which must document all applications of net profits and of extraordinary income. Except for salary levels and job descriptions, which management may define, employees enjoy the protections of civil service status.[15] Plainly, it was the intent of the military regime to make MineroPeru highly responsive to central-state direction.

Note that no comparable restrictions were ever imposed on the managements of Centromin or HierroPeru. Both, of course, were originally private enterprises operating under *derecho de la empresa privada* and enjoying fully autonomous control of their own affairs. When they were nationalized, the government decided not to risk a disruption of their activities that might have resulted from a wholesale reorganization. Hence, although both are nominally

[14] One of the four is the head of the DGM; two others are representatives of the national mediana minería. In consequence, local private capital does have an official voice in MineroPeru's operations, although it is a very weak one.

[15] These protections are not as great in comparison to private employment as the North American or European reader might expect, since permanent job tenure—normally thought of as the sine qua non of civil service status—is guaranteed under current Peruvian law to private-sector employees as well. Indeed, civil service status disadvantages workers in the mining industry (where labor unions are quite powerful), because it restricts their right to unionize. It also disadvantages management, however, in that it disallows transfers of employees among different job categories, thereby introducing rigidities into staffing practices.

subsidiaries of MineroPeru, they function hardly differently from private mining enterprises. The law contemplates that "special" mining enterprises in which MineroPeru participates will enjoy the same degree of independence.

This is the "organization-chart view" of parastatal mining enterprise at the moment of its inception. Organizational structures, however, evolve over time, and as they do the realities of control often have a way of deviating more and more from charted and tabulated institutional formalities. One source of deviation has been changes in government policy. The "second phase" of military rule (1975-1980) moved sharply away from the *dirigisme* and social reconstruction that were hallmarks of the *velasquista* epoch. The post-1980 civilian government, for its part, has sought to revitalize the private economy, to end state entrepreneurial monopolies, and to stress profitability in the parastatal sector. It is especially concerned with the last objective. Having determined to its satisfaction that Peru's high rates of inflation and excessive international borrowings since 1977 are due mostly to the central treasury's chronic budget deficits, it wants all parastatal entities to be fully self-sustaining—i.e., capable of funding their operations and growth out of retained profits, without treasury support.[16]

Such policy changes, notably those of the "second phase," have been taken advantage of by MineroPeru's management in its struggle to increase its de facto autonomy vis-à-vis the mining minister and the central state in general—with some success. The effort began in earnest when MineroPeru's second president, like the first a retired military officer, stepped down and was replaced by a civilian from the private sector, Luis Briceño Arata.[17] Shortly thereafter, Fernández Maldonado relinquished the mining portfolio in order to accept a promotion; later ministers have served for much briefer intervals than his seven years and have been less knowledgeable about sectoral affairs than he was. The subsequent weakening of ministerial control provided MineroPeru's now all-civilian management team with the opening it needed to expand the range and scope of its powers. Management was finally permitted to negotiate agreements with subcontractors and consultants without central government interference, and government officials ceased to pay as much attention as formerly to routine operations. Yet, Briceño and his aides were never satisfied with these concessions and continued during their entire tenure of office to press for full managerial autonomy in all activities that did not involve state subventions or financial contributions.[18]

Management has also sought consistently to get around *trabas burocráticas* (literally, "bureaucratic obstacles"; but read, "political controls") affecting ongoing operations by means of a bifurcation of the organization into two

[16] Interview with Fernando Montero, vice-minister of energy and mines, August 19, 1981.

[17] Prior to his appointment he had been MineroPeru's executive vice-president and one of the directors appointed by the mining ministry (n. 14 and accompanying text). He claimed twenty-four years of professional experience in the industry, all of it in the *mediana minería*.

[18] Interview with Víctor Eyzaguirre, MineroPeru's chief of project planning, December 27, 1977.

levels. It has proposed that *all* operating units (that is, not only Centromin, HierroPeru, and the "associated" and "special" joint ventures, but also units wholly owned by MineroPeru) be transformed into managerially autonomous entities—the lower level; and that MineroPeru headquarters—the upper level—become just a holding company with residual responsibilities for prospecting, exploration, research and development, and new project implementation.[19] The proposal has been justified with the claim that political controls from the center are most appropriate when new projects, involving delicate negotiations with foreign financiers and suppliers, are getting under way; but that once the projects have come on line, the most important consideration should be their profitability—best assured by managerial independence—so that construction loans can be repaid on schedule. This proposed managerial reform has since become the policy of the civilian government but had not yet been implemented as of the end of 1981.

Without doubt, the effect of the reform will be to enable management at the lower of the two levels to escape completely from external control, leaving it free to determine its own entrepreneurial objectives. It is interesting that MineroPeru's top managers instigated this proposal even though their powers would also be reduced if it were to be implemented.

Guillermo Flórez Pinedo, since 1975 the president of Centromin, goes further still. He proposes that the state be legally prevented from interfering at all in routine parastatal management and that it be limited to two tasks: determining once and for all the parastatals' objectives, and holding their managements to account (through their boards of directors) *on the sole basis of results*—profits, plus measurable progress toward attainment of the stated objectives. He aims to give managements full control of their budgets, including the right to shift budgeted sums among line items; to do away with civil service protection of employees, which he sees as having created too many labor cost rigidities; and to make possible managerial salary scales that would be competitive with those in the private sector (at present they are subject to an absolute ceiling imposed in 1977 as an austerity measure). This will be accomplished by reorganizing MineroPeru itself (not just its operating units) as a fully autonomous entrepreneurial entity governed by *derecho de la empresa privada*; indeed, he suggests the same reform for all Peruvian parastatal enterprise. These newly autonomous corporations will then be governed by apolitical directors chosen for their mining or business-financial expertise; they would cease to be, as they are at present, the representatives of the functional ministries—a modality which, according to Flórez Pinedo, encourages directors to defend sectoral interests in opposition to each other instead of concentrating on the welfare of the enterprise. Chief executives and managerial staffs will be completely insulated from politics. This insulation will be strengthened by making the parastatals responsible not to the

[19] Interview with Luis Briceño Arata, October 14, 1977.

state directly but to a master state holding company which will itself be organized along parallel lines.[20] Obviously, Flórez Pinedo's proposals would make over the parastatals into pure state-capitalist institutions.

In sum, MineroPeru's organizational structure has evolved in a direction entirely consistent with the trend of Peruvian governments after 1975, all of which have stressed the efficient rationalization of existing state economic activities in place of bold new initiatives. This evolution is a giant step away from *dirigisme* and a turn toward a more liberal version of state capitalism. In the altered version state enterprise loses whatever potential it had for socioeconomic transformation but gains, presumably, an enhanced ability to coexist peacefully with private enterprise. Significantly, parastatal managers themselves have promoted the evolution described.

The Nature of Management

The class character of MineroPeru's management corps is beyond dispute. When I surveyed it in 1978 I found that every member was a mining engineer and professional corporate manager, a product of the private gran and/or mediana minería; there was not a single government career technocrat among them. Each top manager's professional credentials included, on the average, nearly twenty years of mining-company experience, with eight to ten years spent in positions of managerial responsibility. In every case save Briceño's, most or all of that experience had been gained in the employ of local sub-sidiaries of transnational mining corporations. Cerro was far and away the largest "producer" of MineroPeru managers, followed by Northern Peru Mining. Southern Peru Copper and Marcona, in contrast, had contributed no more than a couple of junior managers to MineroPeru's staff; their relative insignificance as trainers of parastatal managers can be laid to the fact that neither employed Peruvians in high managerial positions until fairly recently. Briceño pointedly mentioned that most of his subordinates had studied in the United States, which, for him, was a source of pride; if their career patterns followed the norm for Peruvian mining professionals (to be elaborated in Chapter 9), this would have consisted of postgraduate study—most probably in mining engineering, possibly in a related technical specialty or in business administration. The background shared by these parastatal managers permits them to relate with ease to private-sector colleagues both at home and abroad.

MineroPeru's upper-level salaries and benefits have never attained full parity with those paid in the private gran minería (the source of Flórez Pinedo's complaint), although they have generally exceeded those in domestic medium mining. It is therefore of interest to investigate whether or not the enterprise has encountered problems in recruiting managers with large-firm experience, for the answer should provide a clue to mining-bourgeois value orientations. That is, a positive reply would tend to show that mining bourgeois seek high

[20] Flórez Pinedo (1981). It may be noted that this is an official Centromin document, not merely an expression of its president's personal views.

incomes and personal financial security even at the price of blocked career ascent in foreign companies and permanent subservience to expatriate superiors, whereas a negative reply would signify that other motives—dedication to the government's reformist objectives, simple nationalism, an opportunity to participate in the building of a new enterprise, a chance to exercise a greater amount of power and authority—are operative.

What we encounter is a mixed picture but one whose broad outlines are reasonably clear. Briceño defined three stages in the evolution of the managerial staff. Stage I spanned the period from 1970 to 1974, when MineroPeru's presidency was occupied by two retired brigadier generals in succession. In those years, recruiting was handicapped by the existence of "a certain prejudice" against any form of state employment, a reflection of then-prevalent bourgeois attitudes toward working conditions in the state administration.[21] (Bear in mind that Peru lacked a tradition of strong, capable parastatal enterprise.) Recruiting was also hindered, Briceño said, by the presence of military officers in the executive suite: Peruvian civilians are not in the habit of ascribing entrepreneurial or managerial leadership qualities to *militares*, and in this instance the generals infuriated their civilian subordinates by running the enterprise *"como un cuartel"* ("like a garrison"; the reference is to a preoccupation with pettyfogging administrative detail). During Stage II, which lasted from 1974 to 1976, the situation changed dramatically for the better: so much so that the enterprise enjoyed a surfeit of qualified applicants. The compilation in the interim of a performance record helped, as did the civilianization of executive authority. Nor were ideological factors absent: aspirants increasingly expressed in their job interviews an interest in working for an enterprise that was helping their country to overcome its condition of underdevelopment and dependency. Still, Briceño admitted, material incentives and status considerations were paramount in this stage. Staff salaries were raised across the board, and construction was begun for a fine new headquarters edifice in the well-to-do Lima suburb of Magdalena del Mar.

Stage III, beginning in 1976, supposedly represents a deterioration resulting from government imposition of salary ceilings.[22] However, the top management cadre was still intact in 1978, so it must be assumed either that Briceño's protestations were self-serving or that the decline in management quality was thus far limited to the lower ranks.

---

[21] State administrative employment before 1968 was characterized by clientelism and corruption, the latter reinforced by low prevailing rates of remuneration. The problems of the state administration before the "revolution" are discussed by Pan-American Union (1966) and by Gomez (1969).

[22] These were imposed as an anti-inflationary measure; but one can reasonably conjecture that their real intent was to win legitimacy for the still greater economic sacrifices demanded at the time from the popular classes. They applied across the board. However, the ceilings were absolute in state and parastatal employment, whereas private firms could exceed them if they did not claim the excess as a deductible business expense.

It appears that however much Peruvian mining managers' political ideals may attract them to national service, they prefer to remain in private employment unless suitable financial inducements are extended to them. On the other hand, once ensconced in their parastatal offices they do not abandon ship in every storm in order to sign on with a more remunerative vessel. To be sure, MineroPeru, like other modern corporations, has a structure of benefits designed to encourage employee loyalty through the accumulation of deferred rewards—vacation allowances, pension rights, longevity bonuses, and so forth; but these merely increase the salary differential required to stimulate a change of jobs. The top managers whom I met would hardly have refused higher pay for their current services. However, they would not have surrendered their considerable authority and resumed playing second fiddle to expatriates in order to get it.

The high salience of managerial concern with remunerations raises the possibility that, as is reportedly true of many Third World parastatals, MineroPeru managers milk the enterprise for incomes and status privileges and so contrive to live in grandiose style—or use their connections and high incomes to found personal businesses.[23] There is some evidence to support the accusation of excessive incomes and privileges: in 1976 MineroPeru listed in its earnings statement $7.58 million in administrative costs, whereas Southern Peru Copper, with a comparable cash flow and total employment, charged off only $1.54 million in general and administrative costs.[24] There is no way of knowing, however, if the two firms followed identical accounting practices in defining the items to be included in this expense category. In addition, as a new enterprise still undergoing rapid growth, MineroPeru may have incurred nonrecurring administrative expenses that would bias the comparison. Briceño proved to be extremely sensitive to charges of administrative waste, and he proudly claimed (a claim I was unable to verify) that the budget for executive perquisites had been cut by 17 percent on top of downward adjustments occasioned by inflation and currency devaluation.[25] My impressionistic observations were that the personal consumption standards of MineroPeru executives did not differ very much from those of private-sector managers employed by the larger mining companies: there were modern homes, but no *palacitos*; new automobiles, but no Mercedes. Neither did I find signs of important new private-sector mining or industrial investment on the part of MineroPeru managerial personnel.

A professional capitalist management may evince a preoccupation with parochial rather than national interests and may be uninterested in maximizing social goods that cannot be recast in economic terms. But it may still somewhat

[23] As is reported, for instance, by Schatz (1977) for Nigeria.

[24] The MineroPeru datum, as is true of all other MineroPeru financial data in this chapter, is taken from a copy of the parastatal's unpublished earnings statement and general balance for 1976 that came into my possession. The Southern Peru Copper datum is from Asarco's "10K" report to the U.S. Securities and Exchange Commission for 1976.

[25] Interview with Luis Briceño Arata, January 10, 1978.

serve the general welfare if it at least brings a high order of technological and organizational expertise to its appointed tasks. It is here where so many Third World parastatal managements fall short. Is the same true of MineroPeru's?

The executives whom I interviewed placed themselves on a par with their colleagues in developed countries as regards their mastery of technical and administrative skills, and we shall shortly see that their technical performance in particular endows that claim with validity. The worst weakness in their collective background, they felt, was a near-total lack of experience in the planning and execution of new projects. This weakness they universally charged (as do I) to the organizational practices of their former employers, the trans-national mining companies. Since the transnationals invariably centralized most of their planning activities in their overseas headquarters, and since none of them ever appointed a Peruvian to its headquarters staff, Peruvian engineers were effectively barred from "learning by doing" in this area.[26] In MineroPeru they were doing so in 1978, and they freely admitted to the errors that went along with the trials.

There is also a second weakness closely related to the foregoing. As project planners and executors advance in their careers, they and their firm build up a series of relationships with and a great deal of "tacit knowledge" about equipment suppliers, engineering consultants, and other outsiders whose goods and services are required for the successful development and implementation of a project plan. The absence of established relationships of this kind has been a source of some difficulty for MineroPeru; large blocks of management time have had to be devoted to cultivating them, and not all of the supplier choices have been optimal.

Other managerial deficiencies were found, but they were relatively minor and should iron themselves out over time. There was nothing whatever to suggest that Peruvians are incapable of structuring and operating a large industrial enterprise, nor that external influences are depriving them of the opportunity to try.

MineroPeru's Economic Performance

It is not easy to evaluate properly MineroPeru's economic performance. Balance sheets and earnings statements are exceedingly difficult for outsiders to come by, and the accuracy of some of the earlier ones is said to be suspect. Officials of the enterprise have publicly acknowledged losses of $6.7 million in 1979 and $15.6 million in 1980, and they have admitted to combined losses of over $25 million as of mid-1981. It is not known whether these figures

[26] Arrow (1962) discusses the economic implications for Third World development of "learning by doing." It may be noted that neither Southern nor Marcona concentrated all of their planning activities in their home offices to the same degree that Cerro did; but at the time that MineroPeru was formed, few Peruvians had yet ascended their hierarchies to levels where project planning is conducted.

take account of payments for recuperation of invested capital, but it is certain that the state has not yet recovered its initial capital investment.

Copper refining is apparently MineroPeru's most profitable line of business. Briceño publicly predicted that the parastatal would contribute $45-50 million in profits to the state in 1977 and perhaps as much as $80 million in 1978, essentially all of it earned in refining.[27] The enterprise enjoys the advantage of a guaranteed flow of feedstocks from Southern Peru Copper's two mines. Political pressure has enabled MineroPeru to charge Southern more than it pays for refining services in the metropoli; yet, the parastatal's refinery operating costs are lower. In 1978 MineroPeru officials privately predicted a return for the year from refining operations of 40 percent on invested capital.[28] Even though the civilian government has dedicated itself to eliminating state entrepreneurial monopolies, its 1981 Mining Code continues to specify that local, state-owned refineries must be given preference over foreign ones. Hence, while Southern's influence is probably sufficiently great to prevent MineroPeru from levying charges that bear no relation at all to those of the metropolitan refineries, the parastatal should be able to go on profiting handsomely from its refining business.

It is also worth noting that the $26.4 million earned by MineroPeru from copper refining in 1975-76 was paid in dollars. Since an equivalent sum would have been paid out abroad if the refinery had not existed, and since there are few imported inputs to the refining process, the total amount represents new foreign exchange acquired by Peru. Moreover, this contribution to bonanza development remains stable regardless of international copper price fluctuations.

The achievement of these results cost MineroPeru $22.3 million in equity investment derived from the state treasury and $34.6 million in borrowed capital, for a total capital expenditure of $56.9 million.[29] This is just over twice the refinery's annual income—a very sound investment.

The only other revenue-generating activity at the time of this writing (late 1981) is the Cerro Verde copper mine. The mine cost $187.4 million, $72.8 million of it in state contributions and the rest borrowed.[30] Production is around 30,000 fine metric tons per year, which means that the mine cost

[27] *El Comercio*, 3 November 1977. Based on past performance, I assume that these figures represent profits *before* taxes and deductions for reinvestment reserves and worker profit-sharing.

[28] MineroPeru's charges to Southern for refining services are based on a formula identical in most respects to those incorporated in the Cuajone sales contracts to determine metropolitan refining charges (see Chapter 5). One of the factors in the formula is intended to account for currency-exchange effects on refining costs, but not to the extent of the rapid devaluations which Peru was already undergoing by this time. When devaluation was factored in, the result was to raise the charges well above those then current in Europe. Southern was prepared to tolerate this situation, but only up to a point. Had the formula not been altered at Southern's insistence (as it was late in 1978), MineroPeru's returns on invested capital from refining would have shot up to over 100 percent. Interview with Frank Archibald, president of Southern Peru Copper, April 1, 1978.

[29] These data are from private MineroPeru documents.

[30] Figures taken from an internal MineroPeru report for limited distribution.

$2.83 per pound of annual production; the corresponding figure for Cuajone is $2.22. Cerro Verde's higher unit investment cost is attributed to a decision to attempt a radical technological innovation in the first phase of the project (Cerro Verde I), as I shall discuss later on. Though the project should become profitable as it moves into the second phase (Cerro Verde II), it has not been thus far. MineroPeru officials maintained in my conversations with them that basic production costs were no greater than Cuajone's and that Cerro Verde's losses were due to three other factors: lower-than-anticipated metal prices; a much shorter loan amortization period than Cuajone's (which means that amortization payments in the early years are proportionately higher); and the fact that Cerro Verde does not share Cuajone's contractual exemption from most duties on imported equipment, from the "windfall" tax on export value enacted in 1976, and from all other post-1969 tax increases.[31] They nevertheless insisted that Cerro Verde I will have returned an average 25-30 percent per year on invested capital by the end of its sixteen-year useful life. They further argued that around $100 million of the Cerro Verde I investment went for mine construction and overburden removal, which are costs chargeable against Cerro Verde II as well; hence, they averred, effective returns during the first phase will be higher when Cerro Verde II goes into operation, allowing these preparation costs to be spread over both phases.[32]

The principal cause of MineroPeru's lack of profitability is its continuing expenditures on exploration, feasibility and engineering studies, etc., relating to nine uncompleted projects under its jurisdiction. Only two of these—a zinc refinery near Lima and a phosphates project, Bayóvar, on the north coast (it is a joint venture with the Soviet Union)—were approaching completion by 1980-81. MineroPeru's problems with the others derive from the fact that, by managerial preference and in accordance with official policy up to 1980, all are to remain under the parastatal's majority control. But overseas banks are not especially eager to extend large project loans to a parastatal enterprise with a weak record of mining performance in a less-developed country whose government is held to be overborrowed internationally. And prospective transnational investors will only participate as minority joint venturers if risks are minimal—meaning that MineroPeru has assumed all exploration, preconstruction, and (possibly) infrastructure construction costs. This the undercapitalized parastatal is in no condition to do.

Faced with this impasse and unwilling to go on financing MineroPeru's expenditures from the central treasury, the civilian government proposes that joint venture arrangements be made more flexible. It suggests that MineroPeru content itself at first with a 25 percent holding and offer its foreign partners majority control in return for their shouldering of most of the preconstruction

---

[31] In other words, the state did not hesitate to wring the maximum in "bonanza" benefits from its own enterprise, where there was no need to compromise with foreign capital or other vested interests.

[32] Interview with Luis Briceño Arata and Víctor Eyzaguirre, December 13, 1977.

costs. Once construction is ready to start, local private capital will be brought in with a 30 percent equity share; that will leave the foreign partner(s) with effective financial control (it or they being the largest shareholder bloc) but will give ultimate control, in the event of a serious conflict with national objectives, to a combination of state and private native capital. Then, after production is under way and the foreigners have recovered their initial investment, MineroPeru will enlarge its holding by reinvesting its profit share or by using it gradually to buy up the foreign stake. In this way the bonanza development goal of state control over vastly expanded mine output will still be attained, albeit after a considerable lapse of time.[33] The priorities of bonanza development, however, counsel such a trade-off of early state control for increased mine exports.

MineroPeru's managers, just as would private corporate managers, have vigorously opposed these proposals. They have also eschewed the seemingly prudent course of "mothballing" the less advanced projects until the financial picture improves. Instead, they prefer to forge as far ahead as they can with their plan to make MineroPeru into a major world nonferrous metals oligopolist with an important market share—as, in their opinion, its reserves warrant. They know full well that if the civilian government's ideas are not implemented, the central state will have to go on subsidizing their preconstruction activities in order to protect wha. it has already invested. Like their U.S. counterparts at the helm of the Chrysler Corporation, they find state subventions a highly preferable alternative to a loss of control over their assets, capital accumulation potential, and oligopoly position.

MineroPeru at Work

Executive officers of the parastatal have always been mindful that the enterprise's master plan of development, based as it is on external financing, "imported" technology, and some planning assistance from abroad, can result in a deepening of Peru's external dependence. They have always understood, too, that dependence is at a maximum when development projects are purchased as integral packages including financing, technology, equipment, and planning and managerial expertise: "turnkey" contracting, as it is called. MineroPeru therefore adopted a policy of foregoing "turnkey" contracting wherever feasible and, instead, attempting to *desintegrar el paquete*—to break up the project package into individual functions, to assume itself such of them as its knowledge and resources permitted, and to contract for each of the others by competitive bidding. The concept was supposed to maximize opportunities for "learning by doing" while assuring that overall project expenditures were as low as could be arranged. Yet, this fundamentally wise policy was compromised on numerous occasions. Compromises were accepted

[33] See n. 16.

in all instances where the alternative would have been to delay the project seriously, either because of a lack of local expertise or because financing could only be concerted as part of a "turnkey" package.

The Ilo Copper Refinery

The copper refinery, MineroPeru's first development project, was built by a consortium of two Japanese firms, Mitsui and Furukawa Electric. It was a "turnkey" project that included a training program for Peruvian supervisors and operatives at a similar installation in Japan. However, the project package did not extend to Japanese management of the completed installation. As we know, the refinery was planned under the assumption that most or all of its "blister" feedstocks would come from Southern Peru Copper's smelter, a mile or so further up the coast.

In this case it was clear from the beginning that MineroPeru's "no-'turnkey'-contracts" policy would have to take a back seat to broader national objectives. We have already seen in Chapter 5 that plans for the refinery were closely interwoven with the complex negotiations over Cuajone. Peru had to display credible evidence of a refining capacity in being before the long-term sales arrangements for Cuajone copper had been finalized; otherwise it would have been unable to win refining rights to that metal and would have been frozen out of access to the new mine's "blister" output for fifteen years. Secondly, it was hoped that possession of a local refinery would enable Peruvian copper to penetrate the rapidly growing markets of the newly industrializing Third World countries;[34] but the transnational oligopolists were not unaware of the business opportunities there, and it seemed as if speed would be essential if the transnationals were not to get to these markets first and lock them up. Lastly, there was little national expertise in refining: the only refinery with which Peruvians had had any experience was Cerro's, and it was both smaller and very much older.

Possibilities for competitive bidding were limited in any event by the fact that the initial discussions with bidders had to be carried on in strictest secrecy lest Southern get wind of them before its role in refining was settled. Even so, a competitive bid was received from Belgian interests. On reviewing them both I conclude that the Japanese offer was indeed superior. The Japanese did not attempt to place any restrictions on the free use of their technology; their price was in line with what the Belgians offered to charge; and, unlike the latter, they were willing to accept payment in cash rather than in copper, which preserved Peru's marketing flexibility. Naturally, for the Japanese the Ilo refinery was a solid business deal, not an aid project. They sold $35 million worth of capital equipment. And, by meeting a key local development requirement that other foreign investors would not, they gained favor with

---

[34] Such a marketing strategy was attractive because it got around the problem of higher developed-country tariffs on finished metal, and because it enabled Peru to expand her world market share without disrupting any of the existing sales patterns of the world copper oligopoly.

MineroPeru and with state authorities—favor that would be of value when the time came for them to bid on gran minería projects that might be tied to Japan's import needs.

Since the refinery has been an unquestioned success in policy and economic terms, even the fiscally conservative post-1975 regime was willing to proceed with its planned expansion from 150,000 to 300,000 fine metric tons of annual output. Inflation, which drove up the cost of the expansion program to $118 million (almost exactly double the cost of the original unit), was no deterrent, as all projections—now founded on actual operating experience—showed that the enlarged refinery would continue to be extremely profitable.[35] After its expansion, the Ilo facility will be the fourth largest electrolytic copper refinery in the Western world.

The refinery would not be able to operate so successfully were it not for Southern Peru Copper's wholehearted cooperation. For, it is not enough that annual "blister" delivery quotas be met; deliveries must also be distributed throughout the year such that refining operations can proceed at full capacity and without pause. Southern has carefully scheduled its deliveries accordingly. Moreover, it has gone to some pains to assure that the frequent strikes at its installations do not interfere with MineroPeru's production schedules; when strikes are anticipated it accelerates "blister" deliveries so that MineroPeru will have a sufficient stock on hand to carry it through the strike period. And in 1978, when the transnational and the parastatal were engaged in acrimonious discussions over refining charges, the former made no move to apply pressure by slowing deliveries.

Southern further recognizes that it shares an interest with MineroPeru in the quality of refined copper produced at Ilo, inasmuch as any sales lost to the one are lost to the other as well. Therefore, when by 1978 normal aging of the refinery began to result in a measurable deterioration of the product, and when MineroPeru engineers proved unable to make the requisite process adjustments unaided, Southern arranged to bring in Asarco refinery experts to assist them. It did so wholly at its own expense.

The Cerro Verde Copper Mine

This open-pit mine, located just twenty-four road kilometers from Arequipa, Peru's second largest city, is MineroPeru's first mining venture. It is small as such mines go, producing slightly over 30,000 fine metric tons per year as compared to 150,000 for Cuajone.

Open-pit copper mines generally exploit ores whose principal constituents are sulfides of the metal. Cerro Verde is unusual in that its reserves of 490

---

[35] Unpublished planning documents, dated 1978, projected gross revenues of $393.2 million over the first ten years of operation, resulting in a net profit plus reinvestment reserve of $156.7 million after payment of $58.9 million in income taxes. Net foreign exchange earnings over the period (after payment of loan amortization, interest, and foreign-exchange operating costs) were projected at $303.5 million.

million metric tons of sulfides are overlain with 36 million tons of copper oxides.[36] Oxides cannot be smelted in the conventional manner, although they can be reduced to metal by using the "lixiviation" process mentioned in Chapter 7 (see p. 197). But in the late sixties and early seventies the process was radically new, having been implemented on a commercial scale only twice before and never in this application. Anaconda, Cerro Verde's former owner and as technologically proficient an international oligopolist as one could ask, had considered employing the "lixiviation" method to produce copper from the oxides rather than merely pushing them aside to get at the sulfides (which is still the customary practice in the industry). It rejected the idea as uneconomic, however. This decision was reversed by MineroPeru when it took Cerro Verde over. Instead, the parastatal's planners, against the unanimous recommendation of outside advisors, determined that the enterprise would go ahead with an oxide-based development. Once the mining operations of the oxide phase, Cerro Verde I, had reached the sulfides, the more conventional second-phase development, Cerro Verde II, would proceed.

Inasmuch as they had conceived Cerro Verde I themselves, MineroPeru officials were firmly resolved to bring the project to completion under their own control rather than turning it over to a "turnkey" contractor. Here the parastatal had the advantage that it already possessed the requisite technology: it had ingeniously assembled a pilot plant to prove out the process at a minimal cost of $1.4 million, which was accomplished by buying bits and pieces of used equipment during "shopping tours" of international mining conventions. Thanks to this technological leverage and to the willingness of COFIDE to guarantee the loans taken out to finance the project, it was in fact possible to undertake and complete it in disaggregated fashion. Three outside consultants were hired to assist MineroPeru in the task: Wright Engineers Ltd. of Canada performed much of the engineering work; British Smelter Constructors Ltd. arranged much of the financing and took charge of design supervision; and Parsons-Jurden of the United States assumed responsibility for planning Cerro Verde II.[37] Nonetheless, MineroPeru engineers intervened actively in all of these assignments, at one point severely modifying Parsons-Jurden's plan for the second phase for the reason that the original version was too grandiose and expensive.

Due partly to its radical technology and partly to its ore composition, Cerro Verde I produces purer copper than does ordinary smelting and refining.

[36] Rodríguez Hoyle (1974:170).

[37] Wright Engineers is a general engineering consulting and civil construction firm founded in 1947 and based in Vancouver; it had some prior Peruvian experience in the area of port development. British Smelter Constructors (BSCL) is a relatively new firm established in 1968 for the specific purpose of building an aluminum smelter in Bahrain (*Peruvian Times*, 23 March 1973); I am given to understand that it submitted a very low bid for the job, undoubtedly in an attempt to build up its business and gain experience in a different part of the world. Parsons-Jurden is a subsidiary of the well-known Los Angeles engineering firm, Ralph M. Parsons Co. Most of its experience is in the petroleum industry, but it was supervising the construction of the giant Sar Chemseh copper mine in Iran before the project was shut down in 1978.

MineroPeru has been awarded a special trademark for it from the LME and claims to be able to sell it at a premium. Still, there have been problems. Unexpected quantities of molybdenum in the ores reduced the yield of the process, limiting the mine's production rate to 80 percent of design capacity. That difficulty was overcome, but its resolution entailed additional expenditures in engineering time. And as was observed earlier, the mine's debt structure and low copper prices have prevented it from turning a profit. Unfortunately for the parastatal, the experience with Cerro Verde I has not been sufficiently reassuring to international lenders; they have declined to finance Cerro Verde II unless the project is under the control of a reputable mine engineering and construction firm. Consequently, Cerro Verde II has had to be converted into another "turnkey" project, on which basis it is now going ahead.

The Cerro Verde experience says much about the way in which MineroPeru executives chose to define their interests. To be sure, they did not hesitate to offer what seemed like sound economic reasons for hinging the success of the project on a risky, unproven technology. Since the country was short of capital, a mining project was needed that would minimize new capital outlays. Provision of infrastructure—road and rail links to a port, electricity and water supply, housing and other residential facilities for workers, etc.—can easily consume half the total cost of new mine development; but thanks to Cerro Verde's near-urban location, these services were already present. Hence, Cerro Verde was bound to be cheaper to develop than any other MineroPeru copper deposit, even after the oxide problem was taken into account. Furthermore, the costs of overburden removal must normally be met out of capital initially paid in and are only recovered later on. But most of Cerro Verde's "overburden" could become a source of early cash flow, further minimizing new capital inputs compared to those demanded for going directly to the sulfides.

It is evident, however, that other kinds of considerations played a role as great or greater in influencing the ultimate decision. Cerro Verde was politically attractive to the military regime because it promised to bring new industrial employment and benefits to a city other than Lima. The majority of Peruvians who do not live in the capital have consistently complained of the tendency to concentrate industry there, and the pledges of previous governments to institute *desarrollo descentralizado* had gone unfulfilled. (This was a particular sore point with *arequipeños*, whose regional economy was largely agricultural despite the city's size; at various times in Peruvian history Arequipa had threatened to secede in protest at Lima's persistent neglect of its economic problems.) The project would thus buttress both national integration and the regime's legitimacy, as it would become the first actually to translate the slogan of decentralized development into a reality. Additionally, since the Cerro Verde I technology is relatively nonpolluting, its use would demonstrate that MineroPeru was socially responsible. Yet, it would simultaneously promote the development of the whole mining industry, in two ways: by demonstrating that its activities could be safely carried on in close proximity to urban areas and agricultural zones;[38] and by pioneering a new technology of evident value in the reduction of polymetal ores mined in the mediana minería.

These broader considerations did not have to be imposed on a reluctant management as external "tool" goals. Indeed, exactly the reverse took place. That is, MineroPeru's managers and project planners themselves conceived the list of political-ideological benefits and utilized it to help sell the idea of the project to the military.

Beyond that, my interviews suggest that parastatal managers were motivated in part by technological interests as well as by personal and national pride. They were eager to experiment with a new mining technology for its own sake; while one assumes that their eagerness might have been dampened had they had to finance their experiment out of profits, their situation at the head of a new enterprise that was not expected to show overnight returns and that could count on state subsidies relieved them of any need to compromise on this score. They were unquestionably anxious to show that they—and Peru— could succeed where a major transnational had not. In short, they wanted to prove that their country was a repository of advanced human skills (of which they were the archetype) and was, therefore, neither inferior nor dependent; and that they, as individuals, were the equals of mining bourgeois anywhere.

The Cajamarquilla Zinc Refinery

Ground was broken in March 1978 for MineroPeru's new zinc refinery, located in the Lima basin about fifteen kilometers northeast of the city. The refinery, completed somewhat later than scheduled in 1981, is designed to accept 199,000 tons per year of zinc concentrates (more than half of what Peru has hitherto exported in unprocessed form) and to produce therefrom 100,000 fine metric tons of electrolytic zinc. It will result in a 145 percent increase over 1977 levels in the country's refined zinc production and a 300 percent increase in its annual output of sulfuric acid.

This project can be questioned on economic grounds. There is doubt that local industry will soon be able to absorb the sulfuric acid production, for which there is no export market. The state's equity investment, $101 million, will yield a return of 13.5 percent—not bad, but less than the returns that could be expected from well-planned mining endeavors. As it is, the investment would have been greater, and returns correspondingly lower, had MineroPeru not decided (with government approval) to site the refinery in

[38] This was potentially a serious political issue. Nationalists had kept alive the memory of Cerro's smelter smoke problem of the early twenties, whose resolution made the company a great landowner (Chapter 2). Southern Peru Copper had to face similar accusations in the late sixties, even though its Ilo smelter is located many miles from any agriculturally productive land; it was eventually absolved of responsibility for crop damage, but only after a long investigation and considerable bad publicity.

the Lima area in order to lower infrastructure costs (zinc refining is highly energy-intensive). But this decision is a setback for *desarrollo descentralizado* and for air pollution control in the Lima basin. It is also a setback for the "no-'turnkey'-contracts" policy of MineroPeru; again, lack of local experience and inability to concert financing independent of a total package caused the entire project to be turned over to SYBETRA, a construction syndicate owned by the mighty Belgian holding company, Société Générale.

We can better understand the zinc refinery by noticing that it sat on a back burner during 1972-1974, when MineroPeru was striving to take advantage of unusually high copper prices, and was only shifted to the forefront in 1975. The shift coincided with a shrill chorus of impending doom from a private— and heavily zinc-producing—mediana minería whose profits had collapsed along with world prices; and with the accession to power of General Morales Bermúdez, whose first political priority was mending fences with the private sector. A local zinc refinery operated by MineroPeru will not put refining profits into the pockets of medium miners. It will, however, answer one of their long-term prayers[39] and in so doing will increase *mine* profits. Greater mediana minería profits on zinc mine production will result from lower refining costs (in this case the benefits *will* be passed on to the mining companies) and from the fact that the refined output will be sold at international posted prices not subject to manipulation by metropolitan buyers. (It was pointed out in Chapter 4 that there is no recognized world market price for zinc concentrates, which are traded internationally by private negotiation between buyer and seller.)

In other words, the zinc refinery subsidizes the local mediana minería. It was prioritized by MineroPeru itself in response to a clear political exigency and was not a state-imposed "tool" goal.

The Tintaya Copper Mine[40]

Tintaya is the other copper deposit that, together with Cerro Verde, was regularly considered for early development because of its low investment requirements (around $200 million). By the time (1975-1977) that MineroPeru was in a position to think about going forward with it, it had become evident that this mine as well could only be built under a "turnkey" contract, for the usual reason: inability to obtain independent financing. Tintaya is meaningful in that it reveals MineroPeru management's attitude toward sharing responsibility and control with outside capital.

When it became plain that MineroPeru would be unable to finance the

---

[39] The demand for a local zinc refinery began to be voiced as early as 1948 and was used to justify the 1950 Mining Code (it was claimed at the time that its enactment would stimulate Cerro to build one). At one point during the late fifties the mediana minería seriously proposed a joint private-state venture to build a zinc refinery—a radical proposal in the economic climate of the era—but the idea came to naught. See Samamé Boggio (1974:1:423-73).

[40] Most of the material in this section is based on a conversation with Alberto Benavides on August 6, 1981.

project alone, the then-minister of economy and finance, Javier Silva Ruete, suggested that Tintaya might be an appropriate avenue of private-sector participation in gran minería development. (His motivation was less that of a "point man" for local medium-mining companies than it was balancing the central state budget by avoiding yet another input of state capital to a new mine. He also wanted to resuscitate the severely depressed construction industry—a politically important employer of large numbers of unskilled workers—by engaging it in less recession-prone activities such as mine construction.) Silva Ruete took the initiative in raising the idea of local private capital participation with Alberto Benavides and a few other noted mining entrepreneurs; and after the World Bank had expressed interest in providing financial assistance, they concluded that the idea might work. Accordingly, they incorporated the Empresa Promotora Tintaya as a private investment vehicle. They also obtained promises of participation from the French government's Bureau de Recherches Géologiques et Minières and from Outokumpu Oy, a Finnish custom refiner.

MineroPeru opposed this idea from the very start and made clear that it would fight at the ministerial level to retain exclusive control of the project. Its argument was that it had taken all of the risks of exploration and preparation; in consequence, private investors had no right to join in for the sole purpose of reaping the rewards. Benavides and the others soon became convinced of MineroPeru's determination to keep them out. They decided that it would be useless to fight on—especially inasmuch as the parastatal appeared to have gained the support of the mining minister—and so they disbanded the Empresa Promotora.

Meanwhile, MineroPeru set up a rival firm, the Empresa Minera Asociada Tintaya S.A. (EMATINSA), as a joint venture with Centromin and COFIDE. COFIDE's backing enabled EMATINSA to concert the financing for Tintaya in Canada (a Canadian firm had been selected as the "turnkey" contractor). The loan contract arrived in Silva Ruete's office on the day before the civilian government was inaugurated; he refused to sign it on the ground that the latter should do so, since it would have to bear the responsibility in any case. In this way the final decision on Tintaya was left to Pedro-Pablo Kuczynski, the new minister of mines.

Kuczynski sought to implement the Belaunde administration's policy of encouraging more foreign investment in Peru, and he was particularly concerned to promote transnational participation in petroleum development. To that end he shepherded through the congress a new law designed to reform the petroleum concession system as requested by the transnationals. His action in that matter, however, provoked virulent attacks from the nationalist Left and, more seriously, rumbles of disapproval from the still-powerful and still-nationalist officer corps. Therefore, Kuczynski concluded that to renew the call for private capital participation in Tintaya *in the face of persistent opposition from MineroPeru* would be too much of a political risk. After some hesitation he signed EMATINSA's financing agreement, allowing the project to proceed as a purely state-owned venture. Canada is lending it $100 million in government funds plus $115 million from private banks.

Other Mining Projects

Soon after its creation MineroPeru began to solicit participation in its many mining projects from entities in the Soviet bloc, apparently believing that this would both serve the regime's declared interest in nonalignment and bring in joint-venture partners who would be more willing than the transnationals to leave control in local hands. In the event Soviet assistance was obtained for the Bayóvar phosphates project; a Polish government agency agreed to join a coal-mining venture, Alto Chicama; and the Rumanian government became a joint venturer in the large Antamina copper project.

Except for Bayóvar, these ventures have come to naught. Although sizable sums were invested in Antamina and Alto Chicama, neither the Poles nor the Rumanians were able to provide the construction financing they had promised when the joint ventures were entered into. Consequently, MineroPeru has been attacked from the Right for proceeding "ideologically" in these instances without regard for economic considerations. More telling, in my opinion, is the argument that the parastatal's failure lay in putting *political* objectives— exclusivity of control, guaranteed by placing itself at the political service of the regime—ahead of economic ones.

The only other mining venture to have reached the stage where construction can be seriously contemplated is Michiquillay, a large copper deposit (it is apparently as large or larger than Cuajone) located in the northern sierra in the department of Cajamarca. It is of great interest to the state because it is in an underdeveloped and deprived area, one of the few in the Andes that has not even seen much medium mining activity. Michiquillay will not bring many new jobs to the region; but the infrastructure associated with it will open up the area to further development. Unfortunately, infrastructure requirements are so great that the project will cost around $1 billion.

Japanese mining companies—most prominently Mitsui, which has some experience in Peru—have shown interest in the project since the early seventies. At a time when world copper prices are low and are predicted to remain that way for some time, only the Japanese interest in secure copper supplies seems sufficient to stimulate investment of such huge scale. However, not even the Japanese are willing to sink up to a billion dollars' worth of capital into a project over which they will have no managerial control. Their response has been to drag out a final decision with endless studies and to suggest that MineroPeru assume the full burden of infrastructure construction—which is, of course, out of the question. Yet again, MineroPeru appears reluctant to give up control, regardless of its inability to press forward on its own.

To summarize: MineroPeru's managers, in their decisions respecting new project development, acted as if they were motivated by three primary goals.

They were: (1) maximizing their control of the projects, both by avoiding "turnkey" contracting where feasible and by disallowing anything other than minority joint-venture participation on the part of private capital, foreign or local; (2) cementing their position by showing that they could voluntarily contribute to the achievement of overriding national political objectives; and (3) securing a position of equality, especially in technical matters, with the international bourgeoisie of the industry. None of these goals was fully met, as the undercapitalized condition of the enterprise continually forced compromises. Nonetheless, the nature of the compromises was always such as to favor control and managerial job security. But this should not be taken solely as a sign of service to self or of an "edifice complex"—a desire to expand for expansion's sake. Managers were, in my view, quite sincere in their nationalism and in their desire to make a contribution to national development. If their efforts have not resulted in a cash contribution, they have brought other rewards: technological employment opportunities for a growing national corps of engineers and technicians; a stronger position in the world metals markets (thanks to refining); and a healthy dose of national pride for a country that has too often seemed to lack it.

THE ISSUE OF SUBORDINATION TO THE METROPOLI

Earlier on it was mentioned that in the dependencista view, Latin American parastatal enterprises often function to foster "dependent development" by forging links between themselves (and local capital, as a junior partner) and metropolitan capital. These links commonly take the form of reliance on transnational corporations for essential technologies, managerial services, and market outlets, as well as on the international banking establishment for financing. Such bonds, once emplaced, subordinate the parastatals and the domestic private firms to metropolitan strategies of capital accumulation. They prevent the pursuit of developmental objectives at variance with metropolitan interests. More seriously still, they coopt parastatal managers, who come to redefine their interests and values—including their perspectives of what development means and how it is best achieved—in metropolitan instead of national terms. Is this true of Peruvian mining parastatals?

Except for the joint ventures that have previously been discussed, in all of which MineroPeru holds a controlling interest, neither MineroPeru nor Centromin is involved in any ongoing partnership arrangement with transnational firms. Foreign consultants and contractors are sometimes employed for specific short-run purposes (of which even "turnkey" project construction is one), as we have seen; but their employment is temporary. All consulting and supply contracts, the "turnkey" ones included, have been awarded only after competitive bids have been received; my investigations failed to turn up any instances where a consultant succeeded in shifting follow-on contracting work to itself or a favored ally through biased evaluation. MineroPeru's and

Centromin's marketing is done via Minpeco alone—a policy that the abolition of the state sales monopoly has not affected. The example of Cerro Verde shows that MineroPeru is not technologically dependent and would be quite able to do much more of its project development work in-house were it not for its financial problems. The examples of Tintaya, Michiquillay, and the other joint ventures indicate that the parastatal seeks above all to maintain control of its activities. As for Centromin, it has embarked upon an extensive program of capital improvements (Chapter 6) under its own supervision.

Linkages with local private mining firms exist, but only to a certain degree. MineroPeru went ahead with the zinc refinery because it saw obvious political advantages for itself in making available to the mediana minería a service that the latter had long desired. However, it otherwise tends to regard the local mining companies as potential competitors and tries to keep them at arm's length. Centromin does not, since it has inherited Cerro's legacy of assistance to native mining capital; its strategy of protection and defense therefore rests on demonstrating that it can perform similarly. Moreover, it has had to proceed under a handicap: as it no longer need compete for the mediana minería's concentrate sales and refining business like Cerro used to do (both are now assigned to it by state fiat), and as its drive to expand and update its facilities places stress on the maximization of reinvestable earnings, it has had to be sterner about the refining charges it exacts than Cerro was. That, needless to say, has led to discontented grumbling among the medium firms. Centromin's response has been to set up its own consulting subsidiary, COMMSA, as a means for making its expertise accessible at low cost to smaller Peruvian firms. COMMSA's capabilities include project evaluation, technical and economic studies, engineering design, purchasing management, project accounting and general supervision, operating management counseling, and personnel training; and it claims to provide these services far more cheaply than they can be bought abroad. In its first year of operation COMMSA had captured two such contracts from firms unaffiliated with Centromin.

We are left with the possibility that the Peruvian mining parastatals, and especially MineroPeru, are rendered dependent or are exploited as a result of their need to resort to external financing. There is the further possibility that their borrowings have contributed to the country's international debt problem, which in 1978 forced it to accept an element of IMF dictation in the area of economic policy.[41]

[41] Copper prices had tumbled late in 1974, seriously disequilibrating the balance of payments and causing a drawdown of foreign-exchange reserves to meet external debt obligations. By 1976 monetary reserves were so low that it was uncertain whether scheduled debt amortization and interest payments would be met. In order to avoid default Peru had no alternative except to call upon the IMF for assistance, and the latter wasted no time in pressuring for adoption of its usual deflationary package of prescriptions: devaluation, drastic reduction of government expenditures, an end to consumption subsidies, more openness toward foreign investment, and less protection for domestic industry. The government, afraid of the social costs and potential for destabilization as well as indignant at this infringement of its sovereignty, resisted valiantly for two years and even managed to extract some interim IMF support; but it was finally forced to

The facts are these: MineroPeru has indeed been diverted from its course of avoiding "turnkey" contracting; but Centromin—whose established reputation was never seriously endangered by its nationalization—has not been. In 1976 MineroPeru had a debt-to-equity ratio of 1.15, twice the average for Asarco, Newmont, and Phelps-Dodge but half the debt load of Southern Peru Copper (then in the midst of financing Cuajone). Its total outstanding long-term debt obligation in that year was $139 million. This obligation was fairly equally spread over banks in Europe, the United States, and Japan. Most of it had been acquired at interest rates ranging from 2 to 2¼ percent above LIBOR (the London interbank offer rate, which is the standard prime rate in the European financial market), but there were also loans funneled through COFIDE that carried lower rates of 1½ to 1¾ percentage points above LIBOR. Long-term Canadian loans to the Tintaya project carry interest rates of 9¾ percent (fixed) for the government contribution and LIBOR plus 1¼ percent for the private.

Do these data suggest dependence? Surely not. They do indicate, however, that the entry barriers which protect the existing world nonferrous metals oligopolists—one such barrier being the difficulty encountered by an inexperienced would-be entrant in concerting outside financing—are just as operative for a parastatal enterprise as they are for a private firm; and that state political power, alone, cannot overcome them.

Do the data imply exploitation? The COFIDE official who monitored MineroPeru's debt obligations in 1978 thought that they did. He felt that the interest rates being charged were not justifiable in terms of actual risk, since neither the Peruvian state nor any of its agencies had defaulted on a loan in modern times (i.e., after the end of the War of the Pacific).[42] On the other hand, Southern Peru Copper was made to pay interest equal to LIBOR plus 1¾ percent on its basic $500 million loan package for Cuajone and an even higher rate of LIBOR plus 2¼ percent on the supplementary $53.4 million borrowing that it needed to finish the mine. Furthermore, Southern's banks subjected its management to a number of restrictions on its freedom of action; nothing of the sort was ever demanded of MineroPeru.

Lower interest rates can be had by Peruvian firms, but only if the loans are secured. Thus, Centromin has been able to borrow for working capital at terms as generous as LIBOR plus ¼ percent when it has given mortgages on capital assets or stocks of unsold metals as security. (This is a common and, for a large enterprise, economically sound practice in the industry.) MineroPeru's problem is that, being a new entity, it lacks sufficient unencumbered assets to use in this manner.

According to the same COFIDE loan officer, there have been a few oc-

give in and enacted a watered-down version of the IMF package in May 1978. Peru's dealings with the IMF from 1976 to 1978 are described by FitzGerald (1979:241-42) and by Stallings (1979). Also see Kuczynski (1981).

[42] But there have been several close calls; see *Business Week*, 21 March 1977, pp. 117-18.

casions where lenders withheld commitments to MineroPeru for reasons that could be described as political—most recently in 1975-76, with the aim of inducing Peru to settle on a compensation formula for Marcona. But despite holding a jaundiced view of the international financial establishment, he was convinced that the banks had never employed their muscle to manipulate the mining policies of either the central government or the parastatals.

Lastly, it is impossible to sustain an argument that the use of foreign debt to build up MineroPeru has measurably affected Peru's overall international debt or its eventual subjugation to the IMF. In the entire period from 1969 to 1976, Peru received a gross inflow of $4.51 billion in new hard-currency loans, or $2.8 billion net of amortization payments made in the interval.[43] MineroPeru's foreign debt in 1976 stood at $101.4 million. To be on the conservative side, let us assume that the state's equity contribution to it, $92.8 million, was also derived from borrowed funds. From the sum of these two figures we then subtract the $26.4 million in foreign exchange earned by MineroPeru from refining operations up to 1976, thereby arriving at $167.8 million as the net amount of borrowed capital poured into the parastatal. That represents a mere 3.7 percent of the gross Peruvian borrowing, or 6 percent of the net, during the years in question—too little to have materially altered the nation's debt picture. If anything, it was wiser to take on loans for financing MineroPeru than for many of the other activities funded from this source— such as covering the general budget deficit.[44] At least MineroPeru's debts are potentially self-amortizing out of the earnings of productive projects.

Conclusions: Parastatal Enterprise and the Bourgeois Class

MineroPeru was formed with the understanding that it would step in where transnational corporations—hardly angels—feared to tread; it would develop mines and refineries that they could or would not. Lacking the advantage of a preexisting base assembled by private effort and acquired after the fact through nationalization, it nevertheless managed to confound the experts with the setting up and profitable running of a large copper refinery as well as with a mining project, Cerro Verde, that stands at the forefront of modern metallurgical technology. It not only became a proving ground for local engineering and managerial talent. More than that, it showed that Peru possessed the technological and organizational wherewithal to develop; that a series of reforms which liberated creative energies in the society and elevated entrepreneurial risk-takers to positions of authority was sufficient to allow development to accelerate; and that external forces are less effective brakes on autonomous capitalist development than is frequently supposed.

[43] My computation from data presented by FitzGerald (1979:307).

[44] FitzGerald's (1979) argument is sound: it is that the crisis was caused less by debt financing of capital construction projects than by the use of borrowed funds for unproductive expenditures and to make up for the unwillingness to increase the low pressure of taxation.

However, MineroPeru's accomplishments might have been fewer had it not had the good fortune to be able to expand into a vacuum. The vacuum had a political dimension: the destruction of the *fuerzas vivas* by the "revolution" eliminated any challenge to bonanza development from above, while authoritarian governance cut off any challenge to it from below. But the key dimension was the economic—the fact that there was empty "economic space" in the mining sector which local private enterprise could not fill and which transnational enterprise, constrained by oligopolistic and market forces, did not wish to fill. The reluctance of foreign mining companies to plunge into the Peruvian gran minería in association with MineroPeru may have been a disguised blessing: had they done so while the parastatal was still new and weak, they might have given rise to another domestic elite with a vested interest in foreign capital penetration of Peruvian society. That did not occur, and MineroPeru's management came instead to preoccupy itself with its own (thence, national) control of the enterprise. It could do so with some hope of success because foreign consultants, equipment suppliers, and banks were concerned with selling their goods and services, not with the effects of MineroPeru's presence on the world capitalist system or on the international nonferrous metals oligopoly.

The class character of MineroPeru is indubitably capitalist (as is that of Centromin). This comes not from the circumstances of its formation nor from the intentions of the military regime but from the thoroughly bourgeois nature of its management and, still more prominently, from the latter's success in freeing the direction of the enterprise from political control. That is to say, its evolution into another bastion of the domestic bourgeoisie was an outcome of a specific set of class practices rather than an ineluctable consequence of systemic dynamics. In order to achieve the aim of autonomy and security of control, MineroPeru's bourgeois managers had to do three things: (1) Build a record of demonstrated performance. Whereas consistently poor results or a major project failure would have been answered (if the military's action in other areas be a guide) by the imposition of yet tighter controls from the center, positive results encouraged central state authorities to loosen the reins. (2) Accept the "tool" goal of bonanza development as their own. They could do so easily enough because the goal could be cast in quantifiable economic terms; because insulation from market forces made it unnecessary to be concerned first and foremost with early profits; and because—one cannot but suppose—they themselves were basically in sympathy with the idea of national development defined in this way. (3) Display great sensitivity to the legitimacy needs of the regime and frame project proposals to meet them. The ability to do this bespeaks a class element that does not share the liberal hostility toward politics mixing into economic affairs.

Peru's mining parastatals are not subservient to metropolitan capital, although MineroPeru's lack of solid capitalization has constrained it in the matter of "turnkey" contracts. Local private capital regards them neither as masters nor as servants but simply as *unas empresas más* ("just a few more companies"). The noncompetitive structure of the industry and the mediana minería or Cerro origins of parastatal managers make this the anticipated outcome. MineroPeru and Centromin have not taken it for granted, however. Both have instead moved actively to build up common interests with local private capital—MineroPeru with its zinc refinery, Centromin with COMMSA. There are instances, such as the one examined in the discussion of Tintaya, where interest differences bring MineroPeru into conflict with the private sector. But these are second-order conflicts of the type that normally arise between firms in a capitalist economy and are no cause for alarm on either side. My conclusion is that the parastatals have promoted bourgeois class formation in a material sense by expanding the ranks of the national manageriat and by vastly enlarging the stock of capital assets under its control; and in an ideological sense by breaking into (MineroPeru) or maintaining a position in (Centromin) the international oligopoly and by engaging in "world-class" technology development. This has been accomplished without "denationalizing" the bourgeoisie in any way.

The payoffs to Peru from the establishment of parastatal mining enterprises have been sufficient to validate the soundness of the measure. Centromin, as seen in Chapter 6, is an unequivocal economic success story. MineroPeru is less so, but its copper refinery has made a noteworthy contribution to increasing local value added, foreign exchange earnings, and marketing flexibility; it remains to be determined what the contributions of the zinc refinery, Cerro Verde II, and Tintaya will be. There are political payoffs as well, and these are at least as significant if not more so. The constitution of parastatals in the mining sector has clearly enhanced the technical and managerial capabilities at the state's disposal, which can only increase its credibility when it seeks to pursue its interests in bargaining bouts with prospective foreign investors.[45] More than that, this act has propitiated (though by no means guaranteed) the attainment of bourgeois ideological hegemony.

Parastatal enterprise under capitalism has an inherently ambiguous nature: its Janus face accurately reflects an underlying reality. On the one hand, the parastatal, left to its own devices, operates on the basis of the same values and criteria animating the ongoing operation of a private business: productive efficiency, authoritarian discipline, cost minimization, and profit maximization. On the other, the parastatal differs in its approach to new investment. As its capital derives from the state treasury, it is not compelled by market forces to look for the highest return on investment from among the options open to it. Projects will not knowingly be given the go-ahead if they result in losses or retard enterprise growth; but, within that limitation, they may be undertaken for the broader development benefits they provide—some directly

---

[45] Stepan (1978:268) makes the same point in relation to Peru's petroleum industry, where PetroPeru, another parastatal enterprise, operates.

economic (e.g., foreign exchange earnings), some indirectly so (e.g., improving the society's stock of technical and managerial expertise).

Whatever these benefits may signify in terms of the class interest of the bourgeoisie, they are undeniably in the general interest of a society that is striving to develop. Consequently, parastatal enterprise is an instrument for demonstrating that the two sets of interests can be brought into harmony. From there it is but a short step to erasing the conceptual distinction between them and making them appear identical—which is what ideological hegemony consists in. One need not worry that the bourgeoisie's ideological apparatus will delay inordinately in taking this step.

PART IV

Mining and Development:
A Class Analysis

UP to this point, our analysis has centered upon institutions—although we have taken pains to demonstrate the salience of institutional structures and relationships in shaping class interests and in constituting vehicles for the expression of class power. Dependency propositions have not fared well. Few signs of structured dependency relationships were discerned in regard to the transnational enterprise sector, where the Peruvian subsidiaries either conformed to local policy dictates of the state or were suitably disciplined; in regard to the domestic private sector, where dynamic corporate growth under national-bourgeois auspices accelerated without furthering dependence on Peruvian or foreign finance capital; or in regard to the public sector, where new parastatal entities advanced the development of the nation's mining industry and placed themselves near the international industry's technological frontier.

On the other hand, nothing in this analysis implies that the ambit of Peruvian state power is unlimited. The state's efforts to project its power *beyond its borders* met some resistance from transnational enterprises and from the international financial establishment, both of them with global interests to protect. Clever negotiating tactics, good knowledge of the international economic environment, and timely exploitation of the latter's contradictions enabled the state to realize many of its economic objectives but could not win total victories in matters such as copper marketing (Cuajone) and the organization of foreign development assistance ("turnkey" contracting).

As institutional analysis, alone, leaves the locus of power and control in the mining industry somewhat ambiguous, so too does it leave unanswered (or better, incompletely answered) the character of the mining bourgeoisie. Given the centrality of the mining industry in the local economy, it is inconceivable that the mining bourgeoisie could be anything other than a leading element of the superordinate local class. Consequently, its character will have much to do with the nature of class domination in postoligarchic Peru. So far, we have found that the particular circumstances of its formation have made the mining bourgeoisie nonstatist, but not anti-statist; nationalist, but not xenophobic; entrepreneurial, but simultaneously "technobureaucratic." In order to comprehend the new form of domination now emerging in the country, we must delve further into the formation and class character of the mining bourgeoisie, with the aim of resolving the apparent contradictions in this description and determining if the class is truly dominant. That is the purpose of Chapter 9.

The fact that the mining bourgeoisie displays "technobureaucratic" features is a clue suggesting that the class element exists in close association with technical and professional middle strata. Chapter 9 argues theoretically that the form of this association is important in establishing the nature of class domination and then proceeds to incorporate it in the empirical investigation of bourgeois class formation and action.

But the Peruvian minería has given rise to more than a bourgeois elite and associated middle strata. It is, in addition, the home of the best organized and most powerful element of the nation's working class. I believe that the growth in the size and organizational capabilities of the Peruvian working class, along with the corresponding numerical shrinkage of the peasantry, have already rendered improbable either a Leninist or a peasant-populist challenge to the present system of class domination. Hence, the developmental prospects available to Peru are, in my opinion, closer to those open to the metropoli than to those available to societies at lower levels of current development. To put it more plainly, the near- to medium-term choice is among three alternatives: a stable political order based on bourgeois economic domination but resting on a structured presence of working-class *material* interests within a "relatively autonomous" state—a presence as likely to be corporatist as liberal in form; a political authoritarianism of the Right—the "bureaucratic-authoritarian state"; or a transition to socialism under true proletarian control rather than under an intellectuals' vanguard party—an evolution without historical precedent. The formation and class character of the proletariat are factors helping to determine which outcome is the most probable.

Thus, not only the mining bourgeoisie and middle strata but also the mine workers and their unions will influence the nature of class domination in Peru in the years to come. The explication of proletarian class formation and action in the mining sector is the task of Chapter 10.

CHAPTER NINE

The Bourgeoisie and
Middle Class of the Minería

A class is defined by a mutual interest in political power and social control. To the degree that a class has a national identity, it is because the common class interest is geographically delimited—not because the members are citizens of a particular country. A national bourgeoisie is one whose concerns derive preponderantly from considerations of a local conjuncture, even if influenced in great measure by external forces. We have observed that the reformed Peruvian state is not a handmaiden of transnational resource corporations' global concerns; that there are also domestic mining firms; and that these, though participants in international markets, do not operate at the sufferance of, or in close partnership with, the transnationals. It follows that the mining bourgeoisie is part of a Peruvian national bourgeoisie.

On the other hand, it does not follow from the mere inclusion of the economically central minería in the national bourgeoisie that the class is necessarily dominant. Dependencistas maintain that Third World national bourgeoisies are not true dominant classes, since their lack of entrepreneurial dynamism deprives them of the image and reality of developmental leadership; and, because their cosmopolitan value system and culture cut them off from their local societies and thus put out of their reach the achievement of cultural-ideological hegemony. Chapters 7 and 8 have exploded the first argument, but the second remains to be dealt with. I shall do so now, by examining mining-bourgeois class formation, ideology, and practice.

Class domination is never exercised by a single elite or functional group, and I make no such claim for the mining bourgeoisie. Rather, I shall treat this class element in two ways: (1) as a *reference group* which is more advanced than most other bourgeois elements but which exhibits in microcosm certain traits likely to become more typical of the whole class in the near future than they are at present; (2) as a *leading stratum* whose activities and values, given the minería's key role in bonanza development, form much of the foundation on which class hegemony (if attained) will have to rest.[1]

With the rise to preeminence of large capitalist enterprises, the criterion for bourgeois class membership becomes less exclusive than "ownership of

[1] As "reference group" and "leading stratum" are not mutually exclusive concepts, it is entirely acceptable to treat the mining bourgeoisie, simultaneously, as both. I shall do so in the following discussion; it will be clear from the context if only one or the other is meant.

the means of material production.'' Another entryway is expertise in the management and administration of corporate enterprises and in the technologies that their profits depend upon.[2] This implies neither that effective enterprise control comes to be vested in a lower-level ''technostructure,''[3] nor that the interests of manager-technocrats are distinct from those of owner-entrepreneurs or of rentiers.[4] It means only that the acquisition of managerial and technical expertise is now an *additional* avenue into the bourgeoisie. Although the paramountcy of the business corporation in the economy catapults managers to the front ranks of the bourgeois class, owner-entrepreneurs and rentiers remain as structural elements and are not automatically precluded from assuming class leadership.

In most of the discussion from here on, the detailed treatment will be confined to managers and technocrats whose class situation is fixed, in the first instance, by control of the organizational resources of the private business corporation and the parastatal enterprise. Inasmuch as the large, dynamic, nationally owned mining corporation is a fairly recent innovation, many are still managed by entrepreneurial founders or by the latter's immediate heirs. But they, too, are for the most part manager-technocrats by training, and it is therefore futile to attempt to distinguish the manageriat from the owner-entrepreneuriat. Rentier investors are another matter. We saw in Chapter 7 that they have little influence over the affairs of the mediana minería, and we know that they have never been present in the gran minería. This chapter will thus deal with them only peripherally.

CLASS STRUCTURATION AND POLITICAL EFFECTIVENESS

The political effectiveness of the bourgeoisie—that is, its success in preserving its power and using it to perpetuate its exclusive privileges against real and potential challenges—is a function of, *inter alia*, its internal cohesiveness and consciousness and the nature of its relationship with the middle strata just below it in the socioeconomic pyramid.

Bourgeois cohesiveness, and a common class consciousness resulting therefrom, are problematical if the class is strongly rent by internal conflicts of

[2] ''Technology is a key resource because those who possess it can be presumed capable of possessing finance capital and other resources as well. . . . [W]ithout technology, even an abundance of other 'factors' of production augurs ill for economic success.

''But technology never exists in a social vacuum; it is owned by identifiable interest groups who may use it as an instrument of social control'' (Goulet 1977:9). ''Possession'' and ''ownership'' ought not to be taken to imply that technology is an external ''thing.'' It is, rather, primordially knowledge and skills, inherent in trained persons and a form of ''human capital.''

[3] As argued by Galbraith (1967).

[4] See Zeitlin (1974); Zeitlin and Norich (1979); and my comments in Chap. 7, n. 36. The latter authors argue that, at least in the United States, ownership rather than managerial interests continue to control the large corporation. In my view, that argument is questionable, not generalizable to other countries, and in any event inessential to sustain the authors' principal thesis.

interest. Various axes of intraclass conflict can be conceived: sectoral (e.g., manufacturing versus mining); role in capital accumulation (finance versus production); nature of property (private versus state)—these are perhaps the three most salient ones. Which of these conflicts, if any, hamper overall class cohesion and give rise to distinctive subclasses or class elements depends on contingent historical factors and is thus a matter for empirical determination. Chapters 7 and 8 showed that the mining bourgeoisie is independent of finance capital and that private versus state capital is not a principal conflict axis. The question of intersectoral conflict cannot be definitively resolved by a study of a single sector, but we may be able to develop some clues by comparing our results with those from counterpart studies of the Peruvian industrial bourgeoisie.

This leaves the issue of the mining bourgeoisie's relationship with the middle strata. The issue is crucial because the middle strata are potentially powerful in their own right. Not only are they numerically larger than the bourgeoisie proper; in addition, they partake of the scarce knowledge resource.[5] I submit: the history of postwar capitalism everywhere in the world makes clear that *a stable political order and bourgeois social domination can only coexist where the bourgeoisie has managed to coopt the bulk of the middle strata and to legitimate its dominant position to them.*

The Nature of the Class Boundary

As the bourgeoisie becomes more of a knowledge-based and less of an ownership-based class, the distinction between it and the middle strata blurs. It is, in fact, increasingly a purely political distinction, one resting on differential access to power maintained by institutional—corporate—forms. But power and control bring economic rewards to their wielders, and the class boundary thus comes to be marked by economic differences. The nature of these differences and their political consequences are not the same in developed and in developing societies, however. We can consider two polar extremes:

1. In the private business corporations of developed, late-capitalist societies, the bourgeoisie receives not only very much higher salaries than the middle strata but also extrasalarial forms of compensation: stock options and "insider" investment tips, profitability bonuses, special tax shelters, etc. These practices are legitimated by referring them to the belief in the social value of private entrepreneurship (viewed ideologically as inhering solely in the top management of the enterprise) and to the myth of equality of opportunity.

[5] Gouldner (1979:12 and passim). Those Marxists who refuse to modify the classical basis of class determination encounter a serious dilemma when they try to describe the class position of scientists, engineers, and technicians in capitalist society. In a society whose production principle is technological innovation, the attempt to resolve the dilemma by falling back on Marx's formalistic distinction between "productive" and "unproductive" labor is strained. Cf. Poulantzas (1975:210-23).

Parastatal enterprises offer their managers comparable rewards, justifying them as necessary to attract and hold scarce talent in competition with the private sector. In the state administrative apparatus, a clear economic superiority of top-ranking officials is more difficult to legitimate and maintain.[6] Relative proximity to the founts of power is the substitute; depending upon local custom, proximity may translate into opportunities for enrichment in the form of favors from private-sector "clients" of the bureau and/or into a second, private-sector career after an early retirement (with a handsome pension) from state service.

The large differential between the bourgeoisie and middle strata in developed capitalist societies has its political reflection. Rather than perceiving themselves as aspirants to full membership in the former, many integrants of the latter acquire a separate political consciousness. This entails, usually, an antagonism toward extremes of upper-class privilege, which may translate into political radicalism—as likely to be a radicalism of the Right as of the Left. Or, it may translate into the particular middle-class interest in individual freedom and quality-of-life issues which has become so much a part of the political currency of the United States.[7]

[6] In classifying state bureaucrats with the bourgeoisie, I am traveling over ground which, while well-plowed by theorists, has yielded an uncertain crop of explanations. Marxist orthodoxy, in particular, is torn by a theoretical contradiction in approaching the problem of bureaucrats' class identification. In insisting on ownership of the means of production as the sole basis of class division, this school has precluded an association of state *administrative* functions with those of the bourgeois class. On the other hand, all Marxists agree that the deployment of state power in a capitalist social formation serves to preserve the capitalist mode of production and to reproduce its structures of domination—which are bourgeois functions.

Examples of this dilemma abound. Miliband (1969:123) argues that state bureaucrats are "conscious or unconscious allies of existing economic and social elites," closely linked to the bourgeoisie by interest and ideology—but not, apparently, a part of it. In a later work (Miliband 1977), he attempts greater precision, now defining (p. 26) "the large and growing army of state employees" as "so to speak, a class apart, whose separateness from other classes is bridged by the factor of *ideology* [emphasis in original]." However, this "class apart" often acts, especially in less-developed countries, such that (pp. 111-12) "the state must be taken to 'represent itself.' " That is, political power is used by the "class apart" for its own enrichment. This suggests that the "state class" is defined not in terms of ownership of the means of production but in Weberian terms—the possession of differential privileges in the market competition for social goods.

Poulantzas (1975) finds that the highest state officials (p. 185) "generally belong to the bourgeois class, not by virtue of their interpersonal relationships with the members of capital itself, but chiefly because, in a capitalist state, they manage the state functions in the service of capital." But for him, the determination of this class situation is (p. 187) "neither direct or immediate"; rather, it "takes place by way of the state apparatus," which is (p. 25) "never anything other than the materialization and condensation of class relations."

The concept of class has ontological significance only when its definition tells unambiguously (1) what a class *is*, and (2) what the class membership of any specified individual is. Neither Miliband nor Poulantzas takes us very far here, although the former is considerably more straightforward in his description of the bureaucrat.

My approach to the definition of the bourgeois class is admittedly tentative; I hope to develop it further in a later work. It has the merit, as I see it, of accounting more fully for the modifications that capitalism has undergone since Marx's day. And, it makes unequivocal the class situation of state elites under capitalism: whether civil or military, they are subgroups of the bourgeoisie.

[7] Lasch (1978).

2. In the least developed capitalist societies, nationalist pride, the absence of a strong local private sector, and the consequent dependence of government revenues on taxes paid by transnational corporations remove much of the social resistance to high economic rewards for state and parastatal managers. Instead, high salaries are legitimated as necessary to elevate these officials to a position of equality vis-à-vis the transnational managers with whom they interact. On the other hand, the scarcity of managerial and technical skills makes it possible for the middle strata to demand and receive remunerations far closer to those of the bourgeoisie than they could command in a more developed context. Lower-level officials in the employ of transnational firms whose superior management slots are filled by expatriates frequently utilize political pressure to raise their level of remuneration close to that of the foreigners, justifying their demands on grounds of nationalism and opposition to (racial, cultural, religious, etc., as circumstances indicate) discrimination.[8]

Closer together in their class privileges, fewer in numbers, and confronting (in many cases) a culturally alien mass, the leading elements of the bourgeoisies and middle classes of these least-developed societies approximate to a cohesive, self-conscious political elite.

In view of its intermediate level of development, we can logically expect Peru to fall somewhere between these polar extremes. The political consequences of the intermediate case will be determined by the manner in which the extreme-case elements are modified and recombined in the intermediate situation.

The Influence of Socioeconomic Mobility

The relationship between the bourgeoisie and the middle strata is also affected by the opportunities for mobility across the boundary separating them. Bourgeois efforts to legitimate class privilege become increasingly unavailing in the absence of such mobility, an absence no longer justifiable once objective class membership qualifications have blurred. Mobility allows the legitimacy of bourgeois power to base itself on *accomplishment* and/or *seniority*. It is the cement that glues the middle strata politically to the existing order; the safety valve that prevents the accumulation of disintegrative pressures arising from the frustrations of the most ambitious and energetic members of the society; and the blood transfusion that enables the bourgeoisie continually to renew itself by accepting into its ranks the "best and brightest" from below. In contrast, a middle class confronted with a situation of "blocked ascent" is ripe for radicalization. Once radicalized it becomes a potent threat to the existing order, since the economic power and organizational expertise of the knowledge-based middle class make it a natural leader of the popular masses.[9] Meanwhile, the dominant bourgeoisie becomes stale and reactionary; the legitimation of its privileges, ever more in question.

[8] Sklar (1975); and Schatz (1977).
[9] See Gouldner (1979:62-63); Giddens (1973:56); and Larson (1977:xvi-xvii, 67-70).

Nonetheless, the political stability which is possible when the middle strata are coopted by the bourgeoisie does not have entirely negative consequences for popular interests. A small, threatened bourgeoisie is likely to take refuge under the shelter of a political authoritarianism of the Right. A more secure bourgeois class, on the other hand, usually opts for liberal or corporate democracy, as it provides institutional means for establishing the general interest of the dominant class.[10] But democracy is an idea not easily contained; once it has been institutionalized, the popular masses sooner or later gain the franchise and, with it, a chance to give effective legal expression to at least some of their most urgent demands.

The Peruvian industrial bourgeoisie has often been portrayed as a closed elite. Furthermore, middle-class "blocked ascent" and resultant radicalism—expressed until recently through the APRA and today through a miscellaneous collection of Left parties—are historical facts in the country.[11] We will want to see if the portrayal of the bourgeoisie is accurate for the mining sector and if the mining middle class is politically radical.

THE CLASS SITUATION OF THE MINING BOURGEOISIE AND MIDDLE STRATA

The bourgeoisie of the minería is composed of the directors and executive officers of locally owned private firms and those controlled or managed by the Hochschild Group (all of whose local officers are Peruvians); Peruvian nationals holding comparable posts in foreign-controlled firms; executive officers of the parastatal entities of the sector; and senior bureaucrats of the Ministry of Energy and Mines. This is a very small group; it consists, by my count, of only about 270 persons. Approximately 220 of them are affiliated with private Peruvian companies. Half of these are managing officers with line authority, usually trained and credentialled as mining engineers, geologists, metallurgical engineers, or chemical engineers; and the remainder are directors representing portfolio investment by rentiers—themselves or others. The next largest subgroup, about 35 persons, is the parastatal executives and senior bureaucrats, all of whom are credentialled professionals (among them a few attorneys specialized in mining law). Finally, there are fifteen or so

[10] On the preference of dominant local bourgeoisies for democratic forms of government when they feel their position in society secure, see Jessop (1978); and Sklar (1977, 1979).

[11] The APRA, discussed briefly in Chapter 2, has always been a vehicle for the expression of the political concerns of the middle classes—for which it has been regularly castigated by Marxists since the time of Mariátegui. (José Carlos Mariátegui, by far the most famous of Peruvian Marxists, participated centrally in the founding of the country's Socialist [later Communist] Party in 1928; his social and political thought will be found in Mariátegui 1971.) Letts (1981) notes the existence of over twenty "parties" of the Marxist Left, which, in the 1980 elections, offered eight separate slates. With the prominent exceptions of the "official" Communist Party, which has strong ties to organized labor, and two or three others with a base among the peasantry, it is safe to say that all of these organizations represent only students and radical intellectuals. That fact may have more than a little to do with their tendency to fractionate over slight disagreements as to strategy, tactics, or "theory."

Peruvians—again, almost all mining professionals—who exercise high-level managerial line authority in foreign-controlled enterprises.

Locating the boundary between the bourgeois stratum and the middle class is made easier for us by a statutory definition of "staff," which, unlike the North American definition, excludes nonhourly personnel whose positions involve minimal knowledge prerequisites and authority.[12] The middle class is thus composed of those employees who are classified as "staff" (the English word is customarily used) but do not meet the qualifications for inclusion in the bourgeois stratum. I estimate that the mining sector supports some 2,000 to 2,500 staff professionals. Some 1,400 to 1,800 of them are mining professionals; the rest are engaged in the provision of ancillary services.[13]

These figures signify a notable growth in professional employment during the seventies; data for 1970 show slightly over 800 mining professionals and 400 others.[14] A second change that has occurred in this decade is that the state and the parastatals have come to loom larger as employers of professionals, in great part as a result of the transfer of Cerro and Marcona from the private to the public sector and the appearance on the scene of MineroPeru. Roelfin de Sulmont found that in 1970 nearly 77 percent of all professionals in the sector were employed in private industry;[15] as of 1981, that percentage can be no greater than 66 and is probably closer to 50.

Economic Situation

Due to the paucity of available data on managerial and staff remunerations, it was not possible to assemble a full set of comparable salary statistics for each group in the same base year. Still, the information obtained from published and private sources allows an approximate comparison after adjustments to reduce them to an equivalent salary base and year. A representative sampling of the adjusted salaries of various bourgeois and middle-class groups is provided in the upper part of Table 9.1; the lower part presents comparative data for selected popular groups.[16]

---

[12] These other nonhourly personnel are called *empleados*; their class position will be taken up in Chapter 10.

[13] The presence of 421 Southern staff members and 712 in Centromin (both data are for 1977) was documented by the enterprises. Neither MineroPeru nor HierroPeru provided the requisite data, but their staffs can be estimated, respectively, as 200 and 150 if it is assumed that their ratios of staff to total employment are comparable to Southern's. The chanciest element of my estimate is the staffs of the mediana minería, the Banco Minero, etc., for which I can offer nothing better than an educated guess: 500 to 1,000. I assume that around 30 percent of the gran minería's staffs, and 15 percent of the mediana minería's, are providers of ancillary services. It may be noted that Oficina Sectoral de Planificación (1975) gives total professional employment in the mining sector as 1,742 in 1975—gratifyingly close to my estimate. Its figure includes mining engineers, geologists, metallurgical engineers, other engineers, physicians, and accountants.

[14] Dirección General de Minería (1970). Oficina Sectoral de Planificación (1975) states that total professional employment in 1968 was 1,100.

[15] R. H. de Sulmont (1972).

[16] Mining camp residents receive many free services from their employers—medical care and hospitalization, housing, community services, family counseling, and others—the value of which

TABLE 9.1 Earnings of Selected Groups Employed in the Peruvian Minería[a]

Data Year[a]	Employer	Employee Category	Monthly Earnings (S/)	($)
1977	Southern Peru	Staff (dollar payroll), min.	169,000[b]	2,000[b]
	Copper	Staff (local payroll), max.	120,000	1,420
		Staff (local payroll), min.	23,000	272
		Gen. foreman/supervisor, max.	85,000	1,006
		Lowest supervisory, max.	43,000	509
		Lowest supervisory, min.	29,000	343
1977	Parastatals	Management and staff, max.	103,000[c]	1,219[c]
1974	Mediana	Management, max.	103,000[c]	1,219[c]
	Minería	Management, median	80,000	947
		Management, min.	56,000	663
		Staff, max.	80,000	947
		Staff, median	24,000	284
1977	All Mining	White-collar workers, avg.	31,505	373
		Blue-collar workers, avg.	18,219	216
1974	All Peru	White-collar workers, avg.	16,000	189
		Blue-collar workers, avg.	6,100	72
1977	All Peru	Income per wage earner, avg.	18,323	157

SOURCES: Compiled by the author from data supplied by Southern Peru Copper Corporation, the Instituto Nacional de Estadística, and the Departamento de Estudios Económicos y Estadística, Sociedad Nacional de Minería y Petróleo. Except for Southern dollar payroll, original data are in soles.
[a] Base earnings excluding vacation and holiday pay, overtime, special bonuses. Value of free services received by mine workers also excluded. Data for 1974 were inflated by 100 percent, the approximate rate of inflation over those three years, prior to entry in the table.
[b] Author's estimate.
[c] Statutory ceiling imposed by the Peruvian government.

We see that the handful of bourgeois employed by Southern Peru Copper—the company's "dollar payroll" staff—is far and away the most economically privileged element of the mining bourgeoisie. It is also in Southern where the economic gap between the bourgeoisie and the middle strata is widest. The size of the gap is due less to the firm's planned salary structure than it is to the ongoing devaluation of the sol; but its existence was starting to produce, in 1978, unmistakable signs of staff alienation from top management.[17]

is not included in the tabulated salaries. The availability of these services must be taken into account whenever mining remunerations are compared to those in other sectors.
[17] I detected such signs as high as the division manager level. The problem was exacerbated

There is little economic distance between the members of the bourgeois elite in parastatal enterprise management and those who manage firms in the medium-mining subsector. A few of the latter probably fare better than the former, especially when extrasalarial compensation possibilities are factored in. Although medium-mine managers do not command an earning potential on a par with their brethren in Southern, they have the offsetting advantage of being big fish in little ponds, not beholden to expatriate superiors and to a home office in another part of the world. On the other hand, parastatal managers are not satisfied, as a rule, to enjoy salary equity with the mediana minería. They prefer, instead, to use Southern as their salary reference. Centromin, it is said, has had to compete in salary by resorting to the dubious expedient of authorizing overtime pay for top management.[18]

Outside of Southern, the gap between elite and middle-stratum remunerations is rather narrow, and the degree of socioeconomic cleavage between the two groups seems smaller than it would be in most developed countries. While staff professionals earn considerably less than they would in the United States, the managers to whom they report do not draw salaries in the six-figure (in dollars) range, as do many of those who direct major transnational mining corporations.[19] A salary administrator for MineroPeru claimed that professional staff (middle stratum) remunerations in the mining sector as a whole had tripled on the average during the Velasco years (1969-1975) as accelerated mining development increased the demand for their services.[20]

Remunerations at the boundary between the mining sector's middle class and the subordinate groups of white- and blue-collar workers below it resemble not at all the salary gap that we expect to find in the least-developed countries. The adjusted earnings of mining white-collar workers average out to more than the median earnings of medium-mining staff, this without even adding in bonuses and overtime; the base pay of blue-collar mine workers averages to 76 percent of the mediana minería staff median and would draw even with it were bonuses and overtime included. What is seen here is the result of labor union pressures, strongly supported by the state in the late sixties and early seventies (Chapter 10). The situation at the middle-class/working-class boundary is similar to conditions in the most heavily unionized U.S. industries. In fact, relative income equality at this boundary, combined with the lack of six-figure managerial salaries at the top, makes the structure of remunerations within the Peruvian mining industry in general somewhat more

by the fact that most of the dollar-payroll expatriates are skilled mechanics and other blue-collar workers whose authority ranks below that of less-well-paid Peruvians on the local currency payroll. In 1978, Southern was searching frantically for a way of restoring salary parity without running afoul of government-imposed salary ceilings.

[18] Centromin expresses its desire to offer higher salaries in its annual report for 1976. The statement about its use of overtime pay comes from a high officer of Southern.

[19] It was reported (*Wall Street Journal*, 1 April 1980, p. 10) that Thomas D. Barrow, board chairman of Kennecott, received $1.2 million in salary and bonuses in 1979 under his five-year contract with the firm.

[20] Interview with Luis Briceño Rodríguez, January 11, 1978.

egalitarian than one finds *either* in highly developed *or* in very underdeveloped settings.

The absence of a conspicuous economic gap separating the popular classes of the sector from the middle class is a recent development.[21] Hence, the continuing capitalist evolution of the industry has gone hand in hand with an improvement in the incomes of the subordinate groups relative to the superordinate. It therefore follows that capitalist industrialization in the world hinterland does not rest in every instance on the "superexploitation" of workers—who, instead, may be among its direct beneficiaries. Still, the economic disarticulation typical of hinterland industrial development marginalizes the mass of workers who remain outside the reach of modern-sector employment. The table shows that the average Peruvian white-collar worker earns two-thirds, and the average blue-collar worker but a fourth, of the median monthly salary of mediana minería staff. A comparison of mining staff salaries with the average income per wage earner leaves no doubt of the privileged position of the middle class in Peruvian society.

Social Origins

Seventeen years ago, William F. Whyte formed the impression that few Peruvian managers originated with either the "criollo class" (by which he meant the oligarchy) or the mestizo and *cholo* masses; most, he concluded, were immigrants or children of immigrants.[22] I cannot state too emphatically that the identification of immigrant entrepreneurship with dependency is pure racism; the test of indigenous development can never be that it arose *ex nihilo*, free from all outside influence whatsoever. Nevertheless, it is possible in practice for an immigrant group to remain socially distinctive and economically monopolistic for generations, as is true in the extreme case of the settler states of Africa. Such a group will often constitute a closed ruling elite, to which the appellation "imperialist" can be applied with some accuracy. Alternatively, immigrant groups can merge, after some years, with the indigenes of their adopted homeland. If that occurs, the infusion of developmental energies can actually increase the upward mobility chances of elements of the native-born population.

The available sociological data, along with impressionistic evidence gathered during my stay in Peru, convince me that Whyte's description is not

---

[21] The historical evolution of Cerro wages is given by DeWind (1977:166). His data indicate that the average miner's wage was S/1.25-1.50 per day in 1906, rising only to S/4.20-18.25 ($0.65-2.81) per day as late as 1945. Wages in the mediana minería were doubtless lower. While the middle class of the period was also deprived, it is difficult to imagine (the requisite data are unavailable) that its situation could have been this poor.

[22] Whyte (1965); a similar view is expressed by Chaplin (1967-68). Chaplin's argument for nonindigenous bourgeois origins is based on his earlier investigation of the Peruvian textile industry (Chaplin 1967). One must be extremely cautious in extrapolating from class characteristics observed in a particular functional group to a class at large.

applicable to the mining bourgeoisie and middle class.[23] On the other hand, his depreciation of "criollo class" production of bourgeois managers remains relevant for professionals in the mining sector. The available data on place of family residence (residence in the sierra being a fairly reliable indicator of nonelite status) and income of mining engineering students in the late sixties and early seventies—today's younger managers—firmly rule out elite social origins.[24] It is of interest to note that the Peruvian pattern of staff professional recruitment from "lower-middle" economic sectors and from smaller towns corresponds remarkably well to recruitment patterns into the engineering profession in the United States.[25]

MOBILITY AND CLASS COHESION

The thrust of the evidence is that the mining industry has for some years represented a major avenue of upward social mobility into the national bourgeois elite for at least a fortunate few from the middle strata of a society not otherwise regarded as an exemplar of equal opportunity. It is doubtful that such mobility chances would have been as available as they are had foreign capital succeeded in monopolizing the mining industry. For it has been in the locally owned mediana minería, only recently supplemented by the parastatal gran minería, where most of the opportunities for upward mobility are found. Yet, the mediana minería could not have provided those opportunities had its enterprises been wholly family-owned and -managed. What has made mobility possible is the evolution of these firms into professionally managed corporations. The ascent to top management may not be free of nepotism and clientelism, but it can be secured by a demonstration of professional com-

[23] I reviewed a listing of 220 surnames of directors and executive officers of Peruvian mining companies, under the assumption that a Spanish surname indicates native birth. I also marked as native-born a few individuals lacking Spanish surnames with whose family history I was familiar. (There has been little recent immigration to Peru from other Hispanic countries, but there are many Peruvians, descendants of earlier immigrants, who retain non-Spanish surnames; consequently, my methodology yields a conservative result for native birth.) Of the 220 individuals listed, 71.4 percent qualified as native-born by my criteria. Note, too, that Hopkins (1967) found very high percentages of indigenous origins and parentage among Peruvian state and parastatal managers. We are on safe ground in assuming that those percentages could not have decreased significantly since he wrote.

[24] In 1966, 43.3 percent of Peruvian university students matriculated in mining engineering were born outside the Lima-Callao metropolitan area, a much larger fraction than for any other academic curriculum. The averge family income of these students, S/6,850 per month, was well below the S/9,171 average for all university students and was, in fact, the second lowest among all academic specialties. In 1971, 39.2 percent of students of mining engineering, metallurgical engineering, and geology came from families with monthly incomes of S/5,000 or less; 91.2 percent of their families earned S/15,000 or less per month. Again, these figures are the second lowest out of all academic specialties (Samamé Boggio 1974:1:136-39).

[25] Data for the United States show that from 1940 to 1950, the proportion of engineers whose fathers were blue-collar workers increased from 30 to 40 percent, while the percentage of those whose fathers were enterprise owners or managers dropped from 30 to 24. Moreover, a disproportionate number were from towns of 5,000 to 50,000 total population (Perrucci 1971).

petence. The basis of managerial professionalism is specialized higher education.

The Nature of Mining Education

The overwhelming majority of the mining professionals received their university education in Peru, most of them at the National Engineering University (UNI).[26] Although the managers and staff members whom I interviewed revealed little awareness of how their own social origins and career patterns compared to those of their peers, all were very conscious of common educational background as a factor promoting group cohesion.[27]

UNI is an elite university, but in the meritocratic sense. It is not and never has been a finishing school for oligarchic *señoritos* in search of humanistic polish and is, thus, a departure from the tradition according to which "in Latin America . . . higher education give[s] greater prominence to classical teaching and to the liberal professions than to courses which are strictly technical or related to industry."[28] The inspiration of its founder, Eduardo Juan de Habich, was unabashedly Saint-Simonian: he defined engineering as a profession devoted to the "rational extract[ion] of natural resources to satisfy the ever-increasing necessities of man and society."[29] He believed that suitable candidates for the profession were to be found at all social levels. Indeed, one of his aims in setting up the school was to make possible the ascendance into that technological meritocracy by anyone, on the basis of individual achievement alone. To that end, he insisted that the school not only be tuition-free but that it extend financial aid to cover other student expenses. While scholarship assistance is no longer provided, the tradition of minimal fees and strict academic standards has been maintained.[30]

Education for development was a watchword of the first Belaunde administration, which greatly expanded technical education in the public university system. In keeping with Belaunde's announced dedication to decentralized development, much of the expansion took place in the provinces: long-dormant provincial universities were reopened, others were revitalized, and all were granted budget increases—with the bulk of the new moneys reserved for

[26] In a survey sample of twenty-four top managers, thirteen reported UNI as the last postsecondary school attended; four, other Lima universities; five, colleges or postgraduate schools in the United States; two, schools in other foreign countries. In a sample of forty-three middle-stratum staff members, twenty-one reported UNI; fourteen, universities in the Peruvian provinces (Sociedad Nacional de Minería y Petróleo 1974).

[27] As one of them put it, "Of course we 'miners' know each other quite well. Most of us, after all, were classmates at UNI." It became obvious to me in very short order that, indeed, many of these individuals are close friends or, at least, social acquaintances.

[28] Cardoso (1967:108).

[29] Samamé Boggio (1974:1:93); see also Chapter 2, n. 30. Samamé states that Habich modeled the university quite deliberately after the major engineering institutes of Paris, Rome, Turin, Freiburg, etc.

[30] Financial aid is provided directly to students by the mining industry. Cerro, Southern, and Atacocha have long had scholarship programs. Other firms have since added them. The programs expanded enormously in the 1970s in response to labor union demands (Chapter 10).

technical programs. The private universities followed suit. By 1971, an aspirant to a professional career in the mining industry could choose from as many as nine schools, depending on his or her preferred specialty, and did not have to migrate to Lima to attend one.[31]

The military regime, while eliminating foreign advisors and instructors, accelerated the expansion of university programs to meet future projected demand for technologically trained manpower. Since mining development was elevated by the military into a national priority, and since government studies regularly predicted a need for additional mining professionals,[32] mining education was strongly pushed. A new school of mines was opened in the sierra at Recuay, and a program of mining career promotion in the secondary schools was instituted.

What the expansion of the country's programs of higher technical education did not do was to make it possible for a larger proportion of applicants to gain entrance. Instead, the fourfold growth in the size of the freshman class from 1960 to 1969 was exactly matched by a corresponding increase in the number of applicants—so that the percentage of applications accepted hardly changed at all. Those would-be technologists who chose the mining specialties were still less fortunate. Successful applications to mining industry engineering programs in all of the country's universities fell from 84.4 percent of solicitations in 1960 to only 37.7 percent in 1968. Successful applications to UNI's mining programs declined comparably in the period in percentage terms, from 90.4 to 40.1 percent.[33] As is true in most developed countries, high academic standards, combined with limited placement opportunities, have become as effective as ascriptive criteria in maintaining a measure of elite exclusivity.[34]

By most accounts, the technical content of the UNI program is, *mutatis mutandis*, as well adapted to the circumstances of the nation's mining industry as are the better schools of mines in the metropoli to theirs. Relatively more

[31] Dirección de Planificación Universitaria (1971).

[32] Consejo Nacional de Investigación (1974). Projected manpower needs for 1980 included 342 new mining engineers, 22 geologists, 250 metallurgical engineers, and 2,104 technicians and paraprofessionals.

[33] Samamé Boggio (1974:1:134).

[34] The statistics omit from consideration those secondary school graduates who, though interested in a mining career, were discouraged from applying to a university by factors relating to family economic circumstances: poor preparation in an inferior secondary school, a home environment unsuited to studying, a need to make an immediate financial contribution, etc. In consequence, the data cannot fully reflect the degree of elitism entailed in the credentialling requirement imposed upon mining professionals. Suleiman's (1974) study is one among many showing how, in societies where academic achievement and credentialling have become significant *billets d'entrée* into elite groups (Suleiman deals with France), stiff academic requirements for entry into the system of higher education can be as effective—more effective, if the prevailing social ideology claims an allegiance to formal equality—as ascriptive criteria such as family wealth in maintaining elite exclusivity. It is more the case in Peru than in most developed countries that the quality of one's primary and secondary education and, thereby, one's chances of being admitted to a more prestigious university, are crucially dependent on the economic situation of one's parents (Paulston 1970).

attention is given to the simple technologies utilized in the medium mines. But the generally good match between the techniques learned in the classroom and those employed by medium-scale industry does not imply a neglect of more advanced topics: though highly technological, Southern Peru Copper has few complaints regarding the training received by Peruvian professionals in its employ, and we already know of the high level of technological expertise exhibited by MineroPeru's and Centromin's all-Peruvian staffs. An index of the adequacy of Peruvian mining education is that locally trained professionals encounter little difficulty in finding jobs abroad.

Were UNI to be true to the *saintsimonisme* of its founder, it would attempt to inculcate in its graduates a belief in a professional ethos of altruism and service to the collectivity.[35] Whether or not such an ethos animates the university's faculty is unknown. What cannot be gainsaid is that the curriculum of the mining engineering program is oriented toward service in a very different cause: the well-being and prosperity of the enterprise. Moreover, that orientation has been reinforced by latter-day curricular modifications, which have added courses in industrial management, general and cost accounting, financial analysis, and other business administration topics.[36] That graduates will tend to identify with the enterprise which employs them rather than with the abstract idea of engineering as a service profession is further propitiated by the high degree of specialization characteristic of modern engineering education, in Peru as much as anywhere else.[37]

A socioeconomic elite which accepts new members from below needs mechanisms whereby its solidarity and cohesion are preserved even as its personnel change. It would appear that technical-professional education in Peru is such a socializing mechanism.

The Influence of Career Advancement Patterns

There are no *Wunderkinder* among the bourgeois elite, all of whose members have attained their current prominence only after serving long apprenticeships. If entrepreneurs, they established their companies in middle life, having first gained experience as staff engineers with other firms. If managers of companies founded by their fathers, they were groomed for top management by being made to learn the business from the ground up. If parastatal managers or state administrators, they began their careers as junior engineers in Cerro and/or the mediana minería. Career progression data obtained in a survey of top medium-mine managers confirm the picture of ascent through the ranks, often with one or more changes of employer: of the twenty-four managers

[35] Comte de Saint-Simon (1952).

[36] Samamé Boggio (1974:1:114). He laments that these courses "sanction as valid, as definitive indicators in a mining project, the concepts of rent, profit, interest, income, costs, risks, etc. There is thus developed in the student a loyalty to the objectives of an enterprise—postponing, with the absence of courses on multisectoral planning (for example), a loyalty toward national objectives."

[37] Perrucci (1971).

sampled, fifteen had previously been employed by at least one other firm, and the median duration of their previous employment was six years.[38]

Most managers started out as apprentice engineers in the mining camps of the sierra.[39] The apprenticeship is vital to the career development of the would-be entrepreneur or top manager, for only in that way can he gain the practical experience lacking in the classroom. Now, a mining-camp apprenticeship entails some real hardships when judged according to the prevailing scale of values of the Peruvian middle and upper classes. In this urban-centered society, assignment to a remote mining camp is a form of cultural exile. It usually implies a separation from family, a considerable sacrifice to a people who tend to find their familial obligations much less onerous than many young North Americans seem to.[40] Camp life is physically rigorous due to the altitude and the nature of the work, but in Peru the rugged outdoor life and pioneering spirit yield no status payoffs.

The trials and tribulations of the mining apprenticeship ought not to be overromanticized; they are much milder than those of the mine worker and come to an end in considerably less than a lifetime. But they are just great enough to constitute a sort of professional initiation. The shared experience fosters a certain camaraderie among the mining professionals of all ages who have passed or are passing through it. It enables them to take pride in *not* being cultured, well-polished *señoritos*: an unmistakable note of condescension creeps into their conversation upon reference to the self-styled *gente decente*. There is just one other Peruvian elite whose formative experiences and resulting cohesion are similar: the military. Though few mining bourgeois evince enthusiasm for the career of arms, the opinions they express of other social groups differ hardly at all from the military attitudes documented by Luigi Einaudi.[41]

Sociologists have sketched the Peruvian oligarchy as an execrable collection of pretended aristocrats oriented toward symbolic status, the enjoyment—not accumulation—of wealth, and the rigorous avoidance of any kind of work tending to *suciarse las manos* ("dirty one's hands").[42] Assuming the accuracy of this portrait, the apprenticeship would have been enough to deter oligarchic scions from embarking upon careers as mining professionals. (Nor, as heirs

[38] Sociedad Nacional de Minería y Petróleo (1974).

[39] According to ibid., eighteen of twenty-four managers in the sample had previously worked in the mining camps of their current employer; their mean time of such service was over three years. (There was no survey item regarding camp experience with another employer.)

[40] Since Peruvian youths usually reside with parents until marriage, the young, unmarried engineering graduate is likely to be leaving them for the first time when he takes up an apprenticeship in a mine. If he is married, the odds are great that he will want his wife to remain in Lima or another city, either to obtain a better education for their children or because a mining camp is not a sufficiently decent environment for a *señora de calidad*. The only notable exceptions are Southern's camps, where excellent facilities, and the example set by expatriate families, encourage Peruvian engineers to keep their wives and children with them.

[41] Einaudi (1969).

[42] Astiz (1969); and Bourricaud (1970).

to great wealth, would they have perceived the need.) There are a very few mining engineers of upper-class origin who hold positions in Lima head offices as family sinecures, having bypassed the apprenticeship on the upward route. Their firms are, with just one exception, fading relics. Their performance records unsullied by financial success, such individuals do not enjoy the career mobility of their better-trained cohorts and are destined to disappear from the scene as corporate concentration advances. They are, naturally, held in contempt by the rest of the mining bourgeoisie.

In sum, the apprenticeship serves to promote intrabourgeois and bourgeois/ middle-class solidarity, to exclude oligarchs from that solidarity, and to enhance the mining entrepreneurs' and managers' self-image of resourcefulness and dedication. A shared apprenticeship experience supplements the educational experience as a mechanism of elite socialization. Once appropriately socialized, new entrants to the profession encounter few mobility barriers.

CLASS FORMATION AND FOREIGN ENTERPRISE

In the days before its expropriation, there was a considerable flow of upwardly mobile professional staff out of Cerro and into the mediana minería. It was made up of more ambitious individuals willing to trade the relative security of the foreign corporation for the opportunity to exercise unrestrained managerial power.[43] Hence, Cerro served the mediana minería as a training ground for some of its brighter lights; it was *la gran universidad minera del país*, the on-the-job educator of as many as 30 to 40 percent of the top managers of the mining sector.[44] It did not debilitate the locally owned mining industry by draining away its best entrepreneurial and managerial talent, as some dependencistas might have predicted.

Cerro's service to the national industry has not, by and large, been repeated by Southern. Its salaries and benefits are so superior to those of other mining firms, and its process technologies are so different, that most of the young engineers whom it hires seem content to live out their professional lives in its embrace. The absence of lateral career mobility between Southern and the rest of the industry does not appear to be a source of resentment among other professionals, however—at any rate, not while the mediana minería and the new parastatals continue to offer alternative opportunities for career development in quantity sufficient to meet the apparent demand. Its most immediate effect is to further Southern's isolation (due in the first instance to its sheer size and the specialized nature of its operations) from the remainder of the industry, to which its relationship is more that of a distant cousin than a big

[43] Movement in the opposite direction, while not impossible, was impeded by Cerro's preference for training its own young Peruvian staff; and there was never any incentive for senior men to trade away their managerial prerogatives in medium firms for the dubious advantages of a staff position in the foreign company.

[44] Interview with Ernesto Baertl Montori, president of Milpo, August 24, 1977.

brother. It is noteworthy that not even MineroPeru's staff has been enriched by a "cross-pollenization" of personnel with Southern—this despite many technical similarities and a close business relationship with respect to copper refining.

Asarco, Southern's parent, has made a certain contribution with its other local subsidiary, Northern Peru Mining. It trained several of MineroPeru's top operations officers and may have given a start to a few medium-mine managers.

BOURGEOIS AND MIDDLE-CLASS ORGANIZATIONAL RESOURCES

Class-based political action is frequently mediated through formal organizations which embody class interests and represent them to the larger society. In the process, such organizations promote class formation in any of several ways: by offering a visible status ratification of class membership—thereby promoting class identification and solidarity while acting as gatekeepers (protectors of class exclusiveness) at the lower boundary; by fostering cross-class cohesion where useful to broader class purposes, as in the case of bourgeois/middle-class solidarity; by resocializing the upwardly mobile in expected elite behaviors; and, of course, by developing and propagating a class ideology. Conservative political parties sometimes perform one or more of these functions, but they are not the only politically salient organizations of the dominant class. Two other common ones are the trade association and the guild association.

Trade associations formally represent the interests of particular bourgeois functional groups. They can, however, become inclusive enough to encompass nearly the whole leading bourgeois stratum.[45] Even if they cannot accomplish this, they facilitate the creation of institutional mechanisms that can. Capitalist societies abound in industrial coordinating committees, political joint-action councils, and the like—organizations that combine individual trade association bases on behalf of mutually shared interests. In addition, trade associations provide much of the financial support for bourgeois political parties.

Guild associations come to the fore in proportion as professional expertise becomes a path of entry into the bourgeoisie. High-status professions often win the privilege of self-regulation through their professional guilds. Guild association membership may be a credential attesting to membership in the profession. The associations engage in ongoing education and assist their members in maintaining their technical competence. To the degree that the bourgeoisie legitimates its social dominance on the basis of a meritocratic managerial ideology, guild associations contribute to its legitimation through their defense of professional ethics and standards and through their propagation

---

[45] The U.S. Chamber of Commerce and the Confederation of British Industries are examples of highly inclusive trade associations.

of an ethos of professional responsibility—a stewardship incorporating the welfare of the collectivity.[46]

Trade and guild associations loom larger in Peruvian bourgeois class formation due to the lack of well-institutionalized class parties of the Right. Guild associations gain importance from the fact that they enjoy grants of official authority under general state supervision without parallel in Anglo-Saxon societies.[47] This custom has enabled the engineering profession in Peru to acquire self-regulating powers that only medicine and law exercise in the United States. Peruvian trade associations, for their part, actually rendered bourgeois class parties superfluous before 1968, since they were the principal mechanisms of corporatist intermediation employed by the *fuerzas vivas*. Consequently, the forms of interest intermediation adopted by the mining sector's trade association after 1968 reveal how the "revolution" has affected the exercise of class power in the society. The study of the mining trade association is additionally useful because the association joins together foreign and local enterprises as well as entrepreneurs, managers, and rentiers. The relative power of each of these should be reflected in the extent to which it shares in controlling the association's affairs.

Guild Associations in Peruvian Mining

Two guild associations are active in the country's mining sector. They are the College of Engineers and the Institute of Mining Engineers (IIM).

The College of Engineers is a quasi-official autonomous body, combining under one roof the stewardship function of a professional guild and the licensing function assigned, in other jurisdictions, directly to the state.[48] The licensing function is implemented by means of examinations administered by the college; those who pass this test of professional competency are enrolled in one of the association's "chapters" according to specialty. The stewardship function is discharged by requiring every enrollee to subscribe his or her allegiance to a set of ethical principles (similar to the physician's Hippocratic Oath) whose enforcement is the college's legal responsibility. In addition, the college attempts to defend the honor of the engineering profession whenever it appears to have been impugned.

The thesis that professional self-regulation and high status are correlated is supported by Peruvian custom: the title *Ingeniero*, the status equivalent of the attorney's *Licenciado* and the physician's *Doctor*, is regularly employed by those eligible to use it.

The power to license, naturally, is no power at all unless the possession

[46] On self-regulation and stewardship notions as attributes of professionalism, see Larson (1977).

[47] Wiarda (1973).

[48] In the United States, the state retains formal licensing powers even in medicine and law, where guilds are strongest. The medical and legal guilds secure their prerogatives by penetrating the state, i.e., by controlling appointments to state licensing boards and by obtaining the assent of state authorities to licensing and disciplinary standards proposed by the guilds.

of a license conveys some patent economic advantage. In contrast to the situation in the United States, where a Professional Engineer license is of value only to civil engineers who approve building plans, the Peruvian engineering profession long ago won enactment of laws requiring the signature of a member of the appropriate chapter of the College of Engineers on a wide variety of documents. In the mining industry, most contracts, statutory declarations, and solicitations to government agencies are invalid unless countersigned by a member of the Mining Chapter.

Many junior engineers inscribe themselves on the rolls of the Mining Chapter for its status and career mobility advantages. But membership is most immediately useful to senior engineers and managers who prepare the documents needing authorized signatures. As of 1979, the rolls of the Mining Chapter contained 566 names, of which about 65 were recognizably those of members of the bourgeois elite. There is also a Geological Engineering Chapter. In 1979 it had 763 members, of whom 7 belonged to the elite.[49]

In contrast to the College of Engineers, the IIM is a voluntary association devoted to the intellectual (technical) content of the mining engineering profession. Its magazine, *Minería*, features technical articles along with summaries and analyses of legislative and regulatory innovations affecting the industry. The association sponsors seminars and technical conferences on topics of current interest to industry professionals. Peruvian mining engineers who wish to advance their careers join the IIM to remain *au courant* and to develop useful personal contacts. Membership probably numbers well over two hundred.[50]

The IIM is instrumental in promoting both intrabourgeois and bourgeois/middle-class cohesiveness within the mining sector. It is effective in this role because it is the only organization in the sector open to all professionals regardless of age, experience, or place of employment. It is the principal forum in which government technocrats and engineers in private enterprise, staff members of Peruvian firms and those of foreign-owned companies, representatives of the gran minería and those of small firms, the managerial-entrepreneurial elite and apprentices, can interact professionally and socially. Its younger members are probably the most ambitious of their age cohort and the most likely to become the next-generation industry elite; participation in IIM affairs is a vital socializing experience preparing them for that ascent.

There is a second service performed for the mining bourgeoisie by the IIM: it is the main institutional contact point between the local and international bourgeoisies of the industry. The association regards itself as the peer of the American Society of Mining, Metallurgical, and Petroleum Engineers and of similar mining societies in the metropoli and maintains fraternal relations with them. It participates in international industry forums and on occasion sponsors them (it hosted the Eighth Annual World Mining Congress in Lima in 1974). *Minería* republishes speeches and articles by leading international mining

[49] *La Minería en el Perú 1979* (1980:O52-O82).
[50] Purser (1971:242) counted "more than 150" members in 1970.

experts. In short, the IIM helps to form, and to propagate in Peru, the joint outlook and community of interests of the international mining bourgeoisie.

The National Mining and Petroleum Society

Two trade associations represent the interests of private capital in the mining sector. The Society for Small Mining Progress lobbies on behalf of the smallest firms but is the pet project of four brothers who operate one of the largest enterprises of the pequeña minería. Although it has successfully forestalled any erosion of the special legal status and promotional benefits awarded to the pequeña minería since 1950, it has proven helpless in the face of the adverse structural conditions which have propelled that subsector into a long-term decline. The National Mining and Petroleum Society is the representative of the gran and mediana minerías. Its 107 members (in 1980) include Southern Peru Copper, the three mining parastatals, all of the private companies in the medium-mining subsector, a few smaller firms, most metal traders and suppliers of industry equipment (many of them local sales offices of North American and European manufacturers), several banks, and some individual entrepreneurs and investors.

"Like business groups everywhere," the Mining Society "is useful to the companies in that a united front is presented to the government, which not only implies unity within the industry but safeguards individual corporations from being singled out for attack."[51] As the industry's employer association it assists member firms in confronting the mine unions at bargaining time. And, as we shall see, it coordinates sectoral planning on its members' behalf.

But the Mining Society has not always been merely a private institution. For years it possessed an official charter and an institutional position in the state apparatus. Along with the other property-owners' associations,[52] it had the right to appoint some of the directors of the Central Reserve Bank, the Banco Minero, and various parastatal entities. Its representatives served on advisory committees within the Ministry of Development, where they were well placed to influence the content and enforcement of mining legislation and regulations.

Though long a potential political heavyweight—thanks to the interests that stood behind it—the Society was weak until it was reorganized in 1940 under Cerro's sponsorship. A new charter was obtained, and the association took on the task of representing all three branches of extractive industry: metal mining, nonmetallic minerals, and petroleum. IPC joined, as did Southern and Marcona from the moment of commencing operations. With this membership lineup, Charles Goodsell's 1974 description of the Society as having "been dominated by [North] American capital for decades" was no exaggeration. He was also correct in asserting that IPC's expropriation changed little, that "the [private] gran minería controlled it even though Cerro, Mar-

---

[51] Goodsell (1974:88).
[52] The National Agrarian Society and the National Society of Industries.

cona, and SPCC [Southern] had only a fifth of the seats on the board of directors.''[53] We shall see shortly how their control was secured without a board majority.

During the 1950-1968 period, the Mining Society generally maintained a low public profile, its quietly effective lobbying enhanced by its institutional links with the state. When necessary, ''[p]ressure was mobilized and applied through commodity subgroups or committees. . . . Lobbying was carried on both before the national legislature and in the pertinent ministries.''[54] But the large North American mining companies were careful not to allow the association to become too obvious a spokesman for foreign capital. When, for example, Southern entered into conflict with the legislature over the Toquepala contract (pp. 53-55), it fought most of the battle alone. The Society, to be sure, vigorously opposed the tightening of investment incentives and higher income tax rates enacted in the sixties. However, the main thrust of its public objections was that the new laws would be disincentives to the expansion of *national* capital in the industry.

From the mid-fifties until the early seventies the Society was the de facto economic planner and coordinator for the whole sector. There was a need for the compilation and analysis of production and economic data, a need which grew hand in hand with the rise of modern mining corporations concerned to plan their activities on a long-range basis. Knowing that mining firms were loath to share sensitive operating data with state bureaucrats whose competence and honesty were then open to serious question, industry technocrats established a division of statistical and economic analysis under the Society's aegis. The information it acquired, aggregated or coded prior to publication so that individual firms were unrecognizable, formed the knowledge base for both private and government planning. Economic analyses were also brought forward in support of the association's legislative proposals. Later, as the DGM finally developed to the point where it could assume the public planning function, its officials worked closely with the Society in setting up a reporting system. In consequence, the system in use today incorporates all of the definitions, reporting categories, and accounting practices previously adopted by the private sector for its own purposes.

The property-owners' associations did not fare well under military rule. Since the generals wanted to enlarge the scope of autonomous state policy-making, their 1969 administrative reforms eliminated most of the institutional representation in the state that those organizations used to enjoy. (In particular, the directors of all parastatal entities were thenceforth selected by the state alone.) In the agricultural and industrial sectors, the associations of property-owners fought the military regime's reforms head-on. They lost.[55] The Mining

---

[53] Goodsell (1974:88).

[54] Ibid., p. 36.

[55] The National Agrarian Society was the principal institutional bastion of the oligarchy—which, of course, opposed the military regime's land reform tooth and nail. The government's

Society, however, eschewed anti-government ideological rhetoric, stressing adaptation and mutual compromise in place of confrontation—which it could do comfortably, since there was no doubt of the importance of private mining capital to the regime's bonanza development plan. Still, the altered political environment had rendered obsolete the concept of an officially chartered trade association with a formal corporate presence inside the state. Having come to view its charter as a devalued asset that might entail some unpleasant obligations—e.g., to accept workers as members—the Society voluntarily surrendered the charter in 1974. Its legal status is now no different from that of any nonprofit private corporate body—but its influence on policy has not disappeared by any means.

This change in the Mining Society's relations with the state coincided in time with an equally dramatic change in the character of the interests it represented. Table 9.2 breaks down the organization's membership list over five-year intervals beginning in 1950. Total membership trended steadily upward until 1970; but except for the 20 percent increase in the number of metal-mining companies between 1950 and 1955 (the years of the growth spurt stimulated by the 1950 Mining Code) and the 19.6 percent increase in 1975-1980, most of the membership gains were accounted for by firms engaged in oil and gas exploration and by suppliers, many of whom were importers of drilling equipment. These were largely foreign businesses, of course, and the international petroleum majors were well represented among them.[56] Had this pattern of membership growth continued, Peruvian companies might have ended up as a numerical minority within "their" trade association. That did not happen. Dry holes and nationalization drove out most of the private oil industry. Expropriation also removed Cerro and Marcona from membership. By the end of 1975, metal-mining companies, all of them but Southern part of the mediana minería and most of them Peruvian-owned, had come to constitute an absolute majority. (They also account for

tolerance for verbal abuse from that source waned when it continued long after the reform was an accomplished fact; on May 12, 1972 the state dissolved the society and seized its assets. Immediately thereafter, it set up a new National Agrarian Confederation made up largely of peasants who were the direct beneficiaries of the agrarian reform (Bourque and Palmer 1975; Harding 1975). To no one's surprise, the new institution was intensely loyal to *velasquismo*. Unfortunately, it did not shift with the winds of the "second phase" of the "revolution"; having become ever more oppositional, it, too, was dissolved, in 1978.

The situation of the National Society of Industries (SNI) was somewhat different. In the early 1970s the larger, more modern firms were cautiously cooperating with the regime's industrial property reforms. Most of them, however, owed a primary loyalty to the Exporters' Association (ADEX). Therefore, it was possible for individuals supported by the more numerous small industrialists to gain control of the SNI. Reflecting the small manufacturers' "liberalism," they moved the SNI into ideological opposition. The regime answered by seeking to compel the SNI to accept workers as members. When its directors refused, the SNI's charter was revoked. It was not, however, formally dissolved and remains today as the Society of Industries. See Bamat (1978:192-219).

[56] In 1970 there were: ARCO; a subsidiary of British Petroleum; Continental Oil; Gulf; Mobil; Occidental Petroleum; Shell; Standard of California; Texaco; and Union Oil.

TABLE 9.2 Mining Society Membership,[a] 1950-1980

| | | Principal Member Activity | | | | | | | | | | | |
| | | Metal Mining | | Other Mining | | Oil & Gas | | Traders & Suppliers | | Banks & Finance | | Natural Persons | |
Year	Total	A	B	A	B	A	B	A	B	A	B	A	B
1950	87	44	50.6	5	5.7	5	5.7	5	5.7	6	6.9	19	21.9
1955	121	53	43.8	7	5.8	17	14.0	11	9.1	6	5.0	27	22.3
1960	132	57	43.2	9	6.8	16	12.1	20	15.2	7	5.3	23	17.4
1965	149	62	41.6	12	8.0	19	12.8	29	19.5	7	4.7	20	13.4
1970	154	65	42.2	12	7.8	24	15.6	31	20.1	7	4.5	15	9.8
1975	97	56	57.7	8	8.2	0	0.0	18	18.6	6	6.2	9	9.3
1980	107	67	62.6	6	5.6	1	0.9	18	16.9	6	5.6	9	8.4

SOURCE: Compiled by the author from the official membership lists of the Mining Society.
NOTE: Columns A = number of members; columns B = percent of total membership.
[a] Except for those listed in the column labeled "natural persons," all members are affiliated business firms.

nearly all of the membership increase since 1975; however, MineroPeru, Centromin, and HierroPeru became members in 1979.)

And yet, *plus ça change.* . . . Neither the changes in its institutional relationship with the state nor the comparably profound changes in the character of its membership seem to have interfered in the least with the Mining Society's ability to keep open channels of communication to the highest organs of the state. Furthermore, by the Society's own reckoning, the communications which flow through these channels have been quite satisfactory from the perspective of their effects on the members' interests. In its contacts with the government after 1968 the Society encountered no serious limitations in regard to the range of matters to be discussed, the ministries and bureaus with whom they could be discussed, or the hierarchical levels at which the discussions could take place. The opinions of the Society have been regularly solicited, just as they had been in years past, on drafts of legislation and administrative regulations prior to their final promulgation.[57]

However, the ability to communicate is only the first step for a lobbying group. Has the Mining Society been able to obtain passage of legislation sought by its members and to veto that to which they are opposed? It has. The first decree-law of the military regime applicable to the mining sector was a long-sought bill aimed at medium-mine promotion. The 1971 and 1981 Mining Codes offer proportionately larger investment incentives to private

[57] Or so the Society claims in its annual reports for all years from 1968 to the present, excepting only 1973 and 1975. Interviews with officials of the Society and with outside observers confirm the claim.

Peruvian enterprise, as compared to foreign enterprise, than did the 1950 Code. Agitation from the Society led in 1975, a crisis year, to a significant increase in the Banco Minero's lending capacity and to the creation of special funds that can be drawn upon for new mine development and for rescuing firms in temporary distress.

In assessing these accomplishments, it must be borne in mind that the Society was not so foolish as to squander its political capital by taking a stand on every state act relevant to private mining business. It was, in fact, judicious in supporting official policy on emotionally charged issues of secondary importance to firms *owned by Peruvians*. Hence, it applauded the expropriation of IPC and also backed, albeit weakly, the later nationalizations of Cerro and Marcona—*even though all three foreign companies were members*. It acquiesced in the expansion of state entrepreneurial activity in the mining industry and encouraged the new parastatals to affiliate. It refrained from combatting the Workers' Community scheme of mandatory comanagement and profit sharing[58] when introduced in 1970. In other words, its success in obtaining preferential treatment for the interests of its national member firms has depended upon a tacit willingness to concede to the state full initiative in policy areas touching on the legitimacy concerns of the government, reserving its aggressiveness for areas where the economic interests of the mediana minería are directly at stake.

Legislative success does not end the tale. The Mining Society's economists and statisticians still work hand in glove with state officials to forecast and plan the future of the industry. In the United States, economic policymaking is said to be dominated by private trade associations (an example being the American Petroleum Association), which control the U.S. government's sources of information.[59] If that is the case in the world's most technologically advanced nation, it should be even more so in a small, late-developing country whose state apparatus is something less than a model of expertise and efficiency. The policy autonomy of the Peruvian government, that is, does not extend to autonomous control over the information on which policy decisions must be based. Therefore, more active state planning in the mining sector cannot become a threat to local private enterprise. Indeed, the converse is true: in proportion as the state becomes a more active planner and promoter of industrial development, policy influence gained through control of the flow of planning data can be far more valuable to private corporations than the old system of organic ties to the state maintained by the property-owners' groups.

Who Controls the Mining Society?

Members of the Mining Society pay annual dues proportional to the value of their production. Before 1969, this arrangement led to a situation whereby IPC's, Cerro's, and Southern's dues contributions each covered about 25

[58] The workings of this scheme are detailed in Appendix D as item VIII.
[59] *Wall Street Journal*, 31 January 1980, p. 10.

percent of the Society's yearly expenditures, with Marcona's share about 20 percent.[60] Their dominance was formalized in the Society's bylaws via a system of weighted voting. Members were divided into three classes according to their dues obligations, and each one's vote was weighted more or less heavily depending upon the class to which it belonged. I am reliably informed that the weighting factors were such as to give the Class A members—the private gran minería and IPC—an absolute veto. The effect was to vest full control of the Society's affairs in the hands of large U.S. capital while shielding that power from public view behind a physical membership and directorial majority of Peruvians. Since Cerro instigated the Society's 1940 rebuilding, and since weighted voting dates from that period, one can only assume that the North American company agreed to bail out the organization in return for the right to control its affairs.

Weighted voting was removed from the bylaws in 1974. Today, each member and each director casts one vote irrespective of firm size. The new arrangement ensures that the nationally owned private companies, who are the numerical majority, have unhindered control of the association. (Were it otherwise, it is inconceivable that the parastatals would have been permitted— let alone encouraged—to affiliate.) Southern, the one remaining private gran minería member, seems perfectly content with the new arrangement; since it relies in any event on one-to-one negotiations with the state to protect its interests, it treats its Society membership as a public relations gambit.

Given the manifest importance of the Mining Society to the Peruvian mining industry, the distribution of its institutional power among professional managers, owner-entrepreneurs, and rentiers should reflect the relative position of each within the bourgeois class. I assume that this power distribution is in turn indicated by the identities of the Society's elected officers, as it is common practice in organizations of this type for the officers to initiate policy and for the members merely to ratify their decisions. I confine myself to officers representing metal-mining interests, since the latter are dominant inside the Society.

My analysis of the Society's officeholders in the thirty-year period 1950-1980 shows a dramatic decline of the rentier element, from 37.5 percent (three of eight officers) in 1950 to just 9.7 percent (three of thirty-one) in 1980. (The decline of rentier power is reflected in Table 9.2 as well, in the decreasing number of individual affiliations since 1965.) Peruvian owner-entrepreneurs have held their own: from 37.5 percent of the officialdom in 1950, their numbers have decreased but slightly, to 32.2 percent in 1980. In contrast, managerial representation has grown significantly, with most of the growth accounted for by managers of Peruvian firms: whereas in 1950 only two of the eight elected officers were salaried managers—one from Atacocha, the other an expatriate—the manageriat in 1980 occupied eighteen of the thirty-

---

[60] Information from private sources who requested anonymity.

one elected offices. Thirteen of these managers (41.7 percent of the elected officers) were from Peruvian-owned companies; two were Peruvian officials of foreign firms, Hochschild and Southern; and three were expatriates.

In sum, a Peruvian manageriat rooted in the locally owned corporations of the mediana minería has displaced U.S. capital from control of the Mining Society. And rentier capital's power in the councils of the Society has diminished to the vanishing point.

IDEOLOGY AND POLITICAL VALUES

Class is a relevant category for the study of social action tending toward domination in that it is "a level or grade" in the social structure, "the members of which tend to think and act as an entity."[61] To put it another way, classes acquire significance *as social actors* insofar as their integrants' objectively shared interests become a foundation for subjective group identification, cohesion, and consciousness; or, in the classical Marxian terminology, when they become classes *für sich*. "While classes are defined in the process of production, they are historical actors only when they establish some consciousness and organized connections between their structural interests and their collective social practices."[62]

The mining bourgeoisie is a functional group, not a class. If it is to be a dominant social force, it must exercise its power as the leading stratum of a larger national bourgeoisie. Are there ideological requirements which the group must satisfy in order to aspire to that status?

1. We have reviewed structuration factors which have the effect of creating a limited group cohesiveness of the mining bourgeoisie and its associated middle strata. Any such cohesive subgroup has a "distinctive identity . . . , manifest behaviorally in the collective actions and attitudes of its members."[63] If the mining bourgeoisie is or can be the leading bourgeois stratum, its "collective actions and attitudes" must not clash fundamentally with other national-bourgeois interests of an essential, long-range character.

2. "Class interests are likely to prevail when they are promoted in the name of national aspirations."[64] The mining bourgeoisie must express and embody broad national goals with which at least the national middle class, and preferably the politically mobilized elements of the popular classes as well, can identify. The ability to do this was labelled *ideological hegemony* by Antonio Gramsci.[65] Ideological hegemony has two components. One op-

---

[61] Sklar (1977).
[62] Castells (1977).
[63] Sklar (1976).
[64] Sklar (1977).
[65] Gramsci defined hegemony as an intellectual and moral leadership exercised over civil society by a dominant class *in addition* to that class's political power exercised through the state. Moreover, he believed that the acquisition of hegemony necessarily *preceded* class political power. "Hegemony . . . is pictured as an equilibrium between civil society and political society—

erates in the realm of belief, referring to "the capacity of a class to present the interests of most classes and fractions of society as convergent with its own interests." The other operates partially in the realm of performance, referring to "an actual capacity of the ruling class to fulfill the immediate interests of most classes and fractions in a better way than any other *possible* alternative."[66] The second component is linked to the first in two ways: in that the systems of belief underlying class ideological hegemony are unlikely to remain firm if performance regularly fails to meet expectations; and in that performance itself is related to belief, which influences interest perceptions and judgments about what is better and what is possible. When a social group is ideologically hegemonic, its pursuit of its own interests appears to be coincidental to the pursuit of a more general interest—we usually call it "the national interest"—held in common by most social groups.[67]

3. If ideological hegemony is to extend to the organized popular classes, the bourgeoisie must not only reconcile its actions with the former's material demands. It must also accommodate to, and incorporate into the *Weltanschauung* it holds and projects, the preexisting organizational activities undertaken by the lower classes to press for *their* interests. Concretely, this means that the bourgeoisie must accept the legitimate presence of labor unions, confining itself to steering the labor movement away from a fundamental and radical critique of the current order. It can be argued that, more than any other of their acts and omissions, the inability or refusal of many Latin American economic and political elites to do this accounts for their incapacity thus far to ratify their dominance with political stability under even a formalistic, limited democracy.[68]

This brings us to the question of the relationship between bourgeois ideology and mode of political organization. The appearance of authoritarian political forms throughout much of the Third World has been duly noted by scholars, most of whom agree that "political monopolies normally consolidate the power of the dominant classes."[69] In those less-developed countries at in-

---

more specifically still, between 'leadership' or 'direction' (*direzione*) based on consent, and 'domination' (*dominazione*) based on coercion in the broadest sense" (Lawner 1973; see also Gramsci 1971:57-58 and passim). I fear that there is a tendency for Marxist structuralists to interpret the concept mechanically, so that it becomes synonymous with the *dominazione* of a particular "class fraction." When I use the term, "hegemony," it is to be taken always in the sense of leadership in civil society. I am not convinced that it invariably precedes the acquisition of class political power or that it is uniformly necessary for class domination, but I do think it necessary for class domination of a *democratic* polity. On this point see Femia (1979).

[66] Castells (1977), emphasis in original.

[67] It follows that the study of bourgeois ideology refers to the class's *political effectiveness*, not its structure. It is well to remember Cardoso's (1976:51) caveat: "Our methodology does not imply . . . discovering in [its] ideology . . . the germ of a national bourgeoisie in order to demonstrate that the latter 'really exists,' nor proving by the same route that the social category is imaginary."

[68] It might be suggested, as a hypothesis for future investigation, that the case of Mexico is the exception that proves the rule.

[69] Sklar (1977); cf. Callaghy (1979).

termediate levels of industrialization where autonomous popular organizations—parties and labor unions—already exist, a chief aim of the authoritarian state is to destroy them.[70] Once that has been done, it is difficult to imagine how the bourgeoisie sheltered under the protective wing of the authoritarian state can ever become ideologically hegemonic—and, so, dispense with political monopoly—as long as the bitter experience of repression, burned into the consciousness of the subordinate societal groups who have suffered it, remains unforgotten. Hence, students of "bureaucratic-authoritarianism" in Latin America are not sanguine about the prospects for an early return to democratic political norms.[71] But not all political authoritarianisms have been as thoroughly brutal as those of South America's Southern Cone in repressing lower-class organizations, and some of them have been replaced in their turn by more limited, participatory forms of government. Peru, where the reestablishment of civilian governance has recently taken place, is one such case. It is said that the reappearance of limited, civilian government, when it occurs, "betokens the existence of dominant social classes, whose members are confident of the their ability to manage the affairs of society."[72] Is this true of Peru?

In responding, I shall have recourse to two bodies of information. The first is an opinion survey of mediana minería managers and middle-class staff professionals taken in 1974. The survey data have neither been analyzed nor published before now, but those who conducted it were kind enough to provide access to the raw completed questionnaires (which I proceeded to analyze myself) on condition that they be granted anonymity.[73] The second is the series of extensive, open-ended discussions that I engaged in during 1977-78 with about twenty-five senior managers from all subsectors of the minería. It is possible and useful to classify the political attitudes and values revealed by these studies into four topical areas: government mining policy; issues of class interest; overall development policy; and the question of military versus civilian rule.

Government Mining Policy

The 1974 survey sampled the attitudes of its respondents regarding various specific acts of the military government which had obviously impacted on the

[70] O'Donnell (1973); see also Collier (1979).

[71] O'Donnell (1979). His pessimism seems justified by recent events in the Southern Cone: it has been reported (*Los Angeles Times*, 11 August 1980, p. 2) that General Pinochet plans elections in Chile—in 1997!

[72] Sklar (1977).

[73] Although hesitant to accept their condition, I felt that the importance of the findings, together with my access to the raw data, justified an exception to customary scholarly strictures. I am in a position to verify that the organizers of the survey are fully qualified. The survey sampled twenty-four top managers and forty-three staff professionals, representative by rank and geographical location of the whole mediana minería. The tables to follow often indicate more than twenty-four or forty-three responses; this is because multiple responses to many of the survey items were fairly common.

operations of mining enterprises. Table 9.3 codifies their replies with reference to the three acts having the greatest political and economic import.

We see from the table that the 1971 Mining Code, the centerpiece of the military regime's bonanza development program, won the general approval of both the bourgeoisie and the middle strata by large majorities. Evidently, medium-mine managers and staff did not object to the state's assumption of an entrepreneurial role in mining, its declaration of a state smelting and refining monopoly, or the institution of worker profit sharing and comanagement (with a qualification to be examined below)—all of which were provisions of the new code. Neither, it seems, did they take serious issue with the tightening of rules for depletion allowances and tax-free profit reinvestment that was also a part of the 1971 law.

Integrants of the two groups appear to have disagreed with each other in regard to labor stability—i.e., guaranteed job tenure for workers, enacted in 1970—and the Cerro expropriation. The small number of responses to these two items, however, raises the possibility that the apparent disagreement is merely a survey artifact. If it is real, it would most likely be connected with the differential impact of the measures. Senior managers, as I verified in my conversations with them, do not perceive much of a productivity loss traceable

TABLE 9.3 Opinions of Mediana Minería Managers and Staff Respecting Aspects of Government Mining Policy in the 1968-1974 Period (*Percent; number of responses in parentheses*)

Law or Policy Measure[a]	Position	Managers	Staff
1971 Mining Code	pro	37	41
(D.L.18880)	con	11	3
Expropriation of Foreign	pro	0	2
Mining Firms (Cerro)	con	0	3
Labor Stability	pro	0	3
(D.L.18471)	con	9	3
Other Aspects of Policy[b]	pro	0	12
	con	37	16
TOTAL		100(35)	100(58)

SOURCE: See n. 73 and accompanying text.

[a] Descriptions of decree-laws D.L.18880 and D.L.18471 will be found in Appendix B, Table B.2.

[b] Managers mentioned, in order of descending frequency: the state monopoly over metal export sales, restrictions on importation of mining machinery, and D.L.20007 regarding housing standards in mining camps. Staff mentioned, in descending order: D.L.20007 (accounts for all positive responses), machinery import restrictions, and the sales monopoly.

to labor stability; but junior supervisors often find themselves transferred to less desirable positions as a consequence of conflict with workers under their command, since the option of discharging the latter has been foreclosed. I would imagine that staff members' disapproval of the Cerro expropriation stemmed from their fears that this historic avenue of upward advance would thenceforth be closed to their like.

In all of my 1977-78 discussions, approval of the 1971 Mining Code was widespread. A few individuals professed a nostalgia for the 1950 Code, but they admitted that such extreme generosity to private capital was no longer politically feasible. Opposition to labor stability, as noted above, was limited and unemotional. Few of the managers registered any opposition to the nationalization of Cerro, which most saw as inevitable in view of its "social debt." In general, the managers seemed secure in the belief that sectoral policy would remain benign from the standpoint of their concerns; all that really worried them were ad hoc measures (such as the 1975 tax on mining exports) adopted, with little evident consideration for their long-term effects on the industry, to combat the post-1975 economic crisis. Parastatal managers and DGM officials held opinions quite similar to those of interviewees from the private sector; there were but a few differences of emphasis, traceable to the particular interests of the institutions with which they were connected.[74]

Issues of Class Interest

Two 1974 survey questions dealt with issues in this category. One asked whether the maintenance of enterprise efficiency did or did not depend on the elimination of labor unions; the class content here is obvious. The other called for suggestions regarding possible changes in the Workers' Community system—profit sharing and comanagement. Under the assumption that anything which promotes working-class solidarity and real worker control of management is to the interest of the working class, we can qualify as "pro-working class" any suggested change that would have: (1) strengthened the comanagement feature of the system; (2) accented profit-sharing distributions in the form of capital stock (at the time, distributed capital shares were held in common by all workers) while deemphasizing cash profit sharing by individual workers; or (3) made it easier for workers, rather than managers or staff members (who also participated in the system if they were not ordinary shareholders in the firm), to control the representative institutions of the Workers' Community—particularly if labor unions shared in that control.

---

[74] These results are reminders that, while the military regime's mining policies never failed to consider duly the needs and interests of domestic private enterprise, the regime did not limit itself to ratifying passively the recommendations of the private sector. Although consultation with representatives of the latter was constant, the regime made its own determination of how public policy should support private capital and of how mining capital's interests should be reconciled with other policy concerns. The relevant political image, again, is that of the "relatively autonomous" capitalist state whose stability depends on its ability to harmonize conflicting class interests without sacrificing the general, long-range interests of the whole dominant class.

Suggestions of an opposite thrust, by contrast, would tend to convert the system into nothing more than a productivity incentive; they can be qualified as "pro-bourgeois." "Class-neutral" responses are also possible, of course.

The upper part of Table 9.4 is a compilation of proposals for change in the Workers' Community system checked off by respondents from a list provided in the survey questionnaire item, with the responses grouped by class content as described above. The lower part of the table summarizes responses to the item regarding the role of labor unions in the enterprise.

As is to be expected, senior managers' orientation toward the Workers' Community system was unanimously and unequivocally "pro-bourgeois." Their main concern was to stave off any erosion of their own authority by completely eliminating the comanagement feature. Second in importance for them were the elimination of sector-wide profit sharing (see note to table)

TABLE 9.4 Opinions of Mediana Minería Managers and Staff Respecting Issues of Class Interest (*Percent; number of responses in parentheses*)

Issue Area and Policy Suggestion	Managers	Staff
Workers' Community:		
Eliminate comanagement aspect	60	14
Improve profit sharing in cash	13	18
Abolish sector-wide profit sharing[a]	13	14
Eliminate labor union influence	7	9
Greater role for staff	0	5
Improve work-incentive aspects	0	4
SUBTOTAL, "Pro-bourgeois" responses:	93(14)	64(14)
More sector-wide profit sharing[a]	0	5
Strengthen comanagement aspect	0	9
SUBTOTAL, "Pro-working-class" responses:	0(0)	14(3)
Better officers and/or regulations	7	18
No changes	0	4
SUBTOTAL, "Class-neutral" responses:	7(1)	22(5)
ISSUE AREA TOTAL:	100(15)	100(22)
Role of Labor Unions in the Enterprise:		
Efficiency compatible with their presence	42	31
Efficiency requires eliminating them	29	36
No response	29	33
ISSUE AREA TOTAL:	100(24)	100(45)

SOURCE: See n. 73 and accompanying text.

[a] Sector-wide profit sharing refers to a scheme by which a portion of shared profits, in both cash and stock certificates, is distributed among all workers of the mining sector rather than just among those of the same firm whose profits are being shared out.

and more emphasis on cash profit sharing—both proposals designed to enhance the system's value as a work incentive. There was some concern over "excessive" labor union influence on the affairs of the Communities, though most managers, it would appear, did not view this as a primary source of difficulty.

Staff members as well revealed a predominantly "pro-bourgeois" attitude toward the system, but theirs was not as pronounced. The most probable explanation for the difference is that middle-class staff members had more to gain personally from it. And, being technical experts, they may have comprehended that they stood an excellent chance of electing their own to the Communities' governing boards and of using that power to advance their interests. One staff member specifically proposed in a handwritten comment that a greater role be provided to professionals in the running of the system; and those who opted for the "better officers" item may well have been thinking of—themselves!

The number of top managers who saw no intrinsic incompatibility between the union presence and enterprise efficiency exceeded the number who did by about 45 percent, thereby tending to verify the hypothesis that modern managerial ideology can accommodate to preexisting tendencies in working-class self-organization. The greater antagonism of staff to the unions is one of the least expected findings of the survey, since in other areas staff members showed somewhat more sensitivity than managers to issues involving social justice. It is my suspicion that what staff opposes is not unions in principle but, instead, the habit that Peruvian labor leaders have of elevating disputes between workers and their immediate supervisors to the level of a *cause célèbre*.

All managers with whom I discussed the Workers' Community issue in 1977-78 favored the idea of profit sharing, even in the form of capital stock distributions. However, there was nary a dissent from the desire to use profit sharing solely as a productivity incentive. Most wanted shares of capital stock to be distributed to workers individually. Everyone totally opposed comanagement, although about half would tolerate some worker input: in routine administrative matters; if limited to certain topics (e.g., reorganizing work assignments to improve output); or if confined to nonbinding suggestions.

None of those whom I interviewed wanted labor unions abolished, but almost all saw them either as "excessively politicized" or as chaotic and undisciplined. A clear majority felt that "political" union leaders were manipulating "unsophisticated" workers. There was a broad consensus to the effect that the government had contributed to labor indiscipline by promoting competition between labor centrals and by giving in too easily to their wage demands (to be discussed in the next chapter). Most regarded labor leaders as personally corrupt and abusive of their prerogatives.[75]

---

[75] But a couple of interviewees, possibly more astute than the rest, observed that leaders who could "get away with" such abuses increased their rank-and-file support thereby. The rank and file, it was said, took pride in such demonstrations of *viveza criolla* ("creole shrewdness") and

About three-fourths of my top management interviewees demonstrated a conscious awareness of class interests by voicing concern over the preservation of private capital's freedom of social action. Still, only two of them supported their arguments with ideological defenses of the sanctity of private property. The rest defended entrepreneurial initiative on the ground that it is an instrumental social good; they drew no distinction between entrepreneurialism as practiced by the private sector and by the state.

Issues of Development Policy

The 1974 opinion survey did not deal with general public policy viewed as part of an overall strategy of national development. I broached a key issue in this category with the managers interviewed in 1977-78: land reform.

The agrarian reform issue proved to be less dormant than the 1976 declaration of its official completion might have implied. Peru in 1977-78 was suffering a severe problem of declining agricultural productivity, as was noted in Chapter 2. Conservative political forces, having reemerged into the open, were attributing agricultural production shortfalls entirely to the *reforma agraria*.

Managerial attitudes toward the reform were equivocal. Only three were firmly set against it, but the rest tended to view it more as an unpleasant historical inevitability than as a bold social initiative. The "peasant problem" was usually regarded, wearily, as one that was bound to persist into the near-term future; it was a problem of *falta de cultura*, as a consequence of which the peasant would neither respond well to market incentives nor restrict his immediate consumption in order to capitalize his productive base.[76] Almost every one of the commentators—it made no difference if he was a private entrepreneur, a parastatal manager, or a state official—believed that the best (or only) solution was the development of an agricultural smallholding bourgeoisie, with its nucleus in the small group of Peruvian kulaks. (But they sharply differentiated such a bourgeoisie from the oligarchy, which few of them admired.) The guiding principle of agricultural development should become the same as that operant in the mining sector: *amparo por el trabajo*. In some unspecified way, the state (or market forces) would encourage the transfer of land into the hands of whomever could demonstrate an ability to produce on it efficiently in units of small to medium scale.

Military versus Civilian Rule

The most salient political issue of all, in 1977-78 as well as in 1974, was the future of civilian participatory government in Peru. To be sure, the circumstances were not the same in both periods: whereas advocates of civilian rule in 1974 had to confront a military establishment apparently intent on

---

believed that their *vivo* union leaders were simply adapting customary upper-class practices to their own purposes.

[76] Note that the Spanish word, *cultura*, cannot be rendered in English as "culture" in this usage. It corresponds more precisely to a modern world view, to an understanding of what is expected of one in a modern society.

retaining power indefinitely, in 1977-78 they had merely to await the 1980 end of the announced transition period and hope that the plans would not be upset by some hard-line military faction. Yet, even in the later period there were those who did not wish to wait two years for a military *salida*. Some were moved to impatience by the regime's seeming incompetence in meeting the economic crisis. Others were loyal supporters of ex-President Belaunde— who, upon returning to Peru, demanded an immediate *salida* and the election of a civilian president under the old 1933 constitution.

In 1974 the issue of a return to civilian governance was so sensitive that the opinion survey dared not allude to it even indirectly. In spite of the omission, two of seventeen managerial respondents inserted handwritten comments demanding free elections at once. Eight staff members used the same technique to express concern with the question. Two called for immediate elections. Four others may have been more interested in democratic content than in electoral formalism; they asked for greater freedom and a wider scope for political participation and dissent.

In 1977-78, few managers, private or parastatal, wanted to do anything that might have upset the ongoing process of transition to civilian government. But the majority had not forgotten the immobilism and ineffectiveness that had helped to bring on the 1968 coup and did not desire the restoration of the constitutional and political status quo ante. While there was little open discussion of what a new civilian regime might look like, those who had opinions on the subject appeared to lean toward a strong presidential system— something, perhaps, on the Gaullist model. (In fact, the 1980 constitution greatly strengthened executive powers.)

The recrudescence of political party activity in the later period made possible, in theory, the use of party affiliation as a guide to political belief. It turned out that none of the interviewees volunteered a party preference, and I formed the distinct impression that they preferred to avoid the question. Nevertheless, two mining managers indicated their preference for the Rightist Popular Christian Party in a more dramatic fashion: they appeared on the party's list of candidates for the 1978 Constituent Assembly, the body which wrote the new constitution. As I anticipated, only a handful of middle-class staff, and no managers, showed sympathy for the parties of the Left; and it was tempered by a belief that these parties were factionalized, dogmatic, and ineffective. Further impressions would be risky. I would suggest—not as a research conclusion but as a hypothesis worthy of investigation—that most managers would describe themselves politically as "centrists" or "reformists" and that their party preference would lean, but without much enthusiasm, toward the APRA and Acción Popular (Belaunde's party).

The Managerial Ideology

In his study of the political behavior of Peruvian industrialists during the 1968-1973 period of the "revolution," Alberto García de Romana challenges the conventional wisdom which depicts their ideological orientation as favoring weak government and laissez faire.[77] He posits instead that the industrial bourgeoisie is divided into "liberals"—predominantly, owners of smaller, family firms—and "developmentalists"—owners and managers of modern corporate enterprises. The "liberals," he maintains, are fearful of any social change and have always opposed the "revolution." In contrast, the "developmentalists" proclaim that today's businesspeople must "abandon the image of the firm as a feudal fief and . . . resign themselves, in the interests of efficiency and [social] solidarity, to the sharing of certain benefits which had been theirs alone until now." The "developmentalists" supported most of the "revolutionary" reforms, excepting only those (e.g., full co-management) that struck directly at managerial authority.

The ideology of military developmentalism, worked out and propagated by the Center for Higher Military Studies (CAEM), rests on the notion that the armed forces are a meritocratic elite in service to the national community. As a service elite, they cannot confine themselves to narrowly military concerns but must further the fundamental interest of the nation: development.[78] The "developmentalist" managerial ideology outlined by García de Romana is remarkably similar in content—including meritocratic elitism—and in the method of propagation via an elite institution. The idea of managerial-entrepreneurial elitism is expressed this way:

> The modern businessman considers himself obligated to the process of national development directed toward the general welfare. "The urgency of change in social and economic structures . . . is obvious to the modern entrepreneur who works to produce and distribute goods efficiently. . . ." [T]he functions of executive and entrepreneur are not exhausted in the board of directors; rather, accounts must also be rendered to the collectivity. The modern concept of management consists in financial responsibility, but also in a social responsibility evaluated according to the general interest.[79]

The institutional mechanism of ideological development and propagation is the Peruvian Institute of Business Administration (IPAE), a private educational organization "whose program has been directed toward satisfying the management training requirements . . . *of the principal mining companies*, local branches of international trading companies [e.g., Hochschild], and the most modern manufacturing companies." IPAE is not a school; run by and for businesspeople, it specializes in setting up training programs inside firms and employs working executives as part-time instructors. It also sponsors a yearly conference of business executives (CADE), where invitees from private

---

[77] García de Romana (1975); cf. Larson and Bergen (1969:273), also Bourricaud (1970:195).
[78] Einaudi and Stepan (1971).
[79] García de Romana (1975:100). The material he quotes is from *Industria peruana*, house organ of the SNI (n. 55).

industry and from government—ministers and high-ranking civil servants participate in the sessions, and the president of the republic usually puts in an appearance—interact and exchange ideas about development strategies.

As is true of the military variant, managerial developmentalism is neither liberal nor socialist; it is corporatist. The national interest in development is to be secured through a partnership of state, business, and labor resting on an elite consensus. The state's role need not be confined to mediation and planning, however. Instead, the establishment of a strong parastatal enterprise sector can be useful in bringing about "an increase in the managerial ambit"— that is, a reinforcement of managerial values and practices—*inside the state apparatus*. It would be necessary only that parastatal enterprise forswear any monopolistic ambitions. "The concept of entrepreneurial spirit" worked out by IPAE "embraced [s]tate entrepreneurial activity properly understood: the [s]tate as one entrepreneur more, with its own risks, rights, and obligations, without usurping functions but competing fairly in order to occupy the positions [in the market] merited by its entrepreneurial capacity." The consensus could be maintained with labor if "[t]he entrepreneur would resign himself to sharing in the fruits and in the administration of the enterprise." But the locus of power need not change; for, the manager would share these things with the workers "*provided that his authority were guaranteed.*"[80]

The predominant themes uncovered in our investigation of mining-bourgeois ideology are those of the managerial ideology identified by García de Romana. The mining bourgeoisie is broadly developmentalist and approves of state planning and entrepreneurship, provided that the state does not become economically monopolistic. There is relatively little overt concern with the "sanctity of private property" or with the other constituents of the liberal viewpoint. Most mining bourgeois do not believe that the attainment of their entrepreneurial goals requires the repression of the working class. They feel able to accommodate to the presence of labor unions so long as union demands are not unconditionally accepted by the government; they are attracted to the idea of sharing profits with workers; and they can tolerate some institutional worker input in enterprise administration if their authority is not eroded. Importantly, most of these attitudes and beliefs are shared by the middle strata of the mining sector.[81]

Besides all this, the mining bourgeoisie appears to be firmly opposed to authoritarian rule and highly supportive of civilian government. This attitude is a constant unaffected by the political and ideological direction of the regime

[80] All quoted material in this and the preceding paragraph is from García de Romana (1975:145-46), emphases added.

[81] Bourgeois/middle-class cohesion, in removing any threat to bourgeois domination from the latter, enables it to play an important mediating role vis-à-vis the working class. With its modest social origins and concern for social justice, the middle class presents to workers the benign, meritocratic face of industrial capitalism. At the same time, it has access to certain forums in which the bourgeoisie also participates, permitting it to project that concern free of intimidation and under circumstances where those with power are more apt to pay heed.

of the moment; it was as strong in 1977-78 under the "conservative" Morales Bermúdez as in 1974 under the "radical" Velasco. The anti-authoritarianism of the mining bourgeoisie contradicts Julio Cotler's assertion that the Peruvian system is drifting toward "bureaucratic-authoritarianism."[82] Bourgeois support for a political monopoly that demobilizes the popular classes is not a feature of Peruvian politics.

Thus, the managerial ideology meets the objectively necessary conditions for ideological hegemony.[83] It expresses a general interest held in common by all advanced bourgeois elements—one that appears far more determinant than the narrow conflict between miners and certain manufacturers over the tactical details of industrial promotion tariffs. It is nationalist and has a developmental thrust. It does not demand the full demobilization of working-class organizations.

The significance of Peruvian managerial ideology goes well beyond the question of the bourgeoisie's potential for establishing a local ideological hegemony, however. It represents *the same ideological viewpoint advanced by the leading spokespersons for the metropolitan class associated with the control of transnational enterprise.*[84] Hence, it is quite consistent with a "postimperialism" in which the "staunch nationalism" of a local dominant bourgeoisie can be reconciled "with the cosmopolitan values of bourgeois leaders abroad who have global interests and perspectives."[85] The military, too, is developmentalist and nationalist; but the prism of military concerns refracts these qualities into a power competition with all other states. As a result, the military alone is structurally incapable of harmonizing local class domination and local development with continued participation in the system of international capitalism. The necessary conclusion: *a capitalist, developmentalist military rule becomes such only to the extent that it is a vehicle for social domination and control by a developmental bourgeoisie.*

CONCLUSIONS: A DOMINANT PERUVIAN BOURGEOISIE

On the one hand, the mining bourgeoisie and its associated technical-professional middle class are numerically small. On the other, they have an economic salience out of all proportion to their numbers, due to the preponderant position of the mining industry in the nation's economy. But neither

[82] Cotler (1979).

[83] Which does not mean that ideological hegemony will in fact be shortly attained. This may be precluded until the structure of Peruvian society has undergone further change. It may also be difficult to achieve because of a weakness in the managerial ideology itself: like most technocratic belief systems, it lacks élan and emotion, without which it is hard to conceive of a bourgeois class "project" of social transformation—"Peru S.A."—capturing the affect, imagination, and voluntary cooperation of the popular classes.

[84] See, for example, Drucker (1968:102-36); Jacoby (1970); and Lodge (1973).

[85] Sklar (1976).

size nor economic salience, alone, determines the political effectiveness of class action. Other factors to be considered are:

    a. Cohesion: based primarily on the perception of interests held in common but reinforced by social and affective bonds. Cohesion usually begins with functional groups. *Class* cohesion, however, requires that integrants of the class, or at least of its leading stratum, forge a broader unity by transcending the contradictions among their parochial functional concerns;

    b. Self-renewal: a function of mobility and the effectiveness of socialization. Classes which cannot periodically renew their energies by accepting dynamic new recruits are doomed to stagnation—the fate of the Peruvian oligarchy. Yet, the preservation of a class identity—the basis of cohesion—requires effective mechanisms for resocializing the *nouveaux arrivés*;

    c. Consciousness: expressed through an ideology which justifies class interests and action intended to secure them;

    d. Nonexclusiveness: the capacity of the class to form coalitions with potential (because they share some of the same interests) allies. The most important such ally for the bourgeoisie is the technical-professional middle class—which forms its natural recruiting ground, lends the element of professional stewardship to its ideology, and is well positioned to project its interests less conflictually to the subordinate classes;

    e. Hegemonic potential: the capability to avoid driving the popular classes into desperate opposition; to justify class interests in terms of widely held national aspirations; and to generate mass acquiescence in a bourgeois class "project" at the national level.

Whether the mining bourgeoisie is viewed figuratively as a reference group or literally as a functional group within a larger bourgeois stratum based in modern industrial enterprise in general, it ranks high on all counts. Cohesion is maintained across divisions of property type, functional role, etc.; and links to the rest of the stratum are sustained through the shared interest in bonanza development and the shared ideology grounded thereupon. The mining bourgeoisie renews itself periodically via upward mobility from the middle class and even, on occasion, from the popular classes; the new recruits are carefully and thoroughly resocialized into their new roles by the system of professional education, the apprenticeship, and the activities of the guild associations. The class has a reasonably acute consciousness of self, expressed in a managerial ideology containing meritocratic, stewardship, and developmentalist themes; it has also evolved institutions for propagating its ideology both within the class and to a wider public. The bourgeoisie is nonexclusive in its relationship with the technical-professional middle class, which has been brought into a very close alliance symbolized by mobility, a common ideology, and the absence of gross status and economic cleavages at the boundary between the two.[86] Finally, the class exhibits a hegemonic potential in the character of its ideological concerns—which downplay the significance of formal property relations while emphasizing values such as development, merit, and entrepreneurship in the guise of an instrumental social good. (I believe that further research would show the Peruvian public at large to be receptive toward these values.) The bourgeois class attitude toward working-class aspirations, too, is one of accommodation rather than confrontation.

Two other characterisitics of the mining bourgeoisie, not listed above because specific to Peru, are its distance from the oligarchy and its affinities with the armed forces. The first quality has contributed to class self-esteem and, thus, to cohesiveness and consciousness; it has also preserved class effectiveness in an epoch of oligarchic decline and fall. The second has removed the only danger to bourgeois social dominance in the period since 1968.

The professional character of the mining bourgeoisie and middle class is the basis of their association with the international bourgeoisie of the industry. It enables local bourgeois to harmonize ideologically their domestic interests with those of international capital without subordinating themselves to the latter. The ability to do so is critical to a scheme of development which includes the continuation of structural ties—but *not* ties of domination and subservience—to the capitalist metropoli. (This is a task from which the military is barred by the nature of its institutional interest in power competition with other states.) Still, and despite its international linkages, the bourgeoisie is nothing other than a true dominant class. Its entrepreneurial dynamism has been amply documented in the two preceding chapters. Now we can add the fact that foreign capital does not control the class organizations—which refused to come to the aid of beleaguered foreign firms even when they were members; and that manager-entrepreneurs, not passive rentiers, are in command of these organizations. I submit, therefore, that class-analytical dependency explanations of post-1968 Peruvian development land well wide of the mark.

I find the structuralist explanation of the 1968 *coup d'état*—that the armed forces seized power because the bourgeoisie "needed" military rule in order to establish its social dominance—to be unpersuasive. Nevertheless, it is clearly the case that military rule consolidated this dominance. By creating strong parastatal enterprises, the generals enlarged the size of the bourgeoisie

[86] Durand (1981) notes that the character of the restored civilian government is entirely middle-class; that "these middle-class interlocutors usually make politics by speaking to the stomachs of the voting majority"; and that neither managers nor entrepreneurs are very promient (although some are present) within the ruling (as of 1982) party coalition—Belaunde's Acción Popular and the Popular Christian Party. This, he feels, raises doubts concerning the ability of the bourgeoisie to realize its class "project" in the current conjuncture. My reply is that middle-class control of the mechanisms of party politics is more the rule than the exception in capitalist polities. The structural factors constraining the capitalist state, together with close bourgeois/middle-class cohesion, are quite sufficient for the former's political purposes and are in some ways preferable to a more overt (and exposed) bourgeois presence in electoral politics.

and gave it another national base in a subsector (the gran minería) which it had not previously colonized. Their expropriation of Cerro and Marcona left the local medium-mining companies in full control of the class organization of greatest economic and political importance. The new parastatal base fortifies the technical-professional nature of the class—the foundation of its cohesion and of its ideology. The quality of the class was protected as it grew, thanks to the military's concern for technical education and manpower development. And military rule, by stressing industrial development in general and mining development in particular, enabled technical and professional personnel to improve materially their economic situation in the marketplace. The military and the bourgeois elite of the mining sector are separated by some very different interests and values. Yet, they were able to establish a mutually satisfactory working relationship—propitiated, I believe, by ideological commonalities and by mutual need stemming from the character of bonanza development. This working relationship rested on the military's deference to the bourgeoisie in matters of essential economic interest; and on the bourgeoisie's deference to the military rulers in purely political matters, especially emotional ones impinging on the latter's legitimacy in power.

The new political order in Peru is corporatist. But it is a consensual corporatism which is neither formally structured nor controlled by a state standing "above" class forces.[87] The truth of this statement is revealed in the alterations that have taken place in the mode of interest intermediation practiced by the core organization of the class. No longer do mining entrepreneurs and managers secure their interests primarily through the Mining Society's corporate presence inside the state. Instead, they rely—like most of their metropolitan counterparts—on the state's economic dependence on the private sector; on the infusion of the managerial ideology within the state apparatus; and on the control of information flows to the state. With this last and with the rise to preeminence in the mining industry of large business corporations, private capital's resistance to state economic planning has diminished. Private corporate planners are assured that this activity will proceed in their interest.

In keeping with the political relationship of mutual deference and exclusivity of spheres that arose between the mining bourgeoisie and the military establishment in power, the former took no action which would have been interpreted as a frontal assault on military rule. However, the bourgeoisie is no supporter of military authoritarianism, *irrespective of its policy content*; for it lacks a threat perception that would lead it to seek such protection. Objectively, there is no threat from the Left: that side of the political spectrum is

[87] Palmer (1973) posits a formally structured corporatism. That the Peruvian state stands "above" civil society is explicit in Stepan's (1978) conception of "organic-statism" and in Quijano's (1974) image of an emerging "state capitalist" power elite which is autonomous of local class forces but subservient to international capital. To my mind, the restoration of civilian governance refutes notions of a Peruvian corporatism resting on a state fully independent of class forces; but it is entirely compatible with a corporatism based on consensus, i.e., the "liberal" or "voluntary" variant discussed by Panitch (1977).

dispersed among a large number of small sectarian parties, whose votaries have demonstrated little talent for collaboration with each other. Subjectively, the bourgeoisie perceives no threat and seems to understand, in its attitude toward agrarian reform and the labor movement, how best to prevent one from arising.[88]

Does all of this mean that we can look forward with confidence to the continuity of civilian governance and to a long period of political stability under a secure bourgeois hegemony? My study supplies no justification for the firmly negative reply offered by Alfred Stepan and various others.[89] Nonetheless, two large question marks stand in the way of an equally firm "Yes." The first has to do with the problem of a stagnating agriculture. A collectivist solution having been tried and apparently failed, is the petty-bourgeois solution suggested by bourgeois leaders a feasible alternative? Can it be implemented on existing foundations without giving simultaneous birth to a still more restive mass of displaced subsistence peasants? Those answers await further research.[90]

The second uncertainty relates to the *structural* requisites (we have examined only the *ideological* requisites) for the establishment of bourgeois

[88] As of late 1982, these lines may seem to reflect undue optimism in view of the activities of the terrorist group known as Sendero Luminoso ("Luminous Path": see *New York Times*, 8 September 1982, p. A2; and *Wall Street Journal*, 22 September 1982, p. 34). There is now considerable concern on the part of Peruvian progressives, as well as on the part of the new political parties of the Left, about this organization's potential for destabilizing the nation's still-fragile democratic order and for producing another military takeover—this time, by some hard-line faction that might be tempted to institute a "Chilean solution." However, the newspaper articles referenced above make clear that Sendero Luminoso's popular support is limited to a few disaffected peasant and student groups in the backward department of Ayacucho, and that its violent acts have cost it the sympathies of potential allies elsewhere in the country. My perception is that the bourgeoisie, too, is concerned but does not regard the problem as one threatening its class dominance. While the bourgeoisie backs strong anti-terrorist measures (as, with some misgivings, does the Left) for dealing with Sendero Luminoso, I sense that the class as a whole remains committed to political democracy and sees no need for generalized repression of progressive social forces.

[89] Stepan (1978); also Cotler (1975, 1979). Stepan seems to imply that he regards the concept of hegemony as having to do with acceptance at the polls; after briefly reviewing supposed debilities of Latin American bourgeoisies, he states (p. 23) that these debilities put "members of the national bourgeoisie in a weak political position to compete—in a nationalist environment—*as an electoral force aiming at hegemonic acceptance for their position* [emphasis added]." Gramsci's position on hegemony, in contrast, has to do but peripherally with electoral outcomes; indeed, for him, bourgeois ideological hegemony is not negated, and may even be promoted, by social-democratic electoral triumphs.

[90] Such research might profitably extend as well to a study of the real class situation of the rapidly growing urban underclass. There is some reason to believe that this group is an incipient petty bourgeoisie par excellence and that it may be more susceptible to the appeals and blandishments of middle-class politics than is the working class. Stepan (1978:158-89, esp. pp. 184-86) notes that the military regime's policies toward the urban underclass—which emphasized home ownership, provision of legal land titles, and other means for regularizing and improving residential conditions in the new urban settlements, or *pueblos jóvenes*—sought, with some moderate success, the incorporation of this social group by treating it as an incipient petty bourgeoisie. I shall return to the issue of the underclass and its significance for bourgeois political objectives in the concluding chapter.

hegemony. One analyst suggests that a hegemonic integration of the working class into a stable capitalist order is possible if

> the bourgeoisie is responsive to the challenge of the workers' movement and responds to it (1) by relying for capital accumulation on higher productivity rather than low pay and (2) by acknowledging the role of the unions in the mediation of collective conflicts. In return, employers ask for and obtain loyalty to the rules of the game both within the factory . . . and in politics. . . .

But:

> [t]his sort of pact requires a specific class structure . . . , a working class both strong and capable of stimulating change through wage demands and other types of pressure. . . . In such systems there is a congruence between the economic and political power of the workers, in the sense that the latters' political strength grows out of and is coexistent with economic development. This is not so in . . . countries where political mobilization is largely the work of revolutionary parties and other factors only indirectly related to the economy. . . .[91]

The mining bourgeoisie appears to meet the requirements laid down for it. Does the working class? To that question we now turn.

[91] Graziano (1980).

CHAPTER TEN

The Mining Industry
and the Claims of Labor

In the advanced capitalist countries, and particularly in the Western European social democracies, politics has largely evolved into an effort to preserve and protect bourgeois ideological hegemony in the face of a more powerful working class while, at the same time, promoting the restructuring of capital and improving the conditions for its accumulation. This is one of the typically contradictory processes of late-capitalist development. The attempt to resolve the contradiction has conduced to a characteristic feature of late capitalism: the rise of corporatist forms of interest intermediation.

Such forms entail a greater presence of working-class interests inside the state, to which extent they are progressive. But the corporatist approach to class collaboration depends as well on arrangements whereby the labor organizations that enjoy this presence are expected to use their authority to discipline the rank and file of the working class—viz., by limiting strikes and restraining "extreme" wage demands. There is thus another dimension to the contradiction, one that cannot be so easily resolved. It is the dimension of class collaboration and self-control versus the fact that class organizations charged with responsibility for self-control are founded on the idea of class struggle, are more democratic than hierarchical in internal structure, and are therefore well equipped to resist discipline imposed by their own higher authority. Labor leadership's ability to deliver on its half of the corporatist bargain is always open to question, and the bargain itself is, in consequence, inherently unstable.[1]

Dependencista class analysis, however, sees little relevance in this discussion for capitalist development in the Third World. There, the most salient feature of dependent capitalism is, precisely, its inability to produce a hegemonic corporatist integration of the working class. Transnational capital, if labor-intensive, depends for accumulation on low-wage "superexploitation," to which no independent labor movement can ever consent. If capital-intensive, it generates a tiny "labor aristocracy," isolated by its inordinate privileges from the working class at large. The only type of corporatism that can exist, then, is authoritarian "state corporatism," where the state assumes

---

[1] Panitch (1981). He points out that class struggle is no less a struggle if it takes an "economistic" form of demands for a larger piece of the economic pie.

direct control of the labor movement in order to keep it subservient.[2] State-controlled labor movements are common enough in Latin America, especially in the bigger and more industrialized countries (such as Argentina, Brazil, and Mexico). It is to those countries that doctrines of "bureaucratic-author-itarianism" (itself a variant of "state corporatism") have applicability.

A corollary is that progress for the popular classes demands, sooner rather than later, a revolutionary overthrow of dependent capitalism. A majoritarian revolutionary movement has to rest on an alliance of the "superexploited" proletariat (that is, the urban masses) and the peasantry; the "labor aristoc-racy" will usually decline to join. Indeed, a few of those who evaluate the situation in such terms have sought to revise the concept of "proletariat" so as to encompass all of these diverse elements while ruling the "labor aris-tocracy" out of the picture.[3] But the revised "proletariat," though it has a permanently revolutionary temperament born of deprivation and nationalism, cannot have undergone the specifically proletarian social experience that Marx held essential for the formation of a self-conscious class able to engage in autonomous action. Hence, a populist strategy of revolution is needed, one in which a radical nationalist intellectual vanguard leads the "proletariat" and "represents" its class interest.

Whatever else those revolutions may accomplish, they are not democratic in any sense. Moreover, the Leninist claim of the vanguard to represent the interest of a class of which it is not really a part has been convincingly shown to rest, even when the proletariat is a true industrial working class, on sheer ideology.[4] And finally, if bourgeois hegemony is actually attainable (as was suggested in Chapter 9), the immediate task of the working class is to free itself from the bourgeois world view and to develop its own; the populist approach to "socialist" revolution, because it ignores the roots of conscious-ness in the collective experience of the working class under capitalism and substitutes poverty and nationalism therefor, does not address this task at all.

We have examined in the foregoing chapters the structures and interrela-tionships of transnational capital, domestic capital, the state, the bourgeoisie, and the middle class in Peruvian bonanza development underwritten by the mining industry. In so doing we have observed much that casts doubt on the applicability to Peru of the dependencista scenario. We shall now complete our study with an investigation of the formation and action of the mining proletariat, in order to determine if that doubt is further confirmed and if, instead, the advanced-country sequence of late-capitalist development may

---

[2] Schmitter (1974) originated the phrase, "state corporatism." The alternative form resting on a measure of consensus and participation (as described by Panitch 1977) he labeled "societal corporatism."

[3] For example, Amin (1980a, 1980b:152-54 and passim). In the latter work he specifically states that (p. 154) "[t]oday we cannot confuse the proletariat with the working class"!

[4] Refer to Chap. 8, n. 6.

apply to this case.[5] Let me suggest, as a point of departure, that we ought not to be surprised should our investigation unearth some apparently unusual kinds of class behavior; for, even a superficial glance at the Peruvian political conjuncture of our day reveals several phenomena that seem unique in Latin America. They include: a virtual explosion of labor militance in the years since 1968; the coincidence of this explosion with military-authoritarian rule; the recent emergence of what is probably the strongest and most radical electoral Left in the hemisphere; and the implementation, under military auspices, of land reform to quiet a numerically declining peasantry.

In all of these developments except the last, mine labor has played a key role—a role that it could not have played were it not for the tremendous economic leverage afforded it by the centrality of mining to bonanza development. Nor does mine labor stand apart from the question of the peasantry's political future. If there is to be a worker-peasant alliance, mine labor would surely be active in forging it. Miners are the only proletarian group that is dispersed in the countryside away from urban centers. And, as we shall see, some of them are close to peasant origins and to current peasant life.

To clarify the issue of the nature and role of the mining proletariat is the purpose of this chapter. It will also expose transnational mining capital's impact, via proletarian class formation, on the negatory side of the dialectic of Peruvian capitalist development.

Should signs of corporatist integration of the working class be found, we may hope to relate them to the contradictions of bonanza development. We will likewise wish to compare them with the pressures toward corporatist integration in advanced capitalist societies. But we ought not to expect yet to see a flowering of the contradictions peculiar to corporatism, since the process of integration (if there is one) will still be in its earliest phase. The best that we will be able to do is to hazard a guess, on the basis of empirical study, as to whether the incorporation of a labor leadership within the state can proceed very far, and whether that leadership has a chance to acquire the kind of control that corporatist arrangements require.

The chapter opens with a description of the legal and institutional environment of the working class, which is necessary to introduce both the actors and some of the factors that constrain and shape their actions. It then looks at the historical process of class formation in the minería, another important constraining and shaping factor. Next it turns to the character of mine workers' militance in pursuit of their class interests; and to the manner in which the class defines those interests—whether "economistically" or in some other

[5] There is no contradiction here between "late" capitalism and Peru's condition of under-development. Late capitalism, in my usage, is not synonymous with economic advancement. It signifies a phase of capitalist development in which oligopolistic corporations dominate the heights of the economy and accumulate capital with the aid of state planning and, sometimes, state entrepreneurship. These conditions can exist even at fairly low levels of development and are common in Latin America. Indeed, it can be suggested that the region's backwardness is to be found primarily in the underdevelopment of the *small business* sector.

way. The character and exercise of the mining proletariat's political power are examined in a final section in the light of recent economic and political events.

THE LEGAL AND INSTITUTIONAL ENVIRONMENT OF THE PERUVIAN WORKING CLASS

Proletarian class formation and action have been decisively affected by state efforts to retard or to guide them by means of legislative-regulatory initiative. On the other hand, laws and institutions have also had to respond to class formation and action. Their ability to do so in a way that achieves state and dominant-class purposes has always been limited and contingent— increasingly so latterly. What has resulted from this interplay is a legal-institutional environment whose chief features are: (1) a tradition of extensive state regulation of working conditions, benefits, and employee rights, together with a reluctance to leave industrial relations to the direct clash of employer-employee interests in the marketplace for labor power; (2) the statutory definition of two distinct working-class strata, *empleados* and *obreros*, each subject to its own set of regulations; and (3) the presence of strict controls over the formation, internal workings, and activities of labor unions—controls which extend, however, across the full gamut of industrial relations and hence interfere as well with management's customary (under capitalism) authority and prerogatives.

Much of the applicable legislation has an ostensibly pro-labor character. It was enacted by politically conservative regimes; the initial advances of labor in the institutionalized political system had nothing to do with working-class political participation, a post-1968 development. The intent of these oligarchic regimes was cooptation pure and simple. That is, there was never any attempt at integrating labor into the political-institutional status quo. The usual hallmarks of "state corporatism" (such as government-sponsored labor unions with controlled access to the state apparatus) were and still are conspicuously missing. Political leaders associated with the oligarchy preferred to believe, one gathers, that economic concessions alone would suffice to destroy any tendency of workers to coalesce and organize around common class concerns. It is probable that the oligarchy's preponderance of nonindustrial interests, along with its intense ideological dedication to laissez faire, barred it from resorting to "state corporatism" in spite of the latter's appeal to other Latin American elites.

The rights and privileges enjoyed under the law by Peruvian workers are outlined in Appendix D.[6] In many areas of the economy these are honored more in the breach than in the observance. The opposite is true, however, in those sectors where labor unions are strong; mining is one such. Most of the

[6] The absence of unemployment insurance is compensated for by the requirement that laid-off employees receive a large amount of severance pay (Appendix D, item IVf).

benefits in question were introduced during the fifties. Two innovations of the "revolution" were guaranteed job tenure, or *estabilidad laboral*; and the Workers' Community system, mentioned in the previous chapter.

The empleado-obrero distinction originated at a time when few workers had attended secondary schools; empleados were those holding jobs, mostly in the white-collar category, for which a secondary education was a prerequisite. But the two categories have long been used somewhat differently in the mining industry. There, most empleados are skilled blue-collar workers, assistant foremen, and foremen. Promotion to empleado status on the sole basis of on-the-job experience was unheard of in the early days but is now fairly common. Empleados are paid a monthly salary, obreros a daily wage. (The daily, rather than hourly, basis of obrero remuneration reflects the fact that time-clock controls are infrequent.) Obreros are paid for their weekly day of rest (the benefit is known as the *dominical*) if they have worked a full eight hours during each of the preceding six days. This provision is designed to discourage tardiness and absenteeism.

Increasing educational attainment among the popular classes, together with the changing conditions of corporate employment, should be rendering this distinction obsolete. However, it retains an effect on proletarian class formation that serves bourgeois ends: in addition to introducing an element of disarticulation into the structuration of the class, it holds forth a prospect of individual upward mobility now that one can be promoted to empleado in later life. (It also implies a promise of transgenerational mobility, since the step up from empleado origins to true middle-class status is less steep than it is starting out in an obrero household.) Furthermore, those who gear their aspirations to the promotion option may well be the most energetic and ambitious workers, otherwise the natural leaders of proletarian protest—notably, if they should see themselves as victims of "blocked ascent." In essence, then, the distinction is a cooptative device which works against proletarian class cohesion. State authorities have all along recognized it as such; regulations prohibit empleados and obreros from belonging to the same local union. (But empleados can organize separately, and most have done so.) Interestingly, the "revolutionary" generals attempted to erase the distinction: they integrated the formerly separate empleados' and obreros' social security and medical care systems.[7] That they did not go further has to do with labor union opposition, not all of it from empleado unions fearing a loss of privileges. It appears that most obreros want to keep the mobility opportunity (even if solely symbolic) that the distinction represents.

Statutes governing labor organization foster bargaining by local unions with individual employers over economic matters while discouraging the solidification of comprehensive class-based organizations. Craft- and industry-wide

---

[7] Formerly, obreros and empleados in the cities had to use separate government hospitals and clinics. The military regime did away with this segregation; now both groups may use the facilities most convenient to their homes or places of work.

unionization is theoretically forbidden; unions are confined to a single plant or work site. Collective bargaining is only permitted at the local level.

Higher-level working-class institutions do exist and ought to help coordinate class action. In practice they form a confused picture, however. There are federations for industries or trades (e.g., the miners' federation, the FTMMP), regions (usually a city or department), and nature of residence (federations of the *pueblos jóvenes*); some local unions belong to several at once. The federations are in turn grouped into no less than four national labor centrals, or confederations—which also accept as members certain local unions lacking federational affiliations. The four are, in descending order of size: the CGTP, a loose associate of the "orthodox," or "Muscovite," Communist Party (the PCP, sometimes referred to as PCP-*Unidad* after its newspaper in order to distinguish it from other Communist factions); the CTP, tightly controlled by the APRA party; the CTRP, which originated in 1973 as the military regime's *oficialista* central; and the CNT, founded by the now-defunct Christian Democratic Party.[8] As if this were not enough, a number of federations, among them the FTMMP, insist on remaining independent of all four centrals. Out of the cacophony of institutions, only the CGTP, the CTP (less since 1968 than before), and the FTMMP have been active in the mines and refineries (the CTRP has some strength in Marcona).

Unions must be formally recognized in order to bargain. Federations and confederations also need recognition before they can discharge their allowed functions: treating with state officials, advising member locals, and engaging in organizing (although semi-clandestine activity by unrecognized entities at all levels occurs often). There are no clear standards for recognition, enabling the government of the day to award, withhold, or withdraw it as a political favor or sanction. Sometimes recognition is de facto. For instance, unions bargain with MineroPeru and HierroPeru managements, even though unionization of state employees is supposedly illegal (unionization in Centromin is legal by special exemption).

All forms of compulsory unionism are prohibited. Dues payments, too, are purely voluntary, even for union members. Nevertheless, contractual agreements resulting from collective bargaining with employers apply without restriction to all similarly situated workers, union members or no. (This might make many workers reluctant to join, for the reasons discussed by Mancur Olson;[9] but in the mining sector, at least, union solidarity has not visibly suffered.) There are no salaried, full-time union officers, except that a few confederation officials and legal advisors are maintained financially by the treasuries of associated political parties. It is therefore the employer who bears most of the costs of supporting the union's officialdom. This is accomplished via the *licencia*: union officers are granted a certain annual number of paid

---

[8] The official ideologies of the four centrals are compared and contrasted by Aparicio Valdez et al. (1975).
[9] Olson (1965).

leaves from their regular jobs to attend to union business and may also be paid travel allowances if that business takes them away from the work site. Starting in 1970, the mine unions have compelled the companies to extend the number of days of leave under this system to the point where it is now possible for some officers to devote all of their time to union affairs while continuing to draw a company wage. In other words, a professional leadership cadre *subsidized by employers* is coming into being.[10]

As is true of union recognition, the right to strike is honored but is hedged about with restrictions. These open legal avenues for the government to outlaw a work stoppage on minor procedural grounds if it so desires. A still more potent weapon in the hands of the state is its authority to intervene in any labor dispute and to impose, at its sole discretion, a binding settlement on any terms at all—without regard to the position of either party. It goes without saying that this discretionary power is more likely to be used the more critical is the branch of industry in which the dispute occurs. Mining is the most critical branch of all. There, wage settlements imposed by the state are the rule, not the exception.

The military regime usually preferred, as will be seen, to tread lightly in dealing with mine strikes unless it was under economic duress. Because their work skills are scarce, miners cannot be readily replaced if their *estabilidad laboral* is withdrawn for striking illegally—for which reason this penalty, if applied at all, is always aimed selectively at strike leaders. And their high wages give them a financial cushion with which to withstand a long work stoppage without worrying about collecting back pay when the strike has ended (the law requires such retroactive pay when a strike is legal). In consequence, the generals had few options in dealing with the mine unions other than conciliation or all-out repression. They never resorted to the latter; we shall seek to find out why.

The civilian government that came to power in 1980 seems intent on moving from dictation to cooperation in industrial relations. We will examine the meaning of its policies in a later section of this chapter.

Changes in total mining employment are shown in Table 10.1, which dissects the 1979 employment total and compares it to the 1967 breakdown. The "revolutionary" years saw a large increase in the numbers of workers employed by the most modern corporate enterprises: the gran minería, the national "big seven" (another tribute to their dynamism), and the U.S. and Japanese mediana minería. On the other hand, we will soon find that labor's power began to be felt in the early 1970s and was most in evidence at Cerro (where the number of jobs has held steady) and at Southern (where the increase

---

[10] DiTella (1981) argues that a "requirement of a representative working-class organization is that it must rely heavily on its own sources of financing, i.e., trade union funds and individual members' quotas." But the development discussed here does not contradict him, as the alternative that he considers is state funding. We shall see that employer subsidization of the unions does not seem to have adversely affected their militancy.

TABLE 10.1 Evolution of Employment in Peruvian Mining, 1967-1979

Subsector/Employer	1967		1979		Percent Change
	Number	Percent	Number	Percent	
Gran Minería:	23,170	27.1	30,077	51.5	29.8
Cerro-Centromin	16,313	19.1	16,513	28.3	1.2
Southern Peru Copper	3,994	4.7	7,472	12.8	87.1
Marcona-HierroPeru	2,863	3.3	3,467	5.9	21.1
MineroPeru	—	—	2,625	4.5	—
Mediana Minería:	23,081	27.0	25,325	43.3	9.7
National:	17,004	19.9	17,473	29.9	2.8
"Big Seven"	7,255	8.5	11,019	18.9	51.9
Other	9,749	11.4	6,454	11.0	−33.8
Foreign:	6,077	7.1	7,852	13.4	29.2
U.S.-owned	3,243	3.8	3,471	5.9	7.0
Japanese-owned	398	0.5	852	1.5	114.1
Other	2,436	2.8	3,529	6.0	44.9
TOTAL, Gran + Mediana	46,251	54.1	55,402	94.8	19.8
Pequeña Minería:	39,166	45.9	3,028	5.2	−92.2
GRAND TOTAL	85,417	100.0	58,430	100.0	−31.6

SOURCES: Compiled by the author from data presented in the consolidated declarations of the companies and supplied by the Departamento de Estudios Económicos y Estadística, Sociedad Nacional de Minería y Petróleo.

only appeared in 1977 with the opening of Cuajone). Consequently, any gains in the power of the mine labor movement will have to be attributed to increases in the work force's economic leverage, not to its numerical growth. The pequeña minería has practically disappeared as an employer of wage labor[11] and will not be further considered herein. As the bulk of its workers have in any case been part-timers, and as the subsector has never been heavily unionized, its near-disappearance means little (in power terms) on the labor front.

The workers of the gran and mediana minerías make up only 2.2 percent of the country's nonagricultural wage earners. This figure has declined by about 0.3 percent since 1967, for employment growth in manufacturing, construction, and services has outstripped that in mining.

THE HISTORY OF PROLETARIAN CLASS FORMATION IN THE MINERÍA

Proletarian class formation is a concrete historical process in which two important variables are the techniques of production and systems of industrial

[11] But the datum may be somewhat misleading: the pequeña minería is not subject to the same reporting requirements governing the gran and mediana minerías, and it is thus possible that the low 1979 employment figure reflects reports from only a few firms.

discipline introduced by capitalist enterprises, and the resistance to proletarianization offered by traditional peasant society. These variables define two epochs of proletarian class formation in Peruvian mining: one associated with Cerro and the mediana minería of the central sierra, the other with the later entrants to the gran minería (i.e., Southern, Marcona-HierroPeru, and MineroPeru), all based in the south or south-center.

Class Formation in the Central Sierra[12]

When they have sought to install capitalist modes of production in newly conquered territories, colonial powers have frequently had to employ coercion in order to force reluctant peasants out of a subsistence economy and into a wage-laboring "vocation." I have already described Cerro as a "colonial company" because it was, among other things, the first to bring large-scale industrial capitalism to then-virgin territory. The woefully weak authority of the state had not yet established itself in the sierra; and Cerro's labor recruiters, once their needs exceeded what the few small, old mining towns could supply, encountered a peasantry that was unwilling to leave the land. It was, moreover, particularly resistant to mine labor, of which it did not lack memories: bitter ones they were, handed down in the folklore from the age of Spanish rule when uncounted Indians sweated and died in the silver mines of the Cerro de Pasco district and the mercury mines of Huancavelica. Were Peru still a colony in the twentieth century, its administrative apparatus would no doubt have cooperated with Cerro by taking steps to destroy the peasant economy (as was done in parts of Africa). But that could not happen in a nominally independent state controlled by landowners. Workers could be fraudulently enticed to the mines by means of the *enganche* (a form of debt peonage where a cash advance had to be repaid by a term of mine labor)[13] and could be kept on the job by force. They could not, however, be prevented from returning to the countryside as soon as their work obligations had been fulfilled. For years the *campo* thus remained a refuge from complete proletarianization in the mines—a circumstance that Cerro and the medium-mining companies, reliant as they then were on pick-and-shovel miners whose replacement entailed minimal loss of manpower training costs, were able to tolerate. Only in 1954 did Cerro put in a modern system of personnel administration suitable for controlling a real proletariat. Save for a core of Cerro smelter and refinery workers, visible from the 1930s onward, a lifelong mine labor "career" did not become the norm in the central sierra until the 1960s.

Proletarianization may correlate with impoverishment but is not the same thing. It consists, rather, in the removal of all means of production (including

[12] In this section I have drawn upon H. Bonilla (1974b); DeWind (1977); Flores Galindo (1974); Kapsoli E. (1975); Kruijt and Vellinga (1979); Morello (1976); and D. Sulmont (1974, 1975, 1977).

[13] The *enganche* system is described in the works cited in the preceding note; see also Chaplin (1967:63-66), where the extent of coerced labor in Peru is documented.

usufruct rights to land) from workers' direct control, and the subsequent ingathering of the now-propertyless proletarians to collective labor under a wage system and centralized direction. In this sense, proletarianization in the mines of the central sierra did not proceed to completion until very recently. Many miners kept family plots in their villages of origin, plots acquired and/ or expanded using cash earned in the pits; these would be farmed by relatives until their owners retired from mine labor. A pattern was consequently established whereby miner families often rose to kulak status and to a position among the village elites.[14] Although not even elite status in a peasant *comunidad* counted for much in an agrarian society ruled over by *latifundistas* and their rural middle-class agents, it sufficed to retard the evolution of a feeling of solidarity with the rest of the working class. Even those miners who did not become kulaks usually refrained from transferring the foci of their aspirations away from the home village and toward the more urbanized world of the mining camps.

To be sure, the Cerro miners had plenty to protest about. In the beginning there were the onerous *enganche* contracts, the all-too-frequent mine accidents, and the abuse meted out by unlettered mine bosses fresh from the rough-and-tumble camps of the North American Wild West. There was the contrast between the miners' barracks and expatriates' residences—the first exposed to the fierce mountain winds and clustered amid the dust and noise of the mineheads, the second far more substantial, well-sheltered, and set off by barbed wire and armed guards—a contrast much like that between the ''settlers' town'' and the ''native town'' pictured by Frantz Fanon in the opening chapter of *The Wretched of the Earth*.[15] There was Cerro's Plant Protection unit (the *huachimanes*), in effect a foreign armed force on Peruvian soil; in enforcing order in the camps it earned a reputation on a par with that of the infamous Pinkerton guards in the labor history of the United States. (Plant Protection was still on the scene in the 1960s. Its job of keeping order having been taken over by the Guardia Civil and, *in extremis*, by the army, it was used for surveillance. Its undercover agents not only reported on union assemblies and protest meetings but also spied upon workers at their posts and in their dwellings, noting down for entry into employment dossiers every minor rule infraction.)[16]

[14] DeWind (1977) analyzes this phenomenon, noting that it was still very much in evidence in the early 1960s in the neighborhood of Cerro's then-new Cobriza mine.

[15] ''The settlers' town is a strongly built town; the streets are covered with asphalt, and the garbage cans swallow all the leavings, unseen, unknown and hardly thought about. . . . The settlers' town is a well-fed town, an easygoing town; its belly is always full of good things. The settlers' town is a town of white people, of foreigners.

''The . . . native town . . . is a place of ill fame, peopled by men of evil repute. . . . It is a world without spaciousness; men live on top of each other, and their huts are built one on top of the other. . . . The native town is a crouching village, a town on its knees, a town wallowing in the mire. . . .'' (Fanon 1963:39).

[16] By this time legislation regulating the conditions under which workers could be dismissed was already on the books. These surveillance measures were intended, therefore, to allow the

While wages and working conditions improved over time, so too did workers' expectations, excited by regular contact with privileged expatriates. Camp conditions did not change much for the better, evolving instead into an ever-greater irritation as workers slowly came to spend more years in them, to bring wives and children into them in larger numbers, and, by the 1970s, finally to weigh them more heavily in defining their aspirations.

Protests, when they occurred, usually took the form of violent outbursts. These typically preproletarian *brotes de violencia* were directed, in Luddite fashion, against company property or against the lives and property of especially hated supervisors.[17] Later on the miners improved their tactics by drawing on the strong indigenous tradition of organized peasant protest—particularly after that tradition was reasserted with the land invasions of the early sixties. One favorite tactic was the *marcha de sacrificio* toward Lima, in which wives, children, and the elderly would also participate; as the capital lies only 177 kilometers down the Central Highway from La Oroya, the marchers could be sure of national publicity and maximal impact on the authorities. But better-disciplined protests are not enough. In order to avail in terms of class interests, they must be part of a sustained strategy backed by effective permanent organization. Proletarian class formation moves to a higher plane when members of the class learn to use the labor union as their principal mechanism of collective self-defense.

Inasmuch as these preproletarians were slow to organize themselves (at the time that the first Cerro unions were formed, anarchosyndicalist unions had been functioning in Lima for thirty years), outsiders—radical middle-class elements from Lima—took over the task. Sent up to La Oroya in 1928 by the just-founded Socialist Party (predecessor of the PCP) and CGTP, they felt ready to call their first strike two years later. Once called off the job, however, the miners would not follow instructions and went off on a violent rampage. The strike was suppressed by troops, with some loss of life; its only lasting result was the proscription of all union activity for fifteen years and the forced dissolution of the CGTP.

Unionization continued in spite of the proscription, led by clandestine organizers sent out by the APRA.[18] It reemerged above ground in 1945 under CTP auspices, thanks to the tolerance of the new president, José Bustamante y Rivero (a progressive by the standards of the day, he had been elected with *aprista* support). Thirty-eight mine unions were formed in Peru between 1945 and 1948, twenty of them in Cerro.[19] It was struck for the second time, but

compilation of demerits so that the company could justify to the labor ministry the firing of almost anyone. The prime targets were the customary "political troublemakers" and "labor agitators." See DeWind (1977).

[17] Preproletarian protest is discussed by Hobsbawm (1959).

[18] Unlike the Socialists, the *apristas* had an effective network of underground cells that could withstand the oppression of the 1933-1945 period.

[19] Remember that, by law, each of the firm's many installations had to have its own union—two, if empleados also organized.

now, due to government acquiescence and the absence of violence, successfully: the company was obliged to bargain, grant a wage increase, and institute the *licencia*. Bustamante's overthrow by General Odría, a virulent anti-*aprista*, marked a setback for labor. But once having driven the CTP underground, Odría turned to cooptation in order to weaken its hold on the labor movement. Local unions in Cerro and elsewhere went on functioning and were rewarded with wage increases if they refrained from striking. Much of the "pro-labor" legislation mentioned in the previous section was enacted. Cooperation was established with efforts then being mounted by the U.S. government and the AFL-CIO to foster "well-behaved" anti-communist unionism in Latin America. In this climate, Cerro thought it wiser to drop its adamant opposition to all labor organization. The company held hopes that better-disciplined, apolitical unions would serve as a social-control adjunct by curbing violence and enforcing workers' compliance with collective bargaining agreements.

The first hope was realized only in part; the second, not at all. Although strikers since the sixties have rarely attacked company property and staff, they have engaged in several bold confrontations with the forces of law and order—one of them at least ending in a small harvest of dead and wounded. As for contract compliance, it soon ceased to exist. Unions regularly accused employers—and still do—of *incumplimiento de pacto*, the second most common cause (after salary issues) of work stoppages. On their side, employers continue to bemoan the tendency of unions to call strikes at any time that they perceive an advantage, even if an agreement is still in force.

As the British Trades Union Congress long ago discovered in its dealings with the Labour Party, the ability of a union to defend the economic interests of its members may be handicapped if union objectives have to take a back seat to the electoral strategy of an allied political party. The contradiction between union and party remained latent so long as the party supplied the unions with their leadership. By the early sixties, though, the Cerro unions at last began to develop their own leadership cadre. The turn from external to internal direction coincided with a revival in Peru of radical political thought, brought on by such events as the Cuban Revolution, the Sino-Soviet split, rural and urban land invasions, and Hugo Blanco's rebellion.[20] In short order a bewildering collection of self-professed Maoists, Trotskyists, Fidelistas et al., had displaced the long-standing APRA-PCP debate from the Left's ideological stage. This reinvigorated ideological climate motivated some young, better-educated, radical mine workers to become active in union affairs, where they soon rose to elected officership by dint of manifest enthusiasm, devotion to duty, and constancy of purpose. (Note that most of the country's mine unions are democratically structured and that participation in assemblies is usually high.) However, the new crop of leaders had to learn the hard way that radical ideology did not furnish an infallible guide to action:

[20] On this last, see Blanco (1972).

many fell from grace after leading their locals into futile solidarity strikes and had to spend seven or eight years regaining the confidence of the rank and file.

Their resurgence was greatly facilitated between 1969 and 1974 by the military regime. Wishing to eliminate decisively the *aprista* influence in the mine labor movement, the generals made it a matter of policy to oppose the demands of CTP-affiliated union leaders while simultaneously granting more extreme ones put forth by the radicals. Whereas this policy did further the eclipse of the CTP and the APRA in the mines of the central sierra, it hardly propitiated a labor movement more tractable to state purposes. We will return to the issue of the military's intentions vis-à-vis organized mine labor.

The home-grown leaders seem to know how to combine rhetorical radicalism with well-planned action aimed at the company's and/or the state's points of maximum vulnerability. In the period between the onset of the "revolution" and Cerro's expropriation, they exploited the firm's checkered history, "social debt," and foreign ownership to win sizable wage and benefit awards. This was accomplished by making it impossible for the generals to be seen supporting Cerro; had they done so, the nationalist basis of their legitimacy in power would have been at risk. Moreover, the unions' ability to generate their own leadership has made them nearly immune to the most common repressive tactic of the state—the arrest and detention of union officers. Whenever this has been tried, new leaders promptly arise to replace the detainees and guide the unions in striking for the latter's freedom. Finally, the current leadership makes the labor confederations and Left political parties bid for its adhesion—it controls, after all, the nation's largest work force and one of the most strategically placed—rather than the other way around. Since 1968 the thirty-two Cerro-Centromin unions have passed through a dizzying series of affiliations and disaffiliations. They have yet to achieve a high level of cooperation among themselves.

Class Formation in the South

Proletarian class formation in the open-pit mines of the south has had little in common with what occurred in the center, although the end point is in certain respects similar. Here the companies needed relatively small numbers of workers, as Table 10.1 indicates. But these had to be trained at considerable expense to operate costly and complex equipment. Employers could not allow this training expense to leak away in high labor turnover. What is more, they were well aware that a few disaffected workers might easily wreak enormous damage through carelessness or sabotage. Hence, a stable and reasonably contented work force was always of great importance to them. They hoped to attain it in part by offering very high wages and salaries by local standards; in part by setting up clean and commodious mining camps fully equipped with modern hospitals and clinics, good schools, and ample sociocultural amenities; and in part by following a policy of benevolent paternalism in labor relations.[21]

These firms had an additional advantage in that they never had to dragoon unwilling peasants into the mines. The camps, wage and benefit levels, and generally decent labor policies were "pull" factors. So too was the nature of the work: open-pit mine labor is not strenuous, takes place out of doors (except for those who man the concentrating plant and smelter), and poses fewer physical and health hazards than does mining below ground. There were also "push" factors. By the mid-fifties, a major out-migration from Puno department was under way. This department, which contains the west-ward extension of the Bolivian *altiplano* (see map, Fig. 2), had long been one of the country's most backward. Land maldistribution was extreme, the *latifundios* antiquated in their production methods; a local tradition of peasant rebellion was very much alive. The region's tenuous socioeconomic equilib-rium had been upset by population growth, by the belated efforts of some *latifundistas* to capitalize their holdings, and by the spread of modern political ideologies. Under this three-pronged assault on its customary way of life, much of the newly "excess" peasantry decided to try its luck elsewhere. Waves of *puneños* flooded into cities and towns all over the southern half of the republic, populating the *pueblos jóvenes*. Upon hearing of the mine con-struction of 1952-1959 in the southern foothills and coast, they flocked there in force. Southern's and Marcona's only recruiting problems were determining whom to hire and damping down complaints from disappointed aspirants.

Despite their general lack of education and experience, the *puneños* proved to be eager learners, were hard workers, and adapted readily to industrial discipline. Unlike their comrades farther north, the option of returning to a better life in the countryside was foreclosed to them; deprived of that outlet, they were far more rapid in redefining their social situation in purely prole-tarian terms. One measure of the difference is job tenure: the percentage of Toquepala and Ilo workers who can claim twenty years' tenure, meaning that they were there at the very start of operations, is exceptionally high; and it is becoming common for workers' sons to fill vacancies left by their fathers' retirement. Another measure is a much greater preoccupation of Southern workers with promotion and job categorization than would have been detected at Cerro when it was of a comparable age. A third is workers' attitudes toward the camps. At Cerro, in spite of gross deficiencies, demands for improvement in family living conditions only started to figure centrally in the unions' *pliegos de reclamos* (collective bargaining proposals) in the early seventies—by which time the Cerro proletariat had been in existence for seventy years. At Southern,

---

[21] The Guggenheim family, founders and, until 1941, owners of Asarco, were among the early U.S. bourgeois critics of the brutalization of labor. Their mines and smelters in Colorado and Mexico operated from the start on a basis of relatively humane labor relations, and that practice remained part of the Asarco managerial tradition (Hoyt 1967; Marcosson 1949). To my knowl-edge, no Asarco installation in Latin America ever became a focal point of insurrectionary violence.

in contrast, the proletariat was less than ten years old when it began to press, through the unions, for equivalent improvements.

Southern workers have also acted with far greater alacrity to seize opportunities for personal upward mobility. Their employer's enlightened promotion policies and training programs encourage this, but the workers have not contented themselves with them. Through their unions they have insisted on still better schools—Southern's are the highest-quality free schools in the country—and on what has become the nation's most extensive program of privately funded college scholarships. Miners can realistically aspire to middle-class status for their children, and occasionally (since the company will grant educational leaves of absence and reimburse the expenses of workers who complete professional or technical courses) for themselves.

Yet, the Puno tradition of resistance did not die out; for Southern's policy of benevolent paternalism gave rise to a different set of resentments. A principal source of irritation was the company's attempt to control rigidly many off-the-job aspects of camp life, including physical movement in and out.[22] This was done in large part, naturally, to keep out "political troublemakers" and "outside agitators." But it was also stimulated by paternalistic concerns. For instance, the company feared that it would be held responsible if it allowed shrewd local tradespeople to enter the camps and cheat its "unsophisticated" work force. Southern also believed it important to promote actively the cultural adaptation of workers and their families to urban conditions; its Division of Social Welfare ran a very intrusive acculturation program that many workers decried as an infringement of their families' privacy rights. Another example of infringement of privacy was the surprise inspections of apartments conducted by the Townsites Division: demerits would be issued for offenses such as unauthorized construction work, overcrowding, improper maintenance and use of sanitary facilities, raising animals on the premises, etc.[23]

Resentment against overweening corporate authority, even when wielded for supposedly benign purposes, spilled over into resistance to work rules. Discipline for clear infractions (e.g., unauthorized absence or gross tardiness) is accepted as just; but workers have increasingly demanded a voice in shift assignments, task organization, job definition, promotion, and appointment

[22] Goodsell (1974) visited Toquepala in the late sixties and describes it (pp. 169-74) as very tightly controlled. In addition to access controls, management exercised a complete communications monopoly; Goodsell avers that Southern made free use of it to indoctrinate workers in political and social values preferred by company officials.

[23] Interview with Peter Graves, Southern Peru Copper townsites manager for Toquepala and Ilo, June 22 and July 1, 1978. He reports that this practice was abolished in the mid-1970s. I can verify that as of 1978, the company no longer held a monopoly over communications. Films shown at Toquepala's company-run cinema were still censored on occasion (for "moral reasons," it was explained), but I was told that this practice would end the next month. (Amusingly, the one film banned in recent years from Toquepala on moral grounds *did* screen in the company cinema at Cuajone!) In any event, Toquepala residents have an alternative—an independent cinema, where the only censorship (again, on moral grounds) is that applied throughout the country by the state.

of supervisors. Exactly as often happens in unionized industries in the United States and Britain, work rules changes instituted unilaterally by management are invariably opposed for that reason alone, irrespective of their effect on workers' routine.

On the other hand, Southern workers have always protested by conducting orderly strikes. They are adept at sit-downs and slowdowns and have also mastered the technique of husbanding their resources by calling out on strike only critical work sections—all signs of a sophisticated tactical capability not yet observed at Centromin. There are few pickets, almost no demonstrations; violence is essentially unheard of. Correspondingly, however, the compact networks of neighborhood associations, wives' and children's support groups, and other forms of autochthonous social organization that Francisco Zapata describes as typical of mining camp life—they *are* typical in the Centromin camps—are missing.[24] Indeed, residential life at Toquepala and Ilo is thought by Southern social-service workers to be quite anomic. They report that the company itself has tried to foster block improvement associations, sport leagues, women's clubs, and a parents' and teachers' group but has encountered limited success.

The process of unionization, too, proceeded differently in Southern than it had in Cerro. Outside organizers were never a factor. Instead, newly hired workers displayed from the start a genius for coordination of action. Unions were formed to protest the firm's announcement that only about a third of the mine and smelter construction workers were to be retained once the installations went into regular operation. A strike was called to defend the fledgling unions when the Guardia Civil, acting without having consulted company officials, arrested their leaders. But Southern immediately recognized the unions (in 1960) without waiting for government approval and went on to bargain amicably with all four of them (one each for empleados and obreros at Toquepala and Ilo; a fifth was later founded by Ilo's metallurgical workers).

During their first decade of existence, the Southern unions, though formally affiliated with the CTP, were led entirely by their own people and zealously guarded their independence. Strikes were called on occasion, but relations with the company were predominantly cooperative. The unions were spectacularly successful in economic terms: the average basic obrero wage tripled, and a host of unprecedented fringe benefits was won.[25]

[24] See Zapata (1980). An excellent description of the political role played in the labor movement by wives of mine workers appears in the testimony of one of them, a Bolivian named Domitila Barrios de Chungara (1979).

[25] Including: annual bonuses amounting to twenty days' basic wages; an allowance of S/500 per month for workers on the waiting list for family apartments; workmen's compensation insurance, funded in equal parts by the company and the unions; low-interest loans from the company for purchases by workers of private homes; reimbursement of workers' expenses for correspondence courses; and college scholarships for workers' children. It may be noted that the unions learned early on that they could win wage increases indirectly by pressing for fringe

Radical ideological ferment reached Southern only after the "revolution" had begun—that is, almost nine years later than Cerro. There was no change in the nonviolent attitude of the rank and file; but, as in the case of the older North American firm, the altered climate brought forth a new crop of idealistic, radical labor leaders. They discovered how, lacking other grievances, to use the issues of authority and paternalism to build a militant following. They discovered as well the tolerance (provided there were payoffs in wage and benefit increases) of the Southern worker for frequent strikes. And they soon found that, as Southern had come to account for the lion's share of Peruvian copper exports and as the company was earning sizable profits, the military government would happily end such strikes by imposing the requisite increases.

A Southern obrero, Víctor Cuadros Paredes, and an attorney who served as an advisor to the CGTP, Ricardo Díaz Chávez, eventually emerged as the leaders of the radicals. They guided the unions out of the CTP and into an affiliation with the CGTP; took over and reconstituted the FTMMP, whose strength has since been based primarily in Southern; and afterward broke with the CGTP to establish the FTMMP as an autonomous political force. The dream of Cuadros Paredes and Díaz Chávez has been to forge the FTMMP into a true nationwide federation with enormous—were it a vehicle for solidarity among all of the nation's mine, smelter, and refinery workers—economic leverage. They enjoyed some momentary successes in 1973-1975, but it was not long before centrifugal tendencies, fed by personal ambition and jealousy as well as by the isolation of the various work groups from each other, brought their project to naught. The FTMMP maintains a tie with the UDP, a small Maoist party that participated in the 1978 and 1980 elections.

Cuajone and the MineroPeru installations have drawn their work forces directly from nearby cities and towns, and sometimes from Lima. Most of these workers were already thoroughly urbanized and had had some industrial or semi-industrial work experience. Most belonged to labor unions before coming to their current jobs, so they promptly organized new ones to represent them. With the partial exception of Cuajone, employers seemed to regard this as a natural course of events and did not oppose unionization;[26] formal (de

---

benefits with cash value, such as the bonuses just mentioned. They refined this tactic in the 1970s and employed it with great success.

[26] Southern hoped that the exceptionally fine conditions which it tried to establish at Cuajone would retard unionization there, although company officials had no illusions that it could be prevented for very long. But if retarding unionization was their aim, they committed a grave error. Deciding to give priority to holding down production costs, they gained government approval for a wage scale significantly lower than Toquepala's (the decision was a controversial one within management circles). Naturally, the lack of wage parity with Toquepala presented union organizers at Cuajone with an entering wedge, which they ably exploited. The mine was struck late in 1978. As management should have foreseen, the government promptly abandoned whatever anti-union alliance that company officials thought they had with it; it immediately recognized the new unions and shortly thereafter granted them wage increases that did, *mutatis mutandis* (there were, after all, large differences in average seniority between the two installations), establish wage parity with Toquepala.

facto, in MineroPeru's case) state recognition was quickly granted. MineroPeru's unions are affiliates of the FTMMP; the Cuajone unions, eschewing a close alliance with Toquepala and Ilo, have chosen to remain independent. Industrial relations in all of these installations are very good when measured by the standards of the mining sector as a whole.

If Cerro's tightly knit camps and Southern's anomic ones at Toquepala and Ilo are representative of two phases in the evolution of camp life as a unique element in mining-based proletarianization,[27] Cuajone and the MineroPeru facilities are a third phase: the virtual disappearance of that factor. There are no camps for Cerro Verde and the Ilo copper refinery, since both are located close to existing population centers; workers receive a cash housing allowance but are otherwise just members of the broad urban working class. Cuajone does have a camp. However, Southern learned from past mistakes in setting it up. Paternalistic controls have been dropped, local tradespeople have been invited to establish businesses in facilities provided for them, large-scale services have been contracted out to domestic providers in order to eliminate an "enclave" appearance,[28] and popular entertainments have been vigorously promoted. Through these means and by virtue of its proximity to the city of Moquegua, Cuajone has acquired a lively, multidimensional social life. In this respect it more closely resembles a "normal" suburban-industrial settlement than it does a mining camp.

In sum, each of the two principal proletarian groups of the mining sector has developed along its own path. The central sierra group, though older, does not show its age as a working class due to the long persistence of preproletarian features. Its origins in the peasantry and its special culture of protest have turned out to be effective weapons for advancing the group's economic interests, particularly when the national sociopolitical environment has been receptive to the peasant tradition. This has been the case, by and large, since the "revolution" unleashed its wave of cultural nationalism. There are indications that since Cerro's conversion into a parastatal enterprise, its new management's attention to housing, schools, etc., and to better communications has begun to undermine the workers' populist attitudes and supporting social infrastructure, if not necessarily their militant pursuit of economic objectives.[29]

[27] Stressed by Zapata (1980).

[28] For example, there is no company store; instead, a supermarket is operated by the government-owned Super/EPSA chain. Policing chores are handled not by a company Plant Protection unit but by the Guardia Republicana, a national military auxiliary force; its budget for this task is underwritten by Southern.

[29] Centromin's annual report for 1980 claims that in seven years under state ownership it has built 178 apartment blocks, has started construction of 126 more, and has begun site grading and infrastructure work for another 120. Eighty-three new schoolrooms have been added; total school enrollment has risen from 10,871 to 27,287. The enterprise has also set up its own television station, which broadcasts news about Centromin's finances, operations, and plans; publicizes social and cultural events in the camps; and, of course, presents management's point of view in labor disputes. Centromin's president, Guillermo Flórez Pinedo, claimed in an in-

The mine and smelter workers of the south have partaken of a less troublesome and more rapid process of proletarianization. They are also well organized and militant in pursuing their core interests, but their protests are usually without emotional fervor; certainly, the treatment they have received at the hands of their employers is not such as to give rise to insurrectionary tendencies. On the contrary: in terms of both wages and benefits they have done very well, and their families face reasonable prospects for upward mobility. These factors, along with workers' preferences for holding on to their privileged employment and their physical separation from other industrial centers, keep the southern group apart from the rest of the national working class and from its counterpart in the central sierra. Cultural differences appear to have further inhibited communication and cooperation between the two groups.

THE NATURE OF MINE WORKERS' MILITANCY

The preceding suggests that appearances—radical leadership rhetoric—to the contrary notwithstanding, Peruvian miners have developed no more than a "trade union consciousness" focusing solely on economic gains for the immediate work group. If so, this is a politically significant finding. For, the workers have been subjected to a steady barrage of Leninist propaganda and political activity designed precisely to overcome that limitation. Much of it, moreover, is delivered not by outsiders but by local union leaders who are otherwise respected and admired.

Workers' Political Opinions

A broad survey of miners' political attitudes and beliefs might settle the question, but the practical obstacles thereto have yet to be surmounted.[30] The best that can be done at present is to draw upon existing measures of relevant attitudes among empleados and obreros in the mediana minería and in MineroPeru's Cerro Verde mine.[31] (Until better information comes along, we

terview on August 22, 1981 that this publicity was proving effective in undercutting once-traditional family backing for strikes: the exposure of wives to the management viewpoint on daytime television often induces them to urge their husbands not to leave the job. One indicator of the impact of these changes and improvements is that productivity, measured in metal output per man-hour worked, has increased by 5.3 percent since 1974 (Centromin 1981).

[30] Workers are usually suspicious of any government or company attempt to get such information from them, and it is my understanding that they have not proved hospitable to North American opinion surveyors. Unions have a vested interest in being able to project an image of proletarian radicalism and would hardly undertake an investigation that might possibly invalidate that claim. Peruvian academics are the obvious ones who should undertake the task, but they are handicapped by lack of research funds.

[31] The mediana minería survey dates from 1974, the Cerro Verde survey from 1977. Both were made available on condition of anonymity (see my comments in Chapter 9, n. 73). The first sampled 10 percent each of empleados and obreros, balanced by employer, region, and job function so as to be accurately representative of the subsector; the second sampled the entire work force.

may view these as reference groups representative to some degree of workers at Centromin and Southern, respectively.) The two opinion surveys are, unfortunately, noncomparable; they were taken three years apart with different instruments. Still, the partial data are useful, especially when combined with impressionistic evidence garnered at Southern.

Medium-mine workers were asked to select from a list the entity or institution which they held most responsible for recent increases (this was in 1974) in the cost of living. Empleados and obreros agreed in assigning culpability primarily to the president and Council of Ministers, secondarily to "property-owners and the wealthy," and thirdly to "middlemen." But, whereas roughly equal percentages of empleados and obreros placed the blame on the propertied classes, significantly more obreros than empleados chose to vest it in the political authorities.[32] The data therefore imply that the least privileged workers perceive their economic adversary as the political "superstructure," not the structure of class domination. In view of the radical nationalism espoused by many union leaders at the time of the survey, it is noteworthy that minuscule proportions of both empleados and obreros felt that responsibility for rising prices lay with "U.S. imperialism."

Empleados alone were asked to describe their own class position and to state the basis for their determination. Just under half used salary as the criterion, while 28 percent opted for educational attainment. On these grounds, 57 percent placed themselves in the "middle class," 12 percent in the "upper middle class," and 22 percent in the "lower middle class." Empleados also gave more emphasis than did obreros to noneconomic, status aspects of work. Asked to state the most important improvement that their employer could make, nearly half of all obreros requested better housing and a fourth, higher wages. Empleados, in contrast, did not mention salary at all, and only 10 percent referred to housing. Instead, a third demanded "improved workplace organization and better employee training," and a like fraction requested more educational support programs. The clear implication is that, at least in the mediana minería, empleados' status concerns cause the distinction between them and obreros to remain a source of proletarian disarticulation.

At Cerro Verde, workers were instructed to indicate whether or not they understood the principal differences among the major politico-economic systems of the modern world, and those who did were encouraged to select their personal preference from among "capitalism," "socialism," and "communism." Two-thirds of the empleados and 31 percent of the obreros replied

---

[32] Obrero data were tabulated by region only, without computed overall averages, in the report that was shown to me. Those blaming the president and Council of Ministers ranged from 40.8 to 70.2 percent (56.9 and 48.6 percent in the two most populous regions, both in the central sierra). The corresponding figures for those blaming the propertied classes were 17.5-29.2 percent (20.6 and 26.8 percent in the two central sierra regions); and for those blaming "middlemen," 2.9-15.6 percent. The empleado data did include overall averages as well as regional breakdowns. The percentages of empleados (there were no major regional differences) blaming the political authorities, the propertied classes, and "middlemen" were 33.7, 20.3, and 14.8, respectively.

in the positive to the first question. The preferences of "knowledgeable" empleados were as follows: for "capitalism," 26 percent; for "socialism," 26 percent; for "communism," none; for "decline to state," 18 percent; for "no preference," 24 percent (6 percent did not respond). "Knowledgeable" obreros chose: "capitalism," 5 percent; "socialism," 39 percent; "communism," 11 percent; "no preference," 43 percent (none declined to state, and 2 percent did not respond). The results suggest that relatively few obreros have a real knowledge of current political ideologies; their expressed preference for alternatives to capitalism therefore comes closer, in all probability, to representing a diffuse alienation from the existing order than it does a strong commitment to something different. Empleados, for their part, seem to have greater knowledge and stronger preferences. However, they are less alienated from the status quo and less attracted to radical alternatives—all of which seems to reflect a belief that the present system offers opportunities for socioeconomic advancement. Again we observe the disarticulating effect of the distinction between the strata.

In the absence of opinion survey data from the Southern installations, I asked a representative selection of foremen and line supervisors to characterize the political orientations of workers under their command.[33] Not one felt that more than a tiny minority of workers were committed to radical ideologies; most described the average worker as largely apolitical—ready to vote for the Left but without great enthusiasm. This impression was confirmed in conversations with randomly selected workers. It was also confirmed by a number of Marxist-Leninists deeply involved in union affairs at Ilo, with whom I was privileged to spend most of a night in freewheeling conversation.

Militancy and Strikes

In developed countries like the United States and Britain, there is often little connection between workers' readiness to undertake militant class action in defense of common interests, on the one hand, and the ideologies claimed by themselves or officially espoused by their unions, on the other. Is the same true in Peru? Has the working class of the minería, whatever its ideological predilections may or may not be, shown increasing militancy *in action* during the "revolution"? The strike record should provide the answer and should additionally permit a determination of the extent to which mine workers have spearheaded the action of the working class at large.

[33] I claim no scientific accuracy for this procedure; it was, simply, the best that could be done in the allotted time. Still, the procedure has value. Union leaders and radical, anti-company intellectuals with whom I spoke agreed that a worker's political opinions would not affect his advancement at Southern; that workers understood this to be so; and that they would freely express such opinions to, or in earshot of, their supervisors. If the latter introduced bias into their characterizations, its direction is uncertain and need not have been influenced by an undue concern for the company's welfare. Most of them were themselves ordinary workers and union members in the mines of the western United States before signing on for jobs in Peru; if anything, top management faults them for being excessively pro-union in their own attitudes and for sympathizing too much with workers under them.

Table 10.2 summarizes Peruvian strike activity in the mines and elsewhere from 1967 to 1979. We see that there is no secular tendency toward an increase or a decrease in the relative weight of mine strikes in the national totals: although strikes in the mining sector mushroomed in 1970-1973 (and again, for reasons to be discussed subsequently, in 1978), they have generally accounted for a constant 6 to 7 percent of the total. That is approximately triple the fraction of mine workers among nonagricultural wage earners; miners have thus formed a disproportionate share of strikers in each of the tabulated years. This share has recently begun to shrink. Other evidence implies that the shrinkage is due mainly to an increase in strike frequency in the rest of the nonagricultural economy. To the degree that the mine strikes of the early seventies were perceived by other workers as successful and, hence, emboldened them to act similarly, the mine unions could be said to have spearheaded greater working-class militancy. However, independent verification of a relationship between the two variables is needed before this hypothesis can be unequivocally accepted.

In Table 10.3 are shown three measures of strike size and intensity. Until the early 1970s, mine strikes tended to involve more workers than did others— for the obvious reason that mining work forces are larger on the average than those in any other industry. But this tendency has reversed since 1975. Inasmuch as there has been neither great industrial growth nor consolidation in 1975-1979, the change can only be attributed to the increasing success of labor federations outside of mining (particularly such militant "middle-class" federations as the teachers' and bank employees') in fomenting industry-wide work stoppages. Contrariwise, the effort mounted by the FTMMP after 1973 (when it came under radical control) to weld all of the local mine unions into a cohesive national force has not borne visible fruit on the strike front.

Mine strikes have always entailed greater losses of labor time than strikes in most other industries. This used to be due, once more, to differences in the average size of work units but now must be laid exclusively to a longer-than-average duration of mine strikes—as the data for labor time lost per striker graphically demonstrate. The latter also reveal a clear secular trend toward *declining* militancy, a trend in evidence throughout the period.[34] It is not, however, confined to mine workers.

Table 10.4, which partially breaks down by enterprise two indicators of mining-sector strike intensity, permits us to correlate militancy with the working-class groups defined earlier. The trend toward decreasing militancy (it appears most vividly in the right half of the table) is here seen to be especially in evidence at Centromin. Indeed, Centromin workers have become less militant on the average than those of the mediana minería, who, except for MineroPeru, make up the "rest of sector." Given that the trend first became plain in 1973, when Cerro's impending expropriation was already public

---

[34] This phenomenon was first noted and commented upon by Zapata (1980).

TABLE 10.2 Strikes in Peru, 1967-1979

Year	Number of Strikes			Number of Strikers			Man-hours Lost to Strikes		
	A Mine	B Other	A/(A+B) Percent	C Mine	D Other	C/(C+D) Percent	E Mine	F Other	E/(E+F) Percent
1967	32	382	7.7	17,818	124,464	12.5	5,269,664	3,103,108	62.9
1968	21	343	5.8	9,426	98,383	8.7	2,825,376	552,425	83.6
1969	24	348	6.5	17,803	73,728	19.5	1,900,748	1,988,552	48.9
1970	66	279	19.1	56,205	54,785	50.6	4,325,853	1,456,003	74.8
1971	76	301	20.2	58,454	102,961	36.2	6,270,632	4,611,320	57.6
1972	33	376	8.1	16,657	113,986	12.7	958,008	5,373,008	15.1
1973	80	708	10.2	59,471	356,780	14.3	3,831,888	11,856,800	24.4
1974	38	532	6.7	27,433	335,304	7.6	1,878,148	11,534,892	14.0
1975	57	722	7.3	50,387	566,733	8.2	2,652,609	17,616,799	13.1
1976	29	411	6.6	31,505	266,596	12.2	572,228	6,249,996	8.4
1977	n/a	234[a]	—	n/a	406,461[a]	—	n/a	6,543,352[a]	—
1978	53	311	14.5	48,596	1,349,791[b]	3.5	4,680,388	31,464,348[b]	12.9
1979	40	537	6.9	25,342	678,141	3.6	1,187,288	9,364,064	11.3

SOURCES: Compiled by the author from data in International Labour Organisation (1980) and Dirección General de Empleo (1973); and from unpublished data furnished by the Departamento de Estudios Económicos y Estadística, Sociedad Nacional de Minería y Petróleo.

[a] Combined data for mine strikes plus other strikes.

[b] Figures include nationwide general strike of May 22-23.

TABLE 10.3 Indicators of Strike Intensity in Peru, 1967-1979

Year	No. of Strikers Per Strike		Man-hours Lost Per Strike[a]		Man-hours Lost Per Striker	
	Mine	Other	Mine	Other	Mine	Other
1967	556.8	325.8	164.7	8.1	296	25
1968	448.9	286.8	134.5	1.6	300	6
1969	741.8	211.9	79.2	5.7	107	27
1970	851.6	196.4	65.5	5.2	77	27
1971	769.1	342.1	82.5	15.3	107	45
1972	504.8	303.2	29.0	14.3	58	47
1973	743.4	503.9	47.9	16.7	64	33
1974	721.9	630.3	49.4	21.7	68	34
1975	884.0	784.9	46.5	24.4	53	31
1976	1,086.4	551.3	19.7	15.2	18	27
1977	n/a	1,737.0[b]	n/a	28.0[b]	n/a	16[b]
1978	916.9	4,340.2	88.3	101.2	96	23
1979	633.6	1,262.8	29.7	17.4	47	14

SOURCE: Computed by the author from data in Table 10.2.

[a] In thousands.

[b] Data are for all strikes, mine and "other."

knowledge, it would appear that the transfer of the firm to national control has definitely helped to reduce strike intensity. Skeptics might argue that the state, as employer, has repressed the labor movement more strenuously than before, or at least that it has lowered the payoffs to militancy by more firmly resisting wage demands. Wage data, to be examined shortly, refute the second accusation. There is a grain of truth to the first; but repression was only seriously felt after 1976, was never extreme, and affected equally the entire mining industry. More important, it seems to me, has been quick action by parastatal management to clear Cerro's "social debt" and to improve its communications with its workers (see n. 29).

Workers at Southern Peru Copper display a greater degree of militancy. It is cyclical, peaking at four- to five-year intervals with little apparent long-term change in the pattern. A comparision with the near-passivity at Marcona-HierroPeru, where workers' backgrounds and other conditions are similar, suggests that those in the employ of a very profitable foreign firm perceive many more opportunities for gains than do those employed by one which is neither profitable nor foreign. In view of what has been learned about the different class-formation histories of the work groups, it can only be concluded that militancy in the Peruvian mines no longer has anything to do with political parties or outside direction, with populist causes (i.e., the reaction of peasants to the disruptive effects of advancing capitalism), or with gross oppression. It must be regarded, rather, as a natural outgrowth of proletarian maturity

TABLE 10.4 Strike Intensity Indicators by Enterprise, 1969-1979

Year	Man-hours Lost Per Strike[a]				Man-hours Lost Per Striker			
	Cerro-Centromin	Southern	Marcona-HierroPeru	Rest of Sector	Cerro-Centromin	Southern	Marcona-HierroPeru	Rest of Sector
1969	169.8	315.3	0.0	25.3	95	146	0	93
1970	92.9	58.2	76.1	34.9	81	66	81	70
1971	82.1	68.8	215.5	73.1	99	69	107	162
1972	4.1	48.2	0.0	16.5	17	86	0	31
1973	131.0	72.9	110.8	35.0	16	91	81	75
1974	282.5	186.2	0.0	30.5	24	216	0	79
1975	59.8	105.9	0.0	25.8	46	75	0	56
1976	147.2	26.7	0.0	11.3	16	22	0	17
1977		92.6				54		
1978		101.6		85.2[b]		117		92[b]
1979		50.6	33.6	21.3[c]		96	16	34[c]

SOURCES: Computed by the author from data presented in the consolidated declarations of the companies and supplied by the Departamento de Estudios Económicos y Estadística, Sociedad Nacional de Minería y Petróleo.

[a] In thousands.

[b] Data are for all enterprises except Southern.

[c] Data are for all enterprises except Southern and HierroPeru.

and as a response to accurate perceptions of the possibilities offered by the employer's profit picture.

"ECONOMISM" AMONG THE WORKING CLASS?

"Economistic" class action is predicated on the assumption that the principal interest of the working class is to augment its share of the economic pie. It therefore abstains from frontal assaults on the structures of political domination and social control which keep the class in its subordinate condition; and it may acquiesce in bourgeois strategies for enlarging the pie. That key elements of the working class incline toward "economistic" patterns of action does not mean that bourgeois hegemony exists. It does mean that the attainment of such hegemony is possible, provided (as noted in Chapter 9) that the bourgeoisie, without excessive sacrifice of its own interest in power and control, can: (1) meet a satisfying portion of the workers' "economistic" demands, and (2) accommodate within its own world view the presence and activities of those indigenous institutions—labor unions, Leftist political parties, etc.—which the working class has constructed and deems essential for its self-protection. The actions of corporate mining enterprises in Peru since 1968 appear to conform to the second requirement. What of the first?

The Evolution of Real Wages and Benefits

Figure 8 displays the post-1967 evolution of average real wages[35] for the nonferrous metal-mining industry as a whole; for Southern; for Cerro-Centromin; and for the mediana minería. Also indicated, for purposes of comparison, is the average nonagricultural wage for metropolitan Lima. Most mine workers experienced a steady increase in real income until the late 1970s. Wages thereafter came under downward pressure in real terms as inflation accelerated. Nonetheless, miners held their own much better than did Lima workers: from 32 percent greater than the latter's in 1968, mining-sector remunerations rose by 1971 to a point 62 percent greater, and were fully 89 percent greater in 1977. Under parastatal management, Centromin's employees have approached one of their most cherished goals: wage parity with Southern. Even miners employed in the mediana minería have advanced further economically than have Lima industrial workers.[36]

Another economic advance that cannot show in the wage data consists in direct and indirect company contributions to the union treasuries, which relieve workers of responsibility for certain expenses that would otherwise come out

[35] Wages include: basic wage or salary; overtime pay; shift differentials; holiday pay; obreros' *dominical*; vacation pay; and deferred payments—employer contributions to social security and employer set-asides for future payment of time-of-service indemnities and other cash benefits.

[36] Mine workers, moreover, receive free services and payments in kind which Lima industrial workers do not. Many of these—especially housing and medical care—increase in value in proportion to inflation. Were they to be figured in, miners' real income would show much less of an inflation-caused deterioration after 1975 than that depicted in Fig. 8.

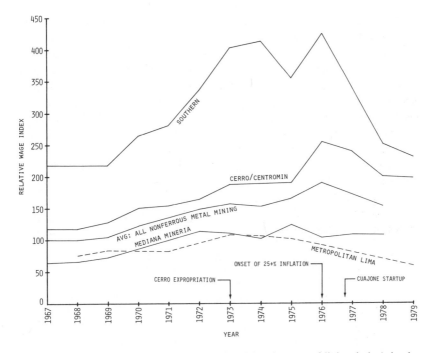

FIGURE 8. Real wages (money wages deflated by the cost-of-living index) in the Peruvian minería and in metropolitan Lima. As data are based on employers' total labor costs, they *include* effects of lost wages due to strikes and stoppages. Also, wage data for Southern in 1977-1979 are based on Toquepala and Ilo only, in order to allow a consistent comparison; wages at Cuajone, where workers have less seniority, are about 20 percent lower. Cost-of-living indices are from the Central Reserve Bank of Peru; wage data are from consolidated declarations and annual reports of the firms. Computations were performed partly by the author and partly by the Departamento de Estudios Económicos y Estadística, Sociedad Nacional de Minería y Petróleo.

of their pay envelopes. This process of employer subsidization of unions is farthest along at Southern but is being imitated elsewhere. Officers of the Southern unions receive a total of 2,140 unrestricted man-days of annual *licencia*—up from 340 man-days with restrictions in 1970. Federation and confederation officers belonging to the empleado unions are granted permanent leaves with full pay. Every officer is awarded a company-paid life and accident insurance policy with a face value of S/1 million (in 1978). The company has had to make $326,000 in cash contributions to the unions' building funds and to donate construction materials and labor; it also pays the unions $19,500 per year in operating and upkeep expenses for their libraries. And it has been induced by union pressure to donate $142,000 to the universities of Tacna and Arequipa.[37]

[37] Because the workers at Southern do so well economically, student groups—which are very

The wage gains accruing to the mining "labor aristocracy" are consistent with E.V.K. FitzGerald's conclusion that, compared to four of the larger, more developed countries of Latin America, Peru in this period showed the least shift of national income toward the top two deciles of the income distribution and the biggest growth in the share captured by the middle four.[38] The military regime, it is true, did little to improve the incomes of the poorest, least mobilized popular sectors; but it was no mainstay of upper-class privilege and did not stand in the way of economic gains by powerful labor groups.

Figure 9 portrays the comparative evolution of empleado versus obrero wages in Cerro-Centromin, in Southern, and in metropolitan Lima. (Full time-series data for MineroPeru and the mediana minería could not be obtained, but I am reliably informed that the trends there are similar.) Observe how the economic differential has become smaller.[39] If one assumes that class cohesion is partly an inverse function of the extent of wage differentials among

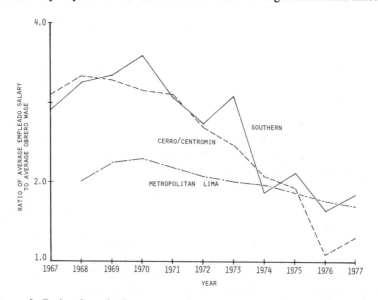

FIGURE 9. Ratio of empleado average salary to obrero average wage for Southern Peru Copper, Cerro-Centromin, and metropolitan Lima, 1967-1977. Data sources and computation as indicated for Fig. 8, except that cost-of-living data are not used here.

radical and which elsewhere seek to maintain ties with the labor movement—have tended to be hostile toward them. It was to overcome this hostility and to form a closer alliance with the students that the unions made the demand for donations to these schools.

[38] FitzGerald (1979:140-41). The other countries are Brazil, Colombia, Mexico, and Venezuela. However, the Peruvian middle sectors have more catching up to do: in 1973-74, only in Brazil did the top 5 percent have a larger share of the total national income.

[39] Mining obreros can today actually earn more than some empleados if they work overtime and/or on night shifts; they may even do better than junior members of the professional staff. The military's attitude toward mine strikes may have been affected by the fact that, by 1975, Southern obreros earned more than an army or air force lieutenant or a navy ensign.

various elements of the working class, then cohesion remains limited by the gran minería-mediana minería gap (although it is narrower than before). However, the economic dimension of empleado-obrero disarticulation has ceased to signify much; the disarticulating effect is now due mainly to the status barrier established by the distinction.

The Question of Control over the Enterprise

Were mine workers' class consciousness of a sort that would lead them to take serious issue with the division of power and authority in the capitalist enterprise, the Workers' Community system, instituted in mining in 1971, presented them with one potential vehicle for expressing such a concern. The Workers' Community was an enterprise reform combining co-ownership with comanagement, both to be gradually achieved through annual reinvestment of corporate profits in capital stock held in common by all workers of the firm. (See Appendix D, item VIII for a description of how the scheme functioned. The distribution, via COCOMI, of shared-out profits over the entire sector was included in order to equalize benefits partially, in compensation for the enormous disparities among companies in profit per employee.)[40] Evelyne Stephens has discussed the theory and practice of the system in considerable detail, with emphasis on its meaning for class relations.[41]

None of the medium or large mining companies, so far as I have been able to determine, ever resorted to borderline or actual fraud in order to evade its obligations under the system—as happened often enough in manufacturing.[42] In fact, some of them sent the corporate directors named by the Community to attend courses (at employer expense) in accounting and business management in order to help them participate more effectively in the conduct of directorial business. Nevertheless, the mine unions, choosing to regard the system as a cooptative device intended to undercut their appeal and to substitute class collaboration for struggle—which, in the minds of the generals, it assuredly was—denounced it and ordered a boycott of its activities.[43] The boycott was fairly well honored for the first two years, during which time empleados alone evinced interest in the scheme. Then, in 1974, workers started to receive very sizable distributions out of the high industry profits of

[40] These are differences due to the high capital intensity of Southern, MineroPeru, and HierroPeru versus the much lower capital intensity of the mediana minería.

[41] Stephens (1980).

[42] Companies were artificially subdivided into chains of "independent" small businesses (exempt from the comanagement requirement). Secret directorial meetings were held in inconvenient locations, to which only the directors representing private capital were invited. Meetings were conducted in languages other than Spanish. Community representatives were presented with doctored accounting data or were deluged with reams of information that they could not possibly assimilate.

[43] They may have been influenced by warnings from sympathetic academics; see, e.g., the analyses of the system by Alberti et al. (1977) and Pásara et al. (1974). However, Pásara and Santistevan (1973) note that nothing in the institutional structure and functioning of the Workers' Community infringes on the bases of union organization.

the previous year. Interest in Community affairs, attendance at its assemblies, and competition for its officerships suddenly increased as a financial impact began to be felt. The unions chose not to buck the trend. This was a wise move, since worker loyalty to organized labor, still the first line of class defense, in no way diminished. Community assemblies, and the Community's access to corporate boards of directors, simply became parallel avenues to unions for advancing the same class concerns. Union leadership cadres, though barred by law from office-holding in the Community, were shortly playing a prominent behind-the-scenes guiding role in the conduct of its affairs.

Community assemblies are democratic and exercise real control over executive officers. Thus, the kinds of concerns that the latter express in their dealings with corporate management accurately reflect rank-and-file desires. It is plain that these concerns have nothing to do with management properly understood, i.e., with controlling the process of capital accumulation and distribution. (Not one of the managers whom I interviewed believed that his authority had been undercut by the Community system.) But they have much to do with the normal process of wage bargaining: according to informants on both sides, Community-appointed directors channel financial information obtained in the course of their duties directly to the unions, where it is used in framing demands and in buttressing labor's position in wage negotiations. The only noneconomic use to which the workers have put the Community is that of bringing personnel matters to the attention of top corporate management. Acting on behalf of petitioners, Community representatives on corporate boards solicit reassignments and promotions, enter objections to the actions of line supervisors, and so forth.[44]

After seven years of experience with the Workers' Communities, the military regime realized that the system had made no observable difference in the character of industrial relations but was acting as a disincentive to new capital investment. Therefore, in November 1978 the system was gutted of its comanagement and communitarian features (see Appendix B, item 33). The maximum workers' share of enterprise ownership was reduced from 50 to 33 percent, guaranteeing to private capital majority control in perpetuity. In addition, shares of capital stock (those already held in the Community's name as well as those to be issued in the future) were thenceforth to be distributed to workers as individual property; these *acciones laborales* are freely traded on the Lima Stock Exchange. Just as one would expect, many workers sell them as soon as received, preferring to have the ready cash.[45]

[44] Managers are happy to have this input, as it gives them a chance to defuse problems that might otherwise blow up in their faces; but they would vastly prefer to see it take place at lower administrative levels.

[45] But the *acciones laborales* have another effect: in the case of Southern, their purchase by Peruvian investors gives the latter an ownership right in the company, thereby tending slowly to nationalize it. Southern's managers are unsure of what this ownership right entails, but they suspect that the Peruvian courts, should they have an opportunity to decide the issue, will attach the same privileges to *acciones laborales* as those conveyed by preferred stock.

It has become possible for firms to implement worker participation in management through *comités de gestión* separate from their boards of directors, if they so choose; these labor-management committees have less power than does a regular directorial board. (Southern rapidly went to the new committee system.)

The gutting of the Workers' Community eliminated the slightest possibility of its being used as a vehicle of class struggle inside corporate enterprise over the question of control. Even so, *the measure brought forth not a whimper of protest from labor leaders or from the rank and file*. The average worker apparently prefers a stock certificate redeemable for currency to an abstract share in the exercise of an authority whose nature he but dimly perceives. Organized labor seems uninterested in helping him to sharpen that perception.

THE POLITICAL POWER OF ORGANIZED MINE LABOR

Labor and National Power

During the "first phase" (the *velasquista* period) of the "revolution," the regime consistently favored the wage demands of the principal mine labor groups. This was done through expanded use of the state's power to impose wage settlements. As soon as it became obvious to the mine unions that the government was on their side in matters of pay and benefits, direct collective bargaining between labor and management degenerated into a *pro forma* exercise empty of content. Unions framed extreme demands and refused compromise, expecting that the labor ministry would ultimately grant them much of what they really sought. Companies likewise avoided compromise in hopes of discouraging the ministry from ceding too much. Labor relations in the mines were thoroughly politicized.

The military's initial favoritism toward mine labor needs explaining. I adduce the following:

1. *Nationalism*. The generals were nationalists by conviction and shared the perception of all Peruvian nationalists that foreign firms had pillaged the country's resource base for many years. Hence, they were not about to do anything to uphold the *short-term* interests of the large foreign mining companies against those of a mobilized, politically vocal group of local citizens. An additional reason for not upholding these corporate interests was that the regime's legitimacy, as viewed by leading *militares*, seemed to be founded in major part on widespread public disgust with the *entreguismo* of previous governments.

2. *Social justice*. Not all of the generals were cynical power-seekers or technocratic elitists; a few, at least, sincerely believed it their duty to help uplift the downtrodden. Fernández Maldonado was one of these. Among his earliest official acts on the labor front were the disarming of private mining-camp police, the prohibition of company interference with free movement of

persons and their goods in and out of the camps, and the removal of guards and barriers around expatriates' camp quarters. Later on he insisted on incorporating into the 1971 Mining Code and supporting regulations the first detailed specifications for working conditions and camp facilities; and under his leadership a decree-law setting standards for housing accommodations was enacted. He frequently interceded with the labor minister in support of union demands.

3. *Bonanza development.* Wage increases, in the generals' view, furthered the strategy of bonanza development in three ways. They represented an increase in the local share of mining value added. They helped to coopt and pacify the work force at foreign capital's expense. And, they linked the mining industry more solidly to the rest of the industrial economy by adding betterpaid mine workers to the market for domestically produced manufactured goods. On the other hand, efforts to accelerate the pace of development pressed ever more heavily on the balance of payments and on the state's finances and international borrowing capacity, all underwritten by mining revenues. Strikes and stoppages that interfered with mine production had therefore to be ended quickly, no matter what the cost.

4. *Anti-aprismo.* The military had a tradition of uncompromising hostility to the APRA and had taken power in 1948, 1962, and 1968 partly to forestall probable *aprista* successes in forthcoming presidential elections (Chapter 2). Until 1968, most of the party's strength lay with its following in the more advanced and better organized sectors of the working class and in the lower elements of the middle class, which are also heavily unionized. *Aprismo* would be gravely weakened by any measures tending to undercut its appeal to organized labor.[46]

All of the mine unions recognized the military disposition for what it was. They therefore concluded that they should station themselves at all times well to the left of the regime; that they should engage in longer and more frequent strikes in order to force accommodation on pay issues; but that they should not persist in such actions for ideological reasons, as the regime would interpret this as a direct threat. These tactics were eminently successful. More than that, they protected the labor movement from co-optation.[47] The unions

[46] Hobsbawm (1971) claims that the military never fully understood the nature of the labor movement and that this failure of understanding led them into major tactical errors in dealing with it. Zapata (1980) echoes this view for the case of mining, adding that the generals overestimated the strength of union-party linkages. They thought to tame labor by getting rid of leaders with visible party affiliations, not realizing that they were thus paving the road to power for more radical leaders—who do *not* maintain close ties with political parties.

[47] For example: the regime decided that a Cerro *marcha de sacrificio* in 1971 should enjoy official protection and support. The marchers were welcomed into Lima along a route provided with a police escort; were encamped in quarters set up for them in the working-class district of San Martín de Porras; and were treated to visits with the president, the labor minister, the mining minister, and other key officials. What was the result of this unprecedented attention? The marchers refused the government's wage offer and threatened to remain in Lima indefinitely unless their demands—which they had already raised beyond what they were at the start of the march—were met in full. They got their way.

cooperated at first with the CGTP, which, having reconstituted itself three months prior to the military seizure of power, was the earliest labor-movement beneficiary of the new government's steadfast opposition to the CTP-APRA. Later, however, the PCP attempted to become the main pro-regime political party and, so, ordered the CGTP to moderate its militancy; the mine unions then broke with it.

Circumstances turned sour in 1975. Falling metals prices translated into falling profits for the mining companies and made them more resistant than ever to union wage demands. In August, Velasco was replaced in the presidency by Morales Bermúdez, ushering in the "second phase" policy of slowing the pace of reform and reassuring private capital. The metals price plunge, together with rising food imports to meet the demand created by the growing and better-paid urban labor force, threw the balance of payments into deficit and drained the nation's foreign currency reserves (see Chapter 8, n. 41). Moreover, food was being sold below cost by state monopolies—another cooptative benefit of bonanza development—and these subsidies helped to unbalance the state budget. Budgetary deficits and devaluation of the sol (which raised local-currency prices of imported consumer and capital goods) resulted in domestic inflation; hitherto much rarer in Peru than in many of the more industrialized Latin American countries, it would reach runaway proportions by the end of the decade.

Had the regime mobilized popular support during the halcyon days of radical reform, it might have been able to ride out the storm sheltered by appeals to patriotic national sacrifice. As it was, the appeals were offered but fell on the deaf ears of a demobilized and apathetic populace whose every attempt to organize politically had been squelched. The sole alternative was repression. Early in 1976 another wave of mine strikes broke out as miners strained to protect their purchasing power against the ravages of inflation by winning extraordinary wage increases. The regime's answer was to declare a state of emergency in the mining sector and to forbid all strikes there. On July 1, 1976 a national state of emergency was put into effect, and six weeks thereafter the strike prohibition was made universal.

The government knew that it was riding a tiger in employing these tactics against mine labor, and it proceeded with caution. Workers in the gran minería, who could best afford the loss of back pay, regularly defied the strike prohibition; but for the occasional and brief detention of leaders, no effort was made to punish them (with one exception, which turned out disastrously for the regime).[48] Importantly, fear of the miners' reaction undoubtedly stiff-

[48] There was a general strike on July 19, 1977. The interior minister, a hard-liner, urged the government to retaliate by jailing its organizers and by allowing employers to fire all workers who had played any active role in the strike besides simply staying off the job. Employers seized the opportunity to pare their work forces in the face of the recession, which *estabilidad laboral* otherwise prevented them from doing; thousands were dismissed. The labor movement hit back with wave after wave of local strikes demanding the *reposición* (rehiring) of all those discharged. Thus, the government had to deal with this turmoil all through the remainder of the year, a

ened the spine of the government in its negotiations over the balance-of-payments problem with the IMF—which was insisting on the imposition of anti-popular, deflationary economic measures as its price for aid. In this the power of the mine unions was deployed, latently but effectively and for the first time, on behalf of the interests of the whole working class and much of the middle class.

Of course, the worsening economic conjuncture made it impossible for the government to hold out forever. Its resistance collapsed in May 1978, and, with many misgivings and after modification to ameliorate its harshest aspects, the package of measures demanded by the IMF was enacted. Labor replied with a very well organized general strike on May 22 and 23—the second time (along with the one-day general strike of the previous year) that mine labor, with its centrally important participation, served broader class interests.[49] The government reimposed the national state of emergency (it had lapsed several months before), but the number of arrests and firings was smaller than it would have been—and was in 1977—had the regime chosen a truly repressive tack.

The year 1978 also witnessed the regime's decision to turn power back to civilians. In order to prepare for a smooth transition as well as to seek the cooperation of all sectors in resolving the economic problem, Morales Bermúdez set up a round of consultations with representatives of political parties, property-owners' associations, professional guilds, *and organized labor*. All of the centrals participated, as did the FTMMP and other important federations. Organized labor's participation in these discussions deserves underscoring, because it was the first time in the nation's history that union representatives were summoned to the presidential palace to be consulted, not dictated to, on affairs of national scope. Labor representatives gained further political participation with the election of the Constituent Assembly: some served as delegates, others acted as committee consultants or were called as witnesses. Thanks in part to their presence, the Assembly placed in the new constitution guarantees of great significance to the popular classes: the right to political liberty, the right to a basic level of material welfare, and the right to organize and act collectively in defense of their material interests.[50]

---

period when it would have much preferred to devote its undivided attention to the economic crisis and to the upcoming transition to civilian rule. The lesson was learned; and the interior minister in question was soon "kicked upstairs" to another, purely military position without government responsibilities.

[49] In the organization of this very important strike, the mine unions once more made their power felt within the labor movement as a whole. The first move toward a general strike was taken by the CGTP in January, but the mine unions withheld their support and the move failed. They thus made it clear that no successful general strike could take place without their backing and approval. They then played a major role in determining the date and duration of the May protest.

[50] State authorities gained something, too, from these events. By serving as proof that the regime was not implacably anti-labor or anti-union, they left it free to draw the line beyond which labor radicalism would not be allowed to pass. When in early 1979 the Toquepala unions

A logical next advance would be for labor and other key economic groups to be brought into formal, regular consultation with state authorities in the making of high economic policy—what the British call "tripartism." The way to such an advance was opened by hyperinflation. The "new bourgeoisie" wants and needs political stability and the survival of civilian rule; but it understands, as do elected officials whose careers are at stake, that neither is likely if the local and the general strike remain labor's only tools for protecting its incomes against inflationary erosion. Consequently, the government has set up a Comisión Tripartidaria of business, labor, and state representatives to look for ways in which wages and salaries might be indexed to the cost of living. Already the Tripartite Commission shows signs of evolving into a permanent consultative body with an institutional role in economic policy making.[51]

An additional advance would be for the labor movement to begin participating in parliamentary politics, which it is now free to do. The necessary mechanisms—Left parties, some of them (notably, the PCP and the UDP) with ties to elements of the movement—already exist. Yet, even though the near-term electoral prospects of the Peruvian Left are probably better than anywhere else in Latin America,[52] the depth of the parties' working-class base is suspect. In a neat reversal of their earlier role as providers of union leadership, a few of the Left parties (e.g., the UDP, one of whose prominent members is Víctor Cuadros Paredes of the FTMMP) now draw their leadership from the unions. But stronger party-union ties, as well as stronger rank-and-

made very stiff wage demands and then went out on strike just as the balance-of-payments situation was beginning to show slight improvement, the government decided that it had had enough and that it was safe to move. Toquepala was occupied by troops, who cut off all communication with the outside world; there were some 55 arrests and 185 dismissals, with warnings of more to come if the strike did not end at once. It did. But there were no solidarity strikes elsewhere, as there surely would have been had other workers and union leaders believed that the move was aimed at the Southern unions as such.

[51] Indeed, a new law reorganizing the labor ministry (whose name becomes "Ministry of Labor and Social Promotion") states that its foremost objective will henceforth be "to promote labor relations within a framework of tripartism, in cooperation with representative organisms of workers and employers, in order to achieve better understanding and harmony in labor affairs." Labor Minister Grados is said to have added a team of economists to the staff of his ministry and to have charged them with the duty of turning the labor portfolio into a "social interlocutor of economic policies." See Torres (1981).

[52] The seven parties of the Left together polled 36.2 percent of the vote in the 1978 election for delegates to the Constituent Assembly. In 1980 the popularity of President Belaunde and the presence on the ballot of his Acción Popular party (which had boycotted the 1978 outing) cut into the Left's electoral totals. These were, however, still very respectable: 16.1 percent in the presidential race, 21.0 percent in contests for the Chamber of Deputies, and 19.9 percent in those for the Senate. A Leftist was elected alcalde (mayor) of Arequipa, the country's second largest city. The Left's future electoral prospects should benefit from recent reforms (Chap. 2, n. 22) that have extended the franchise to include essentially all adult members of the popular classes, along with students—the vast majority of whom are politically radical. As a result of these reforms, the proportion of the population eligible to vote has risen from 18.9 percent in 1963 (the last presidential election before the military takeover) to 34.8 percent in 1980. (All voting and registration data are from Roncagliolo 1980.) Note, too, that the popular classes cannot stay away from the polls, as they often do in the United States; in Peru, voting is mandatory.

file backing, are unlikely to develop so long as the parties continue to insist on ironclad control of associated labor organizations. According to two critics who are otherwise sympathetic to the Left's political purposes, the parties often weaken the labor movement by refusing to broaden its membership, or by expelling those who disagree with them, in their eagerness to gain or retain control.[53] It appears that, in the mining sector, the unions alone will remain for some time to come not only "the primary form of workers' collective life" but also their primary "channel of . . . political expression."[54]

Let us consider the meaning of these events. The military regime's policies of bonanza development and cooptation elevated the importance of the mining industry in the scheme of development and provided the mine unions with greater political and economic leverage than they had hitherto enjoyed. This they used effectively for narrowly self-interested ends, in the process keeping their autonomy and resisting cooptation.[55] A deteriorating economy and the onset of inflation then eroded many of the wage gains of an earlier period. But at the same time they drew mine labor directly into the arena of national politics and economic policy making, since only there is found any hope for workers to overcome inflation's effects on their pocketbooks. The autonomy of organized mine labor, a product of the manner in which the workers of the sector coalesced as a class, ensured that the movement would have to be taken in on a fairly equal basis. Meanwhile, mine labor's national impact was of great value to the popular classes in toto. What has begun to materialize out of all of this is a form of "societal corporatism," rather than the authoritarian "state corporatism" of other Latin American countries where the labor movement has a history of subjugation to state control.

I suggest that disunity in the labor movement—divisions within the mining proletariat, between it and the rest of the working class, and between unions and parties—has propitiated this outcome by calming bourgeois fears of a massive, coordinated challenge to the capitalist order. (Implicit, too, is the further suggestion that, if this outcome is viewed as progressive and desirable in light of the other paths that political developments could have realistically taken, one must be thankful for the *falloff* of the Left's vote in the 1980 election!) On the other hand, such an outcome could not have occurred were

[53] Balbi and Parodi (1981).

[54] Zapata (1980).

[55] DiTella (1981) points out—accurately—that working-class organization has to gain access to elite circles in order to exercise political power within the existing system, but that access comes at the price of distancing labor leadership from the rank and file. (The effect is greater than it is in the case of the superordinate classes, whose integrants are close to elite status to begin with.) This peculiarly working-class situation of leadership estrangement from bases opens the door to the cooptation of the former. DiTella suggests that the value to the labor movement of "ideological militants" is that they limit the degree of estrangement by acting as influence conduits in both directions between leaders and bases, thereby inhibiting the process of cooptation. But we have seen that conditions are fundamentally different in the case of the mine unions. Their economic power is great enough that the government must, in effect, come down to them; their leaders do not have to fight their way into the elite. What is more, the "ideological militants" themselves become leaders of the mine labor movement.

the bourgeoisie unable or unwilling to accommodate to a greater political presence of organized labor.

Labor and Community Power

The experience of the mine labor movement during the Peruvian "revolution" reminds us that a proletariat which chooses to play a national power game may well do so primarily for the purpose of securing its economic interests. Mine labor in Peru made major political gains in that it elbowed its way into the national structure of power. But it was not motivated by a desire to lead or participate in the framing of a viable socialist alternative to that structure, nor even by a yearning to accelerate the pace of reform set by the regime. It sought and attained a measure of power, rather, because its economic concerns had come to be bound up in centralized economic policy making and planning—innovations of the "revolution"—as well as in economic events of national scope.

It can be argued that a proletariat wishing to develop a real capability for political leadership and hegemony, one looking toward the eventual supercession of bourgeois domination, can best begin by involving itself in issues of community power. With specific reference to the situation of mine labor, two reasons may be advanced.

First, there is ample opportunity for mass participation in the organization of the mundane social life of the mining camp, and participation is a sensible alternative to total social dependence on the employer. Becoming active in quotidian camp affairs would inculcate habits of democratic responsibility, helping thereby to overcome (especially in the central sierra) the residual legacy of centuries of peasant subservience; would give the worker a greater feeling of personal effectiveness; and would fortify class cohesion and solidarity. Were the unions to pioneer this effort—which, with their flush treasuries, full-time officials, and reinforced infrastructure, they are now in a position to do—they would reap rewards in firmer rank-and-file allegiance and enhanced political capabilities. This proposal happens to dovetail nicely with the decline of employer paternalism and the new-found desire of the mining companies to unburden themselves of many of the obligations of routine camp operation.

Second, the urban bourgeoisie, no longer restrained by the oligarchy, is physically present at the seats of national power and has few competitors for political influence at the top. Barring a social revolution, any dispersion of power resulting from enlarged working-class political capabilities at the local level thus represents a check on the preeminent position of the bourgeoisie secured with the aid of the central state. Furthermore, the development by the labor movement of a high local political profile may be necessary to any worker-peasant alliance against the system of domination. If Maurice Zeitlin and James Petras are correct in their assessment of the workers' role in Chilean politics, such an alliance was possible there not because peasants were proletarianized, but because they came to share in a socialist political culture cutting across class lines. That culture was propagated by radical unions which were very visible in the affairs of the mining districts and which set examples of organizational skills, political competency, and participatory citizenship.[56]

Having thus stated my belief in the value to the working class of self-help activity, I report with regret that worker self-help in most Peruvian mining camps is conspicuous by its absence. Interviews and observations at Toquepala and Ilo made plain that, in the workers' minds, anything related to the camps was Southern's responsibility. Worker and labor-leader interviewees inevitably complained about the lack of this or that facility; but they were astonished at the suggestion that they themselves might take a hand in providing it. Block and neighborhood associations and sport leagues were starting to appear. However, they had been set up by the Division of Social Welfare in the face of considerable apathy, and their survival as self-sustaining entities was by no means assured. A similar reluctance to become involved seems to have prevailed among the Cerro miners;[57] at Cerro, of course, it is reinforced by workers' lingering tendency to regard the camp as a temporary abode and to identify socially with their places of origin. In Cuajone's case, the camp is too new to allow for firm conclusions; in Toquepala's and Ilo's, further anthropological research is needed to expose the reasons underlying the Southern workers' apparent anomie. In the meantime, it is certain that an opportunity is being missed.

Conclusions: The Rise—and Limitations—of the Labor Movement in the Mines

Some dependencistas still argue that transnational resource corporations conspire with "dependent" Third World elites to keep wages down and the working class politically weak. The resultant "superexploitation" is held to be necessary to the profitability of these enterprises, since "the prices of their products on the world markets . . . [are] a fixed datum to the individual companies. . . ."[58] Coercive controls over labor further the economic exploitation of the less-developed countries, whose bargaining strength vis-à-vis the transnationals is sapped by, *inter alia*, the absence of a powerful and

[56] Zeitlin and Petras (1969); also, Petras and Zeitlin (1967). The ideological hegemony of the *proletariat*, it should be noted, would consist in just this: the evolution of a socialist (hence, originated and propagated by the working class) political culture, or ideology, with cross-class appeal. Gramsci believed that the proletariat would have to develop its hegemony *prior* to taking power and establishing a socialist society; see my remarks in Chap. 9, n. 65.

[57] For instance, Morello (1976:112) found that 41 percent of the camp residents participated in no local social activities of any sort; that 21 percent limited their participation to sports; and that 7 percent attended only holiday celebrations. I have no information that would indicate whether or not this situation has improved since Cerro's expropriation.

[58] Baran (1957:197).

effective labor movement.[59] Wallersteinians add that coerced labor, introduced or maintained by the country's insertion into the capitalist "world-economy," is what consigns the nation to political subservience as a member of the world "periphery."[60]

This study reveals that, if these ideas had applicability to an earlier stage of Peruvian development, they have been rendered obsolete by later events. Cerro's arrival in 1901 *did* articulate Peru more firmly with international capitalism and *was* accompanied by the large-scale "superexploitation" of coerced, preproletarian labor. The difficulty for dependencistas who emphasize "superexploitation" is that the depth of articulation expanded manyfold with the later entry of the modern transnationals, Southern and Marcona. Yet, the modes and relations of production which they introduced led to the formation of a true industrial proletariat, cut off from its peasant origins, protected by its work skills and by high mining technology from the pressures of an "industrial reserve army," and able to organize for the defense of its economic interests without outside assistance.

The discipline and organizational capabilities of this new proletariat made coercive controls counterproductive, and in the mining camps they were progressively dismantled. The new working class secured extremely high (by local standards) remunerations. It took a step toward overcoming one of the debilitating divisions within its ranks by severely reducing the economic differential between empleados and obreros, although it was less successful in eliminating the status differential or in overcoming geographical cleavages. It fortified the labor unions of the sector and made them independent of middle-class party leadership. It resisted attempts at co-optation via the Workers' Community system, which it utilized instead in its own way for its own purposes while ignoring a comanagement feature that did not answer to its self-defined needs.

The political regime and the "new bourgeoisie" lacked both the power and the inclination to adopt a policy of repressing mine labor. Meeting labor's wage demands served the long-term interest of both of these in bonanza development at a price borne mostly by foreign corporations. The latter grumbled but had no choice in the end but to act in accordance with the doctrine of domicile, recognizing the sovereign authority of the Peruvian state to determine labor policy. Southern was not deterred by that policy from going ahead with its Cuajone mine. Domestic mining capital also took important forward strides despite rising mine wages.

Without conscious design but urged along by its internal contradictions as well as by uncontrollable external events, the military regime fostered the institutionalized incorporation of organized labor into the system of power.

---

[59] Barnet and Müller (1974:138). This is a perceptive observation; my only objection to the statement is that the lack of a powerful labor movement is not universal in less-developed countries, as this study has shown.

[60] Wallerstein (1974c).

The regime successfully weakened the APRA, until then the chief popular political force, and thereby created a vacuum on the Left for others to fill. But it deprived itself of mobilized popular support, since to have done otherwise would have risked the elite cohesiveness of the military establishment by politicizing it; it would have tempted generals to compete with each other in currying popular favor. The bourgeoisie, though the main beneficiary of the "revolution," wisely kept its distance from the military and withdrew its tacit support once international economic developments made manifest the consequences of the regime's economic mismanagement. With labor relations already politicized and with national anti-inflationary policy become a necessary preoccupation of the powerful mine unions, labor's incorporation was simply unavoidable.

In relation to labor, as well as to the bourgeoisie, the autonomy of state authorities from class forces was no more than relative. But the balance of class forces was such that the regime, albeit pro-bourgeois, was not hostile to labor. On the other hand, the state's less-than-complete autonomy from local societal forces made it *more* autonomous with respect to external ones. It was able to ignore the wage preferences of transnational mining capital, and it mounted a more valiant resistance to the IMF than is generally admitted—more valiant than seemed possible upon reading Peru's statement of international account. This is the precise opposite of what dependency approaches predict.

Labor's advance within the system was facilitated by its "economism." The arrangement according to which the military ruled was, in effect, that the *economic* interests of mobilized societal groups would be respected so long as they did not openly bid for *political* control. This arrangement was eminently satisfactory from the perspective of a labor movement whose members were alienated from formal politics (which they viewed as a mere competition for spoils) and were not ideologically motivated. It enabled the movement to free itself from subordination to parties and electoral strategies and to pursue uninhibitedly its economic aims. However, the exclusive concern with economic gains had its costs. The question of overall working-class cohesion was largely ignored. Opportunities in the camp community for building self-esteem through self-help and for checking bourgeois power at the center were overlooked. No coalition with other subordinate societal elements was forged. Given these omissions, mine labor could not become a vanguard for socialism.

It is in that light that the supposed radicalism of Peruvian mine labor must be evaluated. In spite of appearances, and in spite of the unquestioned dedication of many of the movement's leaders to Marxism-Leninism, here was no radical movement in any sense. It did nothing to develop a program or ideology based on a root-and-branch critique of the *new* capitalist order that emerged after 1968. (There was no lack of criticism of the *old* order, but there were few returns to be had from castigating the dead.) What is seen instead is the political expression of a group which acquiesces in the system of class domination but is alienated from much of the "superstructure"; which therefore fears political control from the outside and wants to be free to pursue fairly narrow goals of its own choosing. We thus come to a paradox: The "radical" current in the mine labor movement *is actually conservative, since it is even less interested than the party-affiliated leadership that preceded it in subordinating the economic privileges of the mine workers to broad political aims.* Note, however, that the movement is *not* conservative in the sense usually implied by use of the pejorative term, "labor aristocracy." Its actions in the economic crisis have definitely aided the popular classes at large.

"Societal corporatist" incorporation of labor in the developed countries is said to represent a bourgeois response to the postwar condition (in Europe) of full employment,[61] which enhanced the proletariat's economic and political power. It can now be concluded that this argument is too narrow: "societal corporatism" is a possible outcome whenever circumstances of *any* sort produce a dramatic increase in the economic leverage of labor within a capitalist order. In less-developed countries, the most probable such circumstance may be that observed in Peru—the rise in economic impact, under bonanza development, of a key industrial export sector whose productivity depends on scarce (in the local environment) work skills.

We cannot yet be sure whether the corporatist incorporation of labor will proceed, as it must if it is to serve bourgeois ends, to the exercise of greater control by union leaders over the working-class rank and file. We must also reiterate that at the present moment bourgeois ideological hegemony over the working class is still tentative. Nevertheless, there are many indications that this hegemony can be strengthened in the years to come; and there are few signs that the proletariat has built sound ideological defenses against its advance—let alone an effective counterideology that might secure proletarian hegemony over potential working-class allies in the peasantry and the lower strata of the middle class.

The unhappy thought for socialists to contemplate is that, at the current stage of Peru's development, the economic advance of labor is quite compatible with a modernized bourgeois domination.

[61] Panitch (1977).

Conclusions

CHAPTER ELEVEN

The New Bourgeoisie
and the Limits of Dependency

PAUL BARAN was an astute critical observer of the capitalism of his time. Writing at the height of the Cold War, he argued that "the main task of imperialism" was "to prevent, or . . . , to slow down and to control the economic development of underdeveloped countries." He held that Third World development was "profoundly inimical to the interests of foreign corporations producing raw materials for export." It raised "the mortal threat of nationalization. . . ." Worse, it increased the class consciousness and economic bargaining leverage of labor, forcing wages up. This had especially adverse consequences for resource corporations whose methods of production were already highly capital-intensive. Lacking control over market prices and unable to raise productivity by further deepening their technologies, these corporations could not meet the demands of labor except at a sacrifice of profits. Baran therefore concluded that, in order to prevent the erosion of profitability, foreign resource enterprise in less-developed countries

> uses its tremendous power to prop up the backward areas' comprador administrations . . . and to overthrow whatever progressive governments may rise to power. . . . Where and when its own impressive resources do not suffice to keep matters under control . . . , the diplomatic, financial, and, if need be, military facilities of the imperialist power are . . . mobilized to help private enterprise do the required job.[1]

No one who is familiar with the history of Latin America will deny that the neocolonialism described by Baran really existed. Recent events in Central America and the Caribbean suggest that in places it still does. But resource neocolonialism is no longer a *prevailing* mode of capitalist action in the Third World. The demise of neocolonialism was an outgrowth of the continuing evolution of international capitalism. Third World nationalism—*itself a product of capitalism's advance*—hastened the process. Lenin's characterization was premature: capitalism, in its imperialist phase, had not yet reached its "highest stage."

Needed today is a political theory of transnational corporate action in the developing countries whose progressive value commitments do not stand in

[1] Baran (1957:197-98).

the way of comprehending late-capitalist phenomena that have surfaced since the Marxian classics were written. A suitable theory will relate ideas about class formation and practice, institutional behavior, the nature of the local state, and the forms assumed by political power and social control. It will not be deduced in the abstract from philosophical or ideological first principles but will be built up inductively on a groundwork of empirical studies. This study of development in "revolutionary" Peru is offered with the hope that it may serve as a piece of that groundwork.

TRANSNATIONAL CORPORATE ORGANIZATION AND ACTION

The principal resource corporations that have been dealt with in this work are international oligopolists. They accumulate capital globally. Their interests revolve about worldwide control of reserves, production, product flows, and marketing. Particular metropolitan concerns for security of supply are additional variables to be factored into their equations of oligopolistic market stabilization; but, save for the Japanese, those concerns are peripheral to corporate planning. Accordingly, the economic class which in turn controls and benefits from the activities of these institutions must be an *international* bourgeoisie, even though its individual members are cultural and legal nationals of specific countries. Insisting on a strictly national foundation for metropolitan bourgeoisies means ignoring the realities of how control of the means of production is structured and exercised. The basis for that insistence is doctrinaire and untheoretical.

Insofar as capital accumulation becomes fully global, the ties that once bound the economic concerns of transnational corporations to the political concerns of their "home" states are sundered. On the one hand, the corporations' access for business purposes to the territories of various states around the world is facilitated by the separation, for prospective hosts sense less of a peril for their sovereignty when the access-seeker does not seem an agent of a foreign state. On the other hand, the separation denies to the corporations the routine protection of "home"-state political power. Not having military resources of their own, and standing to lose much should their global interests become entrapped in the crossfires of interstate rivalry, transnationals protect themselves in another way: by simultaneously serving the *local* political interests of *all* states within whose boundaries their units function.

In addition to being transnational, modern resource corporations are highly bureaucratized, professionally managed institutions whose survival and prosperity depend upon planning to maximize profits over the long haul. Planning horizons often stretch far into the future: twenty years is not an atypical period for designing and installing a new facility and for recovering the capital invested in it. The necessity for planning that far ahead puts a premium on the stability of the economic, social, and political environments. Development of the host country is of value to resource transnationals because it improves environmental stability. It means a more knowledgeable, competent host state—one administered by persons who understand the national interest in resource exploitation, write it into access agreements, and see to it that those agreements are observed over time. Development also means fewer planning uncertainties regarding the skills and discipline of the work force and the local availability of supervisory cadres.

Stability on this order is not obtained gratis. The foreign investor will be expected to treat the host state, and the societal forces that stand behind it, with genuine respect. When his concerns conflict with theirs, he will be expected to defer to local authorities on political matters in return for access rights and financial incentives. It will be he, in all likelihood, to whom the authorities turn for the financial wherewithal to undertake industrialization and, at the same time, massive cooptation of well-organized popular groups. Nor will his underwriting of bonanza development be a purely voluntary act: the authorities will come to him with laws, taxes, exactions—not with pleas for donations. (If they fully understand the nature of bonanza development, they will not doubt the justice of their exactions—which merely make the investor pay for the development and stability that work to his long-run advantage.) The host state retains the right and the ability, if strong and capable enough, to define "good corporate citizenship" inside its frontiers and to sanction noncompliance with locally determined rules of corporate conduct. As bonanza development entrenches itself, the state acquires an ever greater interest in exercising this right.

Transnational managers' ideological disposition—the doctrine of domicile expresses it—along with the flexibility afforded by global integration, provide them with the tools needed to deal in a mutually satisfactory manner with strong, developmental host states. To place the resource on the world market exclusively and at low enough cost that a profit can be earned is the core concern of a transnational firm. For its part, a host state has a parallel interest in profitable production, tempered by an ideological interest in control. Both sets of interests can be brought into approximate correspondence through joint ventures with state participation, management contracts, sales agency agreements, or, simply, close government oversight and supervision. Transnationals' involvement in resource exploitation is vital to host states that lack, as do most, their own entrée to the market, with its elaborate network of customary and traditional relationships. Transnationals can cement their indispensability by undertaking projects of a scale too large to be locally financed and managed. Large-scale projects are effectively "insured" against expropriation by the participation in them of international complexes of financiers, suppliers, and metal purchasers; and by the host state's oligopolistic interest in preserving and extending "its" share of the international market.[2]

---

[2] Peruvians have long felt that the size of their nonferrous metal reserves entitles them to a greater share of the world market, and the military regime's development strategy sought to attain it. They can also claim advantages in terms of development costs: Takeushi et al. (1977)

To be sure, the international bourgeoisie strives to keep the developing world open to capitalism. But it does so by accommodating as far as it possibly can to the desire for development and by dangling before the eyes of developing societies the material rewards that may be had upon accepting its embrace. We see this in the fact that neither Asarco/Southern nor the international banking consortium behind their Cuajone project rushed to Cerro's aid in its time of troubles. We see it in MineroPeru's ease, limited solely by its undercapitalization, in getting metropolitan suppliers of goods and services to help it draw technologically abreast of one of the world's foremost nonferrous metals transnationals. Only under exceptional circumstances can international capital achieve the conscious unity of purpose required to bring coordinated coercive pressures to bear against a recalcitrant host country. In Peru's case, international capital did not overcome the "Japanese contradiction," which the host state cleverly exploited in order to resolve to its satisfaction a dispute with Asarco/Southern over the latter's uninterest in local refining. Nor could the IFC find general support for its attempted infringement of Peruvian sovereign prerogatives.

As international markets in mineral resources are not wholly monopolized,[3] they support other competitors besides the central oligopolists. Capable—barely—of *economic* survival is an older generation of colonial companies, of which Cerro is the referent in the present work. *Political* survival, however, is a separate issue. Colonial companies differ from central oligopolists in that they do not integrate production in a global frame. Not being far-flung empires, they tend to function under the close control of a home-country management. That limits their flexibility and adaptability to change. They are older and less capital-intensive; their fortunes *do* depend to a considerable extent on cheap labor and low taxes.[4] As their name implies, they were spawned in an earlier epoch, when it was much easier than now to penetrate and exploit weak Third World countries. Unable to conceal their exploitativeness, they had to secure their positions with direct presences in the hosts' political systems—presences achieved through alliances with local comprador elites. They are in great danger whenever and wherever developmentally oriented, industrializing elites succeed in shouldering aside the compradors.

Despite all, colonial companies made a contribution to development. Be-

---

document that, per unit of output, the cost of expanding Peru's productive capacity in copper is lower than that for all but a few less developed countries and the lowest for all CIPEC members. Yet, the required investment remains beyond the country's own capabilities.

[3] Aluminum and (perhaps) nickel are notable exceptions.

[4] Baran (1957) apparently failed to take into account that high productive technology both increases returns on invested capital and reduces the weight of labor costs in total costs of production. The highly capital-intensive producer is *better* able to pay good wages; and it is in his interest to do so, since the result is a more stable (thus, less expensive to train) and efficient work force. The colonial company, whose labor costs are a far greater percentage of total production costs and which lacks a market interest in technification (as its concern is with short-term profits, not long-term protection of a market share) is the one that has the most to lose from rising wages and taxes.

cause they were labor-intensive, they promoted the formation, first, of a local proletariat and, later (once they began to indigenize their staffs), of a local manageriat. The progress of development rendered their contribution superfluous, however. Their profits shrunken by technological obsolescence and rising labor costs, they could ill afford new host-country investment—in which they were uninterested anyway, inasmuch as it was not necessary for protecting their market situations. Without central oligopoly ties, able to offer nothing in managerial or productive technology that a truly developing host country could not provide for itself, incapable of serving as sources of new investment capital in quantity, burdened by "social debts" arising from their previous exploitation and political interference, and made economically dispensable by the presence of other, more modern transnationals, their fate was sealed: if not expropriated by the host government, they were taken over by their more powerful competition. Their local political alliances proved useless in the end. Comprador allies had been so weakened by ongoing development as to be of no assistance any more. Even the managers and entrepreneurs whom they once aided disregarded past services and asked only the proverbial, "But what have you done for us *lately*?" When the answer came up negative, local managers and entrepreneurs remained on the sidelines while state authorities took expropriative action.

In a larger sense, the comparison between Asarco/Southern and Cerro reminds us that the capacity of socioeconomic systems to influence individual and institutional conduct in directions conducive to system maintenance ought not to be exaggerated. Individuals and institutions act on behalf of perceived interests and are not mere "bearers" of systemic relationships. Socioeconomic "laws of motion" *are nothing but statistical aggregates of individual behaviors*. Although corporations with comparable organizational structures and market situations tend to act similarly in similar circumstances, there is about as much reason to expect a given transnational subsidiary to comport itself as predicted by a systemic "law of motion" as there is to expect a person selected at random to behave like a *homo œconomicus*. And rarely, if ever, is the number of transnational subsidiaries engaged in the same line of business in a specified host country large enough to constitute a meaningful statistical aggregate. Therefore, transnational firms and their subsidiaries must be dealt with as concrete institutions embodying economic power. Institutional analysis is not *sufficient* for understanding the nature and loci of power and control, which is why I have opted for a class analaysis. But institutional analysis is a *necessary* step on the way to such an understanding.

TRANSNATIONAL CORPORATIONS AND THE CONDITIONING OF THE SOCIAL ENVIRONMENT

This study has revealed that the bulk of the Peruvian mining bourgeoisie, middle strata, and proletariat draws its sustenance from local private industry, from parastatal industry, and from the central state. Transnational corporate *employment*, in other words, is not a principal factor in local class formation. More significant are the business relationships maintained by the transnationals with local enterprises: Cerro's purchases of ores and concentrates from the mediana minería, together with its financial backing of a few medium-mining companies via loans and equity participation, did help to strengthen the domestic bourgeoisie. However, relationships of that kind are not the norm; we found that Southern Peru Copper conducts its mining business in almost total isolation from the rest of the sector, interacting only with the state and, since the middle of the seventies, with MineroPeru. Thus, the effect of transnational corporate action on class formation—and, thereby, on the character of Peruvian politics and society—is mostly indirect. It takes the form of a conditioning of the social environment; or, to put it less abstractly, of an introduction of new values and new interests which come to animate class action and practice.

Local subsidiaries of transnational firms are efficacious mechanisms for diffusing into the host society the organizational forms and practices, the ways of doing business, and the ideology and values that the transnationals embody. This diffusion process, though, is not automatic; it occurs because, and to the degree that, domestic groups find it in their self-interest. As soon as domestic groups express a desire to learn, officials of the transnationals generally prove to be willing, eager teachers. There are, naturally, certain business secrets that they will avoid revealing. Nevertheless, their expertise per se is not one of those secrets. Much to the contrary: transnational managers sincerely believe that they are meritocrats who have earned their privileges through accomplishment in the face of the best competition that the world can offer; the acquisition of some of their expertise by local citizens does not seem threatening in comparison. Moreover, the managerial ideology is internationalist and universalist; and, like any such creed, its devotees freely proselytize among the uninitiated. In Peru, the avenues of proselytization are IPAE, the domestic fountainhead of the managerial ideology; the guild and trade associations; and the system of higher education—whose shift of emphasis from the liberal arts and professions to scientific and technical fields has been promoted and subsidized by local and transnational private enterprise.[5]

Another avenue of diffusion is that of personal mobility: local citizens trained in the methods and values of the transnationals during employment stints on the latter's staffs take these with them when they shift to employment with state or private domestic firms or go into business for themselves. The

[5] I have mentioned scholarship programs. There are also teacher-training programs and student work-study programs. Although the state has been reluctant to accept corporate donations to public universities, private schools show no such reticence: the Department of Mines at the Catholic University was established with corporate gifts of money and equipment. Note that labor also participates in the diffusion process when it bargains (as at Southern Peru Copper) for more scholarships and for donations to universities.

effectiveness of this avenue depends on: (1) the size of the transnational's local staff, which determines the number of engineers and specialists to whom the avenue is open; (2) the extent of staff indigenization policies; (3) salary levels—which, ideally (from the standpoint of effective diffusion), should be high enough to attract bright, young engineering graduates but not so high as to entice senior personnel to stay on until retirement; and (4) ascent possibilities, since it is "blocked ascent" into higher managerial ranks that most quickly stimulates the "best and brightest" to depart for pastures where they can be masters of the herd. Colonial companies like Cerro met these requirements more completely, as a rule, than do modern transnationals. Being labor-intensive, they tended to have larger supervisory staffs. Seeking to cut costs, they rapidly indigenized their staffs as soon as the availability of trained local personnel permitted. Their salary levels were lower than those of more technological firms. And their tight managerial control at the top cut off upward mobility beyond upper-middle management.

Resource transnationals also condition the environment by making possible modes of development that are attractive to strategically placed domestic groups. Bonanza development with transnational participation separated the interests of the Peruvian mining and industrial bourgeoisies from those of the oligarchy, thus establishing a new economic coalition whose interest in industrialization was not compromised (as was the oligarchy's) by dependence on labor-intensive agriculture. In consequence, the newly dominant mining-industrial bourgeoisie could acquiesce in a solution to the age-old "peasant problem" by way of land reform; no matter that its support was reluctant. Agrarian reform would have been unthinkable for a dominant class if the country's economy depended as much upon agricultural exports as it did before Toquepala.

The mere presence of the transnationals, regardless of how they actually do business, creates new constellations of interests around which classes congeal. State elites begin to recognize that they need a greater knowledge of the purposes and modus operandi of the transnationals, as well as better international market intelligence, in order to maximize the benefits of foreign resource investment for the state; they then recruit into their ranks manager-technocrats from the private sector who possess the necessary expertise. In the process they transform their own class character and further "bourgeois-ify" the state. Domestic industrialists, meanwhile, need an ally to help protect them against transnational competitors and find one in the state. Their "liberal" fear of the state as a restrictor of entrepreneurial initiative diminishes in direct proportion to their self-transformation from an individualist to an organization-based class; to the restructuring of the state apparatus along technical-managerial lines and the infusion within it of the managerial ideology; and to the growth of the "bonanza," which enables them to enjoy the advantages of a strong local state without paying for them.

Let us not overlook the constellation of interests represented by the rise of an industrial proletariat. Colonial companies transform peasants into proletarians. Central oligopolists, whose work forces are far smaller and more stable, play less of a role in this sort of thoroughgoing, necessarily disruptive process of social change—which is a political plus for them, as they avoid accruing a corresponding "social debt." But their high capital intensity, interest in stability, and resultant tendency to yield to union wage demands, propitiate proletarian class formation by lowering the barriers to labor organization. True industrial unions appear, superseding as leaders of the labor movement the violence-prone, protoproletarian unions often found in colonial companies. The newer unions are superior economic bargainers, are aware of the power given them by their strategic placement in the national economy, and are adept at using political means to extract economic concessions. To tame them requires admitting them to the system of power on condition that they accept its legitimacy, or at least tolerate it; their class character conduces toward this type of arrangement.

On the Character of the "New Bourgeoisie"

Metropolitan capitalism is, of course, more dynamic still than the hinterland variety. Yet, structural and institutional innovations pioneered in one or another metropolis soon diffuse to the rest and thence into the hinterland; for, local interest groups, perceiving the competitive advantages that such innovations provide their inventors, rise to the challenge by adopting them themselves (with the modifications necessitated by local conditions). Thus it is that *capitalist development in today's Third World takes the shape of adaptation of the institutional forms, modes of action, and ideologies of organizational, or late, capitalism* as it has developed in the West since World War II.

It is therefore a serious error to expect current Third World bourgeoisies to wreak far-reaching societal transformations in the manner of the individualist, "heroic," market-capitalist bourgeoisies of a century or more ago and to adjudge them deficient—or dependent—if they fail to measure up to that standard. Such a judgment is patently ahistorical. The "heroic" entrepreneur is long gone everywhere save as a marginal presence; outside the United States, not even the fiction of his continued importance figures any more in the legitimation of the capitalist system.[6] The old bourgeoisie's place has been taken by a corporate bourgeoisie. The corporate bourgeois class is professional and organizational in character, not idiosyncratic nor individualist.[7]

[6] The decline of individualism as a legitimating myth in capitalist ideology is discussed by Mellos (1978).

[7] My characterization of the "new bourgeoisie" parallels that of Walzer (1980); it also owes much to Gouldner (1979), although I do not agree with the latter that the "new bourgeoisie" is a universal class (Gouldner qualifies its universality as "flawed") in the Marxian sense. Marx's meaning of the term, "universal class," appears most clearly in Marx (1975a); see also Avineri (1968:41-64).

Credentials and position in the hierarchy of enterprise or state, not amassed wealth nor personal daring, are its stigmata. Positivism, meritocratic elitism, and the notion of professional service-stewardship are its normative and ideological hallmarks; it is not liberal. In the realm of collective action its stance is apolitical rather than anti-political. For it the state is not the natural enemy of civil society and need not be feared; it resolves the essential public-private contradiction of capitalism by "technifying"—depoliticizing—the making of decisions for the collectivity, by exalting the methodology of administration over the clash of competing interests in the political arena.[8]

The nomenclature of class analysis needs a term of reference for this new dominant group. I suggest: *corporate national bourgeoisie*.[9]

A corporate national bourgeoisie *is* entrepreneurial, albeit within an institutional framework. It is assuredly innovative technologically, to the point where some of its members seem enamored of technology and of technological "playthings" for their own sake. Yes, its risk investments are made only after careful planning to reduce uncertainty to a residuum. However, it will venture forth into activities that an *equally cautious* individual investor would ignore. It can do so in relative safety because its institutional basis insulates its members from many of the *personal* consequences of failure (provided, at any rate, that failure is not a regular occurrence). The progress of entrepreneurship is too frequently evaluated by comparison to a personal adventure, e.g., a solo ocean voyage. A more apposite standard of comparison is one of the well-organized technological adventures of our day—e.g., a voyage to the moon—whose success is a function of the planned and coordinated exertions of a cast of thousands.

The corporate national bourgeoisie (remember that the phenomenon is limited to developing countries) is nationalist and developmentalist. Colonialism and neocolonialism, which reserved social and economic privilege to foreigners and their comprador allies, were the historic enemies of its advance. Development—especially when defined as a task to be managed by technical experts—is its forte, its raison d'être, and brings in its wake the aggrandizement of the class in numbers, prestige, and rewards. Yet, the corporate national bourgeoisie is, simultaneously, the most international of all Third

[8] Habermas (1973).

[9] Sklar (1976, 1977) focuses on what he calls the "managerial bourgeoisie"—which is not necessarily, in his usage, a class of managers in the conventional sense. The managerial bourgeoisie is a *transitional* class that emerges in the postcolonial phase of economic reconstruction. Its elements coexist in a state of unstable equilibrium. As development proceeds, he avers, either state or private enterprise will loom as the predominant economic institution. If the former, the class will have evolved into a "state bourgeoisie;" if the latter, into a "corporate" or an "entrepreneurial bourgeoisie," depending on the form of economic organization it adopts.

My term of reference keeps faith with Sklar's approach. The Peruvian "new bourgeoisie" is not a transitional class and has opted for the corporate form of economic organization. "Corporate national bourgeoisie" has the advantage of succinctly displaying the class's commonality with, *as well as* its distinctiveness from, the metropolitan capitalist class—in Sklar's terminology, the "corporate *inter*national bourgeoisie."

World classes at the present time, for the universalistic norms underpinning it are wholly divorced from cultural particularism. *The class articulates nationalism and internationalism complementarily, not contradictorily.* By partaking in universalistic values of technocracy and of the managerial ideology, by participating in international economic, scientific, and engineering forums, and by functioning as junior partners in international markets, corporate national bourgeoisies assert their claim to equality with the international bourgeoisie of the metropoli. Their desire for development under conditions that they control is a logical concomitant of their drive for equality, an attempt to operationalize it in their national practice. Their nationalism will last until that equality is attained.

The rise to power of the corporate national bourgeoisie *may* entail a limited revolutionary restructuring of the old socioeconomic order, but it does not *need* to. Alternatively, a former dominant class of moneyed elites may be overwhelmed and absorbed without being shunted off the societal stage— much as the English bourgeoisie absorbed that country's aristocracy.[10] The Peruvian "new bourgeoisie" has incorporated oligarchic money capital into its enterprises. However, money capital is incorporated in a situation of structural subservience to knowledge capital, which retains effective control.[11] Since the archaic aspects of Peruvian capitalism were, by 1968, already decaying rapidly of their own accord, the full emergence there of the corporate national bourgeoisie required nothing more than a reorganization of state authority so as to institutionalize "new-bourgeois" power and social control. The military establishment, whose basis in expertise makes it a wing of the corporate national bourgeoisie and which was already present within the institutional state, was the logical entity to lead the requisite reorganization.

In any listing of the corporate national bourgeoisie's achievements, pride of place among its positive contributions to development must surely go to the promotion of universal education and its redirection toward the acquisition of socially useful skills. Technical higher education, free and open to all who

[10] Walzer (1980) takes a similar view of bourgeois class formation in the metropoli. There, he feels, "new bourgeoisies" have grown up alongside the old, their advancement having been propitiated by corporate institutions and expanded states. But, since they develop in large part within business corporations, they retain a commitment to private property and are not exclusively associated with state authority. Their life styles repeat established bourgeois patterns of individualism and consumerism. Their rise takes the form of an integration of "new" and "old" bourgeoisies, which has necessitated little political or social dislocation. The old dominant class was joined rather than displaced. "And, since the bourgeoisie was never an exclusive club, the joining was easy. It certainly did not entail a massive shift in power relations."

Peru's historical circumstances, of course, required rather more dislocation and a greater shift in power relations for the "new bourgeoisie" to come into its own. Still, the process fell short of a revolution. Walzer's observations on the metropoli, when compared to the findings of this study, lend powerful confirmation to my assertion above that current Third World capitalist development consists in the local adaptation of the institutions and social modes of late capitalism.

[11] Cf. Parkin (1976), who notes that while occupational achievement and property ownership are distinct principles of privilege in capitalist society, the holders of each fuse into a common class: the bourgeoisie. This agrees with Walzer's conception (n. 10).

can demonstrate scholastic accomplishment, is the generator of the corporate national bourgeoisie and the ratifier of its meritocratic claims. Education of this sort is of obvious value to developing countries and is progressive in that it increases upward mobility opportunities available to members of the popular classes. But, as with many progressive measures, it maintains the status quo *for a while* by relieving pressures from below and by enhancing the dominant class's social legitimacy.

In sum, the corporate national bourgeoisie's ascension to the seat of societal power has its progressive facets. It also, however, has its conservative ones, insofar as it establishes a more durable form of capitalism. How, then, are we to arrive at a judgment of the relative progressiveness of this development?

Some will dismiss as conservative any development that does not immediately lead in a socialist direction. I find that to be an unsatisfactory, doctrine-ridden approach unless one of the following can be shown: that the development has not expanded the productive forces available to the society;[12] or, that socialism *is* within the realm of current national possibility, but the development at issue has hindered its realization. There is no question that the rise of the Peruvian corporate national bourgeoisie has been accompanied by an expansion of the productive forces; this was a principal finding of my institutional analyses of the mediana minería and of parastatal enterprise. As for socialism: My analysis of the proletariat indicates that it has not yet acquired the size and consciousness required to make it a socialist leading class. The declining peasantry is already so far removed from communal traditions as to make improbable a direct transition to socialism on a peasant foundation—if such a narodnik approach has ever been feasible anywhere, which I doubt. There are the urban masses; but, as Marx observed in *The Eighteenth Brumaire*, these can just as easily support a repressive, authoritarian order.[13] Urban intellectuals and students who most avidly articulate radical ideologies have yet to prove that they can transcend their own brand of elitism to forge real links with the popular masses on whose behalf they profess to speak.[14] The Peruvian "revolution" was not a popular movement gone awry or deflected; and if Velasco's fall precipitated a retrocession of certain of its reforms-from-above, it must be recalled that during Velasco's last year in power there was a real danger of a drastic shift to Right authoritarianism under the sponsorship of a cabal of hard-line generals known as "La Misión."[15] Stronger and better labor organization, the one reform that

[12] That capitalism is progressive so long as it expands the productive forces of society was very much Marx's view; so we are reminded by Warren (1980).

[13] Marx (1963b).

[14] Although his rhetoric is florid and, perhaps, uncharitably excessive, Denitch (1979) hits uncomfortably close to the mark when he describes their brand of Marxism as "crude," "anti-democratic," and "anti-working class."

[15] "La Misión"—its makeup, context, and activities—is discussed by Pease García (1977:123-88).

the popular classes won for themselves with minimal assistance from the state, has endured. Authoritarian rule has not.

As I add up the record, I conclude that the ascent of the corporate national bourgeoisie has not arrested what would otherwise have been a broadly based movement of popular liberation and has led to some noteworthy gains for the popular sectors. Hence, this was, in my view, a generally progressive social development. Nonetheless, there is no question but that the corporate national bourgeoisie embodies deeply conservative tendencies in its elitism, its insistence on receiving guild privileges, its uncertain transformatory potential, and, above all, its equivocal attitude toward democracy—the last a point to which I shall shortly return.

How Do We Know that It Is a Dominant Class?

Institutional analysis readily demonstrates that nationalist Third World states exercise political authority. The fact is sometimes presented, alone, as a denial of external domination. It is not; the logic of the proof is undermined by the Marxian concept of relative state autonomy. Fernando Henrique Cardoso and Peter Evans separately show that such an exercise of state authority refutes the idea of "development of underdevelopment" but is consistent with another variant of dependency, "associated-dependent development."[16] The test of local class dominance can only be that the putative dominant class succeeds in putting the authority of the state to work for *its* purpose—assisting it to accumulate capital and maintain its social control. A local dominant class will also use state authority to control relations with foreign capital, so that the latter promotes development without preempting business opportunities that the local class hopes to take advantage of, now or in the future.

This study has documented the repeated deployment of state authority in the "revolutionary" epoch to further the economic interests of Peru's corporate national bourgeoisie. State-guided bonanza development served that class's interest in industrialization and safeguarded it against popular pressures while throwing the cost burden onto foreign investors. The state's recovery of the idle mining concessions from their foreign holders made additional mineral resources available for eventual development by locals (or by foreigners in partnership with locals). A new parastatal mining enterprise became another bastion of the bourgeoisie, a conduit for the introduction of its managerial ideology into the state, and a vehicle for the expression of the class's technological concerns. Its presence, together with the subsequent expropriations of Cerro and Marcona, reduced the foreign threat to domestic preeminence in mining. MineroPeru's zinc refinery satisfied one of the local private industry's wants of longest standing. Parastatal enterprise grew up in a vacuum, alongside rather than in competition with domestic private capital; eschewing monopoly, it has become—exactly as the ideologists of the cor-

[16] Cardoso (1973); Evans (1979).

porate national bourgeoisie had urged—*un empresario más*. Lastly, state economic planning is conducted by technocrats recruited from the corporate national bourgeoisie and with information developed in and controlled by the private sector.

As for social control, it too has been propitiated by state action since 1968— keeping ever in mind that the state did not invariably act at the *behest* of private capital. Organized labor has been integrated into the system in a way that makes less likely in the near future a frontal assault from that quarter on the capitalist status quo. Unions have become better institutionalized and more effective; they have earned the right of participation in tripartite consultation with respect to high economic policy; many of their material demands have been answered. And still, state authority was able, in 1979, to establish and enforce an outer bound of permissible labor radicalism (Chapter 10, n. 50). Comanagement, though largely a fiction, at least opens institutional avenues for the nonconflictual expression of workers' concerns and grievances. The profit-sharing feature of the Workers' Community system is useful to the bourgeoisie as a productivity incentive and has been modified at the latter's urging to make it more so. Agrarian reform has defused a time bomb ticking away beneath the established order. State promotion of technical education in secondary schools and universities improves the cohesion of the bourgeois/middle-class association, enhances the social prestige of both, and facilitates the cooptation of ambitious members of the popular classes.

THE CORPORATE NATIONAL BOURGEOISIE AND THE PROBLEM OF THE STATE

We have found that, although much of the state apparatus is staffed by personnel whose class situation, interests, and action place them in the corporate national bourgeoisie or affiliated middle strata, the new Peruvian state is relatively autonomous in the Marxian meaning. While private capital enjoys a regular policy input and influences both the enactment and the enforcement of legislation, it does not determine absolutely the content of public policy. Labor's voice, too, is heard by the state. Coercive force is applied only when systemic stability is in jeopardy, not whenever it seems profitable from the perspective of narrow bourgeois interests. And even the application of coercive force is performed in a manner such that its class content is not blatant.

The appearance of a more active, relatively autonomous state mirrors the development of the state in metropolitan late capitalism and is the signal *political* achievement of the corporate national bourgeoisie. This kind of state could never have coexisted with oligarchic domination: the oligarchy's interests were excessively particularistic, incapable of legitimation before a wider audience, and intrinsically unsecurable without blocking the advance of other groups' material interests. Lacking, in Alvin Gouldner's words, the "sweet false consciousness" which tells an elite "that it is [its] mission to *serve the people*," the oligarchy was "simply a gang of scoundrels."[17] The corporate national bourgeoisie, in contrast, backs up its societal dominance with legitimacy derived from the universalism of its values and from its desire to impel national development. Inasmuch as it knows itself to be indispensable to the society's realization of widely favored economic goals, it can afford (like all late-capitalist dominant classes) to trade off short-term economic concessions for the opportunity to intensify its essentiality and to further inculcate its *Weltanschauung* into the national consciousness.

The theory of the state in societies undergoing bonanza development requires more elaboration that can be attempted here without straying hopelessly far afield. I do wish, however, to comment on two aspects of the problem, both of which can be addressed concisely within the framework of this study. I refer to bourgeois democracy's near-term capacity for survival; and to the character of the system's latent legitimacy contradiction.

On the Survivability of Bourgeois Democracy

Democratic norms have resurfaced in Peru of late and show signs of considerably greater vitality and operational content than before the "revolution." The franchise has been broadened so that it becomes, for the first time in the country's history, an inalienable right of all adult citizens. The former oligarchic monopoly over the media of political communication has broken up.[18] The widest spectrum of above-ground political parties in Latin America participates in the electoral process; candidates range from representatives of the far Right to those of the Leninist and Trotskyist Left; and victorious Leftist candidates do not encounter threats or intimidation when the time arrives for them to assume their official duties.

On the other hand, the strong technocratic component of the managerial ideology does not permit us to be overly sanguine about the corporate national bourgeoisie's dedication to the democratic political ideal in every circumstance. Democracy is a useful tool for peaceably reconciling interest conflicts among bourgeois functional groups, for taking readings of the level of contentment of the people so that technocratic administrators can monitor their own performance, and for legitimating the corporatist administrative state behind a façade of mass participation. The rub is that the corporate national bourgeoisie's concern with it is purely instrumental and implies no normative attachment to the concept of popular power. Hence, whereas one can properly applaud today's political order as vastly superior to what went before, one can also imagine conjunctures in which the corporate national bourgeoisie

---

[17] Gouldner (1979:87), emphasis in original. His reference is specifically to the oligarchic moneyed elites of developing countries.

[18] The daily press, nationalized by the military regime, has been restored to its former owners—most of them oligarchic families. But in the intervening years, a large number of progressive and radical dailies and weekly news magazines has appeared on the stands. Quite a few of these seem to have secured stable readership bases and adequate amounts of advertising revenue to ensure their continued survival.

would find a form of technocratic authoritarianism—the "bureaucratic-authoritarian state"—more to its liking.[19] Is such a conjuncture on the horizon?

The basic conditions for the viability of bourgeois democracy are these: that the electorate not polarize rigidly along class lines; and that the bourgeoisie perceive a positive benefit-cost balance in opting for an accommodative alternative in place of a repressive one. Recent electoral outcomes, and the subsequent evolution of national politics, indicate that the first condition is satisfied. President Belaunde and his Acción Popular party closely reflect the views of the corporate national bourgeoisie. Indeed, manager-technocrats and forward-looking entrepreneurs are prominent in the Council of Ministers and in *acciopopulista* congressional ranks. Belaunde and his congressional slate nevertheless captured a majority of the vote in the popular districts of the capital and in much of the provinces. Since taking office, Belaunde has had to confront galloping inflation, depressed prices for Peruvian exports, ever-present pressures from the IMF, strikes in the mines and other key sectors of the economy, and an outbreak of terrorism. His skill in maneuvering through these problems is, in my judgment, somewhat uncertain; and his policy choices have at times been unfortunate. But in spite of everything the administration retains, at a minimum, the tolerance of the populace. I have yet to see signs of profound mass disaffection from restored civilian governance.

The second condition obtains due to the character of proletarian class formation and the nature of the labor movement. In much of Latin America—Argentina, Brazil, and Mexico are the stellar examples—the labor movement was formed by a process of "unionization from above" under the aegis of the state, or else its leadership was coopted early on and was admitted to membership in elite circles.[20] By either route the result has been the estrangement of the movement's elitist leadership from disorganized bases. Such "movements" are easily curbed or destroyed by authoritarian regimes at small cost in extended coercive capabilities, for regimes need only lop off the labor politicians at the top in order to reduce the "movements" to virtual political impotence. In contrast, the Peruvian labor movement has grown from the

[19] For O'Donnell (1973, 1978), the "new bourgeoisie" needs "bureaucratic-authoritarianism" because of problems with the import-substitution industrialization model of development. The progress of industrialization, he maintains, eventually comes to require a massive shift of national income upward to the middle- and upper-class consumers of durable goods—something that the disadvantaged majority, given the vote, would never voluntarily accept. I maintain that bonanza development poses fewer difficulties for capital accumulation and that these are unlikely to be related at all to consumption. O'Donnell (1973) additionally insists that technocratic modes and values are always foreign to Latin American societies. Therefore, the technocratic bourgeois stratum (1) is not a part of the national bourgeoisie; (2) must impose technocracy on an unwilling society; and (3) for both reasons lacks legitimacy and must consequently rule coercively. I find, in contrast, that with bonanza development, technocracy arises autochthonously, albeit conditioned by transnational action; because it does, the technocratic stratum *is* an organic part of the larger national bourgeoisie. Hence, bonanza development docs not conduce to "bureaucratic-authoritarianism" by virtue of its inner dynamic.

[20] On Argentina, see Spalding (1977:163-77); on Brazil, Erickson (1977); and on Mexico, Spalding (1977:94-150). Also useful on Mexico is Eckstein (1977:passim).

bottom up. Oligarchic domination held a paradoxical advantage for the working class in that the oligarchy could stomach cooptation but not, thanks to its ideological hostility toward the idea of trade unions, the establishment of an *oficialista* labor movement. In addition, bonanza development stimulated indigenous class organization because access to the benefits of the "bonanza" was never automatic; it was granted solely to those popular groups whose organizational resources enabled them to present themselves as a menace to the system. Unions arose piecemeal at the local level in accordance with the consciousness and combativeness of individual work units and the economic potential of the employer (the last always greatest in the case of foreign enterprises, where workers organized earliest). Local unions were and are self-financed (with the aid of contributions coerced from employers) and are as independent of centrals and political parties as they are of the state. Coopted leaders who do not produce at bargaining time are ousted; those removed by government fiat are promptly replaced from among the rank and file. The suppression of this sort of popular movement would be difficult or impossible short of an extreme—and expensive—augmentation of the state's coercive capabilities. The resultant totalitarianism would impinge as well, as it has in Chile, upon bourgeois interests.

I conclude that bourgeois democracy can survive for the immediate future, so long as the working class goes on treating it with a modicum of respect. To date the portents are positive: the Left minority participates in congressional debates, and its leaders make serious attempts to offer constructive alternatives to official policy within a constitutional framework.

Legitimacy and Its Contradiction

It was suggested that the corporate national bourgeoisie might be able to produce a hegemonic integration of the working class into a stable capitalist order if, *inter alia*, "there is a congruence between the economic and political power of the workers, in the sense that the latters' political strength grows out of and is coexistent with economic development." That describes the Peruvian situation. Hegemonic incorporation is the outgrowth of a kind of class formation process in which *labor's political action is rooted in the real struggle experience of the working class* and is, for that reason, impossible for the authorities to ignore. Bourgeois hegemony does not consist in the mere imposition from on high of "ruling ideas," since ideas cannot be imposed. Rather, it consists in a successful bourgeois ideological and material accommodation to the working class, which occurs because the costs of repression are too large. The corporate national bourgeoisie is more disposed ideologically to make the accommodation than a market-capitalist bourgeoisie would be (unionization per se contradicts its ideal of a free market in labor power) and, having realized scale and other efficiencies of organization, can usually better afford to make it.

(A favorable outlook for hegemonic incorporation does not negate the fact that *all progress of the working class comes about only when it challenges the system of domination*.[21] "Economistic" class action, as practiced by the proletariat of the Peruvian mines and smelters, deserves the support of progressives because it *is* such a challenge.)

The managerial ideology posits a capitalist legitimacy resting, as in the metropoli, on expertise; on the depersonalization of productive property, rendering the corporate exercise of property rights "democratically" justifiable on the ground that it is an instrumental good; on the promise of a technology-induced expansion of material output, eliminating zero-sum competition for scarce goods; and on the dream of a positivistic resolution of class conflict by a nonpartisan administrative state. In the Peruvian case, late-capitalist legitimacy also harmonizes with the Catholic preference for an organic society and rejection of *Gesellschaft* as the basis of social organization. The other side of the coin is the managerial ideology's lack of élan. It suggests that development is, or can be made to be, a painless enterprise. It does not call for universal sacrifice to achieve its vaunted goals; does not delegitimate extremes of elite privilege; and does not motivate enthusiastic, voluntary popular cooperation in a national development "project." In fact, it exacerbates its own difficulties by raising the expectations of all groups sufficiently well organized to present claims against the "bonanza" while providing no ideological mechanism for restraining these claims within the perimeter of what the "bonanza" can realistically supply. *This is the core contradiction of bonanza development.*

The class embodiment of the contradiction is not the proletariat, whose leading element has already enforced its claim on the "bonanza" that it labors to produce. Neither is it the peasantry. Bonanza development marginalizes— reduces to comparative economic insignificance—the entire agricultural sector, whose surplus ceases to figure centrally in the process of capital accumulation. But in Peru, marginalization of agriculture cut the ground out from under oligarchic power and was the sine qua non for a nonviolent yet extensive land reform. Having obviated a squeezing of surplus out of toiling peasants' hides, the corporate national bourgeoisie now allows the peasantry what it has always wanted—to be left alone. This kind of "benign neglect" does not speak well for bourgeois stewardship pretensions. Still, it will probably accomplish its purpose. The "peasant problem" that the bourgeoisie bemoans may, with agrarian reform a fact, solve itself: via "kulakization" and embourgeoisement (for some), agricultural proletarianization (for more), and

[21] See Miliband (1977:53-54). Thus, e.g., Fagen (1977) is quite correct when he criticizes Latin American dominant classes for not redistributing wealth downward; but the critique is irrelevant, since no dominant class has ever done so except under pressure and with perceived benefit—the relief of that pressure—for itself. The real issue is, why redistributive pressures from below have so seldom been effective in Latin America; and the facile answer, "because the classes who embody them are victims of repression," will not do.

urban migration (for the majority). In short, marginalization by the "bonanza" is the condition for the eventual disappearance of the peasantry as a major class actor—in turn a precondition, Barrington Moore has reminded us, for a stable democratic order.[22]

Instead it is the nonproletarian urban masses, the fastest-growing popular sector, who personify the contradiction. With them the danger to the system is manifest: of the several general strikes attempted since 1977, their disruption of urban commerce was a factor in all the successful ones.[23] Urban migrants have previously extracted from the "bonanza" improvements in their residential infrastructure. Soon they will demand meaningful employment; but bonanza development, itself, does not exhibit great potential for job creation.

Members of the corporate national bourgeoisie are not unaware of the problem and have been groping their way toward a solution within the bounds of the status quo. Their reasoning is as follows: Currently, most urban dwellers get by in the "underground economy" (in the more polite United Nations terminology, the "informal sector"). Its activities prosper after a fashion, but they cannot yield income and still meet government regulations and taxes; therefore, they are carried on surreptitiously and do not grow, lest they be brought to the attention of the authorities. Were the informal sector freed from the burdens of taxation and regulation, its operatives would start to compete openly and to strive for growth. Latent entrepreneurial energies would be released. A vital petty-bourgeois sector would then emerge, absorbing the officially unemployed and relieving the direct load on the "bonanza." The corporate economy would assist with technical and managerial advice, financial aid, and other voluntary measures.

In essence, this is a proposal for an economy not unlike those of the metropoli—where corporate oligopolies occupying the economic heights coexist with a multitude of small, competitive businesses "in the valleys," as it were. It is an intriguing but untested proposal, entailing the completion of a late-capitalist economy from the top downward in diametric opposition to the process by which such economies arose in the developed West. Can the idea work?[24] Can the corporate national bourgeoisie thus nurture the "petty-bourgeoisification" of the urban masses and so resolve its latent legitimacy contradiction? We cannot yet know.

[22] Moore (1966:429-30).

[23] Balbi and Parodi (1981) point out that the 1977 and 1978 general strikes succeeded in large part because residents of the *pueblos jóvenes* on the outskirts of Lima and other large cities blocked roads and highways. Bus and *colectivo* drivers, in fear of damage to their vehicles and harm to themselves, then refused to work and, so, brought urban mass transit to a halt. When the urban masses did not riot, as in 1979, general strikes failed.

[24] The crux of the matter is finding a way to: (1) maintain all taxation and regulation currently binding on formally structured businesses, while (2) devising a sliding scale for their gradual imposition as a function of increasing firm size and stability, and yet (3) preventing the sliding scale from becoming a disincentive to growth.

DEPENDENCY AND ITS LIMITS

Throughout this work my judgment of dependency theories has been harsh, for the reason that careful empirical investigation consistently fails to verify them. Some versions are simply not amenable to empirical verification. Others hold rigidly to a turn-of-the-century perspective on capitalism and imperialism, refusing on doctrinal grounds to deal openly with the manifold changes in the structures and institutions of international capitalism since that time. Still others employ "class" approaches that actually take elites or functional groups as their units of analysis. All advance the erroneous claim (false even within the Marxian framework that many have adopted) that political dependency is the automatic, inevitable outcome of economic exploitation.

I have not denied that the rise of the corporate national bourgeoisie incorporates a specific strategy of development, whose selection forecloses—as must *any* selection—the option of choosing otherwise. The dependency paradigm is uncomfortable with the selection: rightly so, perhaps, in normative terms, but less so in theoretical ones. As it wishes to show *theoretically* that the choice was wrong, it

> assumes: a) that there is a latent, suppressed historical alternative to the development that actually took place; b) that the failure of this alternative to materialize was the result primarily of external *imposition*—even if mediated through internal social forces—and not of the *choice* of internal directing groups; c) that the latent (suppressed) alternative would have been more autonomous and therefore would have achieved more rapid development. . . . [But] it cannot be taken for granted that social forces capable of embodying the allegedly suppressed alternative actually exist. . . . [I]t cannot be assumed a priori . . . that autonomous development is always more rapid, or even more "balanced," than dependent development.[25]

Proponents of dependency in Peru are obligated to document, concretely, a better alternative to bonanza development, one that could realistically be adopted were it not for external control. They have not done so. I do not believe that they can.

Neither have I denied that international relations of domination and subordination exist, now as in the past. What I have shown is that, as dependency is not the *general* condition of the Third World (for, it is not the condition of Peru nor, in all probability, of other countries undergoing bonanza development), *it cannot be a systemic product of world capitalism as presently constituted*. The *existence* of dependency—not just its form—in any given instance is contingent upon certain social, economic, and politico-historical variables whose elucidation demands further comparative research.

Where does this leave the issue of human liberation in the developing countries? Liberation is never complete until the norm of egalitarian democ-

---

[25] Warren (1980:166-67), emphasis in original.

racy has been extended into the economic sphere. That is socialism; the word ought not to be employed as a misnomer for a bureaucratic-elitist structure of domination. Socialism, so understood, can only be won by and for working people themselves—who prove by their class practice whether or not they are ready for it. In Peru they are not, in my opinion: the working class is too small, too factionalized, and insufficiently developed in terms of consciousness. Lenin was probably right in asserting that workers cannot transcend "economistic" forms of action unless their class experience is radically interpreted to them by individuals who are just enough removed from daily struggle exigencies that they can form a wider perspective.[26] However, the socialist ideal is negated when those individuals overstep the bounds of the mentor role and come to constitute a counterelite.

Peru, like any other country, will be ready for socialism if and when the working class welds itself—with the aid of socialist teachers but *primarily through its own efforts*—into a consensual, nationally cohesive movement. In the interim, well-wishers may take heart from the fact that bonanza development and the ascendance of the corporate national bourgeoisie have brought with them a fortification of the working class's political power, visible improvement in its material standard of living, and an advance of the productive forces—on which hinges, ultimately, the socialist prospect. But the progress of the working class and of socialism is not likely to be fostered by a dependencia outlook that subordinates class interests to nationalism.

Deficient in explanatory power and unable to stand up to empirical tests, the "theory" of dependency as a systemic outcome of relations with international capitalism is, in reality, an ideology. Dependencista ideology has been useful to political and economic elites striving to free themselves and their nations from subjugation to neocolonialism. That goal has been largely attained. Now the task is to focus on the *national* basis of elitism and domination—which an ideology that blames all evil in the Third World on the metropoli cannot do. The ideology depreciates the drive to institute local participatory democracy (a step forward even in its less-than-perfect bourgeois incarnation) and to extend it beyond formal politics; one searches in vain for a dependencista appreciation that democracy is the only meaningful check on elite power. Accordingly, dependencismo no longer furthers, as it once did, the cause of general human liberation. It is time, therefore, for progressives to lay it to rest.

[26] Lenin (1969).

Appendices

Miscellaneous Data

TABLE A.1 Average Annual Exchange Rate of the Peruvian Sol, 1950-1980
(*Soles per U.S. dollar*)

Year	Rate	Year	Rate	Year	Rate
1950	14.85	1960	27.57	1970	38.70
1951	15.08	1961	26.81	1971	38.70
1952	15.43	1962	26.81	1972	38.70
1953	16.85	1963	26.82	1973	38.70
1954	19.39	1964	26.82	1974	38.70
1955	19.00	1965	26.82	1975	40.80
1956	19.00	1966	26.82	1976	57.43
1957	19.00	1967	27.81	1977	83.81
1958	23.30	1968	38.70	1978	156.34
1959	27.45	1969	38.70	1979	224.55
				1980	288.65

SOURCES: Banco Central de Reserva de Perú, *Boletín* (various issues); International Monetary Fund, *International Financial Statistics* (various issues).

TABLE A.2 Peruvian Consumer Price Index, 1950-1980[a]
(*Base: 1960 = 100*)

Year	Index	Year	Index	Year	Index
1950	47.1	1960	100.0	1970	243.3
1951	51.9	1961	106.0	1971	259.8
1952	55.5	1962	113.0	1972	278.5
1953	60.5	1963	119.8	1973	305.0
1954	63.8	1964	131.6	1974	356.5
1955	66.8	1965	153.2	1975	440.8
1956	70.4	1966	166.8	1976	588.4
1957	75.7	1967	183.1	1977	812.4
1958	81.7	1968	218.1	1978	1,282.2
1959	92.0	1969	231.7	1979	2,150.0
				1980	3,422.0

SOURCES: Computed by the author from data in Banco Central de Reserva del Perú, *Boletín* (various issues) and International Labour Organisation (1980); and from data furnished by the Departamento de Estudios Económicos y Estadística, Sociedad Nacional de Minería y Petróleo.

[a] Consumer price index for metropolitan Lima.

TABLE A.3 Volume of Production of the Peruvian Minería, 1950-1980: Major Non-ferrous Metals (*Metric Tons Fine Content*)

Year	Copper	Lead	Zinc	Silver
1950	33,327	61,837	77,949	417.79
1951	35,446	77,648	89,254	521.46
1952	30,285	83,454	101,521	453.00
1953	33,602	99,245	126,657	556.45
1954	40,123	107,968	129,978	594.15
1955	41,424	121,009	150,464	660.96
1956	45,395	122,610	152,999	602.76
1957	54,818	136,092	136,041	740.65
1958	51,904	125,451	123,177	750.73
1959	50,537	121,259	132,960	865.03
1960	183,988	131,234	157,254	1,015.67
1961	198,052	136,908	170,774	1,055.23
1962	166,790	133,377	183,907	1,031.01
1963	180,064	149,197	194,896	1,094.94
1964	176,445	150,674	236,660	1,070.56
1965	180,336	154,344	254,496	1,134.36
1966	199,999	161,521	283,963	1,149.23
1967	192,688	159,716	304,799	998.64
1968	212,537	154,524	291,404	1,130.98
1969	198,803	154,543	300,303	1,116.19
1970	220,225	156,770	299,136	1,239.02
1971	207,346	165,814	318,073	1,242.64
1972	219,126	184,381	376,129	1,255.66
1973	202,686	183,413	390,576	1,163.64
1974	211,593	165,798	378,029	1,084.91
1975	165,813	154,168	364,915	1,058.35
1976	214,898	161,066	382,693	1,154.86
1977	338,110	170,744	405,250	1,277.28
1978	366,500	170,500	402,600	1,190.19
1979	405,373	174,000	433,000	1,395.71
1980	379,600	176,130	426,200	1,384.75

SOURCE: Compiled by the author from data supplied by the Ministerio de Energía y Minas and by the Departamento de Estudios Económicos y Estadística, Sociedad Nacional de Minería y Petróleo.

TABLE A.4 Value of Production of the Peruvian Minería, 1950-1980: Industry Total and Major Nonferrous Metals (*Millions of dollars*)

Year	Total	Copper	Lead	Zinc	Silver
1950	75.1	11.8	13.0	13.1	12.2
1951	99.7	16.1	24.5	23.7	16.8
1952	111.7	17.5	25.2	24.4	15.7
1953	112.8	18.9	21.6	14.1	17.0
1954	124.0	21.1	25.3	15.7	16.7
1955	151.2	31.8	30.6	22.4	15.9
1956	171.0	34.0	32.6	23.8	14.6
1957	161.7	25.8	31.4	17.0	17.5
1958	151.2	21.1	23.4	13.0	18.7
1959	100.9	25.1	21.3	16.2	21.3
1960	216.2	101.0	23.3	22.9	24.7
1961	224.3	105.0	20.3	20.3	26.9
1962	213.3	93.4	16.6	19.0	32.6
1963	245.9	104.0	24.0	27.7	41.8
1964	299.9	108.7	34.2	50.0	42.6
1965	329.9	132.5	40.7	46.6	44.4
1966	408.4	194.9	38.5	52.8	47.3
1967	447.0	204.8	38.3	57.3	52.6
1968	450.9	211.7	31.7	44.9	72.5
1969	507.1	270.3	37.8	46.4	60.6
1970	520.8	256.5	38.5	58.4	63.9
1971	439.6	193.2	32.8	75.1	54.9
1972	491.8	194.6	44.4	96.8	62.8
1973	730.3	340.8	59.0	144.9	88.1
1974	862.3	330.6	70.8	197.4	143.7
1975	622.4	173.2	46.3	173.1	130.4
1976	667.2	261.1	49.4	140.5	136.7
1977	867.5	367.2	78.6	126.7	166.9
1978	897.4	416.1	85.0	107.0	172.0
1979	1,617.8	726.2	160.4	197.5	398.7
1980	2,004.1	705.5	120.6	194.1	716.0

SOURCE: See Table A.3.

TABLE A.5 Gross Value of Peruvian Mine Production by Subsector, 1963-1980 (*Percentages*)

Year	Gran Minería	Mediana Minería	Pequeña Minería
1963	71.4	28.6[a]	
1964	72.6	27.4[a]	
1965	72.6	27.4[a]	
1966	68.1	31.9[a]	
1967	69.5	30.5[a]	
1968	68.8	28.7	2.5
1969	67.1	30.2	2.7
1970	64.2	32.6	2.2
1971	62.0	35.6	2.4
1972	60.8	35.7	3.5
1973	54.9	39.7	5.4
1974	53.7	42.8	3.5
1975	51.3	45.4	3.3
1976	58.1	38.2	3.7
1977	60.4	37.1	2.5
1978	69.8	27.4	2.8
1979	63.7	33.6	2.7
1980	55.9	40.7	3.4

SOURCE: See Table A.3.

[a] Combined data for the mediana and pequeña minerías.

TABLE A.6 International Price Quotations for Major Nonferrous Metals, 1950-1980[a]
(*Copper, lead, and zinc in U.S. cents per pound; silver in U.S. cents per Troy ounce*[b])

Year	Copper		Lead		Zinc		Silver	
	U.S.	Eur.	U.S.	Eur.	U.S.	Eur.	U.S.[c]	Eur.
1950	21.235	22.353	13.296	13.305	13.866	14.911	74.169	75.614
1951	24.200	27.541	17.500	20.253	18.000	21.458	89.368	90.819
1952	24.200	32.349	16.467	17.049	16.215	18.627	84.941	86.524
1953	28.798	32.180	13.489	11.489	10.855	9.380	85.188	86.660
1954	29.694	31.265	14.054	12.094	10.681	9.814	85.250	85.995
1955	37.491	43.898	15.138	13.192	12.299	11.298	89.099	90.144
1956	41.818	41.072	16.013	14.517	13.494	12.195	90.826	92.179
1957	29.576	27.389	14.658	12.051	11.399	10.173	90.820	91.858
1958	25.764	24.817	12.109	9.130	10.309	8.266	89.044	89.244
1959	31.182	29.823	12.211	8.875	11.448	10.311	91.202	92.243
1960	32.053	30.834	11.948	9.043	12.946	11.192	91.375	92.859
1961	29.921	28.747	10.871	8.033	11.542	9.724	92.449	93.737
1962	30.600	29.344	9.631	7.056	11.625	8.456	108.521	107.065
1963	30.600	29.347	11.137	7.930	11.997	9.588	127.912	128.468
1964	31.960	43.985	13.596	12.621	13.568	14.724	129.300	130.205
1965	35.017	58.648	16.000	14.354	14.500	14.092	129.300	129.990
1966	36.170	69.136	15.115	11.864	14.500	12.717	129.300	130.115
1967	38.226	51.243	14.000	10.285	13.843	12.331	154.968	162.706
1968	41.847	56.012	13.216	10.882	13.500	11.884	214.460	219.026
1969	47.534	66.288	14.895	13.092	14.600	12.927	179.067	180.028
1970	57.700	62.882	15.619	13.523	15.319	13.169	177.082	176.766
1971	51.433	49.273	13.800	11.507	16.128	14.076	154.564	154.195

1972	50.617	48.545	15.029	13.678	17.753	17.118	168.455	168.569
1973	58.852	80.805	16.285	19.382	20.658	38.314	255.756	254.370
1974	76.649	93.097	22.533	26.802	35.945	55.973	470.798	470.600
1975	63.535	56.110	21.529	18.681	38.959	33.792	441.852	441.746
1976	68.824	64.051	23.102	20.502	37.010	32.304	435.346	434.922
1977	65.808	59.460	30.703	28.022	34.392	26.803	462.302	463.310
1978	65.510	61.904	33.653	29.886	30.971	26.914	540.089	541.883
1979	92.334	90.113	52.642	54.574	37.296	33.734	1,109.379	1,110.965
1980	101.374	99.297	42.456	41.213	37.428	34.482	2,063.15	2,085.31

SOURCES: Compiled by the author from data appearing in American Bureau of Metal Statistics, *Non-Ferrous Metal Data* (New York: ABMS); *Engineering and Mining Journal*; and *Metals Week* (various issues).

[a] U.S. prices for copper, lead, and zinc per producers' price (Domestic Refinery) quotes—for copper and lead, FOB New York; for zinc prior to 1972, FOB East St. Louis, Ill.; for zinc 1972 and thereafter, delivered. Europe prices for these three metals per LME Settlement. U.S. silver price per Handy & Harman (New York) quotation. Europe silver price per London 999 Fine Bars quotation.

[b] One Troy ounce = 31.1 grams.

[c] Price for 1950-1961 inclusive is for unrefined metal; for 1962-1980 inclusive, for refined metal.

TABLE A.7 Major Western World Copper Mine Producers, 1977

Rank	Producer's Nationality	Countries Where Mined	Producer	Share of Total Western World Mine Production (%)	(Cum.%)	Share of Privately Owned Western World Mine Production (%)	(Cum.%)
1	Chile	Chile	Chilean State	16.8	16.8		
2	Zambia	Zambia	Zambian State	10.8	27.6		
3	Zaire	Zaire	Zairois State	7.5	35.1		
4	Britain	Canada/S.Africa/Spain/New Guinea	Rio Tinto-Zinc	6.8	41.9	10.5	10.5
5	USA	USA/Australia/Peru/Mexico/Nicaragua	Asarco	6.0	47.9	9.2	19.7
6	USA	USA	Kennecott Copper	5.4	53.3	8.3	28.0
7	Japan	Canada/Peru/Philippines	Consortium: Dowa, Furukawa, Mitsubishi, Mitsui, Nippon, Sumitomo	5.1	58.4	7.9	35.9
8	USA	USA	Phelps-Dodge	4.9	63.3	7.5	43.4
9	USA	Canada/S.Africa/USA	Newmont Mining	3.7	67.0	5.7	49.1
10	USA	Canada/USA	Anaconda	3.4	70.4	5.2	54.3
11	Canada	Canada	INCO	2.4	72.8	3.7	58.0
12	S.Africa	Canada/Namibia/S.Africa/Zimbabwe	Anglo-American Group	2.1	74.9	3.2	61.2
13	USA	USA	Duval Copper div. Pennzoil	1.9	76.8	2.9	64.1

SOURCES: Compiled by the author from data in American Bureau of Metal Statistics, *Non-Ferrous Metal Data 1977* (New York: ABMS, 1977); *Wall Street Journal* (various issues); and various trade journals.

TABLE A.8 Major Western World Primary Refined Copper Producers, 1977
(*Asterisk designates custom refiners*)

Rank	Countries	Producer (Home Country)	Share of Western World Refinery Capacity (%)	(Cum.%)
1	USA, Australia	Asarco (USA)	9.8	9.8
2	Zambia	Zambian State (Zambia)	9.1	18.9
3	Chile	Chilean State (Chile)	7.9	26.8
4	USA, Canada	Kennecott Copper (USA)	6.1	32.9
5	USA	Phelps-Dodge (USA)	5.8	38.7
6	Canada	Noranda Mines (Canada)	5.2	43.9
7	[a]	Nippon Mining* (Japan)	4.3	48.2
8	Belgium	Metallurgie Hoboken-Overpelt*[b] (Belgium)	3.9	52.1
9	[c]	AMAX* (USA)	3.3	55.4
10	Zaire	Zairois State[d] (Zaire)	3.0	58.4
11	[e]	Rio Tinto-Zinc (Britain)	2.9	61.3
12	W. Germany	Norddeutsche Affinerie*[f] (W. Germany)	2.8	64.1
13	Japan	Onahana Smelting & Refining* (Japan)	2.8	66.9
14	USA, Canada	Anaconda (USA)	2.7	69.6
15	Peru	Peruvian State (Peru)	2.3	71.9
16	Canada	INCO (Canada)	2.3	74.2
17	[g]	Newmont Mining* (USA)	2.1	76.3
18	[a]	Sumitomo Metal Mining* (Japan)	2.1	78.4
19	[a]	Mitsubishi Metal Mining* (Japan)	1.9	80.3
20	Yugoslavia	Rudarsko Topionicarski Basen, Bor* (Yugoslavia)	1.8	82.1

SOURCE: Compiled by the author from data in American Bureau of Metal Statistics, *Non-Ferrous Metal Data 1977* (New York: ABMS, 1978).

[a] Basically a custom refiner with all refineries in Japan, but participates in joint mining ventures in Canada, Peru, and the Philippines.

[b] A division of Société Générale de Minerais (SGM), Belgium.

[c] Refines only in the United States; participates in joint mining ventures in Canada, Namibia, South Africa, the United States, and Zimbabwe.

[d] Much of its mine output is refined by SGM under exclusive contract.

[e] Refines copper in Spain; owns mines in Canada and Spain; controls Bougainville Copper Company (Papua New Guinea); participates in joint mining ventures in Canada, Namibia, and South Africa.

[f] A division of Metallgesellschaft AG, West Germany.

[g] Refines copper in the United States; participates in joint mining ventures in Canada, Namibia, and South Africa.

Mining Policy Guidelines and Legislation
of the Military Regime

Table B.1 of this appendix compares the mining sector goals, proposed actions, and guidelines for policymaking that were adopted by the "revolutionary" military regime's two overall plans: the Plan Inca (1974) and the Plan Túpac Amaru (1977). The earlier plan represents the position of the "first phase" of the "revolution" under President Velasco; the later one, the orientation of the "second phase" under President Morales Bermúdez.

Table B.2 is a chronological listing of the major mining legislation enacted by the military regime from its accession to power in 1968 through the end of 1979.

TABLE B.1 A Comparison of the Mining Policy Objectives of the Plan Inca (1974) and the Plan Túpac Amaru (1977)

I. Goals for the Mining Sector
  a. Plan Inca:
  Foster the maximum degree of development of the country's mining potential, putting it at the service of the nation predominantly by means of state activity.
  b. Plan Túpac Amaru:
  Foster the maximum possible degree of development of the country's mineral potential, with the participation of national and foreign private investors and of the state. State participation will be preferentially oriented toward the gran minería.
II. Actions and Guidelines for Policymaking
  a. Plan Inca:
  1. Require mining companies to develop their concessions or lose them; institute the policy of *amparo por el trabajo* for all future mineral exploitation.
  2. Transfer to the state responsibility for refining, export sales, and future development of the gran minería.
  3. Reduce investor incentives to more reasonable levels.
  4. Promote prospecting for minerals throughout the national territory.

(TABLE B.1 cont.)

5. Protect the dignity of the mine worker; improve his job safety conditions and his material welfare.

6. Create a sound state enterprise to take charge of all of the state's activities in the mining sector.

b. Plan Túpac Amaru:

1. Complete and perfect the nation's body of mining legislation.

2. Promote prospecting for minerals throughout the national territory.

3. Draw up a long-term mining development plan, giving first priority to the expansion of refinery capacity.

4. Rationally distribute reserved areas (in which private prospecting is not permitted) and special-rights areas (in which the state becomes a part-owner of any private mineral claim) so as to promote their development by the state or by private capital.

5. Maintain state participation in the gran minería, alone or in association with national and/or foreign private capital.

6. Create incentives to private enterprise to prospect in unrestricted zones and in special-rights areas.

7. Promote to the maximum possible extent the exploration, mining, and smelting of metals in the mediana and pequeña minerías.

8. Promote the highest possible degree of local processing of mine products.

9. Rationalize remunerations in the sector, striking a compromise between the welfare requisites of the mine workers and the profitability and productivity of the enterprises.

10. Rationalize and better integrate the activities of parastatal mining enterprises.

11. Perfect the regulatory and taxation regime of the sector, differentiating between the gran, mediana, and pequeña minerías.

12. Promote greater integration of the metal-mining industry into plans for overall economic development.

13. Promote scientific and technological research and development in the mining sector; improve training and technical education at all employment levels.

14. Improve health and safety conditions in the mines and processing plants.

TABLE B.2 Principal Mining Legislation of the Military Regime

Item	Law	Date	Major Provisions
1.	D.L. 17527	3/21/69	Establishes the organization and functions of the Ministry of Energy and Mines and related agencies, including parastatal enterprises.
2.	D.L. 17712	6/17/69	Authorizes the Central Reserve Bank to become a party to mine development contracts for the purpose of extending guarantees of foreign exchange availability.
3.	D.L. 17774	8/12/69	Sets up the Superior Mining Council as a joint private-state advisory body within the mining ministry; details its membership and functions.
4.	D.L. 17791	9/02/69	Establishes an investment fund, administered by the Banco Minero, for loans to locally owned mining companies; offers these companies accelerated depreciation, duty-free machinery imports, and tax-free reinvestment privileges.
5.	D.L. 17792	9/02/69	Requires mining companies to submit development calendars for idle concessions and to begin their development by April 1, 1970; failure to comply will be penalized by *caducidad* (forfeiture).
6.	D.L. 17793	9/02/69	Reduces the area of concessions that can be combined into a "single economic and administrative entity."
7.	D.L. 18225	4/14/70	The "normative law for the mining sector." Declares a state monopoly over refining and export sales; raises income taxes and lowers investment incentives available to foreign capital; provides for state-private joint ventures; establishes MineroPeru.
8.	D.L. 18368	8/14/70	Tightens requirements for idle-concession development plans, specifying that these must be based on the "critical path" planning method; requires definite proof of project financing.
9.	D.L. 18436	10/13/70	Defines organization and functions of MineroPeru.
10.	D.L. 18471	11/10/70	Law of *estabilidad laboral*. Prohibits discharge of workers for any reason short of *falta*

(TABLE B.2 cont.)

			grave (gross negligence, extreme insubordination, criminal behavior); allows general work force reductions only under exceptional circumstances; all dismissals must be approved by the labor ministry.
11.	D.L.18880	6/08/71	The 1971 Mining Code. Supersedes the 1950 Mining Code and amendments thereto; incorporates previous legislation of the military regime (e.g., items 4-8 above) with minor changes; establishes the Workers' Community system of profit sharing and comanagement; imposes detailed regulations governing working conditions, mining-camp standards, etc.
12.	D.L.19299	2/17/72	Allows mining companies to defer income tax payments when necessary to help them obtain foreign financing for mining projects listed in the national development plan.
13.	D.L.19441	6/20/72	Allows the Banco Minero to take over and operate small mines whose owners have defaulted on their financial obligations.
14.	D.L.19615	11/21/72	Requires foreign state-owned mining entities involved in joint ventures with MineroPeru to renounce all right of diplomatic appeal.
15.	D.L.20007	5/08/73	Establishes new minimum requirements for worker housing in mining camps.
16.	D.L.20492	1/01/74	Expropriates the Peruvian branch of the Cerro Corporation.
17.	D.L.20505	1/15/74	Establishes an ad valorem tax on "traditional" exports such as mine products (later delayed by one year).
18.	D.L.20528	2/19/74	Ratifies the Greene Agreement with the United States as a full settlement of all disputes arising from Peruvian expropriations of U.S. property in 1968-1973.
19.	D.L.20768	10/22/74	Clarifies the interpretation of a certain provision in the Cuajone basic agreement so that MineroPeru can participate in long-term sales of Cuajone copper.
20.	D.L.20784	11/05/74	Establishes Minero Peru Comercial as a separate entity charged with administration of the state metal sales monopoly; it is independent

(TABLE B.2 cont.)

			of the mining ministry and is subject instead to the Ministry of Commerce.
21.	D.L.21094	2/04/75	Redefines the organization and functions of the Ministry of Energy and Mines.
22.	D.L.21106	2/25/75	Requires holiday pay for obreros.
23.	D.L.21117	3/15/75	Defines the organization and functions of Centromin, exempting it from certain provisions governing the operations of other parastatal enterprises in order to take account of its special history and avoid disruption of its activities.
24.	D.L.21228	7/22/75	Exproriates the Marcona Mining Company.
25.	D.L.21237	8/12/75	Sets up a special fund under Banco Minero administration to assist locally owned mining companies in temporary distress due to falling world prices.
26.	D.L.21428	2/24/76	Sets up a special fund enabling the Banco Minero to make risk investments in locally owned mining ventures, new or existing.
27.	D.L.21429	2/24/76	Authorizes the Banco Minero to share in the profits of ventures in which it has made risk investments.
28.	D.L.21435	2/24/76	Defines ''small enterprises'' and exempts them from the Workers' Community system (impact limited to the pequeña minería).
29.	D.L.21462	4/06/76	Declares the mining industry to be in a state of emergency; removes estabilidad laboral of workers who engage in strikes.
30.	D.L.21644	9/28/76	Ratifies compensation agreement with Marcona Mining.
31.	D.L.22126	3/21/78	Alters estabilidad laboral, expanding the legal grounds for dismissal and stiffening penalties imposed on employers for illegal dismissals.
32.	D.L.22197	5/03/78	Makes detail modifications in the 1971 Mining Code; slightly liberalizes investment incentives.
33.	D.L.22333	11/14/78	Modifies the Workers' Community System, as follows: (a) Sector-wide profit sharing now encompasses only the 4 percent of profits dis-

(TABLE B.2 cont.)

tributed in cash and no longer includes the 6 percent distributed in capital shares.

(b) Workers may vote to invest their capital share participation in the firm employing them, in government bonds, or in shares of other corporations; the first and third options are to be implemented via company emissions of special preference stock (*acciones laborales*) with a priority claim against corporate profits; existing Community shares held in common are to be converted to *acciones laborales*. All *acciones laborales* are the individual property of each worker receiving them and may be freely traded to others (but not to anyone who is a regular shareholder of the same firm), used as loan collateral, etc.

(c) Capital participation is reduced from 6 to 5.5 percent; the remaining 0.5 percent is to be paid out to the Workers' Community itself to cover its expenses.

(d) Comanagement provisions are modified: (i) workers' participation does not convey a right to participate in the company's regular annual meeting of shareholders; (ii) if there are two or more worker-directors of the firm, at least one must be an empleado; (iii) worker-directors may not be concurrently, or for three years prior to their selection, officers of any labor union and may not stand for election to union office while holding their directorships; (iv) companies may implement worker participation in management through special committees (*comités de gestión*) separate from their regular directorates.

34. D.L.22390 12/19/78 Amends the 1971 Mining Code; combines the formerly separate geological and mining engineering research institutes into a single en-

(TABLE B.2 cont.)

			tity, INGEMMET; specifies that worker profit sharing and corporate contributions to IN-GEMMET (1 percent of profits) are to be calculated as percentages of profit after deduction of income taxes, not before (as was done previously); states that companies can take a credit against income taxes due in an amount equal to the percentage of their profits distributed as *acciones laborales* multiplied by gross income tax before this adjustment, this amount to be distributed to workers in additional *acciones laborales*.
35.	D.L.22488	4/03/79	Authorizes firms not active in the mining industry to invest a portion of their profits in mining free of income tax.
36.	D.L.22631	8/14/79	Defines organization and functions of IN-GEMMET.

A Comparison of Key Provisions of the Toquepala and Cuajone Basic Agreements

1. Ore Deposits Covered by the Agreement:
   T: Toquepala, but with Cuajone and Quellaveco as possible follow-ons to be developed later. Wording vague as to whether a new agreement will be required for such follow-ons and whether existing contractual terms will be applied to them.
   C: Cuajone only, except that project design is to be such as to accommodate the later development of Quellaveco with minimal modification of the Cuajone installations.
2. Applicable Legal Regime:
   T: 1950 Mining Code Art. 56, on grounds that project is "marginal."
   C: 1950 Mining Code Art. 56 as amended in 1964 and 1968, on grounds that the project is central to the national development plan and that investment incentives and guarantees will help to obtain the needed financing.
3. Foreign Exchange Guarantees:
   T: Free, unrestricted access to foreign exchange for amortization of company's capital investment, amortization and interest payments on outside debt, other loan costs. Company need only submit verification of payments.
   C: Guaranteed access to foreign exchange for above purposes plus payments to foreign consultants. But actual foreign exchange earnings must be credited to Central Reserve Bank, which will then issue offsetting certificates. Guarantee enforced by a complicated system of bank transfers between New York and Peru.
4. Disposition-of-Product Guarantees:
   T: Free disposition of all mine and smelter production.
   C: Free disposition subject to priority sales to local markets as needed. But, state may require some sales to a particular market so long as the price received is no less than that in the market in which the majority of production is sold.
5. Tax Deductions for Depreciation:
   T: Accelerated depreciation of capital-goods costs, including interest costs if financed.

C: Accelerated depreciation at an overall rate between 3 and 12 percent, to be determined as a weighted average of individual depreciation rates. These must bear a reasonable relation to the actual life of equipment being depreciated.

6. Tax Deductions for Depletion:

T: Annual allowance of up to 15 percent of value of production but not more than 50 percent of pretax profit. Unrestricted use of funds deducted for depletion.

C: Annual allowance as above but not more than 33.3 percent of pretax profit. After investment is recuperated, depletion allowances must be reinvested in the Peruvian mining industry within three years, with at least 10 percent committed to prospecting for new ore reserves. Alternatively, company may forego depletion allowances and instead invest tax-free up to 50 percent of pretax profit in smelting and/or refining operations in Peru.

7. Computation of Gross Income for Purposes of Taxation:

T: Gross income equals income actually received.

C: As above, except that if any sales are made at prices below the open-market prices for the market in question, income from such sales will be computed for tax purposes as if the higher price had been received.

8. Tax Rates and Tax Stability:

T: Income tax to be the sole tax, assessed at a 30 percent rate. Actual yearly tax payments not to exceed 10 percent of the previous year's net profit; any balance due is deferred until after investment recuperation. Company will pay 4 percent ad valorem on exports shipped, which will be credited against income taxes due for the year. These rates are guaranteed not to rise during time period specified in item 10 below. (Note: a foreign mining company operating under the general tax regime would have been subject at this time to an income tax rate of 54.5 percent.)

C: Income tax to be the sole tax, assessed at a 47.5 percent rate until after investment recuperation has been completed and at a 54.5 percent rate for the succeeding six years. No deferral of taxes. These rates are guaranteed not to rise during time period specified in item 10 below. (Note: a foreign mining company operating under the general tax regime would have been subject at this time to an income tax rate from 37.7 to 71.5 percent, depending on its ratio of cash flow to net fixed asset value.)

9. Computation of Investment Recuperation:

T: Recuperable investment equals total of invested capital plus loan interest. Only net after-tax profits charged against investment recuperation.

C: Recuperable investment equals total of invested capital plus loan interest but excluding: (i) sums invested after the start of mining operations; (ii) acquisition costs of real estate other than mining concessions; (iii) capital derived from depletion or other reserves of an existing Peruvian mine. Charged against investment recuperation are after-tax profits and allowances for depreciation, depletion, amortization, and corporate reserves (except those for payment of employee benefits). During construction period, company must file quarterly and annual progress reports showing work completed and amounts spent in the reporting period. It must file a final report upon completion of construction showing the total investment and specifying all sources of funds. Company books and records to be available for government verification of data contained in reports. Amount of recuperable investment to be fixed by Supreme Resolution six weeks after submission of final report.

10. Time Limits of Investment Recuperation:
    T: Recuperation period and all contracted benefits and incentives end when eligible investment has been fully recuperated or in fifteen years from date of signing, whichever comes first.
    C: Same as above, except that time limit is ten years and tax stability (but not other contracted benefits and incentives) continues for another six years after recuperation has been completed or the time limit has lapsed. Contract incorporates a projected schedule of results and recuperation. Company may modify this schedule based on actual results but must keep one on file; ten-year time limit is not subject to modification. Government may request or impose modification of the schedule any time that the price of copper varies from 40¢/lb by more than ±10 percent.

11. Imports and Import Duties:
    T: No restriction on importation of equipment and supplies for construction and routine operation. Imports free of duty except for consular fee of 7.5 percent on CIF value. Payment of consular fees may be deferred until after completion of investment recuperation.
    C: Equipment and supplies for construction and routine operation may be imported if locally produced equivalents are unavailable, or inadequate as to quality and function (determined by the company), or priced more than 25 percent above CIF value of equivalent imported items. Imports meeting these requirements are free of duty except for consular fee of 8 percent and a marine transport tax of 4 percent on CIF value. Payments cannot be deferred. Permissible imports are itemized on a list maintained under government supervision.

12. Miscellaneous Provisions to Promote National Development:
    T: None.
    C: Company agrees to make construction equipment available for sale to government after it is no longer needed. Company agrees to purchase some of its electric power from a government-owned hydroelectric facility in the area. Company undertakes specific obligations with respect to training of workers.

13. Grounds for Cancellation of Agreement and Forfeiture of Concession:
    T: None.

C: Failure to submit calendar of operations by April 4, 1970; failure to invest at least $25 million in the first eighteen months; failure to secure promises of full financing within eighteen months; failure to invest at least 60 percent of the amount programmed during any year; failure to complete the project within 6½ years; failure to submit progress reports during construction.

14. Relation to Other Laws and Obligations:

T: Contract is subject to Peruvian law.

C: Same as above, but company renounces right of diplomatic appeal. Government will support company's applications for loans from foreign governments and international agencies as well as application for investment insurance under a U.S. government program; but government will not guarantee nor underwrite such loans or obligations. It is expressly understood that government support of the Cuajone project does not imply the former's acceptance of any financial or other obligation affecting the interests of the Peruvian state.

Statutory Rights and Privileges
of Peruvian Mine Workers

I. Period of Work:

Eight hours per day, forty-eight hours per week. Employer may schedule work in nine-hour days with a corresponding reduction on the sixth day.

II. Overtime:

No more than seven overtime hours can be worked in one day. Overtime is compensated at 1¼ times the regular rate or more. Sunday overtime is compensated at twice the regular rate.

III. Night Work:

No legally mandated shift differential. See item VII(a) for night-work restrictions applicable to younger workers.

IV. Wages, Salaries, and Other Remunerations:

(a) Minimum wage: is established by government for each region and/or industry. It must be sufficient to maintain a minimum living standard and must be periodically readjusted for cost-of-living changes.

(b) Time-of-service benefit (empleados): Those continuously employed by the same employer (including in obrero status) for thirty or more years receive an annual indemnity equal to 30 percent of their basic salary. Indemnity counts as part of salary when computing other benefits.

(c) *Dominical* (obreros): A regular day's pay is received for the weekly rest day, provided that one has worked the entire preceding week excepting holidays, authorized absences, and absences occasioned by *force majeure* or Acts of God.

(d) Holiday pay: Legal holidays are January 1, Holy Thursday (afternoon only), Good Friday, May 1, June 29, July 28-29, August 30, October 9, November 1, December 3, and December 25. Obreros must be paid for all holidays beginning in 1975 (see Table B.2, item 22); previously they had to be paid only for the May 1 Labor Day holiday, but absence on the others did not cause loss of the *dominical*. Empleados, being on monthly salary, are automatically paid for holidays.

(e) Bonuses: are at the employer's option unless governed by a collective bargaining agreement with a labor union. However, under the Peruvian legal doctrine of *derecho adquirido*, any bonus paid for more than two consecutive years becomes a vested employee right. As such it is added to base pay when computing other benefits.

(f) Severance pay: is due all workers who qualify on the basis of time of service regardless of the reason for their departure. Empleados receive one basic monthly salary per year worked (a fractional year is counted as full if it includes at least three months of service) after a three-month probationary period. Obreros receive thirty days' worth of basic daily wages per year worked after 1962; service before that date is compensated at the old rate of fifteen days' worth per year for larger firms, six days' worth for smaller ones. Obreros only must have at least one year of continuous service to qualify if they resign voluntarily; but this is waived if they resign because of illness or incapacity to work. Severance pay is nontaxable and, in the event of the workers' death while still employed, is paid to his or her heirs.

V. Vacation Provisions:

    (a) Empleados: receive thirty days of annual vacation, payable after each year of service. They may elect to take only fifteen days of actual vacation and receive double pay for the remainder.

    (b) Obreros: receive the same vacation allowance under the same conditions except that they must take the full thirty days of vacation.

    (c) Accrual of vacation time: Peruvian workers may accrue up to two years' worth of vacation days if the employer agrees in writing. Expatriates may have any accrual scheme included in their employment contracts so long as the statutory minimum of thirty days per year of service is met.

    (d) Pay rate and indemnity: Vacations are compensated at the employee's basic wage or salary rate as of the date when the vacation begins. Employees who are denied the opportunity to take their vacation days within the year in which they are earned (due usually to employer's pleas based on pressure of business) receive an indemnity equal to thirty days' worth of triple pay.

    (e) Other provisions: Employees must have worked at least 260 days in the year to qualify for vacation benefits. In computing this time the following rules apply: (i) disciplinary suspensions and union leaves under the *licencia* system are counted as days worked; (ii) every day that the worker is on the job for more than four hours counts as a full day worked; (iii) every Saturday, Sunday, and holiday is counted as a day worked; (iv) every overtime stint of more than three hours' duration is counted as a separate, full day worked. If the employee resigns or is dismissed, he or she must be paid for vacation accumulated pro rata; however, the latter is lost if the dismissal is for *falta grave*.

VI. Social Insurance:

All workers are covered by government social security, which provides both a retirement pension (in addition to any provided by the employer) and medical care before and after retirement. Contributions to the system are made only by employers. Employers must also provide each empleado who has put in four years of uninterrupted service with a paid-up life insurance policy whose face amount is equal to one-third of the total salary actually earned in the preceding four years. This policy continues in force and is supplemented by additional policies of a like kind for every four-year block of service time.

VII. Special Provisions for Youth and Women:

(a) The regular minimum age for industrial labor is fifteen, but those under eighteen may be employed only if they pass a physical examination. If the job is classified as one entailing exceptional health risks, physical examinations must be repeated annually by all workers under twenty-one years. Workers younger than eighteen years can work no more than eight hours per day and forty-five hours per week; they may not work on Sundays or holidays and must receive at least a two-hour lunch break. Workers under twenty-one years may not work night shifts. Women are subjected to the same restrictions as are workers under eighteen years of age; their restrictions may be relaxed by the labor ministry if industry conditions require, but this may be done for no more than sixty days in any calendar year (the provision is intended to accommodate seasonal or exceptional conditions).

(b) Mothers' benefits: Pregnant empleados are entitled to forty-two days of unpaid leave prior to the scheduled delivery date and forty-two days of postpartum leave (they are compensated during this time by the social security system). Pregnant obreros receive thirty-six days of pre- and postpartum leave under similar conditions. If the employer has more than twenty-three female workers over eighteen years of age, he must establish and maintain day-care facilities adequate to accommodate all of their infants who are less than one year old; several employers may, if they wish, pool their resources and set up a single day-care facility to service all of their employees, so long as the facility is physically convenient to all of them. Mothers of infants not yet weaned receive a daily nursing leave of one hour with pay, plus free round-trip transportation to the day-care facility (time in transit is in addition to leave time).

VIII. The Workers' Community System—Profit Sharing and Comanagement:[1]

(a) Capital participation: Each firm annually sets aside 6 percent of pretax profits for distribution to workers in the form of capital shares. Of this amount, 20 percent is issued by the firm to its own Workers' Community, which holds the shares in common. The remaining 80 percent is issued to the Mining Compensation Community (COCOMI), which aggregates all such shares received by it and emits participation certificates in amounts equal to that total. These are signed over to each Workers' Community in proportion to the total number of man-days worked in that firm during

---

[1] The following describes the operation of the system as provided for by the 1971 Mining Code and does not consider the effect of post-1978 changes. The latter are outlined in Table B.2, items 33 and 34.

the previous year.[2] Parastatal enterprises issue bonds or COFIDE capital shares rather than shares of their own capital stock.

(b) Cash participation: Each firm annually sets aside 4 percent of pretax profits for distribution to workers in cash. As above, 20 percent goes directly to the firm's Workers' Community and 80 percent is redistributed via COCOMI in proportion to man-days worked. The cash that flows into the Workers' Community by these routes is then distributed among its members: half in equal shares and half in proportion to base wage or salary.

(c) Comanagement: The Workers' Community elects at least one member of the firm's board of directors. (If the board is enlarged after the establishment of the comanagement system, workers are entitled to an additional number of directors as needed to prevent any dilution of their representation.) As the Workers' Community accumulates more of the firm's capital shares via profit distributions, it may elect a number of directors sufficient to give it board representation at least proportional to its share of the firm's total capitalization. Further workers' capital accumulation ceases once the Workers' Community has attained 50 percent ownership and the right to select half of the firm's directors.[3] The board chairman is to be chosen by majority vote of all directors, or by lot in the event of a tie. Worker-directors enjoy the same rights and privileges as regular directors, including the rights to vote on all directorial business and to inspect the firm's books and records.

[2] This provision is a powerful deterrent to strikes, and especially to sectional stoppages planned to paralyze the firm without calling out all of the workers.

[3] The law leaves uncertain how capital participation is to proceed after 50 percent worker ownership has been achieved. It is also uncertain whether, after that time, worker comanagement and share ownership rights are to be exercised collectively by the Workers' Community or individually.

Bibliography

Abusada-Salah, Roberto
   1978   Industrialization Policies in Peru, 1970-1976. Technical Papers Se-
          ries, no. 16. Austin, Texas: Office for Public Sector Studies, In-
          stitute for Latin American Studies, University of Texas at Austin.

Adamson, Walter L.
   1980   *Hegemony and Revolution: Antonio Gramsci's Political and Cul-
          tural Theory*. Berkeley and Los Angeles: University of California
          Press.

Adelman, Irma, and Morris, Cynthia Taft
   1978   Growth and Impoverishment in the Middle of the Nineteenth Cen-
          tury. *World Development* 6 (March):245-73.

Adizes, Ichak
   1975a Autogestión y naciones en desarrollo. *Apuntes* 2, no. 4:115-29.
   1975b On Self-Management: An Organizational Development, a Typology
          of Various Experiments in the World and a Discussion of the Role
          of Professional Management. In *Self-Management: New Dimensions
          to Democracy*, edited by Ichak Adizes and Elisabeth Mann Borghese,
          pp. 3-37. Studies in Comparative Politics, no. 7. Santa Barbara,
          Calif.: American Bibliographical Center-Clio Press.

Ahluwalia, Montek S.
   1976   Inequality, Poverty and Development. *Journal of Development Eco-
          nomics* 3 (December):307-42.

Alberti, Giorgio; Santistevan, Jorge; and Pásara, Luis
   1977   *Estado y clase: la Comunidad Industrial en el Perú*. Lima: Instituto
          de Estudios Peruanos.

Alexander, Robert J.
   1958   *The Bolivian National Revolution*. New Brunswick, N.J.: Rutgers
          University Press.

American Bureau of Metal Statistics
   1978   *Non-Ferrous Metal Data 1977*. New York: ABMS.

Amin, Samir
   1974   *Accumulation on a World Scale: A Critique of the Theory of Un-
          derdevelopment*. Translated by Brian Pearce. New York: Monthly
          Review Press.
   1976   *Unequal Development: An Essay on the Social Formations of Pe-
          ripheral Capitalism*. Translated by Brian Pearce. New York: Monthly
          Review Press.
   1980a The Class Structure of the Contemporary Imperialist System. *Monthly
          Review* 31 (January):9-26.

1980b *Class and Nation, Historically and in the Current Crisis*. Translated by Susan Kaplow. New York: Monthly Review Press.

Andrade, Víctor
1976 *My Missions for Revolutionary Bolivia, 1944-1962*. Pittsburgh: University of Pittsburgh Press.

Aparicio Valdez, Luis; Vásquez, Arturo; and Alcántara, Elsa
1975 Ideología y posición política de las confederaciones de trabajadores. Serie: Documentos de Trabajo, no. 2. Lima: Centro de Investigación, Universidad del Pacífico.

Arrow, Kenneth
1962 The Economic Implications of Learning by Doing. *Review of Economic Studies* 29 (June):155-73.

Astiz, Carlos A.
1969 *Pressure Groups and Power Elites in Peruvian Politics*. Ithaca, N.Y.: Cornell University Press.

————, and García, José Z.
1972 The Peruvian Military: Achievement Orientation, Training, and Political Tendencies. *Western Political Quarterly* 25 (December):667-85.

Avineri, Shlomo
1968 *The Social and Political Thought of Karl Marx*. Cambridge: Cambridge University Press.

Bain, James S.
1956 *Barriers to New Competition: Their Character and Consequences*. Cambridge: Harvard University Press.

Balbi, Carmen Rosa, and Parodi, Jorge
1981 Los Límites de la izquierda: el caso sindical. *La Revista*, no. 5 (July):3-9.

Ballantyne, Janet Campbell
1976 The Political Economy of Peruvian Gran Minería. Ph.D. dissertation, Cornell University.

Ballón Vera, David
1974 Política minera del Perú. Paper presented at the Eighth World Mining Congress, Lima, 3-8 November.

Bamat, Thomas
1977 Relative State Autonomy and Capitalism in Brazil and Peru. *The Insurgent Sociologist* 7 (Spring):74-84.
1978 From Plan Inca to Plan Tupac Amaru: The Recomposition of the

Peruvian Power Bloc, 1968-1977. Ph.D. dissertation, Rutgers University.

Banks, Ferdinand C.
1974 *The World Copper Market: An Economic Analysis.* Cambridge, Mass.: Ballinger Publishing Co.

Baran, Paul A.
1957 *The Political Economy of Growth.* New York: Monthly Review Press.

Barnet, Richard J., and Müller, Ronald E.
1974 *Global Reach: The Power of the Multinational Corporations.* New York: Simon & Schuster.

Basadre, Jorge
1961-1968 *Historia de la República del Perú.* 11 vols. 5th ed. Lima: Ediciones "Historia."

Becker, David G.
1982 "Bonanza Development" and the "New Bourgeoisie": Peru under Military Rule. *Comparative Political Studies* 15 (October):243-88.

Behrman, Jack N.
1971 Taxation of Extractive Industries in Latin America and the Impact on Foreign Investors. In Raymond F. Mikesell et al., *Foreign Investment in the Petroleum and Mineral Industries: Case Studies of Investor-Host Country Relations*, pp. 56-80. Baltimore: Johns Hopkins University Press.

Béjar, Héctor
1969 *Perú 1965: apuntes sobre una experiencia guerrillera.* Havana: Casa de las Américas.
1976 *La Revolución en la trampa.* Lima: Ediciones Socialismo y Participación.

Berle, Adolph A., Jr.
1954 *The Twentieth Century Capitalist Revolution.* New York: Harcourt, Brace.
1959 *Power Without Property: A New Development in American Political Economy.* New York: Harcourt, Brace.

————, and Means, Gardiner C.
1932 *The Modern Corporation and Private Property.* New York: Macmillan Co.

Bernales, Enrique
1980 *Crisis política: ¿solución electoral?* Lima: DESCO.

Berry, Nicholas O.
  1973 The Management of Foreign Penetration. *Orbis* 17 (Summer):598-619.

Bhagwati, Jagdish N., ed.
  1972 *Economics and World Order from the 1970s to the 1990s.* New York: Macmillan Co.

Biersteker, Thomas J.
  1978 *Distortion or Development? Contending Perspectives on the Multinational Corporation.* Cambridge: The MIT Press.

Blanco, Hugo
  1972 *Land or Death: The Peasant Struggle in Peru.* New York: Pathfinder Press.

Block, Fred
  1980 Beyond Relative Autonomy: State Managers as Historical Subjects. In *The Socialist Register 1980*, edited by Ralph Miliband and John Saville, pp. 227-42. London: The Merlin Press.

Bodenheimer, Susanne J.
  1971 *The Ideology of Developmentalism: The American Paradigm-Surrogate for Latin American Studies.* Sage Professional Papers in Comparative Politics, vol. 2. Beverly Hills, Calif.: Sage Publications.

Bonilla, F.
  1974 *Moderna legislación minera del Perú.* Lima: Editorial Mercurio.

Bonilla, Heraclio
  1974a *Guano y burguesía en el Perú.* Lima: Instituto de Estudios Peruanos.
  1974b *El Minero de los Andes: una aproximación a su estudio.* Lima: Instituto de Estudios Peruanos.
  1977 La Emergencia del control norteamericano sobre la economía peruana (1850-1930). *Desarrollo Económico* 16 (January-March):581-600.

Bossio Rotundo, Juan Carlos
  1976 Cambios en la política minero-metalúrgica. In *Cambios estructurales en el Perú*, edited by Ernst-J. Kerbusch, pp. 121-44. Lima: Instituto Latinoamericano de Investigaciones Sociales.

Bosson, Rex, and Varon, Benison
  1977 *The Mining Industry and the Developing Countries.* New York: Oxford University Press.

Bourque, Susan C., and Palmer, David Scott
  1975 Transforming the Rural Sector: Government Policy and Peasant Response. In Lowenthal 1975, pp. 197-219.

Bourricaud, François
  1964   Lima en la vida política peruana. *América Latina* (Rio de Janeiro)
         7 (October-December):89-95.
  1966   Structure and Function of the Peruvian Oligarchy. *Studies in Com-
         parative International Development* 2, no. 2:17-31.
  1967   *Poder y sociedad en el Perú contemporáneo.* Buenos Aires: Edi-
         torial Sur.
  1970   *Power and Society in Contemporary Peru.* Translated by Paul Ste-
         venson. New York: Praeger Publishers.

————, and Simão, Azis
  1965   *El Sindicalismo en Latinoamérica.* Barcelona: Editorial Nova Terra.

Brenner, Robert
  1977   The Origins of Capitalist Development: A Critique of Neo-Smithian
         Marxism. *New Left Review*, no. 104 (July-August):25-92.

Bridges, Amy Beth
  1974   Nicos Poulantzas and the Marxist Theory of the State. *Politics and
         Society* 4 (Winter):161-90.

Brown, Martin S., and Butler, John
  1968   *The Production, Marketing, and Consumption of Copper and Alu-
         minum.* New York: Praeger Publishers.

Brundenius, Claes
  1972   The Anatomy of Imperialism: The Case of Multinational Mining
         Corporations in Peru. *Journal of Peace Research* 9, no. 3:189-206.
  1976   Remuneraciones y redistribución de ingresos. Mimeographed. Lima:
         Instituto Nacional de Planificación.

Burgess, Eugene W., and Harbison, Frederick H.
  1954   *Casa Grace in Peru.* Washington, D.C.: National Planning Asso-
         ciation.

Burneo, José; Ciudad, Adolfo; and Pásara, Luis
  1976   *Empleo y estabilidad laboral.* Lima: DESCO.

Cabieses Cubas, Hugo
  1976   *Comunidad Laboral y capitalismo: alcances y límites.* Lima: DESCO.

————, and Otero, Carlos
  1977   *Economía peruana: un ensayo de interpretación.* Lima: DESCO.

Calderón Cockburn, Julio; Filomeno, Alfredo; and Pease García, Henry
  1975   *Perú 1968-1974: Cronología política.* Vol. III. Lima: DESCO.

Callaghy, Thomas M.
  1979   The Difficulties of Implementing Socialist Strategies of Develop-
         ment in Africa: The "First Wave." In *Socialism in Sub-Saharan*

Africa: A New Assessment, edited by Carl G. Rosberg and Thomas M. Callaghy, pp. 112-29. Research Series, no. 38. Berkeley: Institute of International Studies, University of California, Berkeley.

Cameron, Eugene N., ed.
1973 *The Mineral Position of the United States, 1975-2000*. Madison, Wis.: University of Wisconsin Press.

Caporaso, James A.
1978 Dependence, Dependency, and Power in the Global System: A Structural and Behavioral Analysis. *International Organization* 32 (Winter):13-43.

———, and Zare, Behrouz
1981 An Interpretation and Evaluation of Dependency Theory. In *From Dependency to Development: Strategies to Overcome Underdevelopment and Inequality*, edited by Heraldo Muñoz, pp. 43-56. Boulder, Colo.: Westview Press.

Caravedo, Baltazar
1971 Nacimiento e impacto de la industria minera en el Perú. *Documentos*, no. 1 (November):43-54.

Cardoso, Fernando Henrique
1967 The Industrial Elite. In Lipset and Solari 1967, pp. 94-114.
1972 Dependency and Development in Latin America. *New Left Review*, no. 74 (July-August):83-95.
1973 Associated-Dependent Development: Theoretical and Practical Implications. In *Authoritarian Brazil: Origins, Policies, and Future*, edited by Alfred Stepan, pp. 142-76. New Haven: Yale University Press.
1976 *Ideologías de la burguesía industrial en sociedades dependientes (Argentina y Brasil)*. Mexico, D.F.: Siglo Veintiuno Editores.
1977 The Consumption of Dependency Theory in the United States. *Latin American Research Review* 12, no. 3:7-24.

———, and Faletto, Enzo
1979 *Dependency and Development in Latin America*. Translated by Marjory Mattingly Urquidi. Berkeley and Los Angeles: University of California Press.

Castells, Manuel
1977 Class, State and Dependency in Latin America: Some Theoretical Guidelines. Paper presented at the Plenary Session of the Joint Meeting of the African Studies Association and the Latin American Studies Association, Houston, 11 November.

Centromin
  1981   Gestión de Centromin Perú, 1974-1981. Mimeographed. Lima: Em-
          presa Minera del Centro del Perú.

Chaliand Gérard
  1978   *Revolution in the Third World*. Translated by Diana Johnstone. New
          York: Penguin Books.

Chaplin, David
  1967   *The Peruvian Industrial Labor Force*. Princeton: Princeton Uni-
          versity Press.
  1967-68 Industrialization and the Distribution of Wealth in Peru. *Studies
          in Comparative International Development* 3, no. 3:55-66.
  1976   ed. *Peruvian Nationalism: A Corporatist Revolution*. New Bruns-
          wick, N.J.: Transaction Books.

Charles River Associates
  1969   Economic Analysis of the Copper Industry. Mimeographed. Wash-
          ington, D.C.: Property Management and Disposal Service, General
          Services Administration.

Chilcote, Ronald H.
  1974   Dependency: A Critical Synthesis of the Literature. *Latin American
          Perspectives* 1, no. 1 (Spring):4-29.

Chungara, Domitila Barrios de
  1979   *Let Me Speak! Testimony of Domitila, a Woman of the Bolivian
          Mines*. With Moema Viezzer. New York: Monthly Review Press.

Church, Phillip E.
  1971   Labor Relations in Mineral and Petroleum Resource Development.
          In Raymond F. Mikesell et al., *Foreign Investment in the Petroleum
          and Mineral Industries: Case Studies of Investor-Host Country Re-
          lations*, pp. 81-98. Baltimore: Johns Hopkins University Press.

Cleaves, Peter S., and Scurrah, Martin J.
  1976   State-Society Relations and Bureaucratic Behavior in Peru. SICA
          Occasional Papers, no. 6. Hayward, Calif.: Section on International
          and Comparative Administration, American Society for Public
          Administration.

Collier, David
  1976   *Squatters and Oligarchs: Authoritarian Rule and Policy Change in
          Peru*. Baltimore: Johns Hopkins University Press.
  1979   ed. *The New Authoritarianism in Latin America*. Princeton: Prince-
          ton University Press.

Comisión Bicameral Multipartidaria
   1967   Dictamen de la Comisión Multipartidaria encargada de revisar el
          Convenio entre el Gobierno del Perú y la Southern Peru Copper
          Corporation, para la explotación de las minas de Toquepala y Que-
          llaveco y su ampliación para la Cuajone. Mimeographed. Lima:
          Congreso Nacional.

Comte de Saint-Simon, Henri
   1952   *Selected Writings*. Translated and edited by F.M.H. Markham. New
          York: Macmillan Co.

Consejo Nacional de Investigación (CONACI)
   1974   Recursos humanos científicos y tecnológicos: sector productivo.
          Mimeographed. Lima: CONACI.

Corradi, Juan Eugenio
   1977   Cultural Dependence and the Sociology of Knowledge: The Latin
          American Case. In *Ideology and Social Change in Latin America*,
          edited by June Nash, Juan Corradi, and Hobart Spalding, Jr., pp.
          7-30. New York: Gordon and Breach Science Publishers.

Cotler, Julio
   1967-68   The Mechanics of Internal Domination and Social Change in
          Peru. *Studies in Comparative International Development* 3, no.
          12:229-46.
   1969   El Populismo militar como modelo de desarrollo nacional: el caso
          peruano. Serie: Estudios políticos, no. 1. Lima: Instituto de Estudios
          Peruanos.
   1970   Crisis política y populismo militar en el Perú. *Revista Mexicana de
          Sociología* 32 (May-June):737-84.
   1975   The New Mode of Political Domination in Peru. In Lowenthal 1975,
          pp. 44-78.
   1978   *Clases, estado y nación en el Perú*. Lima: Instituto de Estudios
          Peruanos.
   1979   State and Regime: Comparative Notes on the Southern Cone and
          the "Enclave" Societies. In Collier 1979, pp. 255-82.

Del Prado, Jorge
   1969   *Perú hoy*. Lima: Comisión Nacional de Propaganda, Partido Co-
          munista Peruano.

Denitch, Bogdan
   1979   Legitimacy and the Social Order. In *Legitimation of Regimes: In-
          ternational Frameworks for Analysis*, edited by Bogdan Denitch,
          pp. 5-22. Sage Studies in International Sociology, no. 17. Beverly
          Hills, Calif.: Sage Publications.

DeWind, Adrian W., Jr.
1977   Peasants Become Miners: The Evolution of Industrial Mining Systems in Peru. Ph.D. dissertation, Columbia University.

Dietz, Henry A.
1969   Urban Squatter Settlements in Peru: A Case History and Analysis. *Journal of Inter-American Studies and World Affairs* 11 (July):353-70.

Dirección de Planificación Universitaria
1971   *Profesiones que ofrece la Universidad peruana.* Lima: CONUP, Ministerio de Educación.

Dirección General de Empleo
1973   *Las Huelgas en el Perú, 1957-1972.* Lima: Ministerio de Trabajo.

Dirección General de Minería
1970   Evaluación de recursos humanos para la minería, 1970. Mimeographed. Lima: Ministerio de Energía y Minas.
1975   Estudio de la productividad en la industria minera peruana. Mimeographed. Lima: Ministerio de Energía y Minas.
1976   *Anuario minero 1973.* Lima: Ministerio de Energía y Minas.
1977   *Anuario minero 1975.* Lima: Ministerio de Energía y Minas.

DiTella, Torcuato S.
1965   Populism and Reform in Latin America. In *Obstacles to Change in Latin America*, edited by Claudio Véliz, pp. 47-74. London: Oxford University Press.
1981   Working-Class Organization and Politics in Argentina. *Latin American Research Review* 16, no. 2:33-56.

Dodd, Thomas J.
1975   Peru. In Harold Eugene Davis, Larman C. Wilson, et. al., *Latin American Foreign Policies: An Analysis*, pp. 360-80. Baltimore: Johns Hopkins University Press.

Dore, Elizabeth
1977   Crisis and Accumulation in the Peruvian Mining Industry, 1968-1974. *Latin American Perspectives* 4, no. 3 (Summer):77-102.

Dos Santos, Theotonio
1970   The Structure of Dependence. *American Economic Review* 60 (May):231-36.
1977   Socialism and Fascism in Latin America Today. *The Insurgent Sociologist* 7 (Fall):15-23.

Drucker, Peter F.
1968 *The Age of Discontinuity: Guidelines for Our Changing Society.*
New York: Harper & Row.

Dunning, John H., ed.
1971 *The Multinational Enterprise.* London: George Allen & Unwin.

Durand, Francisco
1981 "Empresarios y política: ser o no ser." *Debate,* no. 9:47-48.

Eckstein, Susan
1977 *The Poverty of Revolution: The State and the Urban Poor in Mexico.*
Princeton: Princeton University Press.

Economic Commission for Latin America (ECLA)
1978 *Economic Survey of Latin America 1977.* Santiago, Chile: United
Nations.

Einaudi, Luigi R.
1969 The Peruvian Military: A Summary Political Analysis. Mimeographed. Santa Monica, Calif.: RAND Corporation.
1970 Peruvian Military Relations with the United States. Mimeographed.
Santa Monica, Calif.: RAND Corporation.
1976 Revolution from Within? Military Rule in Peru since 1968. In Chaplin 1976, pp. 401-27.

————, and Stepan, Alfred C., III
1971 Latin American Institutional Development: Changing Military Perspectives in Peru and Brazil. Mimeographed. Santa Monica, Calif.:
RAND Corporation.

Elliot, William Y., et al.
1937 *International Control in the Non-Ferrous Metals.* New York: Macmillan Co.

Ely, Northcutt
1961 *Summary of Mining and Petroleum Laws of the World.* Washington,
D.C.: U.S. Bureau of Mines.

Empresa Petrolera del Perú (PetroPeru)
1969 *El Petroleo en el Perú: historia de un caso singular para que el
mundo lo juzgue.* Lima: Departamento de Relaciones Públicas,
PetroPeru.

Erickson, Kenneth Paul
1977 *The Brazilian Corporative State and Working-Class Politics.* Berkeley and Los Angeles: University of California Press.

Espinoza Uriarte, Henrique
  1970 Concentración del poder económico en el sector minero. Mimeographed. Lima: Universidad Nacional Federico Villarreal.

———, and Osorio, Jorge
  1971 Dependencia y poder económico: caso minería y pesquería. In Henrique Espinoza Uriarte et al., *Dependencia económica y tecnológica: caso peruano*, pp. 69-230. Lima: Centro de Investigaciones Económicas y Sociales, Universidad Nacional Federico Villarreal.

Evans, Peter
  1971 National Autonomy and Economic Development: Critical Perspectives on Multinational Corporations in Poor Countries. In *Transnational Relations in World Politics*, edited by Robert O. Keohane and Joseph S. Nye, Jr., pp. 325-42. Cambridge: Harvard University Press.
  1979 *Dependent Development: The Alliance of Multinational, State, and Local Capital in Brazil*. Princeton: Princeton University Press.

Fagen, Richard R.
  1977 Studying Latin American Politics: Some Implications of a Dependency Approach. *Latin American Research Review* 12, no. 2:3-26.

Fanon, Frantz
  1963 *The Wretched of the Earth*. Translated by Constance Farrington. New York: Grove Press.

Femia, Joseph V.
  1979 The Gramsci Phenomenon: Some Reflections. *Political Studies* 27 (September):472-83.

Fernández Maldonado Solari, Jorge
  1975 *Plan de Energía y Minas para el bienio 1975-1976*. Lima: Oficina de Relaciones Públicas, Ministerio de Energía y Minas.

Figueroa Arévalo, Adolfo
  1972 Income Distribution, Employment, and Development: The Case of Peru. Ph.D. dissertation, Vanderbilt University.
  1973 El Impacto de las reformas actuales sobre la distribución de ingresos en el Perú. *Revista Interamericana de Planificación* 50 (June):45-63.

Fisher, John
  1977 *Minas y mineros en el Perú colonial*. Lima: Instituto de Estudios Peruanos.

FitzGerald, E.V.K.
  1976   *The State and Economic Development: Peru since 1968*. Cambridge: Cambridge University Press.
  1979   *The Political Economy of Peru 1956-78: Economic Development and the Restructuring of Capital*. Cambridge: Cambridge University Press.

Flores Galindo, Alberto
  1974   *Los Mineros de la Cerro de Pasco, 1900-1930 (un intento de caracterización social)*. Lima: Departamento Académico de Ciencias Sociales, Pontífica Universidad Católica del Perú.

Flórez Pinedo, Guillermo
  1981   Actividad empresarial del Estado. Mimeographed. Lima: Empresa Minera del Centro del Perú.

Form, William H., and Blum, Albert A.
  1965   *Industrial Relations and Social Change in Latin America*. Gainesville, Fla.: University of Florida Press.

Frank, Andre Gunder
  1966   The Development of Underdevelopment. *Monthly Review* 18 (September):17-31.
  1969   *Capitalism and Underdevelopment in Latin America: Historical Studies of Chile and Brazil*. Rev. ed. New York: Monthly Review Press.
  1973   *Lumpenbourgeoisie: Lumpendevelopment: Dependence, Class, and Politics in Latin America*. New York: Monthly Review Press.

Frankman, Myron J.
  1974   Sectoral Policy Preferences of the Peruvian Government, 1946-1968. *Journal of Latin American Studies* 6, no. 2:289-300.

Frontaura Argadoña, Manuel
  1974   *La Revolución nacional*. La Paz: Editorial "Los Amigos del Libro."

Furtado, Celso
  1970   *Economic Development of Latin America: A Survey from Colonial Times to the Cuban Revolution*. Translated by Suzette Macedo. Cambridge Latin American Studies, no. 8. Cambridge: Cambridge University Press.

Galbraith, John Kenneth
  1967   *The New Industrial State*. Boston: Houghton Mifflin Co.

Gall, Norman
  1971   The Master is Dead. *Dissent* 18 (June):281-320.

García de Romana, Alberto
  1975   Comportamiento gremial y político de los empresarios industriales,

1968-73. Mimeographed. Lima: Taller de Estudios Urbano-Industriales, Pontífica Universidad Católica del Perú.

García Sayán, Diego
1977 *El Caso Marcona: análisis histórico-jurídico de los contratos.* Lima: DESCO.

Gerschenkron, Alexander
1962 *Economic Backwardness in Historical Perspective.* Cambridge: Harvard University Press, Belknap Press.

Giddens, Anthony
1973 *The Class Structure of the Advanced Societies.* London: Hutchinson & Co.

Gilbert, Dennis
1980 The End of the Peruvian Revolution: A Class Analysis. *Studies in Comparative International Development* 15 (Spring):15-38.

Gillis, Malcolm
1980 The Role of State Enterprises in Economic Development. *Social Research* 47 (Summer):248-89.

Gilpin, Robert
1975 *U.S. Power and the Multinational Corporation: The Political Economy of Foreign Direct Investment.* New York: Basic Books.

Girvan, Norman
1970 Multinational Corporations and Dependent Underdevelopment in Mineral-Exporting Economies. *Social and Economic Studies* 19 (December):490-526.

Gluschke, Wolfgang; Shaw, Joseph; and Varon, Benison
1979 *Copper: The Next Fifteen Years.* Dordrecht, the Netherlands: United Nations, D. Reidel Publishing Co.

Gobierno Revolucionario de la Fuerza Armada
1975 *Manifiesto, estatuto y Plan Inca del Gobierno Revolucionario de la Fuerza Armada.* Lima: Editorial "Inkari."

Gold, David A.; Lo, Clarence Y. H.; and Wright, Erik Olin
1975 Recent Developments in Marxist Theories of the Capitalist State. *Monthly Review* 27 (October):29-43; and (November):36-51.

Goldrich, Daniel; Pratt, Raymond B.; and Schuller, C. R.
1970 The Political Integration of Lower-Class Urban Settlements in Chile and Peru. In Horowitz 1970, pp. 175-214.

Gomez, Rudolph
    1969   *The Peruvian Administrative System*. Boulder, Colo.: Bureau of
            Governmental Research and Service, University of Colorado.

González Vigil, Fernando, and Parodi Zevallos, Carlos
    1975   Los Grupos financieros internacionales y el sistema financiera na-
            cional: los casos de los proyectos mineros y siderúrgicos en el Perú.
            Serie: Trabajos de Investigación, no. 3. Lima: Centro de Investi-
            gación, Universidad del Pacífico.

Goodsell, Charles T.
    1974   *American Corporations and Peruvian Politics*. Cambridge: Harvard
            University Press.

Gorman, Stephen M.
    1978   Peru Before the Elections for the Constituent Assembly: Ten Years
            of Military Rule and the Quest for Social Justice. *Government and
            Opposition* 13 (Summer):288-306.

Gouldner, Alvin W.
    1979   *The Future of Intellectuals and the Rise of the New Class*. New
            York: Seabury Press.

Goulet, Denis
    1977   *The Uncertain Promise: Value Conflicts in Technology Transfer*.
            New York: IDOC/North America.

Gramsci, Antonio
    1971   *Selections from the Prison Notebooks*. Translated and edited by
            Quintin Hoare and Geoffrey Nowell Smith. New York: International
            Publishers.
    1973   *Letters from Prison*. Translated and edited by Lynne Lawner. New
            York: Harper & Row.

Graziano, Luigi
    1980   The Historic Compromise and Consociational Democracy: Toward
            a "New Democracy"? *International Political Science Review* 1,
            no. 3:345-68.

Greenhill, Robert, and Miller, Rory
    1973   The Peruvian Government and the Nitrate Trade, 1873-1879. *Jour-
            nal of Latin American Studies* 5, no. 1:107-31.

Grunwald, Joseph
    1976   Latin American Resources in the World Economy: Copper and Iron
            Ore. In *Latin America's New Internationalism: The End of Hemi-
            spheric Isolation*, edited by Roger W. Fontaine and James D. The-
            berge, pp. 219-41. New York: Praeger Publishers.

Habermas, Jürgen
  1973 *Legitimation Crisis*. Translated by Thomas McCarthy. Boston: Beacon Press.

Hamilton, Stanley Kerry
  1967 Factors Influencing Investment and Production in the Peruvian Mining Industry, 1940-1965. Ph.D. dissertation, University of Wisconsin.

Handelman, Howard
  1975 *Struggle in the Andes: Peasant Political Mobilization in Peru*. Austin, Texas: University of Texas Press.

Harding, Colin
  1975 Land Reform and Social Conflict in Peru. In Lowenthal 1975, pp. 220-53.

Haya de la Torre, Víctor Raúl
  1936 *El Antimperialismo y el Apra*. 2d ed. Santiago, Chile: Ediciones Ercilla.
  1956 *Treinta años del Aprismo*. Mexico, D.F.: Fondo de Cultura Económica.

Henfrey, Colin
  1981 Dependency, Modes of Production, and the Class Analysis of Latin America. *Latin American Perspectives* 8 (Spring and Fall):17-54.

Herfindahl, Orris C.
  1960 *Copper Costs and Prices: 1870-1957*. Baltimore: Johns Hopkins University Press.

Hilliker, Grant
  1971 *The Politics of Reform in Peru: The Aprista and Other Mass Parties of Latin America*. Baltimore: Johns Hopkins University Press.

Hirschman, Albert O.
  1958 *The Strategy of Economic Development*. New Haven: Yale University Press.
  1971 *A Bias for Hope: Essays on Development in Latin America*. New Haven: Yale University Press.

Hobsbawm, Eric J.
  1959 *Primitive Rebels: Studies in Archaic Forms of Social Movement in the Nineteenth and Twentieth Centuries*. New York: W. W. Norton & Co.
  1967 Peasants and Rural Migrants in Politics. In *The Politics of Conformity in Latin America*, edited by Claudio Véliz, pp. 43-65. Oxford: Oxford University Press.

1971   Peru: The Peculiar Revolution. *New York Review of Books*, 16 December, p. 28.

Hobson, J. A.
1938   *Imperialism: A Study*. Rev. ed. London: George Allen & Unwin.

Hopkins, Jack W.
1967   *The Government Executive of Modern Peru*. Latin American Monographs, 2d ser., no. 3. Gainesville, Fla.: Center for Latin American Studies, University of Florida.

Horowitz, Irving Louis, ed.
1970   *Masses in Latin America*. New York: Oxford University Press.

————, and Trimberger, Ellen Kay
1976   State Power and Military Nationalism in Latin America. *Comparative Politics* 8 (January):223-44.

Hoyt, Edwin P., Jr.
1967   *The Guggenheims and the American Dream*. New York: Funk & Wagnalls.

Hunt, Shane
1973   Growth and Guano in the Nineteenth Century in Peru. Mimeographed. Princeton: Woodrow Wilson School of Public and International Affairs, Princeton University.
1974   Direct Foreign Investment in Peru: New Rules for an Old Game. Mimeographed. Princeton: Woodrow Wilson School of Public and International Affairs, Princeton University.

Huntington, Samuel P.
1968   *Political Order in Changing Societies*. New Haven: Yale University Press.
1973   Transnational Organizations in World Politics. *World Politics* 25 (April):333-68.

Hymer, Stephen Herbert
1972   The Multinational Corporation and the Law of Uneven Development. In Bhagwati 1972, pp. 113-40; also, pp. 54-74 in Hymer 1979.
1979   *The Multinational Corporation: A Radical Approach*. Edited by Robert B. Cohen, Nadine Felton, Jaap van Liere, and Morley Nkosi. Cambridge: Cambridge University Press.

Instituto Nacional de Planificación (INP)
1966   Diagnóstico del sector industrial. Mimeographed. Lima: INP.
1967   *Plan nacional de desarrollo económico y social, 1967-70*. 4 vols. Lima: INP.

1970   *Plan del Perú, 1971-1975.* 5 vols. Lima: INP.

1975a Evaluación del presupuesto de inversión del sector público nacional, bienio 1973-74. Mimeographed. Lima: INP.

1975b *Plan bienal de desarrollo 1975-1976.* 4 vols. Lima: INP.

1975c *Plan nacional de desarrollo, 1975-1978.* Lima: INP.

1977a *Plan nacional de desarrollo para 1977 y 1978.* 2 vols. Lima: INP.

1977b *Tabla de indicadores sociales.* Lima: INP.

International Labour Organisation (ILO)

1980   *Yearbook of Labour Statistics 1980.* Geneva: ILO.

Jacoby, Neal

1970   The Multinational Corporation. *Center Magazine* 3 (May-June):37-55.

Jalée, Pierre

1968   *The Pillage of the Third World.* Translated by Mary Klopper. New York: Monthly Review Press.

Jaquette, Jane S.

1971   The Politics of Development in Peru. Ph.D. dissertation, Cornell University.

1972   Revolution by Fiat: The Context of Policy-Making in Peru. *Western Political Quarterly* 25 (December):648-66.

Jelin, Elizabeth

1974   The Concept of Working-Class Embourgeoisement. *Studies in Comparative International Development* 9 (Spring):1-19.

Jessop, Bob

1978   Capitalism and Democracy: The Best Possible Political Shell? In *Power and the State*, edited by Gary Littlejohn, Barry Smart, John Wakeford, and Nina Yuval-Davis, pp. 10-51. New York: St. Martin's Press.

Jiménez, Luis F.

1974   Propiedad social: el debate. Mimeographed. Lima: DESCO.

Johnson, Terry

1977   What Is to Be Known? The Structural Determination of Social Class. Review Article. *Economy and Society* 6 (May):194-233.

Kahl, Joseph A.

1976   *Modernization, Exploitation, and Dependency in Latin America: Germani, Gonzalez Casanova, and Cardoso.* New Brunswick, N.J.: Transaction Books.

Kantor, Harry
1966   *The Ideology and Program of the Peruvian Aprista Movement.*
       Washington, D.C.: Savile Books.

Kapsoli E., Wilfredo
1975   *Los Movimientos campesinos en Cerro de Pasco, 1800-1963.* Huan-
       cayo: Instituto de Estudios Andinos.

Kindleberger, Charles P., ed.
1970   *The International Corporation.* Cambridge: The MIT Press.

Kissin, S. F.
1972   *Communists: All Revisionists Now?* Fabian Research Series, no.
       299. London: Fabian Society.

Klarén, Peter F.
1973   *Modernization, Dislocation, and Aprismo: Origins of the Peruvian
       Aprista Party, 1870-1932.* Austin, Texas: University of Texas Press.

Klitgaard, Robert E.
1971   Observations on the Peruvian National Plan for Development, 1971-
       1975. *Inter-American Economic Affairs* 25 (Winter):3-22.

Knight, Peter T.
1975   New Forms of Economic Organization in Peru: Toward Workers'
       Self-Management. In Lowenthal 1975, pp. 350-401.

Kolakowski, Leszek
1978   *Main Currents of Marxism.* 3 vols. Translated by P. S. Falla. Ox-
       ford: Oxford University Press.

Krasner, Stephen D.
1978   *Defending the National Interest: Raw Materials Investments and
       U.S. Foreign Policy.* Princeton: Princeton University Press.

Kruijt, Dirk, and Vellinga, Menno
1979   *Labor Relations and Multinational Corporations: The Cerro de
       Pasco Corporation in Peru (1902-1974).* Assen, the Netherlands:
       Van Gorcum & Co.

Kuczynski, Pedro-Pablo
1981   The Peruvian External Debt: Problem and Prospect. *Journal of
       Interamerican Studies and World Affairs* 23 (February):3-27.

Labys, Walter C.
1980   *Market Structure, Bargaining Power, and Resource Price For-
       mation.* Lexington, Mass.: D. C. Heath and Co., Lexington Books.

Laclau, Ernesto
1971   Feudalism and Capitalism in Latin America. *New Left Review*, no.

67 (May-June):19-38; reprinted with an addendum in Laclau 1977, pp. 15-50.

1977   *Politics and Ideology in Marxist Theory: Capitalism-Fascism-Populism.* London: New Left Books.

La Minería en el Perú 1979
1980   Anuario Minero-Comercial, Vol. 16. Lima: Editores Técnicos Asociados.

Larson, Magali Sarfatti
1977   *The Rise of Professionalism: A Sociological Analysis.* Berkeley and Los Angeles: University of California Press.

————, and Bergen, Arlene Eisen
1969   *Social Stratification in Peru.* Politics of Modernization Series, no. 5. Berkeley: Institute of International Studies, University of California, Berkeley.

Lasch, Christopher
1978   *The Culture of Narcissism: American Life in an Age of Diminishing Expectations.* New York: W. W. Norton & Co.

Latham, Earl
1959   The Body Politic of the Corporation. In *The Corporation in Modern Society*, edited by Edward S. Mason, pp. 218-36. Cambridge: Harvard University Press.

Lawner, Lynne
1973   Introduction. In Gramsci 1973, pp. 3-56.

Lenin, V. I.
1933   *Imperialism, the Highest Stage of Capitalism: A Popular Outline.* New York: International Publishers.
1969   *What Is to Be Done? Burning Questions of Our Movement.* New York: International Publishers.

Leonard, H. Jeffrey
1980   Multinational Corporations and Politics in Developing Countries. Review Article. *World Politics* 32 (April):454-83.

Lester, J. M.
1974   *Technology Transfer and Developing Countries: A Selected Bibliography.* Washington, D.C.: George Washington University.

Letts, Ricardo
1981   *La Izquierda peruana: organizaciones y tendencias.* Lima: Mosca Azul Editores.

Lipset, Seymour Martin
  1967   Values, Education, and Entrepreneurship. In Lipset and Solari 1967, pp. 3-60.

————, and Solari, Aldo, eds.
  1967   *Elites in Latin America*. New York: Oxford University Press.

Lodge, George C.
  1973   Multinational Corporations: Make Progress the Product. *Foreign Policy*, no. 12 (Fall):96-112.

Long, Norman
  1975   Structural Dependency, Modes of Production and Economic Brokerage in Rural Peru. In *Beyond the Sociology of Development*, edited by Ivar Oxaal, Tony Barnett, and David Booth, pp. 253-82. London: Routledge & Kegan Paul.

Lowell, J. David
  1970   Copper Resources in 1970. *Mining Engineering* 22 (April):67-73.

Lowenthal, Abraham F.
  1974   Peru's Ambiguous Revolution. *Foreign Affairs* 52 (July):799-817.
  1975   ed. *The Peruvian Experiment: Continuity and Change under Military Rule*. Princeton: Princeton University Press.

Lukoji, Mulumba
  1975   The General Company of Quarries and Mines of Zaire. In *Natural Resources and National Welfare: The Case of Copper*, edited by Ann Seidman, pp. 280-94. New York: Praeger Publishers.

Lynd, Robert S.
  1943   Foreword. In Robert A. Brady, *Business as a System of Power*, pp. vii-xviii. New York: Columbia University Press.

MacLean y Estenós, Percy
  1953   *Historia de una revolución*. Buenos Aires: Editorial E.A.P.A.L.

Maletta, Héctor
  1978   El Subempleo en el Perú: una visión crítica. *Apuntes* 4, no. 8:3-48.

Mallon, Florencia Elizabeth
  1981   The Poverty of Progress: The Peasants of Yanamarca and the Development of Capitalism in Peru's Central Highlands, 1860-1940. Ph.D. dissertation, Yale University.

Malloy, James M.
  1970   *Bolivia: The Uncompleted Revolution*. Pittsburgh: University of Pittsburgh Press.

1974   Authoritarianism, Corporatism, and Mobilization in Peru. *Review of Politics* 36 (January):52-84.

Malpica, Carlos
1975   El Capitalismo extranjero en el modelo de desarrollo del Gobierno peruano. *Revista Interamericana de Planificación* 9 (June):74-86.
1976   *Los Dueños del Perú*. 9th ed. Lima: Ediciones Peisa.
1980   *Los Dueños del Perú*. 11th ed. Lima: Ediciones Peisa.

Mandel, Ernest
1967   International Capitalism and "Supra-Nationality." In *The Socialist Register 1967*, edited by Ralph Miliband and John Saville, pp. 27-41. New York: Monthly Review Press.
1975   *Late Capitalism*. Translated by Joris De Bres. London: New Left Books.

Marcosson, Isaac F.
1949   *Metal Magic*. New York: Farrar, Straus & Co.

Mariátegui, José Carlos
1971   *Seven Interpretive Essays on Peruvian Reality*. Translated by Marjory Urquidi. Austin, Texas: University of Texas Press.

Marsden, Ralph W.
1975   *Politics, Minerals, and Survival*. Madison, Wis.: University of Wisconsin Press.

Marx, Karl
1963a *The Poverty of Philosophy*. New York: International Publishers.
1963b *The Eighteenth Brumaire of Louis Bonaparte*. New York: International Publishers.
1967   *Capital*. Edited by Frederick Engels. 3 vols. New York: International Publishers.
1973   *Grundrisse: Foundations of the Critique of Political Economy (Rough Draft)*. Translated by Martin Nicolaus. London: New Left Books.
1975a Introduction to *Contribution to the Critique of Hegel's Philosophy of Law*. In Karl Marx and Frederick Engels, *Collected Works*, 3:175-87. New York: International Publishers.
1975b *Economic and Philosophical Manuscripts of 1844*. In Karl Marx and Frederick Engels, *Collected Works*, 3:231-346. New York: International Publishers.

————, and Engels, Friedrich (Frederick)
1932   *Manifesto of the Communist Party*. Translated by Samuel Moore. New York: International Publishers.
1961   *The German Ideology*. Edited by R. Pascal. New York: International Publishers.

Matos Mar, José, et al.
  1970 *El Perú actual: sociedad y política.* Mexico, D.F.: Instituto de Investigaciones Sociales, Universidad Nacional Autónoma de México.

Mazzolini, Renato
  1979 *Government Controlled Enterprises: International Strategic and Policy Decisions.* Chichester, England: John Wiley & Sons.

McMahon, A. D.
  1964 *Copper: A Materials Survey.* Washington, D.C.: U.S. Bureau of Mines.

Mellos, Koula
  1978 Developments in Advanced Capitalist Ideology. *Canadian Journal of Political Science* 11 (December):829-60.

Melotti, Umberto
  1977 *Marx and the Third World.* Translated by Pat Ransford. Edited by Malcolm Caldwell. London: Macmillan Press.

Mercado Jarrín, Edgardo
  1974 *Seguridad, estrategia, política.* Lima: Ministerio de Guerra.

Michl, Sara
  1973 Urban Squatter Organization as a National Government Tool: The Case of Lima, Peru. In *Latin American Urban Research*, Vol. 3, edited by Francine F. Rabinovitz and Felicity M. Trueblood, pp. 155-78. Beverly Hills, Calif.: Sage Publications.

Mikdashi, Zuhayr
  1976 *The International Politics of Natural Resources.* Ithaca, N.Y.: Cornell University Press.

Mikesell, Raymond F.
  1971 The Contribution of Petroleum and Mineral Resources to Economic Development. In Raymond F. Mikesell et al., *Foreign Investment in the Petroleum and Mineral Industries: Case Studies of Investor-Host Country Relations*, pp. 3-28. Baltimore: Johns Hopkins University Press.
  1975a *Foreign Investment in Copper Mining: Case Studies of Mines in Peru and Papua New Guinea.* Baltimore: Johns Hopkins University Press.
  1975b *Nonfuel Minerals: U.S. Investment Policies Abroad.* Washington Papers. Beverly Hills, Calif.: Sage Publications.
  1979 *The World Copper Industry: Structure and Economic Analysis.* Baltimore: Resources for the Future, Johns Hopkins University Press.

Miliband, Ralph
  1969 *The State in Capitalist Society: An Analysis of the Western System of Power*. New York: Basic Books.
  1973 Poulantzas and the Capitalist State. *New Left Review*, no. 82 (November-December):83-92.
  1977 *Marxism and Politics*. Oxford: Oxford University Press.

Miller, Rory
  1976 The Making of the Grace Contract: British Bondholders and the Peruvian Government, 1885-1890. *Journal of Latin American Studies* 8, no. 1:73-100.

Ministerio de Economía y Finanzas
  1970 *Plan económico anual 1970*. 4 vols. Lima: Ministerio de Economía y Finanzas.

Ministerio de Energía y Minas
  1974 *La Cerro de Pasco ya es nuestra*. Lima: Oficina de Relaciones Públicas, Ministerio de Energía y Minas.

Moncloa, Francisco
  1977 *Perú: ¿qué pasó? (1968-1976)*. Lima: Editorial Horizonte.

Montalvo V., Abner
  1972 La Participación laboral en la nueva empresa peruana: desarrollo teórico. Serie: Documento de Trabajo, no. 1. Lima: Departamento de Investigación, Escuela Superior de Administración de Negocios (ESAN).

————, and Scurrah, Martin
  1974 Participación laboral en la gestión empresarial: actitudes de los trabajadores peruanos y su comportamiento participativo. Serie: Documento de Trabajo, no. 2. Lima: Departamento de Investigación, Escuela Superior de Administración de Negocios (ESAN).

Montori A., Carlos
  1977 Reflexiones sobre la problemática minera en el Perú. *Minería y Petróleo*, no. 171 (January-April):12-31.

Moore, Barrington
  1966 *Social Origins of Dictatorship and Democracy: Lord and Peasant in the Making of the Modern World*. Boston: Beacon Press.

Moran, Theodore H.
  1973 Transnational Strategies of Protection and Defense by Multinational Corporations: Spreading the Risk and Raising the Cost for Nationalization in Natural Resources. *International Organization* 27 (Spring):273-87.

1974 *Multinational Corporations and the Politics of Dependence: Copper in Chile.* Princeton: Princeton University Press.
1978 Multinational Corporations and Dependency: A Dialogue for Dependentistas and Non-Dependentistas. *International Organization* 32 (Winter):79-100.

Morello, Gino
1976 Los Mineros de la Cerro de Pasco, 1940-1970. Bachelor's thesis, Pontífica Universidad Católica del Perú.

Mouffe, Chantal
1979 Hegemony and Ideology in Gramsci. In *Research in Political Economy*, Vol. 2, edited by Paul Zarembka, pp. 1-31. Greenwich, Conn.: JAI Press.

Müller, Ronald E.
1974 (More) on Multinationals: Poverty Is the Product. *Foreign Policy*, no. 13 (Winter):71-103.

Mytelka, Lynn Krieger
1978 Technological Dependence in the Andean Group. *International Organization* 32 (Winter):101-39.
1979 *Regional Development in a Global Economy: The Multinational Corporation, Technology, and Andean Integration.* New Haven: Yale University Press.

Newcomb, Richard Thomas
1976 Mineral Industry Demands and General Market Equilibrium. In Vogely 1976, pp. 271-316.

Nixon, Charles R.
1979 The Relations between States and Economies in Marx and Weber. Paper presented at the Meeting of the International Political Science Association, Moscow, 12-18 August.

North, Liisa
1966 *Civil-Military Relations in Argentina, Chile, and Peru.* Politics of Modernization Series, no. 2. Berkeley: Institute of International Studies, University of California, Berkeley.

Novoa Monreal, Eduardo
1972 *La Batalla por el cobre: comentarios y documentos.* Santiago, Chile: Empresa Editorial Nacional Quimantu.

Nun, José
1967 The Middle-Class Military Coup. In *The Politics of Conformity in Latin America*, edited by Claudio Véliz, pp. 66-118. Oxford: Oxford University Press.

1968   A Latin American Phenomenon: The Middle-Class Military Coup. In *Latin America: Reform or Revolution?*, edited by James Petras and Maurice Zeitlin, pp. 145-85. Greenwich, Conn.: Fawcett Publications.

1973   *Latin America: The Hegemonic Crisis and the Military Coup.* Politics of Modernization Series, no. 7. Berkeley: Institute of International Studies, University of California, Berkeley.

Ocampo Rodríguez, Esteban
1972   La Cerro Corporation y la penetración imperialista en la economía peruana. *Revista Villarreal* 2, no. 4 (December):41-85.

O'Donnell, Guillermo A.
1973   *Modernization and Bureaucratic-Authoritarianism: Studies in South American Politics.* Politics of Modernization Series, no. 9. Berkeley: Institute of International Studies, University of California, Berkeley.

1978   Reflections on the Patterns of Change in the Bureaucratic-Authoritarian State. *Latin American Research Review* 13, no. 1:3-38.

1979   Tensions in the Bureaucratic-Authoritarian State and the Question of Democracy. In Collier 1979, pp. 285-318.

Oficina Intersectoral de Capacitación
1977   Las Empresas transnacionales de los Estados Unidos de Norteamérica en el Perú, 1966-1974. Mimeographed. Lima: Instituto Nacional de Planificación (INP).

Oficina Intersectoral de Planificación
1973a La Concentración de la producción minera en el Perú. Mimeographed. Lima: Instituto Nacional de Planificación (INP).
1973b El Capital en la minería. Mimeographed. Lima: INP.
1973c Estructura de la propiedad en la minería. Mimeographed. Lima: INP.
1976   Concentración de la producción y estructura de propiedad. Mimeographed. Lima: INP.
1977   El Caso de la deuda pública peruana 1965-1975: las empresas transnacionales y el endeudamiento externo. Mimeographed. Lima: INP.

Oficina Nacional de Estadística y Censos
1974   *Indicadores demográficos, sociales, económicos y geográficos del Perú.* Lima: Instituto Nacional de Estadística.

Oficina Sectoral de Planificación
1975   *Plan sectoral de desarrollo 1975-1978 y 1975-1976.* 2 vols. Lima: Ministerio de Energía y Minas.

Ollman, Bertell
   1968   Marx's Use of "Class." *American Journal of Sociology* 73 (March):573-80.

Olson, Mancur
   1965   *The Logic of Collective Action: Public Goods and the Theory of Groups*. Cambridge: Harvard University Press.

Organisation for Economic Co-operation and Development (OECD)
   1974   *Choice and Adaptation of Technology in Developing Countries: An Overview of Major Policy Issues*. Paris: Development Centre, OECD.

Ossowski, Stanislaw
   1963   *Class Structure in the Social Consciousness*. Translated by Sheila Patterson. New York: Free Press.

Ozawa, Terutomo
   1979   *Multinationalism, Japanese Style: The Political Economy of Outward Dependency*. Princeton: Princeton University Press.

Packenham, Robert A.
   1978   The New Utopianism: Political Development Ideas in the Dependency Literature. Paper presented at the Annual Meeting of the American Political Science Association, New York, 31 August-3 September.

Palma, Gabriel
   1978   Dependency: A Formal Theory of Underdevelopment or a Methodology for the Analysis of Concrete Situations of Underdevelopment? *World Development* 6 (July-August):881-924.

Palmer, David Scott
   1973   "Revolution from Above": Military Government and Popular Participation in Peru, 1968-1972. Ph.D. dissertation, Cornell University.

Pan-American Union
   1966   *La Administración pública como un instrumento de desarrollo, Perú*. Washington, D.C.: Department of Public Affairs, Pan-American Union.

Panitch, Leo
   1977   The Development of Corporatism in Liberal Democracies. *Comparative Political Studies* 10 (April):61-90.
   1981   Trade Unions and the Capitalist State. *New Left Review*, no. 125 (January-February):21-43.

Parkin, Frank
   1976   System Contradiction and Political Transformation. In *Power and*

Control: Social Structures and Their Transformation, edited by Tom R. Burns and Walter Buckley, pp. 127-46. Sage Studies in International Sociology, no. 6. Beverly Hills, Calif.: Sage Publications.

Pásara, Luis, and Santistevan, Jorge
1973 "Industrial Communities" and Trade Unions in Peru: A Preliminary Analysis. *International Labor Review* 108 (August-September):127-42.

————; Bustamante, Alberto; and García Sayán, Diego
1974 *Dinámica de la Comunidad Industrial*. Lima: DESCO.

Paulston, Rolland G.
1970 Estratificación social, poder y organización educacional: el caso peruano. *Aportes* 1, no. 16 (April):91-111.

Payne, James L.
1965 *Labor and Politics in Peru: The System of Political Bargaining*. New Haven: Yale University Press.

Pease García, Henry
1977 *El Ocaso del poder oligárquico: lucha política en la encena oficial*. Lima: DESCO.
1978 *Los Caminos del poder: tres años de crisis en la escena política*. Lima: DESCO.

————, and Filomeno, Alfredo, eds.
1977a *Perú 1975: Cronología política*. Vol. IV. Lima: DESCO.
1977b *Perú 1976: Cronología política*. Vol. V. Lima: DESCO.

————, and Verme Insúa, Olga, eds.
1974 *Perú 1968-1973: Cronología política*. Vols. I and II. Lima: DESCO.

Penrose, Edith
1971 The State and Multinational Enterprises in Less-Developed Countries. In Dunning 1971, pp. 221-39.

Perlmutter, Howard V.
1970 The Tortuous Evolution of the Multinational Corporation. In *World Business: Promise and Problems*, edited by Courtney C. Brown, pp. 66-82. New York: Macmillan Co.

Perrucci, Robert
1971 Engineering: Professional Servant of Power. In *The Professions and Their Prospects*, edited by Eliot Freidson, pp. 119-33. Beverly Hills, Calif.: Sage Publications.

Peruvian Government
1972 Peru's Relations with the United States and National Development Policy. In Sharp 1972, pp. 416-21.

Petras, James, and Havens, Eugene A.
 1979 Peru: Economic Crisis and Class Confrontation. *Monthly Review* 30 (February):25-41.

——, and LaPorte, Robert
 1971 *Perú: ¿transformación revolucionaria o modernización?* Buenos Aires: Amorrortu Editores.

——, and Zeitlin, Maurice
 1967 Miners and Agrarian Radicalism. *American Sociological Review* 32 (August):578-86.

Pike, Frederick B.
 1967 *The Modern History of Peru.* New York: Praeger Publishers.

Pinelo, Adalberto J.
 1973 *The Multinational Corporation as a Force in Latin American Politics: A Case Study of the International Petroleum Company in Peru.* New York: Praeger Publishers.

Poulantzas, Nicos
 1969 The Problem of the Capitalist State. *New Left Review*, no. 58 (November-December):67-78.
 1973 *Political Power and Social Classes.* Translated by Timothy O'Hagan. London: New Left Books.
 1975 *Classes in Contemporary Capitalism.* Translated by David Fernbach. London: New Left Books.
 1976 The Capitalist State: A Reply to Miliband and Laclau. *New Left Review*, no. 95 (January-February):63-83.
 1978 *State, Power, Socialism.* Translated by Patrick Camiller. London: New Left Books.

Prebisch, Raúl
 1962 The Economic Development of Latin America and Its Principal Problems. *Economic Bulletin for Latin America* 7 (February):1-22.
 1963 *Towards a Dynamic Development Policy for Latin America.* New York: United Nations.

Presidencia de la República
 1977 *"Túpac Amaru" Government Plan, 1977-1980.* Lima: Sistema Nacional de Información.

President's Materials Policy Commission
 1952 *Resources for Freedom: A Report to the President.* 5 vols. Washington, D.C.: U.S. Government Printing Office.

Purser, W.F.C.
 1971 *Metal-Mining in Peru, Past and Present.* New York: Praeger Publishers.

Quijano Obregón, Aníbal
  1971 *Nationalism and Capitalism in Peru: A Study in Neo-Imperialism.*
         Translated by Helen R. Lane. New York: Monthly Review Press.
  1972 Imperialismo y capitalismo del Estado. *Sociedad y Política*, no. 1
         (June):5-18.
  1973 La Coyuntura política y las tareas de la clase obrera. *Sociedad y
         Política*, no. 4 (September):12-22.
  1974 Imperialism and International Relations in Latin America. In *Latin
         America and the United States: The Changing Political Realities*,
         edited by Julio Cotler and Richard R. Fagen, pp. 67-91. Stanford,
         Calif.: Stanford University Press.
  1977 Las Nuevas condiciones de la lucha de clases en el Perú. *Sociedad
         y Política*, no. 7 (May):2-15.

Radetzki, Marian
  1977 Where Should Developing Countries' Minerals Be Processed? The
         Country View versus the Multinational Company View. *World De-
         velopment* 5 (April):325-34.

Ramirez, Francisco O., and Thomas, George M.
  1981 Structural Antecedents and Consequences of Statism. In *Dynamics
         of World Development*, edited by Richard Rubinson, pp. 139-64.
         Beverly Hills, Calif.: Sage Publications.

Rodríguez Hoyle, Daniel
  1972 *Perú minero 1971*. Lima: Sociedad Nacional de Minería y Petróleo.
  1974 *Perú minero 1974*. 2d ed. Lima: Sociedad Nacional de Minería y
         Petróleo.

Roël, Virgilio
  1976 *La Actual crisis económica*. Pamphlet. Lima: Editorial Alfa.

Roncagliolo, Rafael
  1980 *¿Quién ganó? elecciones 1931-80*. Lima: DESCO.

Rubio C., Marcial, and Bernales B., Enrique
  1981 *Perú: constitución y sociedad política*. Lima: DESCO.

Saint Pol Maydieu, Patrick
  1973 Minería, empleo y tecnología. Bachelor's thesis, Pontífica Uni-
         versidad Católica del Perú.

Samamé Boggio, Mario
  1974 *Minería peruana: biografía y estrategia de una actividad decisiva*.
         2 vols. 2d ed. Lima: Editorial Gráfica Labor.
  1976 La Minería en nuestra estructura económica y social. Paper pre-
         sented at the Thirteenth Convention of the Instituto de Ingenieros
         de Minas, Arequipa, 8-12 September.
  1979 *El Perú minero: tomo I—Historia*. Lima: INCITEMI.

Sánchez, Fernando
   1975   Las Corporaciones del cobre: un ensayo exploratorio. *Apuntes* 2,
          no. 4:3-34.

Schatz, Sayre P.
   1977   *Nigerian Capitalism.* Berkeley and Los Angeles: University of Cal-
          ifornia Press.

Schmitter, Philippe C.
   1974   Still the Century of Corporatism? *Review of Politics* 36 (January):85-
          131.

————, and Lembruch, Gerhard, eds.
   1979   *Trends Toward Corporatist Intermediation.* Contemporary Political
          Sociology, vol. 1. Beverly Hills, Calif.: Sage Publications.

Schumpeter, Joseph A.
   1935   *The Theory of Economic Development.* Cambridge: Harvard Uni-
          versity Press.
   1942   *Capitalism, Socialism, and Democracy.* New York: Harper & Row.

Schydlowsky, Daniel M., and Wicht, Juan J.
   1980   *Anatomía de un fracaso económico: Perú, 1968-1978.* 5th ed. Lima:
          Centro de Investigación, Universidad del Pacífico.

Scurrah, Martin, and Montalvo, Abner
   1975   Clase social y valores sociales en Perú. Serie: Documento de Tra-
          bajo, no. 8. Lima: Departamento de Investigación, Escuela Superior
          de Administración de Negocios (ESAN).

Sharp, Daniel A., ed.
   1972   *U.S. Foreign Policy and Peru.* Austin, Texas: Institute of Latin
          American Studies, University of Texas at Austin.

Sideri, S., and Johns, S., eds.
   1980   *Mining for Development in the Third World: Multinational Cor-
          porations, State Enterprises and the International Economy.* New
          York: Pergamon Press.

Sigmund, Paul E.
   1980   *Multinationals in Latin America: The Politics of Nationalization.*
          Madison, Wis.: University of Wisconsin Press.

Skidmore, Thomas E.
   1973   Politics and Economic Policy Making in Authoritarian Brazil, 1937-
          71. *In Authoritarian Brazil: Origins, Policies, and Future,* edited
          by Alfred Stepan, pp. 3-46. New Haven: Yale University Press.

Sklar, Richard L.
  1975 *Corporate Power in an African State: The Political Impact of Multinational Mining Companies in Zambia*. Berkeley and Los Angeles: University of California Press.
  1976 Postimperialism: A Class Analysis of Multinational Corporate Expansion. *Comparative Politics* 9 (October):75-92.
  1977 Socialism at Bay: Class Domination in Africa. Paper presented at the Joint Meeting of the African Studies Association and the Latin American Studies Association, Houston, 5 November 1977.
  1979 The Nature of Class Domination in Africa. *Journal of Modern African Studies* 17, no. 4:531-52.
  1982 On the Concept of Power in Political Economy. In *Toward a Humanistic Science of Politics: Essays in Honor of Francis Dunham Wormuth*, edited by Dalmas H. Nelson and Richard L. Sklar, pp. 179-206. Washington, D.C.: University Press of America.
  n.d. Lectures on Socialism and Development. Unpublished draft.

Skocpol, Theda
  1977 Wallerstein's World Capitalist System: A Theoretical and Historical Critique. *American Journal of Sociology* 82 (March):1075-90.
  1979 *States and Social Revolutions: A Comparative Analysis of France, Russia, and China*. Cambridge: Cambridge University Press.

Smith, David N., and Wells, Louis T.
  1975 *Negotiating Third-World Mineral Agreements*. Cambridge, Mass.: Ballinger Publishing Co.

Smith, Sheila
  1980 The Ideas of Samir Amin: Theory or Tautology? *Journal of Development Studies* 17 (October):5-21.

Smith, Tony
  1979 The Underdevelopment of Development Literature: The Case of Dependency Theory. Review Article. *World Politics* 31 (January):247-88.

Sociedad Nacional de Minería y Petróleo
  1974 Estudio integral de actitudes y necesidades de capacitación de los recursos humanos en la minería. 2 vols. Mimeographed. Lima: Sociedad Nacional de Minería y Petróleo.

Sofer, Eugene F.
  1980 Recent Trends in Latin American Labor Historiography. *Latin American Research Review* 15, no. 1:167-76.

Sonquist, John A., and Koenig, Tom
  1976 Examining Corporate Interconnections through Interlocking Direc-

torates. In *Power and Control: Social Structures and Their Transformation*, edited by Tom R. Burns and Walter Buckley, pp. 53-83. Sage Studies in International Sociology, vol. 6. Beverly Hills, Calif.: Sage Publications.

Southern Peru Copper Corporation
1967 *El Contrato de Toquepala*. Lima: Departamento de Relaciones Públicas, Southern Peru Copper Corporation.
n.d. *El Contrato de Cuajone*. Lima: División de Relaciones Públicas, Southern Peru Copper Corporation.

Spalding, Hobart A.
1977 *Organized Labor in Latin America: Historical Case Studies of Urban Workers in Dependent Societies*. New York: Harper & Row.

Spero, Joan Edelman
1977 *The Politics of International Economic Relations*. New York: St. Martin's Press.

Stallings, Barbara
1972 *Economic Dependency in Africa and Latin America*. Comparative Politics Series, vol. 3. Beverly Hills, Calif.: Sage Publications.
1979 Peru and the U.S. Banks: Privatization of Financial Relations. In *Capitalism and the State in U.S.-Latin American Relations*, edited by Richard R. Fagen, pp. 217-53. Stanford, Calif.: Stanford University Press.

Stein, Steve
1980 *Populism in Peru: The Emergence of the Masses and the Politics of Social Control*. Madison, Wis.: University of Wisconsin Press.

Stepan, Alfred
1978 *The State and Society: Peru in Comparative Perspective*. Princeton: Princeton University Press.

Stephens, Evelyne Huber
1980 *The Politics of Workers' Participation: The Peruvian Approach in Comparative Perspective*. New York: Harcourt Brace Jovanovich, Academic Press.

Strassman, W. Paul
1964 The Industrialist. In *Continuity and Change in Latin America*, edited by John J. Johnson, pp. 161-85. Stanford, Calif.: Stanford University Press.

Strauss, Simon D.
1964 Marketing of Nonferrous Metals and Ores. In *Economics of the Mineral Industries*, edited by Edward H. Robie, 1st ed., pp. 281-

304. New York: American Institute of Mining, Metallurgical, and Petroleum Engineers.

1977 Competition in the Non-Ferrous Metal Markets. Address to the Annual Meeting of the American Institute of Mining, Metallurgical, and Petroleum Engineers, Atlanta, 9 March.

1978a Influences that Determine Metals Prices. Paper presented at the Eleventh Commonwealth Mining and Metallurgical Conference, Hong Kong, 8 May.

1978b A View of Commodity Agreements. Paper presented at the Joint Conference of the Australasian Institute of Mining and Metallurgy and the American Institute of Mining, Metallurgical, and Petroleum Engineers, Canberra, 16 May.

1978c Meeting Future Demand for Metals. Address to the Fourteenth Convention of the Instituto de Ingenieros de Minas, Lima, 7 November.

Suleiman, Ezra N.
1974 *Politics, Power, and Bureaucracy in France: The Administrative Elite*. Princeton: Princeton University Press.

Sulmont, Denis
1974 *El Desarrollo de la clase obrera en el Perú*. Lima: Publicaciones CISEPA, Pontífica Universidad Católica del Perú.
1975 Sindicalismo y política en el Peru. Mimeographed. Lima: Taller de Estudios Urbano-Industriales, Pontífica Universidad Católica del Perú.
1977 *Historia del Movimiento obrero peruano (1890-1977)*. Lima: Tarea.

Sulmont, Roelfin Haak de
1972 Estudio exploratorio sobre la situación socio-profesional del ingeniero minero en el Perú. Bachelor's thesis, Pontífica Universidad Católica del Perú.

Sunkel, Osvaldo
1969 National Development Policy and External Dependence in Latin America. *Journal of Development Studies* 6 (October):23-48.
1972 Big Business and "Dependencia": A Latin American View. *Foreign Affairs* 50 (April):517-31.
1973 Transnational Capitalism and National Disintegration in Latin America. *Social and Economic Studies* 22 (March):132-76.

Sweezy, Paul M.
1969 Notes on the Multinational Corporation. *Monthly Review* 21 (October):1-13; and (November):1-13. Reprinted in Paul M. Sweezy and Harry Magdoff, *The Dynamics of U.S. Capitalism*, pp. 88-112. New York: Monthly Review Press, 1972.

Taboada Peña, Sara
  1976   La Inversión directa extranjera en la economía peruana: el caso de
         la minería y de la Southern Peru Copper Corporation. Bachelor's
         thesis, Pontífica Universidad Católica del Perú.

Takeushi, Kenji; Thiebach, Gerhard E.; and Hilmy, Joseph
  1977   Investment Requirements in the Non-Fuel Sector in the Developing
         Countries. *Natural Resources Forum* 1 (April):263-75.

Talledo Araña, María Isabel
  1975   La Distribución del ingreso en el sector minero y la Ley General
         de Minería 18880. Bachelor's thesis, Pontífica Universidad Católica
         del Perú.

Thorndike, Guillermo
  1976   *No, mi General*. Lima: Mosca Azul Editores.

Thorp, Rosemary, and Bertram, Geoffrey
  1978   *Peru 1890-1977: Growth and Policy in an Open Economy*. London:
         Macmillan Press.

Tironi, Ernesto, ed.
  1978a *Pacto Andino: carácter y perspectivas*. Lima: Instituto de Estudios
         Peruanos.
  1978b *Pacto Andino: desarrollo nacional e integración andina*. Lima:
         Instituto de Estudios Peruanos.

Torres Guzmán, Alfredo
  1981   6 Meses de Tripartismo. *Debate*, no. 9:25-32.

Trimberger, Ellen Kay
  1972   A Theory of Elite Revolutions. *Studies in Comparative International
         Development* 7 (Fall):191-207.
  1978   *Revolution from Above: Military Bureaucrats and Development in
         Japan, Turkey, Egypt, and Peru*. New Brunswick, N.J.: Transaction
         Books.

United Nations Department of Economic and Social Affairs
  1973   Multinational Corporations in World Development. Mimeographed.
         New York: United Nations.

U.S. Congress, Senate, Committee on Foreign Relations
  1969   *United States Relations with Peru: Hearings before the Subcom-
         mittee on Western Hemisphere Affairs of the Committee on Foreign
         Relations*. 91st Cong., 1st sess., 14, 16, 17 April.

Valenzuela, J. Samuel, and Valenzuela, Arturo
  1981   Modernization and Dependency: Alternative Perspectives in the Study
         of Latin American Underdevelopment. In *From Dependency to De-*

velopment: Strategies to Overcome Underdevelopment and Inequality, edited by Heraldo Muñoz, pp. 15-41. Boulder, Colo.: Westview Press.

Velasco Alvarado, Juan
    n.d.   *Velasco, la voz de la Revolución*. Lima: Ediciones Peisa.

Vernon, Raymond
    1971   *Sovereignty at Bay: The Multinational Spread of U.S. Enterprises.* New York: Basic Books.
    1977   *Storm over the Multinationals: The Real Issues.* Cambridge: Harvard University Press.

Villanueva, Víctor
    1962   *El Militarismo en el Perú.* Lima: Empresa Gráfica T. Scheuch.
    1969   *¿Nueva mentalidad militar en el Perú?* Lima: J. Mejía Baca.
    1972   *El CAEM y la Revolución de la Fuerza Armada.* Lima: Instituto de Estudios Peruanos.

Vogely, William A., ed.
    1976   *Economics of the Mineral Industries.* 3d ed. New York: American Institute of Mining, Metallurgical, and Petroleum Engineers.

von Clemm, Michael
    1971   The Rise of Corporate Banking. *Harvard Business Review* 49 (May-June):125-42.

Wallerstein, Immanuel
    1974a   *The Modern World-System: Capitalist Agriculture and the Origins of the European World-Economy in the Sixteenth Century.* New York: Harcourt Brace Jovanovich, Academic Press.
    1974b   Dependence in an Interdependent World: The Limited Possibilities for Transformation within the Capitalist World-Economy. *African Studies Review* 17 (April):1-26.
    1974c   The Rise and Future Demise of the World Capitalist System: Concepts for Comparative Analysis. *Comparative Studies in Society and History* 16 (September):387-415.

Walzer, Michael
    1980   Intellectuals to Power? In Michael Walzer, *Radical Principles: Reflections of an Unreconstructed Democrat*, pp. 224-33. New York: Basic Books.

Warren, Bill
    1973   Imperialism and Capitalist Industrialization. *New Left Review*, no. 81 (September-October):3-44

1980   *Imperialism: Pioneer of Capitalism.* Edited by John Sender. London: New Left Books.

Webb, Richard C.
1972a Tax Policy and the Incidence of Taxation in Peru. Mimeographed. Princeton: Woodrow Wilson School of Public and International Affairs, Princeton University.
1972b The Distribution of Income in Peru. Mimeographed. Princeton: Woodrow Wilson School of Public and International Affairs, Princeton University.
1977   *Government Policy and the Distribution of Income in Peru, 1963-73.* Cambridge: Harvard University Press.

————, and Figueroa, Adolfo
1975   *Distribución del ingreso en el Perú.* Lima: Instituto de Estudios Peruanos.

Weber, Max
1958   *The Protestant Ethic and the Spirit of Capitalism.* Translated by Talcott Parsons. New York: C. Scribner's Sons.
1978   *Economy and Society.* 2 vols. Edited by Guenther Roth and Claus Wittich. Berkeley and Los Angeles: University of California Press.

Wells, Louis T.
1971   The Multinational Business Enterprise: What Kind of International Organization? *International Organization* 25 (Summer):447-64.

Wernette, John Philip
1964   *Government and Business.* New York: Macmillan Co.

Wheeler, Harvey
1957   Problems of Stalinism. *Western Political Quarterly* 10 (September):634-74.

Who's Who 1979
1979   London: Adam and Charles Black.

Whyte, William Foote
1965   Common Management Strategies in Industrial Relations—Peru. In Form and Blum 1965, pp. 47-69.

Wiarda, Howard J.
1973   Toward a Framework for the Study of Political Change in the Iberic-Latin Tradition: The Corporative Model. *World Politics* 25 (January):206-35.

Wilkie, James W., and Reich, Peter, eds.
1977   *Statistical Abstract of Latin America, Vol. 18.* Los Angeles: UCLA Latin American Center Publications.

1978   *Statistical Abstract of Latin America, Vol. 19.* Los Angeles: UCLA Latin American Center Publications.
1980   *Statistical Abstract of Latin America, Vol. 20.* Los Angeles: UCLA Latin American Center Publications.

Wils, Frits
1979   *Industrialization, Industrialists, and the Nation-State in Peru.* Research Series, no. 41. Berkeley: Institute of International Studies, University of California, Berkeley.

Zapata, Francisco
1980   Mineros y militares en la coyuntura actual de Bolivia, Chile y Peru (1976-1978). *Revista Mexicana de Sociología* 42 (October-December):1443-64.

Zeitlin, Maurice
1974   Corporate Ownership and Control: The Large Corporation and the Capitalist Class. *American Journal of Sociology* 79 (March):1073-1119.

————, and Norich, Samuel
1979   Management Control, Exploitation, and Profit Maximization in the Large Corporation: An Empirical Confrontation of Managerialism and Class Theory. In *Research in Political Economy*, Vol. 2, edited by Paul Zarembka, pp. 33-62. Greenwich, Conn.: JAI Press.

————, and Petras, James
1969   Los Mineros y el radicalismo de la clase obrera en Chile. *Revista Latinoamericana de Sociología* 5 (March):121-26.

Zimmermann Zavala, Augusto
1974   *El Plan Inca, objectivo: Revolución peruana.* Lima: Empresa Editora del Diario Oficial "El Peruano."

Index

Acción Popular, 270, 337. *See also* Belaunde
agrarian reform, 18, 66, 142, 269, 329; bourgeois attitudes toward, 269. *See also* oligarchy; peasantry
agriculture, 18, 19; bonanza development and, 65-66, 339; declining production in, 18-19; exports, 23, 65-66
AMAX (American Metal Climax Corporation), 74, 77, 353
American Smelting and Refining Company, *see* Asarco, Inc.
Anaconda Copper Corporation, 76, 79, 82-83, 84, 164, 219, 352, 353
Andean Common Market (Pact), 22, 181
apparatus, state, *see* bureaucracy and bureaucrats
APRA (Alianza Popular Revolucionaria Americana), 27, 141, 242, 284, 289, 290, 291, 310. *See also* CTP; Haya de la Torre
aprismo, aprista, see APRA
Archibald, Frank, 106, 133, 151
Asarco, Inc., 35-39, 43, 162; in Cuajone copper sales, 117-22; in financing of Cuajone mining project, 112-14; Guggenheim family and, 35, 292n; internationalization of ownership, 74; and labor, 292n; management character of, 133; Northern Peru Mining Company, a subsidiary of, 35-36, 178, 183; origins of, 35; relations with Cerro de Pasco Corporation, 36-38, 76, 78, 109; in world copper industry, 75, 76, 77, 78, 86, 352, 353. *See also* Southern Peru Copper Corporation; Toquepala copper mine
authoritarianism, 7-8, 263-64, 279-80, 337. *See also* corporatism

Backus and Johnson Company, 31
Banchero, Luis Alberto, 180
Banco Interamericano de Desarrollo (BID), 88
Banco Minero del Perú, 45, 173, 256, 260
banking system, 51, 112, 186n

banks, international, *see* financing of mining projects
Belaunde Terry, Fernando, 55, 67, 68, 98, 135, 141, 142, 223, 248, 270, 275n, 337
Benavides de la Quintana, Alberto, 141, 149, 180-81, 223
Billiton N.V. (a subsidiary of Royal Dutch/Shell), 77, 116, 121, 127, 129
bonanza development, 61-70, 182, 311; authoritarianism and, 337n; bourgeois-military relations and, 276; class formation and, 329; contradiction of, 339-40; and Cuajone mining project, 124; definition of, 64-65; foreign capital and, 52-55, 61-63, 64, 69, 325, 329; military and, 55-56, 61, 67-68, 70; mine labor and, 310, 317; oligarchy and, 65-66, 339; oligopolistic competition and, 86-91; origins of, 55-56, 61; parastatal enterprise and, 68, 206, 214, 216. *See also* mining policy, after 1968
bourgeoisie, 5, 9, 10, 12, 13, 47, 48, 66, 169, 186-87, 195, 200, 237, 328-29; bonanza development and, 66, 329; bureaucrats as members of, 240n, 242, 247n, 255; career advancement, 250-52; Cerro de Pasco expropriation and, 155, 265-66; character of, 238, 275, 330-32, 334; cohesion of, 247-48, 251-52, 335; corporate national, 331-32, 334, 335, 336, 338, 339, 340; delineation of, 237-39, 242-43; democracy and, 7, 276-77, 336-38; economic situation of, 243-46; education and, 248-50, 332-33, 335; financial, 186, 187; foreign enterprise and the formation of, 252-53, 327-29; hegemony of, 6n, 262-64, 273, 275, 277-78, 304, 336, 338-39; ideology and values of, 210-11, 262-73, 274, 328, 332, 339; industrial, 52, 186-87, 329; international, 13, 79, 90-92, 275, 324, 326; labor and, 279, 313-15, 317, 318-19, 335, 338-39; mediana minería and, 171-72, 186-90, 195, 197-200; metropolitan, global interests of, 3-4; middle class and, 239-42, 255, 262, 265, 268, 270, 274-75, 335; military and, 55-56,

bourgeoisie (*cont.*)
    251, 273, 276; mining, as dominant class
    element, 235, 239, 262, 273-78; national,
    colonial institutions and, 164; national,
    components of, 186; national, subservi-
    ence to foreign capital of, 190, 195; new
    (*see* new bourgeoisie); organizational re-
    sources of, 253-62, 271-72; parastatal en-
    terprise and, 170, 203, 210-11, 228-31,
    276, 334-35; political effectiveness of,
    238-39; political opinions of, 264-70, 337;
    size of, in mining sector, 242-43; social
    origins of, 246-47; socioeconomic mobil-
    ity and, 241-42; state and, 6n, 59, 66,
    275-76, 318, 334-40. *See also* capitalism;
    class formation; corporations, entrepre-
    neurs; rentiers
Briceño Arata, Luis, 208, 209n, 210, 211,
    212, 214
British Insulated Callender's Cables (BICC),
    118, 119-20
bureaucracy and bureaucrats, 28, 29, 45, 55-
    60, 71, 207, 208-209, 211, 220; bourgeoi-
    sie and, 240n, 242, 247n, 255. *See also*
    Dirección General de Minería; Instituto
    Nacional de Planificación; Ministry of En-
    ergy and Mines
bureaucratic-authoritarianism (bureaucratic-
    authoritarian state), *see* Corporatism
Bustamante y Rivero, José, 34, 289-90

CAEM, *see* Centro de Altos Estudios Mili-
    tares
Canada, 24, 72, 73, 115, 183, 184, 219,
    223-24
capital, national, *see* bourgeoisie; mediana
    minería
capitalism: bonanza development and, 64-66;
    dependency view of, 1-2, 4, 8, 203-204,
    279-80, 323; international, and develop-
    ment, 3-4, 10, 163; mine workers' prefer-
    ence for, 298-99; oligarchy's conception
    of, 49; Peruvian, 21-24, 29-30, 68, 70-71,
    199-200; as a process of development, 6-
    7, 10, 199-200, 330. *See also* bourgeoisie;
    foreign investment and investors; middle
    class; oligarchy; postimperialism; working
    class
Cardoso, Fernando Henrique, 4, 10, 334
Cartagena Agreement, *see* Andean Common
    Market

Central Reserve Bank of Peru, 151, 256
Centro de Altos Estudios Militares (CAEM),
    58, 143, 271
Centromin (Empresa Minera del Centro del
    Perú), 43, 155-60, 202, 206, 207-208,
    209, 223, 225, 226, 227, 296n; employ-
    ment in, 286; wages in, 305, 306; work-
    ers, 296n, 300-301, 303, 304, 305, 306.
    See also Cerro de Pasco Corporation, na-
    tionalization of; Flórez Pinedo; parastatal
    enterprise
Cerro de Pasco Corporation, 31-39, 41-43,
    46-47, 55, 76; Asarco and, 36-38, 76, 78,
    109; in central sierra, impact on social
    structure of, 137, 140; in Chile, 55, 139,
    142-43, 154; Cobriza copper mine, 34,
    138, 149, 159; as a "colonial company,"
    162-64; doctrine of domicile and, 133,
    160-65; economic performance of, 143,
    144; economic performance of, compared
    to Centromin, 155-57; employment in, 32,
    136, 286; haciendas, 33, 136, 137, 141,
    145; impact on Peruvian society of, 137-
    38, 164; indigenization of staff, 140-41,
    143; joint ventures, 34, 136, 139, 146; la-
    bor unions in, 289-91, 292, 303; manage-
    ment, nature of, 133-36, 162-63; manager
    training by, 210, 252; and manufacturing
    industries, promotion of, 37, 137, 140;
    and mediana minería, 34, 139-40, 175,
    180n; metals production of, 137, 143,
    144; and military regime, attempted ac-
    commodation with, 146-48; mining
    camps, 141-42, 287-89, 292, 316; nation-
    alization of, 132-33, 148-55, 265-66; and
    the National Mining and Petroleum Soci-
    ety, 256, 258, 260-61; origins of, 31-35;
    ownership of, 31, 133, 154-55; postwar
    development of, 138-44; "social debt"
    owed by, 141-42, 145, 153, 155; and
    Southern Peru Copper Corporation, 78,
    109, 139, 149; strikes and protests in,
    288-89, 300-303; wages in, 304-305, 306;
    workers, 141, 287, 288-91, 292; in work-
    ing class formation, 287-91. *See also* Be-
    navides de la Quintana; Fernández Mal-
    donado; Grace, W. R. and Company;
    Koenig; Murphy
Cerro Verde copper mine, *see* MineroPeru
CGTP (Confederación General de Trabaja-
    dores Peruanos), 284, 289, 295, 311. *See*

also Communist Party; FTMMP

Chase Manhattan Bank, financing of Cuajone project, 112-15, 116, 119, 120

Chile, military conflict with Peru, 52, 56

class action: definition of, 15, 262; mediation through organizations, 253. *See also* "economism"

class analysis, 4-15, 170, 235-38, 262, 334; of bourgeoisie and middle class, 237-78; concepts employed in, 14-15; dependencista, 9-12, 279-80, 330, 334, 341; post-imperialist, 12-14, 331n; of working class, 279-319

class dominance, 235-36, 237, 238-39, 334-35

class formation: definition of, 15; bonanza development and, 65-67; Cerro de Pasco's impact on, 47; foreign investment and, 252-53; international, 13; international, mining industry and, 79; of mining bourgeoisie, 235-36; political parties and, 253; transnational corporations and, 327-30; of working class, 282, 287-97, 327-30, 337. *See also* bourgeoisie

CNT (Confederación Nacional de Trabajadores), 284

COAP (Consejo de Asesoría a la Presidencia), 25, 56-57

Cobriza copper mine, *see* Cerro de Pasco Corporation

COCOMI (Comunidad de Compensación Minera), 307, 367-68

COFIDE (Corporación Financiera de Desarrollo), 51, 182, 219, 223, 227

College of Engineers, 254-55

"colonial companies," 163-64, 169, 287, 326-27, 330

COMEX, *see* New York Commodities Exchange

Comisión Tripartidaria, 313

communism: mine workers' preference for, 298-99

Communist Party, Peruvian (PCP), 284, 289, 290, 311, 313

community power, labor and, 315-16

congress, Peruvian, 25, 55, 313n, 337; behavior of Left in, 338; as conservative political institution, 28

Constituent Assembly of 1978-79, 312, 313n

constitution, Peruvian, 7n, 25, 28n, 312

copper, Peruvian industry: exports, 23, 43,

46, 128; exports, bonanza development and, 52, 55-56; and gran minería, 43; origins of, 31-35; production, 347, 348; production, by Centromin, 157, 158; production, by Cerro de Pasco, 137, 144; production, by MineroPeru, 202, 219-20; production, by Southern Peru Copper, 97, 121, 123, 129; refining, 32, 38, 63, 214, 217-18, 228 (*see also* Cuajone copper mining project, refinery controversy); reserves, 19, 36, 55, 106, 146, 218-19, 222, 224 (*see also* Quellaveco copper mine); smelting (*see* smelters and smelting); and U.S. economy, early links to, 33

copper, world industry, 72-84, 86-91; coordinating mechanisms in, 76-77; firms, 352, 353; international class formation and, 79; international politics and, 72; Japanese role in, 79-81, 88, 90, 91; joint ventures in, 77, 89-90; market stabilization practices in, 77-79; monopolization of, barriers against, 75-76; oligopolistic competition in, 86; oligopolistic competition and "bonanza" maximization, 86-90; ownership and control in, 73-77; pricing institutions and practices in, 81-84; structure of, 73-84; transnational firms in, 73-74, 87-88, 90-92, 215; vertical integration in, 74-75, 78

Corporación del Santa, 39

corporations: "entrepreneurial," 161-63; "mature," 161, 162; organization, 4-5

corporatism, 70-71, 272, 276, 279-81, 313-14, 319, 336. *See also* authoritarianism; working class, incorporation of

Council of Ministers, 57, 108, 121, 207

CTP (Confederación de Trabajadores del Perú), 284, 289, 290, 291, 294, 295, 311. *See also* APRA

CTRP (Confederación de Trabajadores de la Revolución Peruana), 284

Cuadros Paredes, Víctor, 295, 313

Cuajone copper mining project, 37, 43, 55, 77, 97-131; basic agreement (contract), 99-112; basic agreement, compared to Toquepala, 110, 361-64; "excess production" controversy, 119, 120; financing of, 112-17, 121, 124, 227; mining camps of, 296, 316; production and productivity of, 123; refinery controversy, 100, 102, 105-106, 111, 118, 120-22; results of, 123-30;

Cuajone copper mining project (*cont.*)
workers, 295, 296. *See also* Asarco, Inc.;
Southern Peru Copper Corporation

democracy, 7-8, 336-38
dependency paradigm (dependencismo, dependencista), 3, 4, 7, 8-14, 197-98, 199,
203-204, 225, 237, 278, 316, 341-42
development: capitalist, nature of, 6-7, 323,
328-30; capitalist, Schumpeterian conception of, 200; class and dependency analyses of, 3-16, 279-80, 316; definition of,
14-15; economic aspect of, 14; oligarchic
domination and, 49-50, 52-53; in Peru,
compared to United States, 18; planning
for, 29, 49, 50-51, 60; policy, opinion
survey on, 269; political aspect of, 4, 8;
social aspect of, 14
developmentalism: bourgeois, 271, 272, 331;
military, 29, 271. *See also* "socialist mercantilism"
Díaz Chávez, Ricardo, 295
Dirección General de Minería (DGM), 45-
46, 57-60; and Cuajone project, 101, 105,
106, 108, 117, 120, 130-31; and Cerro de
Pasco, 147-48, 150-51; and National Mining and Petroleum Society, 257
doctrine of domicile: Cerro de Pasco and,
133, 160-65; definition of, 13; transnational corporations and, 161, 164-65, 325

economic crisis (1975-1980), *see* foreign indebtedness; imports, food; inflation;
strikes, general
economic rent from resource exploitation
(ER): definition of, 172; in mediana minería, 172-73, 174; in mediana minería,
U.S. and Japanese shares of, 191-92
"economism": in theory of class, 200; as a
working-class value orientation, 304-309,
318, 342
economy, Peruvian, 21-25, 29-30
Ecuador, 56, 181
education, technical, 248-50. *See also*
bourgeoisie, education and; Universidad
Nacional de Ingeniería
elections, national, 27-28, 270, 313n
empleados, 282, 283, 365-67; class situation
of, self-specified, 298; political opinions
of, 297-99; wages of, compared to obreros, 306-307
employment in mining industry, 285-86. *See
also* specific companies by name

Empresa Promotora Tintaya, 223
enclave formation in mining, 44-45, 62,
288, 293. *See also* bonanza development,
definition of; Cerro de Pasco Corporation,
"social debt" owed by
enganche, 287, 288
engineering profession, 226, 248-52, 254-56;
class situation of, 239n
entrepreneurs, 52, 189, 195, 198-200, 330;
"heroic" or "Schumpeterian" image of,
199-200, 330; industrial, co-optation of,
52. *See also* bourgeoisie; rentiers
exports, 22-23, 24; as a "bonanza," 52, 55-
56; control of outlets for, 45, 100; dependency and, 61, 100; mineral, in bonanza development, 61, 65
Export-Import Bank (U.S.), 116, 120, 139

Fernández Maldonado Solari, Jorge: and
Cerro de Pasco Corporation, 145-46, 149,
151; in Cuajone project negotiations, 106,
109, 117, 119; DGM staff and, 59; government career of, 59n, 67, 208; as minister of mining, 58-59; political beliefs of,
58-59, 309-310; speech upon Cerro de Pasco's nationalization, 153
financing of mining projects, 75, 78-79;
Centromin's experience with, 227; of Cuajone, 112-17; custom refiners and, 75; international banking and, 78-79; of mediana minería "big seven" firms, 194-95;
MineroPeru's experience with, 215, 220,
222-23, 224, 226-28; in world copper industry, 77. *See also* Banco Minero del
Perú; COFIDE
Fleming, Donald M., 184
Flórez Pinedo, Guillermo, 209-210
foreign indebtedness, Peruvian: and bonanza
development, 62; as factor in economic
crisis, 226-28, 311-12; and financing of
Cuajone project, 107-108, 114; parastatal
enterprises and, 226-28. *See also* International Monetary Fund
foreign investment and investors, 5, 23-24,
29, 58-59; Hochschild Group, 183-85; incentive strategies for, 87-88; in mining,
55, 106, 108, 111, 174-79; Peruvian public opinion toward, 67-68. *See also*
bourgeoisie, international; transnational
corporations; specific companies by name
FTMMP (Federación de Trabajadores Minero-Metalúrgicos del Perú), 284, 295,
296, 300, 312

fuerzas vivas, 49-50, 229. *See also* oligarchy
Furukawa Electric Company, 118, 217, 352

Galbraith, John Kenneth, 161-62
geography, Peruvian, 19-20; political, 26
geology, Peruvian, 19-21
Gobierno Revolucionario de la Fuerza Armada, *see* military establishment; Peruvian government, military (1968-1980)
government, *see* Peruvian government; United States, settlement of claims against Peru
Grace, W. R. and Company, 152n, 180
Gramsci, Antonio, 262; concept of hegemony, 6n, 262
gran minería, 41-44, 46; bonanza development and, 62; definition of, 41; employment in, 285-86; General Mining Law of 1981 and, 69
Greene, James R., 151-52, 153, 154; Mercado-Greene Agreement, 116, 154
gross value of production (GVP): definition of, 172; in mediana minería, 172-73, 174; in mediana minería, U.S. and Japanese shares of, 191-92
guano, 52
Guardia Civil, 288, 294
Guardia, Republicana, 296n
Guggenheim family, 35; approach to labor relations, 292n
guild associations, 253-56. *See also* bourgeoisie, organizational resources of

Habich, Eduardo Juan de, 30n, 248; as propagator of Saint-Simonism, 248
Haggin, James B., 31
Haya de la Torre, Víctor Raúl, 27, 141. *See also* APRA
hegemony, class. *See* bourgeoisie, hegemony of; Gramsci
HierroPeru (Empresa del Hierro del Perú), 43, 202, 207-208; employment in, 286; labor unions in, 284; strikes at, 302, 303. *See also* Marcona Mining Company
Hochschild, "Don" Mauricio, 183-84
Hochschild Group, 177, 183-85, 188, 242
Homestake Mining Company, 84, 85, 109, 183

ideology, *see* bougeoisie, hegemony of; ideology and values of; political opinions of; working class, political opinions of
immigrants, in mining bourgeoisie, 246-47

Imperial Metals Industries (IMI), 118, 119-20
imperialism: in natural resources, 323; U.S., in workers' political opinions, 298. *See also* "colonial companies"; dependency; postimperialism
imports, 24; food, as a factor in economic crisis, 311; from Japan, 24, 40; of mining industry equipment and supplies, 44-45, 62, 104, 107-108, 197
industrial classes, *see* bourgeoisie; middle class; working class
industrialization, 17, 21-22, 29-30, 50; bonanza development and, 65-66. *See also* capitalism; dependency; development
inflation, 24-25, 311, 313, 314; Consumer Price Index, 346; and corporatist integration of labor, 313, 314; and labor militance, 311; and monetary devaluation, 24-25; and Southern Peru Copper staff salary structure, 244; wages as affected by, 304-305; workers' beliefs regarding, 298
institutional analysis, 8-9, 95-96, 170, 235; of parastatal enterprise, 205-213
institutions, policymaking, *see* mining policy
Instituto de Ingenieros de Minas (IIM), 254, 255-56
Instituto Nacional de Planificación (INP), 29, 50, 57
Instituto Peruano de Administración de Empresas (IPAE), 271-72, 328
Inter-American Development Bank, *see* Banco Interamericano de Desarrollo
International Bank for Reconstruction and Development (IBRD, World Bank), 89, 117
international bourgeoisie, *see* bourgeoisie
international capitalism, *see* capitalism; dependency; foreign investment and investors
international debt, *see* foreign indebtedness
International Finance Corporation (IFC), 116-17
international metals markets: prices, 1950-1980, 350-51; pricing institutions and practices, 81-84. *See also* individual metals by name
International Monetary Fund (IMF), 24, 68, 226, 228, 312
International Petroleum Company (IPC), 44, 99, 110, 136, 137, 153; and the National Mining and Petroleum Society, 256, 260-61

iron ore, 40. *See also* HierroPeru; Marcona Mining Company

Japan: banks, in Cuajone financing, 115; as development model for Peru (*el modelo japonés*), 60-61; firms, as suppliers to Peruvian mining industry, 80, 118, 193, 217-18; in international metals markets, 79-81, 88, 91, 118n, 193; in mediana minería, 191-93, 195-96; in mediana minería, employment, 285-86; Peruvian mining investments of, 178, 182n, 183, 224; promotion of lead-zinc mining, 85; trade with Peru, 24, 40, 128
joint ventures, of transnational corporations and host governments, 89-90

Kennecott Copper Company, 74, 76, 79, 84, 162, 352, 353
Koenig, Robert, 34, 134-35, 138-48, 149, 158, 160
Kucynski, Pedro-Pablo, 223-24

labor, *see* working class
"labor aristocracy," 11, 279, 280, 306
labor, organized, 283-84, 286, 289-91; AFL-CIO and, 290; bargaining with employers, 283-84, 290, 292, 294, 305n, 309, 330, 338; bonanza development and, 314, 338; bourgeois acceptance of, 263, 273, 275, 276, 314-15, 317, 338; bourgeois and middle-class attitudes toward, 266-68; in Centromin, 300-301, 303; in Cerro de Pasco, 141, 289-91, 303; confederations and federations, 284, 289-91, 294-96, 300, 305, 311, 312-13; in Constituent Assembly of 1978-79, 312; co-optation of, 52, 310, 314, 317; empleados in, 283, 284; financial support of, 284-85, 290, 304-305; general strikes and, 312; leadership of, 289, 290-92, 294, 295, 314n, 337-38; in Marcona and HierroPeru, 284, 304; militancy of, 281, 296-304, 310, 312; military regime (1968-1980) and, 291, 295, 309-312, 314, 317-18; in MineroPeru, 295-96; obreros in, 283, 284; origins and history of, 289-91, 294, 337-38; participation in electoral politics, 313; participation in policymaking, 312-13, 335; Peruvian, compared to other Latin American, 337-38; political parties and, 284, 289, 290-91, 313-14; proscription of,

289, 290; radicalism in, 290-91, 295, 297, 318-19, 335; in Southern Peru Copper, 291-92, 294-96, 302-303, 312n; state controls over, 282, 283-85, 302, 316-17, 337-38; transnational corporations and, 330; Workers' Community system and, 307-308. *See also* "economism"
land reform, *see* agrarian reform
landed class, *see* oligarchy
landholdings, distribution of (prior to 1969), 18
latifundios, 182, 292
lead, 21; exports, 23, 46; foreign investment in mining of, 84-85; and national mining firms, 180; pricing of, 84-85, 350-51; production of, by Centromin, 157, 158; production of, by Cerro de Pasco, 136, 137, 144; production of, by mediana minería, 43, 180; production of, Peruvian, 43, 137, 144, 157, 347, 348; world industry, 84
legislation, mining, 153, 356-60; as government negotiating lever versus Cerro de Pasco, 146-48, 150; as government negotiating lever versus Southern Peru Copper, 106-108, 122; proposals by National Mining and Petroleum Society, 257, 259-60. *See also* Mining Code
legislature, Peruvian, *see* congress
Leninism, 280, 323, 342
living conditions, in mining centers, *see* mining camps
London Metals Exchange (LME), 82-83, 118, 122, 220

McCune, William A., 31
managerial ideology, 270-73, 328, 339
managers: in parastatal enterprise, 208-213, 221, 225. *See also* bourgeoisie; entrepreneurs
manufacturing, 37, 137, 140, 186, 187-88
Maoism, 290, 295
Marcona Mining Company, 39-43, 47; employment in, 40-41, 286; labor unions in, 284; and the National Mining and Petroleum Society, 256-57, 258, 260, 261; strikes at, 302, 303. *See also* HierroPeru
markets, for nonferrous metals, *see* international metals markets
Marmon Group, 43, 154-55, 179, 183
Marx, Karl, 7, 200n, 333
Marxian ideas, 131, 200, 202-203, 239n,

240n; on class formation, 15, 239n, 280; on international capitalism, 131; on parastatal enterprise, 202-203; on progressiveness of democracy, 7; on relative state autonomy, 6, 334-35; on state monopoly capitalism, 203n

Marxism-Leninism, 12-13, 299, 318. *See also* Communist Pary; Maoism

mediana minería, 41, 43, 44, 171-200; Atacocha Mining Company, 176, 178, 179, 180, 188, 261; bonanza development and, 62-63, 68; bourgeoisie of, 186-90, 195, 198-200; Buenaventura Mining Company, 177, 179, 180, 181; capitalist development and, 199-200; Cerro de Pasco and, 32, 34, 45, 139-40, 175n; definition of, 41; denationalization in, 183; desire for local zinc refinery, 222; dynamics of, 190-98; economic indicators for, 172-73, 174, 191-94; employment in, 285-86; firms, 43, 176-81, 183, 190-96; foreign investment in, 43, 139, 174-79, 181, 183, 185, 190-96; General Mining Law of 1981 and, 69; Hochschild Group, 177-78, 183-85; Japanese investments in, 177-78, 183, 191-93; management and staff salaries in, 244, 245; managers' political opinions, 264-70; national firms, 43, 174-81, 185, 190-96; national firms, "big seven," 176-81, 182-83, 185, 190, 193-96, 199; oligarchy and, 187, 188, 189; ownership structure and control of capital in, 174-86, 187, 188, 189, 194-95; as a polymetal industry, 43, 174, 197; production, 43, 349; state capital in, 43, 182-83; technological development and, 196-98; training of managers for, 252-53; U.S. firms in, 43, 177-79, 191-93; U.S. firms, employment, 285-86; wages in, 304-305; workers, 297-99. *See also* National Mining and Petroleum Society

metals, *see* international metals markets; individual metals by name

middle class: bourgeoisie in mining, relationship to, 235, 239-42, 245, 255, 274; class formation and, 327-28; co-optation of, 52; delineation of, 243; education in formation of, 248-50; international bourgeoisie, relationship to, 275; in late capitalism, 5; as mediator between bourgeoisie and working class, 272n; organizational resources of, 253-62; political opinions of (mediana minería staff), 265-70; radicalization of, 241-42; salaries of, 243-44, 245, 246; size of, in mining sector, 243; social mobility of, 241-42, 247-48, 250-51, 274; technical and scientific personnel in, 239n. *See also* bourgeoisie, middle class and

military establishment: antagonism of civilian managers toward, 211; bourgeoisie and, 55-56, 251, 273, 276; character and beliefs of, 29, 50-51, 56, 59-60; organized labor and, 309-310; political intervention by, 25-26, 27; plans and goals for mining industry, 45, 65, 70, 354-55. *See also* bonanza development; Peruvian government, military

military regimes (as general phenomenon), 28, 30, 273. *See also* authoritarianism

MineroPeru (Empresa Minera del Perú), 41, 43, 68-69, 182; Asarco and, 253; Cerro Verde copper mine, 214-15, 218-21, 228; contracts with outside providers, 216-17, 220, 222, 223, 227; copper production by, 202; copper refining by, 118-21, 214, 217-18, 228; in Cuajone project, 118-21, 123, 125; economic performance of, 212, 213-16; employment in, 286; evaluation of, 228-29; financing of, 225-28; foundation of, 205-206; joint ventures, 68-69, 215-16, 223, 224; management of, 210-13, 216, 220, 252, 253; managerial salaries in, 245; organizational structure of, 207-210; other projects of, 224-25; Southern Peru Copper and, 118-21, 123, 125, 210, 212, 214, 253; Tintaya copper mine, 222-24; workers, 292, 294, 295-96, 297, 298, 299, 316; zinc refinery, 221-22

mining camps, 141-42, 150, 181n; apprentice engineers in, 251; of Cerro de Pasco, 141-42, 288-89, 292, 316; conditions in, as source of labor protest, 288, 293; of Southern Peru Copper, 291-94, 296, 316; working-class participation in life of, 315-16

Mining Code, 99; of 1901, 31, 34; of 1950, 33-35, 52-55, 87, 99, 171, 260; of 1971, 111n, 259-60, 265, 266, 310, 357; of 1981, 69-70, 122, 125, 214, 259-60

mining equipment and supplies, *see* imports; mediana minería, technological development and

mining firms: classification of (*see* gran minería; mediana minería; pequeña minería);

mining firms (*cont.*)
foreign ownership of, 74, 174-76; national ownership of, 176-82
mining industry, international, 72-92
mining industry, Peruvian, 30-48; companies' impact on, 47-48; geography and geology of, 19-21; labor and, 279-319; organization of, 41-46; wages in, 305-306
mining policy: after l968, 49-71, 95, 100; after 1975, 67-71; bourgeois and middle-class opinions on, 265-66; institutions, 56-61. *See also* Plan Inca; Plan Túpac Amaru
mining profession, 248-52
Ministry of Development and Public Works, 29, 45, 256
Ministry of Economy and Finance, 223
Ministry of Energy and Mines, 29, 45, 57-60, 152-53, 206, 207, 208, 223. *See also* Dirección General de Minería
Minpeco (Minero Peru Comercial), 45, 69, 125-27, 228
Mitsui Mining Company, 118, 178, 182n, 183, 217, 224, 352
money and monetary policy, 24-25, 345
Morales Bermúdez Cerutti, Francisco, 67, 68, 106, 117, 222, 273, 311, 312
Morgan, J. P., 31
Murphy, C. Gordon, 134, 135, 148-50, 152-53, 155

National Agrarian Society (SNA), 33, 257n. *See also* oligarchy
National Mining and Petroleum Society (Sociedad Nacional de Minería y Petróleo), 256-62; charter, official, 258; membership of, 258-59, 261-62; voting procedures in, 261
National Society of Industries (SNI), 258n
nationalism: bonanza development and, 65-66; of bourgeoisie, 273, 331-32; of labor leaders, 298; of military, 29, 56; versus mining enclaves, 45
neocolonialism, 13, 323. *See also* "colonial companies"
new bourgeoisie (managers and technical specialists), 5, 312, 317; Cerro de Pasco role in formation of, 140, 145, 210, 252; character of, 330-35
New York Commodities Exchange (COMEX), 82
Newmont Mining Corporation, 37, 38, 39, 43, 84; and Cuajone project, 109, 111; in

world copper industry, 76-77, 78, 352, 353
Nixon, Richard M., 151-52
nonferrous metals: definition of, 72-73; world industries and markets in, 72-92. *See also* individual metals by name
Northern Peru Mining Company (an Asarco subsidiary), 35-36, 178, 183, 210, 253

obreros, 282, 283, 365-67; political opinions of, 297-99; wages, compared to empleados, 306-307
Odría, Manuel, 28, 34, 37, 53n, 111, 290
oligarchy (agro-export class), 21, 23-24, 27-28, 65-66, 186, 246, 247, 269; developmental impact of domination by, 28, 49-50, 52-53; economic policies of, 49-50; foreign investment and, 49-50; as mine managers, 251-52; ownership in mediana minería, 186-89; political control and the state, 27-28, 335-36; and subordinate classes, 28. *See also* agrarian reform; capitalism, oligarchy's conception of; *fuerzas vivas*; rentiers
oligopolistic competition, "bonanza" maximization and, 86-90
oligopoly: in world copper industry, 73-76; in world copper industry, Japanese role in, 79-81
open-pit mines, 54-55, 291-92. *See also* Cuajone copper mining project; Marcona Mining Company; MineroPeru, Cerro Verde copper mine; Toquepala copper mine

Paley Report, 36
parastatal enterprise, 200-231; analysis of, 169-70, 202-205; bourgeoisie and, 228-31, 334; capitalist state and, 203; dependency view of, 203-204; goals of, 205-206; institutional factors in analysis of, 205-213; metropolitan capital and, 225-28; privatization of, 68; socialism and, 202-203. *See also* Centromin; HierroPeru; Minero-Peru; Minpeco
parliament, Peruvian, *see* congress
peasantry, 17; Cerro de Pasco's impact on, 33, 137, 141, 287-89; development and, 339-40; mining managers' view of, 269, 339-40; political unrest among, 53; working class and, 287-89, 292-93, 315-16, 330

pequeña minería, 41, 43-44, 256, 286, 349
Peruvian government, administration and civil service, *see* bureaucracy and bureaucrats
Peruvian government, civilian: 1968 and earlier, 25-28, 39, 55, 98; 1980 and later, 25, 68-70, 122, 208, 209, 215-16, 223-24, 277n, 285, 312-13, 337
Peruvian government, military (1961-63 and earlier), 25, 28
Peruvian government, military (1968-1980), 28-30, 45, 49-71, 136, 144, 145, 259, 268, 275-76; and Banco Minero, 45; bonanza development and, 95, 310; COAP, 25, 56-57; CTRP and, 284; and Cuajone project, 97-112; "first phase" (*velasquista* period, 1968-1975), 28, 135, 208, 273, 311, 333; foreign investment policy of, 67-68; labor and, 309-315; mine strikes and, 285, 291, 311-12; nationalist and developmentalist character of, 29, 309; policies and policymaking, 49-71, 95, 100; presidents, 25; reforms, 29, 55-60, 257 (*see also* "social property"; Workers' Community system); "second phase" (1975-1980), 67-68, 208, 222, 273, 311, 333; social justice and, 309-310; technical education programs of, 249
Phelps-Dodge Corporation, 37, 38-39, 43, 84; Cuajone project and, 109, 111; in world copper industry, 73-74, 352, 353
Plan Inca, 57, 68, 354
Plan Túpac Amaru, 57, 68, 354-55
political opinion: of managers and staff, 264-70; of workers, 297-99. *See also* developmentalism; nationalism
political parties, 27, 312, 336; bourgeois and middle-class, 270, 337; Leftist, in 1978 and 1980 elections, 313n, 314; of old order, 27; organized labor and, 289-91, 294-95, 311, 313-14. *See also* APRA; Communist Party
political power: internal versus external, 7; in mining camps, 315-16; of oligarchy, 27-28, 49; of organized labor, 309-316; popular, 7
political system, *see* Peruvian government
policymakers and institutions in mining, 56-61
"post-dependency," 8-14
postimperialism, 13-14
power, definition of, 14

PPC (Partido Popular Cristiano), *see* political parties, bourgeois and middle-class
Prado Ugarteche, Manuel, 39, 141
proletarianization, definition of, 287-88. *See also* class formation; working class, formation of
proletariat, *see* working class
property owners' associations, *see* National Agrarian Society; National Mining and Petroleum Society; National Society of Industries

Quellaveco copper mine, 97, 104, 106, 107, 110-11; Cuajone project and, 122-23

refineries, for metals, 32, 63, 74-78, 84, 125-26, 137
rentiers, 21, 46, 242; in mediana minería, 188-89; in the National Mining and Petroleum Society, 261-62

St. Joe Minerals Corporation, 84, 85, 183
segmental incorporation, 52
Sendero Luminoso (terrorist organization), 277n
Silva Ruete, Javier, 223
silver, 21; as contributor to company profits, 85, 143; exports, 23, 46; and national mining firms, 180; pricing of, 84, 85, 350-51; production, by Centromin, 157, 158n; production, by Cerro de Pasco, 137, 143, 144; production, by mediana minería, 43, 180; production, Peruvian, 43, 137, 143, 144, 157, 180; purported giveaway by Southern Peru Copper, 102n
Sklar, Richard L., 3, 12-13, 77n; on development, 4, 8; on doctrine of domicile, 133, 160-65. *See also* postimperialism
smelters and smelting, 31, 32, 38; Cerro de Pasco monopoly of, 32; air pollution from, 32-33
social control: in conception of power, 14; by dominant class, state role in, 6, 334; as fundamental class interest, 15; as test of class dominance, 334
"social property," 182
socialism: mine workers' preference for, 298-99; parastatal enterprise and, 202-203; prospects for, in Peru, 333, 342
"socialist mercantilism," 63-64, 70
Sociedad Nacional Agraria, *see* National Agrarian Society

Sociedad Nacional de Industrias (SNI), 258n
Sociedad Nacional de Minería y Petróleo,
    see National Mining and Petroleum Society
Society for Small Mining Progress (Sociedad
    Progreso de la Pequeña Minería), 256
South American Consolidated Enterprises,
    see Hochschild Group
Southern Peru Copper Corporation, 35-39,
    41-43, 47, 77, 78, 327, 328; bonanza development and, 98, 124; Cerro de Pasco
    and, 78, 109, 149, 163; conflict with Peruvian government (1966-67), 53-55; copper production of, 123, 124; economic
    performance of, 38-39, 53-55, 127, 129;
    economic performance, impact on owners'
    consolidated profits, 38, 54, 127; employment in, 39, 123, 286; exports of, 39,
    120, 124, 127, 128; financing of, 36-38,
    102, 111-17, 123, 127, 227; influence of,
    on Peruvian legislation, 69n; joint ventures, 43, 116; labor unions in, 293, 294-
    95; local expenditures by, 124-25, 126,
    127; management and staff salaries in,
    244-45; management structure of, 133;
    and military regime (1968-1980), 97-131,
    317; and MineroPeru, 118-21, 122, 210,
    212, 214, 217-18, 253; mining camps of,
    293, 295n, 296, 316; in the National Mining and Petroleum Society, 256-57, 260-
    61, 262; Odría regime and, 54, 111;
    origins and history of, 35-39; other mining
    companies and, 252-53; ownership and
    control of, 35, 38, 39, 42, 43, 78; sales
    practices of, 117-22; staff, 250, 253;
    strikes in, 294, 295-96, 312n; taxation of,
    39, 53-55, 107, 123-25, 127, 361-63;
    U.S. government and, 99, 116; wages in,
    304-305, 306; workers, 287, 292-94, 295,
    299, 316. *See also* Cuajone copper mining
    project; Quellaveco copper mine; Toquepala copper mine
Soviet Union, 63-64, 70, 215
state: analysis of, 6, 8, 335-36; civil society
    and, 6, 66, 318, 331; in dependency paradigm, 4, 9; development and, 60-65, 66,
    272; legitimacy of, 11; Peruvian, character
    of, 5, 28, 51-53, 55, 335-36; Peruvian,
    and civil society, 59-60, 71, 318, 332,
    334; Peruvian, economic role of, 49-50,
    51, 68, 201, 205-206, 272, 335; Peruvian,
    nurture of mediana minería by, 198-99;

Peruvian, reform and restructuring of, 29,
    30, 51, 335-36; Peruvian, and working
    class, 282, 285, 309, 314, 335; Peruvian,
    in world copper industry, 353; relative autonomy of, 6, 9, 66, 334, 335; transnational corporations and, 6, 9, 71, 329. *See
    also* bonanza development; corporatism;
    doctrine of domicile
state capital in Peru, 29, 45, 51, 182-83,
    272. *See also* Banco Minero del Perú;
    COFIDE; parastatal enterprise
strikes: general, 311n, 312; mine, 285, 289-
    91, 294-95, 299-304, 311-12. *See also* labor, organized
"superexploitation," 5n, 280, 316-17. *See
    also* "colonial companies"

taxation, 50, 52, 88, 92. *See also* "colonial
    companies"; Southern Peru Copper Corporation
technical and scientific personnel, class situation, *see* bourgeoisie, middle class and;
    middle class
technological development, 196-98. *See also*
    MineroPeru, Cerro Verde copper mine
terrorism, 277n
Tintaya copper mine, 222-24
Toquepala copper mine, 36-37, 53-54, 97-
    98, 100, 104, 121, 125, 149; contract,
    compared to Cuajone, 110, 361-64; earnings, compared to Cuajone, 127, 129; production and productivity, 123; workers,
    292, 293, 294, 296, 316
trade, 22-24; partners, 24. *See also* exports;
    imports
trade associations, 253, 254, 256-62
transnational corporations, 34, 45, 46, 88,
    91, 194, 228; bonanza development and,
    53, 62, 64, 71, 92, 325, 329; and class
    analysis, 9; "colonial companies" versus,
    163-64, 169, 326-27; in dependency paradigm, 3-4, 8-9, 131, 225; and doctrine of
    domicile, 13, 96, 161-64, 325; as exploiters of labor, 5n; international bourgeoisie
    and, 13, 79; local class formation and, 13,
    327-30; in mediana minería, 181, 183-85;
    owned and controlled by Peruvians, 180-
    81; in Peru, 23, 41, 43, 46, 95, 97, 131-
    32, 201, 205, 215, 225, 229; postimperialism and, 12-13; and the state, 6, 71,
    130, 164-65, 324-25, 329; theory of, 323-
    29; in world nonferrous metals industries,